Index to Plays in Collections

*An author and title index to plays appearing
in collections published between 1900 and 1962*

By
JOHN H. OTTEMILLER

*Associate University Librarian
Yale University*

Fourth Edition,
Revised and Enlarged

THE SCARECROW PRESS, INC.
New York and London
1964

Copyright 1964

by

John H. Ottemiller

L. C. Card no. 64-11776

"For Instant - tuition"

P. Eichelberger, 1963

DIRECTIONS FOR USE

The main entry is the author entry in the Author Index. The

following information is given: Author's name and dates, title of

the play, the date of first production, and references from variant

titles, e. g.,

Hodge, Merton, 1903-
As it was in the beginning. See The wind and the rain
Grief goes over. 1935. FAMH
The island. 1937. SIXP
The wind and the rain. 1933. FAME
Variant title: As it was in the beginning

Plays of unknown authorship are entered in the Author Index un-

der the general heading, Anonymous plays, e. g.,

Anonymous plays
A comedy called Misogonus. See Misogonus
Common conditions. 1570? FARM
The contract of marriage between wit and
wisdom. 1579? FARM
Variant titles: The marriage of wit and
wisdom; Wit and wisdom
The conversion of St. Paul (Digby). 15th cent.
ADA, MAL, SWIT

Foreign plays translated into English are entered in the Author

Index under the English titles with references from the original

titles, e. g.,

Giacosa, Giuseppe, 1847-1906
As the leaves fall. See Like falling leaves
Come le foglie. See Like falling leaves
Like falling leaves. 1900. Updegraff, E. and
A., trs. MOSQ
Variant titles: As the leaves fall;
Come le foglie

Foreign plays in both the original language and in translation

are entered in the Author Index under the original title with refer-

v

ences from the translated titles. Foreign plays in English are to be distinguished in all cases by translator notes. If no translator appears, it is to be assumed that the play is in the original language.

Destouches, Philippe Néricault, 1680-1754
The conceited count. See Le glorieux
Le glorieux. 1732. BRE
Aldington, R., tr. ALD
Variant title: The conceited count

Symbols (e.g., MOSS1) are used to refer from the Author Index to the List of Collections Analyzed and Key to Symbols, which is arranged alphabetically by symbols. Numbers appended to the symbols and to the titles of the plays in the contents notes are volume numbers and refer to the particular volume of a collection in which the play is printed. When volumes are better identified by year of issue, the year has been used similarly, (e.g., BES41).

In the Title Index reference is made from all titles, variant titles and subtitles to the author and title under which full information is to be found in the Author Index.

CONTENTS

INTRODUCTION

Plays from the earliest times to the present day, from the

Greeks to current Broadway and London successes, which have been

published in play anthologies and collections of literature are in-

dexed and identified in this volume. It is limited to books pub-

lished in England and the United States from 1900 through 1962.

The Index has been prepared for the following purposes: The

location of plays which are not available locally in an author's

works or in separate form; the location of duplicate copies of plays

for class assignments, production groups, reading clubs, Little

Theatre groups, amateur theatricals, and plays made current by re-

vivals, the movies, or television; and the verification and identifica-

tion of authors, dates, production dates, titles (English and foreign,)

partial titles, etc. The List of Collections Analyzed may serve as

a buying guide both for filling in a library's book collection and for

comparison in future buying.

The volume indexes 6993 copies of 2536 different plays by 1300

different authors. There are 814 collections analyzed. Regular

supplements are anticipated to keep the indexing up to date and to

index important collections of plays published in the nineteenth cen-

tury.

A play anthology is defined as a collection of plays by three or

more authors published in book form and usually cited by an edi-

tor's name or by title. Collections of general literature fall within

that definition. Plays in foreign languages published in anthologies in England and the United States have been included. All editions of the same collection have been included when the contents of successive editions vary, (see, for example, in The List of Collections Analyzed, entries under Moses, M.J.). If the contents do not vary, the earliest edition has been cited and indexed.

The index is further limited to dramatic literature, better defined as standard full length plays. Only complete texts of plays are indexed; partial or selected texts have been omitted. Children's plays, amateur plays, one-act plays, radio and television plays, holiday and anniversary plays and pageants, have not been included. But--for the sake of completeness--such plays are indexed when they appear in books as defined above. Anthologies which contain only plays by William Shakespeare plus one-act plays, or fragments, or selections, have been excluded since Shakespeare's plays are so freely available. Anthologies of Chinese, Japanese, Burmese, Cretan, Tibetan and Turkish plays have been omitted because they are in the main selections and are generally of value only from a subject point of view.

An index to plays has two functions: (1) to identify plays indexed, and (2) to indicate their location in books. This Index is therefore arranged in three parts, (1) Author Index, (2) List of Collections Analyzed and Key to Symbols, and (3) Title Index.

For the purposes of identification, the following information is given in the Author Index: Author's name and dates, title of the play, the date of first production, references from both original titles and variant translated titles, references from joint authors and any others who have some connection with the play either as

supposed authors, attributed authors, or translators and adapters.
Plays of unknown authorship are listed in the Author Index under
the general heading Anonymous Plays. The translator is given for
foreign plays translated into English. If an exact date cannot be
determined, an approximate date is given and indicated by a question mark, e.g., 1891? This is particularly true of production
dates. Authorities differ as to the first dates of production in
many instances and anyone familiar with the circumstances of production will realize that errors cannot be totally avoided.

Plays in a foreign language are entered under the original title
with references from translated titles. Foreign plays translated into English are entered under the English titles with references from
the original titles, except when citations are made to plays in both
the original language and in translation. In the latter case, entries
are made under the original title with references from translated
titles. In all cases, foreign plays in English are to be distinguished
by translator notes. If no translator appears, it is to be assumed
that the play is in the original language.

The Title Index helps further to identify the plays. References
have been made freely from all forms of the titles, especially from
variant titles, translated titles, and subtitles.

Each collection analyzed has been given a symbol which is used
to refer from the Author Index to the List of Collections Analyzed
and Key to Symbols. The List of Collections Analyzed is arranged
alphabetically by symbols, and space is allowed so that libraries
can indicate call numbers. Under each book cited is a contents
note of the plays in the volume, arranged alphabetically by authors.

Numbers appended to the symbols in the Author Index (e. g.,
MOSS1) and to the titles of the plays in the contents notes are volume numbers and refer to the particular volume of a collection in
which the play is printed. When volumes are better identified by
year of issue, the year has been similarly used (e. g. BES41).

I wish to thank the many librarians who criticized the original
plans for this work, the first, second, and third editions and
who made the publication of this fourth edition, revised, enlarged
and brought up to date, possible, by their enthusiasm and construc-
tive suggestions. My thanks to Zara Jones Powers and Beverly
Thalberg for their help. Professor Eric Bentley of Columbia University lent his copy of the third edition and his notations of cor-
rections have been incorporated. I am grateful for his interest.
As to my wife, she supervised the entire project and managed to
see to my completing the manuscript.

New Haven, Conn.   John H. Ottemiller
August, 1963.

ABBOTT, GEORGE, 1889- , and
BISSELL, RICHARD
The pajama game (lyrics and
music by Richard Adler and
Jerry Ross; based on the
novel 7-1/2 cents by
Richard Bissell.) 1954.
THEA54

-- and BRIDGERS, ANN PRESTON
Coquette. 1927.　　BES27

--and GLEASON, JAMES
The fall guy. 1925.　　BES24

--See DUNNING, PHILIP; HOLM,
JOHN CECIL; WEIDMAN, JE-
ROME, jt. auths.

ABEL, LIONEL
Absalom. 1956.　　MACH
The death of Odysseus. 1953.
PLAA

ABELL, KJELD, 1901-
Anna Sophie Hedvig. 1939.
Larsen, H., tr.　　SCAN2
Dronning gaar igen. See The
queen on tour
The queen on tour. 1943.
Pearce, J., tr.　　CONT
Variant title: Dronning gaar
igen

ABSE, DANNIE, 1923-
House of cowards. 1960.
PLAN23

ACEVEDO HERNANANDEZ, AN-
TONIO, 1886-
Cabrerita. 1927. Bailey, W.,
tr.　　SSTE

ACHARD, MARCEL, 1889-
Auprès de ma blonde. See

Behrman, Samuel Nathaniel.
I know my love (adapted
from)
Patate. See Rollo
Rollo (adapted by Felicity
Douglas). 1956.　　PLAN20
Variant title: Patate

ACHESON, SAM HANNA, 1900-
We are besieged. 1941.
THX
ACKLAND, RODNEY, 1908-
After October. 1936. FAMI
Before the party (based on a
short story by W. Somer-
set Maugham). 1949.
PLAN2
A dead secret. 1957. PLAN16
The diary of a scoundrel. See
Ostrovsky, Alexander.
The diary of a scoundrel
(tr. and adapted by)
The old ladies. 1935. FAMG
Strange orchestra. 1932.
FAMC
ADAMOV, ARTHUR, 1908-
Professor Toranne. 1953.
Bermel, A., tr.　　FOUF

ADDISON, JOSEPH, 1672-1719
Cato. 1713. DOB, EIGH, HAN,
LIBR, MCM, MCMI, MOR,
NET, STM, TAT, TAU,
TUP, TUQ

ADE, GEORGE, 1866-1944
The college widow. 1904.
COT
The county chairman. 1903.
BES99
ADLER, RICHARD
The pajama game (lyrics and
music by).
See Abbott, George and
Bissell, Richard.

13

The pajama game

A. E., pseud. See Russell,
George William

AESCHYLUS, 525-456 B. C.
Agamemnon. 458 B. C.
   Anon. tr.   EVB1
   Blackie, J., tr. BUCK,
      BUCL, BUCM
   Campbell, L., tr. LAP
   Cookson, G., tr. GRDB5
   Hamilton, E., tr. HAM,
      KRE, TREC1, TREE1
   Lattimore, R., tr. FIFT,
      GREP1, GRER1
   Lucas, F., tr.   LUCA
   MacNeice, L., tr. DEAP,
      DEAR, FIFR, LIND,
      MCKK1, MACJ, MACL1
   Morshead, E., tr., HARC8,
      HOWE, HOWF, LOCM1,
      MAU, OAT1, OATE,
      OATH, ROBJA, THP,
      WARN1
   Murray, G., tr. CAR,
      CARA, FEFT, TEN,
      TRE, TREA2
   Plumptre, E., tr. HIB,
      HIBA, HIBB, HOUS,
      ROB, THOM, THON
   Potter, R., tr.   GREE
   Robinson, C., tr. ROBK
   Thomson, G., tr. AUDE,
      FIFV, ROBI, WEAV1
   Way, A., tr.   PLAG
   The choephori. See Choe-
   phoroe
Choephoroe. 458 B. C.
   Cookson, G., tr. GRDB5
   Lattimore, R., tr. GREP1,
      GRER2
   Morshead, E., tr. HARC8,
      OAT1
   Murray, G., tr. FEFT,
      TEN
   Thomson, G., tr. AUDE,
      FIFV, ROBJ
   Way, A., tr.   PLAG
      Variant titles: The choe-
      phori; The libation-
      bearers; The mourners
Eumenides. 458 B. C.

Cookson, G., tr.   GRDB5
Lattimore, R., tr. GREP1,
   GRER3
Morshead, E., tr. HARC8,
   OAT1, OATE
Murray, G., tr.   FEFT,
   TEN
Plumptre, E., tr. BAT1
Thomson, G., tr. AUDE,
   FIFT, FIFV, ROBJ
Way, A., tr.   PLAG
   Variant titles: The
   furies; The gracious ones
The furies. See Eumenides
The gracious ones. See
   Eumenides
Hepta epi Thebas. See The
   seven against Thebes
Hiketides. See The suppliants
The house of Atreus (trilogy:
   Agamemnon, Choephoroe,
   and Eumenides). See Aga-
   memnon; Choephoroe;
   Eumenides; Oresteia
The libation-bearers. See
   Choephoroe
The mourners. See Choephoroe
Oresteia (trilogy: Agamemnon,
   Choephoroe, and Eumenides).
   458 B. C.
   Morshead, E., tr. (ar-
   ranged for the stage by A.
   V. Griffin).   GRIF
   See also Agamemnon; Choe-
   phoroe; Eumenides
The Persians, 472 B. C.
   Benardete, S., tr. GREP1
   Cookson, G., tr. GRDB5
   Potter, R., tr.   OAT1
Prometheus bound. 478? B. C.
   Anon. tr.   ATT3
   Blackie, J., tr. BUCK,
      BUCL, BUCM, CLF1,
      SEBO, SEBP
   Browning, E., tr. CROS,
      DRA1, GREB2, GREE,
      MAST, MIK7, PLAB1
   Cookson, G., tr. GRDB5
   Grene, D., tr. GREN,
      GREP1, GRER1
   Hamilton, E., tr. DOWN,
      FIFT, HAM
   Havelock, E., tr. BARC

14

Lucas, F., tr.   LUCA
Mendell, C., tr. CLKW, ROBJ
More, P., tr. MURP, OAT1,
    OATE, OATH
Plumptre, E., tr. CROV,
    HARC8, SML
Warner, R., tr.   LIND
Whitelaw, R., tr.   FEET
    Variant titles: Prometheus
    desmotes; Prometheus
    vinctus
Prometheus desmotes. See
    Prometheus bound
Prometheus vinctus. See
    Prometheus bound
Septem contra Thebas. See
    The seven against Thebes
The seven against Thebes. 467 B. C.
    Cookson, G., tr. GRDB5
    Grene, D., tr.   GREP1
    Morshead, E., tr. OAT1
    Variant titles: Hepta epi
    Thebas; Septem contra
    Thebas
The suppliant maidens. See
    The suppliants
The suppliants. 492? B. C.
    Bernadete, S., tr. GREP1
    Cookson, G., tr. GRDB5
    Morshead, E., tr. OAT1
    Variant titles: Hiketides;
    The suppliant maidens

AFINOGENYEV, ALEKSANDR
NIKOLAEVICH, 1904-1941
    Distant point. See Far taiga
    Far taiga. 1935. Bakshy, A.,
    tr.   BAKS
    Variant titles: Distant point;
    Remote
    Fear. 1931. Malamuth, C., tr.
    LYK
    On the eve. 1942. Afinogenova,
    E., tr.   SEVP
    Remote. See Far taiga

AGEE, JAMES
    A death in the family. See
    Mosel Tad. All the way
    home (based on)

AIKEN, GEORGE L., 1820-1876
    Life among the lowly. See

Uncle Tom's cabin
    Uncle Tom's cabin; or, Life
    among the lowly (based on
    the novel by Harriet Beech-
    er Stowe). 1852.   BLAI2,
    CEY, MOSS2

AIKENS, CARROLL
    The god of gods. 1919. MAS2

AKINS, ZOË, 1886-
    Declassee. 1919.   BES19
    The old maid. 1935.   BES34

ALARCÓN Y MENDOZA, JUAN
RUIZ DE. See Ruiz de Alarcón
    y Mendoza, Juan

ALBEE, EDWARD, 1928-
    The sandbox. 1960   CUBH
    The zoo story. 1959.   FAM

ALBERY, JAMES, 1838-1889
    Two roses. 1870.   ROWE

ALBERY, PETER
    Anne Boleyn. 1956.   PLAN14

ALFIERI, VITTORIO, 1749-1803
    Myrrha. 1788?
    Bowring, E., tr.   BAT5
    Saul. 1784   BIN
    Bowring, E., tr.   CLF2

ALFRIEND, EDWARD M., and
WHEELER, ANDREW CARPEN-
TER
    The great diamond robbery.
    1885.   AMP8, CLA

ALI, AKHUND-ZATH FATH'.
See Fath 'Ali, Akhundzadah

ALSINA, ARTURO, 1897-
    La marca de fuego. 1926.
    ALPE

ÁLVAREZ QUINTERO, JOA-
QUIN, 1873-1944. See Álvarez
Quintero, Serafín, jt. auth.

ÁLVAREZ QUINTERO, SERAFIN,
1871-1938, and ÁLVAREZ
QUINTERO, JOAQUÍN

15

An autumn morning. See A
bright morning
A bright morning. 1905.
Castillo, C., and Overman,
E., trs. DIK1
Floyd, L., tr. EDAD
Variant titles: An autumn
morning; Mañana de sol;
A sunny morning
The centenarian. See A hun-
dred years old
Doña Clarines. 1909.
Granville-Barker, H., and
H., trs. CHA, CHAN
A hundred years old. 1909.
Granville-Barker, H., and
H. trs. PLAP3
Variant titles: The cen-
tenarian; Papá Juan:
centenario
Malvaloca. 1912.
Fassett, J., tr. DIE
Mañana de sol. See A bright
morning
Papá Juan: centenario. See A
hundred years old
Pueblo de las mujeres. See
The women's town
A sunny morning. See A
bright morning
The women have their way.
See The women's town
The women's town. 1912.
Turrell, C., tr. TUR
Variant titles: Pueblo de
las mujeres; The women
have their way

ALYOSHIN, SAMUEL
Alone. 1956.
McLean, H., and Vickery,
W., trs. MCKL
Variant title: Odna
Odna. See Alone

AMES, WINTHROP, 1871-1937
A kiss in Xanadu. 1932? LEV,
LEVE

AMESCUA, ANTONIO MIRA DE.
See Mira de Amescua, Antonio

ANCEY, GEORGES, pseud. See

Curnieu, Georges de

ANDERSON, MAXWELL, 1888-
Anne of the thousand days.
1948. BES48, GARW
The bad seed (based on the
novel by William March).
1954. BES54, THEA55
Barefoot in Athens. 1951.
BES51
Both your houses. 1933.
BES32, CORD, CORE,
CORF, LOOA, LOOB
Candle in the wind. 1941.
BES41
Elizabeth the queen. 1930.
BES30, STEI, THO, TRE,
TREA1, TREC2, TREE3,
WATC2, WATI, WHI
The eve of St. Mark. 1942.
BES42
The feast of Ortoland. 1938.
STAT
A girl from Lorraine. See
Joan of Lorraine
Gypsy. 1929. BES28
High Tor. 1937. BES36,
CLDP, CRIT, GAS, GAVE,
GOW, HAP, MERT
Joan of Lorraine. 1946.
BES46
Variant title: A girl from
Lorraine
Journey to Jerusalem. 1940.
GALB
Key Largo. 1940. BES39,
ROLF
Mary of Scotland. 1933.
BES33, CLKW, THF
The masque of kings. 1936.
MOSL
Saturday's children. 1927.
BES26, GASB, TUCD
The star-wagon. 1937. BES37
Storm operation. 1944. BES43
Valley Forge. 1934. BES34,
WARH
The wingless victory. 1936
LOR
Winterset. 1935. BES35,
BROU, CALM, CALN2,
CASS, CHAN, CHAP, COTE,
COTH, CRIT, DAV1, DUR,

16

GAS, GAVE, GRIF, HAT,
HATA, HAVD, HAVE, HIL,
HOLM, MOSH, NELS,
QUIM, QUIN, SIXC, WAIT,
WALB
-- and HICKERSON, HAROLD
Gods of the lightning. 1928.
                        GASB
-- and STALLINGS, LAWRENCE
What price glory? 1924.
   BES24, CHA, GASB,
   MACG, TRE, TREA1,
   TREC2, TREE3, VANM

-- and WEILL, KURT
Lost in the stars (based on the
novel Cry, the beloved
country by Alan Paton).
1949.   BES49, HEWE

ANDERSON, ROBERT WOOD-
RUFF, 1917-
Tea and sympathy. 1953.
   BES53, FAM, GART,
   NEWV, THEA54

ANDERSON, SHERWOOD, 1876-
1941
Textiles. 193-?   ING

ANDREEV, LEONID NIKOLAE-
VICH, 1871-1919
He who gets slapped. 1915.
   Guthrie, J., adapter. HOUG
   MacAndrew, A., tr. GARZJ
   Reeve, F.D., tr.   REEV2
   Zilboorg, G., tr. BES21,
   DIE, MOSG, MOSH, THF,
   TUCG, TUCM, TUCN,
   TUCO, WATI, WATL4
      Variant titles: The knock
      about; The painted laugh
The knock about. See He who
gets slapped
The life of man. 1906.
   Meader, C., and Scott, F.,
   trs.   SML
   Seltzer, T., tr.   DIK2,
   MOSQ
The painted laugh. See He
who gets slapped
Professor Storitsyn. 1912.

Minkoff, I., Noyes, G.,
and Kaun, A., trs. NOY

ANDREYEFF, LEONID NIKOLAE-
VICH. See Andreev, Leonid
Nikolaevich

ANDREYEV, LEONID NIKO-
LAEVICH. See Andreev, Leonid
Nikolaevich

ANDRIEU DE LA VIGNE. See
La Vigne, Andrieu de

ANDRIEV, LEONID NIKOLAE-
VICH. See Andreev, Leonid
Nikolaevich

ÁNGEL PÉREZ DE SAAVEDRA,
RIVAS. See Rivas, Ángel
Pérez de Saavedra

ANNUNZIO, GABRIELE D',
1863-1938
La città morta. See The dead
city
The daughter of Jorio. 1904.
   Porter, C., Isola, P., and
   Henry A., trs.   MOSQ
   Variant title: La figlia di
   Jorio
The dead city. 1898.
   Mantellini, G., tr. SAY
   Variant title: La città
   morta
La figlia di Jorio. See The
daughter of Jorio
Francesca da Rimini. 1902.
   Symons, A., tr.   D1K1,
   TUCG, TUCM, WATL3
Gioconda. 1898.
   Symons, A., tr. DID, SMI

ANONYMOUS PLAYS
Abraham and Isaac (Brome).
   15th cent. ADA, BARD,
   BENY, CAWL, CHI,
   GARZB, GREC1, HOPP,
   IIUD, LIE, MAK, MAT,
   PAR, PARR, POLL, SCW,
   SNYD1, SWIT, TAT, TAU,
   TREA2, TREC1, TREE1
   Variant titles: The Brome

17

Abraham and Isaac; The
sacrifice of Isaac
Abraham, Melchisedec and
Isaac (Chester). 15th cent.
ASH, CHES, EVER, KRE,
POLL
Variant titles: Abraham,
Melchizedek and Lot, with
the sacrifice of Isaac; The
histories of Lot and Abra-
ham; Lot and Abraham;
The sacrifice of Isaac
Abraham, Melchizedek and
Lot, with the sacrifice of
Isaac. See Abraham, Mel-
chisedec and Isaac
Abstraction. 14th cent.?
Chamberlin, B., tr. CLF1,
ORI2
Adam. 1150?
Barrow, S., and Hulme,
W., trs. CROV
Stone, E., tr. CLF1, KRE
Variant titles: Le mystère
d'Adam; The mystery of
Adam; The play of Adam
The adoration of the magi
(Chester). 15th cent. CHES
The adoration of the shep-
herds (Chester). 15th cent.
CHES
Albion, knight. See A moral
play of Albion, knight
All's one, or one of the foure
plaies in one, called A
York-Shire tragedy. See
A Yorkshire tragedy
The annunciation (Coventry).
15th cent. CAWL
The annunciation (Wakefield).
15th cent. LOOM
Antichrist (Chester). 15th cent.
CHES
Apius and Virginia (sometimes
attributed to Richard
Bower). 1563? FARM
Variant title: Appius and
Virginia
Appius and Virginia. See
Apius and Virginia
Arden of Feversham (some-
times attributed to Thomas
Arden; Thomas Kyd; Willi-

am Shakespeare). 1586?
BAS, BRO, MCJ, MIN1,
MIO1, OLH, OLI1, SCH
Variant title: The lament-
able and true tragedy of
Master Arden of Fever-
sham in Kent
Attowell's jig (Francis' new
jig) (sometimes attributed
to George Attowell). 1595?
BAS
Variant title: Mr. Atto-
well's jig
Banns (Coventry). 15th cent.
ADA, SCW
The beauty and good proper-
ties of women (commonly
called Calisto and Meli-
baea). 1530? FARO
The Benediktbeuren play. 13th
cent.
Robinson, D., and Francke,
K., trs. and adapters.
ROBM
The betrayal (Wakefield).
15th cent. HEIL
The betrayal of Christ (Ches-
ter). 15th cent. CHES,
GARZB
The betraying of Christ (Cov-
entry). 15th cent. ADA
The bilker bilk'd. 1742?
HUGH
Bilsen play. See The star
The bird catcher in hell. See
Esashi Jūō. The bird
catcher in hell
The birth of Jesus (York).
15th cent. ADA
The birth of Merlin; or, The
child hath found his father
(sometimes attributed to
William Rowley; William
Shakespeare). 1597? BRO
The book of Job. See Job
The Brome Abraham and
Isaac. See Abraham and
Isaac
Brome plays. See Abraham
and Isaac
The buggbears. See Jeffere,
John (supposed author)
Cain and Abel. 15th cent. CAWL

18

Calisto and Melibaea. See
The beauty and good prop-
erties of women
The castle of perseverance.
1425? ADA, HOPP, POLL
The chalk circle. 13th cent. ?
Van Der Meer, E., tr.
CLF1, KRE
The Chantilly play. See Bour-
let, Katherine. The nativity
Chester play of the deluge;
The deluge
Chester plays. See Abraham,
Melchisedec and Isaac; The
adoration of the magi; The
adoration of the shepherds;
Antichrist; The betrayal of
Christ; Christ's ascension;
Christ's ministry; Christ's
passion; Christ's resurrection; The creation of man;
Adam and Eve; The death
of Herod; The deluge; The
fall of Lucifer; The last
judgment; The magi's oblation; The nativity; The
prophets; The resurrection,
harrowing of hell, and the
last judgment; The sacri-
fice of Isaac; Simon the
leper; The slaying of the
innocents
A Christmas mumming: The
play of Saint [Prince]
George. 15th cent. GARZB
Variant titles: Christmas
play of St. George; The play
of St. George
Christmas play of St. George.
See A Christmas mumming:
The play of Saint [Prince]
George
Christ's ascension (Chester).
15th cent.   CHES
Christ's ministry (Chester).
15th cent.   ADA
Christ's passion (Chester).
15th cent.   CHES
Christ's resurrection (Chester)
15th cent.   CHES
Coliphizacio (Wakefield). 15th
cent.   CAWM
A comedy called Misogonus.

See Misogonus
Common conditions. 1570?
FARM
The contract of marriage be-
tween wit and wisdom.
1579?   FARM
Variant titles: The mar-
riage of wit and wisdom;
Wit and wisdom
The conversion of St. Paul
(Digby). 15th cent. ADA,
MAL, SWIT
The Cornish mystery play of
the three Maries. See The
three Maries
Cornish plays. See The
death of Pilate; The three
Maries
Coventry plays. See The an-
nunciation; Banns; The be-
traying of Christ; The
death of Pilate; The fall of
Lucifer; Herod and the
Magi; The magi, Herod and
the slaughter of the inno-
cents; The mystery of the
redemption; The pageant of
the shearmen and tailors;
The salutation and concep-
tion; The shepherds' play;
The trial of Christ
The creation and the fall of
Lucifer (York). 15th cent.
CAWL, GARZB, POLL
The creation of Adam and Eve
(York) 15th cent.   CAWL
The creation of Eve, with the
expelling of Adam and Eve
out of Paradise. 15th cent.
ADA
The creation of man: Adam
and Eve (Chester). 15th
cent.   CHES
The crucifixion (Wakefield).
15th cent. EVER, GARZB
The crucifixion (York). 15th
cent.   CAWL, HEIL
The dance of death. See
Totentanz
The death of Herod (Chester).
15th cent.   GARZB
The death of Pilate (Cornish).
15th cent. CAWL, GARZB,

19

The death of stone. HAH
Aston, W., tr.   BAT3
The deluge (Chester). 15th
cent. ADA, BENY, CAWL,
CHES, EVER, HOPP, MAK,
MIL, PARR, POLL,
SNYD1, TAT, TAU, WEAT1
Variant titles: Chester
play of the deluge: Noah's
deluge; Noah's flood
The deluge (Wakefield). 15th
cent.   GARZB
Variant title: Noah and his
sons
Depositio cornuti typographici.
See The printer's appren-
tice
The devil and his dame. See
Grim the collier of Croy-
don
Digby plays. See The conver-
sion of St. Paul
Le docteur amoureux. 1691?
LAN
Dr. Kranichs sprechstunde.
See Birmelin, John. Em
Docktor Fogel sei offis
schtunn (based on)
Duk Moraud. 13th cent. ADA
An Easter resurrection play.
10th cent.   GARZB
Edward III. See The reign of
King Edward the third
Elckerlijk. See Everyman
Everyman. 1529? ABRB1,
ADA, ALLE, ASH, BALL,
BARD, BAT4, BENP,
BENY, BIER, BROJ, BROK,
CAWL, CHI, CLF1, CLK1,
COJ, EVE, EVER, FARO,
FIF, GARZB, GASS, GOOD,
GREB1, GREC1, GRIF,
HEIL, HOPP, HOUS, HUD,
KERN, KRE, LEV, LEVE,
LIE, LOOM, MCNI, MOO,
PAR, POLL, REIN, ROB,
RUB, SCW, SHAH1, SHAI1,
SHAJ1, SML, SNYD1, STA,
SWIT, TAT, TAU, TAV,
TRE, TREA2, TREC1,
TREE1, WEAT1, WOOD1,
WOOE1

Variant titles: Elckerlijk;
The moral play of Everyman;
The summoning of Everyman
The extraction of souls from
hell (Wakefield). See The
harrowing of hell
Fair Em. The miller's
daughter of Manchester with
the love of William the con-
queror. 1590?   BRO
The fall of Lucifer (Chester).
15th cent.   CHES
The fall of Lucifer (Coventry).
15th cent. ADA, SCW
The fall of man (York). 15th
cent.   CAWL
The famous victories of Henry
the fifth (sometimes at-
tributed to Richard Tarl-
ton). 1585?   ADA
Variant title: Henry the fifth
La farce de Maître Pathelin.
See La farce de Maitre Pi-
erre Pathelin
La farce de Maître Pierre
Pathelin. 1469? SCN, SET
Allen, J., tr.   ALLE
Holbrook, R., tr.   THO
Jagendorf, M., tr. CAR, CLF1
Variant titles: La farce de
Maître Pathelin; The farce
of the worthy Master Pierre
Patelin; Master Pierre Pa-
telin; Pierre Patelin
The farce of the worthy Mas-
ter Pierre Patelin. See La
farce de Maître Pierre
Pathelin
The fatal error.
McClatchie, T., tr. BAT21
Variant title: Kago-Sodo
The first part of the return
from Parnassus. See The
return from Parnassus; or,
The scourge of Simony
The four elements. See The
nature of the four elements
Francis' new jig. See Atto-
well's jig
Gammer Gurton's needle. See
Stevenson, William (sup-
posed author)
George a Greene, the pinner

of Wakefield. See Greene,
Robert (supposed author)
Godley Queen Hester. 1525?
                FARP
Variant title: An interlude
of Godley Queen Hester
Grim the collier of Croydon;
or, The devil and his dame
(sometimes attributed to
John Tatham). 1600? FARM
The harrowing of hell (Chester). 15th cent.   ADA,
CAWL, POLL
The harrowing of hell; or, The
extraction of souls from
hell (Wakefield). 15th cent.
                EVER
Henry the fifth. See The fam-
ous victories of Henry the
fifth
Herod (Coventry). See The
magi, Herod, and the
slaughter of the innocents
Herod the great (Wakefield).
14th cent.   CAWL
Herod and the magi (Coventry).
See The magi, Herod, and
the slaughter of the inno-
cents
The Hessian Christmas play.
15th cent.
Robinson, D., tr. and
adapter   ROBM
Hickscorner. 1534?   FARO
The histories of Lot and Abra-
ham. See Abraham, Mel-
chisedec and Isaac
The history of Jacob and Esau.
See Jacob and Esau
Impatient poverty. 1560?
                FARN
Variant title: An interlude
of impatient poverty
An interlude of Godley Queen
Hester. See Godley Queen
Hester
An interlude of impatient pov-
erty. See Impatient poverty
The interlude of John the evange-
list. See John the evangelist
An interlude of wealth and
health. See Wealth and
health.

The interlude of youth. See
Youth
Jack Juggler. 1553?   FAR
Jacob and Esau. 1558? FARP
Variant title: The history of
Jacob and Esau
Job. 400? B. C. BUCL, BUCM,
DAVK, SML, TRE, TREA2,
Variant title: The book of
Job
John the evangelist. 1557?
                FARN
Variant titles: The inter-
lude of John the evangelist;
Saint John the evangelist
The judgment. See The judg-
ment day
The judgment day (York).
15th cent. ADA, CAWL, SCW
Variant title: The judgment
Kaga-Sodo. See The fatal er-
ror
The killing of Abel (Wake-
field). 15th cent.   ADA
King Darius. 1565?   FAR
King Edward the third. See
The reign of King Edward
the third
The lamentable and true trage-
dy of Master Arden of
Feversham in Kent. See
Arden of Feversham
The lamentable tragedy of
Locrine (sometimes at-
tributed to George Peele;
William Shakespeare).
1586?   BRO
Variant title: Locrine
The last judgment (Chester).
15th cent.   CHES
The legend of the rood (Corn-
ish). 15th cent.   HAH
Leicestershire St. George
play. 1863.   ADA
The life and death of Lord
Cromwell. See Thomas,
Lord Cromwell
Li tre becchi. See The three
cuckolds
Locrine. See The lamentable
tragedy of Locrine
The London prodigal (some-
times attributed to William

Shakespeare). 1603? BRO
Lot and Abraham. See Abra-
ham, Melchisedec and Isaac
Ludus super iconia Sancti Ni-
colai. 15th cent. POLL
The Maastricht play (adapted
from Paachspel). 14th cent.
Robinson, D., tr. and
adapter ROBM
Mactacio Abel (Wakefield).
15th cent. CAWM, GARZB
Variant title: The murder
of Abel
The magi, Herod, and the
slaughter of the innocents
(Coventry). 15th cent.
ADA, MAK
Variant titles: Herod; Herod
and the magi; The massa-
cre of the innocents; The
slaughter of the innocents
The magi's oblation (Chester).
15th cent. CHES
Magnus Herodes (Wakefield).
15th cent. CAWM
Man's disobedience and the fall
of man (York). 15th cent.
GARZB
Mankind. 1475? ADA, FARN
The marriage of wit and sci-
ence. 1569? FARM
Variant titles: Wit and sci-
ence; Wyt and science
The marriage of wit and wis-
dom. See The contract of
marriage between wit and
wisdom
The martyrdom of Ali
Pelly, L., tr. BAT3
Variant title: Ta'ziya
Mary Magdalene. 15th cent.
ADA, POLL
Mary Magdalene and the apos-
tles. See The mystery of
Mary Magdalene and the
apostles
The massacre of the inno-
cents. See The magi, Herod,
and the slaughter of the in-
nocents
Master Pierre Patelin. See
La farce de Maître Pierre
Pathelin

The merry devil of Edmonton
(sometimes attributed to
Michael Drayton). 1600?
BRO, GAY2, MCI, OLH,
OLI1
The miller's daughter of Man-
chester with the love of
William the conqueror.
See Fair Em
The miracle of Saint Nicholas
and the school-boys. 15th
cent. LOOM
The miracle of Saint Nicholas
and the virgins. 15th cent.
LOOM
Misogonus. 1560? BOND,
FARP
Variant title: A comedy
called Misogonus
Mr. Attowell's jig. See Atto-
well's jig
A moral play of Albion,
knight. 1566? FARP
Variant title: Albion, knight
A most pleasant comedie of
Mucedorus the kings sonne
of Valentia and Amadine,
the kings daughter of Arra-
gon. See Mucedorus
Mucedorus (sometimes at-
tributed to Thomas Lodge;
William Shakespeare).
1588? BAS, BRO, WINN
Variant title: A most pleas-
ant comedie of Mucedorus
the kings sonne of Valentia
and Amadine, the kings
daughter of Arragon
Mundus et infans. See The
world and the child
The murder of Abel (Wake-
field). See Mactacio Abel
(Wakefield)
Le mystère d'Adam. See Adam
Mysterium resurrectionis D. N.
Jhesu Christi. 15th cent.
POLL
The mystery of Adam. See
Adam
The mystery of Mary Magda-
lene and the apostles. 15th
cent. EVER
Variant title: Mary Magda-

lene and the apostles

The mystery of the redemption (Coventry). 15th cent. **LOOM**
Variant title: The redemption

The nativity (The Chantilly play). See Bourlet, Katherine. The nativity

The nativity (Chester). 15th cent. **CHES**

The nativity (Wakefield). See The second shepherd's play

The nativity (York). See The York nativity

Nativity play (Coventry). See The pageant of the shearmen and tailors

The nature of the four elements (sometimes attributed to John Rastell). 1520. **FARO, POLL**
Variant title: The four elements

Nero 1623? **NERO**

New custom. 1573? **FAR**

Nice wanton. 16th cent. **CLKW**
Variant title: A pretty interlude called Nice Wanton

Noah (Wakefield). 15th cent. **ADA, HEIL, SCW**

Noah and his sons. See The deluge (Wakefield)

Noah's deluge. See The deluge (Chester)

Noah's flood. See The deluge

N. Town plays. See Cain and Abel; The woman taken in adultery

Oberufer plays. See The paradise play; The shepherds' play; The three kings' play

Octavia. See Seneca, Lucius Annaeus. Octavia

The Orléans sepulcher. 13th cent. **GARZB**

The Oxfordshire St. George play. 18th cent. **ADA, CHI, PAR**

Paachspel. See The Maastricht play

The pageant of the shearmen and tailors (Coventry). 15th cent. **ALLE, EVER, FIF, GARZB**
Brown, J., adapter. **ROBM**
Variant title: The nativity play

A pantomime for Easter day. **GARZB**

The paradise play (Oberufer). 16th cent.
Harwood, A., tr. **HARW**

Parnassus plays (1598-1601). See The pilgrimage to Parnassus; The return from Parnassus

The passion play of Alsfeld. Katzin, W., tr. **SEVE**

Pharaoh (Wakefield). 15th cent. **ADA**

Le philosophe dupé de l'amour. See The philosopher duped by love

The philosopher duped by love (sometimes attributed to François Dessandrais-Sebire). 17th cent.
Chambers, W., tr. **BAT7**
Variant title: Le philosophe dupé de l'amour

Pierre Patelin. See La farce de Maître Pierre Pathelin

Pilgrimage. See The pilgrimage to Parnassus

The pilgrimage to Parnassus. 16th cent. **LEIS**
Variant title: Pilgrimage

The play of Adam. See Adam

The play of St. George. See A Christmas mumming: The play of Saint [Prince] George

The play of St. George, version reconstructed from memory by Thomas Hardy. 13th cent. ? **CLF1**

The play of the sacrament. 15th cent. **ADA**

A pretty interlude called Nice wanton. See Nice wanton

Prima pastorum (Wakefield). 15th cent. **CAWM**

The printer's apprentice. 1648?

23

Rist, J., tr. (from the
German of William Blades).
BAT4
Variant title: Depositio cor-
nuti typographici
Processus noe cum filiis
(Wakefield). 15th cent.
CAWM
The prophets (Chester). 15th
cent. ADA
The Provençal play. 13th cent.
Robinson, D., tr. and
adapter. ROBM
The puritan; or, The widow of
Watling street (sometimes
attributed to William
Shakespeare). 1606? BRO
Variant title: The puritan
widdow
The puritan widdow. See The
puritan; or, The widow of
Watling street
The quem quaeritis (trope).
9th cent. CHI, GARZB,
HUD, PAR, SCW
Chambers, E., tr. BARH
Querolus. 15th cent. ?
Duckworth, G., tr. DUC2
The raigne of King Edward
the third. See The reign of
King Edward the third
The redemption. See The
mystery of the redemption
The reign of King Edward the
third (sometimes attributed
to Thomas Lodge; Christo-
pher Marlowe; William ⌐
Shakespeare). 1590? BRO,
WINN
Variant titles: Edward III;
King Edward the third; The
raigne of King Edward the
third
Respublica. 1553? FARN
Resurrection (York). 15th
cent. CAWL, SWIT
The resurrection, harrowing
of hell, and the last judg-
ment (synoptic version of
Chester, Coventry, and
Wakefield plays). 15th cent.
GARZB
The resurrection of Christ

(Wakefield). 15th cent.
ADA
The return from Parnassus; or,
The scourge of Simony, pt.
I (1601?). LEIS
pt. II (1602?) LEIS, SCH,
SCI, SCJ
Variant titles: The first
part of the return from
Parnassus; The second part
of the return from Parnas-
sus
The Revesby sword play.
1779. ADA
Rip Van Winkle (as played by
Joseph Jefferson; adapted
by Dion Boucicault). 1865.
CEY, LAW, QUIJ, QUIK,
QUIL, QUIM, QUIN
--See also Burke, Charles.
Rip Van Winkle
Robin Hood and the friar.
15th cent. ADA, CHI, PAR,
SCW
Robin Hood and the knight.
15th cent. CHI
Robin Hood and the potter.
15th cent. CHI
Robin Hood and the sheriff of
Nottingham. 15th cent.
ADA
The sacrifice of Isaac. See
Abraham and Isaac; Abra-
ham, Melchisedec and Isaac
St. George and the dragon.
19th cent. EVER, SCW
St. George plays. See Leices-
tershire St. George play;
The Oxfordshire St. George
play; The play of St.
George, version recon-
structed from memory by
Thomas Hardy; St. George
and the dragon
Saint John the evangelist. See
John the evangelist
Saint Nicholas and the three
scholars. 12th cent. MAK
Variant title: Tres clerici
Saint Nicholas plays. See The
miracle of Saint Nicholas
and the school-boys; The
miracle of Saint Nicholas

24

and the virgins; Saint Nicholas and the three scholars.
The salutation and conception (Coventry). 15th cent. ADA, POLL
Le savetier calbain. 1500? BRN
The sourge of Simony. See The return from Parnassus
The second part of the return from Parnassus. See The return from Parnassus; or, The scourge of Simony
The second play of the shepherds. See The second herd's play
The second shepherd's pageant. See The second shepherd's play
The second shepherd's play (Wakefield). 14th cent. ABRB1, ADA, BARD, BENY, CAWL, CAWM, CHI, CLF1, CLK1, CLKW, COL1, DAV1, EVE, EVER, GARZB, HARW, HEIL, HOPP, HUD, KRE, LIE, LIED1, LIEE1, LOOM, MAK, MAT, PAR, POLL, RUB, SCW, SHAJ1, STA, SPF1, TAT, TAU, TAV, TOBI, TREC1, TREE1, WOO1, WOOD1, WOOE1
Variant titles: The nativity; The second play of the shepherds; The second shepherd's pageant; Secunda pastorum; The shepherds; A Wakefield nativity; The Wakefield second nativity play
Secunda pastorum. See The second shepherd's play
The shepherds. See The second shepherd's play
The shepherds' play (Coventry). 15th cent. EVE, PARR
Shetland sword dance. 18th cent. ADA, PAR
Simon the leper (Chester). 15th cent. CHES
Sir John Oldcastle, pt. I.

(sometimes attributed to Michael Drayton; Richard Hathway; Anthony Munday; Robert Wilson). 1598? BRO
Variant title: The true and honorable historie of the life of Sir John Oldcastle, the good Lord Cobham
Sir Thomas More (An ill Mayday) (sometimes attributed to Anthony Munday). 1590? BRO, SCH, SCI, SCJ
The slaughter of the innocents. See The magi, Herod, and the slaughter of the innocents
The slaying of the innocents (Chester). 15th cent. CHES
The sorrows of Han
Anon, tr. EDAD
Davis, J., tr. ORI4, TAV
The Spanish play. See The wisemen
The star (Bilsen play). 11th cent.
Robinson, D., tr. and adapter. ROBM
The summoning of Everyman. See Everyman
Ta'ziya. See The martyrdom of Ali
Thersites. 1537? FARO, POLL
Thomas, Lord Cromwell. 1592? BRO
Variant titles: The life and death of Lord Cromwell; The true chronical history of the whole life and death of Thomas Lord Cromwell
The three cuckolds. 16th cent.
Katz, L., adapter. BENR1
Variant title: Li tre becchi
The three kings' play (Oberufer). 16th cent. HARW
The three Maries. 15th cent. EVER
Variant title: The Cornish mystery play of the three Maries
Tom Tyler and his wife. 1550? FARP

25

Totentanz. (tr. by Margaret Trinklein from the German text of Martin F. Schloss). 15th cent.   SWIT
Variant title: The dance of death
The Towneley play. 15th cent. Burrell, R., adapter.
                                                ROBM
Tres clerici. See Saint Nicholas and the three scholars
The trial of Christ (Coventry). 15th cent.   ADA
Trial of treasure. 1565? FAR
The true and honorable historie of the life of Sir John Oldcastle, the good Lord Cobham. See Sir John Oldcastle, pt. I
The true chronicle history of the whole life and death of Thomas Lord Cromwell. See Thomas, Lord Cromwell
The two noble kinsmen. See Fletcher, J., and Shakespeare, W.
The Umbrian play. 14th cent. Robinson, D., tr. and adapter.   ROBM
Wakefield plays. See The annunciation; The betrayal; Coliphizacio; The crucifixion; The deluge; The harrowing of hell; Herod the great; The killing of Abel; Magnus Herodes; Noah; Pharaoh; Processus noe cum fillis; The resurrection of Christ; The second shepherd's play
The Wakefield second nativity play. See The second shepherd's play
Wealth and health. 1557?
                                                FARN
Variant title: An interlude of wealth and health
The wept of the wish-ton-wish (based on the novel by James Fenimore Cooper.) 1834   BAT19
The Widow of Watling Street. See The puritan

The wise virgins and the foolish virgins. 1150? Hughes, B., and G., trs.
                                                CLF1
The wisemen (The Spanish play). 12th cent. Robinson, D., tr. and adapter.   ROBM
Wit and science. See The marriage of wit and science; Redford, John. The play of wit and science
Wit and wisdom. See The contract of marriage between wit and wisdom
The woman taken in adultery. 15th cent.   CAWL
The world and the child. 1522?   FARO
Variant title: Mundus et infans
Wyt and science. See The marriage of wit and science; Redford, John. The play of wit and science
The York crucifixion. See The crucifixion (York)
The York nativity. 15th cent. Baird, J., tr.   LEV, LEVE, MAK
Variant title: The nativity
York plays. See The birth of Jesus; The creation and the fall of Lucifer; The creation of Adam and Eve; The crucifixion; The fall of man; The judgment day; The York nativity; Resurrection
A Yorkshire tragedy (sometimes attributed to William Shakespeare). 1605? BRO, OLH, OLI1, RUB
Variant title: All's one, or one of the foure plaies in one, called a York-Shire tragedy
Youth. 1555?   FARP
Variant title: The interlude of youth

ANOUILH, JEAN, 1907-
L'alouette. See The lark
Antigone. 1944.   GRAF

Galantière, L., tr. and
adapter.   BES45, BLOC,
MCNA, SSSU, ULAN, WATE,
WISF
Variant titles: Antigone and
the tyrant; Antigone et le
tyrant
Antigone and the tyrant. See
Antigone
Antigone et le tyrant. See Antigone
Ardèle. 1950.
   Hill, L., tr.   COTK
   Variant titles: Ardèle; ou,
   la Margucrite; The cry of
   the peacock
Ardèle; ou, la Marguerite.
   See Ardèle
Le bal des voleurs. See
   Thicvcs' carnival
Becket; or, The honor of God.
1959.
   Hill, L., tr. BES60, CUBH
   Variant title: Becket; ou,
   L'honneur de Dieu
Becket; ou, L'honneur de Dieu.
   See Becket; or, The honor
   of God
Cecile; or, The school for
   fathers. 1953.
   Klein, L., and A., trs. BENS3
   Variant title: Cécile; ou L'é-
   cole dc pères
Cécile; ou, L'école des pères.
   See Cecile; or, The school
   for fathers
The cry of the peacock. See
   Ardèle
The ermine. 1932.
   John, M., tr.   PLAN13
   Variant title: L'hermine
L'hermine. See The ermine
The lark. 1955.
   Fry, C., tr.   BERM
   Hellman, L., adapter.
   BES55, GARZH, THEA56
   Variant title: L'alouette
Léocadia. See Time remembered
Medea. 1948.
   Klein, L., and A., trs. BENT5
   Small, L., tr.   PLAN15
   Variant title: Médéé
Médéé. See Medea
Thieves' carnival. 1932.

Hill, L., tr. BENT3,
BLOC
Variant title: Le bal des
voleurs
Time remembered. 1954.
   Moyes, P., tr. and
   adapter   BES57
   Variant title: Léocadia
La valse de toréadors. See
   The waltz of the toreadors
Le voyageur sans bagage.
1937?   ROET
The waltz of the toreadors.
1952.
   Hill, L., tr. and adapter.
   BES56, PLAN8
   Variant title: La valse de
   toréadors

ANSKY, S. A., pseud. See Rappoport, Solomon

ANSPACHER, LOUIS KAUFMAN,
1878-1947
   The unchastened woman. 1915.
   BAK, BES09, DIG

ANTHONY, C. L., pseud. See
Smith, Dorothy Gladys

ANZENGRUBER, LUDWIG, 1839-
1889
   The farmer forsworn. 1872.
   Busse, A., tr.   FRA16
   Variant title: Meineidbauer
   The fourth commandment. See
   Das vierte gebot
Meineidbauer. See The farmer
   forsworn
Das vierte gebot. 1877. CAM
   Variant title: The fourth
   commandment

ARBUZOV, ALEXEI
   It happened in Irkutsk. 1959?
   Prokofieva, R., tr.   THY

ARCE, GASPAR NUÑEZ DE. See
Núñez de Arce, Gaspar

ARCHER, WILLIAM, 1856-1924
   The green goddess. 1921.
   BES20, CAR, CEU, LAW,

LOV

ARCHIBALD, WILLIAM, 1919-
The innocents (based on the
novel The turn of the screw
by Henry James). 1950.
BES49
ARDEN, JANE
The party. 1958.   PLAN18

ARDEN, JOHN
Live like pigs. 1958. NEWE3

-- and D'ARCY, MARGRETTA
The happy haven. 1960.
NEWE4
ARDEN, THOMAS, d. 1551
Arden of Feversham (some-
times attributed to). See
Anonymous plays. Arden of
Feversham

ARDREY, ROBERT, 1908-
The murderers. See Stone and
star
Shadow of heroes. See Stone and
star
Stone and star. 1958. BES61
Variant titles: The mur-
derers; Shadow of heroes
Thunder rock, 1939.   FIR

ARENT, ARTHUR
One-third of a nation (edited
by). 1938. FEE, NAGE
Power, a living newspaper.
1937.   FEF

ARIOSTO, LUDOVICO, 1474-1544
I suppositi. See
Gascoigne, George. Sup-
poses (adapted from)
ARISTOPHANES, 446?-385? B. C.
The Acharnians. 425 B. C.
Anon. tr.   OAT2
Casson, L., tr.   CASU
Frere, J., tr.   KRE
Rogers, B., tr. GRDB5
Aves. See The birds
The birds. 414 B. C.
Anon. tr.   FIFV, OAT2
Fitts, D., tr. FEFL, FIFR
Frere, J., tr. CROV, HOUS

MacGregor, M., tr. CLKW
Rogers, B., tr. FEFT,
GRDB5
Variant title: Aves
The clouds. 423 B. C.
Anon. tr. BAT2, MURP,
OAT2, PLAG
Cumberland, R., tr. HOWE,
HOWF
Hickie, W., tr.   GREE
Lucas, F., tr.   LUCA
Mitchell, T., tr.   CLF1
Rogers, B., tr. BARB,
FEFT, GRDB5, MIK7,
ROBJ, WARN1
Variant title: Nubes
The council of women. See The
ecclesiazusae
The ecclesiazusae. 392 B. C.
Anon. tr. BAT21, OAT2
Rogers, B., tr.   GRDB5
Variant title: The council
of women
Equites. See The knights
The frogs. 405 B. C.
Anon. tr.   PLAG
Frere, J., tr. BUCK,
BUCL, BUCM, HIB, HIBA,
HIBB, LAP, MAU, SEBO,
SEBP, SMR, TAV, TEN,
THOM, THON
Hawthorne, J., tr. MCKK1
Murray, G., tr. HOWF,
OAT2, OATH
Rogers, B., tr. FEFT,
GRDB5, HARC8, ROB,
ROBJ, TREC1, TREE1
Variant title: Ranae
The god of riches. See Plutus
The knights. 424 B. C.
Anon. tr.   OAT2
Frere, J., tr. DRA1,
PLAB1
Rogers, B., tr.   GRDB5
Variant title: Equites
Lysistrata. 411 B. C.
Anon. tr. OAT2, PLAG,
WORP
Murphy, C., tr. LIND,
LOCM1, OATE, ROBI
Rogers, B., tr.   GRDB5
Seldes, G., tr. TRE,
TREA2

28

Smolin, D., tr. and
adapter.   PLAM
Nubes. See The clouds
Pax. See Peace
Peace.   421 B. C.
   Anon. tr.   OAT2
   Rogers, B., tr.   GRDB5
   Variant title: Pax
Plutus, the god of riches.
   388 B. C.
   Anon. tr.   OAT2
   Hickie, W., tr.   GREE
   Rogers, B., tr.   GRDB5
   Sandford, D., tr.   TEN
   Variant title: Wealth
Ranae. See the frogs
Thesmophoriazusae. 411 B. C.
   Anon. tr.   OAT2
   Rogers, B., tr.   GRDB5
   Variant title: The women
   celebrating the Thesmophor-
   ia
Vespae. See The wasps
The wasps. 422 B. C.
   Anon. tr.   OAT2
   Rogers, B., tr.   GRDB5
   Variant title: Vespae
Wealth. See Plutus
The women celebrating the
   Thesmophoria. See Thes-
   mophoriazusae

ARLEN, MICHAEL, 1895-1956
   The green hat. 1925.   BES25

ARMSTRONG, ANTHONY, pseud.
See Willis, Anthony Armstrong

ARNOLD, MATTHEW (1822-1888)
   Empedocles on Etna. 1852.
                          PRAT2
   The strayed reveler. 1849.
                          PRAT2
ASHBERY, JOHN
   The heroes. 1953.   MACH

ASHTON, WINIFRED (CLEMENCE
DANE, pseud.)
   A bill of divorcement. 1921.
      BES21, COT, MAP, MOSO
   Granite. 1926. MYB, TUCD
   Moonlight is silver. 1934
                            SEV

Wild Decembers. 1932. SIXH

ATHAS, DAPHNE SPENCER.
See Campbell, Marion
   Gurney, jt. auth.

ATLAS, LEOPOLD LAWRENCE,
1907-
   "L." 1928.   LEV, LEVE
   Wednesday's child. 1934.
                          BES33
ATTOWELL, GEORGE, fl. 1599
   Attowell's jig (sometimes at
   tributed to). See Anony-
   mous plays. Attowell's jig

AUBIGNY, D', pseud. See Bau
douin, Jean Marie Théodore

AUDEN, WYSTAN HUGH, 1907
and ISHERWOOD, CHRIST-
OPHER
   The ascent of F6. 1937.
                           TUCN
   The dog beneath the skin.
   1935.   KOZ, KRE

AUGIER, ÉMILE, 1820-1889
   Le mariage d'Olympe. 1855.
                             BOR
      Clark, B., tr.   SSTG
      Variant title: Olympe's
      marriage
   Olympe's marriage. See Le
      mariage d'Olympe

--and SANDEAU, JULES
   Le gendre de M. Poirier.
   1854. BOR, GRA, SEA
      Clark, B., tr. CLF2, MAU
      Variant titles: M. Poirier's
      son-in-law; The son-in-law
      of M. Poirier
   M. Poirier's son-in-law. See
      Le gendre de M. Poirier
   The son-in-law of M. Poirier.
      See Le gendre de M.
      Poirier

AURTHUR, ROBERT ALAN
   A very special baby. 1956.
                          BES56
AUSTEN, JANE, 1775-1817

Pride and prejudice. See
Jerome, Mrs. Helen (Bur-
ton).
Pride and prejudice (based
on the novel by)

AXELROD, GEORGE, 1923-
The seven year itch. 1952.
GART, NEWV, THEA53

AYALA, ADELARDO LÓPEZ DE.
See López de Ayala, Adelardo

AYMÉ, MARCEL, 1902-
Clérambard. 1950.
Denny, N., tr.   FOUF

B

BABO, JOSEPH MARIUS, 1756-
1822
Dagobert, der franken König.
See Dagobert, king of the
Franks
Dagobert, king of the Franks.
1779.
Thompson, B., tr. BAT12
Variant title: Dagobert,
der franken König

BACKER, WILLIAM A.
The snow goose. See Gallico,
Paul. The snow goose
(adapted by)

BACON, FRANK, 1864-1922.
See Smith, Winchell, jt. auth.

BAGNOLD, ENID
The chalk garden. 1955.
BES55, THEA56
National velvet. 1946. EMB2

BAHR, HERMANN, 1863-1934
The concert. 1909.
Morgan, B., tr.   DID
Variant title: Das konzert
Das konzert. See The Concert

BAKER, ELIZABETH, 1879-
Chains. 1909. DIG, PLAP1

BALDERSTON, JOHN LLOYD,
1889-1954
Berkeley square. 1926.
BES29, GASB
BALE, JOHN, 1495-1563
God's promises. 1538? EVER
Variant title: A tragedy or
interlude manifesting the
chief promises of God unto
man
King John. 1539?   POLL
Variant title: Kynge Johan
Kynge Johan. See King John
A tragedy or interlude mani-
festing the chief promises
of God unto man. See
God's promises

BALZAC, HONORÉ DE, 1799-
1850
Mercadet. 1851.   BOR

BARBA, PRESTON ALBERT,
1883-
An der lumpa parti. 1933.
BUFF
Die verrechelte rechler
(adapted from the novel by
Charles C. More) 1933.
BUFF
BARCA, PEDRO CALDERÓN DE
LA. See Calderón de la Barca,
Pedro

BARING, MAURICE, 1874-1945
The rehearsal. 1911?   WEB

BARKENTIN, MARJORIE
Ulysses in Nighttown (adapted
from the novel Ulysses by
James Joyce). 1958. COTK

BARKER, HARLEY GRANVILLE.
See Granville-Barker, Harley
Granville

BARKER, JAMES NELSON, 1784-
1858
The Indian princess; or, La
belle sauvage. 1808.
MOSS1
Superstition. 1824. HAL,
QUIJ, QUIK, QUIL, QUIM,

30

BARNARD, CHARLES, 1838-
1920. See De Mille, Henry
Churchill, jt. auth.

BARRIE, SIR JAMES MATTHEW,
1860-1937
The admirable Crichton. 1903.
CHAR, CLKW, COTH, DUR,
REDM, SPER, TREC2,
TREE3, WARI
Dear Brutus. 1917. BROW,
WATF2, WATI
The little minister. 1897.
BES94
Mary Rose. 1920. BES20
The old lady shows her
medals. 1921. INGG, INGH
Shall we join the ladies?
1928. WORL4
The twelve pound look. 1910.
BOGO, CONP, DAVI,
MCNA, WEAT2
A well-remembered voice.
1918. FULT
What every woman knows. 1908.
CEU, WATF1, WATI, WATO
The will. 1914. MILL

BARRY, PHILIP, 1896-1949
The animal kingdom. 1932.
BES31, GAS
Foolish notion. 1945. BES44
God bless our home. See The
youngest
Here come the clowns. 1938.
BES38, GARU
Holiday. 1928. BES28, KEY,
MACG, MERW, MOSK,
MOSL
Hotel Universe. 1930. LEV,
LEVE, THF, WATC2,
WATI, WHI
In a garden. 1925. TUCD,
TUCM
The joyous season. 1934.
CATH, DAVI
Paris bound. 1927. BES27,
GASB, QUIL, QUIM, QUIN
Variant title: The wedding
The Philadelphia story. 1939.
BES38, BROU, GARZ,
WAIT, WAIU

Second threshold (revised by
Robert E. Sherwood). 1951.
BES50
Tomorrow and tomorrow.
1931. BES30
The wedding. See Paris bound
You and I. 1923. BES22, HAL
The youngest. 1924. BES24
Variant title: God bless our
home

BASSHE, EMANUEL JO, 1900-
1939
Doomsday circus. See The
dream of the dollar
The dream of the dollar. 1933.
AME5
Variant title: Doomsday
circus

BATEMAN, MRS. SIDNEY
FRANCES (COWELL), 1823-1881
Self. 1857. MOSS2

BATES, ESTHER WILLARD,
1884-
The two thieves. 1925? FED2

BAUDOIN, JEAN MARIE THEO-
DORE (D'AUBIGNY, pseud). See
Caigniez, Louis Charles, jt.
auth.

BAUM, VICKI, 1888-
Grand Hotel. 1930.
Drake, W., tr. BES30,
CEW
Variant title: Menschen im
hotel
Menschen im hotel. See
Grand hotel

BAUS, MANUEL TAMAYO Y.
See Tamayo y Baus, Manuel

BAX, CLIFFORD, 1886-
The rose without a thorn.
1932. FAMB, PLAD
Socrates. 1929. SIXD
The Venetian. 1930. MYB

BAYARD, J. F. A. See Scribe,

31

Augustin Eugène, jt. auth.

BAYÓN HERRERA, LUIS
Santos Vega. 1913.
Fassett, J., tr.   BIES

BEACH, LEWIS, 1891-
The clod. 1914.   GASB
The goose hangs high. 1924.
   BES23, KEY

BEAUMARCHAIS, PIERRE AU-
GUSTIN CARON DE, 1732-1799
The barber of Seville. See
Le barbier de Seville
Le barbier de Seville; ou, La
précaution inutile. 1775.
BOV, BOVE, BRN, STJ1,
ZDA
Bermel, A., tr.   BERM
Fowlie, W., tr.   FOWL
Myrick, A., tr.   MAU
Taylor, W., tr.   CLF2
Variant title: The barber of
Seville
Figarós marriage; or, One
mad day. See Le mariage
de Figaro
Le mariage de Figaro. 1784.
BRE, SEA
Barzun, J., tr.   BENR4
Variant titles: Figarós mar-
riage; or, One mad day;
The marriage of Figaro
The marriage of Figaro. See
Le mariage de Figaro

BEAUMONT, FRANCIS, 1584-
1616, and FLETCHER, JOHN
A king or no king. 1611.
WALL
The knight of the burning
pestle. 1610. ANG, BALD,
BAS, BAT14, BENY, BROC,
HOW, NEI, OLH, OLI2,
SCI, SCJ, SPE, WHE
The maid's tragedy. 1611.
BAS, BROC, CLF1, CLKW,
DUN, MCK, NEI, OLH,
OLI2, RUB, SCH, SCI,
SCJ, SPE
Philaster; or, Love lies a-
bleeding. 1609. BAS, BROC,

HARC47, HOW, HUD, LIE,
MAT, NEI, OLH, OLI2,
PAR, SCH, SCI, SCJ, SPE,
TAT, TAU, THA, WAT,
WHE
--See Fletcher, John, jt. auth.

BECKETT, SAMUEL, 1906-
En attendant Godot. See
Waiting for Godot
Endgame. 1957.
Beckett, S., tr.   BLOC
Variant title: Fin de partie
Fin de partie. See Endgame
Waiting for Godot. 1952.
BES 55
Beckett, S., tr.   SEVD
Variant title: En attendant
Godot

BECQUE, HENRI, 1837-1899
Les corbeaux. 1882. BOR,
GRA, SEA, STJ2
Tilden, F., tr. MOSQ,
TREC2, TREE2, WATL1
Variant titles: The crows;
The ravens; The vultures
The crows. See Les corbeaux
La Parisienne. 1882.
Barzun, J., tr. BENS1,
BENT1
Variant title: The woman of
Paris
The ravens. See Les corbeaux
The vultures. See Les corbeaux
The woman of Paris. See La
Parisienne

BEECHER, CLARE. See Kum-
mer, Mrs. Clare (Beecher)

BEECHER, HARRIET ELIZA-
BETH. See Stowe, Mrs. Harriet (Beecher)

BEERBOHM, MAX, 1872-
A social success. 1913.
BENT6
BEHN, MRS. APHRA (AMIS),
1640-1689
The emperor of the moon.
1687.   HUGH

32

BEHAN, BRENDAN, 1923-
  The hostage. 1958.   BES60
  The quare fellow. 1956? SEVD
BEHRMAN, SAMUEL NATHAN-
IEL, 1893-
  Amphitryon 38 (adapted from
    Amphitryon 38, by Jean
    Giraudoux). 1937. BES37,
    CEW, THH
  Biography 1932. BES32, BROU,
    CET, GARU, MIJY, WAIT,
    WARH, WHI
  Brief moment. 1931. BES31
  The cold wind and the warm.
    1958.   BES58
  End of summer. 1936. BES35,
    CLUR, GAS, WATS
  I know my love (adapted from
    Après de ma blonde by
    Marcel Achard). 1949. BES49
  Jacobowsky and the Colonel
    (adapted from the play by
    Franz Werfel). 1944. BES43,
    GARZH
  Jane (from the story by W.
    Somerset Maugham). 1952.
                        BES51
  No time for comedy. 1939.
    BES38, CER, SIXL
  Rain from heaven. 1934.
    CHAN, CHAP, THF
  The second man. 1927. CAR,
    CARA, GASB, MOSK,
    MOSL

--and LOGAN, JOSHUA
  Fanny (based on the trilogy
    Marius, Fanny and César
    by Marcel Pagnol) (music
    and lyrics by Harold
    Rome). 1954.   THEA55

BEITH, JOHN HAY, 1876-1952.
See Hay, Ian, pseud.

BELASCO, DAVID, 1859-1931
  La belle Russe. 1881. AMP18
  The girl of the golden west.
    1905. MOSJ, MOSK, MOSL
  The heart of Maryland. 1895.
    AMP18, BES94, CLA
  Naughty Anthony. 1899. AMP18
  The return of Peter Grimm.

    1911. BAK, MIL, MOSS3
  The stranglers of Paris.
    1881.   AMP18

-- and DE MILLE, HENRY
CHURCHILL
  The charity ball. 1889.
                      AMP17
  Lord Chumley. 1888. AMP17
  Men and women. 1890.
                      AMP17
  The wife. 1887.   AMP17

--and FYLES, FRANKLIN
  The girl I left behind me.
    1893.   AMP18

--and LONG, JOHN LUTHER
  The darling of the gods.
    1902.   BES99
  Madame Butterfly. 1900.
    QUIG, QUIJ, QUIK, QUIL,
    QUIM, QUIN, QUIO2

BELLOW, SAUL
  The wrecker. 1954? NEWW6

BELLVIS, GUILLEM DE CAST-
RO Y. See Castro y Bellvis.
Guillem

BENAVENTE Y MÁRTINEZ,
JACINTO, 1866-1954
  The bias of the world. See
    the bonds of interest
  The bonds of interest. 1907.
    Underhill, Jr., tr. DID,
    FLOS, MOSQ, WHI
    Variant titles: The bias of
    the world; Los intereses
    creados; Interests created;
    Vested interests
  His widow's husband. 1908?
    Underhill, J., tr. MCCP
    Variant title: El marido de
    su vinda
  Los intereses creados. See
    The bonds of interest
  Interests created. See The
    bonds of interest
  La malquerida. See The pas-
    sion flower
  El marido de su vinda. See

His widow's husband
The nest of another. See El
nido ajeno
El nido ajeno. 1895.   BRET
Variant title: The nest of
another
No fumadores. See No smok-
ing
No smoking. 1904.
Underhill, J., tr.   INGW
Variant title: No fumadores
The passion flower. 1913.
Underhill, J., tr. GARZH,
TUCG, TUCM, TUCN,
TUCO, WATI, WATL3
Variant title: La malquerida
Vested interests. See The
bonds of interest

BENEDICTO, JOAQUIN DICENTA
Y. See Dicenta y Benedicto,
Joaquin

BENEDIX, RODERICH, 1811-1873
Eigensinn. See Obstinacy
Obstinacy. 1864.
Chambers, W., tr.   BAT11
Variant title: Eigensinn

BENELLI, SEM, 1877-1949
L'amore dei tre re. See The
love of the three kings
Le cena delle beffe. See
The jest
A Florentine wager. See The
jest
A fool there was. See The
jest
The jest. 1919.
Sheldon, E., tr. and
adapter.   BES19
Variant titles: La cena
delle beffe; A Florentine
wager; A fool there was;
The jesters' supper; The
love feast; The love thief;
The supper of pranks
The jesters' supper. See The
jest
The love feast. See The jest
The love of the three kings.
1910.
Jones, H., tr.   DIE

Variant title: L'amore dei
tre re
The love thief. See The jest
The supper of pranks. See
The jest

BENGAL, BEN
Plant in the sun. 1937? KOZ

BENNETT, ARNOLD, 1867-1931
Flora. 1933.   FIT
The great adventure. 1913
CHU, COT

--and KNOBLOCK, EDWARD
Milestones. 1912. CEU, COD,
DID, MAP, MOD, PEN,
TUCJ, WAGC4

BENNETT, CLARENCE
A royal slave. 1898? AMP8

BENRIMO, JOSEPH HENRY,
1871-1942. See Hazelton, George
Cochrane, jt. auth.

BENSON, ROBERT HUGH, 1871-
1914
The upper room 191-? PRON

BENSON, MRS. SALLY, 1900-
Junior miss (based on the
book by). See Fields, Jo-
seph and Chodorov, Jerome.
Junior miss

BENTLEY, ERIC RUSSELL
Celestina; or, The tragi-
comedy of Calisto and Me-
libea. See Rojas, Fernan-
do de. Celestina; or, The
tragi-comedy of Calisto and
Melibea (adapted by)
Mary Stuart, See Schiller,
Johann. Mary Stuart
(adapted by)

BEOLCO, ANGELO (called Ruz-
zante), 1502?-1542
Bilora. 1527?
Hughes, B., and G. trs.
CLF2
Il reduce. See Ruzzante re-

34

turns from the wars
Ruzzante returns from the
wars. 1522?
Ingold, A., and Hoffman,
T., trs.   BENR1
Variant title: Il reduce

BERCOVICI, ERIC
The heart of age. 195-?
                            NEWW4
BERG, GERTRUDE, 1900-
Me and Molly. 1948.   BES47

BERGMAN, HJALMAR, 1883-
1931
Herr Sleeman kommer. See
Mr. Sleeman is coming
Mr. Sleeman is coming. 1917.
Alexander, H., tr.   SCAN1
Variant title: Herr Sleeman
kommer
The swedenhielms. 1925.
Alexander, H., and Jones,
L., trs.   SCAN3

BERKELEY, REGINALD CHEYNE,
1890-1935
The lady with a lamp. 1929.
                       FAO, PLAD
The white chateau. 1927. MAP

BERKEY, RALPH. See Denker,
Henry, jt. auth.

BERNARD, JEAN-JACQUES,
1888-
Arver's secret. See Le
secret d'Arvers
Glamour. 1924.
Boyd, E., tr.   DIK2
Katzin, W., tr.   KAT
Variant titles: L'invitation
au voyage; The years be-
tween
L'invitation au voyage. See
Glamour
Martine. 1922.   RHO
Katzin, W., tr.   KAT
Le secret d'Arvers. 1926.
                        GRAF
Variant title: Arver's
secret
The years between. See

Glamour

BERNARD, LAWRENCE J.
Lars killed his son. 1935?
                          TOD
BERNARD, PAUL, 1866-
See Bernard, Tristan, pseud.

BERNARD, TRISTAN (pseud. of
Paul Bernard), 1866-1947
L'anglais tel qu'on le parie.
1899.   SET
Variant titles: English as
it is spoken; French with-
out a master
English as it is spoken. See
L'anglais tel qu'on le parie
French without a master. See
L'anglais tel qu'on le parie

BERNEY, WILLIAM. See Richardson, Howard, jt. auth.

BERNHARD, EMIL (pseud. of
Emil Cohn), 1881-
The Marranos. 1935?
Meyer, B., and Arlet, V.,
trs.   RUA

BERNSTEIN, HENRY, 1876-
1953
Le secret, 1913.   HARV

BERNSTEIN, LEONARD, 1918-
Candide. See Hellman, Lillian. Candide (music by)
Wonderful town. See Fields,
Joseph and Chodorov, Jer-
ome. Wonderful town (mu-
sic by)

BESIER, RUDOLF, 1878-1942
The Barretts of Wimpole
Street. 1930. BES30, CEU,
FAMA, GASS, GOW, INGH,
PLAD, SPER, THO
The virgin goddess. 1906.
                          MAP
BETTI, UGO, 1892-1953
Corruption in the palace of
justice. 1949.
Reed, H., tr.   COTR
Variant title: Corruzione

al palazzo di giustizia
Corruzione al palazzo di gius-
tizia. See Corrpution in
in the palace of justice
La regina e gli insorti. See
The queen and the rebels
The queen and the rebels.
1951.
Reed, H., tr.   ULAN
Variant title: La regina e
gli insorti

BEYNON, RICHARD
The shifting heart. 1957. OBSE

BIGGERS, EARL DERR, 1884-
1933
Seven keys to Baldpate. See
Cohan, George M. Seven
keys to Baldpate (based on
the novel by)

BIRD, ROBERT MONTGOMERY,
1806-1854
The broker of Bogota. 1834.
QUIJ, QUIK, QUIL, QUIM,
QUIN
Caridorf; or, The avenger.
1827?   AMP12
The cowled lover. 1827?
                          AMP12
The gladiator. 1831.   HAL
News of the night; or, A trip
to Niagara. 1929.   AMP12
'Twas all for the best; or,
'Tis all a notion. 1827?
                          AMP12
BIRMELIN, JOHN, 1873-1950
Der gnopp (based on the play
Ein knopf by Julius Rosen).
1935.   BUFF
Em Docktor Fogel sei offis
schtunn (based on the farce
Dr. Kranichs, sprechstunde)
1935?   BUFF

BISSELL, RICHARD PIKE. See
Abbott, George, jt. auth.

BIZET, GEORGES, 1838-1875
Carmencita and the soldier
(based on the opera Car-
men). See Lipskeroff, Kon-

stantin. Carmencita and
the soldier
BJØRNSON, BJØRNSTJERNE,
1832-1910
Between the battles. 1858.
Weingarten, J., tr. MCCP
Variant title: Mellem sla-
gene
Beyond human might. See
Beyond our power
Beyond human power. See
Beyond our power
Beyond our power. 1883.
Björkman, E., tr. TUCG
Hollander, L., tr.   DIC
Variant titles: Beyond hu-
man might; Beyond human
power; Over evne; Pastor
song
A gauntlet. 1883.
Edwards, O., tr.   BAT17
Variant titles: A glove; En
hanske
A glove. See A gauntlet
En hanske. See A gauntlet
Mellem slagene. See Between
the battles
Over evne. See Beyond our
power
Pastor song. See Beyond our
power

BLADES, WILLIAM, 1824-1890
The printer's apprentice, (tr.
from Latin into German by).
See Anonymous plays. The
printer's apprentice

BLITZSTEIN, MARC, 1905-
Another part of the forest (mu-
sic by). See Hellman, Lil-
lian. Another part of the
forest
The cradle will rock. 1937.
                          KOZ
BLOCK, TONI
You must stay to tea. 1948?
                          RUA
BLOK, ALEKSANDR ALEKSAND-
ROVICH, 1880-1921
The puppet show. 1906.
Reeve, F., tr.   REEV2

36

BOCK, JERRY. Fiorello. See
Weidman, Jerome and Abbott,
George. Fiorello (music by)

BOIS-ROBERT, FRANÇOIS LE
MÉTEL DE, 1592-1662
L'amant ridicule. 1655. LAN

BOIS ROBERT, FRANÇOIS. See
Bois-Robert, François Le Métel
de

BOKER, GEORGE HENRY, 1823-
1890
    The bankrupt. 1855.   AMP3
    Francesca da Rimini. 1855.
      ELLI1, HAL, MCDO,
      MOSS3, QUIJ, QUIK, QUIL,
      QUIM, QUIN, QUIO1
    Glacus. 1886   AMP3
    The world a mask. 1851.
            AMP3
BOLAND, BRIDGET
    Cockpit. 1948.   PLAN1
    The prisoner. 1954.   PLAN10
    The return. 1953.   PLAN9

BOLITHO, WILLIAM, pseud. See
Ryall, William Bolitho

BOLT, ROBERT, 1924-
    A man for all seasons. 1960.
    BES61, COTR

BOLTON, GUY REGINALD, 1884-
    Anastasia. See Maurette, Mar-
    celle. Anastasia (adapted
    by)
    Chicken feed. 1923.   BES23
    Variant title: Wages for
    wives
    Don't listen ladies! See Guitry,
    Sacha. Don't listen ladies!
    (adapted by)
    Wages for wives. See Chicken
    feed

-- and MIDDLETON, GEORGE
    Adam and Eva. 1919.   BES19

BOOTHE, CLARE, 1903-
    Kiss the boys good-bye. 1938.
            BES38

    Margin for error. 1939.
      BES39, CER, FIR
    The women. 1936. BES36,
      CET, FAMK, GAS

BORSOOK, HENRY
    Three weddings of a hunch-
    back. 1924.   MAS1

BOTTOMLEY, GORDON, 1874-
1948
    Gruach. 1923.   KRE

BOUICICAULT, DION, 1822-
1890
    Belle Lamar. 1874. LEV,
      LEVE
    Boursiquot. See The Colleen
    Dawn
    The Colleen Bawn; or, The
    brides of Garryowen. 1860.
            ROWE
    Variant title: Boursiquot
    Dot (adapted from The cricket
    on the hearth, by Charles
    Dickens). 1859.   AMP1
    Flying scud; or, A four-
    legged fortune. 1866.
            AMP1, CLA
    Forbidden fruit. 1876. AMP1
    London assurance. 1841.
      BAT22, BENY, MAT,
      MOSN, MOSO
    Louis XI. 1855.   AMP1
    Mercy Dodd; or, Presumptive
    evidence. 1869.   AMP1
    The octoroon; or, Life in
    Louisiana. 1859.   QUIJ,
      QUIK, QUIL, QUIM, QUIN
    Rip Van Winkle (adapted by).
      See Anonymous plays.
      Rip Van Winkle (as played
      by Joseph Jefferson)
    Robert Emmet. 1884. AMP1

BOURLET, KATHERINE, 15th
cent.
    The nativity (The Chantilly
    play). 15th cent.
      Sanchez, E., and Robinson,
      D., trs. and adapters.
            ROBM

BOWEN, MARGARET ELIZA-
BETH
   Crude and unrefined. 194-?
                PROG
BOWER, RICHARD, fl. 1570
   Apius and Virginia (sometimes
   attributed to). See Anony-
   mous plays. Apius and Vir-
   ginia

BOWLES, JANE AUER, 1917-
   In the summer house. 1953.
                BES53
BOX, MURIEL, 1905-
   Angels of war. 1935?   FIN

BOX, SYDNEY, 1907-
   The woman and the walnut
   tree. 1935?   FIN

BRACCO, ROBERTO, 1862-1943
   I fantasmi. See Phantasms
   Phantasms. 1906.
      St. Cyr, D., tr.   TUCG
      Variant title: I fantasmi

BRACKENRIDGE, HUGH HENRY,
1748-1816
   The battle of Bunkers-hill.
   1776?   MOSS1

BRADDON, MARY ELIZABETH,
1837-1915
   Lady Audley's secret. See
   Hazlewood, Colin Hazlewood. Lady Audley's secret
   (from the novel by)

BRADDON, RUSSELL
   Naked island. 1960.   PLAN22

BRADFORD, ROARK, 1896-
   Ol' man Adam and his chillun.
   See Connelly, Marc. The
   green pastures (based on
   the novel by)

BRAND, MILLEN, 1906-
   The outward room. See Kingsley, Sidney. The world we
   make (based on the novel by)

BRANNER, H. C., 1903-

The judge. 1952.
    Roughton, A., tr.   CONT
    Variant title: Søskende
Søskende. See The judge

BRECHT, BERTOLT, 1898-1956
Die ausnahme und die regel.
   See The exception and the
   rule
Der gute mensch von Sezuan.
   See The good woman of
   Setzuan
Dreigroschenoper. See The
   threepenny opera
The exception and the rule.
   1930?
    Bentley, E., tr.   NEW55
    Variant title: Die ausnahme
    und die regel
Galileo. 1947.
    Laughton, C., tr. BENS2
The good woman of Setzuan.
   1943.
    Bentley, E., tr. BLOC,
    REIN, REIP
    Variant title: Der gute
    mensch von Sezuan
Die massnahme. See The
   measures taken
The measures taken. 1930.
    Bentley, E., tr.   BENT6
    Variant title: Die massnahme
Mother Courage. 1941.
    Bentley, E., tr.   BENT2,
    BLOC, KERN
    Hays, H., tr.   NEW41
    Variant titles: Mother Cour-
    age and her children; Mut-
    ter Courage und ihre kinder
Mother Courage and her chil-
   dren. See Mother Courage
Mutter Courage und ihre kin-
   der. See Mother Courage
A penny for the poor. See
   The threepenny opera
The private life of the master
   race. 1944. Bentley, E.,
    tr. TREC2, TREE2
Saint Joan of the stockyards.
   1932?
    Jones, F., tr.   BENS3
The threepenny opera (music
   by Kurt Weill) 1928.

Vesey, D., and Bentley,
E., trs.   BENS1, BENT1
Variant titles: Dreigro-
schenoper; A penny for the
poor
Das verhor des Lukullus.
1939?   FEFH2

BREEN, RICHARD, and
SCHNIBBE, HARRY
"Who ride on white horses,"
the story of Edmund Camp-
ion. 1940.   THEC

BREIT, HARVEY, 1913-   ,
See Schulberg, Budd, jt. author

BRENDLE, THOMAS ROYCE,
1889-
Di hoffning. 19- ?   BUFF
Die mutter. 1934.   BUFF

BRETON DE LOS HERREROS,
MANUEL, 1796-1873
Muérete ¡y verás!   1837.
                    BRET
BRIDGERS, ANN PRESTON. See
Abbott, George, jt. auth.

BRIEUX, EUGENE, 1858-1932
The aim of the law. See La
robe rouge
False gods. 1909.
Fagan, J., tr.   TUCG
Variant title: La foi
La foi. See False gods
The letter of the law. See
La robe rouge
The red robe. See La robe
rouge
La robe rouge. 1900.   GRA
Reed, F., tr. DIC, DIK2,
WHI
Variant titles; The aim of
the law; The letter of the
law; The red robe
The three daughters of M. Du-
pont. See Les trois filles
de M. Dupont
Les trois filles de M. Dupont.
1897.   BER, BOR
Variant title: The three
daughters of M. Dupont

BRIGHOUSE, HAROLD, 1882-
Hobson's choice. 1916.
                  MAP, TUCD
BRITTON, KENNETH PHILLIPS
and HARGRAVE, ROY
Houseparty. 1928?   LEV,
LEVE

BROME, RICHARD, d. 1652?
The antipodes. 1638. GAY3,
KNOW
A jovial crew. 1641.   OLH,
OLI2
A mad couple well matched.
1653?   KNOW, WALL

BRONTË, CHARLOTTE, 1816-
1855
Jane Eyre. See Jerome, Mrs.
Helen (Burton). Jane Eyre
(based on the novel by)

BROOKS, HARRY, 1876-
See Malleson, Miles, jt. auth.

BROUGHAM, JOHN, 1810-1880
The duke's motto; or, I am
here! 1862.   AMP14
Pocahontas; or, The gentle
savage. 1855.   BAT20

BROWN, DAVID PAUL, 1795-
1875
Sertorius; or, The Roman
patriot. 1830.   MOSS2

BROWNE, MAURICE, 1881-1955.
See Nichols, Robert Malise
Boyer, jt. auth.

BROWNE, PORTER EMERSON,
1879-1934
The bad man. 1920.   BES20

BROWNE, ROBERT F. GORE.
See Gore-Browne, Robert F.

BROWNE, WYNYARD, 1911-
The holly and the ivy. 1950.
                      PLAN3
BROWNING, ROBERT, 1812-1889
A blot in the 'scutcheon. 1843.
ASH, GRE, HARC18, MOSN,

39

MOSO, TAT
In a balcony. 1884.　　GREC2

BRUCE, RICHARD, 1905-
Sahdji, an African ballet.
1927.　　LOC

BRUNSON, BEVERLY
A bastard of the blood. 19-?
　　NEWW10
BÜCHNER, GEORG, 1813-1837
Danton's death. 1836.
　Holmstrom, J., tr.　BENT5
　Lustig, T., tr.　LUST
　Spender, S., and Rees, G.,
　trs. BENS1, TREC1,TREE1
　Variant title: Dantons tod
Dantons tod. See Danton's
　death
Leonce and Lena. 1911.
　Bentley, E., tr.　BENS3
Woyzeck. 1879
　Hoffman, T., tr.　BENT1
　Schnitzler, H., and Ulman,
　S., trs.　NEW50
　Variant title: Wozzeck
Wozzeck. See Woyzeck

BUCK, PEARL S., 1892-
Will this earth hold?　INGA

BUCKHURST, LORD. See Sackville, Thomas

BUCKINGHAM, GEORGE VIL-
LIERS, 1628-1687
The rehearsal. 1671. LEV,
　LEVE, MCM, MCMI,
　MOSE1, NET, REST, STM

BUCKSTONE, JOHN BALDWIN,
1802-1879
Luke the labourer; or, The
　lost son. 1826.　MOR

BUECHNER, GEORG. See Büchner, Georg

BULGAKOV, MIKHAIL ALFA-
NASEVICH, 1891-1940
Days of the Turbins. 1926.
　Lyons, E., tr.　LYK
　Reeve, F., tr.　REEV2

Variant title: Last of the
　Turbins
Last of the Turbins. See
　Days of the Turbins

BULKLEY, A.M.
The crown of light. 1934.
　　SEVE
BULWER-LYTTON, EDWARD
GEORGE EARLE LYTTON,
1803-1873
The lady of Lyons; or, Love
　and pride. 1838. STA,
　TAT, TAU
Money. 1840. BAT16, ROWE
Richelieu; or, The conspiracy.
　1839. CROS, DUR, MAT,
　MOSN, MOSO

BUNCE, OLIVER BELL, 1828-
1890
Love in '76. 1857.　MOSS3

BURKE, CHARLES St. THOMAS,
1822-1854
Rip Van Winkle. 1850.
　BAT19, MOSS3
　See also Anonymous plays.
　Rip Van Winkle (as played
　by Joseph Jefferson)

BURNHAM, BARBARA, 1900-
Children in uniform (tr. and
　adapted by). See Winsloe,
　Christa. Children in uni-
　form

BURROWS, ABE. See Burrows,
Abram S.

BURROWS, ABRAM S., 1910-　,
WEINSTOCK, JACK and GIL-
BERT, WILLIE
How to succeed in business
　without really trying (based
　on the book by Shepherd
　Mead) (music by Frank
　Loesser). 1961.　BES61

--See also Swerling, Jo, jt. auth.

BURTON, HELEN. See Jerome,
Mrs. Helen (Burton)

40

BUTLER, RACHEL BARTON
Mamma's affair. 1920. BES19

BYRNE, MRS. DOLLY. See
Varesi, Gilda, jt. auth.

BYRNE, MURIEL ST. CLARE.
See Sayers, Dorothy Leigh, jt.
auth.

BYRON, GEORGE GORDON,
1788-1824
  Cain. 1821.   BARG, KOH2
  Heaven and earth. 1821? KOH2
  Manfred. 1817. BERN,
    GREB2, HAPT2, HARC18,
    SML

C

CABAÑA, AGUSTÍN MORETO Y.
See Moreto y Cavaña, Agustín

CAIGNIEZ, LOUIS CHARLES,
1762-1842, and BAUDOUIN,
JEAN MARIE THÉODORE (d'
Aubigny, pseud.)
  La pie voleuse; ou, La ser-
    vante de Palaiseau. See
    Payne, John Howard. Trial
    without jury (adapted from)

CALDERÓN DE LA BARCA,
PEDRO, 1600-1681
  Amar después de la muerte.
    See Love after death
  Belshazzar's feast. 1632.
    MacCarthy, D., tr. BAT4
    Variant title: La cena de
    Baltasar
  La cena de Baltasar.   See
    Belshazzar's feast
  The constant prince. 1629?
    MacCarthy, D., tr. CLF2,
    STA
    Variant title: El principe
    constante
  El gran teatro del mundo.
    See The great theater of the
    world
  Elvira. See No siempre lo
    peor es cierto

The great theater of the
  world. 1642.
  Singleton, M., tr. FLOR
  Variant title: El gran tea-
  tro del mundo
Guárdate del agua mansa.
  See Keep your own secret
Keep your own secret. 1649.
  Fitzgerald, E., tr. ROB
  Variant title: Guárdate del
  agua mansa
Life a dream. See La vida es
  sueño
Life is a dream. See La vida
  es sueño
Love after death. 1651?
  Campbell, R., tr. BENR3
  Variant title: Amar después
  de la muerte
El magico prodigioso. See
  The wonder-working magi-
  cian
No siempre lo peor es cierto.
  1648?   HILL
  Variant titles: Elvira; The
  worst not always true
El postrer duelo de España.
  See Payne, John Howard.
  The last duel in Spain
  (adapted from)
El principe constante. See
  The constant prince
Such stuff as dreams are
  made of. See La vida es
  sueño
La vida es sueño. 1635. ALP
  Campbell, R., tr. BENR3
  Fitzgerald, E., tr. DRA1,
  HARC26, PLAB1
  Huberman, E., and E.,
  trs.   FLOS
  MacCarthy, D., tr. MAU,
  TAV
  Variant titles: Life a
  dream; Life is a dream;
  Such stuff as dreams are
  made of
The wonder-working magician.
  1637?
  Shelley, P., tr.   BENR3
  Variant title: El magico
  prodigioso
The worst not always true.

See No siempre lo peor es cierto

CALDWELL, ERSKINE, 1903-
See Kirkland, Jack, jt. auth.

CAMPBELL, BARTLEY, 1843-1888
   Fairfax. 1879.   AMP19
   The galley slave. 1879.
                   AMP19
   My partner. 1879.   AMP19
     CLA
   The Virginian. 1873. AMP19
   The white slave. 1882.
                   AMP19
CAMPBELL, MARION GURNEY and ATHAS, DAPHNE SPENCER
   Sit on the earth. 19-? OBSE

CAMPBELL, WILLIAM EDWARD MARCH. See March, William (pseud.)

CAMPISTRON, JEAN GALBERT DE, 1656-1723
   Andronic. See Andronicus
   Andronicus. 1685.
     Lockert, L., tr.   LOCR
     Variant title: Andronic

CAMUS, ALBERT, 1913-1960
   Caligula. 1945.
     Gilbert, S., tr.   BLOC
     O'Brien, J., tr. and
     adapter   BES59
   Le malentendu. 1944. PUCC

ČAPEK, JOSEF, 1887-1927.
See Čapek, Karel, jt. auth.

ČAPEK, KAREL, 1890-1939
   R.U.R. (Rossum's universal robots). 1923.
     Anon. tr.   BROU, STAU
     Selver, P., tr. BES22,
     BROF, BROG, BRR3,
     CALN1, COTH, DIE, DIK1,
     HAV, HAVD, HAVE, HORN
     HUDT, MCD, NAGE, PROX
     TUCG, TUCM, TUCN,
     TUCO, WATI, WATL4,
     WATO

Selver, P., and Playfair, N., trs. CEW, CONG, TREC2, TREE2
--and ČAPEK, JOSEF
   Adam stvoritel. See Adam the creator
   Adam the creator. 1927.
     Round, D., tr. MOSG, MOSH
     Variant title: Adam stvoritel
   And so ad infinitum. 1921.
     Davis, O., tr. and adapter.
                  GARZH
     Selver, P., tr. CHA, CHAN,
     CLKW, INTE
     Variant titles: The insect comedy; The insect play; The life of the insects; The world we live in; Ze zivota honyzu
   The insect comedy. See And so ad infinitum
   The insect play. See And so ad infinitum
   The life of the insects. See And so ad infinitum
   The world we live in. See And so ad infinitum
   Ze zivota honyzu. See And so ad infinitum

CAPOTE, TRUMAN, 1924-
   The grass harp. 1952. WISF

CARRETTE, LOUIS, 1913-
See Marceau, Félicien, pseud.

CARROLL, PAUL VINCENT, 1900-
   Shadow and substance. 1937.
     BES37, CALM, CEW, DUR, FIG, MOSH
   The strings, my Lord, are false. 1943?   NEWR1
   The white steed. 1939. BES38

CARY, FALKLAND L., 1897-
See King, Philip, jt. auth.

CASALIS, JEANNE DE. See De Casalis, Jeanne

CASELLA, ALBERTO, 1891-
   Death takes a holiday. 1929.

42

Ferris, W., tr. and adapter. BES29
Variant title: La morte in vacanze
La morte in vacanze. See Death takes a holiday.

CASIÑO, JESUS. See Sicam, Geronimo D., jt. auth.

CASTRO Y BELLVIS, GUILLEM DE, 1569-1631
Exploits of the Cid. See Las mocedades del Cid
Las mocedades del Cid. 1621. ALP
Anon. tr. BENR4
Variant title: Exploits of the Cid; The youthful adventures of El Cid.
The youthful adventures of El Cid. See Las mocedades del Cid

CAVAN, ROMILLY
All my own work. 1958. OBSE
CAVAÑA, AGUSTÍN MORETO Y. See Moreto y Cavaña, Agustín

CAVERHILL, ALAN, 1910-
See Melville, Alan, pseud.

CAYZER, CHARLES WILLIAM, 1869-
David and Bathshua. 1911? KOH2
CERVANTES SAAVEDRA, MIGUEL DE, 1547-1616
The cave of Salamanca. 1615? Jagendorf, M., tr. CLF2
Variant title: La cueva de Salamanca.
La cueva de Salamanca. See The cave of Salamanca
La guarda cuidadosa. See The vigilant sentinel
La Numance. See La Numancia
La Numancia. 1585. ALP
Campbell, R., tr. BENR3
Variant titles: La Numance; The siege of Numantia

The siege of Numantia. See La Numancia
The vigilant sentinel. 158-?
Flores, A., and Liss, J., trs. FLOS
Variant title: La guarda cuidadosa

CHANDEZON, LÉOPOLD (Léopold, pseud.) and CUVELIER DE TRYE, JEAN GUILLAUME ANTOINE
Mazeppa; ou, Le cheval Tartare. See Payne, John Howard. Mazeppa; or, The wild horse of Tartary (adapted from)

CHAPIN, HAROLD, 1886-1915
Augustus in search of a father. 1910. WEB
The new morality. 1920. MAP

CHAPMAN, GEORGE, 1559?-1634
Bussy D'Ambois. 1604. BAS, BROC, HAPR, MCK, NEI, RYL, SPE
The revenge of Bussy D'Ambois. 1610? WALL

--JONSON, BEN, and MARSTON, JOHN
Eastward ho! 1605. BROC, GAY2, OL11, RUB, SCH, SCI, SCJ, SPE, WALL
Variant title: Eastward hoe
Eastward hoe. See Eastward ho!

CHAPMAN, ROBERT HARRIS. See Coxe, Louis O., jt. auth.

CHASE, MARY COYLE, 1912-
Bernardine. 1952. BES52, THEA 53
Harvey. 1944. BES44, GARU, MIJY
Mr. Thing. See Mrs. McThing
Mrs. McThing. 1952. BES51
Variant title: Mr. Thing

43

CHAUSSÉE, PIERRE CLAUDE
NIVELLE DE LA. See La
Chaussée, Pierre Claude Nivelle
de

CHAYEFSKY, PADDY, 1923-
The dybbuk from Woodhaven.
See The tenth man
Gideon. 1961.   BES61
Marty. 1953? BLAH, BLOC,
MCNA
The tenth man. 1959. BES59,
CEQ, CES
Variant title: The dybbuk
from Woodhaven

CHEKHOV, ANTON PAVLOVICH,
1860-1904
The anniversary. See The
jubilee
The bear. See The boor
The boor. 1888.
Banknage, H., tr. KNIC,
KNID
Clark, B., and Banknage,
H., trs.   HUD
Variant title: The bear
The cherry orchard. 1904.
Anon. tr. BARR, EDAD,
SILM, WORP
Calderon, G., tr. DIC,
HAV, HAVD, MOSG, MOSH,
SSST, THOM, THON,
TUCG, TUCM, TUCN,
TUCO
Covan, J., tr. CAR, CARA,
DEAP, DEAR, MOS,
SCNN, WHI
Daniels, C., and Noyes,
G., trs.   NOY
Garnett, C., tr. ALLI,
CUBE, CUBG, DIK1,
HOUG, KERN, ROET, TRE,
TREA1, TREC2, TREE2,
WHK
Skariatina, I., tr. HIBB,
WEAV2
West, J., tr. STE, WATI,
WATL4, WATR
Yarmolinsky, A., tr.
BLAH, CUBH
Young, S., tr.   BLOC
--See also Logan, Joshua.

The Wisteria trees (adapted
from)
The harmful effects of smok-
ing. See Gassner, John.
Then and now (adapted
from)
Ivanoff. 1887.
Fell, M., tr.   MOSA
Winer, E., tr.   ULAN
The jubilee. 1903.
Roberts, C., tr.   ROE
Variant title: The anniver-
sary
A marriage proposal. 1889.
Chambers, W., tr.   BAT18
Hoffman, T., tr.   ROSS
Variant title: The proposal
--See also Gassner, John.
Then and now (adapted from)
The proposal. See A marriage
proposal
The sea-gull. 1896.
Calderon, G., tr.   MOSQ
Fell, M., tr.   WATL3
Garnett, C., tr. BROK,
CEW, CLKW
Reeve, F., tr.   REEV2
Young, S., tr. BLOC,
DOWN, GARZH, GRIF,
WALJ
The swan song. 1888.
Fell, M., tr. BLAG, BLAH,
The three sisters. 1901.
Covan, J., tr.   MOS
Fen, E., tr. HOGA, REIN,
REIP, SIXB
Garnett, C., tr.   BLOO,
LEG
Guerney, B., tr.   GUE
MacAndrew, A., tr. GARZB
Uncle Vanya. 1897.
Covan, J., tr.   MOS
Fell, M., tr. BARB, HARB,
MIL, WATA, WATI, WATL2
Magarshack, D., tr. MAGA
Young, S., tr.   CLM
Variant title: The wood
demon
The wedding. 1890.
Bentley, E., tr.   FEFL
Roberts, C., tr.   ROE
The wood demon. See Uncle
Vanya

44

CHEN-CHIN HSIUNG. See Hsiung, Cheng-chin

CHETHAM-STRODE, WARREN, 1897-
    Background. 1950.   PLAN4
    Sometimes even now. 1933.
                    FAMD
CHIARELLI, LUIGI, 1884-1947
    La maschera ed il volto. See
        The mask and the face
    The mask and the face. 1916.
        Vic Beamish, N., tr.
                    INTE
        Variant title: La maschera
        ed il volto

CHIKAMATSU (SUGIMORI NOBU-MORI), 1653-1724
    Fair ladies at a game of po-em-cards. 1705.
        Miyamora, A, and Nichols,
        R., trs.   CLF1

CHLUMBERG, HANS, 1897-1930
    The miracle at Verdun. 1931.
        Crankshaw, E., tr. FAMC
        Leigh, J., tr. CHA, CHAN
        Variant title: Wunder um
        Verdun
    Wunder um Verdun. See The
        miracle at Verdun

CHODOROV, EDWARD, 1904-
    Decision. 1944.   BES43
    Kind lady (adapted from a
        story by Hugh Walpole).
        1935.   CART, FREE
    Oh, men! oh, women! 1953.
                THEA54
CHODOROV, JEROME, 1911- .
See Fields, Joseph, jt. auth.

CHRISTIE, AGATHA (MILLER) 1891-
    Witness for the prosecution.
        1953. BES54, FAMO,
                THEA55
CHRISTIE, CAMPBELL, 1893-
See Christie, Dorothy, jt. auth.

CHRISTIE, DOROTHY, 1896- .
and CHRISTIE, CAMPBELL

Carrington, V. C. 1953. FAMO
His excellency. 1950. PLAN4

CHURCH, MRS. VIRGINIA WOOD-SON (FRAME), 1880-
    What men live by. 1924?
        CHU, LAW, SRYG

CIBBER, COLLEY, 1671-1757
    The careless husband. 1704.
             MOSE1, NET
    Hob; or, The country wake
        (sometimes attributed to).
        See Dogget, Thomas. Hob;
        or, The country wake
    Love's last shift: or, The
        fool in fashion. 1695?
        MCM, MCMI, TUQ
    The provoked husband; or, A
        journey to London (from an
        unfinished play by John
        Vanbrugh). 1727? BAT15,
    TICK

CIBBER, THEOPHILUS, 1703-1758. See Jevons, Thomas, jt. auth.

CLARK, MRS. MABEL MARGA-RET (COWIE). See Storm, Les-ley, pseud.

CLARKE, WILLIAM KENDALL
    The ghost patrol (based on a
        story by Sinclair Lewis).
        195- ?   INGB

CLAUDEL, PAUL, 1868-1955
    L'annonce faite à Marie. 1912.
            HARV, RHO
        Sill, L., tr. DIK1, HAV,
                TUCG
        Variant title: The tidings
    brought to Mary
    L'histoire de Tobie et de Sara.
        See Tobias and Sara
    The satin slipper; or, The
        worst is not the worst.
        1919?
        O'Connor, J., tr. HIBB
        Variant title: Le soulier de
    satin; ou, Le père n'est
    pas toujours sûr

The tidings brought to Mary.
See L'annonce faite à Marie
Tobias and Sara. 1942?
Fiske, A., tr.   HAYE
Variant title: L'histoire de
Tobie et de Sara

CLAUSEN, SVEN, 1893-
The bird of contention. 1933?
Thornton, P., and A., trs.
                      CONT
Variant title: Kivflugen
Kivflugen. See The bird of
contention

CLEMENTS, COLIN CAMPBELL,
1894-1948
Columbine. 1922?   SHAY
The siege. 1922?   SHAY
--See Ryserson, Florence, jt.
auth.

CLEMENS, SAMUEL LANG-
HORNE, 1835-1910
The king and the duke. See
Fergusson, Francis. The
king and the duke (based on
the novel Huckleberry Finn
by)

CLINCH, CHARLES POWELL,
1797-1880
The spy, a tale of the neutral
ground. 1822.   AMP14

COCTEAU, JEAN, 1891-
Antigone. See Sophocles.
Antigone (adapted by)
The infernal machine. See La
machine infernale.
Intimate relations. 1938.
Frank, C., tr.   BENS3
Variant titles: Les parents
terribles; The storm within
La machine infernale. 1934.
                      PUCC
Wildman, C., tr. BENS1,
INTE, LOCL, LOCLA,
LOCLB, TUCN, TUCO
Variant title: The infernal
machine
Les mariés de la Tour Eiffel.
1921.

Fitts, D., tr.   NEW37
Les parents terrible. See Inti-
mate relations
Orphée. 1926.
Wildman, C., tr.   BLOC
The storm within. See Inti-
mate relations

COFFEE, LENORE (MRS. W. J.
COWEN), and COWEN, WILLIAM
JOYCE
Family portrait. 1939. BES38,
PLAN1

COFFEY, CHARLES, d. 1745.
See Jevon, Thomas, jt. auth.

COHAN, GEORGE MICHAEL,
1878-1942
Pigeons and people. 1933.
                 BES32, WAGC3
Seven keys to Baldpate (based
on the novel by Earl Derr
Biggers). 1913. BES09,
CART, CONG

COHN, EMIL, 1881- . See
Bernhard, Emil, pseud.

COKAIN, SIR ASTON, 1608-1684
Trappolin suppos'd a prince.
See Tate, Nahum. A duke
or no duke (adapted from)

COKAYNE, SIR ASTON. See
Cokain, Sir Aston

COLETTE, SIDONIE GABRIELLE,
1873-1954
Gigi. See Loos, Anita. Gigi
(from the novel by)

COLLINGS, PIERRE. See Gibney,
Sheridan, jt. auth.

COLMAN, GEORGE, 1732-1794
The jealous wife. 1761. NET,
NIC

--and GARRICK, DAVID
The Clandestine marriage.
1766. BAT15, HAN, MCM,
MCMI, MOR, MOSE2, TWE

46

COLTON, JOHN, 1889-1946, and
RANDOLPH, CLEMENCE
  Rain (based on the story Miss
    Thompson by W. Somerset
    Maugham).1922. BES22,
    GARU, TUCD

COLUM, PADRAIC, 1881-
  The land. 1905.   CAP
  Thomas Muskerry. 1910.
                          MOSN
COMDEN, BETTY
  Wonderful town. See Fields,
    Joseph and Chodorov, Jer-
    ome. Wonderful town (lyrics
    by)

CONGREVE, WILLIAM, 1670-
1729
  Love for love. 1695. BENY,
    CAR, CARA, KRM, MIL,
    STM, TWE
  The way of the world. 1700.
    ABRB1, ASH, BARG, BENY,
    BROJ, BROK, COL1, DEAP,
    DEAR, FOUB, GAY4, GOS,
    GOSA, GREB1, GREC1,
    KRM, KRON, LIE, MAT,
    MCM, MCMI, MEN, MOR,
    MORR, MOSE1, NET,
    REST, ROET, RUB, SHAI1,
    SMO, SPF1, STM, TAT,
    TAU, TRE, TREA2, TREC1,
    TREE1, TUP, TUQ, TWE,
    WALJ, WILS, WOOE

CONKLE, ELLSWORTH PROUTY,
1899-
  Minnie Field. 1928.   GASB
  Prologue to glory. 1938.
    BES37, FEE, SURR

CONNELLY, MARCUS COOK,
1890-
  The green pastures (based on
    the novel Ol' man Adam and
    his chillun, by Roark Brad-
    ford). 1930. BES29, CET,
    CHA, CHAN, CHAP, CONN,
    CORD, CORE, CORF,
    COTE, DUR, FUL, GAS,
    GRD, KNIC, KNID, LOOA,
    LOOB, LOOC, LOOD,

LOOE, MCD4, MOSK,
    MOSL, PROI, SIM, SIXD,
    TRE, TREA1, TREC2,
    TREE3, WATE
  The wisdom tooth. 1926.
                          BES25
  --See also Elser, Frank Ball;
    Kaufman, George S., jt.
    auths.

CONRAD, JOSEPH, 1857-1924
  One day more. 1905. BENT3

CONRAD, ROBERT TAYLOR,
1810-1858
  Jack Cade, the captain of the
    commons. 1835.   MOSS2

CONWAY, HIRAM J.
  The battle of Stillwater; or,
    The maniac. 1840.   AMP14

COOKE, BRITTON, d. 1923
  The translation of John Snaith.
    1923.   MAS1

COOPER, JAMES FENIMORE,
1789-1851
  The wept of the wish-ton-wish
    (based on the novel by).
    See Anonymous plays. The
    wept of the wish-ton-wish

COPEAU, JACQUES, 1879-1949
  The little poor man. 1925 ?
    Thurman, B., tr.   HAYE
    Variant title: Le petit pauvre
  Le petit pauvre. See The little
    poor man

COPPÉE, FRANÇOIS EDOUARD
JOACHIM, 1842-1908
  Le luthier de Crémone. See
    The violin maker of Cre-
    mona
  The violin maker of Cremona.
    1877.
    Jerome, J., tr.   BEAC
    Lord, I., tr.   COOK1
    Variant title: Le luthier de
    Crémone

COPPEL, ALEC

I killed the count. 1939. SIXP

CORMACK, BARTLETT
The racket. 1927.   BES27

CORMON, EUGÈNE, 1811-1903.
See D'Ennery, Adolphe, jt. auth.

CORNEAU, PERRY BOYER
Masks, 1922?   LAW

CORNEILLE, PIERRE, 1606-1684
Le cid. 1636. LYO, SCN, SER,
SERD, STJ1
Anonymous tr.   GAUB
Cooper, F., tr. CLF2,
CROV, GREA, MAU, SMN,
TAV
Fowlie, W., tr.   FOWL
Schevill, J., Goldsby, R.,
and A., trs.   BENR4
Variant title: The cid
The cid. See Le cid
Cinna; or, The mercy of Au-
gustus. 1639.
Landis, P., tr.   KRE
Horace. 1639   SER
The liar. See Le menteur
Le menteur. 1642.   LYO
Variant title: The liar
Polyeucte. 1640.   LYO, SER
Constable, T., tr. HARC26,
LOGG, STA

CORNEILLE, THOMAS, 1625-
1709
Le comte d'Essex. See The
earl of Essex
The earl of Essex. 1678.
Lockert, L., tr.   LOCR
Variant title: Le comte
d'Essex
Laodice. 1668.
Lockert, L., tr.   LOCR

CORWIN, NORMAN LEWIS, 1910-
Ann Rutledge. 1942?   LOVR
El capitan and the corporal.
1942?   NAGE
Good heavens. 1941. BRS,
LOOD
My client Curley. 1942. WATS
The odyssey of Runyon Jones.

1942?   PROD
Radio primer. 1942.   WATS
They fly through the air.
1939?   PROC
We hold these truths. 1941.
BROU

COURTELINE, GEORGES (pseud.
of Georges Moinaux), 1860-1929
Les boulingrin. See These
cornfields
La commissionaire est bon en-
fant. See The commis-
sioner
The commissioner. 1899?
Bermel, A., tr.   FOUF
Variant title: La commis-
sionaire est bon enfant
These cornfields. 1898.
Bentley, E., tr.   BENSA
Variant title: Les boulingrin

COWARD, NOEL PIERCE, 1899-
Blithe spirit. 1941. BES41,
FULT, KRM, TREC2,
TREE3, WALB, WARI
Brief encounter. 1946. GRED
Cavalcade. 1931. CEU, VOAD
Conversation piece. 1934. SEV
Design for living. 1932.
BES32, SIXH
Easy virtue. 1925.   MOSO
Fumed oak. 1936.   ANDE,
COOP
Hay fever. 1925. MOD, MYB
Point Valaine. 1934.   SIXP
Private lives. 1930. CHA,
CHAN, CHAR, LON
The vortex. 1924. TUCD, TUCM
Ways and means. 1935. WATE
The young idea. 1923.   MAP

COWEN, MRS. LENORE (COF-
FEE). See Coffee, Lenore

COWEN, WILLIAM JOYCE. See
Coffee, Lenore, jt. auth.

COWIE, MABEL MARGARET,
1903- . See Storm, Lesley,
pseud.

COWLEY, ABRAHAM, 1618-1677
Cutter of Coleman-street.

COWLEY, MRS. HANNAH
(PARKHOUSE), 1743-1809
The belle's stratagem. 1780.
BAT15
COXE, LOUIS O., 1918-   and
CHAPMAN, ROBERT, 1919-
Billy Budd (based on the novel
by Herman Melville). 1949.
BES50, DAVI, GARW,
HAVG, SSST, SSSU
Variant title: Uniform of
flesh
Uniform of flesh. See Billy
Budd

CRAVEN, FRANK, 1880-1945
The first year. 1920. BES20

CRÉBILLON, PROSPER JOLYOT
DE, 1674-1762
Rhadamiste et Zénobie. 1711.
BRE
Lockert, L., tr.   LOCR
Variant title: Rhadamistus
and Zenobia
Rhadamistus and Zenobia. See
Rhadamiste et Zénobie

CREIGHTON, ANTHONY.   See
Osborne, John, jt. auth.

CROCKER, CHARLES TEMPLE-
TON
The land of happiness. 1917.
BOH3
CROPPER, MARGARET
Two sides of the door. 1925.
FED2
CROTHERS, RACHEL, 1878-
As husbands go. 1931. BES30,
CHA
Expressing Willie. 1924. COT
He and she. 1911. QUIG,
QULJ, QUIK, QUIL, QUIM,
QUIN
Variant title: The Herfords
The Herfords. See He and She
Let us be gay. 1929. BES28
Mary the third. 1923. BES22,
DIG, TUCD, TUCJ, TUCM
Nice people. 1921. BES20,

MOSJ, MOSK, MOSL, QUI
Susan and God. 1937.   BES37
When ladies meet. 1932.
BES32
CROUSE, RUSSEL, 1893-   .
See Lindsay, Howard, jt. auth.

CROWNE, JOHN, 1640?-1712
The destruction of Jerusalem,
pt. 2. 1677.   DOA
Sir Courtly Nice; or, It cannot be. 1685.   SUM

CULBERTSON, ERNEST HOW-
ARD
Rackey. 1919.   LOC

CUMBERLAND, RICHARD, 1732-
1811
The fashionable lover. 1772.
MOSE2
The West Indian. 1771. BENY,
HAN, MCM, MCMI, MIL,
MOR, NET

CUMMINGS, EDWARD ESTLIN,
1894-
him. 1928.   BENS2

CUREL, FRANÇOIS DE, 1854-
1928
L'envers d'une sainte. 1892.
BOR
Variant title: The other side
of a saint
The fossils. 1892.
Clark, B., tr. CLD, WATI,
WATL1
The lion's share. See Le repas
du lion.
The other side of a saint.
See L'envers d'une sainte.
Le repas du lion. 1897. RHO
Variant title: The lion's
share

CURNIEU, GEORGES DE (Georges
Ancey, pseud.), 1860-1917
The dupe. 1891.
Clark, B., tr.   CLD

CURRIE, CARLETON H.
Whither goest thou? 1926. FED2

CUSTIS, GEORGE WASHINGTON
PARKE, 1781-1857
Pocahontas; or, The settlers
of Virginia. 1830. QUIJ,
QUIK, QUIL, QUIM, QUIN

CUVELIER DE TRYE, JEAN
GUILLAUME ANTOINE, 1766-
1824. See Chandezon, Léopold,
jt. auth.

D

DAGERMAN, STIG, 1923-
The condemned. 1947.
Alexander, H., and Jones,
L., trs. SCAN3
Variant title: Den döds-
dömde
Den dösdömde. See The con-
demned

DALY, AUGUSTIN, 1838-1899
The big bonanza (adapted from
Ultimo, by Gustav von
Moser). 1875. AMP20
Divorce. 1871. AMP20
Horizon. 1871. HAL
Man and wife. 1870. AMP20
Needles and pins (adapted
from Starke mitteln, by
Julius Rosen). 1880. AMP20
Pique. 1875. AMP20

DANCHENKO, VLADĪMĪR ĪVANO-
VĪCH NEMĪROVICH. See Nemírovích-Danchenko, Vladímír Ivano-
vích

DANCOURT, FLORENT CARTON,
sieur d'Ancourt, called, 1661-
1725
Les bourgeoises de qualité.
See Woman's craze for titles
Le chevalier à la mode. 1687.
BRE
Woman's craze for titles.
1700.
Chambers, W., tr. BAT8
Variant title: Les bourge-
oises de qualité

DANE, CLEMENCE, pseud. See
Ashton, Winifred

DANIEL, SAMUEL, 1562-1619
The vision of the twelve goddesses. 1604. PAR

D'ANNUNZIO, GABRIELE. See
Annunzio, Gabriele d'

D'ARCY, MARGRETTA. See
Arden, John, jt. auth.

D'AVENANT, SIR WILLIAM,
1606-1668
Love and honor. 1634. WALL
The siege of Rhodes, pt. I.
1661. MCM, MCMI
The wits. 1635. KNOW

-- and DRYDEN, JOHN
The tempest; or, The en-
chanted island. 1667. SUMB

DAVENANT, WILLIAM. See
D'Avenant, Sir William

DAVIDSON, ROBERT, 1808-1876
Elijah. 1860? KOH2

DAVIES, HUBERT HENRY, 1865-
1917
The mollusc. 1907. DIG

DAVIES, MARY CAROLYN
The slave with two faces.
1918? PEN

DAVIOT, GORDON, pseud. See
MacKintosh, Elizabeth

DAVIS, ANDRÉ
Four men, 1938? OBSE

DAVIS, DONALD, 1907- . See
Davis, Owen, jt. auth.

DAVIS, MRS. IRVING KAYE.
See Shelley, Elsa (Mrs. Irving
Kaye Davis).

DAVIS, OWEN, 1874-1956
And so ad infinitum. See
Čapek, Karel and Čapek,
Josef. And so ad infinitum
(adapted by)

50

The detour. 1921. MOSJ,
MOSK, MOSL
Icebound. 1923. BES22, CORD,
CORE, CORF, DIG, HAL
Mr. and Mrs. North (based on
the novel, The Norths meet
murder by Frances and
Richard Lockridge). 1941.

--and DAVIS, DONALD
Ethan Frome (based on the
novel by Edith Wharton).
1936.   BES35, GARU

DAY, CLARENCE, 1874-1935
Life with father. See Lindsay,
Howard and Crouse, Russel.
Life with father (based on
the book by)
Life with mother. See Lindsay,
Howard and Crouse, Russel.
Life with mother (based on
the book by)

DAY, JOHN, 1574-1640?
Humour out of breath. 1608?
NER
The parliament of bees. 1641?
NER

DAYTON, KATHARINE and
KAUFMAN, GEORGE S.
First lady. 1935.   BES35

DE AMESCUA, ANTONIO MIRA.
See Mira de Amescua, Antonio

DEAN, ALEXANDER, 1893-
Just neighborly. 1921.   LAW

DEBENHAM, ARTHUR HENRY,
1881-
Good will toward men. 1934.
SEVE
The prince of peace. 1934.
SEVE
DE CASALIS, JEANNE, 1897- .
See Sherriff, Robert Cedric, jt.
auth.

DECOUR, CHARLES HERBERT
and THÉODORE, ANNE
Le coq de village. See Smith

Richard Penn (adapted
from). The last man

DU CUREL, FRANÇOIS. See
Curel, François de

DE CURNIEU, GEORGES. See
Curnieu, Georges de

DEEVY, TERESA
Kati Roche. 1936.   FAMI

DEKKER, THOMAS, 1570?-1641?
The pleasant comedy of Old
Fortunatus. 1599.   SCH,
SCI
The shoemakers' holiday; or,
The gentle craft. 1599.
BALD, BAS, BENY, BLOO,
DROC, CLKW, COF, DUN,
FOUD, GAY3, GREC1,
HARC47, HAY, HOW,
LAWR, MCCL, MCI, NEI,
PAR, RUB, SCI, SCJ,SCW,
SHAJ1, SPE, SPF1, TAT,
TAU, TAV, WHE, WOO1
--See Ford, John, jt. auth.

--and MIDDLETON, THOMAS
The honest whore, pt. I.
1604. BAS, NEI, SPE,
WALL
The honest whore, pt. II.
1605. NEI, OLH, OLI1,
SPE

DE KOCK, CHARLES PAUL.
See Kock, Charles Paul de

DE KRUIF, PAUL HENRY,
1890- . See Howard, Sidney
Coe, jt. auth.

DE LA BARCA, PEDRO CALDE-
RÓN. See Calderón de la Barca,
Pedro

DELACOUR, ALFRED CHARLE-
MAGNE LARTIGNE, known as,
1817-1883. See Labiche, Eugène
Marin, jt. auth.

DELAFIELD, E.M., pseud. See
51

De La Pasture, Edmée Elizabeth Monica

DELANEY, SHELAGH, 1939.
A taste of honey. 1958.
BES60, SEVD

DE LA PASTURE, EDMÉE
ELIZABETH MONICA (E. M.
Delafield, pseud.), 1890-1943.
To see ourselves. 1930.
FAMA, PLAD

DELAVIGNE, CASIMIR. See
Delavigne, Jean François Casimir

DELAVIGNE, JEAN FRANÇOIS
CASIMIR, 1793-1843
Marino Faliero. 1829. BOR

DELDERFIELD, RONALD FRED-
ERICK, 1912-
Peace comes to Peckham.
1947. EMB3
Worm's eye view. 1945.
EMB1

DELL, FLOYD, 1887-   , and
MITCHELL, THOMAS
Little accident. 1928. BES28

DELL, JEFFREY, 1899-
Payment deferred (based on
the novel by Cecil Fores-
ter). 1934? CART

DE MAUPASSANT, GUY. See
Maupassant, Guy de

DE MILLE, HENRY CHURCH-
ILL, 1850-1893, and BARNARD,
CHARLES
The main line; or, Rawson's
Y. 1886. AMP17

--See Belasco, David, jt. auth.

DE MILLE, WILLIAM CHURCH-
ILL, 1878-1955
The Warrens of Virginia.
1907. AMP16

DENISON, MERRILL, 1893-
Balm. 1923. MAS1
Brothers in arms. 1921.
MAS1
The weather breeder. 1924.
MAS1

DENKER, HENRY
A far country. 1961. BES60

--and BERKEY, RALPH
Breaking point. See Time lim-
it!
Time limit! 1956. THEA56
Variant title: Breaking
point

D'ENNERY, ADOLPHE, 1811-
1899 and CORMON, EUGENE
Les deux orphelines. See The
two orphans
Orphans of the storm. See
The two orphans
The two orphans (adapted by
N. Hart Jackson). 1874.
CEY
Variant titles: Les deux
orphelines; Orphans of the
storm.

DENNEY, REUEL
September lemonade. 1955?
NEWW7

DESSANDRAIS-SEBIRE, FRAN-
ÇOIS
The philosopher duped by love
(sometimes attributed to).
See Anonymous plays. The
philosopher duped by love

DESTOUCHES, PHILLIPPE
NÉRICAULT, 1680-1754
The conceited count. See Le
glorieux
Le glorieux. 1732. BRE
Aldington, R., tr. ALD
Variant title: The con-
ceited count

DEVAL, JACQUES, 1893-
Tovarich. 1936.
Sherwood, R., tr. and
adapter. BES36, CEW

DE VISÉ, JEAN DONNEAU. See
Donneau de Visé, Jean

DIAMANT-BERGER, MAURICE
(André Gillois, pseud.)
   Paddle your own canoe. See
    Regnier, Max A.M. (based
    on)

DICENTA Y BENEDICTO, JOA-
QUIN, 1860-1917
   Juan José. 1895.
    Skidmore, M., tr.   TUR

DICKENS, CHARLES, 1812-1870
   A Christmas carol. See
    Shay, Frank. A Christmas
    carol (adapted from the
    story by)
   The cricket on the hearth.
    See Smith, Albert Richard.
   The cricket on the hearth
    (adapted from the story by)
   Dot. See Boucicault, Dion.
   Dot (adapted from The
    cricket on the hearth)
   Pickwick Papers. See Young,
    Stanley. Mr. Pickwick
    (based on)

DIDEROT, DENIS, 1713-1784
   The father. See Le père de
    famille
   Le père de famille. 1761.
                  BRE
    Variant title: The father

DIGHTON, JOHN, 1909-
   The happiest days of your life.
    1948.   PLAN1
   Who goes there! 1951. PLAN6

DINNER, WILLIAM, and MORUM,
WILLIAM
   The late Edwina Black. 1949.
                   PLAN2
DOBIE, LAURENCE, and SLO-
MAN, ROBERT
   The tinker. 1960.   PLAN24

DODD, LEE WILSON, 1879-1933
   The changelings. 1923. BES23

DOGGET, THOMAS, d. 1721
   Flora; or, Hob in the well.
    See Hob; or, The country
    wake
   Hob; or, The country wake
    (sometimes attributed to
    Colley Cibber). 1711.HUGH
    Variant titles: Flora; or,
    Hob in the well; The opera
    of Flora; or, Hob in the well
   The opera of Flora; or, Hob
    in the well. See Hob; or,
    The country wake

DOHERTY, BRIAN
   Father Malachy's miracle (a-
    dapted from the novel by
    Bruce Marshall). 1945.
                  EMB1
DONNAY, MAURICE CHARLES,
1859-1945
   Les amants. See The lovers
   L'autre danger. See The other
    danger
   The lovers. 1895.
    Clark, B., tr.   MOSQ
    Steeves, H., tr.   STE
    Variant title: Les amants
   The other danger. 1902.
    David, C., tr.   THR
    Variant title: L'autre danger

DONNEAU DE VISÉ, JEAN,
1638?-1710?
   Le gentilhomme guespin. 1670?
                  LAN
DORSET, THOMAS SACKVILLE,
1st earl of. See Sackville,
Thomas

DOSTOEVSKIĬ, FEDOR MIKHAĬL-
OVĬCII, 1821-1881
   The brothers Karamazoff
    (based on the novel by).
    See Nemĭrovĭch-Danchenko,
    Vladímĭr. The brothers
    Karamazoff

DOSTOIEVSKY, FEDOR. See
Dostoevskiĭ, Fedor Mikhaĭlovĭch

DOUGLAS, FELICITY. Rollo.
See Achard, Marcel.

53

Rollo (adapted by)

DOUGLAS, GEORGIA. See Johnson, Mrs. Georgia (Douglas)

DOWLING, JENNETTE and LET-
TON, FRANCIS
Before the throne. See The
young Elizabeth
Princess Elizabeth. See The
young Elizabeth
The young Elizabeth. 1951.
PLAN7
Variant titles: Before the
throne; Princess Elizabeth

DOWN, OLIPHANT, 1885-1917
The maker of dreams. 1912.
BEAC12
DOWSON, ERNEST CHRISTOPHER,
1867-1900
The Pierrot of the minute.
1902.   BENP, SECK

DOYLE, SIR ARTHUR CONANT,
1859-1930
Sherlock Holmes. See Gillette,
William Hooker. Sherlock
Holmes (based on the stor-
ies by)

DRAKE, WILLIAM A. 1899-
Grand hotel (tr. and adapted
by). See Baum, Vicki.
Grand hotel

DRANSFIELD, JANE, 1875-
The lost pleiad. 1910. SHAY

DRAYTON, MICHAEL, 1563-1631
The merry devil of Edmonton
(sometimes attributed to).
See Anonymous plays. The
merry devil of Edmonton
Sir John Oldcastle, pt. I
(sometimes attributed to).
See Anonymous plays. Sir
John Oldcastle, pt. I

DRINKWATER, JOHN, 1882-1937
Abraham Lincoln. 1918.
BES19, DID, PLAP1, SURR
Cophetua. 1911.   PEN

Oliver Cromwell. 1923. DIG

DRUTEN, JOHN VAN. See Van
Druten, John

DRYDEN, JOHN, 1631-1700
All for love; or, The world
well lost. 1677. BAUG,
BENY, CLK1, DOB, GOS,
GOSA, HARC18, KET, LIE,
LIED1, LIEE1, MAL, MAT,
MCCL, MCM, MCMI, MIL,
MOO, MOR, NET, REST,
SHAH1, SHAJ1, SMN,
SNYD1, STM, TUP, TUQ,
TWE, WILS, WOOE1
Almanzor and Almahide; or,
The conquest of Granada by
the Spaniards. 1670. MOR,
NET, TAT, TAU, TUP,
TUQ
Variant titles: The conquest
of Granada; The conquest of
Granada by the Spaniards,
pt. I
Aureng-zebe. 1675. DOA, MEN,
STM, TICK
The conquest of Granada. See
Almanzor and Almahide
The conquest of Granada by
the Spaniards, pt. I. See
Almanzor and Almahide
The secular masque. 1700.
ABRA, HAPT1
The Spanish fryar; or, The
double discovery. 1679.
GAY4, MOSE1
--See D'Avenant, William, jt.
auth.
--and HOWARD, SIR ROBERT
The Indian queen. 1663.
BENY, MCM, MCMI

DUBOIS, WILLIAM EDWARD
BURGHARDT, 1868-
Haiti. 1938.   FEE

DUCANGE, VICTOR HENRY
JOSEPH BRAHAIN, 1783-1833.
See Goubaux, Prosper Parfait,
jt. auth.

DUERRENMATT, FRIEDRICH,

54

1921-
Der besuch der alten dame.
See The visit
The old lady's visit. See The
visit
Time and again. See The visit
Trapps. See Yaffe, James.
The deadly game (adapted
from)
La visite de la vieille dame.
See The visit
The visit. 1956.
Valency, M., tr. and adap-
ter. BES57, BLOC, GOOD
Variant titles: Der besuch
der alten dame; La visite
de la vieille dame; The old
lady's visit; Time and again

DUFFET, THOMAS, fl. 1678
The mock-tempest; or, The
enchanted castle. 1674.
SUMB
DUFFIELD, BRAINERD
The lottery (from the story by
Shirley Jackson). 1953?
LOVR
DUKES, ASHLEY, 1885-1959
The man with a load of mis-
chief. 1925. MAP, PLAP3
The mask of virtue (tr. and
adapted by). See Sternhcim,
Carl. The mask of virtue
Such men are dangerous
(adapted from The patriot,
by Alfred Neumann). 1928.
FAO
DUMAS, ALEXANDRE, père,
1802-1870
Antony. 1831. BOR, COM
Henry III et sa cour. 1829.
BOR, GRA
DUMAS, ALEXANDRE, fils,
1824-1895
Camilla; or, The fate of a co-
quette. See La dame aux
camélias
Camille. See La dame aux
camélias
La dame aux camélias. 1852.
BOR, GRA
Reynolds, E., and Playfair,
N., trs. SSTG

Variant titles: Camilla; or,
The fate of a coquette; Ca-
mille; The lady of the ca-
melias; The queen of the
camelias
Le demi-monde. See The outer
edge of society
The ideas of Madame Aubray.
See Les idées de Madame
Aubray
Les idées de Madame Aubray.
1867. BOR
Variant title: The ideas of
Madame Aubray
The lady of the camelias.
See La dame aux camélias
The outer edge of society.
1855.
Clark, B., tr. MAU
Harper, H., tr. CLFZ
Variant title: Le demi-
monde
The queen of the camelias.
See La dame aux camélias

DUNCAN, RONALD FREDERICK,
1914- .
The death of Satan. 1954.
LOR, SATA

DUNCAN, THELMA
The death dance. 1923. LOC

DUNLAP, WILLIAM, 1766-1839
André. 1798. HAL, MOSS1,
QUIJ, QUIK, QUIL, QUIM,
QUIN
False shame; or, The Ameri-
can orphan in Germany
(adapted from Falsche scham
by August Kotzebue). 1799.
AMP2
Thirty years; or, The gambler's
fate (adapted from Trente
ans, by Prosper Goubaux
and Victor Ducange). 1828.
AMP2
DUNNING, PHILIP HART, 1892-,
and ABBOTT, GEORGE
Broadway. 1926. BES26, CART,
GASB

DUNSANY, EDWARD JOHN MORE-

TON, 1878-
The glittering gate. 1909.
WATF1, WATI
The gods of the mountain.
1911. MOSN, MOSO
If. 1921. HAU
King Argimenes and the un-
known warrior. 1911. DID
The lost silk hat. 1921. CHU,
PROM, PRON, SCWI
A night at an inn. 1916.
BEAC11, BLAG, BLAH,
COOK3, GASS, HUD, PEN,
PROB
The queen's enemies. 1916.
AND
DU RYER, PIERRE, d. 1658
Saul. 1640.
Lockert, L., tr. LOCR
Scaevola. 1644?
Lockert, L., tr. LOCR

D'USSEAU, ARNAUD, 1916- .
See Gow, James Ellis, jt. auth.

DUVAL, ALEXANDRE VINCENT,
1767-1842
La jeunesse de Henri V. See
Payne, John Howard.
Charles the second (adapted
from)
Shakespeare amoureux; ou, La
pièce à l'étude. See Smith,
Richard Penn. Shakespeare
in love (adapted from)

E

E., A., pseud. See Russell,
George William

EBERHART, RICHARD, 1904-
The visionary forms. 1952.
NEWW3
ECHEGARAY Y EIZAGUIRRE,
JOSÉ, 1832-1916
La esposa del vengador. See
The street singer
El gran Galeoto. 1891. BRET
Bontecou, E., tr. CLDM,
DIK2
Lynch, H., tr. FLOS
Nirdlinger, C., tr. and

adapter. MOSQ
Variant titles: The great
Galeoto; Slander; The world
and his wife
The great Galeoto. See El gran
Galeoto
Slander. See El gran Galeoto
The street singer. 1874.
Underhill, J., tr. MCCP
Variant title: La esposa del
vengador
The world and his wife. See
El gran Galeoto

EDWARDS, RICHARD, 1523?-
1566
Damon and Pithias. 1564?
ADA
EGAN, MICHAEL, 1895-1956
The dominant sex. 1934.
FAMG
To love and to cherish. 1938.
FAML
EICHELBAUM, SAMUEL, 1894-
Divorcio nupcial. 1941. ALPE

EIZAGUIRRE, JOSÉ ECHEGARAY
Y. See Echegaray y Eiza-
guirre, José

ELIOT, THOMAS STEARNS,
1888-
The cocktail party. 1949.
BES49
The confidential clerk. 1954.
BES53, THEA54
The family reunion. 1939.
BROS
Murder in the cathedral. 1935.
BALL, BROH, CONP,
CUBH, DEAP, DEAR, HAVG,
TUCO, WARI, WATA
Sweeney Agonistes. 1926.
BENS1
ELSER, FRANK BALL, 1885-
1935, and CONNELLY, MARCUS
COOK
The farmer takes a wife. See
Low bridge
Low bridge. 1934. BES34, LEV
Variant title: The farmer
takes a wife

EMERY, GILBERT, pseud. See
Emery Bemsley

EMIG, EVELYN (MELLON),
1895-
    The china pig. 1920?   SHAY

ENAMAI NO SAYEMON, fl. 1400
    The cormorant fisher. 15th
      cent.
    Waley, A., tr.   TAV

ENNERY, ADOLPHE D'.   See
D'Ennery, Adolphe

ERCKMANN-CHATRIAN. (pseud.
of Erckmann, Emile, 1822-1899
and Chatrain, Alexandre, 1826-
1890, collaborators)
    The Polish Jew. See Lewis,
      Leopold David. The bells
      (adapted from Le juif polo-
      nais by)

ERVINE, ST. JOHN GREER,
1883-
    The first Mrs. Fraser. 1929.
                    BES29
    Jane Clegg. 1913.   BES19,
      PLAP1
    John Ferguson. 1915. BES09,
      CHA, CHAN, CIIAR, DUR,
      THF, TUCD, TUCM, TUCN,
      TUCO
    Mixed marriage. 1911.   DID

ESASHI JŪŌ
    The bird catcher in hell.
      Waley, A., tr. INGW, TAV

ESTABROOK, HOWARD
    The human comedy (screen
      play based on the book by
      William Saroyan). 1943.
                    NAGE
ETHEREGE, SIR GEORGE,
1635?-1691
    The man of mode; or, Sir
      Fopling Flutter. 1675.
      CLKW, GOSA, KRM, MCM,
      MCMI, MOR, MOSE1, NET,
      REST, STM, TUQ, WILS

ÉTIENNE, CHARLES GUIL-
LAUME, 1777-1845
    Les deux gendres. See Payne,
      John Howard. The two sons-
      in-law (adapted from)

EURIPIDES, 480?-406? B. C.
    Alcestis. 438 B. C.
      Aldington, R., tr. ALLI,
      LIND, LOCK, OAT1, OATH
      Browning, R., tr.   MAST
      Coleridge, E., tr. GRDB5
      Fitts, D., and Fitzgerald,
      R., trs.   FIFR, FIFT
      Lattimore, R., tr. GREP3,
      GRER3
      Murray, G., tr.   CLKW
      Potter, R., tr.   CLF1
      Way, A., tr. GREE,
      HOWE, HOWF, THOM,
      THON
    Andromache. 431? B. C.
      Coleridge, E., tr. GRDB5,
      OAT1
      Johnson, V., tr.   FIFV
      Lind, L., tr.   LIND
      Nims, J., tr.   GREP3
    The bacchae. 405 B. C.
      Arrowsmith, W., tr.
      GREP4, GRER3
      Birkhead, H., tr.   LIND
      Coleridge, E., tr. GRDB5
      Lucas, F., tr.   LUCA
      Milman, H., tr.   ROBJ
      Murray, G., tr. HARC8,
      OAT2, OATE
      Variant title: The bac-
      chantes
    The bacchantes. See The bac-
      chae
    The children of Heracles. See
      The Heracleidae
    The cyclops. 5th cent. B. C.
      Arrowsmith, W., tr.
                    GREP3
      Coleridge, E., tr. GRDB5,
      OAT2
      Shelley, P., tr.   PLAG
      Smith, G., tr.   BAT1
    Electra. 413? B. C.
      Coleridge, E., tr. GRDB5,
      OAT2

Murray, G., tr. FEFT,
TEN, TRE, TREA2
Vermeule, E., tr. GREP4,
GRER2
Way, A., tr.   WEAV1
Hecuba. 425? B. C.
    Arrowsmith, W., tr.
                    GREP3
    Coleridge, E., tr.
        GRDB5, OAT1
Helen. 412 B. C.
    Coleridge, E., tr.
        GRDB5, OAT2
    Lattimore, R., tr. GREP3
The Heracleidae. 431? B. C.
    Coleridge, E., tr.
        GRDB5, OAT1
    Gladstone, R., tr. GREP3
    Variant title: The children
    of Heracles
Heracles. 420? B. C.
    Arrowsmith, W., tr. GREP3
    Coleridge, E., tr.
        GRDB5, OAT1
    Variant titles: Heracles
    mad; The madness of
    Heracles.
Heracles mad. See Heracles
Hiketides. See The suppliants
Hippolytus. 428 B. C.
    Coleridge, E., tr. GRDB5,
    OAT1, THP, WARN1
    Grene, G., tr. FIFT,
    GREN, GREP3, GRER1
    Lucas, F., tr.   BARC,
    LUCA
    Murray, G., tr.   FEFT,
    HARC8, MIL, MURP, OATE
    Way, A., tr. ATT2, HOUS,
    ROBI
Ion. 5th cent. B. C.
    Coleridge, E., tr. GRDB5
    Doolittle, H., tr.   KRE
    Potter, R., tr.   OAT1
    Willetts, R., tr. GREP4
Iphigenia among the Tauri.
    See Iphigenia in Tauris
Iphigenia at Aulis. 405 B. C.
    Coleridge, E., tr. GRDB5
    Potter, R., tr. CROS, ROB
    Stawell, F., tr.   OAT2
    Walker, C., tr.   GREP4
    Way, A., tr.   BUCK,

BUCL, BUCM
    Variant title: Iphigenia in
    Aulis
Iphigenia in Aulis. See Iphi-
    genia at Aulis
Iphigenia in Tauris. 420? B. C.
    Bynner, W., tr. GREP3,
    GRER2
    Coleridge, E., tr. GRDB5
    Murray, G., tr.   FEFT,
    TEN
    Potter, R., tr.   OAT1,
    PLAG
    Variant title: Iphigenia a-
    mong the Tauri
The madness of Heracles.
    See Heracles
Medea. 431 B. C.
    Anon. tr.   EVB1
    Agard, W., tr.   MCKK1
    Coleridge, E., tr. EDAD,
    GRDB5, LOCM1, OAT1,
    OATH
    Jeffers, R., tr. and
    adapter. GARW, LOR
    Murray, G., tr. FEFT,
    MAU, ROET, SEBO, SEBP,
    SMP, TEN
    Prokosch, F., tr.   FIFT,
    GOOD
    Robinson, C., tr.   ROBK
    Taylor, J., tr.   TAV
    Trevelyan, R., tr.   ROBI
    Warner, R., tr. GREP3,
    MACJ, MACL1
    Way, A., tr. ATT2, BUCL,
    BUCM, GREE, HOWE,
    HOWF, LAP, PROW,
    ROBJA
    Wodhull, M., tr. DRA1,
    EVA1, HIB, HIBB, MIK7,
    PLAB1
Orestes. 408 B. C.
    Arrowsmith, W., tr.
                    GREP4
    Coleridge, E., tr. GRDB5,
    OAT2
The Phoenician Maidens. See
    The Phoenissae
The Phoenician women. See
    The Phoenissae
The Phoenissae. 413? B. C.
    Coleridge, E., tr. GRDB5,

58

OAT2
  Wyckoff, E., tr. GREP4
  Variant titles: The Phoeni-
  cian maidens; The Phoeni-
  cian women
Rhesus. 5th cent. B. C.
  Coleridge, E., tr. GRDB5
  Lattimore, R., tr. GREP4
  Murray, G., tr.   OAT2
The suppliants. 424 B. C.
  Coleridge, E., tr. GRDB5,
  OAT1
  Jones, F., tr.   GREP4
  Lind, L., tr.   LIND
  Variant titles: Hiketides;
  The suppliant women
The suppliant women. See
  The suppliants
Troades. See The Trojan wo-
  men
The Trojan women. 415 B. C.
  Coleridge, E., tr. GRDB5
  Hamilton, E., tr.   HAM
  Lattimore, R., tr. FIFT,
  GREP3, GRER2, TREC1,
  TREE1
  Murray, G., tr. CAR, CARA,
  OAT1, STA
  Potter, R., tr.   ROBJA
  Raubitschek, I., and A.,
  trs. (assisted by A. Mc-
  Cabe)   ROBJ
  Variant title: Troades

EVREINOV, NIKOLAĬ NIKOLAE-
VICH, 1879-
  The back stage of the soul.
  See The theatre of the soul
The beautiful despot. 1906.
  Roberts, C., tr.   ROE
Behind the curtain of the soul.
  See The theatre of the soul
A merry death, a harlequinade.
  1914.
  Roberts, C., tr.   ROE
The theatre of the soul. 1912.
  Potapenko, M., and St.
  John, C., trs. DIE, HIB,
  HIBA
  Variant titles: The back
  stage of the soul; Behind the
  curtain of the soul

EWING, THOMAS, 1862-
  Jonathan. 1902?   KOH2

F

FAGAN, JAMES BERNARD,
1873-1933
  The improper duchess. 1931.
            FAMA, PLAD
FAIRCHILD, WILLIAM
  The sound of murder. 1959.
            PLAN20
FALKLAND, SAMUEL. See
Heijermans, Herman (pseud. of)

FARJEON, ELEANOR, 1881-
  The plane-tree. 1950.   OULD

--and FARJEON, HERBERT
  The two bouquets. 1936. FAMJ

FARJEON, HERBERT, 1887-
1945. See Farjeon, Eleanor, jt.
auth.

FARQUHAR, GEORGE, 1678-
1707
  The beaux' stratagem. 1707.
    BAT22, BLOO, CLF1,
    CLK1, GOS, GOSA, HUD,
    MAT, MCM, MCMI, MOR,
    MOSE2, NET, REST, STM,
    TAY, TICK, TUP, TUQ,
    TWE, UHL, WEAT1, WILS
  The recruiting officer. 1706.
        GAY4, RUB

FATH'ALI, ĀKHUND-ZADAH,
1812-1878
  The alchemist. 186-?
  Le Strange, G., tr. BAT3
  The magistrates. 186-?
  Wilson, E., tr.   TUQH

FATH ALI, MIRZA. See Faith'-
Ali, Ākhund-zadah

FAUCHOIS, RENÉ, 1882-
  The late Christopher Bean.
  1933.
  Howard, S., tr. and adapter. BES32, GARZH, GASS,

SPES, WARH
Williams, E., tr. and
adapter.   FAMD
Variant titles: Muse of all
work; Prenez garde à la
peinture.
Muse of all work. See The
late Christopher Bean
Prenez garde à la peinture.
See The late Christopher
Bean

FAULKNER, WILLIAM, 1897-
1962. See Ford, Ruth, jt. auth.

FECHTER, CHARLES ALBERT,
1824-1879
Monte Cristo. 1883. AMP16,
CLA

FERBER, EDNA, 1887-   . See
Kaufman, George S., jt. auth.

FERGUSSON, FRANCIS
The king and the duke (based
on Huckleberry Finn by
Samuel Clemens). 1939?
BENS2
FERNÁNDEZ DE MORATÍN,
LEANDRO. See Moratín, Lean-
dro Fernández de

FERRIS, WALTER, 1882-
Death takes a holiday (tr. and
adapted by). See Casella,
Alberto. Death takes a
holiday

FETH-ALI, AKHOUD ZAÏDÉ
MIRZA. See Fath'Ali, Ākhund-
zadah

FEYDEAU, GEORGES LÉON
JULES MARIE, 1862-1921
Breakfast in bed. See Keep
an eye on Amélie!
Keep an eye on Amélie! 1908.
Duffield, B., tr.   BENSA
Variant titles: Breakfast in
bed; Occupe-toi d'Amélie;
Oh, Amelia
Occupe-toi d'Amélie. See Keep
an eye on Amélie!

Oh, Amelia. See Keep an eye
on Amélie!

FIELD, CHARLES KELLOGG,
1873-
The cave man. 1910.   BOH2
The man in the forest. 1902.
BOH1
The owl and cave. 1906.
BOH1
FIELD, EDWARD SALISBURY,
1878-1936
Wedding bells. 1919.   BES19

FIELD, JOSEPH M., 1810-1856
Job and his children. 1852.
AMP14
FIELD, NATHANIEL, 1587-1633
Amends for ladies. 1611. NER
Woman is a weathercock.
1609.   NER

FIELD, RACHEL, 1894-1942
The patchwork quilt. 193-?
COOK2
FIELDING, HENRY (H. Scrible-
rus Secundus, pseud.), 1707-1754
The tragedy of tragedies; or,
The life and death of Tom
Thumb the great. 1731.
EIGH, HAN, NET, STM,
TAT, TAU, TAY, TUP,
TUQ

FIELDS, JOSEPH, 1895-
The doughgirls. 1942.   BES42

--and CHODOROV, JEROME
Junior miss (based on the book
by Mrs. Salley Benson).
1941.   BES41, GOW
My sister Eileen (based on the
stories by Ruth McKenney).
1940.   BES40
The ponder heart (adapted from
the story by Eudora Welty).
1956.   BES55, THEA56
Wonderful town. (based on the
play My sister Eileen; music by Leonard Bernstein;
lyrics by Betty Comden and
Adolph Green). 1953.
BES52, THEA53

FINK, EDITH ROMIG
Nooschens duhn viel. See
Noshions duhn Noshions
duhn. 1950? BUFF
Variant title: Nooschens
duhn viel

FISCHER, LECK, 1904-
The mystery tour. 1949.
Pearce, J., tr. CONT
Variant title: Selskabsrejsen
Selskabsrejsen. See The mys-
tery tour

FITCH, CLYDE, 1865-1909
Barbara Frietchie. 1899.
BES99
Beau Brummell. 1890. COH
Captain Jinks of the horse
marines. 1901. BENT4
The city. 1909. MOSJ, MOSK,
MOSL
The climbers. 1901. BES99,
COT
The girl with the green eyes.
1902. QUIL, QUIM, QUIN,
SHA2
Her great match. 1905. QUIG,
QUIJ, QUIK
The moth and the flame. 1898.
MOSS3
Nathan Hale. 1898. COOK2,
PROF, PROG, PROH,
SCWE
A trip abroad. See Labiche
Eugène Marin and Martin,
Édouard. Le voyage de
Monsieur Perrichon
The truth. 1907. DIC, STA

FITCH, WILLIAM CLYDE. See
Fitch, Clyde

FITZMAURICE, GEORGE
The dandy dolls. 1914? CAP

FLAVIN, MARTIN, 1883-
Amaco. 1932? TOD
The criminal code. 1929.
BES29
FLEMING, Mrs. DOROTHY
(SAYERS). See Sayers, Dorothy

FLETCHER, JOHN, 1579-1625
The chances. 1615. RUB
An equal match. See Rule a
wife and have a wife
The faithful shepherdess.
1609. BAS, GRE, NEI,
SCI, SCJ
The island princess; or, The
generous Portugal. 1621.
BROC
Rule a wife and have a wife.
1624. GAY3, SCH, SCI
Variant title: An equal
match
The wild-goose chase. 1609?
BENY, NEI, SPE, TAT,
TAU, WALL
--See Beaumont, Francis, jt.
auth.

--MASSINGER, PHILIP [and
BEAUMONT, FRANCIS]
Beggars' bush. 1609. BROC

--and SHAKESPEARE, WILLIAM
The two noble kinsmen. 1613.
BRO, PAR, THA

FONTAINE, ROBERT
The happy time. See Taylor,
Samuel. The happy time
(based on the novel by)

FONVIZÍN, DINÍS, IVÁNOVICH,
1744-1792
The choice of a tutor. 1792.
Roberts, C., tr. ROE
The minor. 1782.
Reeve, F., tr. REEV1
The young hopeful. 1782.
Patrick, G., and Noyes,
G., trs. NOY

FOOTE, SAMUEL, 1720-1777
The mayor of Garret. 1764.
MOR
FORBES, JAMES, 1871-1938
The famous Mrs. Fair. 1919.
BES19, MOSJ, MOSK, MOSL

FORBES, KATHRYN
Mama's bank account. See Van
Druten, John. I remember

mama (based on the book
by)

FORD, HARRIET, 1868-1949
Youth must be served. 1926?
TOD
FORD, JOHN, 1586-1640?
The broken heart. 1629?
BALD, BAS, BROC, NEI,
OLH, OLI2, SCI, SCJ, SPE
The chronicle history of Perk-
in Warbeck. 1633? BAS,
SCH
Variant title: Perkin War-
beck
Perkin Warbeck. See The
chronicle history of Perkin
Warbeck
'Tis a pity she's a whore.
1628? BENY, DUN, MCK,
PAR, RUB, RYL, WALL

--DEKKER, THOMAS and ROW-
LEY, WILLIAM
The witch of Edmonton. 1623?
BAS
FORD, RUTH, and FAULKNER,
WILLIAM
Requiem for a nun (adapted
from the novel by William
Faulkner). 1956? BES58

FOREST, LOUIS, 1872-1933
Par un jour de pluie. 192-?
SET
FORESTER, CECIL SCOTT, 1899-
Payment deferred. See Dell,
Jeffrey. Payment deferred
(based on the novel by)

FORSYTH, JAMES, 1913-
Héloise. 1931. COTK

FORTUNE, MRS. JAN ISBELLE,
1892-
The cavalier from France.
194-? PROG

FOX, STEPHEN
Never come Monday. See
Knight, Eric. Never come
Monday (adapted by)

FRAME, VIRGINIA. See Church,
Mrs. Virginia Woodson (Frame)

FRANCE, ANATOLE, 1844-1924
La comédie de celui qui épousa
une femme muette. 1913.
SET
Jackson, W., and E., trs.
SMR
Page, C., tr. LEV, LEVE
Variant title: The man who
married a dumb wife
The man who married a dumb
wife. See La comédie de
celui qui épousa une femme
muette

FRANCIS, ANN
The song of songs which is
Solomon's. 1781? KOH2

FRANK, ANNE, 1929-1945
Diary of a young girl. See
Goodrich, Frances and
Hackett, Albert. The diary
of Anne Frank (based on the
book by)

FRANK, MAUDE MORRISON,
1870-
A mistake at the manor. 1915?
WEB
FRANK, WALDO DAVID, 1889-
New Year's eve. 1928? AME2
FRANKEN, MRS. ROSE D. (Le-
win), 1895-
Another language. 1932. BES31
Claudia. 1940. BES40, CALN1
Outrageous fortune. 1943.
BES43
Soldier's wife. 1944. BES44

FREYTAG, GUSTAV, 1816-1895
The journalists. 1853?
Henderson, E., tr. FRA12
Variant title: Die journalis-
ten
Die journalisten. See The
journalists

FRINGS, KETTI (HARTLEY),
1916-

62

Look homeward, angel (based
on the novel by Thomas
Wolfe). 1957. BES57,
WATA

FRISCH, MAX, 1911-
Biedermann und die brandstifter. See Biedermann and
the firebugs
Biedermann and the firebugs.
1958.
Gorelik, M., tr. BLOC
Variant title: Biedermann
und die brandstifter

FROST, REX
Small hotel. 1955. PLAN13

FROST, ROBERT, 1875-1963
A masque of reason. 1945.
KNID
FRY, CHRISTOPHER, 1907-
The boy with a cart. 1938.
POOL
The dark is light enough.
1954. BES54
Duel of angels. See Giraudoux,
Jean. Duel of angels (adap-
ted by)
A phoenix too frequent. 1946.
BLAH, BROS, FEFL, WARI
Tiger at the gates. See Gi-
raudoux, Jean. Tiger at the
gates (tr. and adapted by)
Venus observed. 1950. BES51,
HAVG, WATE

FULDA, LUDWIG, 1862-1939
Beneath four eyes. See Tête-
à-tête
By ourselves. See Tête-à-tête
Tête-à-tête. 1886.
Townsend, E., tr. FRA17
Variant titles: Beneath four
eyes; By ourselves; Unter
vier augen
Unter vier augen. See Tête-à-
tête

FUNT, JULIAN
Child of Grace. See The mag-
ic and the loss
The magic and the loss. 1954.

BES53
Variant title: Child of
Grace

FYLES, FRANKLIN, 1847-1911.
See Belasco, David, jt. auth.

G

GALANTIÈRE, LEWIS, 1893-
Antigone. See Anouilh, Jean.
Antigone (adapted by)

GALDÓS, BENITO PÉREZ. See
Pérez Galdós, Benito

GALE, ZONA, 1874-1938
Miss Lulu Bett. 1920. CORD,
CORE, CORF

GALLARATI-SCOTTI, TOMMASO,
1878-
Cosi sia. See Thy will be done
Thy will be done. 1923.
Petri, V., tr. SAY
Variant title: Cosi sia

GALLICO, PAUL, 1897-
The snow goose (adapted for
radio by William A. Bacher
and Malcolm Meacham).
195-? INGA, INGB

GALSWORTHY, JOHN, 1867-1933
Escape. 1926. BES27, TRE,
TREA1, TREC2, TREE3
Justice. 1910. BROW, HAU,
HAVD, HAVE, WATF1,
WATI, WATO, WATR
Loyalties. 1922. ANDE, BES22,
BROX, CEU, LEWI, PEN,
SNYD2, SPER, WARI,
WATF2, WATI
The pigeon. 1912. HARB
The silver box. 1906. CHAR,
CLKW, COTH, CROS,
MOSN, MOSO, STAT, TOD
The skin game. 1920. BES20
Strife. 1909. DIC, DUR, INGE,
INGG, MAP, MCCB, MCCD,
MCCF, MCCG, STET,
WATS, WHI, WHK, WOO2

GARCÍA GUTIÉRREZ, ANTONIO, 1813-1884
Juan Lorenzo. 1865. BRET
El trovador. 1835. TRES

GARCIA LORCA, FEDERICO, 1899-1936
Amor de don Perlimplin. See The love of don Perlimplin and Belisa in the garden
Bitter oleander. See Blood wedding
Blood wedding. 1933.
Neiman, G., tr. NEW39
O'Connell, R., and Graham-Luján J., trs. BIER, BLOC, FLOX, LOCLB, TREC2, TREE2, WATA
Variant titles: Bitter oleander; Bodas de sangre
Bodas de sangre. See Blood wedding
La casa de Bernarda Alba. See The house of Bernarda Alba
The house of Bernarda Alba. 1945. PARV
Graham-Lujan, J., and O'Connell, R., trs. ALLI, CLM, HOGA
Variant title: La casa de Bernarda Alba
In the frame of don Cristobal. 193-?
Honig, E., tr. NEW44
The love of don Perlimplin and Belisa in the garden. 1931.
O'Connell, R., and Graham-Luján, J., trs. BENS1
Variant title: Amor de don Perlimplin
The tragicomedy of Don Cristobita and Doña Rosita. 1937.
Oliver, W., tr. NEWW8
Yerma. 1934.
Graham-Luján, J., and O'Connell, R., trs. ULAN

GARCIA VILLA, JOSÉ. See Villa, José Garcia.

GARDEL, JULIO SÁNCHEZ. See Sánchez Gardel, Julio

GARDINER, WREY
The last refuge. 1943? NEWR1

GARDNER, MRS. DOROTHY (Butts)
Eastward in Eden. 1947. BES47

GARDNER, HERB, 1934-
A thousand clowns. 1962. BES61

GARNETT, PORTER, 1871-1950
The green knight. 1911. BOH2

GARRICK, DAVID, 1717-1779
The lying valet. 1741. NET
--See Colman, George, jt. auth.

GASCOIGNE, GEORGE, 1525?-1577
Supposes (adapted from I suppositi, by Ludovico Ariosto). 1566. ADA, BAS, BOA, BON

--and KINWELMERSH, FRANCIS
Jocasta. 1566. CUN

GASCOYGNE, GEORGE. See Gascoigne, George

GASSNER, JOHN, 1903-
Les précieuses ridicules. See Molière, Jean Baptiste Poquelin. Les précieuses ridicules (tr. and adapted by)
Then and now (adapted from The marriage proposal and The harmful effects of smoking, by Anton Chekhov). 19-? GASS

GAY, DELPHINE. See Girardin, Delphine (Gay) de

GAY, JOHN, 1685-1732
The beggar's opera. 1728.
ASH, BARB, EIGH, HAN, KRO, MACK, MCM, MCMI, MOR, MOSE2, NET, SMR, STJM, STM, TAY, TUP,

64

GAZUL, CLARA, pseud. See
Mérimée, Prosper

GAZZO, MICHAEL VINCENTE
A hatful of rain. 1956. FAM,
GART, THEA56

GEDDES, VIRGIL, 1897-
The stable and the grove.
1933.   AME4

GELBER, JACK, 1932-
The connection. 1959. SEVD

GENET, JEAN, 1910-
Le balcon. See The balcony
The balcony. 1960.
Frechtman, B., tr. SEVD
Variant title: Le balcon

GEORGE, ERNEST, pseud. See
Wise, Ernest George

GEORGE, GRACE, 1883-
The nest (tr. and adapted by).
See Geraldy, Paul. The nest

GERALDY, PAUL, 1885-
The nest. 1922.
George G., tr. and adapter.
BES21
Variant titles: Les noces
d'argent; Silver weddings
Les noces d'argent. See The
nest
Silver weddings. See The nest

GERSHWIN, GEORGE, 1899-1937
Of thee I sing (music by). See
Kaufman, George S. and
Ryskind, Morrie. Of thee I
sing

GERSHWIN, IRA, 1896- . See
Kaufman, George S., jt.
auth.

GERSTENBERG, ALICE
Ever young. 1920?   SHAY
Overtones. 1915.   HUD
A patroness. 1917?   SHAY

GHELDERODE, MICHEL DE,
1898-
Escurial. 1929.
Abel, L., tr.   BENT5
Pantagleize. 1930.
Haugher, G., tr.   COTR

GIACOSA, GIUSEPPE, 1847-1908
As the leaves fall. See Like
falling leaves
Come le foglie. See Like fall-
ing leaves
Like falling leaves. 1900.
Updegraff, E., and A.,
trs.   MOSQ
Variant titles: As the
leaves fall; Come le foglie

GIBBS, WOLCOTT, 1902-1958
Season in the sun. 1950.
BES50
GIBNEY, SHERIDAN and COL-
LINGS, PIERRE
The story of Louis Pasteur.
195-?   STAT, STAU

GIBSON, PAULINE, 1908- .
See Gilsdorf, Frederic, jt. auth.

GIBSON, WILFRID WILSON
The family's pride. 1914.
RICH
GIDE, ANDRÉ, 1869-1951
The immoralist. See Goetz,
Ruth and Goetz, Augustus.
The immoralist (based on
the novel by)

GIELGUD, VAL HENRY, 1900-
Away from it all. 1946.
EMB3
Chinese white. 1928.   FIT

GIL Y ZÁRATE, ANTONIO, 1793-
1861
Guzmán el Bueno. 185-?
BRET
GILBERT, MICHAEL FRANCIS,
1912-
The bargain. 1961.   PLAN23
A clean kill. 1959.   PLAN21

GILBERT, WILLIAM SCHWENCK, 1836-1911, [and SULLIVAN, SIR ARTHUR SEYMOUR, composer]
H. M. S. Pinafore; or, The lass that loved a sailor. 1878. COOP, MOSN, MOSO
--See also Moss, Alfred Charles. H. M. S. Pinafore; oder, Das maedle und ihr sailor kerl (based on)
Iolanthe; or, The peer and the peri. 1882. BOWY, HUD, LAW
The mikado; or, The town of Titipu. 1885. MIJ2, PROD
Patience; or, Bunthorne's bride. 1881.   SMR
Pygmalion and Galatea. 1871. MAP, MAT
Sweethearts. 1874. BAT16, COT, WEB

GILBERT, WILLIE. See Burrows, Abram S., and Weinstock, Jack, jt. auths.

GILLETTE, WILLIAM HOOKER, 1855-1937
Secret service. 1896. BES94, QUIG, QUIJ, QUIK, QUIL, QUIM, QUIN
Sherlock Holmes (based on the stories by Sir Arthur Conant Doyle). 1899.   CART

GILLIAT, SIDNEY. See Launder, Frank, jt. auth.

GILLOIS, ANDRÉ, pseud.   See Diamant-Berger, Maurice

GILSDORF, FREDERICH, 1903- , and GIBSON, PAULINE, 1908-
The ghost of Benjamin Sweet. 1956?   WAGC1

GINSBURY, NORMAN, 1903-
The first gentleman. 1935. FIR
John Gabriel Borkman. See Ibsen, Henrik. John Gabriel Borkman (adapted by)
Viceroy Sarah. 1934. FAMG

GIRARDIN, DELPHINE (Gay) de ("Mme. Émile de Girardin"), 1804-1855
La joie fait peur. 1854. BENZ
Variant titles: Sunshine follows rain; Sunshine through the clouds
Sunshine follows rain.   See La joie fait peur
Sunshine through the clouds.   See La joie fait peur

"GIRARDIN, MME. ÉMILE DE."
See Girardin, Delphine (Gay) de

GIRAUDOUX, JEAN, 1882-1944
Amphitryon 38. See Behrman, Samuel Nathaniel. Amphitryon 38 (adapted from)
L'Apollon de Bellac. See The Apollo of Bellac
The Apollo of Bellac. 1942. Valency, M., adapter   GASS
Variant titles: L'Apollon de Bellac; L'Apollon de Marsac
L'Apollon de Marsac.   See The Apollo of Bellac
Cantique des cantiques.   See Song of songs
Duel of angels. 1953. Fry, C., tr. and adapter   BES59
Variant title: Pous Lucrece
Electra. 1937. Smith, W., tr. BENS2, BENT1, BLOC, LOR
Variant title: Electre
Electre.   See Electra
The enchanted (adapted by Maurice Valency). 1950.   BES49
Variant title: Intermezzo
La folle de Chaillot. See The madwoman of Chaillot
La guerre de Troie n'aura pas lieu. See Tiger at the gates.
Intermezzo. See The enchanted.
Judith. 1931. Savacool, J., tr.   BENT3
The madwoman of Chaillot (adapted by Maurice Va-

66

lency). 1948. ALLI, BES48,
BLOC, BROX, GARZH,
GRIF, HAVG, WATE
Variant title: La folle de
Chaillot
Ondine. 1954? (from the novel
Undine by Baron de la Motte
Fouque; adapted by Maurice
Valency). CLM, GARZH,
THEA54
Pour Lucrece. See Duel of
Angels
Siegfried. 1928. GRAF
Sodom and Gomorrah. 1943.
Briffault, H., tr. ULAN
Song of songs. 1938?
Briffault, H., tr. ULAN
Raikes, J., tr. BERM
Variant title: Cantique des
cantiques
Tiger at the gates. 1955.
CLOU, PUCC
Fry, C., tr. BES55,
GARZH, ROET, THEA56,
WAIU
Variant title: La guerre de
Troie n'aura pas lieu

GLASPELL, SUSAN, 1882-1948
Alison's house. 1930. BES30,
CORD, CORE, CORF, SIXD
Trifles. 1916. BEAC11, FREI,
GASB, HUD, PEN, PROD,
PROF, PROG, STAT, STAU,
STAV

GLEASON, JAMES, 1885- .
See Abbott, George, jt. auth.

GLEBOV, ANATOLE GLEBO-
VITCH, 1899-
Inga. 1928.
Malamuth, C., tr. LYK

GLOVER, HALCOTT, 1877-
The king's jewry. 1928. TUCD

GODFREY, THOMAS, 1736-1763
The prince of Parthia. 1767?
MOSS1, QUIJ, QUIK, QUIL,
QUIM, QUIN

GOETHE, JOHANN WOLFGANG

VON, 1749-1832
Egmont. 1791.
Hamburger, M., tr.
BENR2
Lustig, T., tr. LUST
Swanwick, A., tr. CLF2,
HARC19
Faust, pt. I. 1829. EVB2
Anon. tr. DRA2, PLAB2
MacIntyre, C., tr. TREC1,
TREE1
MacNeice, L., tr. MACJ,
MACL2
Priest, G., tr. GRDB47
Swanwick, A., tr. BUCK,
BUCL, BUCM, CROV,
EVA2, FRA1, HARC19,
ROB, THOM, THON,
WEAV2
Taylor, B., tr. IIID, HIBA,
HIBB, LOCM2, TRE,
TREA2, WORP
Faust, pt. II. 1829.
MacNeice, L., tr. MACJ,
MACL2
Priest, G., tr. GRDB47
Swanwick, A., tr. BUCM,
FRA1
Goetz von Berlichingen. 1774.
Scott, W., tr. MAU
Iphigenia in Tauris. 1802.
Swanwick, A., tr. BAT11,
FRA1
Variant titles: Iphigenia of
Tauris; Iphigenie auf
Tauris
Iphigenia of Tauris. See Iphi-
genia in Tauris
Iphigenie auf Tauris. See Iphi-
genia in Tauris
Stella. 1776.
Thompson, B., tr. BAT12
Torquato Tasso. 1807.
Swanwick, A., tr. KRE

GOETZ, AUGUSTUS. See Goetz,
Ruth Goodman, jt. auth.

GOETZ, RUTH GOODMAN, and
GOETZ, AUGUSTUS
The doctor's daughter. See
The heiress
The heiress (based on the

novel Washington Square by
Henry James, Jr.). 1947.
BES47
Variant titles: The doctor's
daughter; Washington Square
The immoralist (based on the
novel by André Gide). 1954.
BES53
Washington Square. See The
heiress

GOGOL, NIKOLAĬ VASILÉVICH,
1809-1852
Gamblers. 1833.
Bentley, E., tr. BENT3
The government inspector.
See The inspector
The inspector. 1836.
Anon. tr. COUR
Davies, T., tr. BAT18
Guerney, B., tr. GUE,
HOUG
MacAndrew, A., tr. GARZE
Magarshack, D., tr. MAGA
Reeve, F., tr. REEV1
Seymour, J., and Noyes,
G., trs. NOY, TREC1,
TREE1
Sykes, A., tr. CLKW,
COUS
Variant titles: The govern-
ment inspector; The inspec-
tor general; Revisor
The inspector general. See
The inspector
The marriage. 1842.
Bentley, E., tr. BENT4
Revisor. See The inspector

GOLD, MICHAEL, 1894-
Hoboken blues; or, The black
Rip Van Winkle. 1927?
AME1
GOLDING, WILLIAM GERALD,
1911-
The brass butterfly. 1958.
BARG
GOLDONI, CARLO, 1707-1793
Un curioso accidente. 1757.
BIN
Zimmern, H., tr. CROV
Variant titles: A curious
mishap; A curious misun-

derstanding
A curious mishap. See Un
curioso accidente
A curious misunderstanding.
See Un curioso accidente
The fan. 1763.
Fuller, H., tr. CLF2
Variant title: Il ventaglio
La locandiera. See The mis-
tress of the inn
Mirandolina. See The mis-
tress of the inn
The mistress of the inn. 1753.
Gregory, I., tr. BENR1
Lohmann, H., tr. LEG
Pierson, M., tr. MAU,
MOSA
Variant titles: La locan-
diera; Mirandolina
L'osteria della posta. See
The post-inn
The post-inn. 1761.
Chambers, W., tr. BAT5
Variant title: L'osteria
della posta
The servant of two masters.
1743?
Dent, E., tr. BENR1
Il ventaglio. See The fan

GOLDSMITH, CLIFFORD, 1900-
What a life. 1938. BES37

GOLDSMITH, OLIVER, 1728-
1774
The good-natured man. 1768.
STM
She stoops to conquer; or,
The mistakes of a night.
1773. BARG, BEAC11,
BENN, BENY, CLF1, COL1,
DEM, DRA1, EIGH, FOUB,
HARC18, HUD, JAFF, KEY,
KRM, MAT, MCM, MCMI,
MOO, MOR, MORR,
MOSE2, NET, PLAB1,
POOL, PROM, RUB, SHAH1,
SMO, SRY, SRYG, STA,
STM, TAT, TAU, TAY,
TUP, TUQ, TWE, UHL

GONNE, FRANCIS
In the city of David. 1934.
SEVE

68

GOODMAN, KENNETH SAWYER
Dust of the road. 1912? FED1

--and HECHT, BEN, 1894-
The hand of Siva. 192-?
STAT, STAU

GOODMAN, PAUL, 1911-
The towel of Babel. 1940.
NEW40

GOODRICH, FRANCES, and
HACKETT, ALBERT
The diary of Anne Frank
(based on the book by Anne
Frank). 1955. BES55, GARU,
THEA56

GOOLD, MARSHALL NEWTON,
1881-
The quest divine. 1925?FED2
St. Claudia. 1924? FED2
The shepherds. 192-? FED2

GORDON, RUTH (MRS. GARSON
KANIN), 1896-
Over 21. 1943. BES43
Years ago. 1946. BES46,
WAGC1, WAGE

GORE-BROWNE, ROBERT F.,
1893- . See Harwood, Harold
Marsh, jt. auth.

GORKI, MAXIM (pseud. of
Aleksiĕl Maksimovich Pĩeskov),
1868-1936
At the bottom. See The lower
depths
Dans les fonds. See The
lower depths
Down and out. See The lower
depths
From the depths. See The
lower depths
In the depths. See The lower
depths
The lower depths. 1902.
Bakshy, A., tr. BLOC,
FOUM
Chambers, W., tr. BAT18
Covan, J., tr. CEW, DIK2,
HAV, HOUG, MOS, TRE,
TREA1, TREC2, TREE2,

TUCN, TUCO, WHI
Guerney, B., tr. GUE
Hopkins, E., tr. DID,
MOSG, MOSH, SMP, TUCG,
WATI, WATL3
MacAndrew, A., tr. GARZJ
Magarshack, D., tr. MAGA
Noyes, G., and Kaun, A.,
trs. NOY
Reeve, F., tr. REEV2
Variant titles: At the bot-
tom; Dans les fonds; Down
and out; From the depths;
In the depths; A night
shelter; Night's lodging;
Submerged
A night shelter. See The
lower depths
Night's lodging. See The
lower depths
Submerged. See The lower
depths
Yegor Bulichov and others.
1932.
Bakshy, A., tr. HOGA
Wixley, A., tr. FOUS

GOUBAUX, PROSPER PARFAIT,
1795-1859, and DUCANGE VIC-
TOR HENRY JOSEPH BRAHAIN
Trente ans; ou, La vie d'un
joueur. See Dunlap, William. Thirty years; or, The
gambler's fate (adapted
from)

GOULDING, EDMUND, 1891- .
See Selwyn, Edgar, jt. auth.

GOW, JAMES ELLIS, 1907-1952
and D'USSEAU, ARNAUD
Deep are the roots. 1945.
BES45
Tomorrow the world. 1942.
BES42, GARZ

GOW, RONALD, 1897-
Ann Veronica (adapted from
the novel by H. G. Wells).
1949. PLAN2
The Edwardians (adapted from
the novel by Victoria Mary
Sackville-West). 1959.
PLAN20

Variant title: Weekend in
May
Weekend in May. See The
Edwardians

GOZZI, CARLO, conte, 1722-
1806
The king stag. 1762?
Wildman, C., tr.   BENR1

GRABBE, CHRISTIAN DIETRICH,
1801-1836
Jest, satire, irony, and
deeper significance. 1827?
Edwards, M., tr. BENS2

GRANVILLE-BARKER, HARLEY
GRANVILLE, 1877-1946
Deburau (tr. and adapted by).
See Guitry, Sacha. Deburau
The Madras house. 1910. DIC,
MOSN, MOSO, WEAL
The Voysey inheritance. 1905.
DIG, PLAP1
Waste. 1909.   TUCD
--See Houseman, Laurence,
jt. auth.
GREEN, ADOLPH, 1915-
Wonderful town. See Fields,
Joseph and Chodorov, Jerome.
Wonderful town (lyrics by)
GREEN, JANET, 1913-
Murder mistaken. 1952. PLAN8
GREEN, JULIEN
South. 1955.   PLAN12
GREEN, PAUL, 1894-
The field god. 1927.   HAL,
TUCD, TUCM, TUCN
The house of Connelly. 1931.
BES31, GARU
Hymn to the rising sun. 1936.
KOZ
In Abraham's bosom. 1927.
BES26, CORD, CORE,
CORF, DIE, LOC, TOD,
WHI
Johnny Johnson (music by Kurt
Weill). 1937. AND, ANDE,
BES36, GAS
The Lord's will. 1925.   LEV,
LEVE
The man who died at twelve
o'clock. 1925.   CHU

The no'count boy. 1924. LOC
Potter's field. See Roll sweet
chariot
Roll sweet chariot. 1934.
CLKW
Variant title: Potter's field
Supper for the dead. 1926?
AME1
Tread the green grass. 1928.
AME3
Unto such glory. 1926?
FLAN, HUDS2
White dresses. 1920.   GASB,
LOC

-- See Wright, Richard, jt.
auth.

GREENE, GRAHAM, 1904-
The complaisant lover. 1959.
BES61
The living room. 1953. BES54
The potting shed. 1957. BES56

GREENE, PATTERSON
Papa is all. 1942.   GALB

GREENE, ROBERT, 1558-1592
Friar Bacon and Friar Bungay.
See The honorable history
of Friar Bacon and Friar
Bungay
George a Greene, The pinner
of Wakefield (supposed au-
thor). 1588?   ADA, BAS,
SCH
Variant title: A pleasant
conceited comedy of [George
a Greene] the pinner of
Wakefield
The honorable history of Friar
Bacon and Friar Bungay.
1589? ASH, BAS, BENY,
BROC, GAY1, HEIL, HOW,
MCI, MIN2, MIO2, NEI,
OLH, OLI1, PAR, SCI,
SCJ, SCW, SPE, TICO
Variant title: Friar Bacon
and Friar Bungay
James the fourth. 1591?
MIN2, MIO2
A pleasant conceited comedy of
[George a Greene] the pin-

70

ner of Wakefield. See
George a Greene, the pin-
ner of Wakefield

GREGORY, ISABELLA AUGUSTA
(Persse), lady, 1859-1932
The Canavans. 1906.   BARF
The dragon. 1917.   WEB
Hyacinth Halvey. 1906.   CAP,
    MIL, WATF1, WATI,
    WATT2
The rising of the moon. 1907.
    BEAC12, DIC, PROB,
    SHAR, SSTA
Spreading the news. 1904.
    BEAC8, FIG, PEN, PROC,
    WATS
The workhouse ward. 1908.
    COD, MOSN, MOSO, TOD,
    TREC2, TREE3

GRESSET, JEAN BAPTISTE
LOUIS, 1709-1777
Le méchant. 1747.   BRE

GRIBOÏEDOV, ALEXANDR
SERGIÉEVICH, 1795-1829
Intelligence comes to grief.
    See Wit works woe
The misfortune of being clever.
    See Wit works woe
The trouble with reason. 1824?
    Reeve, F., tr.   REEV1
Wit works woe. 1831.
    Pares, B., tr.   NOY
    Variant titles: Intelligence
    comes to grief; The misfor-
    tune of being clever; Woe
    from wit
Woe from wit. See Wit works
    woe

GRIBOYEDOV, ALEXSANDER
See Griboïedov, Alexandr Sergié-
evïch

GRIEG, NORDAHL, 1902-1943
The defeat: a play about the
    Paris Commune. 1936.
    Watkins, J., tr.   SCAN2
    Variant title: Nederlaget
Nederlaget. See The defeat

GRIFFIN, ALICE VENEZKY,
1921-
Oresteia. See Aeschylus.
Oresteia (arranged for the
    stage by)

GRIFFITH, HUBERT FREELING,
1896-1953
Youth at the helm (tr. and
    adapted by). See Vulpius,
    Paul. Youth at the helm

GRILLPARZER, FRANZ, 1791-
1872
The fortunes and death of
    King Ottokar. See König
    Ottokars glück und ende
The Jewess of Toledo. 1873.
    Danton, G., and A., trs.
                          FRA6
    Variant title: Die jüdin von
    Toledo
Die jüdin von Toledo. See
    The Jewess of Toledo
König Ottokars glück und ende.
    1825.   CAM
    Variant title: The fortunes
    and death of King Ottokar
Medea. 1821.
    Miller, T., tr.   FRA6
Sappho. 1818.   CAM
    Frothingham, E., tr. SMN
Der traum ein leben. 1834.
                         FEFH1

GROVER, LEONARD
Our boarding house. 1877.
                          AMP4
GRUMBINE, EZRA LIGHT, 1845-
1880
Die inschurens bissness. See
    Die insurance business
Die insurance business. 1880?
                          BUFF
    Variant title: Die inschurens
    bissness

GRUNDY, SYDNEY, 1848-1914
A pair of spectacles. (adapted
    from Les petits loiseaux by
    Eugene Labiche and Dela-
    cour). 1890.   ROWE

GUERRERO, WILFRIDO MARÍA,
1917-
Forever. 1947.   EDAD

GUIMERÁ, ANGEL, 1847-1924
Daniela. 1902.
Underhill, J., tr.   CLDM
Variant titles: La pecadora;
The sinner
La pecadora.   See Daniela
The sinner.   See Daniela

GUINON, ALBERT, 1863-1923,
and MARNIÈRE, JEANNE MARIE
FRANÇOISE
Le joug.   See The yoke
The yoke. 1902.
Anon. tr.   BAT21
Variant title: Le joug

GUITRY, SACHA, 1885-1957
Deburau. 1920.
Granville-Barker, H., tr.
and adapter.   BES20
Don't listen, ladies! (adapted
by Stephen Powys and Guy
Bolton). 1948.   PLAN1
Pasteur. 1919.
Brown, I., tr.   DID

GUTHRIE, J.   He who gets
slapped.   See Andreev, Leonid
Nikolaevich.   He who gets slapped
(adapted by)

GUTHRIE, TYRONE, 1900-
Top of the ladder. 1950.
                     PLAN3
GUTIÉRREZ, ANTONIO GARCÍA.
See García Gutiérrez, Antonio

GUTZKOW, KARL FERDINAND,
1811-1878
Pigtail and sword.   See Sword
and queue
Sword and queue. 1843.
Colbron, G., tr.   FRA7
Variant titles: Pigtail and
sword; Zopf und schwert
Zopf und schwert.   See Sword
and queue

H

HACKETT, ALBERT.   See Goodrich, Frances, jt. auth.

HACKETT, WALTER, 1876-1944.
See Megrue, Roi Cooper, jt. auth.

HAGAN, JAMES, d. 1947
One Sunday afternoon. 1933.
                     BES32

HAINES, WILLIAM WISTER,
1908-
Command decision. 1947.
BES47, CLDP, MIJY,
QUIN, TUCN

HALBE, MAX, 1865-
Mother earth. 1897.
Grummann, P., tr.   FRA20
Variant title: Mutter erde
Mutter erde.   See Mother earth

HALL, HOLWORTHY, 1887-
1936, and MIDDLEMASS, ROBERT
M., 1883-
The valiant. 1921.   BEAC10

HALL, WILLIS
The long and the short and the
tall. 1959.   NEWE3

HAMILTON, PATRICK, 1904-
Angel street. 1941.   BES41,
CART
Variant title: Gaslight
Gaslight.   See Angel street

HAMLIN, Mary P.
The rock. 1921?   FED1

HAMMERSTEIN II, OSCAR,
1895-
Allegro (music by Richard
Rodgers). 1947.   BES47
Oklahoma! (based on Green
grow the lilacs by Lynn
Riggs; music by Richard
Rodgers). 1943.   BES42,
CEY

--and LOGAN, JOSHUA

72

South Pacific (based on Tales
of the South Pacific by
James A. Michener; music
by Richard Rodgers). 1949.
QUIN

HANKIN, ST. JOHN EMILE
CLAVERING, 1869-1909
The Cassilis engagement. 1907.
DIG, MOSN, MOSO
The last of the De Mullins.
1908. CHA, CHAN, CHAR
The return of the prodigal.
1905. MAP, WEAL

HANSBERRY, LORRAINE, 1930-
A raisin in the sun. 1959.
BES58, CEQ, CES

HANSHEW, THOMAS W., 1857-
1914
The forty-niners. 1879. BAT20

HARBURG, EDGAR Y., 1896-
and SAIDY, FRED
Finian's rainbow. 1947. HUDE

HARDT, ERNST, 1876-
Tantris the fool. See Tris-
tram the jester
Tristram the jester. 1907.
Heard, J., tr.   FRA20
Variant title: Tantris the
fool

HARDY, THOMAS, 1840-1928
The play of St. George (reconstructed from memory
by). See Anonymous plays.
The play of St. George

HARGRAVE, ROY. See Britton,
Kenneth Phillips, jt. auth.

HARLAN, WALTER, 1867-1931
The Nüremberg egg. 1913.
Katzin, W., tr.   KAT
Variant title: Das Nürn-
burgisch ei
Das Nürnburgisch ei. See
The Nüremberg egg

HARNICK, SHELDON. See Weidman, Jerome and Abbott, George.

Fiorello (lyrics by)

HARNWELL, MRS. ANNA JANE
(WILCOX) 1872-, and MEAKER,
MRS. ISABELLE (JACKSON)
The alabaster box. 1940.
FED2
HARSHA, SON OF HIRA, 12th
century
Retnavali; or, The necklace.
12th cent.
Wilson, H., tr.   BAT3

HART, MOSS, 1904-
Christopher Blake. 1946.BES46
The climate of Eden (based on
the novel Shadows move a-
mong them by Edgar Mittel-
hölzer). 1952.   BES52,
THEA53
Lady in the dark. 1941.BES40
Light up the sky. 1948. BES48
Winged victory (music by
David Rose). 1943.   BES43

-- See Kaufman, George S.,
jt. auth.

HARTOG, JAN DE, 1914-
The fourposter. 1951. BES51,
GART
Skipper next to God. 1945.
BES47, EMB2

HARTZENBUSCH, JUAN EU-
GENIO, 1806-1880
Los amantes de Teruel. 1837.
BRET
Variant title: The lovers of
Teruel
The lovers of Teruel. See
Los amantes de Teruel

HARWOOD, HAROLD MARSH,
1874-
Old folks at home. 1933.
FAMF
--and GORE-BROWN, ROBERT F.
Cynara. 1930.   BES31

HASTINGS, BASIL MACDONALD,
1881-1928
The new sin. 1912.   PLAP2

HASTINGS, CHARLOTTE
Bonaventure. 1949.   PLAN3
   Variant titles: Mary Bona-
   venture; Sister Cecilia
Mary Bonaventure. See Bona-
   venture
Sister Cecilia. See Bonaven-
   ture
Uncertain joy. 1953.   PLAN12

HASTINGS, HUGH, 1917-
Seagulls over Sorrento. 1950.
                        PLAN4
HASTINGS, MICHAEL
Yes, and after. 1957. NEWE4

HATHWAY, RICHARD, fl. 1602
Sir John Oldcastle, pt. I
   (sometimes attributed to).
   See Anonymous plays. Sir
   John Oldcastle, pt. I

HAUPTMANN, GERHART, 1862-
1946
The assumption of Hannele.
   See Hannele
The beaver coat. 1893.
   Lewisohn, L., tr.   STE,
   WATI, WATL1
   Variant title: Der biberpelz,
   eine diebs komödie
Der biberpelz, eine diebs ko-
   mödie. See The beaver coat
The coming of peace. See Das
   friedensfest
Einsame menschen. 1891. CAM
   Variant title: Lonely lives
The festival of peace. See
   Das friedensfest
Das friedensfest. 1890. STI1
   Variant titles: The coming
   of peace; The festival of
   peace; The reconciliation
Hannele. 1893.
   Archer, W., tr.   BAT12
   Frenz, H., and Waggoner,
   M., trs.   ULAN
   Meltzer, C., tr. HAV, HUD,
   INTE
   Variant titles: The assump-
   tion of Hannele; Hannele's
   assumption; Hanneles him-
   melfahrt; The journey to

heaven of Hannele
Hannele's assumption. See
   Hannele
Hanneles himmelfahrt. See
   Hannele
The journey to heaven of
   Hannele. See Hannele
Lonely lives. See Einsame
   menschen
Michael Kramer. 1900.
                        FEFH2
   Lewisohn, L., tr. FRA18
The rats. 1911.
   Lewisohn, L., tr. TUCG,
   TUCM, TUCN, TUCO
   Variant title: Die ratten
Die ratten. See The rats
The reconciliation. See Das
   friedensfest
The sunken bell. 1896.
   Meltzer, C., tr.   BUCK,
   BUCL, BUCM, FRA18,
   MCCP, MOSQ, WHK
   Variant title: Die versun-
   kene glocke
Die versunkene glocke. See
   The sunken bell
The weavers. 1892.
   Frenz, H., and Waggoner,
   M., trs.   BLOC
   Huebsch, B., tr.   THON
   Morison, M., tr.   CEW,
   DIC, DIK1, FRA18, SMP,
   TRE, TREA1, TREC2,
   TREE2, WHI
   Variant title: Die weber
Die weber. See The weavers
Der weisse heiland. See The
   white saviour
The white redeemer. See The
   white saviour
The white saviour. 1920.
   Muir, W., and E., trs.
                        KRE
   Variant titles: Der weisse
   heiland; The white redeemer

HAUTEROCHE, NOËL LEBRE-
TON, 1617-1707
Crispin médecin. See Ravens-
   croft, Edward and Motteux,
   P. A.   The sham doctor
   (based on)

74

HAWKES, JACQUETTA (HOP-
KINS), 1910- . See Priestley,
John Boynton, jt. auth.

HAWTHORNE, RUTH (WARREN).
See Kennedy, Mary, jt. auth.

HAY, IAN (pseud. of John Hay
Beith), 1876-1952
"Let my people go!" 1948.
EMB3

HAYDEN, JOHN
Lost horizons. 1935. BES34

HAYES, ALFRED, 1911-
Act of love. See The girl on
the Via Flaminia
The girl on the Via Flaminia.
1954. BES53, COTK
Variant title: Act of love

HAYES, JOSEPH, 1918-
The desperate hours. 1955.
BES54, BIER, THEA55

HAZELTON, GEORGE COCHRANE,
JR., 1868-1921
Mistress Nell. 1900. AMP16

-- and BENRIMO, JOSEPH HENRY
The yellow jacket. 1912. DID

HAZELWOOD, COLIN HAZEL-
WOOD, 1820-1875
Lady Audley's secret (from the
novel by Mary Elizabeth
Braddon). 1863. ROWE

HEALEY, FRANCES
The copper pot. 1919? WEB

HEBBEL, CHRISTIAN FRIED-
RICH, 1813-1863
Agnes Bernauer. 1852. CAM
Pattee, L., tr. SMK
Herodes und Mariamne. 1849.
CAM
Maria Magdalena. See Maria
Magdalene
Maria Magdalene. 1844. CAM
Fairley, B., tr. BUCK,
BUCL, BUCM, FEFH1,
TREA2, TREC1, TREE1

Green, P., tr. CLKW,
GRIF
Thomas, P., tr. FRA9,
SMI
Variant title: Maria Mag-
dalena
Siegfried's death. 1862.
Royce, K., tr. FRA9

HECHT, BEN, 1893- . See
Goodman, Kenneth S., jt. auth.

--and MacARTHUR, CHARLES
The front page. 1928. BES28,
CET, GASB

HEGGEN, THOMAS, 1918-1949
and LOGAN, JOSHUA
Mister Roberts. 1948. BES47,
GARW, HATA, SIXC

HEIBERG, GUNNAR EDWARD
RODE, 1857-1929
Kjaerlighedens tragedie. See
The tragedy of love
The tragedy of love. 1904.
Björkman, E., tr. DID
Variant title: Kjaerlighedens
tragedie

HEIJERMANS, HERMAN (Samuel
Falkland, pseud.), 1864-1924
The good hope. 1900?
Saunders, L., and Heijer-
mans-Houwink, C., trs.
GARZH
Variant title: Op hoop van
zegen
Op hoop van zegen. See The
good hope

HELLMAN, LILLIAN, 1905-
Another part of the forest (mu-
sic by Marc Blitzstein).
1946. BES46, WATE
The autumn garden. 1951.
BES50, CLM, FAM, GARW
Candide (based on Candide by
Voltaire; music by Leonard
Bernstein; lyrics by Richard
Wilbur, John Latouche and
Dorothy Parker). 1956.
BES56

75

The children's hour. 1934.
BES34, FIP, GAS, PLAN5
The lark. See Anouilh, Jean.
The lark (tr. and adapted
by)
The little foxes. 1939. BES38,
BLOO, CET, COTE, COTH,
HARB, HAVE, MIJY, SIXC,
SIXL, TREC2, TREE3
Variant title: Regina
Regina. See The little foxes
The searching wind. 1944.
BES43
Toys in the attic. 1960.
BES59, CEQ, CES
Watch on the Rhine. 1941.
BES40, CALN2, CALP,
CALQ, CASS, CRIT, CUBE,
GARZ, GAVE, HAVD,
NAGE

HEMRO.
Poor ostrich. 1948? RUA

HERBERT, FREDERICK HUGH,
1897-
Kiss and tell. 1943. BES42
The moon is blue. 1951.
GARW
HERMITE, l'TRISTAN, 1601-1655
Mariamne. 1636.
Lockert, L., tr. LOCR
Variant title: La Mariane
La Mariane. See Mariamne

HERNANANDEZ, ANTONIO ACE-
VEDO. See Acevedo Hernanandez, Antonio

HERNE, JAMES A., 1839-1901
Drifting apart. 1888. AMP7
Variant title: The fisher-
man's child
The fisherman's child. See
Drifting apart
Margaret Fleming. 1890. QUIL,
QUIM, QUIN
The minute men of 1774-1775.
1886. AMP7
The Reverend Griffith Daven-
port, Act. IV. 1899. AMP7
Shore acres. 1892. DOWM
Within an inch of his life.

1879. AMP7
HERRERA, LUIS BAYÓN. See
Bayón Herrera, Luis

HERREROS, MANUEL BRETÓN
DE LOS. See Bretón de los
Herreros, Manuel

HERSEY, JOHN, 1914-
A bell for Adano. See Osborn,
Paul. A bell for Adano
(based on the novel by)

HERSHADEVA, SRI. See Har-
sha, son of Hira

HERVERA, LUIS BAYÓN. See
Bayón Herrera, Luis

HERVIEU, PAUL ERNEST, 1857-
1915
Connais-toi. See Know thy-
self
La course du flambeau. 1901.
BER
Variant titles: The passing
of the torch; The torch
race; The trail of the torch
Know thyself. 1909.
Cerf, B., tr. DIC
Variant title: Connais-toi
The passing of the torch. See
La course du flambeau
The torch race. See La
course du flambeau
The trail of the torch. See
La course du flambeau

HEYWARD, MRS. DOROTHY
HARTZELL (KUHNS) and HEY-
WARD, DuBOSE
Porgy. 1927. BES27, GASB,
MACG, MIJY, THF

HEYWARD, DuBOSE, 1885-1940.
See Heyward, Mrs. Dorothy
Hartzell (Kuhns), jt. auth.

HEYWOOD, JOHN, 1497?-1580?
The four pp. 1569? ADA, BOA,
GARZB, HOPP, PARR, TAV,
TICO

76

Variant titles: The four p's; The playe called The foure pp

The four p's. See The four pp

Johan Johan. See John, Tyb and Sir John

Johan, Tyb his wife, and Sir Jhan the preest. See John, Tyb and Sir John

John, Tyb and Sir John. 1533. ADA, GAY1, HOPP, LOOM, PAR, RUB

Variant titles: Johan Johan; Johan, Tyb his wife and Sir Jhan the preest; John, Tyb and the curate; A merry play; A mery play betwene Johan Johan, the husbande, Tyb his wyfe, and Syr Jhan, the preest; A mery play be-tweene Johan Johan, Tyb, his wyfe and Syr Jhan, the preest

John, Tyb and the curate. See John, Tyb and Sir John

A merry play. See John, Tyb and Sir John

A mery play betweene Johan Johan, the husbande, Tyb his wyfe, and Syr Jhan, the preest. See John, Tyb and Sir John

A mery play betweene Johan Johan, Tyb, his wyfe and Syr Jhan, the preest. See John, Tyb and Sir John

A mery playe betwene the pardoner and the frere, the curate and neybour Pratte. See The pardoner and the friar

The pardoner and the friar. 1521?   LOOM, POLL

Variant title: A mery playe betwene the pardoner and the frere, the curate and neybour Pratte

The play of the wether. 1521? ADA, GAY1, PARR

The playe called the foure pp. See The four pp

HEYWOOD, THOMAS, 1574?-1641

The fair maid of the west. 1631.   MAL

A woman killed with kindness. 1603. ASH, BAS, BROC, CLF1, DUN, LAWR, MAT, MCJ, NEI, OLH, OLI1, PAR, RYL, SCH, SCI, SCJ, SMI, SPE, TAT, TAU, WALL

HICKERSON, HAROLD. See Anderson, Maxwell, jt. auth.

HILARIUS, 12th century

Ludus super iconia Sancti Nicolai. See The statue of Saint Nicholas

The miracle of Saint Nicholas and the image. 12th cent.   LOOM

The statue of Saint Nicholas. 12th cent.   MAK

Variant title: Ludus super iconia Sancti Nicolai

HILL, LUCIENNE

Paddle your own canoe. See Regnier, Max Albert Marie. Paddle your own canoe (tr. and adapted by)

The waltz of the toreadors. See Anouilh, Jean. The waltz of the toreadors (tr. and adapted by)

HINES, LEONARD JOHN

Simon. 1934.   SEVE

HIVNOR, ROBERT

The ticklish acrobat. 1954.   PLAA

HOADLY, BENJAMIN, 1706-1757

The suspicious husband. 1747.   MOR

HOARE, PRINCE, 1755-1834

No song no supper (music by Stephen Storace). 1790.   HUGH

HOCHWALDER, FRITZ, 1911-

Das heilige experiment. See The strong are lonely

The holy experiment. See The strong are lonely

Der öffentliche ankläger. See
The public prosecutor
The public prosecutor. 1947.
Black, K., tr.   PLAN16
Variant title: Der öffent-
liche ankläger
The strong are lonely. 1942.
LeGallienne, E., tr. PLAN14
Variant titles: Das heilige
experiment; The holy ex-
periment

HODGE, MERTON, 1903-
As it was in the beginning.
See The wind and the rain
Grief goes over. 1935. FAMH
The island. 1937.   SIXP
The wind and the rain. 1933.
                         FAME
Variant title: As it was in
the beginning

HODSON, JAMES LANSDALE,
1891-
Harvest in the north. 1939.
                         FAML
Red night. 1936.   FAMI

HOFFE, MONCKTON, 1880-1951
Many waters. 1926. FAO, PLAD

HOFMANNSTHAL, HUGO HOF-
MANN VON, 1874-1929
Death and the fool. See Der
tor und der tod
The death of Titian. 1892.
Heard, J., tr.   FRA17
Variant title: Der tod des
Tizian
Electra. 1904.
Symons, A., tr.   DIE
Die hochzeit der Sobeide. See
The marriage of Sobeide
The marriage of Sobeide. 1899.
Morgan, B., tr.   FRA20
Variant title: Die hochzeit
der Sobeide
Das Salzburger grosse welt-
heater. 1920.   FEFH2
Der tod des Tizian. See The
death of Titian
Der tor und der tod. 1893.
                         STI1

Hamburger, M., tr. BLOC
Heard, J., tr.   FRA17
Variant title: Death and the
fool

HOGAN, R., and MOLIN, S. E.
The silent woman. See Jonson,
Ben. The silent woman (adapted
by)

HOLBERG, LUDWIG, 1684-1754
Erasmus Montanus. See Ras-
mus Montanus
Jeppe of the hill. 1722.
Jagendorf, M., tr. CLF2
Variant title: Jeppe paa
bjerget
Jeppe paa bjerget. See Jeppe
of the hill
The loquacious barber. 1723.
Chambers, W., tr.   BAT17
Variant title: Mester Gert
Westphaler eller den meget
talende barbeer
Mester Gert Westphaler eller
den meget talende barbeer.
See The loquacious barber
Rasmus Montanus. 1747.
Campbell, O., and Schenck,
F., trs.   MAU
Variant title: Erasmus Mon-
tanus

HOLM, JOHN CECIL, 1906- ,
and ABBOTT, GEORGE
Three men on a horse. 1935.
                         GAS
HOLME, CONSTANCE
"I want!" 1933.   FIT

HOME, JOHN, 1722-1808
Douglas. 1756. BAT14, MCM,
MCMI, MOR, MOSE2, NET,
STM

HOME, WILLIAM DOUGLAS,
1912-
The thistle and the rose. 1949.
                         PLAN4
HOOTE, HORTON
The dancers. 1954? WAGC2

78

HOPKINS, ARTHUR MELANC-
THON, 1878-
Moonshine. 1921. PROF, PROG,
PROH, PROI, TOD

--See Watters, George Manker,
jt. auth.

HOPWOOD, AVERY, 1882-1928.
See Rinehart, Mary Roberts, jt.
auth.

HORACE. See Horatius Flaccus,
Quintus

HORATIUS FLACCUS, QUINTUS
The bore; a dramatic version
of Horace (Satires I, 9)
Ullman, D., tr.   HOWK

HORNE, KENNETH, 1900-
Trial and error. 1953. PLAN9

HOUGHTON, STANLEY, 1881-
1913
Fanny Hawthorne. See Hindle
wakes
Hindle wakes. 1912.   DIG,
PLAP1, TUCD
Variant title: Fanny Haw-
thorne

HOUSMAN, LAURENCE, 1865-
A good lesson! (from Victoria
Regina). 1934.   COOP
Victoria Regina. 1935. BES35,
CEU

--and GRANVILLE-BARKER,
HARLEY GRANVILLE
Prunella; or, Love in a Dutch
garden. 1906.   PLAP2

HOWARD, BRONSON CROCKER,
1842-1908
The banker's daughter. 1873.
AMP10, CLA
Baron Rudolph. 1881. AMP10
The Henrietta. 1887.   HAL
Hurricanes. 1878.   AMP10
Old love letters. 1878. AMP10
One of our girls. 1885. AMP10
Shenandoah. 1888. MOSS3,

QUIG, QUIJ, QUIK, QUIL,
QUIM, QUIN

--See Young, Sir Charles
Lawrence, jt. auth.

HOWARD, SIR ROBERT, 1626-
1698. See Dryden, John, jt. auth.

HOWARD, SIDNEY COE, 1891-
1939
Alien corn. 1933.   BES32,
FAMD
Dodsworth (based on the novel
by Sinclair Lewis). 1934.
BES33, HAT
The late Christopher Bean (tr.
and adapted by). See Fau-
chois, René.   The late
Christopher Bean
Lucky Sam McCarver. 1925.
MOSK, MOSL
Madam, will you walk. 1939.
THEA54
Ned McCobb's daughter. 1926.
MIL
Pi-Pa-Ki. See Lute song
The silver cord. 1926. BES26,
BROW, BROX, CHAN,
CHAP, COTE, DIE, FUL,
JORG, MOSG, MOSH, QUIL,
QUIM, QUIN, THF, TUCD,
TUCM, TUCN, TUCO,
WATC1, WATI, WATO, WHI
They knew what they wanted.
1924.
BES24, CET, CORD, CORE,
CORF, GASB, MACG, MCD,
MERW
--See also Loesser, Frank.
The most happy fella (based
on the play by)

--and De KRUIF, PAUL HENRY
Yellow jack. 1934.   GARU,
MERV, NAGE, SCWI

--and IRWIN, WILLIAM HENRY
Lute song (adapted from the
Chinese classic Pi-Pa-Ki
by Kao-Tong-Kia or Tse-
Tching). 1946.   BES45
Variant title: Pi-Pa-Ki

HOWE, MRS. JULIA (WARD),
1819-1910
Hippolytus. 1911.   AMP16
Leonora; or, The world's own.
1857.   QUIJ, QUIK

HOWELLS, WILLIAM DEAN,
1837-1920
The unexpected guests. 1893?
                           QUIO2
HOYT, CHARLES HALE, 1860-
1900
A bunch of keys; or, The
hotel. 1883.   AMP9
A midnight bell. 1889. AMP9
A milk white flag. 1894.
                           AMP9
A temperance town. 1893.
                           AMP9
A Texas steer; or, "Money
makes the mare go." 1890.
MOSJ, MOSK, MOSL
A trip to Chinatown; or, Idyl
of San Francisco. 1891.
AMP9, CLA

HROSWITHA. See Hrotsvit, of
Gandersheim

HROTSVIT, OF GANDERSHEIM,
935?-1000?
Dulcitius. 10th cent.
Butler, M., tr.   GARZB
Taylor, J., tr.   TAV
Paphnutius. 10th cent.
Butler, M., tr.   GARZB

HSIUNG, CHENG-CHIN
The thrice promised bride.
                           WEB
HUGHES, HATCHER, 1883-1945
Hell-bent for heaven. 1924.
BES23, CORD, CORE,
CORF, COT, MCD, TUCJ

HUGHES, RICHARD ARTHUR
WARREN, 1900-
A high wind in Jamaica. See
Osborn, Paul. The innocent
voyage (based on the novel
by)

HUGHES, Thomas, fl. 1587

The misfortunes of Arthur.
1588.   CUN

HUGO, VICTOR MARIE, 1802-
1885
Hernani. 1830. BOR, COM,
GRA, SEA
Asher, L., tr.   BERM
Crosland, Mrs. N., tr.
CAR, CLF2, MAU
Ruy Blas. 1838. COM, GRA,
SCN, STJ2
Crosland, Mrs. N., tr.
GREA
HUNTER, NORMAN C., 1908-
A day by the sea. 1953.
FAMO
Waters of the moon. 1951.
FAOS
HURLBUT, WILLIAM JAMES,
1883-
The bride of the lamb. 1926.
BES25
HUSSON, ALBERT
La cuisine des anges. See
Spewack, Bella and Spe-
wack, Samuel. My 3 angels
(adapted from)

HUSTON, JOHN. See Koch, Howard, jt. auth.

HUTCHINS, MRS. MAUDE
(PHELPS)
Aunt Julia's Caesar. 195-?
SPC
The case of Astrolable. 1944?
NEW44
A play about Joseph Smith,
jr. 1944?   NEW44
The wandering Jew. 1951?
NEW51
HUTTON, JOSEPH, 1787-1828
Fashionable follies. 1809.
MOSS2
HYDE, DOUGLAS, 1860-
The twisting of the rope. 1901.
CAP
HYMAN, MAC, 1923-
No time for sergeants. See
Levin, Ira. No time for
sergeants (adapted from the
novel by)

I

IBSEN, HENRIK, 1828-1906
Bygmester solness. See The
  master builder
The child wife. See A doll's
  house
A doll's house. 1879.
  Archer, W., tr. CLF2,
  COJ, DRA2, EDAD, HOUS,
  HUD, KNIC, KNID, MAU,
  MCD, PLAB2, PROW,
  THOM, THON, WATI,
  WATL1, WHT
  Variant titles: The child
  wife; Et dukkehjem; Nora
Et dukkehjem. See A doll's
  house
An enemy of society. See An
  enemy of the people
An enemy of the people. 1882.
  Anon. tr., BUCK, BUCL,
  BUCM, DEAR, EVB2,
  GASS, HARB, ROGE, SAND
  Mark-Aveling, E., tr.
  HOLM, MOSA, WALJ, WHK
  Miller, A., adapter. MERV
  Sharp, R., tr. BONA, COD,
  DUR, EVA2, INGW, STA,
  THO
  Variant titles: An enemy of
  society; En folkefiende
En folkefiende. See An enemy
  of the people
Fruen fra havet. See The lady
  from the sea
Gengangere. See Ghosts
Ghosts. 1881.
  Anon. tr. DOWN, SILM
  Archer, W., tr. BARC,
  BAT17, CROV, MIL, ROB,
  SAY, SEBO, SEBP, SMP,
  STE, TREC2, TREE2
  LeGallienne, E., tr. BENU,
  BLOC, LEVI
  Variant title: Gengangere
Hedda Gabler. 1890.
  Anon. tr. LOCL, LOR
  Gosse, E., tr. GPA
  Gosse, E., and Archer,
  W., trs. ALLI, BLAG,
  BLOO, BROF, BROG, BROH,
  CAR, CARA, CLKW, COOP,

FOUM, GRIF, HAV, HAVD,
HAVE, KERN, SMI, TRE,
TREA1, TREC2, TREE2,
WALB, WATA, WATI,
WATL2, WATR
  LeGallienne, E., tr.
  LOCLA, LOCLB
  Legalliene, J., and Leys-
  sac, P., trs. LEG
John Gabriel Borkman. 1897.
  Archer, W., tr. ULAN
  Ginsbury, N., adapter
      PLAN23
Kongsemnerna. See The pre-
  tenders
The lady from the sea. 1888.
  Archer, W., tr. SAY
  Variant title: Fruen fra
  havet
The master builder. 1892.
  Anon. tr. CROS, GUTH, HIB,
  HIBA, HIBB, SIXB
  Gosse, E., and Archer,
  W., trs. WORP
  Variant title: Bygmester
  solness
Nora. See A doll's house
Peer Gynt. 1876.
  Ginsbury, N., tr. BLOC
The pretenders. 1864.
  Archer, W., tr. SMK
  Variant title: Kongsemnerna
Rosmersholm. 1886.
  Anon. tr. BROJ, BROK,
  LOCM2
  Archer, W., tr. TUCN,
  TUCO
  Jellicoe, A., tr. CUBH,
  FOUM
  LeGallienne, E., tr. ROET
Vildanden. See The wild duck
The wild duck. 1885.
  Anon. tr. CEW, SSST,
  SSSU
  Archer, F., tr. BIER,
  CLM, CUBE, CUBG, DEAP,
  LEV, LEVE, MACJ,
  MACL2, MOSQ, WEAV2,
  WHI
  Reinert, O., tr. REIN,
  REIP
  Sharp, R., tr. BARR
  Variant title: Vildanden

IDZUMO, TAKEDA, 1688-1756
Bushido. 1746.
Eliot, S., tr.   LAW

IFFLAND, AUGUST WILHELM,
1759-1814
Conscience. 1800?
Thompson, B., tr. BAT11
Variant title: Das gewissen
Das gewissen. See Conscience

ILYENKOV, VASSILY PAVLOVICH
Campo dei fiori. See The
square of flowers
The square of flowers. 1944.
Bakshy, A., tr.   BAKS
Variant title: Campo dei
fiori

INCHBALD, MRS. ELIZABETH
(SIMPSON), 1753-1821
Adventures of a shawl. See
Appearance is against them
Appearance is against them.
1785.   HUGH
Variant titles: Adventure of
a shawl; Mistake upon mis-
take; or, Appearance is a-
gainst them
Everyone has his fault. 1793.
NIC
Mistake upon mistake; or, Ap-
pearance is against them.
See Appearance is against
them
INGE, WILLIAM, 1913-
Bus stop. 1955. BES54, GART,
HOGA, THEA55
Come back, little Sheba. 1950.
BES49, CUBG, GARW,
NEWV, WATA
The dark at the top of the
stairs. 1957. BES57, CES,
HUDE
Variant title: Farther off
from heaven
Farther off from heaven. See
The dark at the top of the
stairs
Picnic. 1953. BES52, GART,
GAVE, THEA53

IOBST, CLARENCE F., 1894-

Die Calline browierts. 1930.
BUFF
Es Heller's Chrischtdag
(based on the story Es
wasch Heller's Chrischtdag's
zug by Charles C. More).
1931.   BUFF
IONESCO, EUGENE
The bald soprano. 1950.
Allen, D., tr. BLOC,
NEWW9, ULAN
Variant title: La cantatrice
chauve
La cantatrice chauve. See
The bald soprano
The lesson. 1951.
Allen, D., tr. REIN, REIP
Rhinoceros. 1960.
Prouse, D., tr.   BES60,
SEVD

IRELAND, WILLIAM HENRY,
1777-1835
Vortigern. 1796.   BAT22

IRVING, WASHINGTON, 1783-
1859
Rip Van Winkle. See Rauch,
Edward H. Rip Van Winkle
(based on the book by)

--See Payne, John Howard,
jt. auth.

IRWIN, WILL. See Irwin, William Henry

IRWIN, WILLIAM HENRY, 1873-
The Hamadryads. 1904. BOH1

--See Howard, Sidney, jt. auth.

ISHERWOOD, CHRISTOPHER,
1904-
The Berlin stories. See Van
Druten, John. I am a
camera (adapted from the
stories by)

--See Auden, Wystan Hugh, jt.
auth.

JACKSON, ISABELLE. See
Meaker, Mrs. Isabelle (Jackson)

JACKSON, N. HART
The two orphans. See D'Ennery, Adolphe Phillippe and
Cormon, Eugène. The two
orphans (adapted by)

JACKSON, SHIRLEY, 1920
The lottery. See Duffield,
Brainerd. The lottery
(from a story by)

JACOBS, WILLIAM WYMARK,
1863-1943
A love passage. 1897? PEN

JAMES, DAN, 1911-
Winter soldiers. 1942. BES42

JAMES, HENRY, 1843-1916
The American. 1891. HOGA
The turn of the screw. See
Archibald, William. The in-
nocents (based on the novel
by)
Washington Square. See Goetz,
Ruth Goodman and Goetz,
Augustus. The heiress
(based on the novel by)

JAMESON, STORM (née Margaret
Storm Jameson), 1897-
William the defeated. 194-?
OULD

JARRY, ALFRED, 1873-1907
Ubu Roi. 1896.
Wright, B., tr. FOUF

JEANS, RONALD, 1887-
Count your blessings. 1951.
PLAN5
Young wives' tale. 1949.
PLAN3

JEFFERE, JOHN
The buggbears (supposed author). 1561? BOND

JEFFERS, ROBINSON, 1887-
The Cretan woman. 1954.

Medea. See Euripides. Me-
dea (tr. and adapted by)

JEFFERSON, JOSEPH, 1829-1905
Rip Van Winkle. See Anony-
mous plays. Rip Van
Winkle (as played by); see
also Burke, Charles. Rip
Van Winkle

JELLICOE, ANN
The sport of my mad mother.
195-? OBSE

JENNINGS, Gertrude E.
Family affairs. 1934. FAMF

JENNINGS, TALBOT
No more frontier. 1929. TOD

JEROME, MRS. HELEN (BUR-
TON), 1883-
Charlotte Corday. 1939. FIP
Jane Eyre (based on the novel
by Charlotte Brontë). 1936.
FOUP, THH
Pride and prejudice (based on
the novel by Jane Austen).
1935. BES35, FOUP, THH,
VOAD

JERROLD, DOUGLAS WILLIAM,
1803-1857
Black ey'd Susan; or, All in
the downs. 1829. MOSN,
MOSO, ROWE

JESSOP, GEORGE HENRY, d.
1915
Sam'l of Posen; or, The commercial drummer. 1881.
AMP4

JEVON, THOMAS, 1652-1688
Devil of a wife. See The
devil to pay; or, The wives
metamorphos'd (adapted
from)

--and COFFEY, CHARLES;
MOTTLEY, JOHN; CIBBER,
THEOPHILUS
The devil to pay; or, The

wives metamorphos'd (adapted from Devil of a wife by Thomas Jevon). 1731. HUGH

JOAQUÍN, NICK
A portrait of the artist as Filipino. 1952.　　EDAD

JOB, THOMAS, d. 1947
Uncle Harry. 1942.　　BES41

JOHN, ERROL
Moon on a rainbow shawl. 195-?　　OBSE

JOHNSON, CHARLES, 1679-1748
The cobler of Preston. 1716. HUGH
JOHNSON, MRS. GEORGIA (DOUGLAS)
Plumes. 1927?　　LOC

JOHNSON, PAMELA HANSFORD
The duchess at sunset. 1948. OULD
JOHNSON, PHILIP, 1900-
Lovers' leap. 1934.　　FAMG

JOHNSTON, DENIS, 1901-
The moon in the Yellow river. 1931.　　BROT
The old lady says "No!" 1929. CAN
JONES, EDITH NEWBOLD. See Wharton, Mrs. Edith Newbold (Jones)

JONES, HENRY ARTHUR, 1851-1929
The case of rebellious Susan. 1894.　　BES94
The dancing girl. 1891. MAL
Dolly reforming herself. 1908. CHA, CHAN, CHAR
The goal. 1898. HUD, PEN
Judah. 1894.　　RUB
The liars. 1897. DUR, MAP, MAT
The masqueraders. 1894. MOSN, MOSO
Michael and his lost angel. 1896.　　BOWY, DIC
Mrs. Dane's defence. 1900. COT

JONES, JACK
Rhondda roundabout. 1939. SIXL
JONES, JOSEPH STEVENS, 1809-1877
The people's lawyer. See Solon Shingle
Solon Shingle. 1839. BAT20, MOSS2
Variant title: The people's lawyer
The usurper; or, Americans in Tripoli. 1841? AMP14

JONES, PAUL
Birthday honours. 1953. PLAN9
JONES, PETER, 1920-　, and JOWETT, JOHN
The party spirit. 1954. PLAN11
JONSON, BEN, 1572-1637
The alchemist. 1610. ASH, BAS, BENY, BROC, GAY2, GRE, HARC47, HOW, KRM, LIE, LIEE1, NEI, OLH, OLI2, ROET, SPE, TAT, TAU, THA
Bartholomew Fair. 1614. OLH, OLI2, SPE
Epicoene; or, The silent woman. 1609. BALD, BROC, CLKW, GAY2, RUB, STA
Hogan, R., and Molin, S., adapters　　HOGA
Every man in his humour. 1598. ANG, BAS, BAT14, BROC, CLF1, CLK1, GAY2, HAPR, MAT, NEI, PAR, SCI, SCJ, SCW, SPE, WAT
The gipsies metamorphosed. 1621.　　BROC
The hue and cry after cupid. 1608. BAS, SCH, SCI, SCJ
Oberon, the fairy prince. 1611. PAR
The sad shepherd; or, A tale of Robin Hood. 1641? BAS, SCH
Sejanus, his fall. 1603. BAS, NEI, PAR
The silent woman. See Epicoene

84

The vision of Delight. 1617.
ABRA, ABRB1
Volpone; or, The fox. 1606.
ALLI, BARD, BAS, BROC,
DEAO, DEAP, DEAR, DUN,
FOUD, HUD, KRE, KRM,
LIED1, MORR, NEI, OLH,
OLI1, PAR, PARR, SCH,
SCI, SCJ, SPE, SUL, TRE,
TREA2, TREC1, TREE1,
WALL
--See also Zweig, Stefan.
Volpone (adapted by)
--See Chapman, George, jt.
auth.
JOSEPHSON, RAGNAR, 1891-
Kanske en diktare. See Per-
haps a poet
Perhaps a poet. 1932.
Lundbergh, H., tr. SCAN1
Variant title: Kanske en
diktare

JOWETT, JOHN. See Jones,
Peter, jt. auth.

JOYCE, JAMES, 1882-1941. See
Barentin, Marjorie.
Ulysses in Nighttown (based
on the novel by)

JULLIEN, JEAN, 1854-1919
The serenade. 1887.
Clark, B., tr.   CLD

JŪŌ, ESASHI. See Esashi Jūō

JUPP, KENNETH
The socialites. 1961?   SATA

K

KAISER, GEORGE, 1878-1945
Der brand im opernhaus. See
The fire in the opera house
The conflagration of the opera
house. See The fire in the
opera house
The coral. 1917.
Katzin, W., tr. DIK2, TUCG,
TUCM, TUCN, TUCO
Variant title: Die koralle
The fire in the opera house.

1916.
Katzin, W., tr.   KAT
Variant titles: Der brand
im opernhaus; The confla-
gration of the opera house
From morn to midnight. 1916.
Dukes, A., tr. BLOC, DIE,
GARZH, MOSG, MOSH,
ROET
Variant title: Von morgens
bis mitternachts
Gas I. 1918.   STI2
Scheffauer, H., tr. TUCG,
TUCM, TUCN, TUCO
Gas II. 1920.   FEFH2
Katzin, W., tr. TUCG,
TUCM, TUCN, TUCO
Die koralle. See The coral
Von morgens bis mitternachts.
See From morn to midnight

KĀLIDĀSA. 4th century
The fatal ring. See Shakuntala
Sakoontalá. See Shakuntala
Shakuntala. 4th cent.
Jones, W., tr.   TAV
Monier-Williams, M., tr.
BUCK, DUCL, BUCM,
CLF1, EDAD, ORI3, TRE,
TREA2, TREC1, TREE1,
YOHA
Ryder, A., tr.   WARN1
Variant titles: The fatal
ring; Šakoontalá

KANIN, FAY (MITCHELL)
(Michael Kanin), 1917-
Goodbye, my fancy. 1948.
BES48
Variant title: Most likely to
succeed
Most likely to succeed. See
Goodbye, my fancy

KANIN, MICHAEL. See Kanin,
Fay (Mitchell)

KANIN, GARSON, 1912-
Born yesterday. 1946. BES45,
GARZ

KANIN, MRS. GARSON.   See
Gordon, Ruth

KAO, TONG KIA
 Pi-Pa-Ki. See Howard, Sidney
 and Irwin, William Henry.
 Lute song (adapted from)

KATAEV, VALENTĪN PETROVĪCH,
1897-
 Squaring the circle. 1928.
 Malamuth, C., and Lyons,
 E., trs. HAV, HAVE, LYK

KATAYEV, VALENTĪN PETRO-
VĪCH. See Kataev, Valentīn
Petrovich

KATZ, L.
 The three cuckolds. See
 Anonymous plays. The three
 cuckolds (converted by)

KAUFMAN, GEORGE S., 1889-
 The butter and egg man. 1925.
 BES25, LEV, LEVE

 --See Dayton, Katharine;
 Lardner, Ring; Marquand,
 John P.; Teichmann, How-
 ard, jt. auths.

--and CONNELLY, MARCUS COOK
 Beggar on horseback. 1923.
 BES23, CAR, CARA, CHAN,
 CHAP, COT, GASB, WARH,
 WATC1, WATI
 Dulcy. 1921. BES21, COH,
 CONG, MOSJ, MOSK, MOSL
 Merton of the movies (based
 on the novel by Harry L.
 Wilson). 1922. BEAC12,
 BES22, PEN
 To the ladies! 1922. QUI,
 TUCD

--and FERBER, EDNA
 Dinner at eight. 1932. BES32,
 SIXH
 Minich. 1924. BES24
 The royal family. 1927.
 BES27
 Stage door. 1936. BES36,
 CLDP, GAS

--and HART, MOSS

The American way. 1939.
 BES38, PROC
George Washington slept here.
 1940. BES40
The man who came to dinner.
 1939. BES39, CET, DAVK,
 GARZ, SIXC
Merrily we roll along. 1934.
 BES34
Once in a lifetime. 1930.
 BES30, FAMB
You can't take it with you.
 1936. BES36, CLDP,
 CORE, CORF, GAS, LOOC,
 LOOD, LOOE, LOOF,
 MERS, SPES

--and RYSKIND, MORRIE and
GERSHWIN, IRA
 Of thee I sing (music by
 George Gershwin). 1931.
 BES31, CORD, CORE,
 CORF, DUR, FAMD, HIL,
 ROLF, TRE, VAN

--and TEICHMANN, HOWARD
 The solid gold cadillac. 1953.
 GART
KELLY, GEORGE EDWARD,
1887-
 Behold the bridegroom. 1927.
 BES27
 Craig's wife. 1925. BES25,
 CORD, CORE, CORF,
 GASB, HARB, MERW,
 MOSG, MOSH
 Daisy Mayme. 1926. BES26
 The fatal weakness. 1946.
 BES46
 Finders-keepers. 1916?
 WAGC3
 Variant title: The lesson
 The lesson. See Finders-
 keepers
 Poor Aubrey. 1925. GASB,
 PROH, SCWG, THO
 The show-off. 1924. BES23,
 KRM, MOSJ, MOSK, MOSL

KELLY, HUGH, 1739-1777
 False delicacy. 1768. MCM,
 MCMI
KEMP, R . The satire of the

86

three estates. See Lindsay, Sir
David. The satire of the three
estates (modernized by)

KENNEDY, MARGARET, 1896-
Escape me never! 1933. SEV

KENNEDY, MARY and HAW-
THORNE, RUTH (WARREN)
Mrs. Partridge presents. 1925.
BES24
KENYON, CHARLES, 1880-
Kindling. 1911.   DIG

KERR, JEAN (COLLINS)
Mary, Mary. 1961.   BES60

KESSELRING, JOSEPH, 1902-
Arsenic and old lace. 1941.
BES40, CEY, FREE, GARZ
Variant title: Bodies in our
cellar
Bodies in our cellar. See
Arsenic and old lace

KIA, KAO TONG. See Kao,
Tong Kia

KIELLAND, TRYGVE, 1897-
Dronningen og hennes menn.
See Queen Margaret of Nor-
way
Queen Margaret of Norway.
1950.
Malleson, C., tr. MODS

KILLIGREW, THOMAS, 1612-
1683
The parson's wedding. 1640.
KNOW, SUM

KIMBALL, ROSAMOND
The resurrection. 191-? FED1

KIMMINS, ANTHONY, 1901-
The amorous prawn. 1959.
PLAN21
KING, NORMAN
The shadow of doubt. 1955.
PLAN12
KING, PHILIP, 1904-
Serious charge. 1953.   PLAN11

-- and CARY, FALKLAND L.
Sailor, beware! 1955. PLAN12
Watch it, sailor! 1960.
PLAN22
KINGSLEY, SIDNEY, 1906-
Darkness at noon (based on
the novel by Arthur Koestler).
1951. BES50, GARW, GAVE,
WISD
Dead end. 1935. BES35, FREE,
CET, GAS, JAFF
Detective story. 1949. BES48,
GARW, HAVG
Lunatics and lovers. 1954.
THEA55
Men in white. 1934. BES33,
CORD, CORE, CORF,
FAMF, GARU, MERV
Thomas Jefferson. See The
patriots
The patriots. 1943. BES42,
CRIT, GARZ, GAVE
Variant title: Thomas Jeffer-
son
The world we make (based on
the novel The outward room
by Millen Brand). 1939.
BES39
KINOSHITA, JUNJI
Twilight crane. 1949.
Scott, A., tr.   PLAA
Variant title: Yuzuru
Yuzuru, See Twilight crane

KINWELMERSH, FRANCIS, fl.
1570. See Gascoigne, George,
jt. auth.

KIRKLAND, JACK, 1904-   ,
and CALDWELL, ERSKINE
Tobacco road. 1933. CEY,
GAS

KIRSHON, VLADIMIR MIKHAÍL-
OVICH, 1902-
Bread. 1931.
Volochora, S., tr.   LYK

KIYOTSUGU, KWANAMI, 1333-
1384
Sotoba Komachi. 14th cent.
Waley, A., tr. TRE,
TREC1, TREE1

87

KLEIST, HEINRICH BERNT WIL-
HELM VON, 1777-1811
  The broken jug. See Der
    zerbrochene krug
  Kaethchen of Heilbronn; or,
    The test of fire. 1810.
    Pierce, F., tr.   PIE
    Variant title: Das Kätchen
    von Heilbronn; oder, Die
    feuerprobe
  Das Käthchen von Heilbronn;
    oder, Die feuerprobe. See
    Kaethchen of Heilbronn; or,
    The test of fire
  Penthesilea. 1876.
    Trevelyan, H., tr. BENR2
  The Prince of Homburg. See
    Prinz Friedrich von Hom-
    burg
  Prinz Friedrich von Homburg.
    1821.   CAM
    Hagedorn, H., tr. FRA4,
    SMK
    Kirkup, J., tr.   BENR2
    Lustig, T., tr.   LUST
    Variant title: The Prince of
    Homburg
  Der zerbrochene krug. 1808.
                        CAM
    Variant title: The broken jug

KNIGHT, ERIC MOWBRAY, 1897-
1943
  Never come Monday (adapted
    by Stephen Fox). 1939?
                        PROC
KNIGHT, VICK
  Cartwheel. 194-?   PROC

KNOBLOCK, EDWARD, 1874-
1945. See Bennett, Arnold, jt.
auth.

KNOTT, FREDERICK, 1919-
  Dial "M" for murder. 1952.
    BES52, FAOS, THEA53

KNOWLES, JAMES SHERIDAN,
1784-1862
  The love-chase. 1837.   MAL
  Virginius. 1820. MOSN, MOSO

KNOX, FLORENCE CLAY

For distinguished service.
  1918.   SHAY

KOBER, ARTHUR, 1900-
  "Having wonderful time." 1937.
                        CET
  Wish you were here (based on
    "Having wonderful time;"
    music and lyrics by Harold
    Rome). 1953.   THEA53

KOCH, HOWARD and HUSTON,
JOHN
  In time to come. 1941. BES41

KOCHERGA, IVAN, 1885-
  Masters of time. 1934.
    Wixley, A., tr.   FOUS
    Variant title: Watchmaker
    and the hen
  Watchmaker and the hen. See
    Masters of time

KOCK, CHARLES PAUL DE,
1794-1871
  A happy day. 184-?
    Chambers, W., tr.   BAT9
    Variant title: Une journée
    de bonheur
  Une journée de bonheur. See
    A happy day

KOESTLER, ARTHUR, 1905-
  Darkness at noon. See Kings-
    ley, Sidney. Darkness at
    noon (based on the novel by)

KOPIT, ARHTUR L., 1937-
  Oh dad, poor dad, mamma's
    hung you in the closet and
    I'm feelin' so sad. 1960.
                        BES61
KOPS, BERNARD, 1926-
  Enter Solly God. 1961? SATA
  The hamlet of Stepney Green.
    1958.   NEWE1

KORNEICHUK, ALEXANDER EV-
DOKIMOVICH, 1905-
  The front. 1942.
    Anon. tr.   FOUT
    Kotem, B., and Voynow,
    Z., trs.   SEVP

Guerillas of the Ukrainian
Steppes. 1942.
Anon. tr. FOUT
Variant title: Partisans on
the Steppes of the Ukraine
Partisans on the steppes of the
Ukraine. See Guerillas on
the Ukrainian Steppes
Platon Krechet. 1935?
Prokofieva, R., tr. THY

KOSACH, LARISA PETROVNA
(Lesya Ukrainka, pseud.)
The Babylonian captivity. 19th
cent.
Volska, S., tr. ROE

KOTZEBUE, AUGUST FRIEDRICH
FERDINAND VON, 1761-1819
Der egoist und kritikus. See
Egotist and pseudo-critic
Herr Gottlieb Merks
Egotist and pseudo-critic Herr
Gottlieb Merks. 179-?
Chambers, W., tr. BAT11
Variant title: Der egoist und
kritikus
Falsche scham. See Dunlap,
William. False shame
(adapted from)
Das kind der liebe. See
Lovers' vows
Lovers' vows; or, The natural
son. 1798?
Thompson, B., tr. BAT21
Variant title: Das kind der
liebe
Menschenhass und reue. See
The stranger
Pharaoh's daughter. 179-?
Beebe, B., tr. WEB
Variant title: Die tochter
Pharaonis
The stranger. 1789.
Thompson, B., tr. MCM,
MCMI
Variant title: Menschenhass
und reue
Die tochter Pharaonis. See
Pharaoh's daughter

KOZLENKO, WILLIAM, 1908-
This earth is ours. 1937? KOZ

KRAMM, JOSEPH, 1907-
The shrike. 1952. BES51

KRASNA, NORMAN
Dear Ruth. 1944. BES44
John loves Mary. 1947. BES46

KREYMBORG, ALFRED, 1883-
The dead are free. 1935.
AME5
Hole in the wall. 192-?
KRE
Lima beans. 1925? LEV,
LEVE
Manikin and Minikin. 1918.
SHAY
Rocking chairs. 1921? SHAY

KROG, HELGE, 1889-
Konkylien. See The sounding
shell
The sounding shell. 1929.
Campbell, R., tr. SCAN2
Variant title: Konkylien

KUHNS, DOROTHY HARTZELL.
See Heyward, Mrs. Dorothy
Hartzell (Kuhns)

KUMMER, MRS. CLARE
(BEECHER)
Good gracious Annabelle.
1916. DES09
Her master's voice. 1933.
BES33
KURNITZ, HARRY
Reclining figure. 1954.THEA55

KWANAMI KIYOTSUGU. See
Kiyotsugu, Kwanami

KYD, THOMAS, 1558-1594
Arden of Feversham (some-
times attributed to). See
Anonymous plays. Arden
of Feversham
The Spanish tragedy; or, Hier-
onimo is mad again. 1589?
BAS, BROC, HEIL, HOW,
MAT, MCJ, MINI, MIO1,
NEI, OLH, OLI1, PAR,
RUB, SCI, SCJ, SCW,
SPE, TICO

L

LABICHE, EUGÈNE MARIN,
1815-1888, and LEVEAUX, AL-
PHONSE
  La grammaire. 1867. BENZ,
  STOC

--See Legouvé, Ernest, jt.
  auth.

--and DELACOUR, ALFRED
CHARLEMAGNE LARTIGNE
  La cagnolte. See Pots of
  money
  Célimare. 1863.
  Hoffman, L., and T., and
  Bentley, E., trs. BENSA
  Variant title: Célimare le
  bien-aimé
  Célimare le bien-aimé. See
  Célimare
  Les petits oiseaux. See
  Grundy, Sydney. A pair of
  spectacles (adapted from)
  Pots of money. 1864?
  Bermel, A., tr. BERM
  Variant title: La cagnolte

--and MARTIN, ÉDOUARD
  Bluffers. See La poudre aux
  yeux
  Cousin Billy. See Le voyage
  Monsieur Perrichon
  Dust in the eyes. See La
  poudre aux yeux
  Perrichon's voyage. See Le
  voyage de Monsieur Perri-
  chon
  La poudre aux yeux. 1861.
                     SCN
  Variant titles: Bluffers;
  Dust in the eyes
  The 37 sous of M. Montaudoin.
  See Les trente-sept sous de
  M. Montaudoin
  Les trente-sept sous de M.
  Montaudoin. 1862. BRN
  Variant title: The 37 sous
  of M. Montaudoin
  A trip abroad. See Le voyage
  de Monsieur Perrichon
  Le voyage de Monsieur Perri-

chon. 1860.   MCL
  Ward, R., tr.   BENSA
  Variant titles: Cousin Billy;
  Perrichon's voyage; A trip
  abroad

--and MICHEL, MARC ANTOINE
AMÉDÉE
  Haste to the wedding. See An
  Italian straw hat
  An Italian straw hat. 1851.
  Hoffman, L., and T., trs.
                   BENT3
  Variant titles: Haste to the
  wedding; The wedding
  march
  The wedding march. See An
  Italian straw hat

LA CHAUSSÉE, PIERRE CLAUDE
NIVELLE DE, 1692-1754
  Fashionable prejudice. See
  Le préjugé à la mode
  Le préjugé à la mode. 1735. BRE
  Variant title: Fashionable
  prejudice

LA FOSSE, ANTOINE DE, sieur
d'Aubigny, 1653-1708
  Manlius Capitolinus. 1698.
  Lockert, L., tr.   LOCR

LAGERKVIST, PÄR. 1891-
  Låt människan leva. See Let
  man live
  Let man live. 1949.
  Alexander, H., and Jones,
  L., trs.   SCAN3
  Variant title: Låt människan
  leva
  The man without a soul. 1936.
  Kökeritz, H., tr. SCAN1
  Variant title: Mannen utan
  själ
  Mannen utan själ. See The
  man without a soul

LANGLEY, NOEL, 1911- . See
Morley, Robert, jt. auth.

LARDNER, RING WILMER,
1885-1933, and KAUFMAN,
GEORGE S.

90

June moon. 1929.   BES29

LATOUCHE, JOHN TREVILLE,
1917-1956
    Candide. See Hellman, Lilli-
      an. Candide (lyrics by)
    The golden apple (music by
      Jerome Moross). 1954.
      BES53, THEA54

LAUNDER, FRANK, and GILLIAT,
SIDNEY
    The body was well nourished.
      See Meet a body
    Meet a body. 1940.   PLAN10
      Variant title: The body was
      well nourished

LAURENTS, ARTHUR, 1918-
    A clearing in the woods. 1957.
                  BES56
    Home of the brave. 1945.
      BES45, GARZ, HEWE
    The time of the cuckoo. 1952.
      BES52, THEA53

LAVEDAN, HENRI LEON ÉMILE,
1859-1940
    The prince d'Aurec. 1892.
      Clark, B., tr.   THR

LAVERY, EMMET, 1902-
    The magnificent Yankee. 1946.
      BES45, MERT, SPES

--and MURPHY, GRACE
    Kamiano, the story of Damien.
      1938.   THEC

LA VIGNE, ANDRIEU DE, 15th
century
    The miracle of the blind man
      and the cripple. 15th cent.
                  LOOM

LAW, WARNER
    Indomitable blacksmith. 195-?
                  LOVR

LAWLER, RAY
    Summer of the 17th doll.
      1958?   BES57

LAWRENCE, JEROME, 1915- ,
and LEE, ROBERT E.

Inherit the wind. 1955. BES54,
    GART, THEA55

LAWSON, JOHN HOWARD, 1895-
    Processional. 1925.   WATC1,
      WATI
    Roger Bloomer. 1923.   FULT
    Success story. 1932.   LOO

LAYA, JEAN LOUIS, 1761-1833
    L'ami des lois. 1793.   BRE

LEACOCK, JOHN
    The fall of British tyranny; or,
      American liberty triumphant.
      1776?   MOSS1

LEAMON, DOROTHY
    Barabas. 20th cent.   FED2

LEAVITT, JOHN McDOWELL,
1824-
    The Jewish captives. 1876?
                  KOH2

LECOCQ, ALEXANDRE CHARLES,
1832-1918
    The daughter of Madame An-
      got. 1872.
      Seldes, G., and G., trs.
                  PLAM
      Variant title: La fille de
      Madame Angot
    La fille de Madame Angot.
      See The daughter of Mad-
      ame Angot

LEE, JAMES HENRY
    Career. 1956.   COTK

LEE, NATHANIEL, 1653?-1692
    The rival queens; or, The
      death of Alexander the
      great. 1677. MCM, MCMI
    Sophonisba. 1675.   DOA

LEE, ROBERT E. See Law-
rence, Jerome, jt. auth.

LEGOUVÉ, ERNEST, 1807-1903,
and LABICHE, EUGENE MARIN
    La cigale chez les fourmis.
      188-?   BOVE
      Variant title: The grass-

hopper at the home of the
ants
The grasshopper at the home
of the ants. See La cigale
chez les fourmis

LEMAÎTRE, JULES, 1853-1914
Forgiveness. See The pardon
Le pardon. See The pardon
The pardon. 1895.
    Clark, B., tr.   THR
    Variant titles: Forgiveness;
    Le pardon

LENNOX, GILBERT
Close quarters. See Somin,
    W. O.   Close quarters (tr.
    and adapted by)

LENORMAND, HENRI RENÉ,
1882-1938
The coward. 1925.
    Orna, D., tr. CHA, CHAN
    Variant title: La lâche
Crépuscule du théâtre. See
    In Theatre street
The devourer of dreams. See
    The dream doctor
The dream doctor. 1922.
    Orna, D., tr.   MOSG,
    MOSH
    Variant titles: The devourer
    of dreams; Le mangeur de
    rêves
L'homme et ses fantômes.
    1924.   RHO
    Variant title: Man and his
    phantoms
In Theatre street. 1936.
    Dukes, A., tr.   FAMK
    Variant title: Crépuscle du
    théâtre
Le lâche. See The coward
Man and his phantoms. See
    L'homme et ses fantômes
Le mangeur de rêves. See
    The dream doctor
Simoom. See Le simoun
Le Simoun. 1920.   HARV
    Variant title: Simoom
Le temps est un songe. See
    Time is a dream
Time is a dream. 1919.

Katzin, W., tr. DIE, HAV
Variant title: Le temps est
un songe

LEONOV, LEONID MAXIMO-
VICH, 1899-
Invasion. 1943.
    Anon. tr.   FOUT
The orchards of Polovchansk.
    1938.
    Robbins, J., tr.   SEVP

LÉOPOLD, pseud. See Chandezon, Léopold

LERNER, ALAN JAY, 1918-
Brigadoon (music by Frederick
    Loewe). 1947.   BES46
My fair lady (adapted from
    Bernard Shaw's Pygmalion;
    music by Frederick Loewe).
    1956.   BES55

LE SAGE, ALAIN RENÉ, 1668-
1747
Crispin, rival de son maître.
    See Crispin, rival of his
    master
Crispin, rival of his master.
    1707
    Chambers, W., tr. BAT8
    Variant title: Crispin,
    rival de son maitre
The financier. See Turcaret
Turcaret. 1709. BRE, ZDA
    Aldington, R., tr.   ALD
    Merwin, W., tr. BENR4
    Variant titles: The finan-
    cier; Turcaret; or, The
    financier
Turcaret; or, The financier.
    See Turcaret

LESSING, DORIS MAE, 1919-
Each his own wilderness.
    1958.   NEWE1

LESSING, GOTTHOLD EPHRAIM,
1729-1781
Minna von Barnhelm; or, The
    soldier's fortune. 1767.
    Bell, E., tr. BAT10, CROV,
    GREA, HARC26, MAU

Miss Sara Sampson. 1753.
   Bell, E., tr.   CLF2
Nathan der weise. See
   Nathan the wise
Nathan the wise. 1783.
   Frothingham, E., tr.KOH2
   Lustig, T., tr.   LUST
   Variant title: Nathan der
   weise

LETTON, FRANCIS. See Dowling, Jennette, jt. auth.

LEVEAUX, ALPHONSE, b. 1810.
See Labiche, Eugène Marin, jt.
auth.

LEVIN, IRA
   No time for sergeants (adapted
   from the novel by Mac Hyman). 1955. BES55, GART,
   THEA56

LEVITT, SAUL
   The Andersonville trial. 1959.
   BES59, CEQ

LEVY, BENN WOLF, 1900-
   Clutterbuck. 1949.   BES49
   The devil passes. 1932. BES31
   Mrs. Moonlight. 1928.   FAO
   Springtime for Henry. 1931.
      LEV, LEVE

LEWIN, ROSE D. See Franken,
Mrs. Rose D. (Lewin)

LEWIS, LEOPOLD DAVID, 1828-
1890
   The bells (adapted from Le
   juif Polonais by Erckmann-
   Chatrian). 1871.   ROWE
   Variant title: The Polish Jew
   The Polish Jew. See The
   bells

LEWIS, SAUNDERS
   King's daughter. See Siwan
   Siwan. 1954.
      Humphreys, E., tr.PLAN21
      Variant title: King's daugh-
      ter

LEWIS, SINCLAIR, 1885-1951
   Dodsworth. See Howard, Sidney. Dodsworth (based on
   the novel by)
   The ghost patrol. See Clarke,
   William Kendall. The ghost
   patrol (based on the story
   by)

LILLO, GEORGE, 1693-1739
   The London merchant; or, The
   history of George Barnwell.
   1731. BENY, BROJ, BROK,
   EIGH, HAN, MCM, MCM1,
   MOR, NET, SMI, STM,
   TAU, TUQ

LINARES RIVAS, MANUEL, 1866-
   The claws. 1914.
      Turrell, C., tr.   TUR
      Variant title: La garra
   La garra. See The claws

LINDSAY, SIR DAVID, 1490-1555
   The satire of the three es-
   tates. 1540.
      Kemp, R., modernizer
             ROET
LINDSAY, HOWARD, 1889- ,
and CROUSE, RUSSEL
   Life with father (based on the
   book by Clarence Day).
   1939. BES39, CASS, CET,
   CEY, COOP, GARZ,
   LOVR, MERS, SPER
   Life with mother (based on
   the book by Clarence Day).
   1948.   BES48
   Remains to be seen. 1951.
             BES51
   State of the union. 1945.
   BES45, GARW

LIPSCOMB, WILLIAM PERCY,
1887- , and MINNEY, RU-
BEIGH J.
   Clive of India. 1934.   FAME

LIPSKEROFF, KONSTANTIN,
1899-
   Carmencita and the soldier
   (based on the opera Carmen
   by Georges Bizet; libretto

by Prosper Mérimée.) 1923.
Seldes, G., and G., trs.
PLAM
LIVING NEWSPAPER. See Staff
of the Living Newspaper

LIVINGS, HENRY
Stop it, whoever you are.
1961.   NEWE5

LOCHER, JENS, 1889-1952
Tea for three. 1943.
Anon. trs. (revised by Fur-
bank, P., and Bredsdorff,
E.)   CONT
Variant title: Tre maa man
vaere
Tre maa man vaere. See Tea
for three

LOCKRIDGE, FRANCES (MRS.
RICHARD LOCKRIDGE) and
LOCKRIDGE, RICHARD
The Norths meet murder. See
Davis, Owen. Mr. and
Mrs. North (based on the
novel by)

LOCKRIDGE, RICHARD, 1898- ,
See Lockridge, Frances, jt. auth.

LODGE, THOMAS, 1558?-1625
Mucedorus (sometimes attributed to). See Anonymous
plays. Mucedorus
The reign of King Edward the
third (sometimes attributed
to). See Anonymous plays.
The reign of King Edward
the third

LOESSER, FRANK, 1910-
Guys and dolls. See Swerling,
Jo, and Burrows, Abe.
Guys and dolls (music and
lyrics by)
How to succeed in business
without really trying. See
Burrows, Abram S. How to
succeed in business without
really trying (music and
lyrics by)
The most happy fella (based on

Sidney Howard's play They
knew what they wanted).
1956.   THEA56

LOEWE, FREDERICK
Brigadoon. See Lerner, Alan
Jay. Brigadoon (music by)
My fair lady. See Lerner,
Jay. My fair lady (music
by)

LOGAN, JOSHUA, 1908-
The wisteria trees (based on
the Cherry orchard by An-
ton Chekhov). 1950. BES49

--See Behrman, Samuel Na-
thaniel; Hammerstein II,
Oscar; Heggen, Thomas;
Kober, Arthur, jt. auths.

LONG, JOHN LUTHER, 1861-
1927. See Belasco, David, jt.
auth.

LONGFELLOW, HENRY WADS-
WORTH, 1807-1882
The Spanish student. 1843?
BAT19
LONGFORD, CHRISTINE
Mr. Jiggins of Jigginstown.
1933.   CAN

LONGFORD, EDWARD ARTHUR
HENRY, 1902-
Yahoo. 1933.   CAN

LONSDALE, FREDERICK, 1881-
1954
Aren't we all? 1923.   SEV
Half a loaf. See Let them eat
cake
The last of Mrs. Cheyney.
1925.   BES25
Let them eat cake. 1959.
PLAN19
Variant titles: Half a loaf;
Once is enough
Once is enough. See Let them
eat cake

LOOS, ANITA, 1893-
Gigi (from the novel by Col-

94

ette). 1951.   BES51

LOPE DE RUEDA. See Rueda,
Lope de

LOPEZ, SABATINO, 1867-1951
    Il passero. See The sparrow
    The sparrow. 1918.
        Goldberg, I., tr.   GOL
        Variant title: Il passero

LÓPEZ DE AYALA, ADELARDO,
1828-1879
    Consuelo. 1878.   BRET

LORCA, FEDERICO GARCIA.
See Garcia Lorca, Federico

LOS HERREROS, MANUEL BRE-
TÓN DE. See Bretón de los
Herreros, Manuel

LOW, SAMUEL, b. 1765
    The politician out-witted. 1789.
                          MOSS1
LUDWIG, OTTO, 1813-1865
    Der erbförster. 1850.   CAM
        Remy, A., tr.   FRA9
        Variant title: The hereditary
        forester
    The hereditary forester. See
        Der erbförster
LYLY, JOHN, 1554?-1606
    Alexander and Campaspe. See
        Campaspe
    Campaspe. 1584. ADA, GAY1,
        MCI, OLH, OLI1
        Variant title: Alexander and
        Campaspe
    Endimion. See Endymion, the
        man in the moon
    Endymion, the man in the
        moon. 1588. BAS, BROC,
        MIN2, MIO2, NEI, PAR,
        SCH, SCI, SCJ, SCW, SPE
        Variant title: Endimion
    Midas. 1589.   WINN
    Mother Bombie. 1589? TAT,
        TAU
LYNDON, BARRÉ, 1896-
    The amazing Dr. Clitterhouse.
        1936.   FOUP, THH
    The man in Half moon street.

1939.   SIXL
They came by night. 1937.
                    FIP
LYTTON, EDWARD GEORGE
BULWER. See Bulwer-Lytton,
Edward George Earle Lytton

M

MacARTHUR, CHARLES, 1895-
1956. See Hecht, Ben, jt. auth.

McCARTHY, JUSTIN HUNTLEY,
1861-1936
    If I were king. 1901. BES99
        Variant title: The vagabond
        king
    The vagabond king. See If I
        were king

McCAULEY, CLARICE VALL-
ETTE
    The conflict. 1920.   SHAY
    The seeker. 1919.   FED1

McCLOSKEY, JAMES J.
    Across the continent; or,
        Scenes from New York life
        and the Pacific railroad.
        1870.   AMP4

McCRACKEN, MRS. ESTHER
(ARMSTRONG), 1902-
    Quiet wedding. 1938.   SIXL

McCULLERS, MRS. CARSON
(SMITH), 1917-
    The member of the wedding.
        1950. BES49, GARW,
        GAVE, HEWE, MIJY

MacDONAGH, DONAGH, 1912-
    Happy as Larry. 1947. BROS,
        NEWW6
    Step-in-the-hollow. 1957.
                          BROT
MacDOUGALL, ROGER, 1910-
    The gentle gunman. 1950.
                          PLAN5
    To Dorothy, a son. 1950.
                          PLAN4
McENROE, ROBERT EDWARD,
1916-

Oliver Erwenter. See The
silver whistle
The silver whistle. 1948.
BES48
Variant title: Oliver Er-
wenter

McEVOY, CHARLES, 1879-1929
The likes of her. 1923. MAP

McGEEHAN, MRS. SOPHIE
(TREADWELL). See Treadwell,
Sophie

McGUIRE, WILLIAM ANTHONY,
1885-1940
Six cylinder love. 1921. BES21

McHARDY, AIMÉE. See Stuart,
Mrs. Aimée (McHardy)

MACHIAVELLI, NICCOLO, 1469-
1527
La mandragola. See Mandra-
gola
Mandragola. 1525?
Hale, J., tr. BARB
May, F., and Bentley, E.,
trs. BENR1
Young, S., tr. HAYD
Variant titles: La mandra-
gola; The mandrake
The mandrake. See Mandra-
gola

MACKAY, CONSTANCE D'ARCY
Benjamin Franklin, journey-
man. 1912? LAW
Counsel retained. 1915? PEN
The prince of court painters.
1915? WEB

MACKAY, MRS. ISABEL (MAC-
PHERSON) ECCLESTONE, 1875-
1928
The second lie. 1921. MAS1

MACKAY, L. A.
The freedom of Jean Guichet.
1925. MAS2

MacKAYE, PERCY WALLACE,
1875-

Napoleon crossing the Rockies.
1924. CHU
The pilgrim and the book.
1920. FED1
Sam Average. 1911. BEAC11
The scarecrow. 1910. DIC,
FLAN, GASS, MOSJ, MOSK,
MOSL, QUIG, QUIJ, QUIK,
QUIL, QUIM, QUIN

MacKAYE, STEELE, 1842-1894
An arrant knave. 1889. AMP11
Hazel Kirke. 1880. QUIG,
QUIJ, QUIK, QUIL, QUIM,
QUIN
In spite of all. 1885. AMP11
Paul Kauvar; or, Anarchy.
1890. MOSS3
Rose Michel. 1875. AMP11
Won at last. 1877. AMP11

McKENNEY, RUTH, 1911-
My sister Eileen (based on the
stories by). See Fields,
Joseph and Chodorov, Je-
rome. My sister Eileen
Wonderful town. See Fields,
Joseph and Chodorov, Je-
rome. Wonderful town
(based on the stories My
sister Eileen by)

MacKENZIE, RONALD, 1903-
1932
The Maitlands. 1934. FAMF
Musical chairs. 1931. FAMB,
PLAD

MACKIE, PHILIP
The whole truth. 1955. PLAN13

MacKINTOSH, ELIZABETH
(Gordon Daviot, pseud.)
The laughing woman. 1934.
FAME
Richard of Bordeaux. 1933.
FAMD
Queen of Scots. 1934. FAMF

MacLEISH, ARCHIBALD, 1892-
Air raid. 1938. MCCF
The fall of the city. 1937.
BROU, BRR3, GAS, KERN,

96

KRE, LOOB, LOOC, LOOD,
LOOE, NELS, VOAD, WAIT
J. B. 1958.   BES58
The music crept by me upon
the waters. 1953?   SUL

McLELLAN, C. M. S. (Hugh Morton, pseud.), 1865-1916
Leah Kleschna. 1904. BES99

MacMILLAN, DOUGALD, 1897-
Off Nags head; or, The bell
buoy. 1922?   LAW

MACMILLAN, MARY LOUISE,
1870-
The pioneers. 1917?   LAW

MACNEICE, LOUIS, 1907-
The dark tower. 1946. ANDE,
BENS2

MacOWAN, NORMAN, 1877-
Glorious morning. 1938.FAML

MACPHERSON, ISABEL. See
Mackay, Mrs. Isabel (Macpherson) Ecclestone

MACRAE, ARTHUR, 1908-
Both ends meet. 1954. PLAN10

MAETERLINCK, MAURICE, 1862-
1949
The death of Tintagiles. 1899.
Sutro, A., tr. BAT21, SHAY
Variant title: La mort de
Tintagiles
Home. See Interior
L'intérieur. See Interior
Interior. 1894.
Archer, W., tr.   MCCP,
MIL
Variant titles: Home; L'in-
térieur
The intruder. 1890.
Block, H., tr.   BLOC
Hovey, R., tr. BENP, CAR,
CARA, HUD, TREC2,
TREE2
Variant title: L'intruse
L'intruse. See The intruder.

Monna Vanna. 1903.
Sutro, A., tr.   MOSQ
La mort de Tintagiles. See
The death of Tintagiles
Pelléas and Mélisande. See
Pelléas et Mélisande
Pelléas et Mélisande. 1892.
RHO
Hovey, R., tr. DIC, DIK1,
HAV, SMN, TUCG, TUCM,
TUCN, TUCO, WATI,
WATL2, WATR, WHI
Variant title: Pelléas and
Mélisande

MAIRET, JEAN DE, 1604-1686
Sophonisba. 1634.
Lockert, L., tr.   LOCR

MALLESON, MILES, 1888-
Le malade imaginaire. See
Molière, Jean Baptiste
Poquelin. Le malade
imaginaire (tr. and adapted
by)
The misanthrope. See Molière,
Jean Baptiste Poquelin.
Le misanthrope (tr. and
adapted by)
The miser. See Molière,
Jean Baptiste Poquelin. The
miser (tr. and adapted by)
The prodigious snob. See
Molière, Jean Baptiste
Poquelin. Le bourgeois
gentilhomme (tr. and adap-
ted by)
School for wives. See Molière,
Jean Baptiste Poquelin.
L'école des femmes (tr.
and adapted by)
Sganarelle. See Molière, Jean
Baptiste Poquelin. Sgana-
relle (tr. and adapted by)
Tartuffe. See Molière, Jean
Baptiste Poquelin. Tartuffe
(tr. and adapted by)

--and BROOKS, HARRY
Six men of Dorset. 1938.
FAML
MALTZ, ALBERT, 1908-
Private Hicks. 1935?   KOZ

MANCO, SILVERIO
    Juan Moreira. 1886.
        Fassett, J., tr.   BIE

MANN, HEINRICH, 1871-
Madame Legros. 1914.
    Katzin, W., tr.   KAT

MANNERS, JOHN HARTLEY,
1870-1928
    Peg o' my heart. 1912.   CEY

MANNING, MARY
    Youth's the season...? 1931.
                              CAN
MARCEAU, FÉLICIEN (pseud. of
Louis Carrette), 1913-
    The egg. 1957?
        Schlitt, R., tr. and adapter
                             BES61
        Variant title: L'oeuf
    L'oeuf. See The egg

MARCEL, GABRIEL, 1887-
    Ariadne. 1936?
        Heywood, R., tr.   ULAN
        Variant title: Le chemin de
        Crête
    Le chemin de Crête.   See
    Ariadne

MARCH, WILLIAM (pseud. of
Wm. Edward March Campbell),
1894-
    The bad seed. See Anderson,
    Maxwell. The bad seed
    (based on the novel by)

MARC-MICHEL (pseud. of Marc
Antoine Amédee Michel,) 1812-
1868. See Labiche, Eugène, jt.
auth.

MARIVAUX, PIERRE CARLET DE
CHAMBLAIN DE, 1688-1763
    The false confessions. 1737.
        Merwin, W., tr.   BENR4
        Variant title: Les fausses
        confidences
    Les fausses confidences. See
    The false confessions
    The game of love and chance.
    See Le jeu de l'amour et

    du hazard
    Le jeu de l'amour et du hazard.
    1730. BRE, SEA, STJ1,
    ZDA
        Aldington, R., tr.   ALD
        Fowlie, W., tr.   FOWL
        Variant title: The game of
        love and chance

MARKS, MRS. L. S. See Peabody, Josephine Preston

MARLOWE, CHRISTOPHER,
1564-1593
    Doctor Faustus. See The
    tragical history of Doctor
    Faustus
    Edward II. See The trouble-
    some reign and lamentable
    death of Edward the second
    Faustus. See The tragical
    history of Doctor Faustus
    The Jew of Malta. 1589?
        BROC, NEI, PAR, SPE,
        THA
    The reign of King Edward the
    third (sometimes attributed
    to). See Anonymous plays.
    The reign of King Edward
    the third
    Tamburlaine the great. 1587?
        BROC, HOW, SCW
    Tamburlaine the great, pt. I.
        1587? BALD, BAS, KRE,
        NEI, RYL, SCI, SCJ, SPE,
        TICO
    The tragical history of Doctor
        Faustus. 1588? ABRB1,
        BALL, BARD, BAS, BAUG,
        BENY, BROC, BROK, CLF1,
        CLK1, COF, COJ, COL1,
        DEAN, DOWN, DEAO, DUN,
        FOUD, GREB1, GREC1,
        GRIF, HARC19, HAY, HEIL,
        HOW, HUD, LIE, LIED1,
        LIEE1, LOCK, LOCL,
        MCNI, MIL, MOO, NEI,
        OLH, OLI1, PAR, RUB,
        SCH, SCI, SCJ, SCW,
        SHAH1, SHAI1, SHAJ1, SMI,
        SNYD1, SPE, SPF1, STA,
        TOBI, TREC1, TREE1,
        WAT, WEAT1, WCO1,

98

WOOD1, WOOE1
Variant titles: Doctor Faustus; The tragical history of the life and death of Doctor Faustus
The tragical history of the life and death of Doctor Faustus. See The tragical history of Doctor Faustus
The troublesome reign and lamentable death of Edward the second. 1592? ASH, BAS, BROC, CLKW, GRE, HARC46, MAT, NEI, OLH, OLI1, PAR, RUB, SCH, SCI, SCJ, SPE, TAT, TAU
Variant title: Edward II

MARNI, JEANNE, pseud. See Marnière, Jeanne Marie Françoise

MARNIÈRE, JEANNE MARIE FRANÇOISE (Jeanne Marni, pseud.), 1854-1910. See Guinon, Albert, jt. auth.

MARQUAND, JOHN PHILLIPS, 1893- , and KAUFMAN, GEORGE S.
The late George Apley. 1944. BES44, COTE, COTH
Point of no return. See Osborn, Paul. Point of no return (adapted from the novel by)

MARQUINA, EDUARDO, 1879-
Cuando florez can las rosales. See When the roses bloom again
When the roses bloom again. 1913.
Turrell, C., tr. TUR
Variant title: Cuando florez can las rosales

MARQUIS, DON, 1787-1937
The old soak. 1922. BES22

MARSHAK, SAMUIL IAKOVLE-VICII, 1887-
Twelve months. 1943?

Bakshy, A., tr. BAKS

MARSHALL, BRUCE, 1899-
Father Malachy's miracle.
See Doherty, Brian. Father Malachy's miracle (based on the novel by)

MARSTON, JOHN, 1575?-1634
The Dutch courtesan. 1603.
WALL
--and WEBSTER, JOHN
The malcontent. 1604. BAS, BROC, HAPR, LAWR, NEI, SPE

MARTENS, ANNE COULTER
Blue beads. 1938? LOVR

MARTIN, ÉDOUARD, 1828-1866.
See Labiche, Eugène Marin, jt. auth.

MARTÍNEZ, JACINTO BENA-VENTE Y. See Benavente y Martínez, Jacinto

MARTÍNEZ SIERRA, GREGORIO, 1881-1947, and MARTÍNEZ SI-ERRA, MARIA
Canción de cuna. See The cradle song
The cradle song. 1911.
Underhill, J., tr. BES26, CEW, HAV
Variant title: Canción de cuna
The kingdom of God. 1916.
Granville-Barker, H., and H., trs. BES28
Variant title: El reino de Dios
A lily among thorns. 1911.
Granville-Barker, H., and H., trs. DIE
Variant title: Lirio entre espinas
Lirio entre espinas. See A lily among thorns
Los pastores. See The two shepherds
El reino de Dios. See The kingdom of God

99

The two shepherds. 1913.
Granville-Barker, H., and
H., trs.   LEV, LEVE
Variant title: Los pastores

MARTÍNEZ SIERRA, MARÍA,
1880-   . See Martínez Sierra,
Gregorio, jt. auth.

MARTYN, EDWARD, 1859-1923
Maeve. 1900.   CAP

MASEFIELD, JOHN, 1878-
The tragedy of Pompey the
great. 1910. MOSN, PLAP2

MASON, HARRY SILVERNALE
At the gate beautiful. 1925?
FED2
MASSEY, EDWARD
Plots and playwrights. 1917?
BAK
MASSINGER, PHILIP, 1583-1640
The bondman. 1623.   RUB
The maid of honor. 1621?
BAS
A new way to pay old debts.
1625? ANG, BAS, BAT13,
BROC, DUN, GAY3,
HARC47, HOW, KRE,
LAWR, MAT, NEI, OLH,
OLI2, PAR, RUB, SCH, SCI,
SCJ, SMO, SPE, TAV,
WALL, WHE
The Roman actor. 1626. MCK

--See Fletcher, John, jt. auth.

MATHEUS, JOHN
'Cruiter. 1926?   LOC

MAUGHAM, WILLIAM SOMER-
SET, 1874-
Before the party. See Ack-
land, Rodney. Before the
party (based on a short
story by)
The breadwinner. 1930. CHA,
CHAN, CHAR
The circle. 1921. BES21,
BROH, CEU, CLM, COT,
COTH, DIG, DUR, HAVE,
KRM, MAP, MCD, MOSG,

MOSH, MYB, TREC2,
TREE2, TUCD, TUCM,
WALB, WATF2, WATI,
WATO, WEE
The colonel's lady. See Sher-
riff, Robert Cedric. The
colonel's lady (based on the
story by)
The constant wife. 1927.
BES26, HAU, LOR, WARI
For services rendered. 1932.
MOD
Jane. See Behrman, Samuel
Nathaniel. Jane (based on
the story by)
Loaves and fishes. 1911.
WEAL
Our betters. 1917. DID, MOSO,
SMO, WHI
Sheppey. 1933.   SIXH
Miss Thompson. See Colton,
John and Randolph, Clem-
ence. Rain (based on the
story by)

MAUPASSANT, GUY DE, 1850-
1893
The household peace. 1893.
Chambers, W., tr. BAT9
Variant title: La paix du
ménage
La paix du ménage. See The
household peace

MAURETTE, MARCELLE
Anastasia. 1953?
Bolton, G., adapter.
PLAN9, THEA55

MAUREY, MAX, 1868-1947
Rosalie. 1900.   SET

MAURIAC, FRANÇOIS, 1885-
Asmodée. 1938.
Thurman, B., tr.   HAYE

MAYAKÓVSKY, VLADÍMIR
VLADIMÍROVICH, 1894-1930
The bathhouse. 1929?
MacAndrew, A., tr. GARZJ
The bedbug. 1929.
Reeve, F., tr.   REEV2
Mystery-bouffe. (Second vari-

ant). 1921.
Noyes, G., and Kaun, A.,
trs.   NOY

MAYER, EDWIN JUSTUS, 1897-
Children of darkness. 1930.
AMI, GARV, KRM
The firebrand. 1924. BES24

MAYNE, RUTHERFORD, pseud.
See Waddell, Samuel

MAYOR, BEATRICE
The pleasure garden. 1924.
PLAP3
MEACHAM, MALCOLM
The snow goose. See Gallico,
Paul. The snow goose
(adapted by)

MEAD, SHEPHERD, 1914-
How to succeed in business
without really trying. See
Burrows, Abram S. How
to succeed in business without really trying (based on
the book by)

MEAKER, MRS. ISABELLA (JACK-
SON), 1874- . See Harnwell,
Mrs. Anna Jane (Wilcox), jt. auth.

MEDWALL, HENRY, fl. 1486-
1500
Fulgens and Lucrece. 1497?
BOA
Nature. 1495?   FARN

MEGRUE, ROI COOPER, 1883-
1927
Under cover. 1914.   CART

--and HACKETT, WALTER
It pays to advertise. 1914.
MOSJ, MOSK, MOSL

MELDON, MAURICE
Purple path to the poppy field.
1953.   NEWW5

MELL, MAX, 1882-
The apostle play. 1934.
White, M., tr.   SEVE

MELLON, EVELYN EMIG. See
Emig, Evelyn

MELVILLE, ALAN (pseud. of
Alan Caverhill), 1910-
Castle in the air. 1949.
PLAN3
Dear Charles. 1952. PLAN8
Simon and Laura. 1954.
PLAN11
MELVILLE, HERMAN, 1819-
1891
Billy Budd. See Coxe, Louis
O., and Chapman, Robert.
Billy Budd (based on the
novel by)

MENANDER, OF ATHENS, 342?-
292? B. C.
The arbitration. 4th cent. B. C.
Allinson, F., tr.   HOWE,
HOWF
Casson, L., tr.   CASU
Post, L., tr. OAT2, OATE
Variant title: Epitrepontes
Dyskolos. See The grouch
Epitrepontes. See The arbi-
tration
The girl from Samos. 4th
cent. B. C.
Casson, L., tr.   CASU
Post, L., tr.   OAT2
Variant titles: Samia; The
woman of Samos
The grouch. 317 B. C.
Casson, L., tr.   CASU
Variant title: Dyskolos
The perikeiromene. See The
shearing of Glycera
Samia. See The girl from
Samos
The shearing of Glycera. 4th
cent. B. C.
Casson, L., tr.   CASU
Post, L., tr.   OAT2
Variant titles: The perikei-
romene; She who was shorn
She who was shorn. See The
shearing of Glycera
The woman of Samos. See
The girl from Samos

101

MENDOZA, JUAN RUIZ DE
ALARCÓN. See Ruiz de Alarcón
y Mendoza, Juan

MENOTTI, GIAN-CARLO, 1911-
The saint of Bleecker Street.
1954. THEA55

MÉRIMÉE, PROSPER (Clara Gazul, pseud.), 1803-1870
Carmencita and the soldier
(based on the opera Carmen,
by Georges Bizet). See
Lipskeroff, Konstantin.
Carmencita and the soldier
Inez Mendo; or, The triumph
of prejudice. 1825. BAT21

MERRILL, JAMES, 1926-
The bait. 1953. MACH
The immortal husband. 1955.
PLAA
MESSAGER, CHARLES. See
Mildrac, Charles, pseud.

METASTASIO, PIETRO ANTONIO
DOMENICO BUONAVENTURA
(pseud. of Pietro Trepassi),
1698-1782
Achilles in Scyros. 1800?
Hoole, J., tr. JOH
Attilo Rigolo. 1740. BIN
The dream of Scipio. 1800?
Hoole, J., tr. BAT5
Variant title: Il sogno di
Scipione
Il sogno di Scipione. See The
dream of Scipio

MICHEL, MARC ANTOINE
AMEDÉE. See Labiche, Eugène,
jt. auth.

MICHENER, JAMES, 1907-
Tales of the South Pacific.
See Hammerstein II, Oscar
and Logan, Joshua. South
Pacific (adapted from)

MICK, HETTIE LOUISE
The maid who wouldn't be
proper. 1921? LAW

MIDDLEMASS, ROBERT M.,
1883- . See Hall, Holworthy,
jt. auth.

MIDDLETON, GEORGE, 1880-
See Bolton, Guy Reginald, jt.
auth.

MIDDLETON, THOMAS, 1580-
1627
A chaste maid in Cheapside.
1612? WALL
A game at chess. 1624. BROC
Michaelmas term. 1606?
SCI, SCJ
A trick to catch the old one.
1606? BAS, NEI, SPE
Women beware women. 1623?
OLH, OLI2

--See Dekker, Thomas, jt.
auth.

--and ROWLEY, WILLIAM
The changeling. 1623? BAS,
BROC, LAWR, NEI, OLH,
OLI2, SCH, SCI, SCJ, SPE,
TAT, TAU
A fair quarrel. 1617?
OLH, OLI2
The Spanish gipsie. 1623.
GAY3
MILLAR, RONALD, 1919-
Waiting for Gillian. 1954.
PLAN10
MILLAY, EDNA ST. VINCENT,
1892-
Aria da capo. 1919. CHU,
GASB, KRE
The king's henchman. 1927.
TUCD
The lamp and the bell. 1921.
SHAY
MILLER, ARTHUR, 1915-
All my sons. 1947. BES46,
BROH, GARW, GAVE,
HATA, HEWE, SIXB
The crucible. 1953. BES52,
COOP, GART, GUTH, LOR,
MLJY, SUL, THEA53,
WATA
Variant title: Those familiar
spirits

102

Death of a salesman. 1949.
  BENU, BES48, BIER, BLOC,
  BROX, CALQ, FOUM,
  GARW, GAVE, HUNT,
  MCNA, NEWV, STEI, STJM,
  TREC2, TREE3, TUCO,
  WARH, WATE, WISE, WISF
An enemy of the people. See
  Ibsen, Henrik. An enemy
  of the people (adapted by)
The man who had all the luck.
  1943.   CROZ1
Pussycat and the expert plumb-
  er who was a man. 194-?
                            PROX
Those familiar spirits. See
  The crucible
A view from the bridge. 1955.
  BES55, CLM, CUBH, GART,
  REIN, THEA56, ULAN

MILLER, CINCINNATUS HEINE,
1841-1913. See Miller, Joaquin,
pseud.

MILLER, DANIEL, 1843-1909?
  En gespräch zwischer zweb
    demokrate über politiks.
    18-?   BUFF
  Noch eppes vom Peter seim
    handwerk.   BUFF
  Der Peter soil en handwerk
    lernen. 18-?   BUFF

MILLER, JOAQUIN (pseud. of
Cincinnatus Hiner (or Heine)
Miller), 1841-1913
  The Danites in the Sierras.
    1877.   HAL

MILLER, SIGMUND STEPHEN
  One bright day. 1956. PLAN14

MILLS, HUGH
  The little glass clock. 1954.
                            PLAN11
  The house by the lake. 1956.
                            PLAN14
MILMAN, HENRY HART, 1791-
1868
  Belshazzar. 1822?   KOH2
  The fall of Jerusalem. 1820?
                            KOH2

MILNE, ALAN ALEXANDER,
1882-1956
  The boy comes home. 1918.
    SRY, SRYG
  The Dover road. 1922. BES21,
    DIE, MOD, WATT2
  The great Broxopp. 1923. CHU
  The ivory door. 1927.   TUCJ
  Michael and Mary. 1929.
                            BES29
  Mr. Pim passes by. 1919.
    CALM, CEU, MCD, THF,
    WATF2, WATI
  Success. 1923.   COT, MYB
  The truth about Blayds. 1921.
    MOSG, MOSH, TUCD, TUCM

MILTON, JOHN, 1608-1674
  Comus. 1634. CLK1, HARC4,
    OLH, OLi2, PAR, RICH
  Samson Agonistes. 1670?
    BARD, GREB1, GREC1,
    GRED, HAPT2, HARC4,
    KOH2, SML

MINNEY, RUBEIGH J., 1895-   .
See Lipscomb, William Percy, jt.
auth.

MIRA DE AMESCUA, ANTONIO,
fl. 1600
  El esclavo del demonio. 1612.
                            ALP
MIRBEAU, OCTAVE, 1850-1917
  Les affaires sont les affaires.
    1903.   BER
    Variant title: Business is
    business
  Business is business. See Les
    affaires sont les affaires
  The epidemic. 1898?
    Barzun, J., tr.   BENS2
    Variant title: L'epidémie
  L'epidémie. See The epidemic

MIRZA FATH-ALĪ. See Fath'Alī,
Ākhund-zadah

MIRZA FETH-ALĪ AKHOUD
ZAIDÉ. See Fath'Alī, Ākhund-
zadah

"MR. PUNCH," pseud.

A dramatic sequel to Hamlet; or, The new wing at Elsinor, 19th cent.   BAT22
A dramatic sequel to The lady of Lyons; or, In the Lyons den. 19th cent.   BAT22
Omar and oh my! 19th cent.   BAT21
"MR. S. MR. OF ART," pseud. See Stevenson, William
MITCHELL, LANGDON ELWYN, 1862-1935
Becky Sharp. 1899.   AMP16
The New York idea. 1906. BENT4, BLAI2, HAL, MOSS3, QUIG, QULJ, QUIK, QUIL, QUIM, QUIN, WATC1
MITCHELL, THOMAS, See Dell, Floyd, jt. auth.
MITCHELL, YVONNE, 1925-
Here choose I. See The same sky
The same sky. 1951.   PLAN6
Variant title: Here choose I
MITTELHOLZER, EDGAR
Shadows move among them. See Hart, Moss. The climate of Eden (based on the novel by)
MOELLER, PHILIP, 1880-
Helena's husband. 1915. BEAC12
Madame Sand. 1917.   HAL, TUCD

MOINAUX, GEORGES, 1861-1929. See Courteline, George (pseud. of)

MOLIÈRE, JEAN BAPTISTE PO-QUELIN, 1622-1673
The affected young ladies. See Les précieuses ridicules
L'avare. See The miser
Le bourgeois gentilhomme. 1670.   SCN
Anon. tr.   GAUB
Baker, H., and Miller, J., trs. CLF2, MACL2, MACJ
Malleson, M., tr. and adapter   PLAN6
Porter, M., tr.   LOCLA
Variant titles: The bourgeois gentleman; The cit turned gentleman; The prodigious

snob; The would-be gentleman
The bourgeois gentleman. See Le bourgeois gentilhomme
The cit turned gentleman. See Le bourgeois gentilhomme
The doctor in spite of himself. 1666.
Anon. tr.   COPB, INGW, SHAR
Clark, B., tr. LEV, LEVE
Van Laun, H., tr. WEAV2
Wall, C., tr.   SMR
Variant titles: Le médecin malgré lui; The physician in spite of himself
Doctor's delight. See Le malade imaginaire
L'école de maris. 1661.
Anon. tr.   BAT7
Variant title: School for husbands.
L'école des femmes. 1662.
Malleson, M., tr. and adapter.   PLAN10
Variant title: School for wives
Les femmes savantes. See The intellectual ladies
The gay invalid. See Le malade imaginaire
The high-brow ladies. See Les précieuses ridicules
The hypochondriac. See Le malade imaginaire
The hypocrite. See Le Tartuffe
The imaginary invalid. See La malade imaginaire
The imposter. See Le Tartuffe
The intellectual ladies. 1672.
Fowlie, W., tr.   FOWL
Variant title: Les femmes savantes
Le malade imaginaire. 1673.
Baker, H., and Miller, J., trs.   LOGG
Bishop, M., tr.   DEAR
Jackson, B., tr. and adapter   PLAN5
Malleson, M., tr. and adapter   PLAN19

104

Marmur, M., tr.   BERM
Variant titles: Doctor's de-
light; The gay invalid; The
hypochondriac; The imagin-
ary invalid; The robust in-
valid; The would-be invalid
Le médicin malgré lui.
See The doctor in spite of
himself
Le misanthrope. 1666.   LYO,
SER, STJ1
Anon. tr. CAR, CARA,
CROV, EDAD, GRIF, HOUS
Baker, H., and Miller, J.,
trs.   ROB
Bentley, G., tr.   MIL
Grebanier, D., tr. GREC1
Guth, H., tr.   GUTH
Malleson, M., tr. and
adapter   PLAN11
Page, C., tr. KRE, WALJ
Van Laun, H., tr. BUCK,
BUCL, BUCM, DEAP, HIB,
HIBA, HIBB, LOCM2, TRE,
TREA2, TREC1, TREE1
Wall, C., tr. DRA1, PLAB1
Wilbur, R., tr.   BENR4,
FEFL, GOOD, KERN, ROET
Variant title: The misan-
thrope
The misanthrope. See Le
misanthrope
The miser. 1668.
Anon. tr.   CROS, THO
Barnet, S., Berman, M.,
and Burto, W., trs. BARB
Malleson, M., tr. and
adapter   PLAN1
Parks, L., tr. ALLI, BENU
Van Laun, H., tr. THOM,
THON
Wall, C., tr.   CLKW
Wormeley, K., tr.   STA
Variant title: L'avare
The physician in spite of him-
self. See The doctor in
spite of himself
Les précieuses ridicules. 1659.
LYO, SER, SERD
Anon. tr.   COOP,
SEBO, SEBP
Gassner, J., tr. and
adapter   GASS

Variant titles: The affected
young ladies; The high-brow
ladies; The pretentious
ladies; The ridiculous pré-
cieuses
The pretentious ladies. See
Les précieuses ridicules
The prodigious snob. See Le
bourgeois gentilhomme
The ridiculous précieuses.
See Les précieuses ridicu-
les
The robust invalid. See Le
malade imaginaire
School for husbands. See
L'école de maris
School for wives. See L'école
des femmes
Sganarelle. 1660.
Malleson, M., tr. and
adapter.   PLAN11
Le Tartuffe; ou, L'imposteur.
1669.   LYO, SER
Anon. tr. EVB2, SMO
Hartle, R., tr.   DOWN
Hogan, R., and Molin, S.,
trs.   HOGA
Page, C., tr. HARC26,
HUD, MAU
Van Laun, H., tr. BUCK,
BUCL, BUCM, EVA2,
WEAV2
Malleson, M., tr. and
adapter.   PLAN3
Waldinger, R., tr. REIN
Wall, C., tr. BLAG, GREA
Variant titles: The hypo-
crite; The imposter; Tar-
tuffe
Tartuffe. See Le Tartuffe
The would-be gentleman. See
Le bourgeois gentilhomme
The would-be invalid. See Le
malade imaginaire

MOLIN, S. E. See Hogan, R.,
jt. auth.

MOLINA, TIRSO DE, pseud. See
Téllez, Gabriel

MOLLOY, MICHAEL J.
The king of Friday's men.

1948.   PLAN2

MOLNÁR, FERENC, 1878-1952
The daisy. See Liliom
Liliom. 1909.
    Glazer, B., tr. BES20,
    CEW, DIE, DIK1, HAV,
    LEV, LEVE, MOSG, MOSH,
    STE, THF, TRE, TREA1,
    TREC2, TREE2, TUCG,
    TUCM, TUCN, TUCO, WHI
    Variant titles: The daisy;
    The lily
The lily. See Liliom
The play in the castle. See
    The play's the thing
The play's the thing. 1926.
    Wodehouse, P., tr. and
    adapter. BES26, GARZH
    Variant title: The play in
    the castle
The swan. 1914.
    Baker, M., tr.   BES23
    Glazer, B., tr. CHA, CHAN

MONKHOUSE, ALLAN NOBLE,
1858-1936
The conquering hero. 1924.
                         HAU
First blood. 1926.   MOSO
The grand cham's diamond.
    1924. BEAC10, COOK2,
    PROB
    Variant title: The grand
    cham's necklace
The grand cham's necklace.
    See The grand cham's dia-
    mond
Mary Broome. 1911.   PLAP2

MONTANO, SEVERINO
Sabina. 195-?   EDAD

MONTELLANO, BERNARDO OR-
TIZ DE. See Ortiz de Montellano, Bernardo

MONTENOY, CHARLES PALIS-
SOT DE. See Palissot de Montenoy, Charles

MONTHERLANT, HENRY DE,
1896-

Le maître de Santiago. See
    The master of Santiago
The master of Santiago. 1947.
    Griffin, J., tr.   ULAN
    Variant title: La maître de
    Santiago
Port-Royal. 1954.
    Griffin, J., tr.   HAYE
Le reine morte. 1942.   PUCC

MONZAEMON CHIKAMATSU.
See Chikamatsu

MOOCK, ARMANDO.   See Moock
Bousquet, Armando

MOOCK BOUSQUET, ARMANDO,
1894-1942
La serpiente. 1920.   ALPE

MOODY, WILLIAM VAUGHN,
1869-1910
The death of Eve. 1912? KRE
The faith healer. 1909. QUIG,
    QUIJ, QUIK, QUIL, QUIN
The great divide. 1906.
    BES99, DIC, DOWN
    Variant title: A Sabine wo-
    man
A Sabine woman. See The
    great divide

MORATÍN, LEANDRO FER-
NÁNDEZ DE, 1760-1828
The girls acquiescence. See
    El sí de las niñas
El sí de las niñas. 1805.
                         BRET
    Davis, W., tr.   FLOS
    Variant titles: The girls'
    acquiescence; When a girl
    says yes
When a girl says yes. See
    El sí de las niñas

MORAE, JOSÉ ZORRILLA Y.
See Zorrilla y Morae, José

MORE, CHARLES C.
Die verrechelte rechler. See
    Barba, Preston Albert. Die
    verrechelte rechler (adapted
    from the novel by)

106

Es wasch Heller's Chrischtdag's zug. See Iobst,
Clarence F. Es Heller's
Chrischtdag (based on the
story by)

MORE, HANNAH, 1745-1833
Belshazzar. 1782?   KOH2
Daniel. 1782?   KOH2
David and Goliath. 1782? KOH2
Moses in the bulrushes. 1782?
                          KOH2
MORETO Y CABAÑA, AGUSTÍN.
See Moreto y Cavaña, Agustín.
MORETO Y CAVANA, AGUSTÍN.
1618-1669
El desdén con el desdén. 1654.
                          ALP
    Variant titles: Donna Diana;
    Love's victory; or, The
    school for pride
Donna Diana. See El desdén
    con el desdén
Love's victory; or, The school
    for pride. See El desdén
    con el desdén

MORGAN, DIANA, 1913-
A house in the square. 1940.
                          FIR
MORLEY, CHRISTOPHER DAR-
LINGTON, 1890-1957
Good theatre. 1926?   CHU
Really, my dear...1928?
                          WEE
Rehearsal. 1922?   SHAY
Thursday evening. 1922? PEN
Wagon-lits. 1928?   WEE

MORLEY, ROBERT, 1908-   ,
and LANGLEY, NOEL
Edward, my son. 1948. BES48

MOROSS, JEROME, 1913-
The golden apple. See La-
    touche, John. The golden
    apple (music by)

MORRIS, MRS. ELIZABETH
(WOODBRIDGE), 1870-
The crusade of the children.
    1923?   FED1

MORRIS, LLOYD, 1893-   . See
Van Druten, John, jt. auth.

MORSELLI, ERCOLE LUIGI,
1882-1921
Acqua sul fuoco. See Water
    upon fire
Il domatore Gastone. See
    Gastone the animal tamer
Gastone the animal tamer,
    1923.
    Goldberg, I., tr.   GOL
    Variant title: Il domatore
    Gastone
Water upon fire. 1920.
    Goldberg, I., tr.   GOL
    Variant title: Aqua sul fuoco

MORTIMER, LILLIAN
No mother to guide her. 1905.
                          AMP8
MORTIMER, JOHN CLIFFORD,
1923-
The dock brief. 1958. PLAN17
What shall we tell Caroline?
                          PLAN17
MORTON, HUGH, pseud. See
McClellan, C. M. S.

MORTON, JOHN MADDISON,
1811-1891
Box and Cox. 1847.   THO

MORTON, THOMAS, 1764?-1838
Speed the plough. 1800. MOR,
NIC

MORUM, WILLIAM. See Dinner,
William, jt. auth.

MOSEL, TAD
All the way home (based on A
    death in the family by
    James Agee). 1960. BES60

MOSER, GUSTAV VON, 1825-
1903
Ultimo. See Daly, Augustin.
    The big bonanza (adapted
    from)

MOSS, ALFRED CHARLES and
NEWHARD, ELWOOD L.

107

H. M. S. Pinafore; oder, Das maedle und ihr sailor kerl (based on the opera by W. S. Gilbert and Sir A. S. Sullivan). 1882. BUFF

MOSS, HOWARD
No strings attached. 1944? NEW44

MOTOKIYO, SEAMI. See Seami, Motokiyo

MOTTE FOUQUÉ, HENRI AUGUSTE, BARON DE LA, 1698-1774
Undine. See Giraudoux, Jean. Ondine. (from the novel by)

MOTTEUX, PETER ANTHONY, 1663-1718. See Ravenscroft, Edward, jt. auth.

MOTTLEY, JOHN, 1692-1750. See Jevon, Thomas, jt. auth.

MOWATT, MRS. ANNA CORA (OGDEN) RITCHIE. See Ritchie, Mrs. Anna Cora (Ogden) Mowatt

MOYES, P. Time remembered. See Anouilh, Jean. Time remembered (tr. and adapted by)

MULVAY, TIMOTHY J.
Letter to Tuffy. 194-? PROI

MUNDAY, ANTHONY, 1553-1633
Sir John Oldcastle, pt. I (sometimes attributed to). See Anonymous plays. Sir John Oldcastle, pt. I
Sir Thomas More (sometimes attributed to). See Anonymous plays. Sir Thomas More

MUNK, KAJ, 1898-1944
Egelykke. 1939.
  Jones, L., tr. MODS
Herod the king. 1933.
  Keigwin, R., tr. CONT
  Variant title: En idealist
En idealist. See Herod the king

Niels Ebbesen. 1942.
  Larsen, H., tr. SCAN2

MUNRO, CHARLES KIRKPATRICK, 1889-
At Mrs. Beam's. 1923.
  MAP, MOSO, PLAP3
The rumour. 1922. MYB

MURDOCH, FRANK HITCHCOCK, 1843-1872
Davy Crockett; or, Be sure you're right, then go ahead. 1872. AMP4, CLA

MURPHY, ARTHUR, 1727-1805
All in the wrong. 1761. MOR
The way to keep him. 1760. NIC

MURPHY, GRACE. See Lavery, Emmet, jt. auth.

MURRAY, THOMAS C., 1873-
Birthright. 1910. CAP

MUSSET, ALFRED DE, 1810-1857
Les caprices de Marianne. 1851. BOR
  Variant title: The follies of Marianne
The chandelier. 1847.
  Chambers, W., tr. BAT9
A door should be either open or shut. 1848.
  Barzun, J., tr. BENS3
  Variant title: Il faut qu'une porte soit ouverte ou fermée
Fantasio. 1834.
  Baring, M., tr. BENS1, BENT2, CLOU
The follies of Marianne. See Les caprices de Marianne
Il faut qu'une porte soit ouverte ou fermée. See A door should be either open or shut
Lorenzaccio. 1896.
  Bruce, R., tr. BENT6
No trifling with love. See On ne badine pas avec l'amour
On ne badine pas avec l'amour. 1861. COM, GRA

108

Pellissier, R., tr. TREC1,
TREE1
Variant title: No trifling
with love

MYGATT, TRACY DICKINSON
The sword of the Samurai.
1925?   FED2

MYRTLE, FREDERICK S.
Gold. 1916.   BOH3

N

NAGEL, URBAN, BROTHER,
1905-
Savonarola, the flame of
Florence. 193-?   THEC

NAHARRO, BARTOLOMÉ TOR-
RES DE. See Torres de Naharro,
Bartolomé de

NAJAC, ÉMILE DE, 1828-1889.
See Sardou, Victorien, jt. auth.

NEMÍROVÍCH-DANCHENKO,
VLADÍMIR ÍVANOVICH, 1848-1936
The brothers Karamazoff
(based on the novel by Fedor
Dostoevskii) 1922?
Covan, J., tr.   MOSA
Love and death, featuring
"Aleko," by Rachmaninoff
(based on the story by
Aleksandr Pushkin). 1891.
Seldes, G. and G., trs.
                       PLAM
NEUMANN, ALFRED, 1895-1952
The patriot. See Dukes, Ash-
ley. Such men are danger-
ous (adapted from)

NEWHARD, ELWOOD L. See
Moss, Alfred Charles, jt. auth.

NEWSPAPER, STAFF OF THE
LIVING. See Staff of the Living
Newspaper

NICHOLS, ANNE
Abie's Irish rose. 1922. CEY

NICHOLS, DUDLEY
The informer. See O'Flaherty,
Liam. The informer
(adapted by)

NICHOLS, ROBERT MALISE
BOYER, 1893-1944, and BROWNE,
MAURICE
Wings over Europe. 1928.
BES28, CHU, MCCG,
MOSG, MOSH

NIGGLI, JOSEPHINA
This bull ate nutmeg. 1937?
                       GALB
NIRDLINGER, CHARLES FRED-
ERIC, 1863-1940
The world and his life. See
Echegaray y Eizaguirre,
José. The great Galeoto
(tr. and adapted by)

NIVELLE DE LA CHAUSSÉE,
PIERRE CLAUDE. See La
Chaussée, Pierre Claude Nivelle
de

NIVOIX, PAUL. See Pagnol,
Marcel, jt. auth.

NOAH, MORDECAI MANUEL,
1785-1851
She would be a soldier; or,
The plains of Chippewa.
1819.   MOSS1

NOBUMORI, SUGIMORI. See
Chikamatsu

NORTON, THOMAS, 1532-1584.
See Sackville, Thomas, jt. auth.

NO SAYEMON, ENAMAI. See
Enamai No Sayemon

NUGENT, ELLIOTT, 1900- .
See Thurber, James, jt. auth.

NÚÑEZ DE ARCE, GASPAR,
1834-1903
The face of wood. See El haz
de leña
El haz de leña. 1872. BRET

109

Variant title: The face of
wood

O

OBEY, ANDRÉ, 1892-
Noah. 1931.
Wilmurt, A., tr. and
adapter   GARZH
Venus and Adonis. 1932?
Becker, W., tr.   BENS2

O'BRIEN, J.   Caligula. See
Camus, Albert.   Caligula
(adapted by)

O'BRIEN, LIAM
The remarkable Mr. Penny-
packer. 1953.   THEA54

O'CASEY, SEAN, 1884-
Cock-a-doodle dandy. 1949.
BENT5, BLOC
The end of the beginning.
1939. FREI, STAV
Juno and the paycock. 1925.
ALLI, BARR, BLOC, CAP,
CLM, COT, CUBE, CUBG,
DIE, DUR, FIG, HAVG,
KRM, SNYD2, WARI,
WATF2, WATI, WHI
The plough and the stars.
1926. BES27, HOGA,
TREC2, TREE3, TUCN,
TUCO, WORP
Purple dust. 1953. BARF,
COTK, ULAN, WATA
Red roses for me. 1943. SIXB
The shadow of a gunman.
1923.   MERC

O'CONNOR, FRANK. See
O'Donovan, Michael (pseud. of)

O'CONOR, JOSEPH, 1916-
The iron harp. 1955. BES56,
BROT

ODETS, CLIFFORD, 1908-1963
Awake and sing. 1935. BES34,
BLOC, CER, CLOR, FAMI,
GARU, GRIF, HAT, MOSL,
TREA1

The big knife. 1954.   FAMO
Variant title: A winter
journey
The country girl. 1950.
BES50, CLM
The flowering peach. 1954.
BES54
Golden boy. 1937. BES37,
FAML, GAS, MERT,
MOSH, TREC2, TREE3
Rocket to the moon. 1938.
BES38
Till the day I die. 1935.
FAMJ
Waiting for Lefty. 1935.
CASS, CET, DUR, HIL,
KOZ, WARH
A winter journey. See The
big knife

O'DONOVAN, MICHAEL (Frank
O'Connor, pseud.), 1903-
In the train. 1937.   BARF

OFFENBACH, JACQUES, 1819-
1880
La périchole. 1868.
Seldes, G. and G., trs.
PLAM
Variant title: Singing birds
Singing birds. See La péri-
chole

O'FLAHERTY, LIAM, 1897-
The informer (adapted by Dud-
ley Nichols). 1935. HAU,
HAVD

OGDEN, ANNA CORA. See
Ritchie, Mrs. Anna Cora (Ogden)
Mowatt

O'HARA, FRANK
Try! Try! 1953.   MACH

OHNET, GEORGES, 1848-1918
The forge master. See The
iron manufacturer
The iron manufacturer. 1883.
Leslie, G., tr.   BAT9
Variant titles: The forge
master; The iron master;
Le maître de forges

The iron master. See The
  iron manufacturer
Le maître de forges. See
  The iron manufacturer

OLESHA, YURI, 1899-1960
  A list of assets. 1931?
    MacAndrew, A., tr. GARZJ

O'NEILL, EUGENE GLADSTONE,
1888-1953
  Ah, wilderness! 1933. BES33,
    CET, DAVK, HAVG, HIL,
    HOLM, JAFF, WATA
  Anna Christie. 1921. ASH,
    BES21, BLAG, CASS, CHAN,
    CHAP, CORD, CORE, CORF,
    COTE, COTH, CUBG,
    RICK2, TRE, TREA1,
    TREC2, TREE3
  Before breakfast. 1916. SHAY
  Beyond the horizon. 1920.
    BES19, CORD, CORE, CORF,
    FULT, HAPD, HAT, HAVD,
    HAVE, LOOA, LOOB, LOOC,
    LOOD, LOOE, LOOF, MILL,
    QUIG, QUIK, QUIL, QUIM,
    QUIN, ROB, WHK
  Bound east for Cardiff. 1916.
    BLAH, CONP, GPA, NELS,
    SAND
  Desire under the elms. 1924.
    BARC, BES24, CUBH,
    GASB, MCCP, MIJY, MOSG,
    MOSH, RAY2, WALJ
  Diff'rent. 1920.   COT
  The dreamy kid. 1919. LOC
  The Emperor Jones. 1920.
    BES20, BLOC, BROX, CHU,
    CLK2, COJ, CUBE, DEAP,
    DIE, DOWN, ELLK, FOUM,
    HARB, HATA, HUBA2,
    HUD, HUTC, LOC, LOCK,
    MCCA, MCCB, MCCD,
    MCCF, MCCG, MCD,
    MIJA1, MOSJ, MOSK, MOSL,
    QUI, SCWG, SIXC, TUCJ,
    UNTE2, WAR, WATC1,
    WATI, WORP
  The great god Brown. 1926.
    BES25, DUR, HAL, POCH2,
    STE, STEI, TUCD, TUCM,
    TUCN, TUCO

The hairy ape. 1922. AND,
  ANDE, BLAI2, BLAJ,
  BLOO, BRAC2, BRAD,
  BROU, CLDP, CLKW,
  DAV1, DIG, DOWM, FUL,
  GASB, HARA, HIB, HIBA,
  HIBB, LEVI, MIL, SHA2,
  STL4, TREC2, TREE3,
  WAIT, WAIU, WALB,
  WATC2, WATO, WHI
The iceman cometh. 1946.
  BES46, BLOC, GARW,
  MIKE2
"Ile." 1916. BEC12, GASB,
  KNIC, KNID, PEN
In the zone. 1917. BROW,
  GRED, HAP, THO, WAGC2
Lazarus laughed. 1928. NELS,
  OXF, QUIO2
Long day's journey into night.
  1956.   BES56
The long voyage home. 1919.
  CARA, COOP, LOCL,
  LOCLA, LOCLB, RAY2,
  ULAN
Marco millions. 1928. CHA,
  HUB, HUDS2, HUDT
A moon for the misbegotten.
  1947. BES56, GART, LOR
The moon of the Caribbees.
  1918. LEV, LEVE, LOO,
  MACG
Mourning becomes Electra.
  1931. BES31, WARH
The rope. 1919.   ELLI2
Strange interlude. 1928.
  BES27, CORD, CORE,
  CORF, THF
A touch of the poet. 1958.
                          BES58
Where the cross is made.
  1918. BENP, COD, ING,
  INGA, PROW, SCWE, TOD

ORRERY, ROGER BOYLE, 1st
earl of, 1621-1679
  The tragedy of Mustapha, the
    son of Solyman the mag-
    nificent. 1665.   DOA

ORTIZ DE MONTELLANO, BER-
NARDO, 1899-
  Salome's head. 1944?

Mallan, L., tr.   NEW44

OSBORN, PAUL, 1901-
A bell for Adano (based on the
novel by John Hersey). 1944.
                            BES44
The innocent voyage (based on
the novel A high wind in
Jamaica by Richard Hughes).
1943.   BES43
Morning's at seven. 1939.
BES39, GARU, KRM
On borrowed time (based on
the novel by Lawrence E.
Watkin). 1938. BES37, GARU,
GOW
Point of no return (adapted
from the novel by John P.
Marquand). 1950. BES51,
WAGC3

OSBORNE, JOHN, 1929-
The entertainer. 1958? BES57
Look back in anger. 1956.
BES57, BLOC

--and CREIGHTON, ANTHONY
Epitaph for George Dillon.
1958. BES58, NEWE2

OSBORNE, MARIAN
The point of view. 1923. MAS1

OSGOOD, PHILLIPS ENDECOTT,
1882-
A sinner beloved. 192-? FED1

OSTROVSKIĬ, ALEKSANDR NIK-
OLAEVICH, 1823-1886
The diary of a scoundrel.
1868.
Ackland, R., tr.   BENT2
Kasherman, P., tr. MOSA
Variant titles: Enough stu-
pidity in every wise man;
Even a wise man stumbles
A domestic picture. 18-?
Voynich, E., tr.   COUR
Easy money. 1870?
Magarshack, D., tr.BENS2
Variant title: Fairy gold
Enough stupidity in every wise
man. See The diary of a

scoundrel
Even a wise man stumbles. See
The diary of a scoundrel
Fairy gold. See Easy money
The poor bride. 1852.
Seymour, J., and Noyes,
G., trs.   NOY
The storm. See The thunder-
storm
The thunderstorm. 1860.
MacAndrew, A., tr. GARZE
Magarshack, D., tr. MAGA
Reeve, F., tr.   REEV1
Whyte, F., and Noyes, G.,
trs.   CLF2
Variant title: The storm
OSTROVSKY, ALEKSANDER.
See Ostrovskiĭ, Aleksandr Nikol-
aevich
OTIS, MERCY. See Warren,
Mrs. Mercy (Otis)

OTWAY, THOMAS, 1652-1685
Venice preserv'd; or, A plot
discover'd. 1682. DOB,
GOS, GOSA, MAT, MCM,
MCMI, MEN, MOR, MOSE1,
NET, REST, RUB, STM,
TAT, TAU, TICK, TUP,
TUQ, TWE, WILS

OULESS, E.U.
Our pageant. 1926?   THU

OWEN, ALUN
Progress to the park. 1961.
                      NEWE5

P

PAGNOL, MARCEL, 1899-
Marius, Fanny and César.
See Behrman, Samuel Na-
thaniel and Logan, Joshua.
Fanny (based on the trilogy
by)

--and NIVOIX, PAUL
Les marchands de gloire.
1925.   GRAF

PAILLERON, EDOUARD JULES
HENRI, 1834-1899

112

The art of being bored. See
Le monde où l'on s'ennuie
The cult of boredom. See Le
monde où l'on s'ennuie
Le monde où l'on s'ennuie.
1881.   BOR, BOV
Variant titles: The art of
being bored; The cult of
boredom; This bored world;
The world of boredom
This bored world. See Le
monde où l'on s'ennuie
The world of boredom. See
Le monde où l'on s'ennuie

PAKINGTON, MARY AUGUSTA,
1878-
The queen of hearts. 1926?
                          THU
PALARCA, JULIA
Other tomorrows. 195-? EDAD

PALISSOT DE MONTENOY,
CHARLES, 1730-1814
Les philosophes. 1760.   BRE

PARKER, DOROTHY (ROTHS-
CHILD), 1893-
Candide. See Hellman, Lillian.
Candide (lyrics by)

PARKER, LOUIS NAPOLEON,
1852-1944
Disraeli. 1911.   BES09
A minuet. 1915.   CAR

PARKHOUSE, HANNAH. See
Cowley, Mrs. Hannah (Parkhouse)

PATON, ALAN
Cry, the beloved country. See
Anderson, Maxwell and
Weill, Kurt. Lost in the
stars (based on the novel by)

PATRICK, JOHN, 1907-
The hasty heart. 1945. BES44,
GARZ
The story of Mary Surratt.
1947.   BES46
Variant title: This gentle
ghost
The teahouse of the August

moon (based on the novel
by Vern Sneider). 1953.
BES53, GARU, GAVE,
THEA54
This gentle ghost. See The
story of Mary Surratt

PAUL, MRS. CLIFFORD
The fugitive king. 1926? THU

PAULDING, JAMES KIRKE,
1778-1860
The bucktails; or, Americans
in England. 1847.   HAL

PAYNE, JOHN HOWARD, 1791-
1852
The black man; or, The
spleen. 181-?   AMP6
The boarding schools; or, Life
among the little folks. 1841?
                          AMP5
Brutus; or, The fall of Tar-
quin. 1818. GRE, MOSS2,
The Italian bride. 1832?
                          AMP6
The last duel in Spain (adapted
from El postrer duelo de
España, by Calderón de la
Barca). 1822?   AMP6
Mazeppa; or, The wild horse
of Tartary (adapted from
Mazeppa, by Léopold Chan-
dezon and Jean Cuvilier de
Trye). 1825?   AMP5
Mount Savage (adapted from
Le mont sauvage, by René
Pixérécourt). 1822. AMP5
Romulus, the shepherd king.
1839?   AMP6
The Spanish husband; or, First
and last love. 1830.AMP5
Thérèse, the orphan of Gen-
eva. 1821.   BAT19
Trial without jury; or, The
magpie and the maid (adap-
ted from La pie voleuse,
by Louis Caigniez and Jean
Marie Théodore Baudouin).
1815?   AMP5
The two sons-in-law (adapted
from Les deux gendres, by
Charles Étienne). 1824?
                          AMP5

Woman's revenge. 1832.AMP6

--and IRVING, WASHINGTON
Charles the second; or, The
merry monarch (adapted
from the book La jeunesse
de Henri V by Alexandre
Duval). 1824. QUIJ, QUIK,
QUIL, QUIM, QUIN, TAFT

PEABODY, JOSEPHINE PRES-
TON (MRS. L. S. MARKS), 1874-
1922
The piper. 1910. BRIK, DID,
MOSJ, MOSK, MOSL

PEACOCK, MRS. BARBARA
(BURNHAM). See Burnham,
Barbara

PEACOCK, THOMAS LOVE,
1785-1866
Nightmare abbey. See Sharp,
Anthony. Nightmare abbey
(adapted from the frolic by)

PEARSE, PADRIAC, 1880-1916
The singer. 1915   CAP

PEELE, GEORGE, 1558?-1597?
The arraignment of Paris.
1584?   BAS, BROC
David and Bethsabe. 1593.
MIN1, MIO1
The lamentable tragedy of Lo-
crine (sometimes attributed
to). See Anonymous plays.
The lamentable tragedy of
Locrine
The old wives' tale. 1593?
BAS, BROC, GAY1, MCI,
MIN2, MIO2, NEI, OLH,
OLI1, PAR, PARR, RUB,
SCI, SCJ, SCW

PÉREZ DE SAAVEDRA RIVAS,
ÁNGEL. See Rivas, Angel Pérez
de Saavedra

PÉREZ GALDÓS, BENITO, 1845-
1920
La de San Quintín. 1894.BRET
Hayden, P., tr.   CLDM

Variant title: The duchess
of San Quentin
The duchess of San Quentin.
See La de San Quintín
Electra. 1901.
Anon. tr.   BUCK
Turrell, C., tr.   TUCG,
TUR
Variant title: The nun and
the barbarian
The nun and the barbarian.
See Electra

PERTWEE, MICHAEL. See Pertwee, Roland, jt. auth.

PERTWEE, ROLAND, 1885-
Heat wave. 1929.   FIT

--and PERTWEE, MICHAEL
The paragon. 1948.   PLAN1

PERYALIS, NOTIS
Masks of angels. 195-?
Finer, L., tr.   COTR

PESHKEV, ALEXEI MAXIMO-
VITCH. See Pîeskov, Aleksîeï
Maksimovich

PETERS, PAUL
Nat Turner. 1940.   CROZ1

PETERSON, LOUIS STAMFORD,
1922-
Take a giant step. 1953.
BES53
PHILLIPS, STEPHEN, 1868-1915
Paolo and Francesca. 1902.
DIG, SMN

PICARD, LOUIS BENOIT, 1769-
1828
The rebound. See Les rico-
chets
Les ricochets. 1807.   BOR
Variant title: The rebound

PICASSO, PABLO, 1881-
Le désir attrapé par la queue.
See Desire trapped by the
tail
Desire trapped by the tail. 195-?

114

Briffault, H., tr. NEWW2
Variatn title: Le désir
attrapé la queue

PIESHKOV, ALEXEI. See Pĭeskov, Aleksĭeĭ Maksimovĭch

PĬESKOV, ALEKSĬEĬ MAKSIMO-
VICH, 1868-1936. See Gorki,
Maxim, pseud.

PIETRO TREPASSI. See Metastasio, Pietro Antonio Domenico
Buonaventura, pseud.

PILLOT, JOSEPH EUGENE
My lady dreams. 1922? SHAY
Two crooks and a lady. 1917.
COOK3
PINERO, SIR ARTHUR WING,
1855-1934
The gay Lord Quex. 1899.
MOSN, MOSO, SMO
Iris. 1901.   COT
The magistrate. 1885. BENS3,
SMR
Mid-channel. 1909. HAU, SMI,
WATF1, WATI, WEAL,
WHI
The second Mrs. Tanqueray.
1893. BENY, BOWY, CEU,
CLK2, COF, DIC, DUR,
FULT, HUD, MAT, STE,
TAU, WATT2
The thunder-bolt. 1908. CHA,
CHAN, CHAR, TUCD,
TUCM, TUCN, TUCO
Trelawny of the "Wells." 1898.
BES94, MAP

PINTER, HAROLD, 1930-
The birthday party. 1958.
SEVD
The caretaker. 1960. BES61
The dumb waiter. 1960.
NEWE3
PIRANDELLO, LUIGI, 1867-1936
And that's the truth. See
Right you are! If you think
so
As you desire me. 1931.
Alba, M., tr.   GARZH
Putnam, S., tr.   HAV

Variant title: Come tu mi
vuoi
Ciascuno a suo modo. See
Each in his own way
Come tu mi vuoi. See As
you desire me
Cosi è se vi pare! See Right
you are! If you think so
Each in his own way. 1924.
Livingston, A., tr. CHA,
CHAN
Variant title: Ciascuno a
suo modo
Enrico IV. See Henry IV
Henry IV. 1922.
Storer, E., tr. BLOC,
ULAN, WATA, WATI,
WATL4
Variant titles: Enrico IV;
The living mask; The mock
emperor
The jar. 1917.
Livingston, A., tr. HIBB
The living mask. See Henry
IV
Lumie di Sicilia. See Sicilian
limes
The mock emperor. See
Henry IV
Naked. 1922.
Livingston, A., tr. CLKW,
DIE
Variant title: Vestire
gl'ignudi
Our lord of the ships. 1925.
Anon. tr.   MCCP
Variant title: La sagra del
signore della nave
Right you are! If you think
so. 1918.
Livingston, A., tr. MOSG,
MOSH
Variant titles: And that's
the truth; Cosi è se vi pare!
La sagra del signore della
nave. See Our lord of the
ships
Sei personaggi in cerca
d'autore. See Six charac-
ters in search of an author
Sicilian limes. 1910.
Goldberg, I., tr.   GOL
Variant title: Lumie di

Sicilia
Six characters in search of an
author. 1921.
Storer, E., tr. BARR,
CEW, DIK2, REIP, TRE,
TREA1, TREC2, TREE2,
WHI
Variant title: Sei person-
aggi in cerca d'autore
Vestire gl'ignudi. See Naked

PISEMSKIĬ, ALEKSIĔI FEOFIL-
AKTOVICH, 1820-1881
A bitter fate. 1859.
Kagan, A., and Noyes, G.,
trs. NOY
Variant titles: Cruel fate;
A hard fate
Cruel fate. See A bitter fate
A hard fate. See A bitter fate

PIXÉRÉCOURT, RENÉ CHARLES
GUILBERT DE, 1773-1844
Coelina; ou, L'enfant du mys-
tère. 1800. BOR
Le mont sauvage; ou, Le
solitaire. See Payne, John
Howard. Mount Savage
(adapted from)

PIXLEY, FRANK, 1865-1919
Apollo. 1915. BOH3

PLAUTUS, TITUS MACCIUS,
254?-184? B. C.
Amphitryon. 186? B. C.
Anon. tr. BAT21
Alison, R., tr. DUC1
Sugden, E., tr. LOCM1
Variant title: Jupiter in dis-
guise
Asinaria. See The comedy of
asses
Aulularia. 194? B. C.
Alison, R., tr. DUC1
Bennett, C., tr. CLKW
Riley, H., tr. BUCM
Rogers, H., tr. SEBO
Sugden, E., tr. STA
Variant titles: The crock of
gold; The pot of gold
The braggart captain. See
Miles gloriosus

The braggart soldier. See
Miles gloriosus
The braggart warrior. See
Miles gloriosus
The captives. 2d cent. B. C.
Anon. tr. CROV
Alison, R., tr. DUC1
Riley, H., tr. MIK8
Sugden, E., tr. CLF1,
HOUS, MAU, ROB, THOM,
THON
Variant title: Captivi
Captivi. See The captives
The Carthaginian. 2d cent.
B. C.
Duckworth, G., tr. DUC1
Variant title: The poenulus
Casina. 185? B. C.
Duckworth, G., tr. DUC1
The casket. 2d cent. B. C.
Duckworth, G., tr. DUC1
Variant title: Cistellaria
The churl. See Truculentus
Cistellaria. See The casket
The comedy of asses. 2d cent.
B. C.
Sugden, E., tr. DUC1
Variant title: Asinaria
The crock of gold. See Aulu-
laria
Curculio. 194? B. C.
Duckworth, G., tr. DUC1
Variant title: The weevil
Epidicus. 2d cent. B. C.
Duckworth, G., tr. DUC1
The girl from Persia. 2d
cent. B. C.
Murphy, C., tr. DUC1
Variant title: The Persa
The haunted house. 2d cent.
B. C.
Anon. tr. MCKK2
Bassett, E., Jarcho, L.,
and Murphy, C., trs.
Casson, L., tr. CASU
Mitchell, L., tr. DUC1,
GRIF
Nixon, P., tr. MIL
Variant title: Mostellaria
Jupiter in disguise. See
Amphitryon
The Menaechmi. 2d cent. B. C.
Anon. tr. HOWJ, TREA2,

116

TREC1, TREE1
Hyde, R., and Wiest, E.,
trs. BROJ, BROK, DUC1,
EDAD, GUI, GUIN, HAPV
Nixon, P., tr.   HUD
Riley, H., tr. CROS, MIK8,
SEBP
Taylor, J., tr.   TAV
Thornton, B., and Warner,
R., trs.   SMR
Variant titles: The twin
brothers; The twin Menaech-
mi
Mercator. See The merchant
The merchant. 2d cent. B. C.
Murphy, C., tr.   DUC1
Variant title: Mercator
Miles gloriosus. 205? B. C.
Anon. tr.   PAR
Duckworth, G., tr. DUC1,
ROET
Riley, H., tr.   MIK8
Suskin, A., tr.   HOWK
Variant titles: The braggart
captain; The braggart sol-
dier; The braggart warrior
Mostellaria. See The haunted
house
The Persa. See The girl
from Persia
The poenulus. See The Cartha-
ginian
The pot of gold. See Aulularia
Pseudolus. 2d cent. B. C.
Murphy, C., tr.   DUC1
Variant title: The trickster
The rope. 2d cent. B. C.
Casson, L., tr.   CASU
Chase, C., tr. DUC1, GUI,
GUIN, HAPV
Variant titles: The rudens;
The slipknot
The rudens. See The rope
The slipknot. See The rope
Stichus. 200 B. C.
Workman, J., tr.   DUC2
The three penny day. 2d cent.
B. C.
Duckworth, G., tr.   DUC2
Variant titles: The three
pieces of money; Trinum-
mus
The three pieces of money.

See The three penny day
The trickster. See Pseudolus
Trinummus. See The three
penny day
Truculentus. 2d cent. B. C.
Duckworth, G., tr. DUC2
Variant title: The churl
The twin brothers. See The
Menaechmi
The twin Menaechmi. See
The Menaechmi
The two bacchides. 189? B. C.
Sugden, E., tr.   DUC1
The weevil. See Curculio

POGODIN, NIKOLAĬ FEDERO-
VICH, 1900-
Aristocrats. 1935.
Wixley, A., and Carr, R.,
trs.   FOUS
The chimes of the Kremlin.
1941.
Bakshy, A., tr.   BAKS
Shoett, A., tr.   THY
Variant title: Kremlin
chimes
Kremlin chimes. See The
chimes of the Kremlin
Tempo. 1930.
Talmadg, I., tr.   LYK

POLLOCK, CHANNING, 1880-
1946
The enemy. 1925.   BES25
The fool. 1922.   BES22

POLLOCK, RICHARD
Zoo in Silesia. 1945. EMB1

POPPLEWELL, JACK
Dead on nine. 1955. PLAN13
Dear delinquent. 1957.
                        PLAN16
POPPLEWELL, OLIVE M.
This bondage. 1935.   FIN

PORTER, HENRY, fl. 1599
The pleasant history of the
two angry women of Abing-
ton. 1598? GAY1, NER,
OLH, OLI1
Variant title: The two angry
women of Abington

The two angry women of Abington. See The pleasant history of the two angry women of Abington

PORTO-RICHE, GEORGES DE, 1849-1930
Amoureuse. 1891.   RHO
    Crawford, J., tr.   DID
    Variant titles: Cupid's rival; The impassioned wife; A loving wife; The tyranny of love
La chance de Françoise. See Françoise' luck
Cupid's rival. See Amoureuse
Françoise' luck. 1888.
    Clark, B., tr.   CLD
    Variant title: La chance de Françoise
The impassioned wife. See Amoureuse
A loving wife. See Amoureuse
The tyranny of love. See Amoureuse

POTTLE, EMERY BEMSLEY (GILBERT EMERY, pseud.), 1875-
The hero. 1921. BES21, QUI, TUCD
Tarnish. 1923.   BES23

POWYS, STEPHEN (MRS. BUY BOLTON) (née Virginia de Lanty). See Guitry, Sacha. Don't listen, ladies! (adapted by)

PRAGA, MARCO, 1862-1929
The closed door. 1913.
    MacDonald, A., tr.   SAY
    Variant title: La porta chiusa
La porta chiusa. See The closed door

PRESTON, JOHN
The brave Irishman (sometimes attributed to). See Sheridan, Thomas. The brave Irishman

PRESTON, THOMAS, 1537-1598
Cambises, King of Persia.

1569. ADA, BAS, MIO1
Variant titles: Cambyses; The life of Cambises, King of Percia
Cambyses. See Cambises, King of Persia
The life of Cambises, King of Percia. See Cambises, King of Persia

PRÉVERT, JACQUES, 1900-
La famille tuyare de poile; ou, Une famille bien unie. See A united family
A united family. 1955?
    Allen, J., tr.   BENSA
    Variant title: La famille tuyare de poile; ou, Une famille bien unie

PRIESTLEY, JOHN BOYNTON, 1894-
Cornelius. 1935.   SIXP
Dangerous corner. 1932.
    CEU, SIXH
An inspector calls. 1945.
    BES47, HUDE
Laburnum grove. 1933. SEV

--and HAWKES, JACQUETTA
Dragon's mouth. 1952. COTK, FAOS

PRYCE, RICHARD, 1864-1942
Frolic wind. 1935.   FAMG

"PUNCH." See "Mr. Punch," pseud.

PUSHKIN, ALEKSANDR SERGIÈ-EVICH, 1799-1837
Boris Godunov. 1870.
    Reeve, F., tr.   REEV1
Love and death featuring "Aleko," by Rachmaninoff. (based on the story by). See Nemirovich-Danchenko, Vladímĭr Ĭvanovĭch. Love and death
The stone guest. 1847.
    MacAndrew, A., tr. GARZE

118

Q

QUINTANA, EDUARDO DE
ZAMACOIS Y. See Zamacois,
Eduardo

QUINTERO, JOAQUÍN ÁLVEREZ.
See Álvarez Quintero, Joaquín

QUINTERO, SERAFÍN ÁLVAREZ.
See Álvarez Quintero, Serafín

R

RACHMANINOFF, SERGEI, 1873-
1943
Aleko. See Nemirovich-Dan-
chenko, Vladīmīr Īvanovich.
Love and death featuring
"Aleko, " by Rachmaninoff

RACINE, JEAN BAPTISTE, 1639-
1699
Andromache. See Andromaque
Andromaque. 1667. LYO, SCN,
SER, SERD, STJ1
Abel, L., tr.   BERM
Boswell, R., tr.   CLKW
Variant title: Andromache
Athaliah. 1691.
Anon. tr.   GAUB, HOUS
Boswell, R., tr.   DUCK,
BUCL, BUCM, GREA,
KOH2, KRE
Bérénice. 1670.
Boswell, R., tr.   CLF2
Masefield, J., tr.   STA
Esther. 1689.   SER
Phaedra. See Phèdre
Phèdre. 1677.   LYO, SER
Anon. tr.   GAUB, EVB2
Boswell, R., tr. CAR,
CARA, DRA1, HARC26,
LOCM2, LOGG, MACJ,
MACL2, MAU, MIL, PLAB1,
ROB, SEBO, SEBP, SMP
Fowlie, W., tr.   FOWL
Henderson, R., tr. EVA2,
HIB, HIBB, THOM, THON,
TRE, TREA2, TREC1,
TREE1, WALJ
Lockert, L., tr.   WEAV2
Lowell, R., tr.   BENR4

Muir, K., tr.   ROET
Variant titles: Phaedra;
Phèdre and Hippolyte
Phèdre and Hippolyte. See
Phèdre
Les plaideurs. 1668.
Browne, I., tr.   BAT7
Variant title: The suitors
The suitors. See Les plai-
deurs

RAISIN, JACQUES, 1653?-1702
Merlin gascon. 1690.   LAN

RANDOLPH, CLEMENCE. See
Colton, John, jt. auth.

RAPHAELSON, SAMSON, 1896-
Accent on youth. 1934.
BES34, FAMH
Jason. 1942.   BES41
Skylark. 1939   BES39

RAPPOPORT, SOLOMON (A. S.
ANSKY, pseud.), 1863-1920
The dybbuk. 1913?
Alsberg, H., and Katzin,
W., trs. BES25, CEW,
DIE, GARZH

RASTELL, JOHN, d. 1536
The nature of the four elements (sometimes attributed
to). See Anonymous plays.
The nature of the four elements

RATTIGAN, TERENCE, 1911-
After the dance. 1939.   SIXL
The Browning version. 1949.
HAMI
The deep blue sea. 1952.
FAOS
French without tears. 1936.
FIP, THH
Love in idleness. See O mis-
tress mine
O mistress mine. 1946.
BES45
Variant title: Love in idle-
ness
Separate tables. 1956. BES56
The Winslow boy. 1946.

BES47, BOGO, REDM, SPER, WAGC2

RAUCH, EDWARD H. (PIT SCHWEFFELBRENNER, pseud.), 1826-1902
Rip Van Winkle; oder, Die shpooks fun Blowa Barrick (based on the book by Washington Irving). 18-? BUFF

RAVENSCROFT, EDWARD, fl. 1671-1697
The London cuckolds. 1681. SUM
--and MOTTEUX, PETER ANTHONY
The anatomist; or, The sham doctor... with the loves of Mars and Venus (based upon Crispin médecin by Hautroche). 1696. HUGH

RAYNAL, PAUL
The tomb beneath the Arc de triomphe. See Le tombeau sous l'Arc de triomphe
Le tombeau sous l'Arc de triomphe. 1924. RHO
Variant titles: The tomb beneath the Arc de triomphe; The unknown warrior
The unknown warrior. See Le tombeau sous l'Arc de triomphe

READE, CHARLES, 1814-1884. See Taylor, Tom, jt. auth.

REDDING, JOSEPH DEIGHN, 1859-
The atonement of Pan. 1912. BOH2
REDFORD, JOHN, fl. 1535
The play of wit and science. 1541? ADA, FARN
Variant titles: Wit and science; Wyt and science
Wit and science. See The play of wit and science
Wyt and science. See The play of wit and science
-- See also Anonymous plays.

The marriage of wit and science

REED, MARK WHITE, 1893-
Yes, my darling daughter. 1937. BES36, GAS

REELY, MARY KATHERINE, 1881-
Flittermouse. 1927. GALB

REGNARD, JEAN FRANÇOIS, 1655-1709
Le légataire universel. 1708. BRE
Aldington, R., tr. ALD
Variant title: The residuary légatee
The residuary légatee. See Le légataire universel

REGNIER, MAX ALBERT MARIE, 1908-
The headshrinkers. See Paddle your own canoe
Paddle your own canoe (based on the scenario by André Gillois), 1957?
Hill, L., tr. and adapter PLAN17
Variant title: The headshrinkers

REID, ARTHUR
People in love. 1937. FAMK

REID, BEN
The fourth room. 1944? NEW44

REID, LESLIE
Trespassers. 1923. MAS2

REIZENSTEIN, ELMER. See Rice, Elmer L.

REXROTH, KENNETH, 1905-
Iphigenia at Aulis. 1944? NEW44
Phaedra. 1944? NEW44

REYNOLDS, FREDERIC, 1764-1841
The dramatist; or, Stop him

120

who can! 1789. MOR, NIC

RICARDO DE LA VEGA. See Vega, Ricardo de la

RICE, ELMER L. (formerly Elmer Reizenstein), 1892-
The adding machine. 1923.
    DAV1, DIG, DUR, GARU,
    HAT, HATA, JORG, MOSJ,
    MOSK, MOSL, SCNN, THF
Counsellor-at-law. 1931. FAMC
Dream girl. 1945.   BES45,
    GARZ
Flight to the west. 1940.
                        BES40
Judgment day. 1934. FAMK
The left bank. 1931.   BES31
On trial. 1914. BES00, CART
See Naples and die. 1929.
                        FAMB
Street scene. 1929. BES28,
    CER, CHA, CHAN, CHAP,
    CLDP, CORD, CORE, CORF,
    COTE, COTH, FULT,
    GASB, GRIF, MACG,
    MERU, SIXD, WATC2,
    WATI, WATO
We, the people. 1933. BES32

RICHARDS, IVOR ARMSTRONG, 1893-
A leak in the universe. 1954.
                        PLAA
RICHARDSON, HOWARD, and BERNEY, WILLIAM
Barbara Allen. See Dark of the moon
Dark of the moon. 1945.
                        PLAN2
Variant title: Barbara Allen

RICHARDSON, WILLIS, 1889-
The broken banjo. 1925. LOC
The flight of the natives. 1927.
                        LOC
RICHE, GEORGES DE PORTO.
See Porto-Riche, Georges de

RICHMAN, ARTHUR, 1886-1944
Ambush. 1921.   BES21

RICHMOND, SAMUEL S.

Career for Ralph. 1949?
                        LOVR
RICKERT, VAN DUSEN, JR.
The bishop's candlesticks.
    1945?   GALB

RIGGS, LYNN, 1899-1954
Green grow the lilacs. 1931.
    BES30, CLDP, GARU,
    LEV, LEVE, SIM
--See also Hammerstein II,
    Oscar. Oklahoma! (based
    on)
Knives from Syria. 1927.
    BENP, TOD
Roadside. 1930. TUCN, TUCO

RINEHART, MRS. MARY (RO-BERTS), 1876- and HOPWOOD, AVERY
The bat. 1920. CART, CEY
    Variant title: The circular
    staircase
The circular staircase. See
    The bat

RITCHIE, MRS. ANNA CORA (OGDEN) MOWATT, 1819-1870
Fashion; or, Life in New York.
    1845. HAL, MOSS2, QUIJ,
    QUIK, QUIL, QUIM, QUIN

RIVAS, ÁNGEL PEREZ DE SAA-VEDRA, 1791-1865
Don Álvaro; ó la fuerza del
    sino. 1835. BRET, PATT,
    TRES
    Variant title: Don Álvaro;
    or, The force of destiny;
    La forza del destino
Don Alvaro; or, The force of
    destiny. See Don Alvaro
    ó la fuerza del sino
La forza del destino. See
    Don Álvaro

RIVAS, MANUEL LINARES. See
Linares Rivas, Manuel

RIVES, AMÉLIE. See Troubets-koy, Amélie (Rives) Chanler

121

ROBERT, FRANÇOIS LE MÉTEL
DE BOIS. See Bois-Robert,
François Le Métel de

ROBERTS, CYRIL
Tails up. 1935?   GALB

ROBERTSON, LOUIS ALEX-
ANDER, 1856-
Montezuma. 1903.   BOH1

ROBERTSON, THOMAS WILL-
IAM, 1829-1871
Caste. 1867. BOWY, COD,
COT, DUR, MAP, MAT,
MOSN, MOSO, ROWE, TAU
Society. 1865. BAT16, RUB

ROBINSON, LENNOX, 1886-
The big house. 1926.   CAP
Church street. 1934.   CAN
The far-off hills. 1928. CHA,
CHAN, CHAR
The whiteheaded boy. 1916.
MYB, PLAP3

RODGERS, RICHARD, 1902-
Allegro (music by). See
Hammerstein II, Oscar.
Allegro
Oklahoma! (music by). See
Hammerstein II, Oscar.
Oklahoma!
South Pacific (music by). See
Hammerstein II, Oscar.
South Pacific

ROGERS, JOHN WILLIAM, JR.
Judge Lynch. 1924.   LOC,
PROG
Where the dear antelope play.
1941.   THX

ROGERS, ROBERT, 1731-1795
Ponteach; or, The savages of
America. 1766?   MOSS1

ROJAS, FERNANDO DE, d. 1541
Celestina; or, The tragi-
comedy of Calisto and Me-
libea. 16th cent.
Mabbe, J., tr. and Bent-
ley, E., adapter   BENR3

ROJAS, RICARDO, 1882-
Ollántay. 1938.   ALPE

ROJAS ZORRILLA, FRANCISCO
DE, 1607-1648
Del rey abajo, ninguno. 1650.
ALP
Variant title: None beneath
the King
None beneath the King. See
Del rey abajo, ninguno

ROKK, VSEVOLOD
Engineer Sergeyev. 1941.
Moss, H., tr.   SEVP

ROMAINS, JULES, 1885-
Cromedeyre-le-vieil. 1920.
RHO
Dr. Knock. 1923.
Granville-Barker, H., tr.
BENS3
ROME, HAROLD JACOB, 1908-
Fanny. See Behrman, Samuel
Nathaniel and Logan, Josh-
ua. Fanny (music and
lyrics by)
Wish you were here. See
Kober, Arthur and Logan,
Joshua. Wish you were
here (music and lyrics by)

RONDER, JACK
This year, next year. 1960.
PLAN22
Variant title: Wedding day
Wedding day. See This year,
next year

ROSE, DAVID
Winged victory (music by).
See Moss, Hart. Winged
Victory

ROSEN, JULIUS, 1833-1892
Ein knopf. See Birmelin,
John. Der gnopp (based on
the play by)
Starke mitteln. See Daly,
Augustin. Needles and pins
(adapted from)

ROSENBERG, JEROLD. See

Ross, Jerry (pseud.)

ROSENTHAL, ANDREW
    Third person. 1951.   PLAN7

ROSS, GEORGE, 1907- , and
SINGER, CAMPBELL
    Any other business. 1957.
                        PLAN18
    Guilty party. 1960.   PLAN24
        Variant title: Refer to
        drawer
    Refer to drawer. See Guilty
        party

ROSS, JERRY (pseud. of JEROLD
ROSENBERG) 1926-1955
    The pajama game. See Abbott,
        George and Bissell, Rich-
        ard. The pajama game
        (lyrics and music by)

ROSSO DI SAN SECONDO, PIER-
MARIA, 1889-
    La scala. See The stairs
    The stairs. 1925.
        Katzin, W., tr.   KAT
        Variant title: La scala

ROSTAND, EDMOND, 1868-1918
    Cyrano de Bergerac. 1897.
        BOR, GRA, SEA
        Anon. tr.   WISD
        Dole, H., tr.   SMN
        Hall, G., tr. COTH, DID,
        DIK2, HAV, HUDS2, MCCD,
        MCCF, MCCG, MOSQ,
        TUCG, TUCM, TUCN,
        TUCO, WATI, WATL2,
        WATO, WATR, WHI, WHK
        Henderson, D., tr.   HUD
        Hooker, B., tr. BLOO,
        CARA, CEW, KNIC, TREC2,
        TREE2, WALJ, WISE
        Kingsbury, H., tr. BLOD1,
        COJ, LEV, LEVE, TREA1
        Thomas, G., and Guille-
        mard, M., trs.   MIL
        Whitehall, H., tr.   WORP
        Wolfe, H., tr. BENU,
        FOUM
    La dernière nuit de Don Juan.
        See The last night of Don Juan.

Don Juan's last night. See
    The last night of Don Juan
The fantasticks. See The ro-
    mancers
The last night of Don Juan. 1922.
    Riggs, T., tr.   KRE
    Variant titles: La dernière
    nuit de Don Juan; Don
    Juan; Don Juan's last night
The romancers. 1894.
    Anon. tr.   COOK2
    Clark, B., tr.   BERM
    Hendee, M., tr.   COD
    Variant titles: The fantas-
    ticks; The romantics;
    Les romanesques
Les romanesques. See The
    romancers
The romantics, See The
    romancers

ROSTEN, NORMAN
    Mister Johnson. 1955. THEA56

ROSTROU, JEAN, 1609-1650
    Chosroes. 1648.
        Lockert, L., tr.   LOCR
        Variant title: Cosroès
    Cosroès. See Chosroes
    Venceslas. See Wenceshaus
    Wenceshaus. 1647.
        Lockert, L., tr.   LOCR
        Variant title: Venceslas
ROSWITHA VON GANDERSHEIM,
See Hrotsvit, of Gandersheim
ROTTER, FRITZ, and VINCENT,
ALLEN
    Letters to Lucerne. 1941.
                            BES41
ROWE, NICHOLAS, 1674-1718
    The fair penitent. 1703. DOB,
        MCM, MCMI
    The tragedy of Jane Shore.
        1713. EIGH, HAN, MOSE2,
        NET, STM, TUQ

ROWLEY, WILLIAM, 1585?-
1642?
    The birth of Merlin (some-
        times attributed to). See
        Anonymous plays. The
        birth of Merlin

--See Ford, John; Middleton, Thomas, jt. auths.

ROYLE, EDWIN MILTON, 1862-1942
The squaw man. 1905. BES99

RUEDA, LOPE DE, 1510?-1565
The olives. 1560?
    Flores, A., tr.   FLOS
    Variant title: El paso de
    las olivas
El paso de las olivas. See
    The olives
Paso séptimo. See The
    seventh farce
The seventh farce. 16th cent.
    Chambers, W., tr. BAT6,
    PATT
    Variant title: Paso séptimo

RUIZ DE ALARCÓN Y MENDOZA, JUAN, 1581?-1639
No hay mal que por bien no
    venga (Don Domingo de Don
    Blas). 161-?   HILL
Las paredes oyen. 161-?
                     PATT
The suspecting truth. See La
    verdad sospechosa
The truth suspected. See La
    verdad sospechosa
La verdad sospechosa. 1619.
                     ALP
    Ryan, R., tr.   FLOS
    Variant titles: The suspect-
    ing truth; The truth sus-
    pected

RUNYAN, DAMON, 1884-1946
Idyll of Miss Sarah Brown.
    See Swerling, Jo and Bur-
    rows, Abe. Guys and dolls
    (based on the story by)

RUSSELL, GEORGE WILLIAM
(A. E., pseud.), 1867-1935
    Deirdre. 1902.   CAP

RUZZANTE. See Beolco, Angelo

RYALL, WILLIAM BOLITHO
(William Bolitho, pseud.), 1890-

1930
Overture. 1930.   BES30

RYE, ELIZABETH
The three-fold path. 1935.
                     FIN
RYERSON, FLORENCE, 1894-
(MRS. COLIN CLEMENTS), and
CLEMENTS, COLIN CAMPBELL
    Harriet. 1943.   BES42

RYSKIND, MORRIE, 1895-   .
    See Kaufman, George S., jt. auth.

S

"S., MR., MR. OF ART," See
    Stevenson, William

SAAVEDRA, MIGUEL DE CER-
    VANTES. See Cervantes Saa-
    vedra, Miguel

SAAVEDRA RIVAS, ÁNGEL
PEREZ DE. See Rivas, Ángel
    Pérez de Saavedra

SACHS, HANS, 1494-1576
Der fahrende schüler im Para-
    dies. See The wandering
    scholar from Paradise
Der fahrende schüller mit dem
    teufelbanner. See Raising
    the devil
The horse thief. 1553.
    Leighton, W., tr.   INGW
Raising the devil. 155-?
    Chambers, W., tr. BAT10
    Variant titles: Der fahrende
    schüller mit dem teufel-
    banner; The wandering
    scholar and exorcist
The wandering scholar and
    exorcist. See Raising the
    devil
The wandering scholar from
    Paradise. 1550.
    Eliot, S., tr. CLF1, KRE,
    PROW
    Variant title: Der fahrende
    schüller im Paradies

SACKVILLE, THOMAS (LORD

BUCKHURST, 1st Earl of Dorset), 1536-1608, and NORTON,
THOMAS
    Gorboduc; or, Ferrex and
        Porrex. 1561. ADA, BAS,
        CUN, GARZB, MCJ, MIN1,
        MIO1, SCW, TAV
        Variant title: The tragidie
        of [Gorboduc; or of] Ferrex
        and Porrex
    The tragidie of [Gorboduc; or
        of] Ferrex and Porrex. See
        Gorboduc; or, Ferrex and
        Porrex

SACKVILLE-WEST, VICTORIA
MARY, 1892-
    The Edwardians. See Gow,
        Ronald. The Edwardians
        (adapted from)

ST. JOSEPH, ELLIS
    A passenger to Bali. 1940.
                            HAT
SAIDY, FRED. See Harburg,
Edgar Y., jt. auth.

SÁNCHEZ, FLORENCIO, 1875-
1910
    Los derechos de la salud.
        1907.   ALPE
    The foreign girl. See La
        gringa
    La gringa. 1904.
        Coester, A., tr.   SSTE
        Variant title: The foreign
        girl

SÁNCHEZ GARDEL, JULIO, d.
1937
    La montaña de las brujas. See
        The witches' mountain
    The witches' mountain. 1912?
        Fassett, J., tr.   BIE
        Variant title: La montaña de
        las brujas

SANDEAU, JULES, 1811-1883.
See Augier, Émile, jt. auth.

SAN SECONDO, PIERMARIA
ROSSO DI. See Rosso di San
Secondo, Piermaria

SAPINSLEY, ALVIN,   1921-
    Even the weariest river.
        1957?   GRED

SARDOU, VICTORIEN, 1831-1908
    Fatherland. See Patrie!
    Patrie! 1869.
        Clark, B., tr. LEV, LEVE
        Variant title: Fatherland
    Les pattes de mouche. 1860.
        Gilmour, L., tr. DRA2,
        PLAB2, SSTG
        Variant title: A scrap of
        paper
    A scrap of paper. See Les
        pattes de mouche

--and NAJAC, ÉMILE DE
    Divorçons. See Let's get a
        divorce!
    Let's get a divorce! 1880.
        Goldsby, A., and R., trs.
                            BENSA
        Variant title: Divorçons

SARMENT, JEAN, 1897-
    The most beautiful eyes in
        the world. See Les plus
        beaux yeux du monde
    Le pêcheur d'ombres. 1921.
                            HARV
        Variant title: The shadow
        fisher
    Les plus beaux yeux du monde.
        1925.   RHO
        Variant title: The most
        beautiful eyes in the world
    The shadow fisher. See Le
        pêcheur d'ombres

SAROYAN, WILLIAM, 1908-
    Hello out there. 1942. WATE
    The human comedy. See Esta-
        brook, Howard. The human
        comedy (screen play based
        on the book by)
    The man with the heart in the
        Highlands. See My heart's
        in the highlands
    My heart's in the highlands.
        1939. BENT4, TREC2,
        TREE3, VOAD
        Variant title: The man with

the heart in the highlands
The people with light coming
out of them. 1942.   GALB
The time of your life. 1939.
BES39, BIER, BLOC, CET,
CLUR, CRIT, GARZ,
GAVE, HATA, KERN,
MERU, STEI

SARTRE, JEAN-PAUL, 1905-
The flies. 1943.
Gilbert, S., tr. TREC2,
TREE2
Variant title: Les mouches
Huis clois. 1946?   CLOU
Stuart, S., tr.   BLOC,
GARZH, HAMI
Variant titles: In camera;
No exit
In camera. See Huis clois
Les mains sales. 1948. PUCC
Les mouches. See The flies
No exit. See Huis clois

SASTRE, ALFONSO, 1926-
Anna Kleiber. 1961.
Pronko, L., tr.   COTR

SAUNDERS, LOUISE
The knave of hearts. BEAC7,
COOK1

SAVORY, GERALD, 1909-
George and Margaret. 1937.
FIP, THH

SAVOY(!), GERALD. See Savory,
Gerald

SAYEMON, ENAMAI NO. See
Enamai No Sayemon

SAYERS, DOROTHY LEIGH
(MRS. DOROTHY FLEMING),
1893-
The zeal of thy house. 1937.
FAML

--and BYRNE, MURIEL ST.
CLARE
Busman's honeymoon. 1936.
FAMK
SCHARY, DORE, 1905-

The devil's advocate (based on
the novel by Morris L.
West). 1961.   BES60
Sunrise at Campobello. 1958.
BES57, CES

SCALA, FLAMINO, fl. 1620
The faithful friend. 17th cent. ?
Chambers, W., tr. BAT5
Variant title: Il fido amico
Il fido amico. See The faith-
ful friend
The portrait. 1575?
Van Der Meer, E., tr.
CLF2, LEV, LEVE
Variant title: Il rittrato
Il rittrato. See The portrait

SCHAUFFLER, MRS. ELSIE
(TOUGH), 1888-1935
Parnell. 1936.   FAMJ

SCHEFFAUER, HERMAN
GEORGE, 1876-
The sons of Baldur. 1908.
BOH1
SCHILDT, RUNAR, 1888-1925
Galgamannen: en midvinter-
saga. See The gallows
man: a midwinter story
The gallows man; a midwinter
story. 1922.
Alexander, H., tr. SCAN1
Variant title: Galgamannen:
en midvintersaga

SCHILLER, JOHANN CHRISTOPH
FRIEDRICH   VON, 1759-1805
The camp of Wallenstein. 1798.
Churchill, J., tr.   BAT10
Variant titles: Das lager;
Wallenstein; Wallensteins
lager
The death of Wallenstein. 1799.
Coleridge, S., tr.   FRA3,
KRE
Variant titles: Wallenstein;
Wallensteins tod
Don Carlos. 1787.
Kirkup, J., tr.   BENR2
The homage of the arts. 1804.
Coleman, A., tr.   FRA3
Variant title: Die huldigung

des künste

Die huldigung des künste. See
The homage of the arts

Das lager. See The camp of
Wallenstein

Mary Stuart. 1801.
Lustig, T., tr.   LUST
Mellish, J., tr., and Bent-
ley, E., adapter. BENR2,
DRA2, PLAB2

Wallenstein (trilogy). See The
camp of Wallenstein; The
death of Wallenstein

Wallensteins lager. See The
camp of Wallenstein

Wallensteins tod. See The
death of Wallenstein

Wilhelm Tell. See William
Tell

William Tell. 1804.
Martin, T., tr.   CLF2,
FRA3, GREA, HARC26,
MAU, SMK, STA, WEAV2
Variant title: Wilhelm Tell

SCHLITT, R . The egg. See
Marceau, Felicien. The egg
(tr. and adapted by)

SCHLOSS, MARTIN F.
Totentanz. See Anonymous
plays. Totentanz (from the
German text of)

SCHLÜTER, KARL, 1883-
Afsporet. See Off the rails
Off the rails. 1932.
Born, A., tr.   CONT
Variant title: Afsporet

SCHNIBBE, HARRY. See Breen,
Richard, jt. auth.

SCHNITZLER, ARTHUR, 1862-
1931
The affairs of Anatol. See
Anatol
Anatol. 1893.
Colbron, G., tr.   CEW
Granville-Barker, H., tr.
BENS3
Variant title: The affairs of
Anatol

--See also A farewell supper
(from Anatol)

The duke and the actress.
See The green cockatoo

Der einsame weg. See The
lonely way

A farewell supper (from Ana-
tol). 1893.
Granville-Barker, H., tr.
MILL

Flirtation. See Light-o'-love

Die frage an das schicksal.
See Questioning the irre-
vocable

The green cockatoo. See Der
gruene kakadu

Der gruene kakadu. 1899.
FEFH2
Samuel, H., tr.   FRA20
Van Der Meer, E., tr.
LEV, LEVE
Variant titles: The duke and
the actress; The green
cockatoo

Hands around. See Round
dance

Intermezzo. 1905.
Björkman, E., tr.   STE
Variant title: Zwischenspiel

Lebendige stunden. 1902. STI1
Colbron, G., tr.   DID
Variant title: Living hours

Liebelei. See Light-o'-love

Light-o'-love. 1895.
Morgan, B., tr. DIK1,
TUCG, TUCM, TUCN,
TUCO, WATI, WATL1
Variant titles: Flirtation;
Liebelei; Playing with love;
The reckoning

Literatur. See Literature

Literature. 1902.
Coleman, A., tr.   FRA20
Variant title: Literatur

Living hours. See Lebendige
stunden

The lonely way. 1904.
Björkman, E., tr. MOSQ
Leigh, J., tr.   WHI
Variant title: Der einsame
weg

Merry go round. See Round
dance

Playing with love. See Light-
o'-love.
Professor Bernhardi. 1912.
Borell, L., and Adam, R.,
trs.   FAMJ
Questioning the irrevocable.
1893.
Chambers, W., tr. BAT12
Variant title: Die frage an
das schicksal
The reckoning. See Light-o'-
love
Reigen. See Round dance
La ronde. See Round dance
Round dance. 1897.
Bentley, E., tr.   BENT2
Wallis, K., tr.   BENS1
Weigert, H., and Newhall,
P., trs.   BLOC
Variant titles: Hands a-
round; Merry go round;
Reigen; La ronde
Zwischenspiel. See Intermezzo

SCHÖNHERR, KARL, 1869-
Faith and fireside. 1910.
Mach, E., tr.   FRA16
Variant title: Glaube und
heimat
Glaube und heimat. See Faith
and fireside

SCHULBERG, BUDD, 1914-   ,
and BREIT, HARVEY
The disenchanted (adapted
from the novel by Budd
Schulberg). 1958.   BES58

SCHWARTZ, DELMORE, 1914-
Choosing company. 1936?
AME5
Paris and Helen. 1941?
NEW41
Shenandoah. 1941?   KRE

SCHWEFFELBRENNER, PIT.
See Rauch, Edward H. (pseud. of)

SCOTT, DUNCAN CAMPBELL,
1862-
Pierre. 1921.   MAS1

SCOTT, PAUL

Pillars of salt. 1947? RUA

SCOTTI, TOMMASO GALLA-
RATI. See Gallarati-Scotti,
Tommaso

SCRIBE, AUGUSTIN EUGÈNE,
1791-1861
Les doigts de fée. 1858.
BENZ
Variant titles: Frocks and
thrills; Lady Margaret
Frocks and thrills. See Les
doigts de fée
A glass of water. See Le
verre d'eau
Lady Margaret. See Les
doigts de fée
Le verre d'eau. 1840. BOR
Bodee, D., tr.   SSTG
Variant title: A glass of
water

--and BAYARD, J. F. A.
La frontière de savoie. See
A peculiar position
A peculiar position. 1837.
Planche, J., tr.   SSTG
Variant title: La frontière
de savoie

SCRIBE, EUGÈNE. See Scribe,
Augustin Eugène

SCRIBLERUS SECUNDUS, pseud.
See Fielding, Henry

SEAMI, MOTOKIYO, 1363-1444
Atsumori. 14th cent.
Waley, A., tr. TAV, YOHA
Nakamitsu. 15th cent.
Chamberlain, B., tr.
CLF1, KRE, ORI2

SEBIRE, FRANÇOIS DESSAND-
RAIS. See Dessandrais-Sebire,
François

SECOND, LOUIS, pseud.
Apollinaris. 1942?   NEW42

SECONDO, PIERMARIA ROSSO
DI SAN. See Rosso di San Se-

condo, Piermaria

SECUNDUS, H. SCRIBLERUS,
pseud. See Fielding, Henry

SEDAINE, MICHEL JEAN, 1719-
1797
Le philosophe sans le savoir.
1765. BRE, ZDA

SEGURA, MANUEL ASCENSIO,
1805-1871
Na Catita. 1856. ALPE

SELWYN, EDGAR, 1875-1944,
and GOULDING, EDMUND
Dancing mothers. 1924.BES24

SENECA, LUCIUS ANNAEUS, 4?
B.C.-65 A.D.
Agamemnon. 1st cent.
Miller, F., tr. DUC2
Hercules furens. See Mad
Hercules
Hercules Oetaeus. See Her-
cules on Oeta
Hercules on Oeta. 1st cent.
Harris, E., tr. DUC2
Variant title: Hercules
Oetaeus
Mad Hercules. 1st cent.
Miller, F., tr. DUC2
Variant title: Hercules
furens
Medea. 1st cent.
Anon. tr. MCKK2
Harris, E., tr. CROS,
CROV, GUIN, HAPV
Miller, F., tr. CLF1,
DUC2
Taylor, J., tr. TAV
Octavia. 1st cent.
Miller, F., tr. DUC2,
HOWJ, HOWK
Oedipus. 1st cent.
Mendell, C., tr. LEVI
Miller, F., tr. DUC2
Phaedra. 1st cent.
Bradshaw, W., tr. MIK8
Harris, E., tr. HAPV
Miller, F., tr. DUC2
The Phoenician women. 1st
cent.

Harris, E., tr. DUC2
Variant title: Phoenissae
Phoenissae. See The Phoeni-
cian women
Thyestes. 1st cent.
Harris, E., tr. DUC2,
HAPV, PAR
Heywood, L., tr. MCJ
Troades. See The Trojan
women
The Trojan women. 1st cent.
Miller, F., tr. DUC2
Variant title: Troades

SERLING, ROD
Patterns. 1955. HUNT

SETTLE, ELKANAH, 1648-1724
The Empress of Morocco.
1673. DOA

SHADWELL, THOMAS, 1642?-
1692
Bury fair. 1689? MOR,
STM
The Lancashire witches and
Tegue O. Divelly, the
Irish priest. 1681? BAT22
The squire of Alsatia. 1688.
MCM, MCMI

SHAFFER, PETER, 1926-
Five finger exercise. 1958.
BES59, NEWE4

SHAIRP, MORDAUNT, 1887-1939
The green bay tree. 1933.
BES33, CEU

SHAKESPEARE, WILLIAM,
1564-1616
All's well that ends well.
1595? GRDB27
Antony and Cleopatra. 1606?
BROG, BROH, CROS,
DOWN, GRDB27, GUTH,
MIL, OLI2, WOOE1
Arden of Feversham (some-
times attributed to). See
Anonymous plays. Arden of
Feversham
As you like it. 1599? BRIK,
GRDB26, HOUS, OLI1,
SCW1

The birth of Merlin (sometimes attributed to). See Anonymous plays. The birth of Merlin
The comedy of errors. 1592? GRDB26, TAV
Coriolanus. 1607? GRDB27, OLI2
Cymbeline. 1609. GRDB27, OLI2
Hamlet. 1600? DAVK, GRDB27, HAPD, HAPS1, HAPT1, HARC26, KERN, LOCM1, MACL1, OLI1, RICH, ROGE, STA, THOM, THON, TRE, TREA2, TREC1, TREE1, WALJ, WARN2
Variant title: The tragedy of Hamlet, Prince of Denmark
Henry IV. See King Henry the fourth
Julius Caesar. 1599? BEAC11, BENP, COOK3, GRDB26, KET, OLI1, REDM, WORL2
King Henry the eighth. 1613? GRDB27
King Henry the fifth. 1598? GRDB26
King Henry the fourth, pt. I. 1597? ABRA, ABRB1, BEAL, BOGO, BROJ, BROK, COL1, DAV1, DEAN, GRDB26, HAPS1, HAPT1, KERN, OLI1, PRAT1, SMK, STJM
Variant title: Henry IV
King Henry the fourth, pt. II. 1597? GRDB26
King Henry VI, pt. I. 1591? GRDB26
King Henry VI, pt. II. 1591? GRDB26
King Henry VI, pt. III. 1591? GRDB26
King John. 1596? GRDB26
King Lear. 1605? BARC, BROK, DEAN, DEAO, GRDB27, GRED, HARC46, HIB, HIBA, HIBB, HOGA, HOUS, OLI1, PRAT1, ROB, RUSS
Variant title: The tragedy of

King Lear
King Richard II, 1595? GRDB26
Variant title: The tragedy of King Richard II
King Richard II. 1592? CONG, GRDB26
Variant title: The tragedy of King Richard III
The lamentable tragedy of Locrine (sometimes attributed to). See Anonymous plays. The lamentable tragedy of Locrine
The London prodigal (sometimes attributed to). See Anonymous plays. The London prodigal
Love's labour's lost. 1594? GRDB26
Macbeth. 1605? BARD, BEAC12, BENN, BRIG, GOOD, GRDB27, HARC46, INGE, INGG, KNID, MIJ2, MIJA2, NEVI, OLI2, POOL, PROM, PRON, REIN, ROSS, SHAR, SRY, SRYG, WAGC4, WORL4
Variant title: The tragedy of Macbeth
Measure for measure. 1604? GRDB27, KRE
The merchant of Venice. 1596? BEAC10, GRDB26, OLI1
The merry wives of Windsor. 1600? GRDB27
A midsummer night's dream. 1595? BEAC9, BONA, GRDB26, HUDE, OLI1
Mucedorus (sometimes attributed to). See Anonymous plays. Mucedorus
Much ado about nothing. 1598? GRDB26
Othello, the Moor of Venice. 1604? BEAR, BENU, BIER, BLOO, COOP, GRDB27, GREC1, JAFF, LEVI, OLI1, SCNN, SMP
Pericles, Prince of Tyre. 1609? GRDB27
The puritan; or, The widow of Watling street (sometimes

attributed to). See Anonymous plays. The puritan; or, The widow of Watling street

The reign of King Edward the third (sometimes attributed to). See Anonymous plays. The reign of King Edward the third

Romeo and Juliet. 1594? BLAH, EDAD, EVA2, EVB2, GASS, GPA, GRDB26, GRIF, JORG, OLI1, SHAW, SMN, THO

The taming of the shrew. 1593? GRDB26, SMR

The tempest. 1611? CONN, GRDB27, HAPS1, HAPT1, HARC46, SSST, SSSU

Timon of Athens. 1607?
GRDB27

Titus Andronicus. 1593?
GRDB26

The tragedy of Hamlet, Prince of Denmark. See Hamlet

The tragedy of King Lear. See King Lear

The tragedy of King Richard II. See King Richard II

The tragedy of King Richard III. See King Richard III

The tragedy of Macbeth. See Macbeth

Troilus and Cressida. 1602?
GRDB27

Twelfth night; or, What you will. 1599. BARB, BENU, BIER, FEFL, GRDB27, MIL, OLI1, WALJ

The two gentlemen of Verona. 1594?   GRDB26

The winter's tale. 1610. GRDB27, OLI2, PRAT1

A Yorkshire tragedy (sometimes attributed to). See Anonymous plays. A Yorkshire tragedy

--See Fletcher, John, jt. auth.

SHARP, ANTHONY
Nightmare abbey (adapted from

the frolic by Thomas Love Peacock). 1952.   PLAN7

SHAW, GEORGE BERNARD, 1856-1950
Androcles and the lion. 1913. KRM, SAND, WISF

Arms and the man. 1894. ABRA, ABRB2, BARB, BEAL, BEAR, BOWY, CUBG, GASS, HAVI, JORG, LOOF, REIN, REIP, SCNN

Caesar and Cleopatra. 1899. BIER, GAED, FREI, KET, LOR

Candida. 1895. BARR, BONA, COOP, HAVG, KNIC,KNID, LOCLB, STEI, TRE, TREA1, TREC2, TREE3

The devil's disciple. 1897. CLM, CUBH, LOCLA, SUL

The doctor's dilemma. WARI

Don Juan in hell (from Man and superman). 1907. BALL

Getting married. 1909. ULAN, WEAL

John Bull's other island. 1904. BARF

Major Barbara. 1905. BARG, BLOC, WAIU

Man and superman. 1903. BLOC, HAPS2, HAPT2, ROET, WATA

The man of destiny. 1897. DANI, FEFL, STEI

Mrs. Warren's profession. 1902.   SIXB

Pygmalion. 1912. DEAR, EAVE, FOUM, KRM, SHAW, WATE, WISE

--See Lerner, Alan Jay. My fair lady (adapted from)

The shewing up of Blanco Posnet. 1909.   BARH

The six of Calais. 1934.
HOGA

Saint Joan. 1923. THF, WAGC4

SHAW, IRWIN, 1912-
Bury the dead. 1936. AND, EDAD, FAMJ, GAS, KOZ

131

SHAY, FRANK, 1888-
A Christmas carol (adapted
from the story by Charles
Dickens). 1929?   LEV,
LEVE

SHEINEN, LEV ROMANOVICH,
1905-   . See Tur, Leonid
Davidovich, jt. auth.

SHELDON, EDWARD BREWSTER,
1886-1946
The boss. 1911. QUIG, QUIJ,
QUIK, QUIL, QUIM, QUIN
The jest. See Benelli, Sem.
The jest (tr. and adapted
by)
Romance. 1913. BAK, BES09

SHELLEY, ELSA (MRS. IRVING
KAYE DAVIS)
Pick-up girl. 1944.   BES43

SHELLEY, PERCY BYSSHE,
1792-1822
The Cenci. 1886. HARC18,
KRE, MOSE2, SMP, TAT,
TAU, TRE
Prometheus unbound. 1820.
BERN, GREB2, HAPT2,
PRAT2, SML

SHERIDAN, RICHARD BRINSLEY
BUTLER, 1751-1816
The critic; or, A tragedy re-
hearsed. 1779. ASH, COP,
COPC1, FEFL, NET, STM
The duenna. 1775.   STM
The rivals. 1775. ALLI,
BENP, CLK1, DEM, DRA2,
EIGH, HOUS, KEY, MOR,
NET, PLAB2, ROB, SHAI2,
SHAJ2, SNYD1, STM, TUP,
TUQ, TWE, UHL, WEAT1,
WOO1
The school for scandal. 1777.
ABRB1, BAUG, BENY,
BRIG, BROJ, BROK, CLF1,
CLKW, COF, COJ, CONP,
DAV1, DEM, FOUB, GASS,
GRE, GREB1, GREC1,
HARC18, HUD, KRM, KRO,
LIE, LIED1, LIEE1, MAT,

MCCL, MCM, MCMI, MOO,
MORR, MOSE2, NET, RUB,
RUSS, SMO, SPF1, STA,
STM, TAT, TAU, THO,
TREC1, TREE1, TUP,
TUQ, TWE, UHL, WATT2,
WOOD1, WOOE1

SHERIDAN, THOMAS, 1719-1788
The brave Irishman; or, Captain O'Blunder (sometimes
attributed to John Preston).
1746.   HUGH
Variant title: Captain O'-
Blunder; or, The brave
Irishman
Captain O'Blunder; or, The
brave Irishman. See The
brave Irishman

SHERRIFF, ROBERT CEDRIC,
1896-
Badger's green. 1930. SIXD
The colonel's lady (screen
play based on the story by
W. Somerset Maugham).
JORG
Journey's end. 1928. BES28,
CEU, CHA, CHAN, CHAR,
FAO, FREI, FUL, HUDS2,
LOV, MOD, PLAD, STAT,
STAU, STAV, TRE,
TREA1, TREC2, TREE3
The long sunset. 1955. PLAN12
A shred of evidence. 1960.
PLAN22
The telescope. 1957. PLAN15

--and DE CASALIS, JEANNE
St. Helena. 1935.   BES36,
FAMI

SHERWOOD, ROBERT EMMET,
1896-1955
Abe Lincoln in Illinois. 1938.
BES38, BIER, BROX,
CALG, CALP, CASS,
CLDP, COOJ, CORF,
COTE, COTH, GARZ, GOW,
HAT, HATA, HAVD, HAVE,
NAGE, PROD, ROLF,
WAT1, WATO
Idiot's delight. 1936. BES35,

132

CLUR, CORE, CORF, GAS,
HIL, MERU, MOSH, SIXP
The petrified forest. 1935.
  BES34, CET, DOWM,
  MOSL, WATC2
Reunion in Vienna. 1931.
  BES31, FAME, THF
The road to Rome. 1926.
  BES26, GASB
The rugged path. 1945. BES45
Second threshold. See Barry,
  Philip. Second threshold
  (revised by)
There shall be no night. 1940.
  BES39, DUR
Tovarich. See Deval, Jacques.
  Tovarich (tr. and adapted
  by).

SHIELS, GEORGE, 1886-1949
  The new gossoon. 1930. CAN

SHIELS, J. WILSON
  Nec-natama. 1914.   BOH3

SHIRLEY, JAMES, 1596-1666
  The cardinal. 1641. BAS,
    BROC, NEI, PAR, WALL
  The lady of pleasure. 1635.
    BAS, KNOW, NEI, SCH,
    SCI, SCJ, SPE
  The royall master. 1638. GAY3
  The traitor. 1631. OLH, OLI2,
    TAV
  The wedding. 1626.   KNOW

SHKVARKIN, VASILII VASIL'-
EVICH, 1893-
  Father unknown. 1933.
    Bakshy, H., tr.   BAKS

SHULMAN, MAX, 1919- and
SMITH, ROBERT PAUL
  The tender trap. 1954.
                         THEA55
SHVARTS, EVGENII L'VOVICH,
1897-1958
  The shadow. 1940.
    Reeve, F., tr.   REEV2

SICAM, GERONIMO D., and
CASIÑO, JESUS
  Mir-i-nisa (based on the story

by Jose García Villa).
  195- ?   EDAD

SIDNEY, SIR PHILIP, 1554-1586
  The lady of May. 1579? PAR

SIERRA, GREGORIO MARTÍNEZ.
See Martínez Sierra, Gregorio

SIERRA, MARIA MARTÍNEZ.
See Martínez Sierra, Maria

SIEVEKING, LANCELOT DE
GIBERNE, 1896-
  The strange case of Dr. Jekyll
    and Mr. Hyde (adapted from
    the novel by Robert Louis
    Stevenson). 1956.   PLAN15

SIFTON, CLAIRE, and SIFTON,
PAUL
  Give all thy terrors to the
    wind. 1936?   KOZ

SIFTON, PAUL. See Sifton,
Claire, jt. auth.

SIGURJÓNSSON, JÓHANN, 1880-
1919
  Bjaerg-Ejvind og hans hustru.
    See Eyvind of the hills
  Eyvind of the hills. 1911.
    Schanche, H., tr.   DIE
    Variant title: Bjaerg-Ejvind
    og hans hustru

SIMONOV, KONSTANTIN, 1915-
  The Russian people. See The
    Russians
  The Russians. 1942.
    Odets, C., tr.   SEVP
    Shelley, G., and Guthrie,
    T., trs.   FOUT
    Variant title: The Russian
    people

SIMPSON, ELIZABETH. See
Inchbald, Mrs. Elizabeth (Simpson)

SIMPSON, NORMAN FREDERICK
  A resounding tinkle. 1957.
    NEWE2, OBSE

133

SINGER, CAMPBELL. See Ross, George, jt. auth.

SISSON, ROSEMARY ANNE
The Queen and the Welshman. 1957. PLAN18
The splendid outcasts. 1959. PLAN19
SKELTON, JOHN, 1460-1529
Magnyfycence. 1516? POLL

SKINNER, CORNELIA OTIS, 1901- . See Taylor, Samuel, jt. auth.

SLOMAN, ROBERT. See Dobie, Laurence, jt. auth.

SMEE, LILLIAN
No thoroughfare. 1935. FIN

SMITH, ALBERT RICHARD, 1816-1860
The cricket on the hearth (adapted from the story by Charles Dickens). 1859. CAR
SMITH, BETTY, 1904-
Fun after supper. 1940. GALB

SMITH, DODIE, pseud. See Smith, Dorothy Gladys

SMITH, DOROTHY GLADYS (Dodie Smith; C. L. Anthony, pseuds.), 1896-
Autumn crocus. 1931. FAMA, PLAD
Call it a day. 1935. BES35, FAMI
Service. 1932. FAMC
Touch wood. 1934. FAMF

SMITH, HARRY JAMES, 1880-
Mrs. Bumpstead-Leigh. 1911. BES09, MOSJ, MOSK, MOSL

SMITH, HOWARD FORMAN
Blackberryin'. 1922? SHAY

SMITH, RICHARD PENN, 1799-1854

The bombardment of Algiers. 1829? AMP13
The last man; or, The cock of the village (adapted from Le coq de village, by Charles Décour and Anne Théodore). 1822. AMP13
The sentinels; or, The two sergeants. 1829. AMP13
Shakespeare in love (adapted from Shakespeare amoureux, by Alexandre Duval). 1804. AMP13
The triumph at Plattsburg. 1830. QUIJ, QUIK
A wife at a venture. 1829. AMP13
William Penn. 1829. AMP13

SMITH, ROBERT PAUL. See Shulman, Max, jt. auth.

SMITH, WINCHELL, 1871-1933, and BACON, FRANK
Lightnin'. 1918. CEY

SMOLIN, DMITRY
Lysistrata. See Aristophanes. Lysistrata (tr. and adapted by).

SNEIDER, VERN
The teahouse of the August moon. See Patrick, John. The teahouse of the August moon (adapted from the novel by)

SOLOVEV, VLADIMIR ALEK-SANDROVICH, 1907-
Field Marshal Kutuzov. 1939. Robbins, J., tr. SEVP

SOLOVYOV, VLADIMIR A. See Solovev, Vladimir Aleksandrovich

SOMIN, W. O.
Attentat. See Close quarters
Close quarters. 1935. Lennox, G., tr. and adapter. FAMH
Variant title: Attentat

SØNDERBY, KNUD, 1909-
En kvinde er overfl∅dig. See
A woman too many
A woman too many. 1942.
Roughton, A., tr.   CONT
Variant title: En kvinde er
overfl∅dig

SOPHOCLES, 496-406 B. C.
Ajax. 5th cent. B. C.
Jebb, R., tr.   GRDB5
Moore, J., tr.   GREP2
Trevelyan, R., tr. OAT1
Antigone. 441 B. C.
Anon. tr.   EVB1
Cocteau, J., adapter and
Wildman, C., tr. BENU,
CLM
Fitts, D., and Fitzgerald,
R., trs. BEAR, BONA,
CONG, CONP, COOP, FIFT,
GUTH, HOGA, KERN,
SSST, SSSU, SUL
Francklin, T., tr.   MIK7
Gassner, J., tr.   GASS
Jebb, R., tr. GRDB5,
GREE, HUD, KNID, OAT1,
OATE, OATH, THO, TRE,
TREA2
Lucas, F., tr.   LUCA
Neufeld, M., tr.   MCKK1
O'Sheel, S., tr.   LIND
Plumptre, E., tr. BAT1,
BUCK, BUCL, BUCM,
EVA1, HARC8, HAVI, HIB,
HIBB, HOUS, HUDS2,
HUDT, INGW, MAST,
THOM, THON
Robinson, C., tr.   ROBK
Roche, P., tr.   BARH
Watling, E., tr.   BLOO
Way, A., tr.   STA
Whitelaw, R., tr. ATTI,
CLM, FEFT, ROBI, ROBJA,
TEN
Wyckoff, E., tr. GREP2,
GRER1
Young, G., tr. CLF1,
CROS, PLAG, SEBO, SEBP
Electra. 5th cent.
Anon. tr.   HAPD
Campbell, L., tr.   FEFT
Ferguson, F., tr.   FIFT

Grene, D., tr.   GREP2,
GRER2
Jebb, R., tr. GRDB5,
OAT1
Plumptre, E., tr. CLKW
Whitelaw, R., tr. ATT3
Young, G., tr.   PLAG
King Oedipus. See Oedipus
the king
Oedipus at Colonus. 401 B. C.
Anon. tr.   GRER3
Campbell, L., tr. FEFT,
ROBJA
Fitzgerald, R., tr. FIFT,
GREP2
Jebb, R., tr. GRDB5,
OAT1
Plumptre, E., tr.   ROBJ
Young, G., tr.   KRE
Variant title: Oedipus
coloneus
Oedipus coloneus. See Oedipus
at Colonus
Oedipus, King of Thebes. See
Oedipus the king
Oedipus rex. See Oedipus the
king
Oedipus the king. 5th cent.
B. C.
Anon. tr.   EVB1, SCNN
Cook, A., tr. DAVK, LIND
Fitts, D., and Fitzgerald,
R., trs. ALLI, BIER,
DEAR, DOWN, FIFR, JAFF,
LEVI, REIN
Francklin, T., tr.   GREE
Gassner, J., tr. TREC1,
TREE1
Grene, D., tr. BEAL,
BLAG, BLAH, GPA, GREN,
GREP2, GRER1, LOCL,
LOCLA, LOCLB, ROBI
Jebb, R., tr. BROK,
GRDB5, GREC1, LOCM1,
MAU, MURP, OAT1, OATE,
OATH, THP, WARN1
Lucas, F., tr.   LUCA
Mendell, C., tr. ROBJA,
WALJ
Murray, G., tr. CAR,
CARA, COJ, FEFT, MIL,
TEN
Plumptre, E., tr. BUCK,

BUCL, BUCM, DRA1,
EVA1, HARC8, PLAB1,
SMP
Sheppard, J., tr.   BARC,
WEAV1
Starr, F., tr.   LAP
Whitelaw, R., tr.   ATT1,
HOWE, HOWF
Yeats, W., tr.   DEAP,
FIFT, MACJ, MACL1,
ROET
Young, G., tr.   PLAG
Variant titles: King Oedipus;
Oedipus, King of Thebes;
Oedipus rex; Oedipus tyran-
nus; Oedipus turannos
Oedipus turannos. See Oedipus
the king
Oedipus tyrannus. See Oedipus
the king
Philoctetes. 409 B. C.
Chase, A., tr.   FIFV
Francklin, T., tr.   OAT1
Freeman, K., tr.   LIND
Grene, D., tr.   GREP2,
GRER3
Jebb, R., tr.   GRDB5
Workman, J., tr.   ROBJ
The trachiniae. 5th cent. B. C.
Jameson, M., tr.   GREP2
Jebb, R., tr.   GRDB5,
OAT1
Variant title: The women of
Trachis
The women of Trachis. See
The trachiniae

SOUTHERNE, THOMAS, 1660-1746
Oroonoko. 1696.   DOB

SOWERBY, KATHERINE GITHA
Rutherford and son. 1912.
DIG, PLAP2

SOYA, C. E., 1896-
To traade. See Two threads
Two threads. 1943.
Anon. tr. (revised by P. N.
Furbank)   CONT
Variant title: To traade

SPENCE, EULALIE
The starter. 1927.   LOC

SPEWACK, MRS. BELLA
(COHEN), 1899-   , and SPE-
WACK, SAMUEL
Boy meets girl. 1935. BES35,
CET, FAMJ, GAS
My 3 angels (adapted from La
cuisine des anges by Albert
Husson). 1953. BES52,
GARZH, THEA53

SPEWACK, SAMUEL, 1899-
Two blind mice. 1949. BES49
Under the sycamore tree.
1952.   PLAN7

--See Spewack, Mrs. Bella
(Cohen), jt. auth.

SRI-HARSHADEVA. See Harsha,
son of Hira

STAFF OF THE LIVING NEWS-
PAPER
Triple-A plowed under. 1936.
FEF
STALLINGS, LAURENCE, 1894- .
See Anderson, Maxwell,
jt. auth.

STEELE, SIR RICHARD, 1672-
1729
The conscious lovers. 1722.
COF, EIGH, MCM, MCMI,
MOR, MOSE1, NET, STM,
TAT, TAU, TAY, TUP,
TUQ

STEELE, RUFUS, 1877-
The fall of Ug. 1913.   BOH3

STEELE, SILAS SEXTON
The crock of gold; or, The
toiler's trials. 1845.
AMP14
STEELE, WILBUR DANIEL,
1886-
The giant's stair. 1924? THO

STEIN, GERTRUDE, 1874-1946
Daniel Webster eighteen in
America. 1937?   NEW37,
SPC

STEINBECK, JOHN, 1902-
The moon is down. 1942.
BES41
Of mice and men. 1937. BES37,
CLUR, CRIT, GAS, GAVE

STEPHENS, HENRY MORSE,
1857-1919
St. Patrick at Tara. 1909.
BOH2
STERNHEIM, CARL, 1878-1942
Die marquise von Arcis. See
The mask of virtue
The mask of virtue. 1920.
Dukes, A., tr. and adapter.
FAMH
Variant title: Die marquise
von Arcis
A pair of drawers. See The
underpants
A place in the world. 1913.
Bentley, E., tr. BENS1
Clark, B., and Katzin, W.,
trs. KAT
Variant title: Der snob; The
snob
Der snob. See A place in the
world
The snob. See A place in the
world
The underpants. 1911.
Bentley, E., tr. BENT6
Variant title: A pair of
drawers

STEVENSON, ROBERT LOUIS,
1850-1894
The strange case of Dr. Jekyll
and Mr. Hyde. See Sieve-
king, Lance. The strange
case of Dr. Jekyll and Mr.
Hyde (adapted from)

STEVENSON, WILLIAM ("MR. S.
MR. of ART." pseud.), fl. 1551-
1561
Gammer Gurton's nedle. See
Gammer Gurton's needle
Gammer Gurton's needle (sup-
posed author). 1552? ADA,
BAS, BOA, FAR, GARZB,
GAY1, HEIL, LEV, LEVE,
MAL, WATT2

Variant title: Gammer Gurton's nedle

STEWART, DONALD OGDEN,
1894-
Rebound. 1930. BES29

STIRLING, GEORGE
The triumph of Bohemia. 1906.
BOH1
STONE, JOHN AUGUSTUS, 1800-
1834
Metamora; or, The last of
the Wampanoags. 1829.
AMP14, CLA
Tancred, King of Sicily; or,
The archives of Palermo.
1831. AMP14

STORACE, STEPHEN
No song no supper. See
Hoare, Prince. No song
no supper (music by).

STOREY, ROBERT
Touch it light. 1957. PLAN18

STORM, LESLEY (pseud. of Mrs.
Mabel Margaret (Cowie) Clark),
1903-
Black chiffon. 1949. PLAN2

STOWE, MRS. HARRIET ELIZA-
BETH (BEECHER), 1811-1896
Uncle Tom's cabin. See Aiken,
George L. Uncle Tom's
Cabin (based on the novel
by)

STRINDBERG, AUGUST, 1849-
1912
Brott och brott. See There
are crimes and crimes
Comrades. 1888.
Öland, E., and W., trs.
TUCG, TUCM, TUCN,
TUCO
Variant title: Kamraterna;
Marodörer
Countess Julie. See Miss Julia
Creditors. 1889.
Sprigge, E., tr. PLAN21
Variant title: Fordringsägare

To Damescus, part 1. 1900.
Paulson, A., tr.　ULAN
The dance of death. 1901?
Locock, C., tr.　ROET
The dream play. 1902.
Björkman, E., tr. WALJ,
WATA, WATI, WATL3
Locock, C., tr.　DIK2
Variant title: Ett drömspel
Ett drömspel. See The dream
play
Fadren. See The father
The father. 1887.
Erichsen, M., tr. DIC, SMI
Öland, E., and W., trs.
TRE, TREA1, TREC2,
TREE2, WHI
Variant title: Fadren
Fordringsagare. See Creditors
Fröken Julie. See Miss Julia
The ghost sonata. 1907.
Anon. tr.　REIP
Palmstierna, E., and Fa-
gan, J., trs.　HAV
Sprigge, E., tr.　BENY,
BLOC, REIN
Variant titles: Spogelses-
sonaten; The spook sonata
The great highway. 1910.
Paulson, A., tr.　MODS
Variant title: Stora lands-
vägen
Kamraterna. See Comrades
Lady Julie. See Miss Julia
Marodörer. See Comrades
Miss Julia. 1888.
Björkman, E., tr. CAR,
HAV
Locock, C., tr.　BARC,
INTE
Sprigge, E., tr.　BLOC,
CLM
Variant titles: Countess
Julie; Fröken Julie; Lady
Julie; Miss Julie
Miss Julie. See Miss Julia
Moderskärlek. See Motherly
love
Motherly love. 1893.
Ziegler, F., tr.　SHAY
Variant title: Moderskärlek
Spogelses-sonaten. See The
ghost sonata

The spook sonata. See The
ghost sonata
Stora landsvägen. See The
great highway
The stronger. See The stronger
woman
The stronger woman. 1890.
Anon. tr.　SHAY
Sprigge, E., tr.　KERN
Variant title: The stronger
There are crimes and crimes.
1899.
Björkman, E., tr. MOSG,
MOSH, TREC2, TREE2
Variant title: Brott och
brott

STRODE, WARREN CHETHAM.
See Chetham-Strode, Warren

STRONG, AUSTIN, 1881-1952
The drums of Oude. 1906.
LEV, LEVE, MIL

STUART, MRS. AIMÉE (Mc-
HARDY), 1890-
Jeannie. 1940.　FIR
Lace on her petticoat. 1950.
PLAN5
Sixteen. 1934.　FAME

STURGES, PRESTON, 1898-1959
Strictly dishonorable. 1929.
BES29, GASB

SUDERMANN, HERMANN, 1857-
1928
Casa paterna. See Magda
The fires of St. John. 1900.
Swickard, C., tr.　MOSQ
Variant title: Johannisfeuer
Das glück im winkel. See The
vale of content
Happiness in a nook. See The
vale of content
Heimat. See Magda
Home. See Magda
Johannes. See John the Bap-
tist
Johannisfeuer. See The fires
of St. John
John the Baptist. 1898.
Marshall, B., tr.　FRA17

138

Variant title: Johannes
Magda. 1893.
  Winslow, C., tr. WATI,
  WATL2
  Variant titles: Casa paterna;
  Heimat; Home
The vale of content. 1895.
  Leonard, W., tr. DIC
  Variant titles: Das glück im
  winkel; Happiness in a nook

SUGIMORI NOBUMORI. See
Chikamatsu

SULLIVAN, SIR ARTHUR SEY-
MOUR, 1842-1900 (composer).
See Gilbert, William Schwenck

SUNDGAARD, ARNOLD
  Spirochete. 1938. FEF

SUNDUKĬANTS, GAVRIĬL NIKI-
TOVICH, 1825-1911
  The ruined family. 1888.
    Collins, F., tr. ARM
    Variant title: Die ruinerte
    Familie
  Die ruinerte Familie. See
  The ruined family

SUTRO, ALFRED, 1863-1933
  John Glayde's honour. 1907.
    DIG
  A marriage has been ar-
    ranged. 1902. PEN
  The walls of Jericho. 1904.
    MAP

SVEINBJÖRNSSON, TRYGGI,
1891-
  Bishop Jón Arason. 1950.
    Hollander, L., tr. MODS

SWERLING, JOSEPH, BURROWS,
ABRAM, and LOESSER, FRANK
  Guys and dolls (based on the
    story Idyll of Miss Sarah
    Brown by Damon Runyan).
    1950. BENT4, BES50

SYLVAINE, VERNON
  As long as they're happy.
    1953. PLAN9

SYNGE, JOHN MILLINGTON,
1871-1909
  Deidre of the sorrows. 1910.
    BARF
  In the shadow of the glen.
    1903. BALL, LOCLA,
    MERC
  The playboy of the western
    world. 1907. BLOC, CEW,
    CLKW, COL2, CUBE, CUBG,
    DUR, FIG, GREC2, GRED,
    HAU, KRM, LIED2, LIEE2,
    MACL2, STEI, WALJ
  Riders to the sea. 1904.
    ALLI, BLOC, BRIG, CAP,
    CAR, CARA, COD, CONN,
    DAV1, DIC, FIG, HAVI,
    HUD, INGE, INGG, INGH,
    LOOA, LOOB, LOOC, LOOD,
    LOOE, LOOF, MCCA,
    MCCB, MILL, MOSN,
    MOSO, PROW, SSTA, STEI,
    TOBI, TRE, TREA1,
    TREC2, TREE3, TUCN,
    TUCO, WARI, WATA,
    WATF1, WATI, WATT2,
    WEAT2, WHI, WHK,
    WOOD2, WOOE2
  The well of the saints. 1905.
    ULAN

T

TABORI, GEORGE, 1914-
  The emperor's clothes. 1953.
    BES52
TAKEDA IDZUMO. See Idzumo,
Takeda

TAMAYO Y BAUS, MANUEL,
1829-1898
  Un drama nuevo. 1867. BRET

TARKINGTON, BOOTH, 1869-
1946
  Clarence. 1919. BES19, GARU
  The intimate strangers. 1921.
    COH
  Monsieur Beaucaire. 1901.
    PEN, PROB
  The tyrsting-place. 1923?
    SCWE, SCWG

--and WILSON, HARRY LEON
The Gibson upright. 1919.
WEB
The man from home. 1908.
BES99, CEY

TARLTON, RICHARD, d. 1588
The famous victories of Henry
the fifth (sometimes attributed to). See Anonymous
plays. The famous victories
of Henry the fifth

TASSO, TORQUATO, 1544-1595
Aminta. 15-?
Oldmixon, J., tr. HAYD

TATE, NAHUM, 1652-1715
A duke and no duke; or, Trapolin's vagaries (adapted
from Trappolin suppos'd a
prince by Sir Aston Co-
kain). 1684. HUGH
The history of King Lear.
1681? SUMB

TATHAM, JOHN, fl. 1600
Grim the collier of Croydon;
or, The devil and his dame
(sometimes attributed to).
See Anonymous plays. Grim
the collier of Croydon; or,
The devil and his dame

TAYLEURE, CLIFTON W.
Horse-shoe Robinson. 1856.
MOSS2
TAYLOR, CHARLES A., 1864-
1942
From rags to riches. 1903.
AMP8
TAYLOR, SAMUEL, 1912-
The happy time (based on the
novel by Robert Fontaine).
1950. BES49
Sabrina fair. 1953. THEA54

--and SKINNER, CORNELIA OTIS
The pleasure of his company.
1958. BES58

TAYLOR, TOM, 1817-1880
The ticket-of-leave man. 1863.

MOSN, MOSO, ROWE

--and READE, CHARLES
Masks and faces; or, Before
and behind the curtain.
1852. ROWE

TCHEKOFF, ANTON. See Chekhov, Anton Pavlovich

TCHING, TSE. See Kao, Tong
Kia

TEICHMANN, HOWARD, and
KAUFMANN, GEORGE S.
The solid gold Cadillac. 1953.
GART, THEA54

TEJADA, LUIS VARGAS. See
Vargas Tejada, Luis

TÉLLEZ, GABRIEL (TIRSO DE
MOLINA, pseud.), 1570?-1648
El burlador de Sevilla. 1630.
ALP, BRAG, HILL
Campbell, R., tr. BENR3,
FLOR
O'Brien, R., tr. FLOS
Variant titles: The love-
rogue; The rogue of Se-
ville; The trickster of Se-
ville; The trickster of Se-
ville and his guest of stone
The love-rogue. See El bur-
lador de Sevilla
The rogue of Seville. See
El burlador de Sevilla
The trickster of Seville. See
El burlador de Sevilla
The trickster of Seville and
his guest of stone. See El
burlador de Sevilla

TEMPLE, JOAN
No room at the inn. 1945.
EMB2
TENNYSON, ALFRED, 1809-
1892
Becket. 1893. MOSN, SMK

TERENCE. See Terentius Afer,
Publius

140

TERENTIUS AFER, PUBLIUS,
195?-159 B. C.
  Adelphi. 160 B. C.
    Anon. tr. DUC2, TREC1,
    TREE1
    Casson, L., tr.   CASU
    Oldfather, W., tr. GUI,
    GUIN, HAPV
    Riley, H., tr.   MIK8
    Suskin, A., tr.   HOWK
    Variant title: The brothers
  The Andria. See The woman
    of Andros
  Andria, the fair Andrian. See
    The woman of Andros
  The brothers. See Adelphi
  The eunuch. 161 B. C.
    Anon. tr.   DUC2
    Colman, G., tr.   BAT2
    Variant title: Eunuchus
  Eunuchus. See The eunuch
  Heautontimorumenos. 163 B. C.
    Anon. tr.   DUC2
    Riley, H., tr.   MIK8
    Variant titles: The self
    avenger; The self-tormentors
  Hecyra. See The mother-in-
    law
  The mother-in-law. 165 B. C.
    Anon. tr.   DUC2
    Variant title: Hecyra
  Phormio. 161 B. C.
    Anon. tr.   CLF1, HOWJ
    Casson, L., tr.   CASU
    Clark B., tr. DUC2, WEAV1
    Morgan, M., tr. CLKW, MAU
    Oldfather, W., tr. GUI,
    GUIN, HAPV
  The self-avenger. See Heau-
    tontimorumenos
  The self-tormentors. See
    Heautontimorumenos
  The woman of Andros. 166 B. C.
    Anon. tr. DUC2, MCKK2
    Riley, H., tr.   CROS,
    SEBO, SEBP
    Variant titles: The Andria;
    Andria, the fair Andrian

THARP, NEWTON J.
  The quest of the Gorgon.
    1905.   BOH1

THÉODORE, ANNE. See Décour,
  Charles Hébert, jt. auth.

THOMA, LUDWIG, 1867-1921
  Champions of morality. See
    Moral
  Moral. 1908.
    Recht, C., tr.   DID
    Variant title: Champions of
    morality

THOMAS, ALBERT ELLSWORTH,
1872-1947
  No more ladies. 1934. BES33

THOMAS, AUGUSTUS, 1857-1934
  As a man thinks. 1911. BAK
  The copperhead. 1918.   COH
  In Mizzoura. 1893.   MOSS3
  The witching hour. 1907.
    BES99, DIC, MOSJ, MOSK,
    MOSL, QUIG, QUIJ, QUIK,
    QUIL, QUIM, QUIN

THOMAS, DYLAN, 1914-1953
  The doctor and the devils.
    1953.   BEAR
  Under milk wood. 1953.
                      BES57
THOMAS, GWYN, 1913-
  The keep. 1961.   PLAN24

THOMPSON, DENMAN, 1833-
1911
  Joshua Whitcomb. See The
    old homestead
  The old homestead. 1875. CEY
    Variant title: Joshua Whit-
    comb

THURBER, JAMES, 1894-
  A Thurber carnival. 1960.
                      BES59
--and NUGENT, ELIOT
  The male animal. 1940.
    BES39, BLOO, GARZ,
    HARB, KRM, LOCK, MIJY,
    ROLF, WISD

TIECK, JOHANN LUDWIG,
1773-1853
  Der gestiefelte kater. 1844
                      CAM

141

Winter, L., tr.   FRA4
Variant title: Puss in boots
Puss in boots. See Der gestie-
felte kater

TIRSO DE MOLINA, pseud. See
Téllez, Gabriel

TOBIN, JOHN, 1770-1804
The honeymoon. 1805. BAT16

TOLLER, ERNST, 1893-1939
Hoppla! See Hoppla! Such is
life!
Hoppla! Such is life! 1927?
Ould, H., tr.   ULAN
Variant titles: Hoppla!;
Hoppla, wir leben
Hoppla, wir leben. See Hop-
pla! Such is life
The machine-wreckers. 1922.
Dukes, A., tr.   MOSG,
MOSH
Variant title: Die maschinen-
stuermer
Man and the masses. See
Masse mensch
Die maschinen-stuermer. See
The machine-wreckers
Masse mensch. 1921.   STI2
Untermeyer, L., tr. WATI,
WATL4
Variant title: Man and the
masses
Nie wieder friede. See No
more peace!
No more peace! 1937.
Crankshaw, E., and Auden,
W., trs.   CALM
Variant title: Nie wieder
friede
Transfiguration. 1919.
Crankshaw, E., tr. HAV
Variant titles: Transforma-
tion; Wandlung
Transformation. See Trans-
figuration
Wandlung. See Transfiguration

TOLSTOÍ, ALEKSIÉÏ KONSTANT-
INOVICH, 1817-1875
The death of Iván the terrible.
1867.

Noyes, G., tr.   NOY
Tsar Fyodor Ivanovitch. 1868?
Covan, J., tr.   MOS

TOLSTOÍ, LEV NICHOLAEVICH,
1828-1910
Condemnation. 18-?
Maude, L., and Aylmer,
trs.   COUR
The dominion of darkness.
See The power of darkness
The live corpse. 1911.
Anon. tr.   GARZH
Maude, L., and A. trs.
CHA, CHAN
Variant titles: The living
corpse; The man who was
dead; Redemption
The living corpse. See The
live corpse
The man who was dead. See
The live corpse
The power of darkness; or, If
a claw is caught the bird is
lost. 1895.
Anon. tr.   DIK1
MacAndrew, A., tr. GARZE
Magarshack, D., tr. MAGA
Noyes, G., and Patrick, G.,
trs. HOUG, NOY, TREC2,
TREE2
Reeve, F., tr.   REEV1
Variant title: The dominion
of darkness
Redemption. See The live
corpse
Taxes. 18-?
Maude, L., and Aylmer,
trs.   COUR

TOLSTOY. See Tolstoí

TOMPKINS, F. G.
Sham. 1920?   MIJA1

TONG KIA, KAO. See Kao, Tong
Kia

TOOMER, JEAN, 1894-
Balo. 1924.   LOC

TORRENCE, FREDERIC RIDGE-
LY, 1875-

142

The danse Calinda. 1922. LOC
Granny Maumee. 1917. LOC
The rider of dreams. 1917.
LOC
TORRES NAHARRO, BARTOLO-
MÉ DE, fl. 1517
Comedia Himenea. See Hymen
Hymen. 1517?
Chambers, W., tr. BAT6
Variant title: Comedia Hi-
menea

TOTHEROH, DAN, 1894-
Wild birds. 1925. BES24

TOUGH, ELSIE. See Schauffler,
Mrs. Elsie (Tough)

TOURNEUR, CYRIL, 1575?-1626
The revenger's tragedy. 1606?
OLH, OLI2, RYL

TOWNLEY, JAMES, 1714-1778
High life below stairs. 1759
BAT16, MOR

TREADWELL, SOPHIE (MRS.
SOPHIE McGEEHAN)
Hope for a harvest. 1941.
BES41
Machinal. 1928. BES28, GASB

TRENEV, KONSTANTIN FEDOR-
OVICH, 1900-
Lyubov Yarovaya. 1926.
Bakshy, A., tr. BAKS

TRENYOV, KONSTANTIN FYO-
DOROVICH. See Trenev, Konstantin Fedorovich

TREPASSI, PIETRO. See Metastasio, Pietro Antonio Domenico
Buonaventura, pseud.

TROUBETSKOY, AMÉLIE (RIVES)
CHANLER, 1863-1945
Herod and Mariamne. 1888?
KOH2
TRYE, JEAN GUILLAUME AN-
TOINE CUVELIER DE. See
Cuvelier de Trye, Jean Guillaume
Antoine

TSE-TCHING. See Kao, Tong
Kia

TUR, LEONID DAVIDOVICH,
1905- ; TUR, PETR DAVIDO-
VICH, and SHEININ, LEV RO-
MANOVICH
Smoke of the fatherland. 1942.
Feinberg, A., tr. SEVP

TUR, PETR DAVIDOVICH, 1907-.
See Tur, Leonid David-
ovich, jt. auth.

TURGENEV, IVAN SERGIEE-
VICH, 1818-1883
A month in the country. 1872.
MacAndrew, A., tr. GARZE
Mandell, M., tr. FAMK
Noyes, G., tr. NOY, TREC1,
TREE1
Williams, E., adapter
GARZH, HOUG

TURNEY, CATHARINE
Bitter harvest. 1936. FOUP

TURNEY, ROBERT, 1900-
Daughter of Atreus. 1936.
BES36

TURQUE, MICHAEL, 1933-
Shoptalk. 19-? GRED

TYLER, ROYALL, 1757-1826
The contrast. 1787. BLAI1,
CADY, DOWM, ELLI1, HAL,
MOSS1, QUIJ, QUIK, QUIL,
QUIM, QUIN, QUIO1, SPI,
STL1
The island of Barrataria. 18th
cent. AMP15
Joseph and his brethren. 18th
cent. AMP15
The judgment of Solomon.
18th cent. AMP15
The origin of the feast of Pur-
im; or, The destinies of
Haman and Mordecai. 18th
cent. AMP15

U

UDALL, NICHOLAS, 1505-1556

143

Ralph Roister Doister. 1566?
ADA, BAS, BAT13, BOA,
GARZB, GAY1, MAT,
MIN2, MIO2, PAR, SCW,
TAV
Variant title: Roister Doister
Roister Doister. See Ralph
Roister Doister

UKRAINKA, LESYA, pseud. See
Kosach, Larisa Petrovna

UNRUH, FRITZ VON, 1885-
Heinrich aus Andernach. 1925.
STI2
UPSON, WILLIAM HAZLETT,
1891-
The master salesman. 1924.
GALB
USSEAU, ARNAUD D'. See
D'Usseau, Arnaud

USTINOV, PETER, 1921-
The love of four colonels.
1953. BES52, THEA53

V

VALENCY, MAURICE JACQUES,
1903-
The Apollo of Bellac. See
Giraudoux, Jean. The
Apollo of Bellac (adapted by)
The enchanted. See Giraudoux,
Jean. The enchanted
(adapted by)
The madwoman of Chaillot.
See Giraudoux, Jean. The
madwoman of Chaillot (adap-
ted by)
Ondine. See Giraudoux, Jean.
Ondine (adapted by)
The Visit. See Duerrenmatt,
Friedrich. The visit (tr.
and adapted by)

VAN DOREN, MARK, 1894-
The last days of Lincoln. 1961.
SURR
VANBRUGH, SIR JOHN, 1664-
1726
The confederacy. 1705. KRM
A journey to London (ms.

completed by C. Cibber).
1728.   BAT15, TICK
Variant title: The provoked
husband
The provoked husband. See A
journey to London
The provok'd wife. 1697.
GAY4, GOS, GOSA, MAT,
MOSE1, RUB, TWE
The relapse; or, Virtue in
danger. 1696. MCM, MCMI,
MOR, NET, REST, TUQ

VAN DRUTEN, JOHN, 1902-
After all. 1929. FAMA, MYB,
PLAD
Behold we live. 1932. FAMC
Bell, book and candle. 1950.
BES50, GARW
The distaff side. 1933.
BES34, FAME
Flowers of the forest. 1934.
FAMG
I am a camera (adapted from
the Berlin stories by
Christopher Isherwood).
1951. BES51, FAMO, GART
GAVE
Variant title: Sally Bowles
I remember mama (based on
the book Mama's bank ac-
count by Kathryn Forbes).
1944. BES44, DAVI,
GARZ, MERS, REDM,
SPES, STAV
London wall. 1931.   FAMA
Sally Bowles. See I am a
camera
Somebody knows. 1932. FAMB
There's always Juliet. 1931.
FAMB
The voice of the turtle. 1943.
BES43, GARZ, KRM
Young Woodley. 1925. BES25,
FAO, PLAD

--and MORRIS, LLOYD
The damask cheek. 1942.
BES42
VANE, SUTTON, 1888-1943
Outward bound. 1923. BES23,
CEU, MAP

144

VARESI, GILDA, 1887-   , and
BYRNE, MRS. DOLLY
Enter madame. 1920. BES20

VARGAS TEJADA, LUIS, 1802-
1829
Las convulsiones. 1828.
Bailey, W., tr.   SSTE
Variant title: My poor
nerves
My poor nerves. See Las
convulsiones

VEGA, RICHARDO DE LA, 1829-
1910
Pepa la frescachona. 190-?
BRET
VEGA, VENTURA DE LA, 1807-
1865
El hombre de mundo. 1845.
BRET
Variant title: A man of the
world
A man of the world. See El
hombre de mundo

VEGA CARPIO, LOPE FÉLIX DE,
1562-1635
The dog in the manger. 1613?
Chambers, W., tr. BAT6
Variant titles: The garden-
er's dog; El perro del
hortelano
La estrella de Sevilla. 1617?
ALP
Hayden, F., tr. CLKW,
CROV, MAU
Variant title: The star of
Seville
Fuenteovejuna. 1619.   ALP
Campbell, R., tr. BENR3
Flores, A., and Kittel M.,
trs. FLOR, FLOS, TREC1,
TREE1
Underhill, J., tr. DOWN,
KRE, WARN2
Variant title: The sheep well
The gardener's dog. See The
dog in the manger
The king, the greatest Alcalde.
1620?
Underhill, J., tr. CLF2,
LOCM1, WEAV1

Variant title: El mejor Al-
calde el rey
El mejor Alcalde el rey. See
The king, the greatest Al-
calde
Peribanez and the commander
of Ocana. See Peribáñez y
el commendador de Ocaña
Peribáñez y el commendador
de Ocaña. 1610?   HILL
Variant title: Peribanez and
the commander of Ocana
El perro del hortelano. See
The dog in the manger
The sheep well. See Fuenteo-
vejuna
The star of Seville. See La
estrella de Sevilla

VEILLER, BAYARD, 1869-1916
The thirteenth chair. 1916.
CART
Within the law. 1912.   CART

VENTURA DE LA VEGA. See
Vega, Ventura de la

VERGA, GIOVANNI, 1840-1922
La caccia al lupo. See The
wolf-hunt
Cavalleria rusticana. 1880?
Bentley, E., tr.   BENT1
The wolf-hunt. 1901.
Goldberg, I., tr.   GOL
Variant title: La caccia al
lupo

VERHAEREN, ÉMILE, 1855-1916
Les aubes. See The dawn
The dawn. 1898.
Symons, A., tr.   MOSQ
Variant title: Les aubes

VERNEUIL, LOUIS, 1893-1952
Affairs of state. 1950. BES50,
PLAN8
Variant title: Irene
Irene. See Affairs of state

VIDAL, GORE, 1925-
The best man. 1960. BES59
Visit to a small planet. 1957.
BES56

145

VIGNE, ANDRIEU DE LA. See
La Vigne, Andrieu de

VIGNY, ALFRED VICTOR DE,
1797-1863
Chatterton. 1835. BOR, COM,
GRA

VILDRAC, CHARLES (pseud. of
CHARLES MESSAGER), 1882-
Michel Auclair. 1922.
Howard, S., tr. LEV,
LEVE
Le paquebot Tenacity. 1920.
HART, HARV
Howard, S., tr.   TUCG,
TUCM
Newberry, J., tr.   DIE
Variant titles: S. S. Tenacity;
The steamer Tenacity; The
steamship Tenacity
S. S. Tenacity. See Le paque-
bot Tenacity
The steamer Tenacity. See
Le paquebot Tenacity
The steamship Tenacity. See
Le paquebot Tenacity

VILLA, JOSE GARCIA
Mir-i-nisa. See Sicam, Geronimo D., and Casiño,
Jesus. Mir-i-nisa (based
on the story by)

VILLA, LILIA A.
Educating Josefina. 195-?
EDAD
VILLIERS, CLAUDE DES-
CHAMPS, 1600?-1681
L'apoticaire devalisé. 1658?
LAN
VILLIERS, GEORGE. See Buck-
ingham, George Villiers

VINCENT, ALLEN. See Rotter,
Fritz, jt. auth.

VISÉ, JEAN DONNEAU DE. See
Donneau de Visé, Jean

VĪSHNEVSKIĬ, VSEVOLOD VITA-
LÉVICH
An optimistic tragedy. 1933.

Scott, H., and Carr, R.,
trs.   FOUS

VIZIN, DENIS VON. See Fonvízin, Dinís Ivanovich

VOLLMER, LULA, 1898-1955
Sun-up. 1923. BES23, LOW,
QUIG, QUIK, QUIL, QUIM,
QUIN, TUCD, TUCM

VOLLMOLLER, KARL GUSTAV,
1878-1948
Uncle's been dreaming. 192-?
Katzin, W., tr.   KAT

VOLTAIRE, FRANÇOIS MARIE
AROUET DE, 1694-1778
Candide. See Hellman, Lilli-
an. Candide (based on)
Mahomet. 1741.
Leigh, O., tr.   BAT8
Nanine. 1749.   BRE
Socrates. 1759.
Leigh, O., tr.   BAT8
Zaïre. 1732. BRE, LOCR,
SEA

VULPIUS, PAUL
Youth at the helm. 1934.
Griffith, H., tr. and adap-
ter.   FAMH

W

WADDELL, SAMUEL (RUTHER-
FORD MAYNE, pseud.), 1878-
Bridge head. 1934.   CAN

WALKER, STUART, 1880-1941
The medicine show. 1917.
BEAC11
WALLACK, LESTER, 1820-1888
Rosedale; or, The rifle ball.
1863.   AMP4

WALPOLE, SIR HUGH, 1884-
1941
Kind lady. See Chodorov, Edward. Kind lady (adapted
from a story by)

WALTER, EUGENE, 1874-1941

146

The easiest way. 1908. BES09,
DID, MOSS3

WARD, JULIA. See Howe, Mrs.
Julia (Ward)

WARREN, MRS. MERCY (OTIS),
1728-1814
The group. 1775?   MOSS1

WARREN, RUTH. See Haw-
thorne, Ruth (Warren)

WATKIN, LAWRENCE EDWARD,
1901-
On borrowed time. See Os-
born, Paul. On borrowed
time (based on the novel by)

WATKINS, MAURINE
Chicago. 1926.   BES26

WATKYN, ARTHUR
Not in the book. 1958. PLAN17
For better, for worse. 1952.
PLAN8

WATTERS, GEORGE MANKER,
1891-1943, and HOPKINS, ARTHUR
MELANCTHON
Burlesque. 1927.   BES27

WEBBER, CECIL EDWIN
Be good, sweet maid. 1957.
PLAN15

WEBBER, JAMES PLAISTED,
1878-1930
Frances and Francis. 1923.
WEB

WEBSTER, JOHN, 1580?-1625?
The Duchess of Malfi. 1613.
BALD, BAS, BROC, DEAN,
DEAO, DUN, FOUD, HARC47,
HOW, MAT, MCK, NEI,
OLH, OLI2, ROET, SCH,
SCI, SCJ, SPF1, TAT, TAU,
THA, TRE, TREA2, TREC1,
TREE1, WATT2, WHE
Variant title: The tragedy of
the Duchess of Malfi
The tragedy of the Duchess of
Malfi. See The Duchess of
Malfi
The white devil; or, Vittoria

corombona. 1610? BENY,
HAPR, KRE, OLH, OLI2,
PAR, RUB, RYL, SPE,
WALL, WHE

--See Marston, John, jt. auth.

WEDEKIND, FRANK, 1864-1918
The court singer. See Der
kammersänger
The earth-spirit. See Erdgeist
The epicurean. See The Mar-
quis of Keith
Erdgeist. 1895.
Eliot, S., tr.   DIK2
Variant title: The earth-
spirit
Frühlingserwachen. See
Spring's awakening
Der kammersänger. 1899.
STI1
Boesche, A., tr. FRA20
Tridon, A., tr. HUDE,
TREC2, TREE2
Variant titles: The court
singer; The tenor
König Nikolo. See Such is
life
The Marquis of Keith. 1900?
Gottlieb, B., tr. BENS2,
BLOC
Variant title: The epicurean
So ist des leben. See Such is
life
Spring's awakening. 1906.
Bentley, E., tr.   BENT6
Variant title: Frühlingser-
wachen
Such is life. 1902.
Ziegler, F., tr. DIE, TUCG
Variant titles: So ist das le-
ben; König Nikolo
The tenor. See Der kammer-
sänger

WEIDMAN, JEROME, 1913-   and
ABBOTT, GEORGE
Fiorello! (music by Jerry
Bock; lyrics by Sheldon Har-
wick). 1959.   BES59

WEILL, KURT, 1900-1950
Johnny Johnson. See Green,

147

Paul. Johnny Johnson (music by)
The threepenny opera. See Brecht, Bertolt. The threepenny opera (music by)

--See Anderson Maxwell, jt. auth.

WEINSTOCK, JACK. See Burrows, Abram S., jt. auth.

WEITZENKORN, LOUIS, 1893-1943
Five star final. 1930. BES30

WELLS, HERBERT GEORGE, 1866-1946
Ann Veronica. See Gow, Ronald. Ann Veronica (adapted from the novel by)

WELTY, EUDORA, 1909-
The ponder heart. See Fields, Joseph and Chodorov, Jerome. The ponder heart (adapted from the novel by)

WERFEL, FRANZ, 1890-1945
Bockgesang. See Goat song
Goat song. 1921.
Langner, R., tr.   THF
Variant title: Bockgesang
Jacobowsky and the Colonel.
See Behrman, Samuel Nathaniel. Jacobowsky and the Colonel (adapted from the play by)

WERNER, FRIEDRICH LUDWIG ZACHARIAS, 1768-1823
The twenty-fourth of February.
See Der vierundzwanzigste Februar
Der vierundzwanzigste Februar. 1809.   CAM
Chambers, W., tr.   BAT10
Variant title: The twenty-fourth of February

WESKER, ARNOLD, 1932-
Chicken soup with barley.
1958.   NEWE1

The kitchen. 1959.   NEWE2

WEXLEY, JOHN, 1902-
The last mile. 1930.   BES29
Running dogs. 1938?   KOZ
They shall not die. 1934.   BES33

WHARTON, MRS. EDITH NEWBOLD (JONES), 1862-1937
Ethan Frome. See Davis, Owen and Davis, Donald.
Ethan Frome (based on the novel by)

WHEELER, ANDREW CARPENTER, 1835-1903. See Alfriend, Edward M., jt. auth.

WHEELER, HUGH CALLINGHAM, 1913-
Big fish, little fish. 1961.   BES60

WHITE, LUCY
The bird child. 1922.   LOC

WHITING, JOHN
Marching song. 1954. NEWE3
Saint's day. 1951.   PLAN6

WHITTINGTON, ROBERT, 1912-
The death of Garcia Lorca.
1940.   CROZ1

WIEAND, PAUL R.
Die huchzich um kreitz waig?
18-?   BUFF
Der parra kumpt, 18-? BUFF
Tzu forwitsich. 18-?   BUFF

WIECHERT, ERNST EMIL, 1887-
Das spiel vom deutschen bettelmann. 1933.   STI2

WIED, GUSTAV JOHANNES, 1858-1914
Ranke viljer. See 2 x 2 = 5
2 x 2 = 5. 1906.
Boyd, E., and Koppel, H., trs.   LEG
Variant title: Ranke viljer

148

WILBRANDT, ADOLF VON,
1837-1911
   The master of Palmyra. 1889.
      Stork, C., tr.   FRA16
      Variant title: Der meister
      von Palmyra
   Der meister von Palmyra.
     See The master of Palmyra

WILBUR, RICHARD, 1921-
   Candide. See Hellman, Lillian. Candide (lyrics by)

WILCOX, ANNA JANE. See
Harnwell, Mrs. Anna Jane (Wilcox)

WILDE, OSCAR, 1854-1900
   An ideal husband. 1895. JAFF
   The importance of being ear-
   nest. 1895. ASH, BARB,
   BARG, BARR, BENU,
   BOWY, BROG, CAR, CARA,
   CEU, CRAN2, EDAD, FEFL,
   FOUM, GREB2, GREC2,
   HOUS, KRM, LOO, LOOA,
   MOSN, MOSO, NEV1, SHAJ2,
   SMR, STE, STEI, THOM,
   THON, TRE, TREA1,
   TREC2, TREE3, TUCD,
   TUCM, TUCN, TUCO,
   WATA, WHI, WOO2, WOOD2,
   WOOE2
   Lady Windermere's fan. 1892.
   BAUG, BENY, BROJ, BROK,
   DAV1, DIC, HUD, LIE,
   LIED2, LIEE2, MAT,
   MCCL, MOO, RUB, SMO,
   TAT, TAU
   A woman of no importance.
   1893.   COT

WILDE, PERCIVAL, 1887-1953
   Blood of the martyrs. 191-?
              STAU
   Confessional. 1916. BENP,
   PEN
   The traitor. 191-?   RICH

WILDENBRUCH, ERNST VON,
1845-1909
   Heinrich und Heinrich's geschlecht. See King Henry

Henry IV of Germany, pt. I.
   See King Henry
King Henry. 1896.
   Wernaer, R., tr. FRA17
   Variant titles: Heinrich und
   Heinrich's geschlecht; Henry
   IV of Germany, pt. I.

WILDER, THORNTON NIVEN,
1897-
   The angel on the ship. 1928?
              CIIU
   The happy journey to Trenton
   and Camden. 1931. COOP,
   GALB, WATE
   The long Christmas dinner.
   1931. DOWM, MILL, SHAW
   The matchmaker. 1955. BES55,
   BLOC, GART, THEA56
   Variant title: The merchant
   of Yonkers
   The merchant of Yonkers.
   See The matchmaker
   Our town. 1938. BES37,
   BLOD1, BRR1, BRS, CATH,
   CET, COOJ, CORF, CROX,
   EDAD, FULT, HAT, ING,
   INGA, INGB, MCDL, NAGE,
   ROGE, SIM, TREC2,
   TREE3, WORL3
   Pullman car Hiawatha. 1931?
             BENT4
   The skin of our teeth. 1942.
   BES42, CUBE, CUBG,
   CUBH, HEWE, WATA

WILKINS, JOHN H., 1836?-1853
Signor Marc. 1854.   AMP14

WILLARD, JOHN, 1885-1942
   The cat and the canary. 1922.
             CART

WILLCOX, HELEN LIDA, 1883-
   Larola. 1917?   FED1

WILLIAMS, CHARLES, 1886-
1945
   Thomas Cranmer of Canterbury. 1936.   BROS

WILLIAMS, EMLYN, 1905-
   The corn is green. 1938.
   BES40, CEU, EDAD,

GREC2, PROX
The late Christopher Bean.
See Fauchois, René. The
late Christopher Bean (tr.
and adapted by)
A month in the country. See
Turgenev, Ivan. A month
in the country (adapted by)
Night must fall. 1935. CART,
FAMH

WILLIAMS, HUGH, 1904-   ,
and WILLIAMS, MARGARET
(VYNER)
By accident. 1959.   PLAN21
Variant title: Special provi-
dence
Double yolk. 1960.   PLAN21
The grass is greener. 1958.
PLAN19
The happy man. 1957. PLAN17
The irregular verb to love.
1961.   PLAN23
Plaintiff in a pretty hat. 1956.
PLAN15
A sparrow falls. See With in-
tent
Special providence. See By
accident
With intent. 1959.   PLAN21
Variant title: A sparrow
falls

WILLIAMS, JESSE LYNCH, 1871-
1929
And so they were married.
See Why marry?
Why marry? 1917. BES09,
CORD, CORE, CORF, QUI
Variant title: And so they
were married
Why not? 1922.   BES22

WILLIAMS, MARGARET (VYNER).
See Williams, Hugh, jt. auth.

WILLIAMS, TENNESSEE (b.
Thomas Lanier Williams), 1914-
Camino real. 1953. CES, FAM,
MIJY, ULAN
Cat on a hot tin roof. 1955.
BES54, GART, GAVE,
THEA55

The glass menagerie. 1944.
BES44, BLOC, BONA,
CLDP, COOP, CUBE,
CUBG, CUBH, DOWM,
GARZ, GASS, GAVE, HATA,
HAVI, KNIC, KNID, MCNA,
REIP, SIXB, SIXC, SPES,
STEI, TREC2, TREE3,
WAIT, WAIU, WALB,
WARH, WATE
I rise in flame, cried the
Phoenix. 1951?   NEWW1
The night of the iguana. 1959.
BES61
Orpheus descending. 1957.
BES56
Period of adjustment. 1960.
BES60
Dos ranchos; or, The purifi-
cation. 1944?   NEW44
The rose tattoo. 1951. BES50,
CLM, GART, GRED
Something unspoken. 1953?
SUL
A streetcar named desire.
1947. BES47, GAVE, GARW,
GOOD, NEWV, TUCO
Summer and smoke. 1948.
HAVG, GARW
Sweet bird of youth. 1959.
BES58
27 Wagons full of cotton. 1955.
HALU, SPC

WILLIAMS, THOMAS LANIER.
See Williams, Tennessee

WILLIAMS, WILLIAM CARLOS,
1883-
The first president. 1936?
AME5
Trial horse no. 1: Many loves.
1942?   NEW42

WILLIAMSON, HAROLD
Peggy. 1919.   HUD

WILLIAMSON, HUGH ROSS, 1901-
Diamond cut diamond. 1952.
PLAN7
Gunpowder, treason and plot.
1951.   PLAN6
Heart of Bruce. 1959. PLAN20

A question of obedience. See
  Teresa of Avila
Teresa of Avila. 1961. PLAN24
  Variant title: A question of
  obedience

WILLIS, ANTHONY ARMSTRONG
(ANTHONY ARMSTRONG, pseud.)
1897-
  Ten minute alibi. 1933. FAMD

WILLIS, NATHANIEL PARKER,
1806-1867
  Bianca Visconti; or, The heart
    overtasked. 1837.   HAL
  Tortesa, the usurer. 1839.
    MOSS2, QUIJ, QUIK, QUIL,
    QUIM, QUIN

WILMOT, ROBERT, fl. 1568-1608
  Tancred and Gismund; or, Gis-
    mond of Salerne. 1591?
                          CUN
WILMURT, ARTHUR. See Obey,
André. Noah (tr. and adapted by)

WILSON, FRANK H., 1886-1956
  Sugar cane. 1925.   LOC

WILSON, HARRY LEON, 1867-
1939
  Merton of the movies. See
    Kaufman, George S., and
    Connelly, Marc. Merton of
    the movies (based on the
    novel by)

  --See Tarkington, Booth, jt.
    auth.

WILSON, ROBERT, d. 1600
  Sir John Oldcastle, pt. I (some-
    times attributed to). See
    Anonymous plays. Sir John
    Oldcastle, pt. I

WILSON, SANDY, 1924-
  The boy friend. 1953. BES54

WILSON, THEODORA WILSON
  Champion north. 1933.   FIT

WINCELBERG, SHIMON

The enemy. See Kataki
Kataki. 1959.   BES58
  Variant title: The enemy

WINSLOE, CHRISTA
  Children in uniform. 1932.
    Burnham, B., tr. and
    adapter   FAMC
  Variant titles: Gestern und
    heute; Girls in uniform;
    Maedchen in uniform
  Gestern und heute. See Chil-
    dren in uniform
  Girls in uniform. See Chil-
    dren in uniform
  Maedchen in uniform. See
    Children in uniform

WINTER, JOHN KEITH, 1906-
  The rats of Norway. 1933.
                          SIXH
  The shining hour. 1934.
    BES33, SEV

WISE, ERNEST GEORGE (ER-
NEST GEORGE, pseud.), 1894-
  Down our street. 1930. SIXD

WISHENGRAD, MORTON
  The rope dancers. 1957.
                          BES57
WITHERSPOON, KATHLEEN
  Jute. 1930.   THX

WODEHOUSE, PELLHAM GREN-
VILLE, 1881-
  The play's the thing. See
    Molnar, Ferenc. The play's
    the thing (adapted by)

WOLFE, HUMBERT, 1885-1940
  The silent knight. 1939. SIXP

WOLFE, THOMAS, 1900-1938
  Look homeward, angel. See
    Frings, Ketti. Look home-
    ward, angel (based on the
    novel by)

WOLFSON, VICTOR
  Excursion. 1937.   BES36

WOLLENWEBER, LUDWIG AUGUST

Ein gesprach. 18-? BUFF
Das lied von der union. 18-?
BUFF
Die Margareth und die Lea.
18-? BUFF
Eb Refschneider un Susi Leim-
bach. 18-? BUFF
Die Sara und die Betz. 18-?
BUFF
WOOD, MRS. HENRY, 1813-1887
East Lynne. 1863. CEY
Variant title: The marriage
bells; or, The cottage on
the cliff
The marriage bells; or, The
cottage on the cliff. See
East Lynne

WOODBRIDGE, ELIZABETH. See
Morris, Elizabeth (Woodbridge)

WOODS, WALTER
Billy the kid. 1906. AMP8

WOOLF, BENJAMIN EDWARD,
1836-1901
The almighty dollar. See The
mighty dollar
The mighty dollar. 1875. CLA
Variant title: The almighty
dollar

WOOLL, EDWARD, 1878-
Libel! 1934? SEV

WOUK, HERMAN, 1915-
The Caine mutiny court-mar-
tial. 1953. BES53, GART,
NEWV, THEA54

WRIGHT, RICHARD, 1909, and
GREEN, PAUL
Native son. 1941. BES40

WUCHTER, ASTOR CLINTON
An der lumpa parti. See
Barba, Preston Albert
(based on the poem by)

WYCHERLEY, WILLIAM, 1640?-
1716
The country wife. 1674?
FOUB, GOS, GOSA, KRM,

REST, TUQ, TWE, WILS
The plain-dealer. 1676. GAY4,
MAT, MCMI, MOR, MOSE1,
NET

Y

YAFFE, JAMES, 1927-
The deadly game (adapted
from the novel Trapps by
Friedrich Duerrenmatt).
1960. BES59

YEATS, JACK BUTLER, 1871-
1957
La la noo. 1942. BARF

YEATS, WILLIAM BUTLER,
1865-1939
At the hawk's well. 1916?
BLOC
Variant title: The well of
immortality
Cathleen ni Houlihan. 1902.
DUR, MERC, MILL, MOSN,
MOSO
The Countess Cathleen. 1892.
BOWY, SECK
Deirdre. 1906. SSTA
The dreaming of the bones.
1931. STEI
A full moon in March. 1935.
BENS1
The hour-glass. 1903. DIC
The king's threshold. 1903.
KRE
The land of heart's desire.
1894. HUD, MCCP, WATT2
On Baile's strand. 1904.
BARC, CAP, ULAN
The only jealousy of Emer.
1921? CAP
Purgatory. 1939? BARH,
BENT2, REIN, REIP, ULAN
The resurrection. 1934. MERC
The well of immortality. See
At the hawk's well.
The words upon the window
pane. 1935. BARF, CAN

YEVREINOV, NIKOLAÍ. See
Evreinov, Nikolaí

152

YORDAN, PHILIP, 1914-
Anna Lucasta. 1944. BES44

YOUNG, SIR CHARLES LAW-
RENCE, 1839-1887, and HOWARD,
BRONSON CROCKER
Knave and queen. 1882?AMP10

YOUNG, STANLEY, 1906-
Mr. Pickwick. (based on
Charles Dickens' Pickwick
papers). 1952. THEA53

Z

ZAMACOIS, EDUARDO (EDUAR-
DO DE ZAMACOIS Y QUINTANA),
1873-
The passing of the magi. 1912.
Turrell, C., tr. TUR
Variant title: Los reyes pa-
san
Los reyes pasan. See The
passing of the magi

ZAMACOIS Y QUINTANA, ED-
UARDO DE. See Zamacois,
Eduardo

ZÁRATE, ANTONIO GIL Y. See
Gil y Zárate, Antonio

ZOLA, ÉMILE, 1840-1902
Thérèse Raquin. 1873.
Boutall, K., tr. BENS3

ZORRILLA, FRANCISCO DE
ROJAS. See Rojas Zorrilla,
Francisco de

ZORRILLA Y MORAE, JOSÉ,
1817-1893
Don Juan Tenorio. 1844. BRET,
TRES

ZUCKMAYER, CARL, 1896-
The devils general. 1946.
Gilbert, I., and W., trs.
BLOC

ZWEIG, STEFAN, 1881-1942
Volpone (adapted from the play
by Ben Jonson)
Langner, R., tr. GARZH

ABRA   Abrams, Meyer Howard;
Donaldson, E. Talbot; Smith,
Hallett; Adams, Robert M.;
Monk, Samuel Holt; Ford,
George H. and Daiches,
David, eds.   The Norton
anthology of English litera-
ture... New York, W. W.
Norton [c1962] 2024p.
Dryden, J.   The secular
masque
Jonson, B.   The vision of de-
light
Shakespeare, W.   King Henry
the fourth, pt. I
Shaw, G.   Arms and the man

ABRB   Abrams, Meyer Howard;
Donaldson, E. Talbot; Smith,
Hallett; Adams, Robert M.;
Monk, Samuel Holt; Ford,
George H. and Daiches,
David, eds.   The Norton
anthology of English litera-
ture... New York, W. W.
Norton [c1962] 2v
Everyman   1
The second shepherds' play 1
Congreve, W.   The way of
the world.   1
Jonson, B.   The vision of de-
light.   1
Marlowe, C.   The tragical
history of the life and death
of Doctor Faustus.   1
Shakespeare, W.   King Henry
the fourth, pt. I.   1
Shaw, G.   Arms and the man.2
Sheridan, R.   The school for
scandal.   1

ADA   Adams, Joseph Quincy, ed.
Chief pre-Shakespearean
dramas... Boston, Houghton

Mifflin [c1924] 712p
Banns
The betraying of Christ
The birth of Jesus
The castle of perseverance
Christ's ministry
The conversion of St. Paul
The creation of Eve, with the
expelling of Adam and Eve
out of Paradise
The deluge
Duk Moraud
Edwards, R.   Damon and
Pithias
Everyman
The fall of Lucifer
The famous victories of Henry
the fifth
Gammer Gurton's nedle
Gascoygne, G.   Supposes
George a Greene, the pinner
of Wakefield
The harrowing of hell
Heywood, J.   A mery play be-
twene Johan Johan, the hus-
band, Tyb his wife and Syr
Johan the preest
Heywood, J.   The playe called
the four pp
Heywood, J.   The play of the
wether
The judgment day
The killing of Abel
Leicestershire St. George
play
Lyly, J.   Campaspe
The magi, Herod, and the
slaughter of the innocents
Mankind
Mary Magdalene
Noah
Norton, T., and Sackville, T.
Gorboduc; or, Ferrex and
Porrex

ADA (continued)
Oxfordshire St. George play
Pharaoh
The play of the sacrament
Preston, T. Cambises, king
of Persia
The prophets
The resurrection of Christ
The Revesby sword play
Robin Hood and the friar
Robin Hood and the sheriff of
Nottingham
The sacrifice of Isaac
The salutation and conception
The shepherds
Shetland sword dance
The trial of Christ
Udall, N. Roister Doister
Wyt and science

ALD Aldington, Richard, ed.
French comedies of the
XVIIIth century... London,
Routledge [1923] 347p
Destouches, P. The conceited
count
Le Sage, A. Turcaret; or,
The Financier
Marivaux, P. The game of
love and chance
Regnard, J. The residuary
légatee

ALLE Allen, John, ed. Three
medieval plays... London...
Heineman [c1953] 54p
The farce of Master Pierre
Pathelin
The pageant of the shearmen
and taylors
The summoning of Everyman

ALLI Allison, Alexander W.;
Carr, Arthur J., and East-
man, Arthur M., eds.
Masterpieces of the drama
... New York, Macmillan
[c1957] 693p
Chekhov, A. The cherry or-
chard
Euripides. Alcestis
Garcia Lorca, F. The house
of Bernda Alba

Giraudoux, J. The madwoman
of Chaillot
Ibsen, H. Hedda Gabler
Jonson, B. Volpone, or the
fox
Moliére, J. The miser
O'Casey, S. Juno and the
paycock
Sheridan, R. The rivals
Sophocles. Oedipus rex
Synge, J. Riders to the sea

ALP Alpern, Hymen and Martel,
José, eds. Diez comedias
del siglo de oro... New
York, Harper [c1939] 859p
Calderón de la Barca, P. La
vida es sueño
Castro y Bellvis, G. Las
mocedades del Cid
Cervantes Saavedra, M. La
Numancia
Mira de Amescua, A. El es-
clavo del demonio
Moreto y Cabaña, A. El des-
dén con el desdén
Rojas Zorilla, F. Del rey
abajo, ninguno
Ruiz de Alacrón y Mendoza,
J. La verdad sospechosa
Téllez, G. El burlador de
Sevilla
Vega Carpio, L. La estrella
de Seville
Vega Carpio, L. Fuenteovej-
una

ALPE Alpern, Hyman and Mar-
tel, José, eds. Teatro his-
panoamericano... [1st ed.]
New York, Odyssey Press
[c1956] 412p
Alsina, A. La marca de fuego
Eichelbaum, S. Divorcio nup-
cial
Moock Bousquet, A. La ser-
piente
Rojas, R. Ollántay
Sánchez, F. Los derechos de
la salud
Segura, M. Na Catita

AME American caravan, a yearbook of American literature... Edited by Van Wyck Brooks, Alfred Kreymborg, Lewis Mumford and Paul Rosenfeld. New York, Macaulay [c1927-c1936] 5v Title varies: 1927, The american caravan; 1928, The second American Caravan; 1929, The new American caravan; 1931, American caravan IV; 1936, The new caravan.

Basshe, E. The dream of the dollar. 5

Frank, W. New Year's eve. 2

Geddes, V. The stable and the grove. 4

Gold, M. Hoboken blues. 1

Green, P. Supper for the dead. 1

Green, P. Tread the green grass. 3

Kreymborg, A. The dead are free. 5

Schwartz, D. Choosing company. 5

Williams, W. The first president. 5

AMERICAN LITERATURE: a period anthology; Oscar Cargill, general editor. See MCDO McDowell, Tremaine, ed. The romantic triumph... NELS Nelson, John Herbert and Cargill, Oscar, eds. Contemporary trends.. SPI Spiller, Robert Ernest, ed. The roots of national culture...

AMI American omnibus, with an introduction by Carl Van Doren. New York, Literary guild [c1933] v.p.
Mayer, E. Children of darkness

AMP America's lost plays... Barrett H. Clark, general editor. Princeton, N.J., Princeton university press,

1940-41. 20v
Alfriend, E., and Wheeler, A. The great diamond robbery.

Belasco, D. La belle russe. 18

Belasco, D. The heart of Maryland. 18

Belasco, D. Naughty Anthony. 18

Belasco, D. The stranglers of Paris. 18

Belasco, D. and De Mille, H. The charity ball. 17

Belasco, D., and De Mille, H. The wife. 17

Belasco, D., and Fyles, F. The girl I left behind me. 18

Bennett, C. A royal slave. 8

Bird, R. Caridorf; or, The avenger. 12

Bird, R. The cowled lover. 12

Bird, R. News of the night; or, A trip to Niagara. 12

Bird, R. 'Twas all for the best; or, 'Tis all a notion. 12

Boker, G. The bankrupt. 3

Boker, G. Glaucus. 3

Boker, G. The world a mask. 3

Boucicault, D. Dot. 1

Boucicault, D. Flying scud. 1

Boucicault, D. Forbidden fruit. 1

Boucicault, D. Louis XI. 1

Boucicault, D. Mercy Dodd. 1

Boucicault, D. Robert Emmet. 1

Brougham, J. The duke's motto; or, I am here! 14

Campbell, B. Fairfax. 19

Campbell, B. The galley slave. 19

Campbell, B. My partner. 19

Campbell, B. The Virginian. 19

ASH (continued)
Congreve, W. The way of the
world
Everyman
Gay, J. The beggar's opera
Greene, R. Friar Bacon and
Friar Bungay
Heywood, T. A woman killed
with kindness
Jonson, B. The alchemist
Marlowe, C. Edward II
O'Neill, E. Anna Christie
Sheridan, R. The critic
Wilde, O. The importance of
being earnest

ATKINSON, BROOKS. See
FOUB Four great comedies
of the restoration and 18th
century; See
NEWV New voices in the
American theatre...

ATT Attic tragedies... Boston,
Bibliophile society, 1927.
3v
Aeschylus. Prometheus bound.
3
Euripides. Hippolytus.   2
Euripides. Medea.   2
Sophocles. Antigone.   1
Sophocles. Electra.   3
Sophocles. Oedypus the king.1

AUDE Auden, Wystan Hugh, ed.
The portable Greek reader
...New York, Viking, 1948.
726p
Aeschylus. Agamemnon
Aeschylus. Choephoroe
Aeschylus. Eumenides

AYLIFF, H.K. See
MAL Malvern festival
plays...

B

BAK Baker, George Pierce,
comp. Modern American
plays... New York, Harcourt,
Brace and Howe, 1920.
544p

Anspacher, L. The unchastened
woman
Belasco, D. The return of
Peter Grimm
Massey, E. Plots and play-
wrights
Sheldon, E. Romance
Thomas, A. As a man
thinks

BAKS Bakshy, Alexander, comp.
and tr. Soviet scene; six
plays of Russian life... New
Haven, Yale university
press, 1946. 348p
Afinogenov, A. Far taiga
Ilyenkov, V. The square of
flowers
Marshak, S. Twelve months
Pogodin, N. The chimes of
the Kremlin
Shkvarkin, V. Father unknown
Trenyov, K. Lyubov Yarovaya

BALD Bald, Robert Cecil, ed.
Six Elizabethan plays...
Boston, Houghton Mifflin
[c1963]
Beaumont, F., and Fletcher,
J. The knight of the burn-
ing pestle
Dekker, T. The shoemakers'
holiday
Ford, J. The broken heart.
Jonson, B. Epicolne; or, The
silent woman
Marlowe, C. Tamburlaine the
great (Part 1)
Webster, J. The duchess of
Malfi

BALL Ball, John, ed. From
Beowulf to modern British
writers. Based on Robert
Shafer's From Beowulf to
Thomas Hardy. [One-vol-
ume ed.] New York, Odys-
sey Press [1959] 1364p
Everyman
Eliot, T. Murder in the ca-
thedral
Marlowe, C. The tragical his-
tory of Doctor Faustus

Shaw, G.   Don Juan in hell
Synge, J.   In the shadow of
    the glen

BARB   Barnet, Sylvan; Berman,
    Morton and Burto, William,
    eds.   Eight great comedies
    [New York] New American
    Library [c1958] 472p
Aristophanes.   The clouds
Chekhov, A.   Uncle Vanya
Gay, J.   The beggar's opera
Machiavelli, N.   Mandragola
Molière, J.   The miser
Shakespeare, W.   Twelfth night;
    or, What you will
Shaw, G.   Arms and the man
Wilde, O.   The importance of
    being earnest

BARC   Barnet, Sylvan; Berman,
    Morton and Burto, William,
    eds.   Eight great tragedies
    ...[New York] New Ameri-
    can Library [1957] 443p
Aeschylus.   Prometheus bound
Euripides.   Hippolytus
Ibsen, H.   Ghosts
O'Neill, E.   Desire under the
    elms
Shakespeare, W.   King Lear
Sophocles.   Oedipus the king
Strindberg, A.   Miss Julie
Yeats, W.   On Baile's strand

BARD   Barnet, Sylvan; Berman,
    Morton and Burto, William,
    eds.   The genius of the early
    English theater...[New York]
    New American Library
    [c1962] 453p
Abraham and Isaac
Everyman
The second shepherd's play
Jonson, B.   Volpone
Marlowe, C.   Doctor Faustus
Milton, J.   Samson Agonistes
Shakespeare, W.   Macbeth

BARF   Barnet, Sylvan; Berman,
    Morton and Burto, William,
    eds.   The genius of the Irish
    theater...[New York] New

American Library [c1960]
    366p
Gregory, I.   The Canavans
O'Casey, S.   Purple dust
O'Donovan, M.   In the train
Shaw, G.   John Bull's other
    island
Synge, J.   Deidre of the sor-
    rows
Yeats, J.   La la noo
Yeats, W.   The words upon the
    windowpane

BARG   Barnet, Sylvan; Berman,
    Morton and Burto, William,
    eds.   The genius of the
    later English theater...
    [New York] New American
    Library [c1962] 536p
Byron, G.   Cain
Congreve, W.   The way of the
    world
Golding, W.   The brass butter-
    fly
Goldsmith, O.   She stoops to
    conquer; or, The mistakes
    of a night
Shaw, G.   Major Barbara
Wilde, O.   The importance of
    being earnest

BARH   Barnet, Sylvan; Berman,
    Morton and Burto, William,
    eds.   An introduction to lit-
    erature...Boston, Little,
    Brown [c1961] 491p
Quem quaeritis
Sophocles.   Antigone
Shaw, G.   The shewing up of
    Blanco Posnet
Yeats, W.   Purgatory

BARR   Barrows, Herbert; Heff-
    ner, Hubert; Ciardi, John
    and Douglas, Wallace, eds.
    An introduction to litera-
    ture...Boston, Houghton
    Mifflin [c1959] 1331p
Chekhov, A.   The cherry or-
    chard
Ibsen, H.   The wild duck
O'Casey, S.   Juno and the pay-
    cock

161

BARR (continued)
Pirandello, L. Six characters
in search of an author
Shaw, G. Candida
Wilde, O. The importance of
being earnest

BARNES, JOHN R. See
PROW Prose and poetry
of the world...

BAS Baskervill, Charles Read;
Heltzel, Virgil B., and
Nethercot, Arthur H., eds.
Elizabethan and Stuart plays
...New York, Holt [c1934]
1660p
Arden of Feversham
Attowell's jig (Francis' new
jig)
Beaumont, F., and Fletcher,
J. The knight of the burn-
ing pestle
Beaumont, F., and Fletcher,
J. The maid's tragedy
Beaumont, F., and Fletcher,
J. Philaster
Chapman, G. Bussy d'Ambois
Dekker, T. The honest whore,
pt. I
Dekker, T. The shoemakers'
holiday
Fletcher, J. The faithful shep-
herdess
Ford, J. The broken heart
Ford, J. Perkin Warbeck
Ford, J., Dekker, T., and
Rowley, W. The witch of
Edmonton
Gascoigne, G. Supposes
Greene, R. Friar Bacon and
Friar Bungay
Greene, R. George a Greene
Heywood, T. A woman killed
with kindness
Jonson, B. The alchemist
Jonson, B. Every man in his
humor
Jonson, B. The hue and cry
after cupid
Jonson, B. The sad shepherd
Jonson, B. Sejanus, his fall
Jonson, B. Volpone

Kyd, T. The Spanish tragedy
Lyly, J. Endymion
Marlowe, C. Doctor Faustus
Marlowe, C. Edward II
Marlowe, C. Tamburlaine, pt.
I
Marston, J., and Webster, J.
The malcontent
Massinger, P. The maid of
honor
Massinger, P. A new way to
pay old debts
Middleton, T. A trick to
catch the old one
Middleton, T., and Rowley, W.
The changeling
Mucedorus
Norton, T., and Sackville, T.
Gorboduc
Peele, G. The arraignment of
Paris
Peele, G. The old wives' tale
Preston, T. Cambises
Shirley, J. The cardinal
Shirley, J. The lady of pleas-
ure
Stevenson, W. Gammer Gur-
ton's needle
Udall, N. Roister Doister
Webster, J. The Duchess of
Malfi

BAT Bates, Alfred...The drama;
its history, literature and
influence on civilization...
London, Athenian society,
1903-04. 22v
Aeschylus. Eumenides.   1
Alfieri, V. Myrrha.   5
Aristophanes. The clouds.   2
Aristophanes. Ecclesiazusae.
                            21
Babo, J. Dagobert, king of
the Franks.   12
Beaumont, F., and Fletcher,
J. The knight of the burn-
ing pestle.   14
Benedix, R. Obstinacy.   11
Bjørnson, B. A gauntlet. 17
Boucicault, D. London assur-
ance.   22
Brougham, J. Pocahontas. 20
Bulwer-Lytton, E. Money. 16

162

BAT (continued)
Tobin, J. The honeymoon. 16
Torres Naharro, B. Hymen. 6
Townley, J. High life below
stairs.   16
Udall, N. Ralph Roister
Doister.   13
Vanbrugh, J. The provoked
husband.   15
Vega Carpio, L. The dog in
the manger.   6
Voltaire, F. Mahomet.   8
Voltaire, F. Socrates.   8
The wept of the wish-ton-wish.
                                19
Werner, F. The twenty-fourth
of February.   10

BAUG Baugh, Albert C., and
McClelland, George W.,
eds. English literature...
New York, Appleton-Century
-Crofts [c1954] 1480p
Dryden, J. All for love
Marlowe, C. The tragical his-
tory of Doctor Faustus
Wilde, O. Lady Windermere's
fan

BAYLISS, JOHN See
NEWR New road...

BEAC Beacon lights of litera-
ture...[Edited by] Marquis
E. Shattuck...Rudolph W.
Chamberlain...Edwin B.
Richards...[Books six-
twelve] Syracuse, N.Y.,
Iroquois, 1940. 7v
Coppée, F. The violin maker
of Cremona.   8
Down, O. The maker of
dreams.   12
Dunsany, E. A night at an
inn.   11
Glaspell, S. Trifles.   11
Goldsmith, O. She stoops to
conquer.   11
Gregory, I. The rising of the
moon.   12
Gregory, I. Spreading the
news.   8
Hall, H., and Middleman, R.

The valiant.   10
Kaufman, G., and Connelly,
M. Merton of the movies,
                                12
MacKaye, P. Sam Average.11
Moeller, P. Helena's husband.
                                12
Moorhouse, A. The grand
cham's diamond.   10
O'Neill, E. Ile.   12
Saunders, L. The knave of
hearts.   7
Shakespeare, W. Julius Cae-
sar.   11
Shakespeare, W. Macbeth. 12
Shakespeare, W. The mer-
chant of Venice.   10
Shakespeare, W. A midsum-
mer night's dream,   9
Walker, S. The medicine show.
                                11

BEAL Beal, Richard S., and
Korg, Jacob, eds. The
complete reader. Englewood
Cliffs, N.J., Prentice-Hall,
1961. 630p
Shakespeare, W. The chronicle
history of King Henry the
fourth, pt. one
Shaw, G. Arms and the man
Sophocles. Oedipus the King

BEAR Beardsley, Monroe C.;
Daniel, Robert and Leggett,
Glenn, eds. Theme and
form...Englewood Cliffs,
N.J. Prentice-Hall, 1956.
725p
Shakespeare, W. Othello
Shaw, G. Arms and the man
Sophocles. Antigone
Thomas, D. The doctor and
the devils

BECHHOFER, CARL ERIC. See
ROE Roberts, Carl Eric
Bechhofer, tr. Five Rus-
sian plays...

BENÉT, WILLIAM ROSE. See
OXF Oxford anthology of
American literature...

164

edited by William Rose Benét and Norman Holmes
Pearson.

BENN Bennett, Henry Garland,
ed. ... English literature...
N. Y. , American book company [c1935] 603p
Goldsmith, O. She stoops to
conquer
Shakespeare, W. Macbeth

BENP Bennett, Henry Garland
...On the high road...N. Y. ,
American book company
[c1935] 600p
Dowson, E. The Pierrot of
the minute
Everyman
Maeterlinck, M. The intruder
O'Neill, E. Where the cross
is made
Riggs, L. Knives from Syria
Shakespeare, W. Julius Caesar
Sheridan, R. The rivals
Wilde, P. Confessional

BENR Bentley, Eric Russell,
ed. The classic theatre
[1st ed.]...Garden City,
N. Y. , Doubleday, 1958-61.
4v
The three cuckolds,   1
Beaumarchais, P. Figaro's
marriage; or, One mad
day,   4
Beolco, A. Ruzzante returns
from the wars,   1
Calderón de la Barca, P.
Life is a dream,   3
Calderón de la Barca, P.
Love after death,   3
Calderón de la Barca, P.
The wonder-working ma-
gician,   3
Castro y Bellvis, G. Exploits
of the Cid,   4
Cervantes Saavedra, M. The
siege of Numantia,   3
Corneille, P. The cid,   4
Goethe, J. Egmont,   2
Goldoni, C. Mirandolina,   1
Goldoni, C. The servant of

two masters,   1
Gozzi, C. The king stag,   1
Kleist, H. Penthesilea,   2
Kleist, H. The Prince of
Homburg,   2
Lesage, A. Turcaret,   4
Machiavelli, N. The man-
drake,   1
Marivaux, P. The false con-
fessions,   4
Molière, J. The misan-
thrope,   4
Racine, J. Phaedra   4
Rojas, F. Celestina; or, The
tragi-comedy of Calisto
and Melibea,   3
Schiller, J. Don Carlos,   2
Schiller, J. Mary Stuart,   2
Téllez, G. The trickster of
Seville and his guest of
stone,   3
Vega Caprio, L. Fuente
Ovejuna,   3

BENS Bentley, Eric Russell, ed.
From the modern repertoire.
Series one - three. [Denver,
Col.] University of Denver
press; Bloomington, Ind.,
Indiana university press.
[c1949-1956] 3v
Anouilh, J. Cecile; or, The
school for fathers,   3
Becque, H. La Parisienne. 1
Brecht, B. Galileo,   2
Brecht, B. Saint Joan of the
stockyards,   3
Brecht, B. The threepenny
opera,   1
Büchner, G. Danton's death 1
Büchner, G. Leonce and
Lena,   3
Cocteau, J. The infernal ma-
chine,   1
Cocteau, J. Intimate rela-
tions,   3
Cummings, E. him,   2
Eliot, T. Sweeney Agon-
istes,   1
Fergusson, F. The king and
the duke,   2
Garcia Lorca, F. The love
of Don Perlimplin and

165

BENS (continued)
Belisa in the garden. 1
Giraudoux, J. Electra. 2
Jeffers, R. The Cretan wo-
man. 3
Macneice, L. The dark
tower. 2
Mirbeau, O. The epidemic. 2
Musset, A. A door should be
either open or shut. 3
Musset, A. Fantasio. 1
Obey, A. Venus and
Adonis. 2
Ostrovsky, A. Easy money. 2
Pinero, A. The magistrate. 3
Romains, J. Dr. Knock. 3
Schnitzler, A. Anatol. 3
Schnitzler, A. Round dance. 1
Sternheim, C. The snob. 1
Wedekind, F. The Marquis
of Keith. 2
Yeats, W. A full moon in
March. 1
Zola, E. Thérèse Raquin. 3

BENSA Bentley, Eric Russell,
ed. Let's get a divorce!
and other plays. New York,
Hill and Wang [c1958] 364p
Courteline, G. These corn-
fields
Feydeau, G. Keep an eye on
Amélie!
Labiche, E. and Delacour, A.
Célimare
Labiche, E. and Martin, É.
A trip abroad
Prévert, J. A united family
Sardou, V. and Najac, E.
Let's get a divorce!

BENT Bentley, Eric Russell, ed.
The modern theatre. [Plays]
Garden City, N. Y., Double-
day [c1955]-1960. 6v
Anouilh, J. Medea. 5
Anouilh, J. Thieves' carni-
val. 3
Becque, H. Woman of Paris. 1
Beerbohm, M. A social
success. 6
Brecht, B. The measures
taken. 6

Brecht, B. Mother courage. 2
Brecht, B. The threepenny
opera. 1
Büchner, G. Woyzeck. 1
Büchner, G. Danton's
death. 5
Conrad, J. One day more. 3
Fitch, C. Captain Jinks of
the horse marines. 4
Ghelderode, M. Escurial. 5
Giraudoux, J. Electra. 1
Giraudoux, J. Judith. 3
Gogol, N. Gamblers. 3
Gogol, N. The marriage. 5
Labiche, E., and Marc-
Michel. An Italian straw
hat. 3
Mitchell, L. The New York
idea. 4
Musset, A. Fantasio 2
Musset, A. Lorenzaccio. 6
O'Casey, S. Cock-a-doodle
dandy. 5
Ostrovsky, A. The diary of
a scoundrel. 2
Saroyan, W. The man with
the heart in the Highlands.
4
Schnitzler, A. La ronde. 2
Sternheim, C. The under-
pants. 6
Swerling, J., Burrows, A.,
and Loesser, F. Guys
and dolls. 4
Verga, G. Cavalleria rusti-
cana. 1
Wedekind, F. Spring's
awakening. 6
Wilder, T. Pullman car
Hiawatha. 4
Yeats, W. Purgatory. 2

BENU Bentley, Eric Russell,
ed. The play; a critical
anthology... New York,
Prentice-Hall, 1951. 774p
Ibsen, H. Ghosts
Miller, A. Death of a sales-
man
Molière, J. The miser
Rostand, E. Cyrano de Berge-
rac
Shakespeare, W. Othello

166

Shakespeare, W. Twelfth night
Sophocles. Antigone
Strindberg, A. The ghost
sonata
Wilde, O. The importance of
being earnest

BENY Bentley, Gerald Eades,
ed. The development of
English drama... New York,
Appleton-Century-Crofts
[c1950] 823p
Abraham and Isaac
Beaumont, F., and Fletcher,
J. The knight of the burn-
ing pestle
Boucicault, D. London assur-
ance
Congreve, W. Love for love
Congreve, W. The way of the
world
Cumberland, R. The West In-
dian
Dekker, T. The shoemakers'
holiday
The deluge; or, Noah's flood
Dryden, J. All for love; or,
The world well lost
Dryden, J., and Howard, R.
The Indian queen
Everyman
Fletcher, J. The wild-goose
chase
Ford, J. 'Tis a pity she's a
whore
Goldsmith, O. She stoops to
conquer
Greene, R. Friar Bacon and
Friar Bungay
Jonson, B. The alchemist
Lillo, G. The London merchant
Marlowe, C. Doctor Faustus
Pinero, A. The second Mrs.
Tanqueray
The second shepherds' play
Sheridan, R. The school for
scandal
Webster, J. The white devil
Wilde, O. Lady Windermere's
fan

BENZ Benton, Charles William,
ed. Easy French plays...

Chicago, Scott, Foresman,
1901. 236p
Girardin, É. de. La joie fait
peur
Labiche, E. La grammaire
Scribe, E. Les doigts de fée

BERGH, ALBERT ELLERY. See
DRA Dramatic master-
pieces...

BER Bergin, Thomas Goddard
and Anderson, Theodore,
eds. French plays... New
York, American book co.
[c1941] 452p
Brieux, E. Les trois filles de
M. Dupont
Hervieu, P. La course du
flambeau
Mirbeau, O. Les affaires sont
les affaires

BERM Bermel, Albert, ed. The
genius of the French the-
ater... New York, New A-
merican Library [c1961]
574p
Anouilh, J. The lark
Beaumarchais, P. The barber
of Seville
Giraudoux, J. Song of songs
Hugo, V. Hernani
Labiche, E., and Delacour, A.
Pots of money
Molière, J. The imaginary in-
valid
Racine, J. Andromache
Rostand, E. The romantics

BERN Bernbaum, Ernest, ed.
Anthology of romanticism
... New York, Ronald
[c1948] 1238p
Byron, G. Manfred
Shelley, P. Prometheus un-
bound

BES Best plays of 1894/1899-
1961/62; and The yearbook of
the drama in America... Edited by R. B. Mantle... G. P.
Sherwood... John Chapman...

168

172

BLAG Blair, Walter, and Ger-
ber, John C., eds. ...
Literature (Better Reading
vol. 2). Chicago, Scott,
Foresman [c1949] 778p
Note: Also published in one vol-
ume under the title, The Col-
lege Anthology.
Chekhov, A. The swan song
Dunsany, E. A night at an
inn
Ibsen, H. Hedda Gabler
Molière, J. Tartuffe
O'Neill, E. Anna Christie
Sophocles. Oedipus the king

BLAH Blair, Walter and Ger-
ber, John, eds. Repertory
... Chicago, Scott, Fores-
man [1960] 1173p
Chekhov, A. The cherry or-
chard
Chekhov, A. The swan song
Chayefsky, P. Marty
Dunsany, E. A night at an inn
Fry, C. A phoenix too fre-
quent
O'Neill, E. Bound east for
Cardiff
Shakespeare, W. Romeo and
Juliet
Sophocles. Oedipus the king

BLAI Blair, Walter; Hornberger,
Theodore, and Stewart,
Randall, eds. The litera-
ture of the United States...
Chicago, Scott, Foresman
[c1946-47] 2v
Aiken, G. Uncle Tom's cab-
in; or, Life among the
lowly.   2
Mitchell, L. The New York
idea.   2
O'Neill, E. The hairy ape. 2
Tyler, R. The contrast.   1

BLAJ Blair, Walter; Hornberger,
Theodore and Stewart, Ran-
dall. The literature of the
United States... Single vol-
ume edition. Chicago, Scott,
Foresman [c1949] 1313p

O'Neill, E. The hairy ape

BLOC Block, Haskell M., and
Shedd, Robert G., eds.
Masters of modern drama
... New York, Random
House [c1962] 1198p
Anouilh, J. Antigone
Anouilh, J. Thieves' carnival
Beckett, S. Endgame
Brecht, B. The good woman
of Setzuan
Brecht, B. Mother courage
and her children
Camus, A. Caligula
Chayefsky, P. Marty
Chekhov, A. The cherry or-
chard
Chekhov, A. The sea gull
Cocteau, J. Orphée
Duerrenmatt, F. The visit
Frisch, M. Biedermann and
the firebugs
García Lorca, F. Blood wed-
ding
Giraudoux, J. Electra
Giraudoux, J. The madwoman
of Chaillot
Gorki, M. The lower depths
Hauptmann, G. The weavers
Hofmannsthal, H. Death and
the fool
Ibsen, H. Ghosts
Ibsen, H. Peer Gynt
Ionesco, E. The bald soprano
Kaiser, G. From morn to
midnight
Maeterlinck, M. The intruder
Miller, A. Death of a sales-
man
O'Casey, S. Cock-a-doodle
dandy
O'Casey, S. Juno and the pay-
cock
Odets, C. Awake and sing!
O'Neill, E. The Emperor
Jones
O'Neill, E. The iceman
cometh
Osborne, J. Look back in
anger
Pirandello, L. Henry IV
Saroyan, W. The time of your

life
Sartre, J.   No exit
Schnitzler, A.   La ronde
Shaw, G.   Major Barbara
Shaw, G.   Man and superman
Strindberg, A.   The ghost
    sonata
Strindberg, A.   Miss Julie
Synge, J.   The playboy of the
    western world
Synge, J.   Riders to the sea
Wedekind, F.   The Marquis of
    Keith
Wilder, T.   The matchmaker
Williams, T.   The glass me-
    nagerie
Yeats, W.   At the hawk's well
Zuckmayer, C.   The devil's
    general

BLOD   Blodgett, Harold William
    and Johnson, Burges, eds.
    Readings for our times...
    Boston, Ginn [c1942] 2v
Rostand, E.   Cyrano de Ber-
    gerac.   1
Wilder, T. Our town.   1

BLOO   Bloomfield, Morton W.
    and Elliott, Robert C., eds.
    Ten plays...New York,
    Rinehart [c1951] 719p
Chekhov, A.   Three sisters
Dekker, T.   The shoemaker's
    holiday
Farquhar, G.   The beaux'
    stratagem
Hellman, L.   The little foxes
Ibsen, H.   Hedda Gabler
O'Neill, E.   The hairy ape
Rostand, E.   Cyrano de Ber-
    gerac
Shakespeare, W. Othello
Sophocles. Antigone
Thurber, J., and Nugent, E.
    The male animal

BOA   Boas, Frederick Samuel,
    ed.   Five pre-Shakespearean
    comedies (early Tudor peri-
    od)...London, Oxford uni-
    versity press [1934] 343p
    (The world's classics)

Gascoigne, G.   Supposes
Heywood, J.   The four pp
Medwall, H.   Fulgens and Lu-
    crece
"Mr. S. Mr. of Art." Gam-
    mer Gurton's needle
Udall, N.   Ralph Roister
    Doister

BOGO   Bogorad, Samuel N. and
    Trevithick, Jack, eds. The
    college miscellany...New
    York, Rinehart [c1952]
    621p
Barrie, J.   The twelve-pound
    look
Rattigan, T.   The Winslow boy
Shakespeare, W.   King Henry
    the fourth, pt. I

BOH   Bohemian club, San Fran-
    cisco. The Grove plays of
    the Bohemian club; edited
    by Porter Garnett...San
    Francisco, The club, 1918.
    3v
Crocker, C.   The land of
    happiness.   3
Field, C.   The cave man.   2
Field, C.   The man in the
    forest.   1
Field, C.   The owl and care.
                               1
Garnett, P.   The green knight.
                               2
Irwin, W.   The Hamadryads.
                               1
Myrtle, F.   Gold.   3
Pixley, F.   Apollo.   3
Redding, J.   The atonement
    of Pan.   2
Robertson, L.   Montezuma. 1
Scheffauer, H.   The sons of
    Baldur.   1
Shiels, J.   Nec-natama.   3
Steele, R.   The fall of Ug.   3
Stephens, H.   St. Patrick at
    Tara.   2
Stirling, G.   The triumph of
    Bohemia.   1
Tharp, N.   The quest of the
    Gorgon.   1

American tradition in literature...New York, Norton
[c1956] 2v
O'Neill, E. The hairy ape. 2

BRAD Bradley, Edward Sculley;
Beatty, Richmond Croom,
and Long, E. Hudson, eds.
The American tradition in
literature...Shorter edition.
New York, W.W. Norton
[c1956] 1575p
O'Neill, E. The hairy ape

BRAG Brady, Agnes Marie and
Turk, Laurel Herbert, eds.
...Romantic Spanish read-
ings...New York, D. Apple-
ton-Century [c1939] 274p
Téllez, G. El burlador de
Sevilla

BRE Brenner, Clarence Dietz,
and Goodyear, Nolan, A.,
eds. Eighteenth century
French plays...New York,
Century [c1927] 561p
Beaumarchais, P. Le mariage
de Figaro
Crébillon, P. Rhadamiste et
Zénobie
Dancourt, F. Le chevalier à
la mode
Destouches, P. Le glorieux
Diderot, D. Le père de famille
Gresset, J. Le méchant
La Chaussée, P. Le préjugé
à la mode
Laya, J. L'ami des lois
Lesage, A. Turcaret
Marivaux, P. Le jeu de
l'amour et du hazard
Palissot de Montenoy, C. Les
philosophes
Regnard, J. Le légataire uni-
versel
Sedaine, M. Le philosophe
sans le savoir
Voltaire, F. Nanine
Voltaire, F. Zaïre

BRET Brett, Lewis Edward,
ed. ...Nineteenth century

Spanish plays...New York,
Appleton-Century [c1935]
889p
Benavente y Martínez, J. El
nido ajeno
Bretón de los Herrerós, M.
Muérete ¡y verás!
Echegaray y Eizaguirre, J.
El gran Galeoto
Garcia Guitérrez, A. Juan
Lorenzo
Gil y Zárate, A. Guzmán el
Bueno
Hartzenbusch, J. Los amantes
de Teruel
López de Ayala, A. Consuelo
Moratín, L. El sí de las
niñas
Núñez de Arce, G. El haz
de leña
Pérez Galdós, B. La de San
Quintín
Rivas, A. Don Alvaro
Tamayo y Baus, M. Un drama
nuevo
Vega, R. Pepa la fresca-
chona
Vega, V. El hombre de mun-
do
Zorrilla y Morae, J. Don
Juan Tenorio

BRIG Briggs, Thomas Henry;
Herzberg, Max J., and
Bolenius, Emma Miller,
eds. ...English literature
...Boston, Houghton Miff-
lin [c1934] 770p (Literature
in the senior high school.
v4)
Shakespeare, W. The tragedy
of Macbeth
Sheridan, R. The school for
scandal
Synge, J. Riders to the sea

BRIK Briggs, Thomas Henry;
Herzberg, Max J., and
Bolenius, Emma Miller,
eds. ...Romance...Boston,
Houghton Mifflin [c1932]
770 p (Literature in the
senior high school v2)

BRIK (continued)
Peabody, J. The piper
Shakespeare, W. As you like
it

BRN Brodin, Sylvie Bostsarron
and Vigneras, Marcel, eds.
En scène; trois comédies
avec musique... New York,
Dryden press [c1942] 295p
Beaumarchais, P. Le barbier
de Séville
Labiche, E., and Martin, E.
Les trente--sept sous de
M. Montaudoin
Le savetier Calbain

BRO Brooke, Charles Frederick
Tucker, ed. The Shake-
speare apocrypha... Oxford,
Clarendon press, 1918.
455p
Arden of Feversham
The birth of Merlin
Edward III
Fair Em
Locrine
The London prodigal
The merry devil of Edmonton
Mucedorus
The puritan
Sir John Oldcastle
Sir Thomas More
Thomas, lord Cromwell
The two noble kinsmen
A Yorkshire tragedy

BROC Brooke, Charles Frede-
rick Tucker and Paradise,
Nathaniel Burton, eds.
English drama, 1580-1642
... Boston, Heath [c1933]
1044p
Beaumont, F., and Fletcher,
J. The knight of the burn-
ing pestle
Beaumont, F., and Fletcher,
J. The maid's tragedy
Beaumont, F., and Fletcher,
J. Philaster
Chapman, G. Bussy d'Ambois
Chapman, G., Jonson, B.,
and Marston J. Eastward

ho!
Dekker, T. The shoemakers'
holiday
Fletcher, J. The island
princess
Fletcher, J., and Massinger,
P. Beggars' bush
Ford, J. The broken heart
Greene, R. Friar Bacon and
Friar Bungay
Heywood, T. A woman killed
with kindness
Jonson, B. The alchemist
Jonson, B. Epicoene; or, The
silent woman
Jonson, B. Every man in his
humour
Jonson, B. The gipsies meta-
morphosed
Jonson, B. Volpone; or, The
fox
Kyd, T. The Spanish tragedy
Lyly, J. Endymion
Marlowe, C. Doctor Faustus
Marlowe, C. Edward II
Marlowe, C. The Jew of
Malta
Marlowe, C. Tamburlaine,
pt I
Marston, J. The malcontent
Massinger, P. A new way to
pay old debts
Middleton, T. A game at
chess
Middleton, T., and Rowley,
W. The changeling
Peele, G. The arraignment of
Paris
Peele, G. The old wives tale
Shirley, J. The cardinal
Webster, J. The Duchess of
Malfi

BROF Brooks, Cleanth; Purser,
John Thibaut and Warren,
Robert Penn. An approach
to literature. Baton Rouge,
Louisiana university press,
1936. 578p
Čapek, K. R.U.R. (Rossum's
universal robots)
Ibsen, H. Hedda Gabler

BROG Brooks, Cleanth; Purser, John Thibaut and Warren, Robert Penn. An approach to literature. Rev. ed. New York, Crofts, 1939. 634p
Čapek, K. R.U.R. (Rossum's universal robots)
Ibsen, H. Hedda Gabler
Shakespeare, W. Antony and Cleopatra
Wilde, O. The importance of being earnest

BROH Brooks, Cleanth; Purser, John Thibaut and Warren, Robert Penn. An approach to literature. Third edition. New York, Appleton-Cen tury-Crofts [c1952] 820p
Eliot, T.S. Murder in the cathedral
Ibsen, H. Hedda Gabler
Maugham, W. The circle
Miller, A. All my sons
Shakespeare, W. Antony and Cleopatra

BROJ Brooks, Cleanth, and Heilman, Robert B., eds. Understanding drama...New York, Holt [c1945] 515p
Congreve, W. The way of the world
Everyman
Lillo, G. The London merchant
Ibsen, H. Rosmersholm
Plautus. The twin Menaechmi
Shakespeare, W. Henry IV, pt. I
Sheridan, R. The school for scandal
Wilde, O. Lady Windermere's fan

BROK Brooks, Cleanth and Heilman, Robert B. Under-standing drama; twelve plays...New York, Holt [c1948] 674, +64p
Chekhov, A. The sea gull

Congreve, W. The way of the world
Everyman
Ibsen, H. Rosmersholm
Lillo, G. The London merchant; or, The history of George Barnwell
Marlowe, C. Dr. Faustus
Plautus. The twin Menaechmi
Shakespeare, W. Henry IV, pt. I
Shakespeare, W. King Lear
Sheridan, R. The school for scandal
Sophocles. Oedipus the king
Wilde, O. Lady Windermere's fan

BROOKS, VAN WYCK. See AME American caravan...

BROWNE, ELLIOTT MARTIN. See also NEWE New Eng-lish dramatists...

BROS Browne, Elliott Martin, ed. Four modern verse plays...[Harmondsworth, Middlesex] Penguin Books [1957] 269p
Eliot, T. The family reunion
Fry, C. A phoenix too fre-quent
MacDonagh, D. Happy as Larry
Williams, C. Thomas Cran-mer of Canterbury

BROT Browne, Elliott Martin, ed. Three Irish plays... Baltimore, Penguin Books [1960, c1959] 236p
Johnston, D. The moon in the Yellow river
MacDonagh, D. Step-in-the-hollow
O'Conor, J. The iron harp

BROWN, IVOR. See FOUP Four plays of 1936...

BROU Brown, Leonard Stanley; Waite, Harlow O., and

181

BROU (continued)
    Atkinson, Benjamin P., eds.
    Literature for our time...
    New York, Holt [c1947]
    951p
    Anderson, M. Winterset
    Barry, P. The Philadelphia
    story
    Behrman, S. Biography
    Čapek, K. R.U.R.
    Corwin, N. We hold these
    truths
    MacLeish, A. The fall of the
    city
    O'Neill, E. The hairy ape

BROW Brown, Leonard Stanley,
    and Perrin, Porter Gale,
    eds. A quarto of modern
    literature... New York,
    Scribner [c1935] 436p
    Barrie, J. Dear Brutus
    Galsworthy, J. Justice
    Howard, S. The silver cord
    O'Neill, E. In the zone

BROX Brown, Leonard Stanley,
    and Perrin, Porter Gale,
    eds. A quarto of modern
    literature... Third edition.
    New York, Scribner [c1950]
    631p
    Galsworthy, J. Loyalties
    Giraudoux, J. The madwoman
    of Chaillot
    Howard, S. The silver cord
    Miller, A. Death of a sales-
    man
    O'Neill, E. The Emperor Jones
    Sherwood, R. Abe Lincoln in
    Illinois

BRR Brown, Sharon Osborne, ed.
    Present tense... New York,
    Harcourt, Brace, 1941. 3v
    Čapek, K. R.U.R. (Rossum's
    universal robots)   3
    MacLeish, A. The fall of the
    city.   3
    Wilder, T. Our town.   1

BRS Brown, Sharon Osborne, ed.
    Present tense. Rev. ed.

    New York, Harcourt,
    Brace, 1945. 762p
    Corwin, N. Good heavens
    Wilder, T. Our town

BRYSON, LYMAN. See THP
    Three great Greek plays...

BUCK Buck, Philo M., jr., ed.
    An anthology of world litera-
    ture... New York, Macmill-
    an, 1934. 1016p
    Aeschylus. Agamemnon
    Aeschylus. Prometheus bound
    Aristophanes. The frogs
    Euripides. Iphigenia at Aulis
    Goethe, J. Faust, pts. I and
    II
    Hauptmann, G. The sunken
    bell
    Hebbel, F. Maria Magdalena
    Ibsen, H. An enemy of the
    people
    Kalidasa. Śakoontalá
    Molière, J. The misanthrope
    Molière, J. Tartuffe
    Pérez Galdós, B. Electra
    Racine, J. Athaliah
    Sophocles. Antigone
    Sophocles. Oedipus the king

BUCL Buck, Philo M., jr., and
    Alberson, Hazel, eds. An
    anthology of world litera-
    ture. Revised edition... New
    York, Macmillan, 1940.
    1148p
    Aeschylus. Agamemnon
    Aeschylus. Prometheus bound
    Aristophanes. The frogs
    Book of Job
    Euripides. Iphigenia at Aulis
    Euripides. Medea
    Goethe, J. Faust, pts. I and
    II
    Hauptmann, G. The sunken
    bell
    Hebbel, F. Maria Magdalena
    Ibsen, H. An enemy of the
    people
    Kalidasa. Śakoontalá
    Molière, J. The misanthrope
    Molière, J. Tartuffe

Racine, J. Athaliah
Sophocles. Antigone
Sophocles. Oedipus the king

BUCM Buck, Philo M., Jr.,
and Alberson, Hazel Stew-
art, eds. An anthology of
world literature. Third
edition... New York, Mac-
millan [c1951] 1150p
Aeschylus. Agamemnon
Aeschylus. Prometheus bound
Aristophanes. The frogs
Book of Job
Euripides. Iphigenia at Aulis
Euripides. Medea
Goethe, J. Faust
Hauptmann, G. The sunken
bell
Hebbel, F. Maria Magdalena
Ibsen, H. An enemy of the
people
Kalidasa. Shakuntala
Molière, J. The misanthrope
Molière, J. Tartuffe
Plautus. Aulularia
Racine, J. Athaliah
Sophocles. Antigone
Sophocles. Oedipus the king

BUFF Buffington, Albert F.,
ed. The Reichard collection
of early Pennsylvania Ger-
man plays... Lancaster, Pa.,
1962. 439p (v61, Pennsyl-
vania German Society)
Barba, P. An der lumpa parti
Barba, P. Die verrechelte
rechler
Birmelin, J. Der gnopp
Birmelin, J. Em Docktor Fogel
sei offis schtunn
Brendle, T. Di hoffning
Brendle, T. Die mutter
Fink, E. Noshions duhn
Grumbine, E. Die insurance
business
Iobst, C. Die Calline browierts
Iobst, C. Es Heller's Chrischt-
dag
Miller, D. Der Peter soll en
handwerk lernen
Miller, D. En gespräch zwis-

chen zweb demokrate über
politiks
Miller, D. Noch eppes vom
Peter seim handwerk
Moss, A., and Newhard, E.
H. M. S. Pinafore; oder,
Das maedle und ihr sailor
kerl
Rauch, E. Rip Van Winkle;
oder, Die shpooks fum
Blowa Barrick
Wieand, P. Der parra kumpt
Wieand, P. Die huchzich um
kreitz waig
Wieand, P. Tzu forwitsich
Wollenweber, L. Das lied von
der union
Wollenweber, L. Die Marga-
reth und die Lea
Wollenweber, L. Die Sära
und die Betz
Wollenweber, L. Eb Refsch-
neider un Susi Leimbach
Wollenweber, L. Ein ges-
präch

THE BURNS MANTLE YEAR-
BOOK... See BES Best
plays of 1894/99... etc.

C

CADY Cady, Edwin H., ed.
Literature of the early re-
public... New York, Rine-
hart [c1950] 495p
Tyler, R. The contrast

CALG Campbell, Gladys and
Thomas, Russell Brown,
eds. Reading American
literature... Boston, Little,
Brown, 1944. 912p
Sherwood, R. Abe Lincoln in
Illinois

CALM Campbell, Oscar James;
Van Gundy, Justine and
Shrodes, Caroline, eds.
Patterns for living. New
York, Macmillan, 1940.
1306p
Anderson, M. Winterset

CALM (continued)
Carroll, P. Shadow and substance
Milne, A. Mr. Pim passes by
Toller, E. No more peace!

CALN Campbell, Oscar James;
Van Gundy, Justine and
Shrodes, Caroline, eds.
Patterns for living... Alternate edition... New York,
Macmillan [c1943, c1947] 2v
Anderson, M. Winterset. 2
Capek, K. R.U.R. 1
Franken, R. Claudia. 1
Hellman, L. Watch on the 2
Rhine.

CALP Campbell, Oscar James;
Van Gundy, Justine and
Shrodes, Caroline, eds.
Patterns for living... Third
edition. New York, Macmillan, 1949. 951p
Hellman, L. Watch on the
Rhine
Sherwood, R. Abe Lincoln in
Illinois

CALQ Campbell, Oscar James;
Van Gundy, Justine and
Shrodes, Caroline, eds.
Patterns for living... Fourth
edition. New York, Macmillan [c1955] 975p
Hellman, L. Watch on the
Rhine
Miller, A. Death of a salesman

CAM Campbell, Thomas Moody,
ed. German plays of the
nineteenth century... New
York, Crofts, 1930. 437p
Anzengruber, L. Das vierte
gebot
Grillparzer, F. König Ottokars glück und ende
Hauptmann, G. Einsame menschen
Hebbel, C. Agnes Bernauer
Hebbel, C. Herodes und Mariamne

Hebbel, C. Maria Magdalene
Kleist, B. Der zerbrochene
krug
Kleist, B. Prinz Friedrich
von Homburg
Ludwig, O. Der erbförster
Tieck, J. Der gestiefelte
kater
Werner, Z. Der vierundzwanzigste Februar

CANADIAN PLAYS FROM HART
HOUSE THEATRE. See
MAS Massey, Vincent, ed.

CAN Canfield, Curtis, ed.
Plays of changing Ireland.
New York, Macmillan,
1936. 481p
Johnston, D. The old lady
says 'No!'
Longford, C. Mr. Jiggins of
Jigginstown
Longford, E. Yahoo
Manning, M. Youth's the season... ?
Mayne, R. Bridge head
Robinson, L. Church street
Shiels, G. The new gossoon
Yeats, W. The words upon the
windowpane

CAP Canfield, Curtis, ed. Plays
of the Irish renaissance,
1880-1930... New York,
Ives Washburn, 1929. 436p
Colum, P. The land
Fitzmaurice, G. The dandy
dolls
Gregory, I. Hyacinth Halvey
Hyde, D. The twisting of the
rope
Martyn, E. Maeve
Murray, T. Birthright
O'Casey, S. Juno and the paycock
Pearse, P. The singer
Robinson, L. The big house
Russell, G. Deirdre
Synge, J. Riders to the sea
Yeats, W. On Baile's strand
Yeats, W. The only jealousy
of Emer

184

CARGILL, OSCAR. See American literature: a period anthology; Oscar Cargill, general editor

CAR Carpenter, Bruce, comp. A book of dramas, an anthology of nineteen plays... New York, Prentice-Hall, 1929. 1111p
Aeschylus. Agamemnon
Archer, W. The green goddess
Behrman, S. The second man
Chekhov, A. The cherry orchard
Congreve, W. Love for love
Dickens, C. The cricket on the hearth
Euripides. The Trojan women
The farce of the worthy master Pierre Patelin
Hugo, V. Hernani
Ibsen, H. Hedda Gabler
Kaufman, G., and Connelly, M. Beggar on horseback
Maeterlinck, M. The intruder
Molière, J. The misanthrope
Parker, L. A minuet
Racine, J. Phaedra
Sophocles. Oedipus, King of Thebes
Strindberg, A. Miss Julia
Synge, J. Riders to the sea
Wilde, O. The importance of being earnest

CARA Carpenter, Bruce, ed. A book of dramas... [Rev. ed.] New York, Prentice-Hall, 1949. 992p
Aeschylus. Agamemnon
Behrman, S. The second man
Chekhov, A. The cherry orchard
Congreve, W. Love for love
Euripides. The Trojan women
Ibsen, H. Hedda Gabler
Kaufman, G., and Connelly, M. Beggar on horseback
Maeterlinck, M. The intruder
Molière, J. The misanthrope
O'Neill, E. The long voyage home
Racine, J. Phaedra
Rostand, E. Cyrano de Bergerac
Sophocles. Oedipus, King of Thebes
Synge, J. Riders to the sea
Wilde, O. The importance of being earnest

CARTMELL, VAN H. See CEY Cerf, Bennett Alfred and Cartmell, Van H., comps. S.R.O. ...

CART Cartmell, Van H., and Cerf, Bennett Alfred, comps. Famous plays of crime and detection... Philadelphia, Blakiston, 1946. 910p
Cohan, G. Seven keys to Baldpate
Chodorov, E. Kind lady
Dell, J. Payment deferred
Dunning, P., and Abbott, G. Broadway
Gillette, W. Sherlock Holmes
Hamilton, P. Angel street
Megrue, R. Under cover
Rice, E. On trial
Rinehart, M., and Hopwood, A. The bat
Veiller, B. The thirteenth chair
Veiller, B. Within the law
Willard, J. The cat and the canary
Williams, E. Night must fall

CASS Cassidy, Frederic G., ed. Modern American plays... New York, Longmans, Green, 1949. 501p
Anderson, M. Winterset
Hellman, L. Watch on the Rhine
Lindsay, H., and Crouse, R. Life with father
Odets, C. Waiting for Lefty
O'Neill, E. Anna Christie
Sherwood, R. Abe Lincoln in Illinois

185

CASU   Casson, Lionel, ed. and tr.
Masters of ancient comedy
...New York, Macmillan,
1960. 424p
Aristophanes. The Acharnians
Menander. The arbitration
Menander. The grouch
Menander. She who was shorn
Menander. The woman of
Samos
Plautus, T. The haunted house
Plautus, T. The rope
Terentius Afer, P. The
brothers
Terentius Afer, P. Phormio

CATH   Catholic University of
America.   Committee for
the revision of English cur-
ricula...American profile.
(The Catholic high school
literature series. Book III)
New York, W.H. Sadlier
[c1944] 752p
Barry, P. The joyous season
Wilder, T. Our town

CAWL   Cawley, Arthur C., ed.
Everyman and medieval
miracle plays...New York,
Dutton [c1959] 266p
Abraham and Isaac
The annunciation
Cain and Abel
The creation, and the fall of
Lucifer
The creation of Adam and Eve
The crucifixion
The death of Pilate
Everyman
The fall of man
The harrowing of hell
Herod the great
The judgment
Noah's flood
The resurrection
The second shepherds' pageant
The woman taken in adultery

CAWM   Cawley, Arthur C., ed.
The Wakefield pageants in
the Towneley cycle...[Man-
chester] Manchester Uni-

versity Press [c1958] 187p
(Old and Middle English
texts)
Coliphizacio
Mactacio Abel
Magnus Herodes
Prima pastorum
Processus Noe cum filiis
Secundus pastorum

CERF, Bennett Alfred.
See also CART Cartmell,
Van H., and Cerf, Bennett
Alfred, comps. Famous
plays of crime and detec-
tion...

CEQ   Cerf, Bennett Alfred,
comp. Four contemporary
American plays...New
York, Vintage Books [c1961]
386p
Chayefsky, P. The tenth man
Hansberry, L. A raisin in the
sun
Hellman, L. Toys in the attic
Levitt, S. The Andersonville
trial

CER   Cerf, Bennett Alfred, ed.
The pocket book of modern
American plays...New
York, Pocket books [1942]
430p
Behrman, S. No time for
comedy
Boothe, C. Margin for error
Odets, C. Awake and sing
Rice, E. Street scene

CES   Cerf, Bennett Alfred, ed.
Six American plays for to-
day...New York, Modern
Library [c1961] 599p
Chayefsky, P. The tenth man
Hansberry, L. A raisin in
the sun
Hellman, L. Toys in the at-
tic
Inge, W. The dark at the top
of the stairs
Schary, D. Sunrise at Campo-
bello

Williams, T. Camino Real

CET Cerf, Bennett Alfred and
     Cartmell, Van H., eds.
     Sixteen famous American
     plays... Garden City, N. Y.,
     Garden City publishing co.
     [c1941] 1049p
Behrman, S. Biography
Boothe, C. The women
Connelly, M. The green pas-
     tures
Hart, M., and Kaufman, G.
     The man who came to din-
     ner
Hecht, B., and MacArthur, C.
     The front page
Hellman, L. The little foxes
Howard, S. They knew what
     they wanted
Kingsley, S. Dead end
Kober, A. "Having wonderful
     time"
Lindsay, H., and Crouse, R.
     Life with father
Odets, C. Waiting for Lefty
O'Neill, E. Ah, wilderness!
Saroyan, W. The time of
     your life
Sherwood, R. The petrified
     forest
Spewack, B., and Spewack,
     S. Boy meets girl
Wilder, T. Our town

CEU Cerf, Bennett Alfred and
     Cartmell, Van H., comps.
     Sixteen famous British
     plays... Garden City, N. Y.,
     Garden City publishing co.
     [1942] 1000p
Archer, W. The green god-
     dess
Barrie, J. What every woman
     knows
Bennett, A., and Knoblock,
     E. Milestones
Besier, R. The Barretts of
     Wimpole street
Coward, N. Cavalcade
Galsworthy, J. Loyalties
Housman, L. Victoria Regina
Maugham, W. The circle

Milne, A. Mr. Pim passes
     by
Pinero, A. The second Mrs.
     Tanqueray
Priestley, J. Dangerous
     corner
Shairp, M. The green bay
     tree
Sherriff, R. Journey's end
Vane, S. Outward bound
Wilde, O. The importance of
     being earnest
Williams, E. The corn is
     green

CEW Cerf, Bennett Alfred, and
     Cartmell, Van H., comps.
     Sixteen famous European
     plays... Garden City, N. Y.,
     Garden City publishing co.
     [1943] 1052p
Ansky, S. The dybbuk
Baum, V. Grand hotel
Capek, K. R. U. R.
Carroll, P. Shadow and sub-
     stance
Chekhov, A. The sea gull
Deval, J. Tovarich
Giraudoux, J. Amphitryon 38
Gorky, M. The lower depths
Hauptmann, G. The weavers
Ibsen, H. The wild duck
Martínez Sierra, G. The
     cradle song
Molnár, F. Liliom
Pirandello, L. Six characters
     in search of an author
Rostand, E. Cyrano de Ber-
     gerac
Schnitzler, A. Anatol
Synge, J. The playboy of the
     western world

CEY Cerf, Bennett Alfred, and
     Cartmell, Van H., comps.
     S. R. O.; the most success-
     ful plays in the history of
     the American stage... Gar-
     den City, N. Y., Doubleday,
     Doran, 1944. 920p
Aiken, G. Uncle Tom's cabin
Boucicault, D. Rip Van
     Winkle

CEY (continued)
D'Ennery, A., and Cormon,
E. The two orphans
Hammerstein, O., and
Rodgers, R. Oklahoma!
Kesselring, J. Arsenic and
old lace
Kirkland, J. Tobacco road
Lindsay, H., and Crouse, R.
Life with father
Manners, J. Peg o' my heart
Nichols, A. Abie's Irish Rose
Rinehart, M., and Hopwood,
A. The bat
Smith, W., and Bacon, F.
Lightnin'
Tarkington, B., and Wilson,
H. The man from home
Thompson, D. The old home-
stead
Wood, Mrs. H. East Lynne

CHA Chandler, Frank Wadleigh
and Cordell, Richard Al-
bert, eds. Twentieth cen-
tury plays... New York,
Nelson, 1934. v.p.
Álvarez Quintero, S., and
Álvarez Quintero, J. Doña
Clarines
Anderson, M., and Stallings,
L. What price glory
Čapek, K., and Čapek, J.
And so ad infinitum
Chlumberg, H. The miracle
at Verdun
Connelly, M. The green
pastures
Coward, N. Private lives
Crothers, R. As husbands go
Ervine, St. J. John Ferguson
Hankin, St. J. The last of the
De Mullins
Jones, H. Dolly reforming
herself
Lenormand, H. The coward
Maugham, W. The bread-
winner
Molnár, F. The swan
O'Neill, E. Marco Millions
Pinero, A. The thunderbolt
Pirandello, L. Each in his
own way

Rice, E. Street scene
Robinson, L. The far-off
hills
Sherriff, R. Journey's end
Tolstoy, L. The live corpse

CHAN Chandler, Frank Wad-
leigh and Cordell, Richard
Albert, eds. Twentieth
century plays... Rev. New
York, Nelson, 1939. v.p.
Álvarez Quintero, S., and
Álvarez Quintero, J. Doña
Clarines
Anderson, M. Winterset
Behrman, S. Rain from
heaven
Čapek, K., and Čapek, J.
And so ad infinitum
Chlumberg, H. The miracle
at Verdun
Connelly, M. The green
pastures
Coward, N. Private lives
Ervine, St. J. John Ferguson
Hankin, St. J. The last of
the De Mullins
Howard, S. The silver cord
Jones, H. Dolly reforming
herself
Kaufman, G., and Connelly,
M. Beggar on horseback
Lenormand, H. The coward
Maugham, W. The bread-
winner
Molnár, F. The swan
O'Neill, E. Anna Christie
Pinero, A. The thunderbolt
Pirandello, L. Each in his
own way
Rice, E. Street scene
Robinson, L. The far-off
hills
Sherriff, R. Journey's end
Tolstoy, L. The live corpse

CHAP Chandler, Frank Wadleigh and Cordell, Richard
Albert, eds. Twentieth
century plays, American
...Rev. New York, Nelson,
1939. 295p
Anderson, M. Winterset

Behrman, S. Rain from
heaven
Connelly, M. The green pas-
tures
Howard, S. The silver cord
Kaufman, G., and Connelly,
M. Beggar on horseback
O'Neill, E. Anna Christie
Rice, E. Street scene

CHAR Chandler, Frank Wadleigh,
and Cordell, Richard Al-
bert, eds. Twentieth cen-
tury plays, British...Rev.
and enl. New York, Nel-
son, 1941. 399p
Barrie, J. The admirable
Crichton
Coward, N. Private lives
Ervine, St. J. John Ferguson
Galsworthy, J. The silver box
Hankin, St. J. The last of the
De Mullins
Jones, H. Dolly reforming
herself
Maugham, S. The breadwinner
Pinero, A. The thunderbolt
Robinson, L. The far-off hills
Sherriff, R. Journey's end

CHAPMAN, JOHN ARTHUR See
BES Best plays of 1894/99
...etc.; THEA Theater.
1953/56...

CHES The Chester Mystery
Plays...Adapted into modern
English by Maurice P. Hus-
sey. London, William
Heinemann [c1957] 160p
The fall of Lucifer
The creation of man: Adam
and Eve
Noah's deluge
Abraham and Isaac
The nativity
The adoration of the shepherds
The adoration of the magi
The magi's oblation
The slaying of the innocents
Simon the leper
The betrayal of Christ
Christ's passion

Christ's ascension
Antichrist
The last judgment

CHI Child, Clarence Griffin,
ed. and tr. The second
shepherd's play, Everyman,
and other early plays...
Boston, Houghton Mifflin
[c1910] 138p
The Brome Abraham and Isaac
Everyman
The Oxfordshire St. George
play
The Quem quaeritis
Robin Hood and the friar
Robin Hood and the knight
Robin Hood and the potter
The second shepherds' play

CHU Church, Mrs. Virginia
Woodson (Frame), ed. Cur-
tain! A book of modern
plays...New York, Harper,
1932. 504p
Bennett, A. The great adven-
ture
Church, V. What men live by
Dunsany, E. The lost silk hat
Green, P. The man who died
at twelve o'clock
MacKaye, P. Napoleon cross-
ing the Rockies
Millay, E. Aria da capo
Milne, A. The great Broxopp
Morley, C. Good theatre
Nichols, R., and Brown, M.
Wings over Europe
O'Neill, E. The Emperor
Jones
Wilder, T. The angel on the
ship

CLARK, BARRETT HARPER.
See also AMP America's
lost plays.

CLA Clark, Barrett Harper, ed.
Favorite American plays of
the nineteenth century...
Princeton, N.J., Princeton
university press, 1943.
553p

CLA (continued)
Alfriend, E., and Wheeler, A.
The great diamond robbery
Belasco, D. The heart of
Maryland
Boucicault, D. Flying scud;
or, A four-legged fortune
Campbell, B. My partner
Fechter, C. Monte Cristo
Howard, B. The banker's
daughter
Hoyt, C. A trip to Chinatown;
or, An idyll of San Fran-
cisco
Murdoch, F. Davy Crockett;
or, Be sure you're right,
then go ahead
Stone, J. Metamora; or, The
last of the Wampanoaga
Woolf, B. The mighty dollar

CLD Clark, Barrett Harper, tr.
Four plays of the Free
theater... Cincinnati, Stew-
art & Kidd, 1915. 257p
Ancey, G. The dupe
Curel, F. The fossils
Julien, J. The serenade
Porto-Riche, G. Françoise'
luck

CLDM Clark, Barrett Harper,
ed. Masterpieces of mod-
ern Spanish drama... New
York, Duffield, 1917. 290p
Echegaray [y Elizaguirre], J.
The great Galeoto
Guimerá, A. Daniela
Pérez Galdós, B. The Duchess
of San Quentin

CLDP Clark, Barrett Harper,
and Davenport, William H.,
eds. Nine modern plays...
New York, Appleton-Century
-Crofts [c1951] 432p
Anderson, M. High Tor
Ferber, E., and Kaufman, G.
Stage door
Haines, W. Command deci-
sion
Hart, M., and Kaufman, G.
You can't take it with you

190

O'Neill, E. The hairy ape
Rice, E. Street scene
Riggs, L. Green grow the
lilacs
Sherwood, R.E. Abe Lincoln
in Illinois
Williams, T. The glass me-
nagerie

CLF Clark, Barrett Harper,
ed. World drama... New
York, Appleton, 1933. 2v
Abstraction.   1
Adam.   1
Aeschylus. Prometheus
bound.   1
Alfieri, V. Saul.   2
Aristophanes. The clouds.   1
Augier, E., and Sandeau, J.
M. Poirier's son-in-
law.   2
Beaumarchais, P. The
barber of Seville.   2
Beaumont, F., and Fletcher,
J. The maid's tragedy.   1
Beolco, A. Bilora.   2
Calderón de la Barca, P.
The constant prince.   2
Cervantes Saavedra, M. The
cave of Salamanca.   2
The chalk circle.   1
Chikamatsu Monzaemon.
Fair ladies at a game of
poemcards.   1
Corneille, P. The cid.   2
Dumas, A. fils. The demi-
monde.   2
Euripides. Alcestis.   1
Everyman.   1
The farce of the worthy
Master Pierre Patelin.   1
Farquhar, G. The beaux-
stratagem.   1
Goethe, J. Egmont.   2
Goldoni, C. The fan.   2
Goldsmith, O. She stoops
to conquer.   1
Heywood, T. A woman
killed with kindness.   1
Holberg, L. Jeppe of the
hill.   2
Hugo, V. Hernani.   2
Ibsen, H. A doll's house.   2

Jonson, B. Every man in his humour. 1
Kālidāsa. Śakoontalá. 1
Lessing, G. Miss Sara Sampson. 2
Marlowe, C. The tragical history of Dr. Faustus. 1
Molière, J. The cit turned gentleman. 2
Ostrovsky, A. The thunderstorm. 2
Plautus, T. The captives. 1
The play of St. George. 1
Racine, J. Berenice. 2
Sachs, H. The wandering scholar from Paradise. 1
Scala, F. The portrait. 2
Schiller, J. William Tell. 2
Seami, M. Nakamitsu. 1
The second shepherds' play. 1
Seneca. Medea. 1
Sheridan, R. The school for scandal. 1
Sophocles. Antigone. 1
Terence. Phormio. 1
Vega Carpio, L. The king, the greatest Alcalde. 2
The wise virgins and the foolish virgins. 1

CLK Clark, David Lee; Gates, William Bryan and Leisy, Ernest Erwin, eds. The voices of England and America...New York, Nelson, 1939. 2v
Dryden, J. All for love. 1
Everyman. 1
Farquhar, G. The beaux' stratagem. 1
Jonson, B. Every man in his humor. 1
Marlowe, C. The tragical history of Doctor Faustus. 1
Milton, J. Comus. 1
O'Neill, E. The Emperor Jones. 2
Pinero, A. The second Mrs. Tanqueray. 2
The second shepherds' play. 1
Sheridan, R. The rivals. 1

CLKW Clark, William Smith II, ed. Chief patterns of world drama...[Boston] Houghton Mifflin [c1946] 1152p
Aeschylus. Prometheus bound
Anderson, M. Mary of Scotland
Aristophanes. The birds
Barrie, J. The admirable Crichton
Beaumont, F., and Fletcher, J. The maid's tragedy
Čapek, J., and Čapek, K. The life of the insects
Chekhov, A. The sea-gull
Dekker, T. The shoemakers' holiday
Euripides. Alcestis
Etherege, G. The man of mode; or, Sir Fopling Flutter
Galsworthy, J. The silver box
Gogol, N. The inspector-general
Green, P. Roll sweet chariot
Hebbel, J. Maria Magdalena
Ibsen, H. Hedda Gabler
Jonson, B. Epicoene; or, The silent woman
Marlowe, C. The troublesome reign and lamentable death of Edward the Second
Molière, J. The miser
Nice wanton
O'Neill, E. The hairy ape
Pirandello, L. Naked
Plautus. The pot of gold
Racine, J. Andromache
The second shepherds' play
Sheridan, R. The school for scandal
Sophocles. Electra
Synge, J. The playboy of the western world
Terence. Phormio
Vega, Lope de. The star of Seville

CLM Clayes, Stanley A., and Spencer, David G., eds. Contemporary drama... New York, Scribner [c1962] 512p

CLM (continued)
Chekhov, A. Uncle Vanya
García Lorca, F. The house
of Bernarda Alba
Giraudoux, J. Ondine
Hellman, L. The autumn
garden
Ibsen, H. The wild duck
Maugham, W. The circle
Miller, A. A view from the
bridge
O'Casey, S. Juno and the
paycock
Odets, C. The country girl
Shaw, G. The devil's disciple
Sophocles. Antigone (Cocteau,
J. adapter)
Sophocles. Antigone
Strindberg, A. Miss Julie
Williams, T. The rose tattoo

CLOU Clouard, Henri, and
Leggewie, Robert, eds.
Anthologie de la litterature
française. Tome II...New
York, Oxford University
Press, 1960. 468p
Giraudoux, J. La guerre de
Troie n'aura pas lieu
Musset, A. Fantasio
Sartre, J. Huis clos

CLUR Clurman, Harold, ed.
Famous American plays of
the 1930s...[New York,
Dell publishing co. c1959]
480p (Laurel drama series)
Behrman, S. End of summer
Odets, C. Awake and sing!
Saroyan, W. The time of your
life
Sherwood, R. Idiot's delight
Steinbeck, J. Of mice and
men

CLURMAN, HAROLD. See also
SEVD Seven plays of the
modern theatre

COD Coffman, George Raleigh,
ed. ...A book of modern
plays...Chicago, Scott,
Foresman [c1925] 490p

Bennett, A., and Knoblock,
E. Milestones
Gregory, I. The workhouse
ward
Ibsen, H. An enemy of the
people
O'Neill, E. Where the cross
is made
Robertson, T. Caste
Rostand, E. The romancers
Synge, J. Riders to the sea

COF Coffman, George Raleigh,
ed. Five significant Eng-
lish plays...New York,
Nelson, 1930. 433p
Dekker, T. The shoemakers'
holiday
Marlowe, C. Dr. Faustus
Pinero, A. The second Mrs.
Tanqueray
Sheridan, R. The school for
scandal
Steele, R. The conscious
lovers

COH Cohen, Helen Louise, ed.
Longer plays by modern
authors (American)...New
York, Harcourt, Brace
[c1922] 353p
Fitch, C. Beau Brummell
Kaufman, G., and Connelly,
M. Dulcy
Tarkington, B. The intimate
strangers
Thomas, A. The copperhead

COJ Cohen, Helen Louise, ed.
Milestones of the drama.
New York, Harcourt, Brace
[c1940] 580p
Everyman
Ibsen, H. A doll's house
Marlowe, C. Doctor Faustus
O'Neill, E. The Emperor
Jones
Rostand, E. Cyrano de Ber-
gerac
Sheridan, R. The school for
scandal
Sophocles. Oedipus, king of
Thebes

192

THE COLLEGE OMNIBUS. See
MCCA, MCCB, MCCD,
MCCF, MCCG McCallum,
James Dow, ed. See also
FUL Fullington, James
Fitz-James. The new col-
lege omnibus.

COL College survey of English
literature...[Edited by B.J.
Whiting; Fred B. Millett;
Alexander M. Whitherspoon
and others] New York,
Harcourt, Brace, 1942. 2v
Congreve, W. The way of the
world.   1
Goldsmith, O. She stoops to
conquer.   1
Marlowe, C. The tragical
history of Doctor Faustus. 1
The second play of the shep-
herds (Wakefield)   2
Shakespeare, W. King Henry
IV, pt. I.   1
Synge, J. The playboy of
the western world.   2

COLLETTE, ELIZABETH. See
WORL The world in literature.

COMFORT, ALEX See NEWR
New road...

COM Comfort, William Wistar,
ed. French romantic plays
...New York, Scribner
[c1933] 628p
Dumas, A. père. Antony
Hugo, V. Hernani
Hugo, V. Ruy Blas
Musset, A. On ne badine pas
avec l'amour
Vigny, A. Chatterton

CONG Congdon, S. Perry, ed.
The drama reader...New
York, Odyssey Press [c1962]
418p
Čapek, K. R.U.R.
Cohan, G. Seven keys to
Baldpate
Kaufman, G., and Connelly,

M. Dulcy
Shakespeare, W. Richard III
Sophocles. Antigone

CONN Connolly, Francis Xavier,
ed. Literature, the chan-
nel of culture...New York,
Harcourt, Brace, 1948.
714p
Connolly, M. The green pastures
Shakespeare, W. The tempest
Synge, J. Riders to the sea

CONP Connolly, Francis X.,
ed. The types of litera-
ture...New York, Harcourt,
Brace [c1955] 810p
Barrie, J. The twelve-pound
look
Eliot, T. Murder in the ca-
thedral
O'Neill, E. Bound east for
Cardiff
Sheridan, R. The school for
scandal
Sophocles. Antigone

CONT Contemporary Danish
plays...London, Thames
and Hudson, 1955. 557p
Abell, K. The Queen on tour
Branner, H. The judge
Clausen, S. The bird of con-
tention
Fischer, L. The mystery tour
Locher, J. Tea for three
Munk, K. Herod the king
Schüter, K. Off the rails
Sønderby, K. A woman too
many
Soya, C. Two threads

CONTINENTAL DRAMA. See
HARC Harvard classics,
v26

COOJ Cook, Luella Bussey; Lo-
ban, Walter; McDowell,
Tremaine and Stauffer,
Ruth M., eds. America
through literature...Har-
court, Brace, 1948. 750p

193

COOJ (continued)
(Living literature)
Sherwood, R. Abe Lincoln in
Illinois
Wilder, T. Our town

COOK Cook, Luella Bussey;
Norvell, George W., and
McCall, William A., eds.
Hidden treasures in litera-
ture... New York, Harcourt,
Brace, 1934. 3v
Coppée, F. The violin-maker
of Cremona.   1
Dunsany, E. A night at an
inn.   3
Field, R. The patchwork
quilt.   2
Fitch, C. Nathan Hale.   2
Monkhouse, A. The grand
cham's necklace.   2
Pillot, E. Two crooks and
a lady.   3
Rostand, E. The romancers 2
Saunders, L. The knave of
hearts.   1
Shakespeare, W. Julius
Caesar.   3

COOP Cooper, Charles W.
Preface to drama... New
York, Ronald press [c1955]
773p
Coward, N. Fumed oak
Gilbert, W. H. M. S. Pinafore
Housman, L. "A good lesson!"
Ibsen, H. Hedda Gabler
Lindsay, H., and Crouse, R.
Life with father
Miller, A. The crucible
Molière, J. The ridiculous
précieuses
O'Neill, E. The long voyage
home
Shakespeare, W. Othello
Shaw, G. Candida
Sophocles. Antigone
Wilder, T. The happy journey
to Trenton and Camden
Williams, T. The glass me-
nagerie

COOPER, LANE. See

TEN Ten Greek plays...

COP Copeland, Charles Townsend, ed. The Copeland
reader. New York, Scrib-
ner, 1926. 1687p
Sheridan, R. The critic; or,
A tragedy rehearsed

COPB Copeland, Charles Townsend, ed. The Copeland
translations... New York,
Scribner, 1934. 1080p
Molière, J. The physician in
spite of himself

COPC Copeland, Charles Townsend, ed. Copeland's
treasury for booklovers...
New York, Scribner, 1927.
5v
Sheridan, R. The critic; or,
A tragedy rehearsed.   1

CORD Cordell, Kathryn (Coe)
and Cordell, William How-
ard, eds. The Pulitzer
prize plays, 1918-1934...
New York, Random House
[1935] 856p
Anderson, M. Both your
houses
Connelly, M. The green pas-
tures
Davis, O. Icebound
Gale, Z. Miss Lulu Bett
Glaspell, S. Alison's house
Green, P. In Abraham's
bosom
Howard, S. They knew what
they wanted
Hughes, H. Hell-bent for
heaven
Kaufman, G., and Ryskind, M.
Of thee I sing
Kelly, G. Craig's wife
Kinglsey, S. Men in white
O'Neill, E. Anna Christie
O'Neill, E. Beyond the hori-
zon
O'Neill, E. Strange interlude
Rice, E. Street scene
Williams, J. Why marry?

194

CORE Cordell, Kathryn (Coe) and Cordell, William Howard, eds. The Pulitzer prize plays...New ed. New York, Random house [1938?] 983p
Anderson, M. Both your houses
Connelly, M. The green pastures
Davis, O. Icebound
Gale, Z. Miss Lulu Bett
Glaspell, S. Alison's house
Green, P. In Abraham's bosom
Hart, M., and Kaufman, G. You can't take it with you
Howard, S. They knew what they wanted
Hughes, H. Hell-bent fer heaven
Kaufman, G., and Ryskind, M. Of thee I sing
Kelly, G. Craig's wife
Kingsley, S. Men in white
O'Neill, E. Anna Christie
O'Neill, E. Beyond the horizon
O'Neill, E. Strange interlude
Rice, E. Street scene
Sherwood, R. Idiot's delight
Williams, J. Why marry?

CORF Cordell, Kathryn (Coe) and Cordell, William Howard, eds. A new edition of the Pulitzer prize plays ...New York, Random house [1940] 1091p
Anderson, M. Both your houses
Connelly, M. The green pastures
Davis, O. Icebound
Gale, Z. Miss Lulu Bett
Glaspell, S. Alison's house
Green, P. In Abraham's bosom
Hart, M., and Kaufman, G. You can't take it with you
Howard, S. They knew what they wanted
Hughes, H. Hell-bent fer heaven
Kaufman, G., and Rysking, M. Of thee I sing
Kelly, G. Craig's wife
Kinglsey, S. Men in white
O'Neill, E. Anna Christie
O'Neill, E. Beyond the horizon
O'Neill, E. Strange interlude
Rice, E. Street scene
Sherwood, R. Abe Lincoln in Illinois
Sherwood, R. Idiot's delight
Wilder, T. Our town
Williams, J. Why marry?

CORDELL, RICHARD ALBERT. See also CHA, CHAN, CHAP, CHAR Chandler, Frank Wadleigh and Cordell, Richard Albert, eds. Twentieth century plays...

COT Cordell, Richard Albert, ed. Representative modern plays...New York, Nelson, 1929. 654p
Ade, G. The college widow
Bennett, A. The great adventure
Crothers, R. Expressing Willie
Dane, C. A bill of divorcement
Fitch, C. The climbers
Gilbert, W. Sweethearts
Hughes, H. Hell-bent fer heaven
Jones, H. Mrs. Dane's defence
Kaufman, G., and Connelly, M. Beggar on horseback
Maugham, W. The circle
Milne, A. Success
O'Casey, S. Juno and the paycock
O'Neill, E. Diff'rent
Pinero, A. Iris
Robertson, T. Caste
Wilde, O. A woman of no importance

195

COTE   Cordell, Richard Albert,
ed. Twentieth century
plays, American...Third
edition. New York, Ronald
press [c1947] 329p
Anderson, M. Winterset
Connelly, M. The green pas-
tures
Hellman, L. The little foxes
Howard, S. The silver cord
Marquand, J., and Kaufman,
G. The late George Apley
O'Neill, E. Anna Christie
Rice, E. Street scene
Sherwood, R. Abe Lincoln in
Illinois

COTH   Cordell, Richard Albert,
ed. Twentieth century
plays, British, American,
Continental...Third edition.
New York, Ronald press
[c1947] 447p
Anderson, M. Winterset
Barrie, J. The admirable
‿ Crichton
Čapek, K. R.U.R.
Galsworthy, J. The silver box
Hellman, L. The little foxes
Maugham, W. The circle
Marquand, J., and Kaufman,
G. The late George Apley
O'Neill, E. Anna Christie
Rice, E. Street scene
Rostand, E. Cyrano de Ber-
gerac
Sherwood, R. Abe Lincoln in
Illinois

COTK   Cordell, Richard Albert,
and Matson, Lowell, eds.
The off-Broadway theatre...
New York, Random house
[c1959] 481p
Anouilh, J. Ardèle
Barkentin, M. Ulysses in
Nighttown
Forsyth, J. Héloise
Hayes, A. The girl on the
Via Flaminia
Lee, J. Career
O'Casey, S. Purple dust
Priestley, J., and Hawkes, J.

Dragon's mouth

COTR   Corrigan, Robert W.,
ed. The new theatre of
Europe...[New York, Dell
Publishing Co., c1962]
399p
Betti, U. Corruption in the
palace of justice
Bolt, R. A man for all sea-
sons
Ghelderode, M. Pantagleize
Peryalis, N. Masks of angels
Sastre, A. Anna Kleiber

COUR   Cournos, John, ed. A
treasury of classic Russian
literature...New York,
Capricorn Books [c1961]
580p and index
Gogol, N. The inspector-
general
Ostrovskiĭ, A. A domestic
picture
Tolstoi, L. Condemnation
Tolstoi, L. Taxes

COUS   Cournos, John, ed. A
treasury of Russian life
and humor...New York,
Coward-McCann [c1943]
676p
Gogol, N. The inspector

CRAN   Crane, William Garrett
[and others] eds. Twelve
hundred years; the literature of England...Harris-
burg, Pa., Stackpole and
Heck, 2v [c1949]
Wilde, O. The importance of
being earnest,   2

CRIT   The Critics' prize plays.
Introduction by George
Jean Nathan. Cleveland,
Ohio, World publishing co.
[c1945] 377p
Anderson, M. High Tor
Anderson, M. Winterset
Hellman, L. Watch on the
Rhine
Kingsley, S. The patriots

Saroyan, W. The time of
your life
Steinbeck, J. Of mice and
men

CROS Cross, Ethan Allen, ed.
World literature. New York,
American book co. [c1935]
1396p
Aeschylus. Prometheus bound
Bulwer-Lytton, E. Richelieu;
or, The conspiracy
Euripides. Iphigenia in Aulis
Galsworthy, J. The silver box
Ibsen, H. The master builder
Molière, J. The miser
Plautus. Menaechmi; or, The
twin brothers
Seneca. Medea
Shakespeare, W. Antony and
Cleopatra
Sophocles. Antigone
Terence. Andria

CROV Cross, Tom Peete and
Slover, Clark H., eds.
Heath readings in the lit-
erature of Europe... Boston,
Heath [c1933] 1194p
Adam, The play of
Aeschylus. Prometheus bound
Aristophanes. The birds
Corneille, P. Le cid
Goethe, J. Faust, pt. I
Goldoni, C. A curious mis-
hap
Ibsen, H. Ghosts
Lessing, G. Minna von Barn-
helm
Molière, J. The misanthrope
Plautus. The captives
Seneca. Medea
Vega Carpio, L. The star of
Seville

CROX Cross, Tom Peete; Smith,
Reed; Stauffer, Elmer C.,
and Collette, Elizabeth.
American writers. Revised
edition... Boston, Ginn
[c1955] 708p
Wilder, T. Our town

CROZ Cross-section... Edited by
Edwin Seaver. New York,
L. B. Fischer [c1944-48]
4v
Miller, A. The man who had
all the luck.   1
Peters, P. Nat Turner.   1
Whittington, R. The death
of García Lorca.   1

CUBE Cubeta, Paul M., ed. ...
Modern drama for analy-
sis. New York, William
Sloane Associates [c1950]
584p
Chekhov, A. The cherry or-
chard
Hellman, L. Watch on the
Rhine
Ibsen, H. The wild duck
O'Casey, S. Juno and the
paycock
O'Neill, E. The Emperor
Jones
Synge, J. The playboy of the
western world
Wilder, T. The skin of our
teeth
Williams, T. The glass me-
nagerie

CUBG Cubeta, Paul M. Modern
drama for analysis. Re-
vised edition. [New York,
Dryden, c1955] 785p
Chekhov, A. The cherry or-
chard
Ibsen, H. The wild duck
Inge, W. Come back, little
Sheba
O'Casey, S. Juno and the
paycock
O'Neill, E. Anna Christie
Shaw, G. Arms and the man
Synge, J. The playboy of the
western world
Wilder, T. The skin of our
teeth
Williams, T. The glass me-
nagerie

CUBH Cubeta, Paul M. Modern
drama for analysis... 3rd

CUBH (continued)
ed. New York, Holt,
Rinehart and Winston [c1962]
613p
Albee, E. The sandbox
Anouilh, J. Becket; or, The
honor of God
Chekhov, A. The cherry or-
chard
Eliot, T. Murder in the ca-
thedral
Ibsen, H. Rosmersholm
Miller, A. A view from the
bridge
O'Neill, E. Desire under the
elms
Shaw, G. The devil's disciple
Wilder, T. The skin of our
teeth
Williams, T. The glass me-
nagerie

CUN Cunliffe, John William, ed.
Early English classical
tragedies... Oxford, Claren-
don press, 1912. 352p
Gascoigne, G., and Kinwel-
mersh, F. Jocasta
Hughes, T. The misfortunes
of Arthur
Norton, T., and Sackville, T.
Gorboduc; or, Ferrex and
Porrex
[Wilmot, R., and others]
Gismond of Salerne

D

DANA, H. W. L. See SEVP
Seven Soviet plays...

DANI Daniel, Robert Woodham,
and Leggett, G. H., eds.
The written word... Englewood Cliffs, N. J., Pren-
tice Hall, 1960. 726p
Shaw, G. The man of destiny

DAV Davenport, William H.;
Wimberley, Lowry C., and
Shaw, Harry, eds. Domi-
nant types in British and
American literature... New

York, Harper [c1949] 2v
Anderson, M. Winterset   1
Barrie, J. The twelve-pound
look   1
O'Neill, E. The hairy ape   1
Rice, E. The adding ma-
chine   1
The second shepherds'
play   1
Shakespeare, W. King Henry
the fourth   1
Sheridan, R. The school for
scandal   1
Synge, J. Riders to the sea
1
Wilde, O. Lady Winder-
mere's fan   1

DAVI David, Sister Mary Ag-
nes, Modern American
Drama... New York, Mac-
millan [c1961] 235p (The
pageant of literature)
Barry, P. The joyous season
Coxe, L., and Chapman,
R. Billy Budd
Van Druten, J. I remember
mama

DAVK Davis, Earle R., and
Hummel, William C., eds.
Readings for enjoyment.
Englewood Cliffs, N. J.,
Prentice-Hall, 1959. 611p
The book of Job
Kaufman, G., and Hart, M.
The man who came to din-
ner
O'Neill, E. Ah, wilderness
Shakespeare, W. Hamlet,
Prince of Denmark
Sophocles. Oedipus rex

DEAN Dean, Leonard, ed. ...
Elizabethan drama... New
York, Prentice-Hall, 1950.
334p (English masterpieces.
v2)
Marlowe, C. Doctor Faustus
Shakespeare, W. Henry the
fourth, pt. I
Shakespeare, W. King Lear
Webster, J. The Duchess

198

of Malfi

DEAO Dean, Leonard Fellows,
ed. Elizabethan drama...
Second edition. Englewood
Cliffs, N. J., Prentice-Hall,
1961. 364p (English master-
pieces. v2)
Jonson, B. Volpone; or, The
fox
Marlowe, C. The tragical his-
tory of Doctor Faustus
Shakespeare, W. King Lear
Webster, J. The Duchess of
Malfi

DEAP Dean, Leonard Fellows,
ed. Nine great plays from
Aeschylus to Eliot. New
York, Harcourt, Brace
[c1950] 595p
Aeschylus. Agamemnon
Chekhov, A. The cherry or-
chard
Congreve, W. The way of the
world
Eliot, T. Murder in the ca-
thedral
Ibsen, H. The wild duck
Jonson, B. Volpone; or, The
fox
Molière, J. The misanthrope
O'Neill, E. The Emperor
Jones
Sophocles. King Oedipus

DEAR Dean, Leonard, F., ed.
Nine great plays, from
Aeschylus to Eliot. Revised
edition... New York, Har-
court Brace [c1956] 695p
Aeschylus. Agamemnon
Chekhov, A. The cherry or-
chard
Congreve, W. The way of the
world
Eliot, T. Murder in the ca-
thedral
Ibsen, H. An enemy of the
people
Jonson, B. Volpone
Molière, J. The would-be in-
valid

Shaw, G. Pygmalion
Sophocles. Oedipus Rex

DEBENHAM, A. H. See SEVE
Seven sacred plays...

DEM De Mille, Alban Bertram,
ed. Three English come-
dies... Boston, Allyn and
Bacon [c1924] 479p
Goldsmith, O. She stoops to
conquer
Sheridan, R. The rivals
Sheridan, R. The school for
scandal

DENSMORE, H. B. See TEN
Ten Greek plays...

DIC Dickinson, Thomas Herbert,
ed. Chief contemporary
dramatists... [first series]
Boston, Houghton Mifflin
[c1915] 676p
Barker, G. The Madras house
Bjørnson, B. Beyond human
power
Brieux, E. The red robe
Chekhov, A. The cherry or-
chard
Fitch, C. The truth
Galsworthy, J. Strife
Gregory, A. The rising of
the moon
Hauptmann, G. The weavers
Hervieu, P. Know thyself
Jones, H. Michael and his
lost angel
MacKaye, P. The scarecrow
Maeterlinck, M. Pélléas and
Mélisande
Moody, W. The great divide
Pinero, A. The second Mrs.
Tanqueray
Strindberg, A. The father
Sudermann, H. The vale of
content
Synge, J. Riders to the sea
Thomas, A. The witching
hour
Wilde, O. Lady Windermere's
fan
Yeats, W. The hour-glass

DID Dickinson, Thomas Herbert, ed. Chief contemporary dramatists, second series...Boston, Houghton Mifflin [c1921] 734p
Annunzio, G. d'. Gioconda
Bahr, H. The concert
Benavente (y Martínez), J. The bonds of interest
Bennett, A., and Knoblock, E. Milestones
Drinkwater, J. Abraham Lincoln
Dunsany, E. King Argimenes and the unknown warrior
Ervine, St. J. Mixed marriage
Gorki, M. The lower depths
Guitry, S. Pasteur
Hazelton, G., and Benrimo, J. The yellow jacket
Heiberg, G. The tragedy of love
Maugham, W. Our betters
Peabody, J. The piper
Porto-Riche, G. de. A loving wife
Rostand, E. Cyrano de Bergerac
Schnitzler, A. Living hours
Thoma, L. Moral
Walter, E. The easiest way

DIE Dickinson, Thomas Herbert, ed. Chief contemporary dramatists, third series...Boston, Houghton, Mifflin [c1930] 698p
Álvarez Quintero, S., and Alvarez Quintero, J. Malvaloca
Andreyev, L. He who gets slapped
Ansky, S. The dybbuk
Benelli, S. The love of the three kings
Čapek, K. R.U.R.
Green, P. In Abraham's bosom
Hofmannsthal, H. von. Electra
Howard, S. The silver cord
Kaiser, G. From morn to midnight
Lenormand, H. Time is a dream
Martínez Sierra, G., and Martínez Sierra, M. A lily among thorns
Milne, A. The Dover road
Molnár, F. Liliom
O'Casey, S. Juno and the paycock
O'Neill, E. The Emperor Jones
Pirandello, L. Naked
Sigurjónsson, J. Eyvind of the hills
Vildrac, C. The steamship Tenacity
Wedekind, F. Such is life
Yevreinov, N. The theatre of soul

DIG Dickinson, Thomas Herbert, and Crawford, Jack Randall, eds. Contemporary plays...Boston, Houghton Mifflin [c1925] 650p
Anspacher, L. The unchastened woman
Baker, E. Chains
Crothers, R. Mary the third
Davies, H. The mollusc
Davis, O. Icebound
Drinkwater, J. Oliver Cromwell
Granville-Barker, H. The Voysey inheritance
Hankin, St. J. The Cassilis engagement
Houghton, S. Hindle wakes
Kenyon, C. Kindling
Maugham, W. The circle
O'Neill, E. The hairy ape
Phillips, S. Paolo and Francesca
Rice, E. The adding machine
Sowerby, G. Rutherford and son
Sutro, A. John Gladye's honour

DIK Dickinson, Thomas Herbert, ed. ...Continental plays...Boston, Houghton Mifflin [c1935] 2v (Types

200

contemporary drama)
Álvarez Quintero, S., and
Álvarez, Quintero, J.   A
bright morning.   1
Andreyev, L. The life of
man.   2
Annunzio, G. d'. Francesca
da Rimini.   1
Bernard, J. L'invitation au
voyage.   2
Brieux, E. The red robe.   2
Čapek, K. R.U.R.   1
Chekhov, A. The cherry or-
chard.   1
Claudel, P. The tidings
brought to Mary.   1
Echegaray [y Eizaguirre], J.
The great Galeoto.   2
Gorky, M. The lower
depths.   2
Hauptmann, G. The weavers.
1
Kaiser, G. The coral.   2
Maeterlinck, M. Pelléas
and Mélisande.   1
Molnár, F. Liliom.   1
Pirandello, L. Six characters
in search of an author.   2
Rostand, E. Cyrano de Ber-
gerac.   2
Schnitzler, A. Light-o'-
love.   1
Strindberg, A. A dream
play.   2
Tolstoy, L. The power of
darkness.   1
Wedekind, F. Erdgeist.   2

DOA Dobrée, Bonamy, ed. Five
heroic plays... London, Ox-
ford University Press, 1960.
417p
Crowne, J. The destruction
of Jerusalem
Dryden, J. Aureng-zebe
Lee, N. Sophonisba
Orrery, R. The tragedy of
Mustapha, the son of Soly-
man the magnificent
Settle, E. The Empress of
Morocco

DOB Dobrée, Bonamy, ed. Five

restoration tragedies...
[London] Oxford university
press [1928] 450p (The
world's classics)
Addison, J.   Cato
Dryden, J. All for love
Otway, T. Venice preserv'd
Rowe, N. The fair penitent
Southerne, T. Oroonoko

DOWM Downer, Alan S., ed.
American drama... New
York, Thomas Y. Crowell
[c1960] 261p (American
literary forms)
Herne, J. Shore acres
Moody, W. The great divide
O'Neill, E. The hairy ape
Sherwood, R. The petrified
forest
Tyler, R. The contrast
Wilder, T. The long Christ-
mas dinner
Williams, T. The glass me-
nagerie

DOWN Downer, Alan S.   The
art of the play... New York,
Henry Holt [c1955] 451p
Aeschylus. Prometheus bound
Chekhov, A. The sea gull
Ibsen, H. Ghosts
Marlowe, C. Doctor Faustus
Molière, J. Tartuffe
O'Neill, E. The Emperor
Jones
Shakespeare, W. Antony and
Cleopatra
Sophocles. Oedipus rex
Vega Carpio, L.   Fuente ove-
juna

DRA Dramatic masterpieces by
Greek, Spanish, French,
German and English drama-
tists; with a special intro-
duction by Albert Ellery
Bergh. Rev. ed. New York,
Collier [c1900] 2v (The
world's greatest literature)
Aeschylus. Prometheus
bound.   1
Aristophanes. The knights. 1

DRA (continued)
Calderón de la Barca, P.
  Life is a dream. 1
Euripides. Medea. 1
Goethe, J. Faust. 2
Goldsmith, O. She stoops
  to conquer. 1
Ibsen, H. A doll's house. 2
Molière, J. The misan-
  thrope. 1
Racine, J. Phaedra. 1
Sardou, V. Les pattes de
  mouche. 2
Schiller, F. Mary Stuart. 2
Sophocles. Oedipus rex. 1
Sheridan, R. The rivals. 2

DUC Duckworth, George Eckel,
  ed. The complete Roman
  drama... New York, Ran-
  dom house [c1942] 2v
Plautus. Amphytryon. 1
Plautus. The braggart
  warrior. 1
Plautus. The captives. 1
Plautus. The Carthaginian. 1
Plautus. Casina. 1
Plautus. The casket. 1
Plautus. The comedy of
  asses. 1
Plautus. Curculio. 1
Plautus. Epidicus. 1
Plautus. The girl from
  Persia. 1
Plautus. The haunted
  house. 1
Plautus. The merchant. 1
Plautus. The pot of gold. 1
Plautus. Pseudolus. 1
Plautus. The rope. 1
Plautus. Stichus. 2
Plautus. The three penny
  day. 2
Plautus. Truculentus. 2
Plautus. The twin Menaech-
  mi. 1
Plautus. The two bacchides. 1
Querolus. 2
Seneca. Agamemnon. 2
Seneca. Hercules on Oeta. 2
Seneca. Mad Hercules. 2
Seneca. Medea. 2
Seneca. Octavia. 2

Seneca. Oedipus. 2
Seneca. Phaedra. 2
Seneca. The Phoenician
  women. 2
Seneca. Thyestes. 2
Seneca. The Trojan wo-
  men. 2
Terence. The brothers. 2
Terence. The eunuch. 2
Terence. The mother-in-
  law. 2
Terence. Phormio. 2
Terence. The self-tor-
  mentor. 2
Terence. The woman of
  Andros. 2

DUN Dunn, Esther Cloudman,
  ed. Eight famous Eliza-
  bethan plays... New York,
  Modern library [1932]
  721p
Beaumont, F., and Fletcher,
  J. The maid's tragedy
Dekker, T. The shoemakers'
  holiday
Ford, J. 'Tis a pity she's a
  whore
Heywood, T. A woman killed
  with kindness
Jonson, B. Volpone; or, The
  fox
Marlowe, C. The tragical
  history of Doctor Faustus
Massinger, P. A new way to
  pay old debts
Webster, J. The Duchess of
  Malfi

DUR Durham, Willard Higley
  and Dodds, John W., eds.
  British and American plays,
  1830-1945... New York, Ox-
  ford university press, 1947.
  796p
Anderson, M. Winterset
Barrie, J. The admirable
  Crichton
Bulwer-Lytton, E. Richelieu
Carroll, P. Shadow and sub-
  stance
Connelly, M. The green pas-
  tures

Ervine, St. J. John Ferguson
Galsworthy, J. Strife
Ibsen, H. An enemy of the people
Jones, H. The liars
Kaufman, G., and Ryskind, M. Of thee I sing
Maugham, W. The circle
O'Casey, S. Juno and the paycock
Odets, C. Waiting for Lefty
O'Neill, E. The great god Brown
Pinero, A. The second Mrs. Tanqueray
Rice, E. The adding machine
Robertson, T. Caste
Sherwood, R. There shall be no night
Synge, J. The playboy of the western world
Yeats, W. Cathleen ni Houlihan

DUSE, ELEONORA. See SAY
Sayler, Oliver Martin, ed.
The Eleonora Duse series of plays...

E

EAVE Eaves, Thomas Cary
Duncan and Kimpe, Ben D., eds. The informal reader
... New York, Appleton-Century-Crofts [c1955] 743p
Shaw, G. Pygmalion

EDAD Edades, Jean and Fosdick, Carolyn E., eds.
Drama of the east and west.
Manila, Bookman, 1956.
656p
Alvarez Quintero, S., and J.
A sunny morning
Chekhov, A. The cherry orchard
Euripides. Medea
Guerrero, W. Forever
Ibsen, H. A doll's house
Joaquín, N. A portrait of the artist as Filipino
Kālidāsā. Shakuntala

Molière, J. The misanthrope
Montano, S. Sabina
Palarca, J. Other tomorrows
Plautus. The menaechmi
Shakespeare, W. Romeo and Juliet
Shaw, I. Bury the dead
Sicam, G., and Casiño, J. Mir-i-nisa
The sorrows of Han
Villa, L. Educating Josefina
Wilde, O. The importance of being earnest
Wilder, T. Our town
Williams, E. The corn is green

EIGH Eighteenth-century plays with an introduction by Ricardo Quintana... New York, Modern library [c1952] 484p
Addison, J. Cato
Fielding, H. The tragedy of tragedies
Gay, J. The beggar's opera
Goldsmith, O. She stoops to conquer
Lillo, G. The London merchant
Rowe, N. The tragedy of Jane Shore
Sheridan, R. The rivals
Steele, R. The conscious lovers

THE ELEONORA DUSE SERIES OF PLAYS. See SAY
Sayler, Oliver Martin, ed.

ELEVEN PLAYS OF THE GREEK DRAMATISTS. See PLAG
Plays of the Greek dramatists...

ELIOT, CHARLES W. See HARC
Harvard classics...

ELLI Ellis, Harold Milton; Pound, Louise, and Spohn, George Weida, eds. A college book of American literature... New York,

203

ELLI (continued)
American book co. [c1939]
2v
Boker, G. Francesca de
Rimini.   1
O'Neill, E. The rope.   2
Tyler, R. The contrast.   1

ELLK Ellis, Harold Milton;
Pound, Louise; Spohn,
George Weida and Hoffman,
Frederick J., eds. A col-
lege book of American lit-
erature... Second edition.
New York, American book
co. [c1949] 1107p
O'Neill, E. The Emperor
Jones

ELLIS, HAVELOCK. See NER
Nero (Tragedy); Nero and
other plays...

ELIZABETHAN DRAMA. See
HARC Harvard classics,
v46-7

EMB Embassy successes...
London, Sampson, Low,
Marston [1946-48] 3v
Bagnold, E. National vel-
vet.   2
Delderfield, R. Peace comes
to Peckham.   3
Delderfield, R. Worm's eye
view.   1
Doherty, B. Father Malachy's
miracle.   1
Gielgud, V. Away from it
all.   3
Hartog, J. Skipper next to
God.   2
Hay, I. "Let my people
go!"   3
Pollock, R. Zoo in Silesia. 1
Temple, J. No room at the
inn.   2

ENGLISH MASTERPIECES. v2.
See DEAN Dear, Leonard,
ed. Elizabethan drama; v5.
See MACK Mack, Maynard,
ed. The Augustans...

EVA Everett, Edwin Mallard;
Brown, Calvin S., and
Wade, John D., eds.
Masterworks of world lit-
erature... New York, Dry-
den press [c1947] 2v
Euripides. Medea.   1
Goethe, J. Faust, pt. I.   2
Ibsen, H. An enemy of the
people.   2
Molière, J. Tartuffe.   2
Racine, J. Phaedra.   2
Shakespeare, W. Romeo and
Juliet.   2
Sophocles. Antigone.   1
Sophocles. Oedipus the king.1

EVB Everett, Edwin Mallard;
Brown, Calvin S., and
Wade, John D., eds.
Masterworks of world lit-
erature ... Revised edition
... New York, Dryden
[c1955] 2v
Aeschylus. Agamemnon   1
Euripides. Medea   1
Goethe, J. Faust, pt. I   2
Ibsen, H. The enemy of
the people   2
Molière, J. Tartuffe   2
Racine, J. Phaedra   2
Shakespeare, W. Romeo and
Juliet   2
Sophocles. Antigone   1
Sophocles. Oedipus the king
                               1

EVE Everyman and other plays.
[London] Chapman and
Hall, 1925. 201p
Everyman
The nativity
The shepherds' play

EVER "Everyman," with other
interludes, including eight
miracle plays. London,
Dent [1928] 198p (Every-
man's library)
Abraham, Melchisedec, and
Isaac
Bale, J. God's promises
The crucifixion
The deluge

205

FAMG   Famous plays of 1934-
35... London, Gollancz,
1935. 695p
Ackland, R. The old ladies
Egan, M. The dominant sex
Ginsbury, M. Viceroy Sarah
Johnson, P. Lovers' leap
Pryce, R. Frolic wind
Van Druten, J. Flowers of
the forest

FAMH   Famous plays of 1935...
London, Gollancz, 1935.
622p
Hodge, M.   Grief goes over
Raphaelson, S. Accent on
youth
Somin, W. Close quarters
(Attentat)
Sternheim, C. The mask of
virtue
Vulpius, P. Youth at the helm
Williams, E. Night must fall

FAMI   Famous plays of 1935-36
... London, Gollancz, 1936.
701p
Ackland, R. After October
Anthony, C. Call it a day
Deevy, T. Katie Roche
Hodson, J. Red night
Odets, C. Awake and sing
Sherriff, R., and De Casalis,
J.   St. Helena

FAMJ   Famous plays of 1936...
London, Gollancz, 1936.
568p
Farjeon, E., and Farjeon, H.
The two bouquets
Odets, C. Till the day I die
Schauffler, E. Parnell
Schnitzler, A. Professor
Bernhardi
Shaw, I. Bury the dead
Spewack, B., and Spewack,
S. Boy meets girl

FAMK   Famous plays of 1937...
London, Gollancz, 1937.
775p
Boothe, C. The women
Lenormand, H. In Theatre

street
Reid, A. People in love
Rice, E. Judgment day
Sayers, D., and Byrne, M.
Busman's honeymoon
Turgenev, I. A month in the
country

FAML   Famous plays of 1938-
39... London, Gollancz,
1939. 661 p.
Egan, M. To love and to
cherish
Hodson, J. Harvest in the
north
MacOwan, N. Glorious morn-
ing
Malleson, M., and Brooks, H.
Six men of Dorset
Odets, C. Golden boy
Sayers, D. The zeal of thy
house

FAMO   Famous plays of 1954...
London, Gollancz, 1954.
592p
Christie, A. Witness for the
prosecution
Christie, D., and C. Car-
rington, V. C.
Hunter, N.   A day by the sea
Odets, C. The big knife
Van Druten, J. I am a
camera

FAO   Famous plays of to-day...
London, Gollancz, 1929.
671p
Berkeley, R. The lady with
a lamp
Dukes, A. Such men are
dangerous
Hoffe, M. Many waters
Levy, B. Mrs. Moonlight
Sherriff, R. Journey's end
Van Druten, J. Young Wood-
ley

FAOS   Famous plays of today...
London, Gollancz, 1953.
373p
Hunter, N. Waters of the
moon

Knott, F. Dial "M" for
 murder
Priestley, J., and Hawkes, J.
 Dragon's mouth
Rattigan, T. The deep blue
 sea

FAR Farmer, John Stephen, ed.
 ...Anonymous plays. 3rd
 series...London, Early
 English drama society,
 1906. 302p (Early English
 dramatists)
Gammer Gurton's needle
Jack Juggler
King Darius
New custom
Trial of treasure

FARM Farmer, John Stephen,
 ed. ...Five anonymous
 plays. 4th series...Lon-
 don, Early English drama
 society, 1908. 328p (Early
 English dramatists)
Appius and Virginia
Common conditions
Grim the collier of Croydon
The marriage of wit and science
The marriage of wit and wisdom

FARN Farmer, John Stephen,
 ed. ...Recently recovered
 "lost" Tudor plays with
 some others. London,
 Early English drama society,
 1907. 472p (Early English
 dramatists)
An interlude of impatient
 poverty
The interlude of John the
 evangelist
An interlude of wealth and
 health
Mankind
Medwall, H. Nature
Redford, J. The play of wit
 and science
Respublica

FARO Farmer, John Stephen,

ed. ...Six anonymous
 plays. 1st series (c1510-
 1537)...London, Early English drama society, 1905. 286p
 (Early English dramatists)
The beauty and good properties of women (commonly
 called Calisto and Meli-
 baea)
Hickscorner
The nature of the four elements
The summoning of Every man
Thersites
The world and the child

FARP Farmer, John Stephen,
 ed. ...Six anonymous
 plays. 2d series. ...Lon-
 don, Early English drama
 society, 1906. 478p (Early
 English dramatists)
A comedy called Misogonus
The history of Jacob and
 Esau
An interlude of godly Queen
 Hester
The interlude of youth
A moral play of Albion, knight
Tom Tyler and his wife

FAY, W. G. See FIT Five
 three-act plays...

FED Federal council of the
 churches of Christ in A-
 merica. Committee on re-
 ligious drama. Religious
 dramas, 1924-25...New
 York, Century [c1923-26]
 2v
Bates, E. The two thieves.
 2
Cropper, M. Two sides of
 the door. 2
Currie, C. Whither goest
 thou? 2
Goodman, K. Dust of the
 road. 1
Goold, M. The quest divine.
 2
Goold, M. St. Claudia. 2
Goold, M. The shepherds. 2

207

Thebes

FIF   Fifteenth century prose
and verse, with an intro-
duction by Alfred W. Pol-
lard. New York, Dutton
[1903] 324p (An English
garner. [v1])
Everyman
The pageant of the shearmen
and tailors

FIFR   Fitts, Dudley, ed. Four
Greek plays...New York,
Harcourt, Brace [c1960]
310p
Aeschylus. Agamemnon
Aristophanes. The birds
Euripides. Alcestis
Sophocles. Oedipus rex

FIFT   Fitts, Dudley, ed. Greek
plays in modern translation
...New York, Dial press,
1947. 596p (The permanent
library series)
Aeschylus. Agamemnon
Aeschylus. Eumenides
Aeschylus. Prometheus bound
Euripides. Alcestis
Euripides. Hippolytus
Euripides. Medea
Euripides. The Trojan women
Sophocles. Antigone
Sophocles. Electra
Sophocles. King Oedipus
Sophocles. Oedipus at Colonus

FIFV   Fitts, Dudley, ed. Six
Greek plays in modern
translation...New York,
Dryden [c1955] 294p
Aeschylus. Agamemnon
Aeschylus. Choephoroe
Aeschylus. Eumenides
Aristophanes. The birds
Euripides. Andromache
Sophocles. Philoctetes

FIG   Five great modern Irish
plays...with a foreword by
George Jean Nathan. New
York, Modern Library

[1941] 332p
Carroll, P. Shadow and sub-
stance
Gregory, I. Spreading the
news
O'Casey, S. Juno and the
paycock
Synge, J. The playboy of the
western world
Synge, J. Riders to the sea

FIN   Five new full-length plays
for all-women casts...
London, Dickson & Thomp-
son [1935] 375p
Box, M. Angels of war
Box, S. The woman and the
walnut tree
Popplewell, O. This bondage
Rye, E. The three-fold path
Smee, L. No thoroughfare

FIP   Five plays of 1937...
[London] Hamilton [1937]
v.p.
Hellman, L. The children's
hour
Jerome, H. Charlotte Corday
Lyndon, B. They came by
night
Rattigan, T. French without
tears
Savory, G. George and
Margaret

FIR   Five plays of 1940...Lon-
don, Hamilton [1940] v.p.
Ardrey, R. Thunder rock
Boothe, C. Margin for error
Ginsbury, N. The first gentle-
man
Morgan, D. A house in the
square
Stuart, A. Jeannie

FIT   Five three-act plays; fore-
word by W.G. Fay. [Lon-
don] Rich and Cowan
[1933] 448p
Bennett, A. Flora
Gielgud, V. Chinese white
Holme, C. "I want!"
Pertwee, R. Heat wave

FIT (continued)
Wilson, T. Champion north

FLAN Flanagan, John Theodore
and Hudson, Arthur Palmer,
eds. Folklore in Ameri-
can literature... Evanston,
Ill., Rowe, Peterson
[c1958] 511p
Green, P. Unto such glory
MacKaye, P. The scarecrow;
or, The glass of truth

FLOR Flores, Angel, ed.
Masterpieces of the Span-
ish golden age... New York,
Rinehart [c1957] 395p
Calderón de la Barca. The
great theater of the world
Téllez, G. The trickster of
Seville and the guest of
stone
Vega Carpio, L. Fuenteove-
juna

FLOS Flores, Angel, ed.
Spanish drama... New York,
Bantam Books [c1962] 473p
(Library of world drama)
Benavente y Martínez, J.
The bonds of interest
Calderón de la Barca, P.
Life is a dream
Cervantes Saavedra, M. The
vigilant sentinel
Echegaray y Eizaguirre, J.
The great Galeoto
Garcia Lorca, F. Blood wed-
ding
Moratín, L. When a girl says
yes
Rueda, L. The olives
Ruiz de Alarcón y Mendoza,
J. The truth suspected
Téllez, G. The rogue of
Seville
Vega Carpio, L. Fuenteovej-
una

FOUB Four great comedies of
the restoration and 18th
century... With an introduction by Brooks Atkinson.

New York, Bantam Books
[c1958] 321p
Congreve, W. The way of
the world
Goldsmith, O. She stoops to
conquer; or, The mistakes
of a night
Sheridan, R. The school for
scandal
Wycherley, W. The country
wife

FOUD Four great Elizabethan
plays. With an introduc-
tion by John Gassner.
New York, Bantam Books
[c1960] 316p
Dekker, T. The shoemakers'
holiday; or, A pleasant
comedy of the gentle craft
Jonson, B. Volpone; or, The
fox
Marlowe, C. The tragical
history of Doctor Faustus
Webster, J. The Duchess of
Malfi

FOUF Four modern French
comedies... With an intro-
duction by Wallace Fowlie.
New York, Capricorn
Books [c1960] 256p
Adamov, A. Professor Tor-
anne
Aymé, M. Clérambard
Courteline, G. The commis-
sioner
Jarry, A. Ubu Roi

FOUM Four modern verse
plays. First [and] second
series... ed. by Henry
Popkin. New York, Holt,
Rinehart and Winston
[c1957, 1961] 2v
Gorky, M. The lower depths
Ibsen, H. Hedda Gabler
Ibsen, H. Rosmersholm
Miller, A. Death of a sales-
man
O'Neill, E. The Emperor
Jones
Rostand, E. Cyrano de

210

Bergerac
Shaw, G. Pygmalion
Wilde, O. The importance of
being earnest

FOUP Four plays of 1936...
with an introduction by Ivor
Brown. [London] Hamilton
[1936] 624p
Jerome, H. Jane Eyre
Jerome, H. Pride and preju-
dice
Lyndon, B. The amazing Dr.
Clitterhouse
Turney, C. Bitter harvest

FOUS... Four... Soviet... plays
.... New York, Interna-
tional publishers, 1937.
427p
Gorky, M. Yegor Bulichov
and others
Kocherga, I. Masters of time
Pogodin, N. Aristocrats
Vishnevskiĭ, V. An optimistic
tragedy

FOUT Four Soviet war plays
... London, Hutchinson
[1944] 208p
Korneichuk, A. The front
Korneichuk, A. Guerillas of
the Ukrainian Steppes
Leonov, L. Invasion
Simonov, K. The Russians

FOWLIE, WALLACE. See also
FOUF Four modern French
comedies...

FOWL Fowlie, Wallace, ed.,
and tr. Classical French
drama... New York, Ban-
tam Books [c1962] 277p
Beaumarchais, P. The barber
of Seville
Corneille, P. The cid
Marivaux, P. The game of
love and chance
Molière, J. The intellectual
ladies
Racine, J. Phaedra

FRA Francke, Kuno, ed. The
German classics of the
nineteenth and twentieth
centuries... New York,
German publication society
[c1913-14] 20v
Anzengruber, L. The farmer
foresworn.   16
Freytag, G. The journal-
ists.   12
Fulda, L. Tête-à-tête.   17
Goethe, J. Faust, pt. I   1
Goethe, J. Faust, pt. II   1
Goethe, J. Iphigenia in
Tauris.   1
Grillparzer, F. The Jewess
of Toledo.   6
Grillparzer, F. Medea.   6
Gutzkow, K. Sword and
queue.   7
Halbe, M. Mother earth.   20
Hardt, E. Tristram the
jester.   20
Hauptmann, G. Michael
Kramer.   18
Hauptmann, G. The sunken
bell.   18
Hauptmann, G. The
weavers.   18
Hebbel, F. Maria Magda-
lena.   9
Hebbel, F. Siegfried's
death.   9
Hofmannsthal, H. Death and
the fool.   17
Hofmannsthal, H. The death
of Titian.   17
Hofmannsthal, H. The mar-
riage of Sobeide.   20
Kleist, H. The prince of
Homburg.   4
Ludwig, O. The hereditary
forester.   9
Schiller, F. The death of
Wallenstein.   3
Schiller, F. The homage of
the arts.   3
Schiller, F. William Tell.   3
Schnitzler, A. The green
cockatoo.   20
Schnitzler, A. Literature. 20
Schönherr, K. Faith and
fireside.   16

211

FRA (continued)
Sudermann, H. John the
   Baptist.   17
Tieck, J. L. Puss in boots. 4
Wedekind, F. The court
   singer.   20
Wilbrandt, A. The master of
   Palmyra.   16
Wildenbruch, E. King
   Henry.   17

FREE Freedley, George, ed.
   Three plays about crime
   and criminals... New York,
   Washington Square Press
   [c1962] 278p
Chodorov, E. Kind lady
Kesselring, J. Arsenic and
   old lace
Kingsley, S. Detective story

FREI Freier, Robert, Lazarus,
   Arnold Leslie and Potell,
   Herbert, eds. Adventures in
   modern literature. Fourth
   edition. New York, Harcourt,
   Brace [c1956] 690p (Adven-
   tures in literature series)
Glaspell, S. Trifles
O'Casey, S. The end of the
   beginning
Shaw, G. Caesar and Cleo-
   patra
Sherriff, R. Journey's end

FULLINGTON, JAMES FITZ-
   JAMES. See also MCCA,
   MCCB, MCCD, MCCF,
   MCCG McCallum, James
   Dow, ed. The college omni-
   bus...

FUL Fullington, James Fitz-
   James; Reed, Harry B., and
   McCorkle, Julia Norton,
   eds. The new college omni-
   bus... New York, Harcourt,
   Brace, 1938. 1241p
Connelly, M. The green pas-
   tures
Howard, S. The silver cord
O'Neill, E. The hairy ape
Sherriff, R. Journey's end

FULT Fulton, Albert Rond-
   thaler, ed. Drama and
   theatre, illustrated by seven
   modern plays... New York,
   Holt [c1946] 556p
Barrie, J. A well-remembered
   voice
Coward, N. Blithe spirit
Lawson, J. Roger Bloomer
O'Neill, E. Beyond the hori-
   zon
Pinero, A. The second Mrs.
   Tanqueray
Rice, E. Street scene
Wilder, T. Our town

               G

GALB Galbraith, Esther E., ed.
   Plays without footlights...
   New York, Harcourt, Brace
   [c1945] 358p
Anderson, M. Journey to
   Jerusalem
Greene, P. Papa is all
Niggli, J. This bull ate nut-
   meg
Reely, M. Flittermouse
Rickert, V. The bishop's
   candlesticks
Roberts, C. Tails up
Saroyan, W. The people with
   light coming out of them
Smith, B. Fun after supper
Upson, W. The master sales-
   man
Wilder, T. The happy journey
   to Trenton and Camden

GARNETT, PORTER. See BOH
   Bohemian club, San Francisco. The Grove plays of
   the Bohemian club...

GASSNER, JOHN. See also
   FOUD, Four great Elizabethan plays; TRE, TREA,
   TREC, TREE. A treasury
   of the theatre...

GART Gassner, John, ed. Best
   American plays. Fourth series... 1951-57... New York,

212

Crown [c1958] 648p
Anderson, R. Tea and sympathy
Axelrod, G. The seven year itch
Gazzo, M. A hatful of rain
Hartog, J. The fourposter
Inge, W. Bus stop
Inge, W. Picnic
Kaufman, G., and Teichman, H. The solid gold Cadillac
Lawrence, J., and Lee, R. Inherit the wind
Levin, I. No time for sergeants
Miller, A. The crucible
Miller, A. A view from the bridge
O'Neill. E. A moon for the misbegotten
Van Druten, J. I am a camera
Wilder, T. The matchmaker
Williams, T. Cat on a hot tin roof
Williams, T. The rose tattoo
Wouk, H. The Caine mutiny

GARU Gassner, John, ed. Best American plays; supplementary vol., 1918-58... New York, Crown [c1961] 687p
Barry, P. Here come the clowns
Behrman, S. Biography
Chase, M. Harvey
Colton, J. Rain
Davis, O., and Davis, D. Ethan Frome
Goodrich, F., and Hackett, A. The diary of Anne Frank
Green, P. The house of Connelly
Howard, S., and DeKruif, P. Yellow jack
Kingsley, S. Men in white
Mayer, E. Children of darkness
Odets, C. Awake and sing
Osborn, P. Morning's at seven
Osborn, P. On borrowed time

Patrick, J. The teahouse of the August moon
Rice, E. The adding machine
Riggs, L. Green grow the lilacs
Tarkington, B. Clarence

GARW Gassner, John, ed. Best American plays. Third series - 1945-51... New York, Crown [c1952] 707p
Anderson, M. Anne of the thousand days
Coxe, L., and Chapman, R. Billy Budd
Euripides. Medea
Heggen, T., and Logan, J. Mister Roberts
Hellman, L. The autumn garden
Herbert, F. The moon is blue
Inge, W. Come back, little Sheba
Kingsley, S. Darkness at noon
Kingsley, S. Detective story
Lindsay, H., and Crouse, R. State of the union
McCullers, C. The member of the wedding
Miller, A. All my sons
Miller, A. Death of a salesman
O'Neill, E. The iceman cometh
Van Druten, J. Bell, book and candle
Williams, T. A streetcar named Desire
Williams, T. Summer and smoke

GARZ Gassner, John, ed. Best plays of the modern American theatre: Second series ... New York, Crown [c1947] 776p
Barry, P. The Philadelphia story
Gow, J., and D'Usseau, A. Tomorrow the world
Hellman, L. Watch on the Rhine
Kanin, G. Born yesterday

GARZ (continued)
Kaufman, G., and Hart, M.
The man who came to
dinner
Kesselring, J. Arsenic and
old lace
Kingsley, S. The patriots
Laurents, A. Home of the
brave
Lindsay, H., and Crouse, R.
Life with father
Patrick, J. The hasty heart
Rice, E. Dream girl
Saroyan, W. The time of your
life
Sherwood, R. Abe Lincoln in
Illinois
Thurber, J., and Nugent, E.
The male animal
Van Druten, J. I remember
mama
Van Druten, J. The voice of
the turtle
Williams, T. The glass me-
nagerie

GARZB Gassner, John, ed.
Medieval and Tudor drama
...New York, Bantam Books
[c1963] 457p (Library of
world drama)
Abraham and Isaac
The betrayal of Christ
A Christmas mumming; the
play of Saint (Prince) George
The creation and the fall of
Lucifer
The crucifixion
The death of Herod
The death of Pilate
The deluge
An Easter resurrection play
Everyman
Man's disobedience and the
fall of man
The murder of Abel
The Orléans sepulcher
The pageant of the shearmen
and tailors
A pantomime for Easter day
The quem quaeritis
The resurrection, harrowing
of hell, and the last judg-

ment
The second shepherds' play
Heywood, J. The play called
the four pp
Hrotsvit. Dulcitius
Hrotsvit. Paphnutius
Sackville, T., and Norton, T.
Gorboduc
Stevenson, W. Gammer Gur-
ton's needle
Udall, N. Ralph Roister
Doister

GARZE Gassner, John, ed. 19th
century Russian drama...
with introduction and prefaces by Marc Slonin. New
York, Banton Books [c1963]
342p (Library of world
drama)
Gogol, N. The inspector general
Ostrovsky, A. The thunderstorm
Pushkin, A. The stone guest
Tolstoy, L. The power of
darkness
Turgenev, I. A month in the
country

GARZH Gassner, John, ed.
Twenty best European plays
on the American stage...
New York, Crown [c1957]
733p
Anouilh, J. The lark
Behrman, S. Jacobowsky and
the Colonel
Benavente y Martínez, J. The
passion flower
Čapek, J., and Čapek, K.
The world we live in
Chekhov, A. The sea gull
Giraudoux, J. The madwoman
of Chaillot
Giraudoux, J. Ondine
Giraudoux, J. Tiger at the
gates
Heijermans, H. The good hope
Howard, S. The late Christo-
pher Bean
Kaiser, G. From morn to mid-
night

214

Molnár, F. The play's the thing
Obey, A. Noah
Pirandello, L. As you desire
me
Rappoport, S. The dybbuk
Sartre, J. No exit
Spewack, S. My three angels
Tolstoy, L. Redemption
Turgenev, I. A month in the
country
Zweig, S. Volpone

GARZJ Gassner, John, ed. 20th
century Russian drama.
Translated with an introduc-
tion and prefaces by Andrew
R. MacAndrew. New York,
Bantam Books [c1963] 376p
(Library of world drama)
Andreyev, L. He who gets
slapped
Chekhov, A. The three sisters
Gorky, M. The lower depths
Mayakóvsky, V. The bathhouse
Olesha, Y. A list of assets

GAS Gassner, John, ed. Twenty
best plays of the modern
American theatre... New
York, Crown [c1939] 874p
Abbott, G., and Holm, J.
Three men on a horse
Anderson, M. High Tor
Anderson, M. Winterset
Barry, P. The animal king-
dom
Behrman, S. End of summer
Boothe, C. The women
Connelly, M. Green pastures
Ferber, E., and Kaufman, G.
Stage door
Green, P. Johnny Johnson
Hart, M., and Kaufman, G.
You can't take it with you
Hellman, L. The children's
hour
Kingsley, S. Dead end
Kirkland, J., and Caldwell, E.
Tobacco road
MacLeish, A. The fall of the
city
Odets, C. Golden boy
Reed, M. Yes, my darling

daughter
Shaw, I. Bury the dead
Sherwood, R. Idiot's delight
Spewack, B., and Spewack, S.
Boy meets girl
Steinbeck, J. Of mice and
men

GASB Gassner, John, ed.
Twenty-five best plays of
the modern American the-
atre: Early series... New
York, Crown [c1949] 756p
Anderson, M., and Hickerson,
H. Gods of the lightning
Anderson, M. Saturday's
children
Balderston, J. Berkeley Square
Barry, P. Paris bound
Beach, L. The clod
Behrman, S. The second man
Conkle, E. Minnie Field
Dunning, P., and Abbott, G.
Broadway
Glaspell, S. Trifles
Green, P. White dresses
Hecht, B., and MacArthur, C.
The front page
Heyward, D., and Heyward,
D. Porgy
Howard, S. They knew what
they wanted
Kaufman, G., and Connelly,
M. Beggar on horseback
Kelly, G. Craig's wife
Kelly, G. Poor Aubrey
Millay, E. Aria da Capo
O'Neill, E. Desire under the
elms
O'Neill, E. The hairy ape
O'Neill, E. Ile
Rice, E. Street scene
Sherwood, R. The road to
Rome
Stallings, L., and Anderson,
M. What price glory?
Sturges, P. Strictly dishonor-
able
Treadwell, S. Machinal

GASS Gassner, John, and Sweet-
kind, Morris, eds. Intro-
ducing the drama... New

GASS (continued)
York, Holt, Rinehart and
Winston [1963] 583p
Everyman
Besier, R. The Barretts of
Wimpole Street
Dunsany, E. A night at an inn
Gassner, J. Then and now
Giraudoux, J. The Apollo of
Bellac
Howard, S. The late Christo-
pher Bean
Ibsen, H. An enemy of the
people
MacKaye, P. The scarecrow
Molière, J. The pretentious
ladies
Shakespeare, W. The tragedy
of Romeo and Juliet
Shaw, G. Arms and the man
Sheridan, R. The school for
scandal
Sophocles. Antigone
Williams, T. The glass me-
nagerie

GAUB   Gaubert, Helen A. Four
classic French plays... New
York, Washington Square
Press [c1961] 260p
Corneille, P. The cid
Molière, J. The would-be
gentleman
Racine, J. Athaliah
Racine, J. Phaedra

GAVE   Gaver, Jack, ed. Critics'
choice. New York Drama
Critics' Circle prize plays
1935-55... New York, Haw-
thorn books [c1955] 661p
Anderson, M. High tor
Anderson, M. Winterset
Hellman, L. Watch on the
Rhine
Inge, W. Picnic
Kingsley, S. Darkness at noon
Kingsley, S. The patriots
McCullers, C. The member of
the wedding
Miller, A. All my sons
Miller, A. Death of a sales-
man

Patrick, J. The teahouse of
the August moon
Saroyan, W. The time of your
life
Steinbeck, J. Of mice and men
Van Druten, J. I am a camera
Williams, T. Cat on a hot tin
roof
Williams, T. The glass me-
nagerie
Williams, T. A streetcar
named Desire

GAY   Gayley, Charles Mills, ed.
Representative English
comedies... New York,
Macmillan, 1903-36. 4v
Brome, R. The antipodes.   3
Chapman, G.; Jonson, B.,
and Marston, J. East-
ward hoe.   2
Congreve, W. The way of
the world.   4
Cowley, A. Cutter of Coleman-street.   4
Dekker, T. The shoemakers
holiday.   3
Dryden, J. The Spanish
fryar.   4
Farquhar, G. The recruit-
ing officer.   4
Fletcher, J. Rule a wife and
have a wife.   3
Greene, R. The honorable
historie of Frier Bacon
and Frier Bungay.   1
Heywood, J. A mery play betweene Johan Johan, Tyb,
his wyfe, and Syr Jhan
the preest.   1
Heywood, J. The play of the
wether.   1
Jonson, B. The alchemist. 2
Jonson, B. Epicoene; or, The
silent woman.   2
Jonson, B. Every man in his
humour.   2
Lyly, J. Alexander and
Campaspe.   1
Massinger, P. A new way to
pay old debts.   3
The merry devill of Edmonton.   2

216

Middleton, T., and Rowley,
W. The Spanish gipsie. 3
Peele, G. The old wives'
tale. 1
Porter, H. The two angry
women of Abington. 1
Shirley, J. The royall
master. 3
Stevenson, W. Gammer Gur-
ton's nedle. 1
Udall, N. Roister Doister. 1
Vanbrugh, J. The provok'd
wife. 4
Wycherley, W. The plain-
dealer. 4

GEST, MORRIS. See MOSA
Moscow art theatre series
of Russian plays...

GOL Goldberg, Isaac, tr. Plays
of the Italian theatre...
Boston, Luce, 1921. 202p
Lopez, S. The sparrow
Morselli, E. Gastone the ani-
mal tamer
Morselli, E. Water upon fire
Pirandello, L. Sicilian limes
Verga, G. The wolf-hunt

GOOD Goodman, Randolph, ed.
Drama on stage...New
York, Holt, Rinehart and
Winston [c1961] 475p
Everyman
Duerrenmatt, F. The visit
Euripides. Medea
Molière, J. The misanthrope
Shakespeare, W. The tragedy
of Macbeth
Williams, T. A streetcar
named Desire

GORDON, DUDLEY CHADWICK,
See TOD Today's litera-
ture...

GOS Gosse, Edmund William.
Restoration plays from Dry-
den to Farquhar. London,
Dent [1929] 431p (Every-
man's library)
Congreve, W. The way of the

world
Dryden, J. All for love
Farquhar, G. The beaux-
stratagem
Otway, T. Venice preserved
Vanbrugh, J. The provok'd
wife
Wycherley, W. The country
wife

GOSA Gosse, Edmund William.
Restoration plays from Dry-
den to Farquhar. London,
Dent [1932] 509p (Every-
man's library)
Congreve, W. The way of the
world
Dryden, J. All for love
Etherege, G. The man of
mode
Farquhar, G. The beaux-
stratagem
Otway, T. Venice preserved
Vanbrugh, J. The provok'd
wife
Wycherley, W. The country
wife

GOW Gow, J. Rodger and Han-
lon, Helen J., eds. Five
Broadway plays...New
York, Harper [c1948] 432p
Anderson, M. High Tor
Besier, R. The Barretts of
Wimpole Street
Chodorov, J., and Fields, J.
Junior miss
Osborn, P. On borrowed time
Sherwood, R. Abe Lincoln in
Illinois

GPA Graham, Cary B. Fresh-
man English program...
Chicago, Scott, Foresman
[c1960] 946p
Ibsen, H. Hedda Gabler
O'Neill, E. Bound east for
Cardiff
Shakespeare, W. Romeo and
Juliet
Sophocles. Oedipus the king

217

GRA   Grant, Elliott Mansfield,
ed. Chief French plays of
the nineteenth century...
New York, Harper, 1934.
934p
Augier, É. Le gendre de M.
Poirier
Becque, H. Les corbeaux
Brieux, E. La robe rouge
Dumas, A. fils. La dame aux
camélias
Dumas, A. père. Henri III et
sa cour
Hugo, V. Hernani
Hugo, V. Ruy Blas
Musset, A. On ne badine pas
avec l'amour
Rostand, E. Cyrano de Berge-
rac
Vigny, A. Chatterton

GRAF   Grant, Elliott Mansfield,
ed. Four French plays of
the twentieth century... New
York, Harper [c1949] 338p
Anouilh, J. Antigone
Bernard, J. Le secret d'Ar-
vers
Giraudoux, J. Siegfried
Pagnol, M., and Nivoix, P.
Les marchands de gloire

GRD   Great American parade.
Garden City, N.Y., Doubleday, Doran, 1935. 611p
Connelly, M. The green pastures

GRDB   Great books of the west-
ern world...[Robert May-
nard Hutchins, editor in
chief]...[Chicago] W. Ben-
ton [1952] 54v
Aeschylus. Agamemnon.   5
Aeschylus. Choephoroe.   5
Aeschylus. Eumenides.   5
Aeschylus. The Persians.   5
Aeschylus. Prometheus bound.
5
Aeschylus. The seven against
Thebes.   5
Aeschylus. The suppliant
maidens.   5

Aristophanes. Acharnians.   5
Aristophanes. Birds.   5
Aristophanes. Clouds.   5
Aristophanes. Ecclesiazusae.
5
Aristophanes. Frogs.   5
Aristophanes. Knights.   5
Aristophanes. Lysistrata.   5
Aristophanes. Peace.   5
Aristophanes. Plutus.   5
Aristophanes. Thesma-
phoriazusae.   5
Aristophanes. Wasps.   5
Euripides. Alcestis.   5
Euripides. Andromache.   5
Euripides. The bacchantes. 5
Euripides. The cyclops.   5
Euripides. Electra.   5
Euripides. Helen.   5
Euripides. Hecuba.   5
Euripides. Heracleidae.   5
Euripides. Heracles mad.   5
Euripides. Hippolytus.   5
Euripides. Ion.   5
Euripides. Iphigenia among
the Tauri.   5
Euripides. Iphigenia at Aulis.
5
Euripides. Medea.   5
Euripides. The Phoenician
maidens.   5
Euripides. Rhesus.   5
Euripides. The suppliants. 5
Euripides. The Trojan wo-
men.   5
Goethe, J. Faust.   47
Shakespeare, W. All's well
that ends well.   27
Shakespeare, W. Antony and
Cleopatra.   27
Shakespeare, W. As you like
it.   26
Shakespeare, W. The comedy
of errors.   26
Shakespeare, W. Coriolan-
us.   27
Shakespeare, W. Cymbe-
line.   27
Shakespeare, W. Hamlet,
Prince of Denmark.   27
Shakespeare, W. Julius
Caesar.   26
Shakespeare, W. King Henry

GREB (continued)
Aeschylus. Prometheus
 bound. 2
Byron, G. Manfred. 2
Congreve, W. The way of
 the world. 1
Everyman. 1
Marlowe, C. The tragical his-
 tory of Doctor Faustus. 1
Milton, J. Samson Agon-
 istes. 1
Molière, J. The misan-
 thrope. 1
Shelley, P. Prometheus
 unbound. 2
Sheridan, R. The school for
 scandal. 1
Wilde, O. The importance of
 being earnest. 2

GREC Grebanier, Bernard D. N.;
 Middlebrook, Samuel;
 Thompson, Stith, and Watt,
 William, eds. English lit-
 erature and its backgrounds.
 Revised edition... New York,
 Dryden press [c1949] 2v
Abraham and Isaac. 1
Browning, R. In a balcony. 2
Congreve, W. The way of
 the world. 1
Dekker, T. The shoemaker's
 holiday. 1
Everyman. 1
Marlowe, C. Doctor Faustus.
 1
Milton, J. Samson Agon-
 istes. 1
Molière, J. The misan-
 thrope. 1
Shakespeare, W. Othello. 1
Sheridan, R. The school for
 scandal. 1
Sophocles. Oedipus the
 king. 1
Synge, J. The playboy of the
 western world. 2
Wilde, O. The importance of
 being earnest. 2
Williams, E. The corn is
 green. 2

GRED Grebanier, Bernard D. N.,
220

and Reiter, Seymour, eds.
 Introduction to imaginative
 literature. New York,
 Thomas Y. Crowell Com-
 pany...[c1960] 969p
Coward, N. Brief encounter
Milton, J. Samson Agonistes
O'Neill, E. In the zone
Sapensley, A. Even the weari-
 est river
Shakespeare, W. King Lear
Shaw, G. Caesar and Cleo-
 patra
Synge, J. The playboy of the
 western world
Turque, M. Shoptalk
Williams, T. The rose tattoo

GREE Greek dramas... with
 biographical notes and a
 critical introduction by
 Bernadotte Perrin...[Aldine
 ed.] New York, Appleton,
 1900. 390p (The world's
 great books)
Aeschylus. Agamemnon
Aeschylus. Prometheus bound
Aristophanes. The clouds
Aristophanes. Plutus
Euripides. Alcestis
Euripides. Medea
Sophocles. Antigone
Sophocles. Oedipus tyrannus

GREN Grene, David, tr. Three
 Greek tragedies in trans-
 lation... Chicago, Univer-
 sity of Chicago press
 [c1942] 228p
Aeschylus. Prometheus bound
Euripides. Hippolytus
Sophocles. Oedipus the king

GREP Grene, David, and Latti-
 more, Richmond, eds. The
 complete Greek tragedies
 ...[Chicago] University of
 Chicago Press [1959] 4v
Aeschylus. Agamemnon. 1
Aeschylus. The eumenides. 1
Aeschylus. The libation
 bearers. 1
Aeschylus. The Persians 1

Aeschylus. Prometheus
bound. 1
Aeschylus. Seven against
Thebes. 1
Aeschylus. The suppliant
maidens. 1
Euripides. Alcestis. 3
Euripides. Andromache. 3
Euripides. The bacchae. 4
Euripides. The cyclops, 3
Euripides. Electra. 4
Euripides. Hecuba. 3
Euripides. Helen. 3
Euripides. The Heracleidae.3
Euripides. Heracles. 3
Euripides. Hippolytus, 3
Euripides. Ion. 4
Euripides. Iphigenia in
Aulis. 4
Euripides. Iphegenia in
Tauris. 3
Euripides. The Medea. 3
Euripides. Orestes. 4
Euripides. The Phoenician
women, 4
Euripides. Rhesus, 4
Euripides. The suppliant
women. 4
Euripides. The Trojan wo-
men, 3
Sophocles. Ajax, 2
Sophocles. Antigone, 2
Sophocles. Electra. 2
Sophocles. Oedipus at
Colonus, 2
Sophocles. Oedipus the king 2
Sophocles. Philoctetes, 2
Sophocles. The women of
Trachis. 2

GRER Grene, David, and Latti-
more, Richmond, eds.
Greek tragedies...[Chicago]
University of Chicago
Press [1960] 3v
Aeschylus. Agamemnon. 1
Aeschylus. The eumenides, 3
Aeschylus. The libation
bearers. 2
Aeschylus. Prometheus
bound. 1
Euripides. Alcestis. 3
Euripides. The bacchae. 3

Euripides. Electra. 2
Euripides. Hippolytus. 1
Euripides. Iphigenia in
Tauris. 2
Euripides. The Trojan wo-
men. 2
Sophocles. Antigone. 1
Sophocles. Electra. 2
Sophocles. Oedipus at
Colonus. 3
Sophocles. Oedipus the
king. 1
Sophocles. Philoctetes. 3

GRIF Griffin, Alice Sylvia (Ven-
ezky), ed. Living theatre
...New York, Twayne
[c1953] 510p
Aeschylus. Oresteia
Anderson, M. Winterset
Chekhov, A. The sea gull
Everyman
Giraudoux, J. The madwoman
of Chaillot
Hebbel, F. Maria Magdalena
Ibsen, H. Hedda Gabler
Marlowe, C. Faustus
Molière, J. The misanthrope
Odets, C. Awake and sing
Plautus, T. Mostellaria
Rice, E. Street scene
Shakespeare, W. Romeo and
Juliet

THE GROVE PLAYS OF THE
BOHEMIAN CLUB. See
BOH Bohemian club, San
Francisco.

GUE Guerney, Bernard Guilbert,
ed. A treasury of Russian
literature...New York,
Vanguard press [c1943]
1048p
Chekhov, A. The three sisters
Gogol, N. The inspector general
Gorki, M. The lowest depths

GUI Guinagh, Kevin and Dor-
jahn, Alfred Paul, eds.
Latin literature in transla-

221

GUI (continued)
tion... New York, Longmans,
Green, 1942. 822p
Plautus, T. The menaechmi
Plautus, T. The rudens; or,
The rope
Terence. The Adelphi; or, The
brothers
Terence. The Phormio

GUIN Guinagh, Kevin and Dor-
jahn, Alfred P., eds. Latin
literature in translation...
Second edition. New York,
Longmans, Green [c1952]
822p
Plautus. The menaechmi
Plautus. The rudens
Seneca. Medea
Terence. The Adelphi
Terence. The Phormio

GUSTAFSON, ALRIK. See SCAN
Scandinavian plays of the
twentieth century...

GUTH Guth, Hans Paul. Idea
and image... Belmont, Calif.,
Wadsworth Pub. Co. [c1962]
838p
Ibsen, H. The master builder
Miller, A. The crucible
Molière, J. The misanthrope
Shakespeare, W. Antony and
Cleopatra
Sophocles. Antigone

H

HAH Halliday, Frank Ernest,
ed. The legend of the rood
... London, Gerald Duck-
worth [c1955] 142p
The death of Pilate
The legend of the rood
The three Maries

HALLINE, ALLAN GATES See
also SIXC Six modern
American plays...

HAL Halline, Allan Gates, ed.
American plays. New York,

American book co. [c1935]
787p
Barker, J. Superstition
Barry, P. You and I
Bird, R. The gladiator
Boker, G. Francesca da Ri-
mini
Daly, A. Horizon
Davis, O. Icebound
Dunlap, W. André
Green, P. The field god
Howard, B. The Henrietta
Miller, J. The Danites in the
Sierras
Mitchell, L. The New York
idea
Moeller, P. Madame Sand
Mowatt, A. Fashion
O'Neill, E. The great god
Brown
Paulding, J. The bucktails; or,
Americans in England
Tyler, R. The contrast
Willis, N. Bianca Visconti

HALU Hamalian, Leo, and
Volpe, Edmond L., eds.
Pulitzer prize reader...
New York, Popular Library
[c1961] 607p
Williams, T. 27 wagons full of
cotton

HAM Hamilton, Edith, tr. Three
Greek plays... New York,
Norton [c1937] 239p
Aeschylus. Agamemnon
Aeschylus. Prometheus bound
Euripides. The Trojan women

HAMI Hamilton (Hamish) ltd.,
London Majority; 1931-52...
London, Hamish Hamilton
[1952] 1035p
Rattigan, T. The Browning
version
Sartre, J. In camera

HAN Hampden, John, comp.
Eighteenth century plays.
... London, Dent [1928]
408p (Everyman's library)
Addison, J. Cato

Colman, G., and Garrick, D.
The clandestine marriage
Cumberland, R. The West
Indian
Fielding, H. The tragedy of
tragedies; or, Tom Thumb
the great
Gay, J. The beggar's opera
Lillo, G. The London mer-
chant; or, George Barnwell
Rowe, N. Jane Shore

HAP Harbrace omnibus... edited
by H.B. Reed, J.N. Mc-
Corkle, W.H. Hildreth,
and J.D. McCallum.   New
York, Harcourt, Brace,
1942. v.p.
Anderson, M. High Tor
O'Neill, E. In the zone

HAPD Harding, Helen Elizabeth,
ed. ...Tragedies old and
new... New York, Noble &
Noble [c1939] 486p
Note: Also published under the
title, Hamlet and other tragedies...
O'Neill, E. Beyond the horizon
Shakespeare, W. Hamlet
Sophocles. Electra

HAPR Harrier, Richard C., ed.
The Anchor anthology of
Jacobean drama.   Volume
1. ...New York, Doubleday,
1963. 517p
Chapman, G. Bussy D'Ambois
Jonson, B. Every man in his
humour
Marston, J., and Webster, J.
The malcontent
Webster, J. The white devil;
or, The tragedy of Paulo
Giordano Ursini, Duke of
Brachiano, and Vittoria
Corombona

HAPS Harrison, G.B., ed.
Major British Writers... New
York, Harcourt [c1954] 2v
Shakespeare, W. Hamlet,

Prince of Denmark
Shakespeare, W. King Henry
the fourth, pt. I
Shakespeare, W. The tempest
Shaw, G. Man and superman

HAPT Harrison, George Bag-
shawe [and others], eds.
Major British writers...
Enl. ed., New York, Har-
court, Brace [c1959] 2v
Byron, G. Manfred.   2
Dryden, J. The secular
masque.   1
Milton, J. Samson Agon-
istes.   1
Shakespeare, W. Hamlet.   1
Shakespeare, W. Henry IV,
part I.   1
Shakespeare, W. The tem-
pest.   1
Shaw, G. Man and super-
man.   2
Shelley, P. Prometheus un-
bound.   2

HAPV Harsh, Philip Whaley,
ed. An anthology of Roman
drama... New York, Holt,
Rinehart and Winston
[c1960] 317p
Plautus, T. The rope
Plautus, T. The twin Menaech-
mi
Seneca, L. The Medea
Seneca, L. The Phaedra
Seneca, L. The Thyestes
Terentius Afer, P. The
brothers
Terentius Afer, P. The Phor-
mio

HARA Hart, James David, and
Gohdes, Clarence, eds.
America's literature. New
York, Dryden [c1955] 958p
O'Neill, E. The hairy ape

HARB Hartley, Lodwick Charles
and Ladu, Arthur Irish,
eds. Patterns in modern
drama... New York, Pren-
tice-Hall, 1948. 496p

HARW Harwood, A. C., tr.
Christmas plays from Obe-
rufer... London, Anthropo-
sophical publishing co.
[1944] 64p
The Paradise play.
The Shepherds' play.
The Three kings' play.

HAT Hatcher, Harlan Henthorne,
ed. Modern American
dramas... New York, Har-
court, Brace, 1941. 394p
Anderson, M. Winterset
Howard, S. Dodsworth
Odets, C. Awake and sing
O'Neill, E. Beyond the hori-
zon
Rice, E. The adding machine
St. Joseph, E. A passenger
to Bali
Sherwood, R. Abe Lincoln in
Illinois
Wilder, T. Our town

HATA Hatcher, Harlan Hen-
thorne, ed. Modern Ameri-
can dramas. New edition...
New York, Harcourt, Brace
[c1949] 378p
Anderson, M. Winterset
Heggen, T. Mister Roberts
Miller, A. All my sons
O'Neill, E. The Emperor
Jones
Rice, E. The adding machine
Saroyan, W. The time of your
life
Sherwood, R. Abe Lincoln in
Illinois
Williams, T. The glass me-
nagerie

HAU Hatcher, Harlan Henthorne,
ed. Modern British dramas
... New York, Harcourt,
Brace, 1941. 374p
Dunsany, E. If
Galsworthy, J. Justice
Maugham, W. The constant
wife
Monkhouse, A. The conquer-
ing hero

O'Flaherty, L. The informer
Pinero, A. Mid-channel
Synge, J. The playboy of the
western world

HAV Hatcher, Harlan Henthorne,
ed. Modern continental
dramas... New York, Har-
court, Brace, 1941. 747p
Capek, K. R. U. R.
Chekhov, A. The cherry or-
chard
Claudel, P. The tidings
brought to Mary
Gorky, M. The lower depths
Hauptmann, G. Hannele
Ibsen, H. Hedda Gabler
Katayev, V. Squaring the
circle
Lenormand, H. Time is a
dream
Maeterlinck, M. Pelléas and
Mélisande
Martínez Sierra, G. The
cradle song
Molnár, F. Liliom
Pirandello, L. As you desire
me
Rostand, E. Cyrano de Ber-
gerac
Strindberg, A. The ghost
sonata
Strindberg, A. Miss Julia
Toller, E. Transfiguration

HAVD Hatcher, Harlan Hen-
thorne, ed. Modern dra-
mas. Shorter edition...
New York, Harcourt, Brace
[c1944] 495p
Anderson, M. Winterset
Capek, K. R. U. R.
Chekhov, A. Cherry orchard
Galsworthy, J. Justice
Hellman, L. Watch on the
Rhine
Ibsen, H. Hedda Gabler
O'Flaherty, L. The informer
O'Neill, E. Beyond the hori-
zon
Sherwood, R. Abe Lincoln in
Illinois

HAVE   Hatcher, Harlan Hen-
thorne, ed. Modern dra-
mas. New shorter edition.
New York, Harcourt, Brace
[c1948] 479p
Anderson, M. Winterset
Capek, K. R.U.R.
Galsworthy, J. Justice
Hellman, L. The little foxes
Ibsen, H. Hedda Gabler
Katayev, V. Squaring the
circle
Maugham, W. The circle
O'Neill, E. Beyond the hori-
zon
Sherwood, R. Abe Lincoln in
Illinois

HAVG   Hatcher, Harlan Hen-
thorne... A modern reper-
tory. New York, Harcourt,
Brace [c1953] 714p
Coxe, L., and Chapman, R.
Billy Budd
Eliot, T. Murder in the ca-
thedral
Fry, C. Venus observed
Giraudoux, J. The madwoman
of Chaillot
Kingsley, S. Detective story
O'Casey, S. Juno and the pay-
cock
O'Neill, E. Ah, wilderness!
Shaw, G. Candida
Williams, T. Summer and
smoke

HAVI   Havighurst. Walter; Almy,
Robert F., Wilson, Gordon
D., and Middlebrook, L.
Ruth, eds. ... Selection; a
reader for college writing.
New York, Dryden [c1955]
740p
Shaw, G. Arms and the man
Sophocles. Antigone
Synge, J. Riders to the sea
Williams, T. The glass me-
nagerie

HAY   Hayden, Hiram Collins, ed.
The portable Elizabethan
reader... New York, Viking,

1946. 688p
Dekker, T. The shoemaker's
holiday; or, A pleasant
comedy of the gentle craft
Marlowe, C. Doctor Faustus

HAYD   Haydn, Hiram and Nel-
son, John Charles, eds.
...A renaissance treasury
...New York, Doubleday,
1953. 432p
Machiavelli, N. Mandragola
Tasso, T. Aminta

HAYES, HELEN See GRIF
Griffin, Alice Sylvia (Venezky), ed. Living theatre...

HAYE   Hayes, Richard, ed.
Port-Royal, and other
plays... New York, Hill and
Wang [c1962] 267p (Mer-
maid dramabook)
Claudel, P. Tobias and Sara
Copeau, J. The little poor
man
Mauriac, F. Asmodée
Montherlant, H. Port-Royal

HEIL   Heilman, Robert B., ed.
An anthology of English
drama before Shakespeare
...New York, Rinehart
[c1952] 405p
The betrayal
The crucifixion
Everyman
Greene, R. The honorable his-
tory of Friar Bacon and
Friar Bungay
Kyd, T. The Spanish tragedy
Marlowe, C. The tragical his-
tory of Dr. Faustus
Noah the second shepherds' play
Stevenson, W. Gammer Gur-
ton's needle

HEWES, HENRY. See also
BES Best plays of 1894/
99-1961/62...

HEWE   Hewes, Henry, ed.
Famous American plays of

226

the 1940's...[New York,
Dell. c1960] 447p (Laurel
drama series)
Anderson, M., and Weil, K.
Lost in the stars
Laurents, A. Home of the
brave
McCullers, C. The member
of the wedding
Miller, A. All my sons
Wilder, T. The skin of our
teeth

HIB Hibbard, Clarence Addison,
ed. Writers of the western
world. Boston, Houghton,
Mifflin [c1942] 1261p
Aeschylus. Agamemnon
Aristophanes. The frogs
Euripides. Medea
Evreinov, N. The theatre of
the soul
Goethe, J. Faust, pt. I
Ibsen, H. The master builder
Molière, J. The misanthrope
O'Neill, E. The hairy ape
Racine, J. Phaedra
Shakespeare, W. King Lear
Sophocles. Antigone

HIBA Hibbard, Clarence Addi-
son, ed. ...Writers of the
western world...[Rev. ed.]
Boston, Houghton, Mifflin
[c1946] 1033p. (United
States Naval Academy edi-
tion edited by Cyril B.
Judge)
Aeschylus. Agamemnon
Aristophanes. The frogs
Evreinov, N. The theatre of
the soul
Goethe, J. Faust, pt. I
Ibsen, H. The master builder
Molière, J. The misanthrope
O'Neill, E. The hairy ape
Shakespeare, W. King Lear

HIBB Hibbard, Clarence Addison, and Frenz, Horst, eds.
Writers of the western
world...Second edition...
Boston, Houghton Mifflin

[c1954] 1239p
Aeschylus. Agamemnon
Aristophanes. The frogs
Chekhov, A. The cherry or-
chard
Claudel, P. The satin slipper;
or, The worst is not the
surest
Euripides. Medea
Goethe, J. Faust, pt. I
Ibsen, H. The master builder
Molière, J. The misanthrope
O'Neill, E. The hairy ape
Pirandello, L. The jar
Racine, J. Phaedra
Shakespeare, W. King Lear
Sophocles. Antigone

HILDRETH, WILLIAM HENRY.
See also HAP Harbrace
omnibus...

HIL Hildreth, William Henry
and Dumble, Wilson Randle,
eds. Five contemporary
American plays...New York,
Harper [c1939] 410p
Anderson, M. Winterset
Kaufman, G., and Ryskind,
M. Of thee I sing
Odets, C. Waiting for Lefty
O'Neill, E. Ah, wilderness
Sherwood, R. Idiot's delight

HILL Hill, John McMurray and
Harlan, Mabel Margaret,
eds. Cuarto comedias...
New York, Norton [c1941]
699p
Calderón de la Barca, P. No
siempre lo peor es cierto
Ruiz de Alarcón y Mendoza,
J. No hay mal que por bien
no venga (Don Domingo de
Don Blas)
Téllez, G. (Tirso de Molina
[pseud.]). El burlador de
Sevilla
Vega [Carpio], L. de. Peri-
báñez y el comendador de
Ocaña

227

HOGA   Hogan, Robert Goode
and Molin, Sven Eric, eds.
Drama; the major genres.
...New York, Dodd, Mead,
1962. 652p
Chekhov, A. The three sisters
Garcia Lorca, F. The house
of Bernarda Alba
Gorky, M. Yegor Bulychov
and the others
Inge, W. Bus stop
James, H. The American
Jonson, B. The silent woman
Molière, J. Tartuffe
O'Casey, S. The plough and
the stars
Shakespeare, W. The tragedy
of King Lear
Shaw, G. The six of Calais
Sophocles. Antigone

HOLM   Holmes, John Albert and
Towle, Carroll S., eds.
A complete college reader
...Boston, Houghton, Miff-
lin [c1950] 1063p
Anderson, M. Winterset
Ibsen, H. An enemy of the
people
O'Neill, E. Ah, wilderness!

HOPP   Hopper, Vincent Foster,
and Lahey, Gerald B., eds.
Medieval mystery plays...
morality plays...and inter-
ludes. Great Neck, N.Y.,
Barron's Educational Series
[c1962] 299p
Abraham and Isaac
The castle of perseverance
Everyman
Noah's flood
The second shepherd's play
Heywood, J. Johan Johan
Heywood, J. The play called
the four pp

HORN   Horn, Gunnar. A cavalcade of world writing...
Boston, Allyn and Bacon,
1961. 718p
Capek, K. R.U.R. (Ros-
sum's universal robots)

HORNE, HERBERT P.   See
NER Nero (Tragedy).
Nero & other plays...

HOUG   Houghton, Norris, ed.
Great Russian plays...
[New York, Dell, c1960]
511p (Laurel drama series)
Andreyev, L. He who gets
slapped
Chekhov, A. The cherry or-
chard
Gogol, N. The inspector gen-
eral
Gorky, M. The lower depths
Tolstoy, L. The power of
darkness
Turgenev, I. A month in the
country

HOUS   Houston, Percy Hazen
and Smith, Robert Metcalf,
eds. Types of world litera-
ture...Garden City, N.Y.,
Doubleday, Doran [c1930]
1200p
Aeschylus. Agamemnon
Aristophanes. The birds
Euripides. Hippolytus
Everyman
Ibsen, H. A doll's house
Molière, J. The misanthrope
Plautus, T. The captives
Racine, J. Athaliah
Shakespeare, W. As you like
it
Shakespeare, W. King Lear
Sheridan, R. The rivals
Sophocles. Antigone
Wilde, O. The importance of
being earnest

HOW   Howard, Edwin Johnson,
ed. Ten Elizabethan plays
...New York, Nelson,
1931. 451p
Beaumont, F., and Fletcher,
J. The knight of the burn-
ing pestle
Beaumont, F., and Fletcher,
J. Philaster
Dekker, T. The shoemakers'
holiday

228

Greene, R. The honorable history of Friar Bacon and Friar Bungay
Jonson, B. The alchemist
Kyd, T. The Spanish tragedy
Marlowe, C. Tamburlaine the great
Marlowe, C. The tragical history of Dr. Faustus
Massinger, P. A new way to pay old debts
Webster, J. The Duchess of Malfi

HOWE   Howe, George and Harrer, Gustave Adolphus, eds. ...Greek literature in translation...New York, Harper [c1924] 642p
Aeschylus. Agamemnon
Aristophanes. The clouds
Euripides. Alcestis
Euripides. Medea
Menander. The arbitration
Sophocles. Oedipus the king

HOWF   Howe, George, and Harrer, Gustave Adolphus, eds. Greek literature in translation...Revised edition by Preston Herschel Epps. New York, Harper [c1948] 903p
Aeschylus. Agamemnon
Aristophanes. The clouds
Aristophanes. The frogs
Euripides. Alcestis
Euripides. Medea
Menander. The arbitration
Sophocles. Oedipus the king

HOWJ   Howe, George, and Harrer, Gustave, eds. ... Roman literature in translation...New York, Harper, 1924. 630p
Plautus. Menaechmi
Seneca. Octavia
Terence. Phormio

HOWK   Howe, George, and Harrer, Gustave, eds. Roman literature in translation...

Revised by Albert Suskin ...New York, Harper [c1959] 649p
Horatius Flaccus, Q. The bore; a dramatic version of Horace (Satires I, 9)
Plautus, T. The braggart soldier
Seneca, L. Octavia
Terentius Afer, P. The brothers

HUB   Hubbell, Jay Broadus, ed. American life in literature ...New York, Harper [c1936] 849p
O'Neill, E. Marco millions

HUBA   Hubbell, Jay Broadus, ed. American life in literature...New York, Harper [c1949] 2v
O'Neill, E. The Emperor Jones.   2

HUD   Hubbell, Jay Broadus and Beatty, John Owen, eds. An introduction to drama ...New York, Macmillan, 1927. 838p
Abraham and Isaac
Beaumont, F., and Fletcher, J. Philaster
Chekhov, A. The boor
Dunsany, E. A night at an inn
Everyman
Farquhar, G. The beaux' stratagem
Gerstenberg, A. Overtones
Gilbert, W., and Sullivan, A. Iolanthe
Glaspell, S. Trifles
Goldsmith, O. She stoops to conquer
Hauptmann, G. The assumption of Hannele
Ibsen, H. A doll's house
Jones, H. The goal
Jonson, B. Volpone
Maeterlinck, M. The intruder
Marlowe, C. Doctor Faustus
Molière, J. Tartuffe

HUD (continued)
O'Neill, E. The Emperor
Jones
Pinero, A. The second Mrs.
Tanqueray
Plautus, T. Menaechmi
Quem quaeritis
Rostand, E. Cyrano de Ber-
gerac
The second shepherds' play
Sheridan, R. The school for
scandal
Sophocles. Antigone
Synge, J. Riders to the sea
Wilde, O. Lady Windermere's
fan
Williamson, H. Peggy
Yeats, W. The land of heart's
desire

HUDE Huberman, Edward, and
Raymo, Robert R., eds.
Angles of vision...Boston,
Houghton Mifflin [c1962]
679p
Harburg, E., and Saidy, F.
Finian's rainbow
Inge, W. The dark at the top
of the stairs
Priestley, J. An inspector
calls
Shakespeare, W. A midsum-
mer night's dream
Wedekind, F. The tenor

HUDS Hudson, Arthur Palmer;
Hurley, Leonard Buswell
and Clark, Joseph Deadrick,
eds. Nelson's college cara-
van...New York, Nelson,
1936. 4v
Green, P. Unto such glory. 2
O'Neill, E. Marco millions.2
Rostand, E. Cyrano de
Bergerac. 2
Sherriff, R. Journey's end. 2
Sophocles. Antigone. 2

HUDT Hudson, Arthur Palmer;
Hurley, Leonard Buswell
and Clark, Joseph Deadrick,
eds. Nelson's college caravan...3rd ed. New York,

Nelson, 1942. 1418p (4v
in 1)
Capek, K. R.U.R.
O'Neill, E. Marco millions
Sophocles. Antigone

HUGH Hughes, Leo, and Scou-
ten, A.H., eds. Ten Eng-
lish farces...Austin, Texas, University of Texas
press, 1948. 286p
Behn, A. The emperor of the
moon
The bilker bilk'd.
Dogget, T. Hob; or, The
country wake
Hoare, P. No song no supper
Inchbald, E. Appearance is
against them
Jevon, T.; Coffey, C.; Mottley, J., and Cibber, T.
The devil to pay; or, The
wives metamorphos'd
Johnson, C. The cobbler of
Preston
Ravenscroft, E., and Mot-
teux, P. The anatomist;
or, The sham doctor
Sheridan, T. The brave Irishman
Tate, N. A duke and no duke

HUNT Hunt, Kellogg, W., and
Stoakes, Paul, eds. Our
living language...Boston,
Houghton Mifflin [c1961]
631p
Miller, A. Death of a sales-
man
Serling, R. Patterns

HUSSEY, MAURICE P. See
CHES Chester mystery
plays

HUTC Hutchens, John K., ed.
The American twenties...
Philadelphia, Lippincott
[c1952] 480p
O'Neill, E. The Emperor
Jones

HUTCHINS, ROBERT MAYNARD.

230

See GRDB Great books of
the western world...

I

ING Inglis, Rewey Belle; Gehl-
mann, John; Bowman, Mary
Rives and Foerster, Nor-
man, eds. Adventures in
American literature. 3rd
ed. ... New York, Harcourt,
Brace, 1941. v. p.
Anderson, S. Textiles
O'Neill, E. Where the cross
is made
Wilder, T. Our town

INGA Inglis, Rewey Belle; Bowman, Mary Rives; Gehl-
mann, John and Schramm,
Wilbur. Adventures in A-
merican literature... Fourth
... edition. New York,
Harcourt, Brace [c1947]
811p
Buck, P. Will this earth hold?
Gallico, P. The snow goose
O'Neill, E. Where the cross
is made
Wilder, T. Our town

INGB Inglis, Rewey Belle; Gehlmann, John; Bowman, Mary
Rives and Schramm, Wilbur,
eds. Adventures in Ameri-
can literature. Mercury
edition. [5th edition] New
York, Harcourt, Brace.
1952. 783p
Clarke, W. The ghost patrol
Gallico, P. The snow goose
Wilder, T. Our town

INGE Inglis, Rewey Belle;
Cooper, Alice Cecilia;
Sturdevant, Marion A., and
Benêt, William Rose, eds.
Adventures in English lit-
erature. Rev. ed. ... New
York, Harcourt, Brace,
1938. 1178p
Galsworthy, J. Strife
Shakespeare, W. Macbeth

Synge, J. Riders to the sea

INGG Inglis, Rewey Belle;
Cooper, Alice Cecilia; Op-
penheimer, Celia, and Be-
nêt, William Rose, eds.
Adventures in English lit-
erature... Fourth edition.
New York, Harcourt, Brace
[c1946] 775p
Barrie, J. The old lady shows
her medals
Galsworthy, J. Strife
Shakespeare, W. Macbeth
Synge, J. Riders to the sea

INGH Inglis, Rewey Belle;
Stauffer, Donald A., and
Larsen, Cecil Evva, eds.
Adventures in English lit-
erature. Mercury edition.
New York, Harcourt,
Brace. 1952. 782p
Barrie, J. The old lady
shows her medals
Besier, R. The Barretts of
Wimpole Street
Synge, J. Riders to the sea

INGW Inglis, Rewey Belle, and
Stewart, William Kilbourne,
eds. Adventures in world
literature... New York,
Harcourt, Brace, 1936.
1268p
Benavente y Martínez, J.
No smoking
The bird-catcher in hell
Ibsen, H. An enemy of the
people
Molière, J. The physician in
spite of himself
Sachs, H. The horse thief
Sophocles. Antigone

INTE International modern
plays... London, Dent [1950]
304p (Everyman's library)
Čapek, K., and Čapek, J.
The life of the insects
Chiarelli, L. The mask and
the face
Cocteau, J. The infernal machine

231

INTE (Continued)
Hauptmann, G. Hannele
Strindberg, A. Lady Julie

J

JACKSON, SIR BARRY. See
MAL Malvern festival
plays...

JAFF Jaffe, Adrian H., and
Weisinger, Herbert, eds.
The laureate fraternity...
Evanston, Ill., Row, Peter-
son [c1960] 720p
Goldsmith, O. She stoops to
conquer; or, The mistakes
of a night
Kingsley, S. Detective story
O'Neill, E. Ah, wilderness!
Shakespeare, W. Othello, the
Moor of Venice
Sophocles. Oedipus rex
Wilde, O. An ideal husband

THE JOHNS HOPKINS STUDIES
IN ROMANCE LITERATURE
AND LANGUAGES v29.
See LAN Lancaster, Henry
Carrington, ed. Five French
farces, 1655-1694?...

JOH [Johnson, Rossiter] ed. An
anthology of Italian authors
from Cavalcanti to Fogaz-
zaro (1270-1907)...[New
York] National alumni
[c1907] 388p (The literature
of Italy, 1265-1907)
Metastasio, P. Achilles in
Scyros

JORG Jorgenson, Paul A., and
Shroyer, Frederick B.,
eds. A college treasury...
New York, Charles Scrib-
ner's sons [c1956] 598p
Howard, S. The silver cord
Rice, E. The adding machine
Shakespeare, W. Romeo and
Juliet
Shaw, G. Arms and the man
Sherriff, R. The colonel's

lady

K

KAT Katzin, Mrs. Winifred,
comp. Eight European
plays...New York, Bren-
tano, 1927. 426p
Bernard, J. Glamour
Bernard, J. Martine
Harlan, W. The Nüremberg
egg
Kaiser, G. The fire in the
opera house
Mann, H. Madame Legros
Rosso di san Secondo, P.
The stairs
Sternheim, C. A place in the
world
Vollmöller, K. Uncle's been
dreaming

KERN Kernan, Alvin B., ed.
Character and conflict: An
introduction to drama...
New York, Harcourt,
Brace [c1963] 757p
Everyman
Brecht, B. Mother Courage
and her children
Chekhov, A. The cherry or-
chard
Ibsen, H. Hedda Gabler
MacLeish, A. The fall of the
city
Molière, J. The misanthrope
Saroyan, W. The time of your
life
Shakespeare, W. King Henry
the fourth, part 1
Shakespeare, W. The tragedy
of Hamlet, Prince of Den-
mark
Sophocles. Antigone
Strindberg, A. The stronger

KET Ketchum, Roland and Gil-
lis, Adolph, eds. Three
masters of English drama
...New York, Dodd, Mead,
1934. 469p
Dryden, J. All for love
Shakespeare, W. Julius

232

Caesar
Shaw, G. Caesar and Cleo-
patra

KEY Keyes, Rowena Keith and
Roth, Helen M., eds. ...
Comparative comedies pres-
ent and past...New York,
Noble & Noble [c1935] 628p
Barry, P. Holiday
Beach, L. The goose hangs
high
Goldsmith, O. She stoops to
conquer
Sheridan, R. The rivals

KING, VERNON RUPERT. See
TOD Today's literature...

KNIC Knickerbocker, Kenneth
L., and Reninger, H. Wil-
lard, eds. ...Interpreting
literature. New York,
Henry Holt [c1955] 850p
Chekhov, A. The boor
Connelly, M. The green pas-
tures
Ibsen, H. A doll's house
O'Neill, E. Ile
Rostand, E. Cyrano de Berge-
rac
Shaw, G. Candida
Williams, T. The glass me-
nagerie

KNID Knickerbocker, Kenneth L.,
and Reninger, H. Willard,
eds. Interpreting literature,
Revised edition...New York,
Holt, Rinehart and Winston
[c1960] 832p
Chekhov, A. The boor
Connelly, M. The green pas-
tures
Ibsen, H. A doll's house
O'Neill, E. Ile
Frost, R. A masque of reason
Shakespeare, W. The tragedy
of Macbeth
Shaw, G. Candida
Sophocles. Antigone
Williams, T. The glass me-
nagerie

KNOW Knowland, A.S., ed.
Six Caroline plays...Lon-
don, Oxford University
Press, 1962. 553p
Brome, R. The antipodes
Brome, R. The mad couple
well matched
D'Avenant, W. The wits
Killigrew, T. The parson's
wedding
Shirley, J. The lady of plea-
sure
Shirley, J. The wedding

KOH Kohut, George Alexander,
ed. A Hebrew anthology.
...Cincinnati, Bacharach,
1913. 2v
Byron, G. Cain.   2
Byron, G. Heaven and
earth.   2
Cayzer, C. David and
Bathshua.   2
Davidson, R. Elijah.   2
Ewing, T. Jonathan.   2
Francis, A. The song of
songs which is Solomon's.
2
Leavitt, J. The Jewish cap-
tives.   2
Lessing, G. Nathan the
wise.   2
Milman, H. Belshazzar.   2
Milman, H. The fall of
Jerusalem.   2
Milton, J. Samson Agon-
istes.   2
More, H. Belshazzar.   2
More, H. Daniel.   2
More, H. David and Go-
liath.   2
More, H. Moses in the
bulrushes.   2
Racine, J. Athaliah.   2
Rives, A. Herod and Mari-
amne.   2

KOZ Kozlenko, William, ed.
The best short plays of the
social theatre...New York,
Random house [c1939] 456p
Auden, W., and Isherwood, C.
The dog beneath the skin

233

KOZ (continued)
Bengal, B. Plant in the sun
Blitzstein, M. The cradle will
  rock
Green, P. Hymn to the rising
  sun
Kozlenko, W. This earth is
  ours
Maltz, A. Private Hicks
Odets, C. Waiting for Lefty
Shaw, I. Bury the dead
Sifton, C., and Sifton, P.
  Give all thy terrors to the
  wind
Wexley, J. Running dogs

KREYMBORG, ALFRED. See
  also AME American cara-
  van...

KRE Kreymborg, Alfred, ed.
  Poetic drama... New York,
  Modern age [c1941] 855p
Abraham, Melchisedec, and
  Isaac
Adam
Aeschylus. Agamemnon
Aristophanes. The Acharnians
Auden, W., and Isherwood, C.
  The dog beneath the skin
Buttomley, G. Gruach
The chalk circle
Corneille, P. Cinna
Euripides. Ion
Everyman
Goethe, J. Torquato Tasso
Hauptmann, G. The white
  saviour
Jonson, B. Volpone
Kreymborg, A. Hole in the
  wall
MacLeish, A. The fall of the
  city
Marlowe, C. Tamburlaine the
  great, pt. I
Massinger, P. A new way to
  pay old debts
Millay, E. Aria da capo
Molière, J. The misanthrope
Moody, W. The death of Eve
Racine, J. Athaliah
Rostand, E. The last night of
  Don Juan

Sachs, H. The wandering
  scholar from Paradise
Schiller, F. The death of
  Wallenstein
Schwartz, D. Shenandoah
Seami. Nakamitsu
The second shepherds' play
Shakespeare, W. Measure for
  measure
Shelley, P. The Cenci
Sophocles. Oedipus coloneus
Vega Carpio, L. de. The
  sheep well
Webster, J. The white devil
Yeats, W. The king's thresh-
  old

KRONENBERGER, LOUIS See
  also BES Best plays of
  1894/99-1961/62

KRM Kronenberger, Louis, ed.
  Cavalcade of comedy...
  New York, Simon and Schu-
  ster [c1953] 715p
Congreve, W. Love for love
Congreve, W. The way of the
  world
Coward, N. Blithe spirit
Etherege, G. The man of
  mode
Goldsmith, O. She stoops to
  conquer
Jonson, B. The alchemist
Jonson, B. Volpone
Kelly, G. The show-off
Maugham, W. The circle
Mayer, E. Children of dark-
  ness
O'Casey, S. Juno and the pay-
  cock
Osborn, P. Morning's at sev-
  en
Shaw, G. Androcles and the
  lion
Shaw, G. Pygmalion
Sheridan, R. The school for
  scandal
Synge, J. The playboy of the
  western world
Thurber, J., and Nugent, E.
  The male animal
Vanbrugh, J. The confederacy

234

Van Druten, J. The voice of the turtle
Wilde, O. The importance of being earnest
Wycherley, W. The country wife

KRO Kronenberger, Louis, ed. An eighteenth century miscellany... New York, Putnam, 1936. 578p
Gay, J. The beggar's opera
Sheridan, R. The school for scandal

KRON Kronenberger, Louis, ed. The pleasure of their company... New York, Knopf, 1946. 653p
Congreve, W. The way of the world

L

LAN Lancaster, Henry Carrington, ed. ... Five French farces, 1655-1694?... Baltimore, Johns Hopkins press, 1937. 141p (The Johns Hopkins studies in Romance literatures and languages, v29)
Boisrobert, F. L'amant ridicule
Le docteur amoureux
Donneau de Visé, J. Le gentilhomme guespin
Raisin, J. Merlin gascon
Villiers, C. L'apoticaire devalisé

LAP Landis, Paul Nissley, ed. Four famous Greek plays ... New York, Modern library [1929] 285p
Aeschylus. Agamemnon
Aristophanes. The frogs
Euripides. Medea
Sophocles. Oedipus the king

LAUGHLIN, JAMES. See NEW
New directions in prose and poetry...

LAUREL DRAMA SERIES. See HEWE Hewes, Henry, ed. Famous American plays of The 1940's... HOUG Houghton, Norris, ed. Great Russian plays... MACG Macgowan, Kenneth, ed. Famous American plays of the 1920's...

LAW Law, Frederick Houk, ed. Modern plays, short and long... New York, Century, 1924. 429p
Archer, W. The green goddess
Church, V. What men live by
Corneau, P. Masks
Dean, A. Just neighborly
Gilbert, W. Iolanthe
Idzumo, T. Bushido
Mackay, C. Benjamin Franklin, journeyman
MacMillan, D. Off Nags head
Macmillan, M. The pioneers
Mick, H. The maid who wouldn't be proper
Rip van Winkle

LAWR Lawrence, Robert G., ed. Early seventeenth century drama... New York, Dutton [c1963] 390p
Dekker, T. The shoemakers' holiday; or, The gentle craft
Heywood, T. A woman killed with kindness
Marston, J., and Webster, J. The malcontent
Massinger, P. A new way to pay old debts
Middleton, T., and Rowley, W. The changeling

LEG Le Gallienne, Eva, ed. Eva Le Gallienne's Civic repertory plays... New York, Norton [c1928] 327p
Chekhov, A. Three sisters
Goldoni, C. La locandiera
Ibsen, H. Hedda Gabler
Wied, G. 2 x 2 = 5

LEIS   Leishman, J. B., ed.
The three Parnassus plays
(1598-1601)... London, Ivor
Nicholson & Watson, 1949.
398p
The first part of the return
from Parnassus.
The pilgrimage to Parnassus.
The second part of the return
from Parnassus.

LEV   Leverton, Garrett Hasty,
ed.   Plays for the college
theater... New York, French,
1932. 629p
Ames, W.   A kiss in Xanadu
Atlas, L.   "L"
Barry, P.   Hotel Universe
Boucicault, D.   Belle Lamar
Britton, K., and Hargrave, R.
Houseparty
Buckingham, G.   The rehearsal
Elser, F.   Low bridge
Everyman
France, A.   The man who
married a dumb wife
Gammer Gurton's needle
Green, P.   The Lord's will
Ibsen, H.   The wild duck
Kaufman, G.   The butter and
egg man
Kreymborg, A.   Lima beans
Levy, B.   Springtime for Henry
Martínez Sierra, G.   The two
shepherds
Molière, J.   The doctor in
spite of himself
Molnár, F.   Liliom
O'Neill, E.   The moon of the
Caribbees
Riggs, L.   Green grow the
lilacs
Rostand, E.   Cyrano de Ber-
gerac
Sardou, V.   Patrie!
Scala, F.   The portrait
Schnitzler, A.   The green
cockatoo
Shay, F.   A Christmas carol
Strong, A.   The drums of Oude
Vildrac, C.   Michel Auclair
The York nativity

LEVE   Leverton, Garrett Hasty,
ed.   Plays for the college
theater... New York, French,
1934. 601p
Ames, W.   A kiss in Xanadu
Atlas, L.   "L"
Barry, P.   Hotel Universe
Boucicault, D.   Belle Lamar
Britton, K., and Hargrave, R.
Houseparty
Buckingham, G.   The re-
hearsal
Everyman
France, A.   The man who
married a dumb wife
Gammer Gurton's needle
Green, P.   The Lord's will
Ibsen, H.   The wild duck
Kaufman, G.   The butter and
egg man
Kreymborg, A.   Lima beans
Levy, B.   Springtime for
Henry
Martínez Sierra, G.   The two
shepherds
Molière, J.   The doctor in
spite of himself
Molnár, F.   Liliom
O'Neill, E.   The moon of the
Caribbees
Riggs, L.   Green grow the
lilacs
Rostand, E.   Cyrano de Ber-
gerac
Sardou, V.   Patrie!
Scala, F.   The portrait
Schnitzler, A.   The green
cockatoo
Shay, F.   A Christmas carol
Strong, A.   The drums of
Oude
Vildrac, C.   Michel Auclair
The York nativity

LEVI   Levin, Richard Louis, ed.
Tragedy; Plays, theory,
criticism... New York, Har-
court, Brace & World
[c1960] 217p
Ibsen, H.   Ghosts
O'Neill, E.   The hairy ape
Seneca, L.   Oedipus
Shakespeare, W.   Othello

Sophocles. Oedipus rex

LEWI Lewisohn, Ludwig, ed. A-
mong the nations... New York,
Farrar. Strauss [c1948] 270p
Galsworthy, J. Loyalties

LIBRARY OF BEST AMERICAN
PLAYS See GARW, GARZ,
GAS, GASB Gassner, John,
ed. ...

LIBRARY OF WORLD DRAMA. See
FLOS Flores, Angel, ed.
Spanish drama... GARZB
Gassner, John, ed. Medieval
and Tudor drama... GARZE
Gassner, John, ed. 19th cent.
Russian drama... GARZJ
Gassner, John, ed. 20th cent.
Russian drama.

LIBR Library of universal literature... New York, Alden bros.
[c1906] [701]p
Addison, J. Cato

LIE Lieder, Paul Robert; Lovett,
Robert Morss and Root, Ro-
bert Kilburn, eds. British
drama... Boston, Houghton
Mifflin [c1929] 374p
Beaumont, F., and Fletcher, J.
Philaster; or, Love lies a-
bleeding
The Brome Abraham and Isaac
Congreve, W. The way of the
world
Dryden, J. All for love; or, The
world well lost
Everyman
Jonson, B. The alchemist
Marlowe, C. The tragical his-
tory of Dr. Faustus
The second shepherds' play
Sheridan, R. The school for
scandal
Wilde, O. Lady Windermere's fan

LIED Lieder, Paul Robert; Lovett,
Robert Morss and Root, Robert Kilburn, eds. British
prose and poetry. Revised ed.
Boston, Houghton Mifflin
[c1938] 2v

Dryden, J. All for love.   1
Jonson, B. Volpone.   1
Marlowe, C. Dr. Faustus.   1
Second shepherds' play.   1
Sheridan, R. The school for
scandal.   1
Synge, J. The playboy of
the western world.   2
Wilde, O. Lady Winder-
mere's fan.   2

LIEE Lieder, Paul Robert;
Lovett, Robert Morss and
Root, Robert Kilburn, eds.
British poetry and prose.
Third edition... Boston,
Houghton Mifflin [c1950]
2v
Dryden, J. All for love.   1
Jonson, B. Alchemist.   1
Marlowe, C. Dr. Faustus.   1
The second shepherd's
play.   1
Sheridan, R. The school for
scandal.   1
Synge, J. Playboy of the
western world.   2
Wilde, O. Lady Windermere's
fan.   2

LIND Lind, Levi Robert, ed.
Ten Greek plays in con-
temporary translations...
Boston, Houghton Mifflin
[c1957] 419p
Aeschylus. Agamemnon
Aeschylus. Prometheus bound
Aristophanes. Lysistrata
Euripides. Alcestis
Euripides. Andromache
Euripides. Bacchae
Euripides. Suppliants
Sophocles. Antigone
Sophocles. Oedipus rex
Sophocles. Philoctetes

THE LITERATURE OF ITALY,
1265-1907. See JOH
Johnson, Rossiter, ed.
An anthology of Italian au-
thors from Cavalcanti to
Fogazzaro...

LOC Locke, Alain Le Roy, and
Montgomery, Gregory, eds.
Plays of Negro life... New
York, Harper, 1927. 430p
Bruce, R. Sahdji, an African
ballet
Culbertson, E. Rackey
Duncan, T. The death dance
Green, P. In Abraham's bosom
Green, P. The no'count boy
Green, P. White dresses
Johnson, G. Plumes
Matheus, J. 'Cruiter
O'Neill, E. The dreamy kid
O'Neill, E. The Emperor
Jones
Richardson, W. The broken
banjo
Richardson, W. The flight of
the natives
Rogers, J. Judge Lynch
Spence, E. The starter
Toomer, J. Balo
Torrence, R. The danse Ca-
linda
Torrence, R. Granny Maumee
Torrence, R. The rider of
dreams
White, L. The bird child
Wilson, F. Sugar cane

LOCK Locke, Louis Glenn; Gib-
son, William M., and
Arms, George, eds. Intro-
duction to literature... New
York, Rinehart [c1948]
592p (Readings for liberal
education. v2)
Euripides. Alcestis
Marlowe, C. Doctor Faustus
O'Neill, E. The Emperor
Jones
Thurber, J., and Nugent, E.
The male animal

LOCL Locke, Louis Glenn;
Gibson, William M., and
Arms, George, eds. Intro-
duction to literature... Re-
vised edition. New York,
Rinehart [c1952] 749p
(Readings for liberal edu-
cation, v2)

Cocteau, J. The infernal ma-
chine
Ibsen, H. Hedda Gabler
Marlowe, C. The tragical
history of Doctor Faustus
O'Neill, E. The long voyage
home
Sophocles. Oedipus the king

LOCLA Locke, Louis Glenn;
Gibson, William M., and
Arms, George, eds. Intro-
duction to literature. Third
edition... New York, Rinehart [c1957] 864p (Read-
ings for liberal education,
v2)
Cocteau, J. The infernal machine
Ibsen, H. Hedda Gabler
Molière, J. The bourgeois
gentleman
O'Neill, E. The long voyage
home
Shaw, G. The devil's disciple
Sophocles. Oedipus the king
Synge, J. In the shadow of
the glen

LOCLB Locke, Louis Glenn;
Gibson, William and Arms,
George, eds. Introduction
to literature. Fourth edi-
tion... New York, Holt,
Rinehart and Winston [c1962]
(Readings for liberal educa-
tion, v2)
Cocteau, J. The infernal ma-
chine
Garcia Lorca, F. Blood wed-
ding
Ibsen, H. Hedda Gabler
O'Neill, E. The long voyage
home
Shaw, G. Candida
Sophocles. Oedipus the king

LOCM Locke, Louis Glenn;
Kirby, John P., and Porter,
M. E., eds. Literature of
western civilization... New
York, Ronald [c1952] 2v
Aeschylus. Agamemnon.   1

238

Aristophanes. Lysistrata. 1
Euripides. Medea. 1
Goethe, J. Faust, pt. I. 2
Ibsen, H. Rosmersholm. 2
Molière, J. The misanthrope.
 2
Plautus, T. Amphitryon. 1
Racine, J. Phaedra. 2
Shakespeare, W. Hamlet. 1
Vega Carpio, L. The king
 the greatest Alcalde. 1
Sophocles. Oedipus the king. 1

LOCR Lockert, Lacy, ed., and
 tr. The chief rivals of
 Corneille and Racine...
 Nashville, Vanderbilt Uni-
 versity Press; c1956. 605p
Campistron, J. Andronicus
Corneille, T. The earl of
 Essex
Corneille, T. Laodice
Crebillon, P. Rhadamistus
 and Zenobia
Du Ryer, P. Saul
Du Ryer, P. Scaevola
Hermite, T. Mariamne
La Fosse, A. Manlius Capi-
 tolinus
Mairet, J. Sophonisba
Rotrou, J. Chosroes
Rotrou, J. Wenceshaus
Voltaire, F. Zaire

LOGG Loggins, Vernon, ed.
 Three great French plays...
 Greenwich, Connecticut,
 Fawcett [c1961] 256p
Corneille, P. Polyeucte
Molière, J. The hypochondri-
 ac
Racine, J. Phèdre

LON London omnibus, with an
 introduction by Carl Van
 Doren, Garden City, N.Y.,
 Doubleday, Doran, 1932.
 v.p.
Coward, N. Private lives

LOO Loomis, Roger Sherman
 and Clark, Donald Leman,
 eds. Modern English read-

ings...New York, Farrar
 and Rinehart, 1934. 892p
Lawson, J. Success story
O'Neill, E. The moon of the
 Caribbees
Wilde, O. The importance of
 being earnest

LOOA Loomis, Roger Sherman,
 and Clark, Donald Leman,
 eds. Modern English readings. Rev. ed. ...New
 York, Farrar and Rine-
 hart, 1936. 1074p
Anderson, M. Both your
 houses
Connelly, M. The green pastures
O'Neill, E. Beyond the horizon
Synge, J. Riders to the sea
Wilde, O. The importance of
 being earnest

LOOB Loomis, Roger Sherman,
 and Clark, Donald Leman,
 eds. Modern English readings. 3rd ed. ...New
 York, Farrar and Rinehart,
 1939. 1147p
Anderson, M. Both your
 houses
Connelly, M. The green pastures
MacLeish, A. The fall of the
 city
O'Neill, E. Beyond the horizon
Synge, J. Riders to the sea

LOOC Loomis, Roger Sherman,
 and Clark, Donald Leman,
 eds. Modern English readings. 4th ed. ...New
 York, Farrar and Rine-
 hart, 1942. 968p
Connelly, M. The green pastures
Hart, M., and Kaufman, G.
 You can't take it with you
MacLeish, A. The fall of the
 city
O'Neill, E. Beyond the hori-

LOOC (continued)
zon
Synge, J. Riders to the sea

LOOD Loomis, Roger Sherman,
and Clark, Donald Leman,
eds. Modern English read-
ings. Fifth edition... New
York, Rinehart [c1946]
1062p
Connelly, M. The green pas-
tures
Corwin, N. Good heavens
Hart, M., and Kaufman, G.
You can't take it with you
MacLeish, A. The fall of the
city
O'Neill, E. Beyond the hori-
zon
Synge, J. Riders to the sea

LOOE Loomis, Roger Sherman,
and Clark, Donald Leman,
eds. Modern English read-
ings. Sixth edition... New
York, Rinehart [c1950]
1061p
Connelly, M. The green pastures
Hart, M., and Kaufman, G.
You can't take it with you
MacLeish, A. The fall of the
city
O'Neill, E. Beyond the horizon
Synge, J. Riders to the sea

LOOF Loomis, Roger Sherman;
Clark, Donald Leman, and
Middendorf, John Harlan,
eds. Modern English read-
ings. Seventh edition...
New York, Rinehart [c1956]
1097p
Hart, M., and Kaufman, G.
You can't take it with you
O'Neill, E. Beyond the hori-
zon
Shaw, G. Arms and the man
Synge, J. Riders to the sea

LOOM Loomis, Roger Sherman
and Wells, Henry Willis,

eds. Representative med-
ieval and Tudor plays,
translated and modernized
...New York, Sheed &
Ward, 1942. 301p
The annunciation
Heywood, J. John, Tyb, and
Sir John
Heywood, J. The pardoner
and the friar
Hilarius. The miracle of
Saint Nicholas and the im-
age
La Vigne, Andrieu de. The
miracle of the blind man
and the cripple
The miracle of Saint Nichol-
as and the school boys
The miracle of Saint Nichol-
as and the virgins
The mystery of the redemp-
tion
The second shepherds' play
The summoning of Everyman

LOR Lovell, Ernest James,
and Pratt, Willis W., eds.
Modern drama: An anthol-
ogy of nine plays...Boston,
Ginn [c1963] 425p
Anderson, M. The wingless
victory
Duncan, R. The death of Sa-
tan
Euripides. Medea
Giraudoux, J. Electra
Ibsen, H. Hedda Gabler
Maugham, W. The constant
wife
Miller, A. The crucible
O'Neill, E. A moon for the
misbegotten
Shaw, G. Caesar and Cleo-
patra

LOV Lovett, Robert Morss,
and Jones, Howard Mum-
ford, eds. The college
reader...Boston, Houghton
Mifflin [c1936] 1099p
Archer, W. The green god-
dess
Sherriff, R. Journey's end

LOVR Lovrien, Marian; Potell,
Herbert and Bostwich,
Prudence, eds. Adventures
in living... New York, Har-
court, Brace, 1955. 626p
(Adventures in literature
series)
Corwin, N. Ann Rutledge
Duffield, B. The lottery
Law, W. Indomitable black-
smith
Lindsay, H., and Crouse, R.
Life with father
Martens, A. Blue beads
Richmond, S. Career for
Ralph

LOW Lowe, Orton, ed. Our
land and its literature...
New York, Harper, 1936.
666p
Vollmer, L. Sun-up

LUCA Lucas, Frank Laurence.
Greek drama for everyman
... London, J.M. Dent
[1954] 454p
Aeschylus. Agamemnon
Aeschylus. Prometheus bound
Aristophanes. The clouds
Euripides. The bacchae
Euripides. Hippolytus
Sophocles. Antigone
Sophocles. Oedipus the king

LUCAS, HARRIET MARCELLA.
See PROD Prose and po-
etry for appreciation...

LUST Lustig, Theodore H., tr.
Classical German drama...
With an introduction by
Victor Lange... New York,
Bantam Books [c1963] 466p
Büchner, G. Danton's death
Goethe, J. Egmont
Kleist, H. The prince of
Homburg
Lessing, G. Nathan the wise
Schiller, J. Mary Stuart

LYMAN, WILLIAM WHITTING-
HAM. See TOD Today's

literature...

LYK Lyons, Eugene, ed. ...
Six Soviet plays... Boston,
Houghton Mifflin, 1934.
[469]p
Afinogenyev, A. Fear
Bulgakov, M. Days of the
Turbins
Glebov, A. Inga
Katayev, V. Squaring the
circle
Krishon, V. Bread
Pogodin, N. Tempo

LYO Lyons, John Coriden and
Searles, Colbert, eds.
Eight French classic plays
... New York, Holt [c1932]
609p
Corneille, P. Le cid
Corneille, P. Le menteur
Corneille, P. Polyeucte
Molière, J. Le misanthrope
Molière, J. Les précieuses
ridicules
Molière, J. Le Tartuffe; ou
L'imposteur
Racine, J. Andromaque
Racine, J. Phèdre

M

MACG Macgowan, Kenneth, ed.
Famous American plays of
the 1920's... [New York,
Dell, c1959] 511p (Laurel
drama series)
Anderson, M., and Stallings,
L. What price glory?
Barry, P. Holiday
Heyward, D., and Heyward,
D. Porgy
Howard, S. They knew what
they wanted
O'Neill, E. The moon of the
Caribbees
Rice, E. Street scene

MACH Machiz, Herbert, ed.
Artists' theatre: four plays
... New York, Grove
[c1960] 224p

MACH (continued)
  Abel, L. Absalom
  Ashbery, J. The heroes
  Merrill, J. The bait
  O'Hara, F. Try! Try!

MACJ Mack, Maynard [and
  others], eds. The conti-
  nental edition of world
  masterpieces... New York,
  W. W. Norton [c1962]
  1971p
  Aeschylus. Agamemnon
  Euripides. Medea
  Goethe, J. Faust, pts. 1 & 2
  Ibsen, H. The wild duck
  Molière, J. The bourgeois
    gentleman
  Racine, J. Phaedra
  Sophocles. King Oedipus

MACK Mack, Maynard, ed. ...
  The Augustans... New York,
  Prentice-Hall, 1950. 343p
  (English masterpieces. v5)
  Gay, J. The beggar's opera

MACL Mack, Maynard [and
  others] eds. World master-
  pieces... New York, W. W.
  Norton [c1956] 2v
  Aeschylus. Agamemnon.   1
  Euripides. Medea.   1
  Goethe, J. Faust, pts. 1
    & 2   2
  Ibsen, H. The wild duck.   2
  Molière, J. The bourgeois
    gentleman.   2
  Racine, J. Phaedra.   2
  Shakespeare, W. Hamlet,
    Prince of Denmark.   1
  Sophocles. King Oedipus.   1
  Synge, J. The playboy of
    the western world.   2

MAGA Magarshack, David, tr.
  The storm, and other Rus-
  sian plays... New York,
  Hill and Wang [c1960] 362p
  (Mermaid dramabook)
  Chekhov, A. Uncle Vanya
  Gogol, N. The government
    inspector

Gorky, M. The lower depths
Ostrovsky, A. The storm
Tolstoy, L. The power of
  darkness

MAK Malcolmson, Anne (Bur-
  nett), adapter. Miracle
  plays; seven medieval
  plays for modern players
  ... Boston, Houghton Miff-
  lin [c1956, 1959] 142p
  Abraham and Isaac
  Herod and the magi
  The nativity
  Noah's flood
  Saint Nicholas and the three
    scholars
  The shepherds' play
  Hilarius. The statue of Saint
    Nicholas

MALINE, JULIAN L. See PROI
  Prose and poetry of A-
  merica...

MALLON, WILFRED M. See
  PROI Prose and poetry of
  America...

MAL Malvern festival plays
  MCMXXXIII, arranged for
  production by H. K. Ayliff.
  With an introduction by
  Hugh Walpole and a pref-
  ace by Sir Barry Jackson.
  London, Heath Cranton,
  1933. 343p
  The conversion of St. Paul
  Dryden, J. All for love
  Heywood, T. The fair maid
    of the west
  Jones, H. The dancing girl
  Knowles, J. The love-chase
  "Mr. S., master of arts."
  Gammer Gurton's needle

MANTLE, R. BURNS. See BES
  Best plays of 1894/1899...
  etc. See also TRE, TREA
  A treasury of the theatre
  ...

MARNAU, FRED. See NEWR

242

MAT (continued)
  reign and lamentable death
  of Edward the second
Massinger, P. A new way to
  pay old debts
Otway, T. Venice preserved;
  or, A plot discovered
Pinero, A. The second Mrs.
  Tanqueray
Robertson, T. Caste
The second shepherds' play
Sheridan, R. The school for
  scandal
Udall, N. Ralph Roister
  Doister
Vanbrugh, J. The provoked
  wife
Webster, J. The Duchess of
  Malfi
Wilde, O. Lady Windermere's
  fan
Wycherley, W. The plain
  dealer

MAU Matthews, Brander, ed.
  The chief European drama-
  tists... Boston, Houghton
  Mifflin [c1916] 786p
Aeschylus. Agamemnon
Aristophanes. The frogs
Augier, É., and Sandeau, J.
  The son-in-law of M.
  Poerier
Beaumarchais, P. The barber
  of Seville
Calderón de la Barca, P.
  Life is a dream
Corneille, P. The cid
Dumas, A. fils. The outer
  edge of society
Euripides. Medea
Goethe, J. Goetz von Ber-
  lichingen
Goldoni, C. The mistress of
  the inn
Holberg, L. Rasmus Mon-
  tanus
Hugo, V. Hernani
Ibsen, H. A doll's house
Lessing, G. Minna von Barn-
  helm
Molière, J. Tartuffe
Plautus, T. The captives

Racine, J. Phaedra
Schiller, J. William Tell
Sophocles. Oedipus the king
Terence, P. Phormio
Vega Carpio, L. de. The star
  of Seville

McCALLUM, JAMES DOW.
  See also HAP Harbrace
  omnibus...

MCCA McCallum, James Dow,
  ed. The college omnibus
  ... New York, Harcourt,
  Brace, 1933. 832p
O'Neill, E. The Emperor
  Jones
Synge, J. Riders to the sea

MCCB McCallum, James Dow,
  ed. The college omnibus
  ... New York, Harcourt,
  Brace [c1934] 982p
Galsworthy, J. Strife
O'Neill, E. The Emperor
  Jones
Synge, J. Riders to the sea

MCCD McCallum, James Dow,
  ed. The 1936 college omni-
  bus... in collaboration with
  Marston Balch, Percy
  Marks... [and others]. New
  York, Harcourt, Brace
  [c1936] 1193p
Galsworthy, J. Strife
O'Neill, E. The Emperor
  Jones
Rostand, E. Cyrano de Ber-
  gerac

MCCF McCallum, James Dow,
  ed. The revised college
  omnibus... in collaboration
  with Marston Balch, Ralph
  P. Boas, Percy Marks
  [and others]. New York,
  Harcourt, Brace, 1939.
  1258p
Galsworthy, J. Strife
MacLeish, A. Air raid
O'Neill, E. The Emperor
  Jones

244

Rostand, E. Cyrano de Bergerac

MCCG McCallum, James Dow, ed. The college omnibus. 6th edition... in collaboration with Marston Balch, Ralph P. Boas, Percy Marks, Benfield Pressey, Louis Untermeyer. New York, Harcourt, Brace [c1947] 1288p
Galsworthy, J. Strife
Nichols, R., and Browne, M. Wings over Europe
O'Neill, E. The Emperor Jones
Rostand, E. Cyrano de Bergerac

MCCL MacClelland, George William, and Baugh, Albert Croll, eds. Century types of English literature chronologically arranged... New York, Century, 1925. 1144p
Dekker, T. The shoemakers' holiday
Dryden, J. All for love
Sheridan, R. The school for scandal
Wilde, O. Lady Windermere's fan

MCCP McClintock, Marshall, ed. The Noble prize treasury... Garden City, N. Y., Doubleday, 1948. 612p
Benavente, J. His widow's husband
Bjørnson, B. Between the battles
Echegaray, J. The street singer
Hauptmann, G. The sunken bell
Maeterlinck, M. Interior
O'Neill, E. Desire under the elms
Pirandello, L. Our lord of the ships
Yeats, W. The land of heart's desire

McCORKLE, J. N. See HAP Harbrace omnibus...

MCD McDermott, John Francis, ed. Modern plays... New York, Harcourt, Brace ᴗ [c1932] 427p
Capek, K. R. U. R.
Howard, S. They knew what they wanted
Hughes, H. Hell bent fer heaven
Ibsen, H. A doll's house
Maugham, W. The circle
Milne, A. Mr. Pim passes by
O'Neill, E. The Emperor Jones

MCDL McDowell, Tremaine, ed. America in literature ... New York, Crofts, 1944. 540p
Connelly, M. The green pastures
Wilder, T. Our town

MCDO McDowell, Tremaine, ed. The romantic triumph; American literature from 1830 to 1860... New York, Macmillan, 1933. 744p (American literature: a period anthology; Oscar Cargill, general editor. v2)
Boker, G. Francesca da Rimini

McGRAW, H. WARD. See PROB Prose and poetry for appreciation... PROF, PROG, PROH Prose and poetry of America... PROM, PRON Prose and poetry of England...

MCI McIlwraith, Archibald Kennedy, ed. Five Elizabethan comedies... London, Oxford university press [1934] 308p (The world's classics)

MCI (continued)
Dekker, T. The shoemakers'
holiday
Greene, R. Friar Bacon and
Friar Bungay
Lyly, J. Campaspe
The merry devil of Edmonton
Peele, G. The old wives' tale

MCJ McIlwraith, Archibald Ken-
nedy, ed. Five Elizabethan
tragedies... London, Oxford
university press [1938]
399p (The world's classics)
Arden of Feversham
Heywood, T. A woman killed
with kindness
Kyd, T. The Spanish tragedy
Norton, T., and Sackville, T.
Gorboduc
Seneca, L. Thyestes

MCK McIlwraith, Archibald Ken-
nedy, ed. Five Stuart
tragedies... London, Oxford
university press [1953]
497p (The world's classics)
Beaumont, F., and Fletcher,
J. The maid's tragedy
Chapman, G. Bussy D'Ambois
Ford, J. 'Tis pity she's a
whore
Massinger, P. The Roman
actor
Webster, J. The Duchess of
Malfi

MCKK MacKendrick, Paul, and
Howe, Herbert M., eds.
Classics in translation.
Madison, Wisconsin, The
university of Wisconsin
press, 1952. 2v
Aeschylus. Agamemnon.   1
Aristophanes. Frogs.   1
Euripides. Medea.   1
Plautus. The haunted house. 2
Seneca. Medea.   2
Sophocles. Antigone.   1
Terence. Woman from
Andros.   2

MCKL McLean, Hugh and Vick-

ery, Walter N., eds. and
trs. The year of protest,
1956: An anthology of So-
viet literary materials...
New York, Random House
[c1961] 269p
Alyoshin, S. Alone

MCL McMahon, Agnes; Krauss,
Franklin Brunell, and
Carter, James Franklin,
eds. Explorations in
French literature... New
York, Nelson, 1939. 538p
Labiche, E. Le voyage de
Monsieur Perrichon

MCM MacMillan, Dougald, and
Jones, Howard Mumford,
eds. Plays of the restora-
tion and eighteenth century
... New York, Holt, 1931.
896p
Addison, J. Cato
Cibber, G. Love's last shift
Colman, G., and Garrick, D.
The clandestine marriage
Congreve, W. The way of the
world
Cumberland, R. The West
Indian
D'Avenant, W. The siege of
Rhodes, pt. I
Dryden, J. All for love
Dryden, J., and Howard, R.
The Indian queen
Etherege, G. The man of
mode
Farquhar, G. The beaux'
stratagem
Gay, J. The beggar's opera
Goldsmith, O. She stoops to
conquer
Home, J. Douglas
Kelly, H. False delicacy
Kotzebue, A. The stranger
Lee, N. The rival queens
Lillo, G. The London mer-
chant
Otway, T. Venice preserved
Rowe, N. The fair penitent
Shadwell, T. The squire of
Alsatia

Sheridan, R. The school for
scandal
Steele, R. The conscious
lovers
Vanbrugh, J. The relapse
Villiers, G., and others. The
rehearsal

MCMI MacMillan, Dougald and
Jones, Howard Mumford,
eds. Plays of the restora-
tion and eighteenth century
...New York, Holt [1938]
961p
Addison, J. Cato
Cibber, C. Love's last shift
Colman, G., and Garrick, D.
The clandestine marriage
Congreve, W. The way of the
world
Cumberland, R. The West
Indian
D'Avenant, W. The siege of
Rhodes, pt. I
Dryden, J. All for love
Dryden, J., and Howard, R.
The Indian queen
Etherege, G. The man of
mode
Farquhar, G. The beaux'
stratagem
Gay, J. The beggar's opera
Goldsmith, O. She stoops to
conquer
Home, J. Douglas
Kelly, H. False delicacy
Kotzbue, A. The stranger
Lee, N. The rival queens
Lillo, G. The London mer-
chant
Otway, T. Venice preserved
Rowe, N. The fair penitent
Shadwell, T. The squire of
Alsatia
Sheridan, R. The school for
scandal
Steele, R. The conscious
lovers
Vanbrugh, J. The relapse
Villiers, G., and others. The
rehearsal
Wycherley, W. The plain-
dealer

MCNA McNamee, Maurice B.;
Cronin, James E., and
Rogers, Joseph A., eds.
Literary types and themes.
New York, Rinehart
[c1960] 705p
Anouilh, J. Antigone
Barrie, J. The twelve-pound
look
Chayefsky, P. Marty
Miller, A. Death of a sales-
man
Williams, T. The glass me-
nagerie

MCNI McNiff, William T., ed.
The beginnings of English
literature...New York,
Macmillan [c1961] 198p
Everyman
Marlowe, C. The tragedy of
Doctor Faustus

MEN Mendenhall, John Cooper,
ed. English literature,
1650-1800...Chicago, Lip-
pincott [c1940] 1166p
Congreve, W. The way of the
world
Dryden, J. Aureng-zebe
Otway, T. Venice preserv'd

MERC Mercier, Vivian, and
Greene, David H., eds.
1000 years of Irish prose.
Part I. The literary re-
vival...New York, Devin-
Adair, 1952. 607p
O'Casey, S. The shadow of a
gunman
Synge, J. In the shadow of
the glen
Yeats, W. Cathleen ni Houli-
han
Yeats, W. The resurrection

MERS Mersand, Joseph E., ed.
Three comedies of Ameri-
can family life..New York,
Washington Square Press
[c1961] 314p
Kaufman, G., and Hart, M.
You can't take it with you

MERS (continued)
Lindsay, H., and Crouse, R.
Life with father
Van Druten, J. I remember
mama

MERT Mersand, Joseph E., ed.
Three dramas of American
individualism... New York,
Washington Square Press
[c1961] 266p
Anderson, M. High Tor
Lavery, E. The magnificent
Yankee
Odets, C. Golden boy

MERU Mersand, Joseph E., ed.
Three dramas of American
realism... New York, Washington Square Press [c1961]
312p
Rice, E. Street scene
Saroyan, W. The time of your
life
Sherwood, R. Idiot's delight

MERV Mersand, Joseph E., ed.
Three plays about doctors
... New York, Washington
Square Press [c1961] 294p
Howard, S., and DeKruif, P.
Yellow jack
Ibsen, H. An enemy of the
people
Kingsley, S. Men in white

MERW Mersand, Joseph E., ed.
Three plays about marriage
... New York, Washington
Square Press [c1962] 298p
Barry, P. Holiday
Howard, S. They knew what
they wanted
Kelly, G. Craig's wife

MLJ Miller, Edwin Lillie, ed.
Explorations in literature
... Chicago, Lippincott
[c1933-34] 2v
Gilbert, W. The mikado.   2
Shakespeare, W. Macbeth.   2

MLJA Miller, Edwin Lillie, ed.

Explorations in literature
... Rev. ed. ... Chicago,
Lippincott [c1937-38] 2v
O'Neill, E. The Emperor
Jones.   1
Shakespeare, W. Macbeth.   2
Tompkins, F. Sham.   1

MLJY Miller, Jordan Yale, ed.
American dramatic litera-
ture... New York, McGraw-
Hill, 1961. 641p
Behrman, S. Biography
Chase, M. Harvey
Haines, W. Command deci-
sion
Hellman, L. The little foxes
Heyward, D., and Heyward,
D. Porgy
McCullers, C. The member
of the wedding
Miller, A. The crucible
O'Neill, E. Desire under the
elms
Thurber, J., and Nugent, E.
The male animal
Williams, T. Camino real

MIK Miller, Marion Mills, ed.
The classics, Greek &
Latin... New York, V.
Parke [c1909-10] 15v
Aeschylus. Prometheus bound.
                             7
Aristophanes. The clouds.   7
Euripides. Medea.   7
Plautus, T. Captivi.   8
Plautus, T. Menaechmi.   8
Plautus, T. Miles glori-
osus.   8
Seneca, L. The phaedra; or,
Hippolytus.   8
Sophocles. Antigone.   7
Terence. Adelphi.   8
Terence. Heautonimoru-
menos.   8

MIKE Miller, Perry [and
others], eds. Major writers
of America... New York,
Harcourt, Brace & World
[c1962] 2v
O'Neill, E. The iceman

248

MIL Millett, Fred Benjamin,
and Bentley, Gerald Eades,
eds. The play's the thing
... New York, Appleton-
Century [c1936] 571p
Belasco, D. The return of
Peter Grimm
Chekhov, A. Uncle Vanya
Chester play of the deluge
Congreve, W. Love for love
Cumberland, W. The West
Indian
Dryden, J. All for love
Euripides. Hippolytus
Gregory, I. Hyacinth Halvey
Howard, S. Ned McCobb's
daughter
Ibsen, H. Ghosts
Maeterlinck, M. Interior
Marlowe, C. Doctor Faustus
Molière, J. The misanthrope
O'Neill, E. The hairy ape
Plautus, T. The haunted
house
Racine, J. Phaedra
Rostand, E. Cyrano de Berge-
rac
Shakespeare, W. Antony and
Cleopatra
Shakespeare, W. Twelfth night
Sophocles. Oedipus, king of
Thebes
Strong, A. The drums of Oude

MILL Millett, Fred Benjamin.
Reading drama; a method of
analysis with selections
for study... New York,
Harper, [c1950] 252p
Barrie, J. The will
O'Neill, E. Beyond the hori-
zon
Schnitzler, A. A farewell
supper
Synge, J. Riders to the sea
Wilder, T. The long Christ-
mas dinner
Yeats, W. Cathleen ni Houli-
han

MIN Minor Elizabethan drama

... London, Dent [1913]
2v (Everyman's library)
Arden of Feversham. 1
Greene, R. Friar Bacon and
Friar Bungay. 2
Greene, R. James the
fourth. 2
Kyd, T. The Spanish
tragedy. 1
Lyly, J. Endimion. 2
Norton, T., and Sackville,
T. (Lord Buckhurst)
Gorboduc. 1
Peele, G. David and Beth-
sabe. 1
Peele, G. The old wives'
tale. 2
Udall, N. Ralph Roister
Doister. 2

MIO Minor Elizabethan drama
... London, Dent [1939] 2v
(Everyman's library)
Arden of Feversham. 1
Greene, R. Friar Bacon and
Friar Bungay. 2
Greene, R. James the
fourth. 2
Kyd, T. The Spanish
tragedy. 1
Lyly, J. Endimion. 2
Norton, T., and Sackville,
T. (Lord Buckhurst)
Gorboduc. 1
Peele, G. David and Beth-
sabe. 1
Peele, G. The old wives'
tale. 2
Preston, T. Cambyses. 1
Udall, N. Ralph Roister
Doister. 2

MOD Modern plays... London,
Dent [1937] 354p (Every-
man's library)
Bennett, A., and Knoblock,
E. Milestones
Coward, N. Hay fever
Maugham, W. For services
rendered
Milne, A. The Dover road
Sherriff, R. Journey's end

MODERN ENGLISH DRAMA.
See HARC Harvard clas-
sics, v18

MODS Modern Scandinavian
plays... New York, Live-
right [c1954] 366p
Kielland, T. Queen Margaret
of Norway
Munk, K. Egelykke
Strindberg, A. The great
highway
Sveinbjörnsson, T. Bishop Jón
Arason

MOO Moore, John Robert, ed.
Representative English
dramas... Boston, Ginn
[c1929] 461p
Dryden, J. All for love
Everyman
Goldsmith, O. She stoops to
conquer
Marlowe, C. The tragical his-
tory of Doctor Faustus
Sheridan, R. The school for
scandal
Wilde, O. Lady Windermere's
fan

MOR Morgan, Arthur Eustace,
comp. English plays,
1660-1820... New York,
Harper, 1935. 1157p
Addison, J. Cato
Buckstone, J. Luke, the
labourer
Colman, G., and Garrick, D.
The clandestine marriage
Congreve, W. The way of the
world
Cumberland, R. The West
Indian
Dryden, J. All for love; or,
The world well lost
Dryden, J. Almanzor and
Almahide; or, The conquest
of Granada by the Spaniards
Etherege, G. The man of
mode; or, Sir Fopling
Flutter
Farquhar, G. The beaux'
stratagem

Foote, S. The mayor of Gar-
ret
Gay, J. The beggar's opera
Goldsmith, O. She stoops to
conquer; or, The mistakes
of a night
Hoadly, B. The suspicious
husband
Home, J. Douglas
Lillo, G. The London mer-
chant
Morton, T. Speed the plough
Murphy, A. All in the wrong
Otway, T. Venice preserv'd;
or, A plot discover'd
Reynolds, F. The dramatist;
or, Stop him who can!
Shadwell, T. Bury-fair
Sheridan, R. The rivals
Steele, R. The conscious
lovers
Townley, J. High life below
the stairs
Vanbrugh, J. The relapse; or,
Virtue in danger
Wycherley, W. The plain-
dealer

MORR Morrell, Janet M., ed.
Four English comedies of
the 17th and 18th centuries
... Baltimore, Penguin
[Harmondsworth, Middle-
sex, 1950,... 1962] 414p
Congreve, W. The way of
the world
Goldsmith, O. She stoops to
conquer; or, The mistakes
of a night
Jonson, B. Volpone; or, The
fox
Sheridan, R. The school for
scandal

MOS Moscow art theatre series of Russian plays, ed.
by Oliver M. Sayler...
New York, Brentano
[c1923] v.p.
Chekhov, A. The cherry orchard
Chekhov, A. The three sisters

Chekhov, A. Uncle Vanya
Gorky, M. The lower depths
Tolstoĭ, A. Tsar Fyodor
Ivanovitch

MOSA Moscow art theatre series of Russian plays, direction of Morris Gest, ed. by Oliver M. Sayler. [2nd series] New York, Brentano [c1923] v.p.
Chekhov, A. Ivanoff
Dostoievsky, F. The brothers Karamazoff
Goldoni, C. The mistress of the inn
Ibsen, H. An enemy of the people
Ostrovsky, A. Enough stupidity in every wise man

MOSE Moses, Montrose Jonas, ed. British plays from the restoration to 1820...Boston, Little, Brown, 1929. 2v
Cibber, C. The careless husband.   1
Colman, G., and Garrick, D. The clandestine marriage.   2
Congreve, W. The way of the world.   1
Cumberland, R. The fashionable lover.   2
Dryden, J. The Spanish Fryar; or, The double discovery.   1
Etherege, G. The man of mode; or, Sir Fopling Flutter.   1
Farquhar, G. The beaux' stratagem.   2
Gay, J. The beggar's opera.   2
Goldsmith, O. She stoops to conquer; or, The mistakes of a night.   2
Home, J. Douglas.   2
Otway, T. Venice preserv'd; or, A plot discover'd.   1
Rowe, N. Jane Shore.   2
Shelley, P. The Cenci.   2

Sheridan, R. The school for scandal.   2
Steele, R. The conscious lovers.   1
Vanbrugh, J. The provok'd wife.   1
Villiers, G. The rehearsal.   1
Wycherley, W. The plaindealer.   1

MOSG Moses, Montrose Jonas, ed. Dramas of modernism and their forerunners ...Boston, Little Brown, 1931. 741p
Andreyev, L. He who gets slapped
Čapek, K., and Čapek, J. Adam the creator
Chekhov, A. The cherry orchard
Gorky, M. Night's lodging (The lower depths)
Howard, S. The silver cord
Kaiser, G. From morn to midnight
Kelly, G. Craig's wife
Lenormand, H. The dream doctor
Maugham, W. The circle
Milne, A. The truth about Blayds
Molnár, F. Liliom
Nichols, R., and Browne, M. Wings over Europe
O'Neill, E. Desire under the elms
Pirandello, L. Right you are! (If you think so)
Strindberg, A. There are crimes and crimes
Toller, E. The machine wreckers

MOSH Moses, Montrose Jonas and Campbell, Oscar James, eds. Dramas of modernism and their forerunners...Rev. ed. ... Boston, Little, Brown, 1941. 946p
Anderson, M. Winterset

MOSH (continued)
Andreyev, L. He who gets
  slapped
Čapek, K., and Čapek, J.
  Adam the creator
Carroll, P. Shadow and sub-
  stance
Chekhov, A. The cherry or-
  chard
Gorky, M. Night's lodging
  (The lower depths)
Howard, S. The silver cord
Kaiser, G. From morn to
  midnight
Kelly, G. Craig's wife
Lenormand, H. The dream
  doctor
Maugham, W. The circle
Milne, A. The truth about
  Blayds
Molnár, F. Liliom
Nichols, R., and Browne, M.
  Wings over Europe
Odets, C. Golden boy
O'Neill, E. Desire under the
  elms
Pirandello, L. Right you are!
  (If you think so)
Sherwood, R. Idiot's delight
Strindberg, J. There are
  crimes and crimes
Toller, E. The machine-
  wreckers

MOSJ Moses, Montrose Jonas,
  ed. Representative Ameri-
  can dramas, national and
  local...Boston, Little,
  Brown, 1926. 681p
Belasco, D. The girl of the
  golden west
Crothers, R. Nice people
Davis, O. The detour
Fitch, C. The city
Forbes, J. The famous Mrs.
  Fair
Hoyt, C. A Texas steer
Kaufman, G., and Connelly,
  M. Dulcy
Kelly, G. The show-off
MacKaye, P. The scarecrow
Megrue, R., and Hackett, W.
  It pays to advertise

O'Neill, E. The Emperor
  Jones
Peabody, J. The piper
Rice, E. The adding machine
Smith, H. Mrs. Bumpstead-
  Leigh
Thomas, A. The witching
  hour

MOSK Moses, Montrose Jonas,
  ed. Representative Ameri-
  can dramas, national and
  local...Rev. ed. Boston,
  Little, Brown, 1933. 890p
Barry, P. Holiday
Behrman, S. The second man
Belasco, D. The girl of the
  golden west
Connelly, M. The green pas-
  tures
Crothers, R. Nice people
Davis, O. The detour
Fitch, C. The city
Forbes, J. The famous Mrs.
  Fair
Howard, S. Lucky Sam Mc-
  Carver
Hoyt, C. A Texas steer
Kaufman, G., and Connelly,
  M. Dulcy
Kelly, G. The show-off
MacKaye, P. The scarecrow
Megrue, R., and Hackett, W.
  It pays to advertise
O'Neill, E. The Emperor
  Jones
Peabody, J. The piper
Rice, E. The adding machine
Smith, H. Mrs. Bumpstead-
  Leigh
Thomas, A. The witching
  hour

MOSL Moses, Montrose Jonas
  and Krutch, Joseph Wood,
  eds. Representative American dramas, national and
  local...Rev. and brought
  up-to-date...Boston, Little,
  Brown, 1941. 1041p
Anderson, M. The masque of
  kings
Barry, P. Holiday

252

Behrman, S. The second man
Belasco, D. The girl of the
golden west
Connelly, M. The green pas-
tures
Crothers, R. Nice people
Davis, O. The detour
Fitch, C. The city
Forbes, J. The famous Mrs.
Fair
Howard, S. Lucky Sam Mc-
Carver
Hoyt, C. A Texas steer
Kaufman, G., and Connelly,
M. Dulcy
Kelly, G. The show-off
MacKaye, P. The scarecrow
Megrue, R., and Hackett, W.
It pays to advertise
Odets, C. Awake and sing
O'Neill, E. The Emperor
Jones
Peabody, J. The piper
Rice, E. The adding machine
Sherwood, R. The petrified
forest
Smith, H. Mrs. Bumpstead-
Leigh
Thomas, A. The witching
hour

MOSN Moses, Montrose Jonas,
ed. Representative British
dramas, Victorian and
modern...Boston, Little,
Brown, 1918. 861p
Barker, G. The Madras house
Boucicault, D. London assur-
ance
Browning, R. A blot in the
'scutcheon
Bulwer-Lytton, E. Richelieu;
or, The conspiracy
Colum, P. Thomas Muskerry
Dunsany, E. The gods of the
mountain
Galsworthy, J. The silver box
Gilbert, W. H.M.S. Pina-
fore; or, The lass that
loved a sailor
Gregory, I. The workhouse
ward
Hankin, St. J. The Cassilis

engagement
Jerrold, D. Black-ey'd Susan;
or, All in the downs
Jones, H. The masqueraders
Knowles, J. Virginius
Masefield, J. The tragedy of
Pompey the Great
Pinero, A. The gay Lord
Quex
Robertson, T. Caste
Synge, J. Riders to the sea
Taylor, T. The ticket-of-
leave man
Tennyson, A. Becket
Wilde, O. The importance of
being earnest
Yeats, W. Cathleen ni Houli-
han

MOSO Moses, Montrose Jonas,
ed. Representative British
dramas, Victorian and
modern. New rev. ed.
...Boston, Little, Brown,
1931. 996p
Boucicault, D. London assur-
ance
Browning, R. A blot in the
'scutcheon
Bulwer-Lytton, E. Richelieu;
or, The conspiracy
Coward, N. Easy virtue
Dane, C. A bill of divorce-
ment
Dunsany, E. The gods of the
mountain
Galsworthy, J. The silver box
Gilbert, W. H.M.S. Pina-
fore; or, The lass that
loved a sailor
Granville-Barker, H. The
Madras house
Gregory, I. The workhouse
ward
Hankin, St. J. The Cassilis
engagement
Jerrold, D. Black-ey'd Susan;
or, All in the downs
Jones, H. The masqueraders
Knowles, J. Virginius
Maugham, W. Our betters
Monkhouse, A. First blood
Munro, C. At Mrs. Beam's

253

MOSO (continued)
Pinero, A. The gay Lord
Quex
Robertson, T. Caste
Synge, J. Riders to the sea
Taylor, T. The ticket-of-
leave man
Wilde, O. The importance of
being earnest
Yeats, W. Cathleen ni Houli-
han

MOSQ Moses, Montrose Jonas,
ed. Representative conti-
nental dramas, revolution-
ary and transitional...Bos-
ton, Little, Brown, 1924.
688p
Andreyeff, L. The life of
man
Annunzio, G. d'. The daugh-
ter of Jorio
Becque, H. The vultures
Benavente y Martínez, J. The
bonds of interest
Chekhov, A. The sea-gull
Donnay, M. Lovers
Giacosa, G. Like falling
leaves
Hauptmann, G. The sunken
bell
Ibsen, H. The wild duck
Maeterlinck, M. Monna Vanna
Nirdlinger, C. The world and
his wife
Rostand, E. Cyrano de Ber-
gerac
Schnitzler, A. The lonely way
Sudermann, H. The fires of
St. John ,
Verhaeren, E. The dawn.

MOSS Moses, Montrose Jonas,
ed. Representative plays
by American dramatists...
New York, Dutton, 1918-
25. 3v
Aiken, G. Uncle Tom's cabin. 2
Barker, J. The Indian princess; or, La belle sauvage.
1
Bateman, Mrs. S. Self.   2

Belasco, D. The return of
Peter Grimm.   3
Boker, G. Francesca da Ri-
mini.   3
Brackenridge, H. The battle
of Bunkershill.   1
Brown, D. Sertorius; or,
The Roman patriot.   2
Bunce, O. Love in '76.   3
Burke, C. Rip Van Winkle. 3
Conrad, R. Jack Cade.   2
Dunlap, W. André.   1
Fitch, C. The moth and
the flame.   3
Godfrey, T. The prince of
Parthia.   1
Howard, B. Shenandoah.   3
Hutton, J. Fashionable
follies.   2
Jones, J. The people's
lawyer.   2
Leacock, J. The fall of
British tyranny; or,
American liberty.   1
Low, S. The politician out-
witted.   1
MacKaye, S. Paul Kauvar;
or, Anarchy.   3
Mitchell, L. The New York
idea.   3
Mowatt, Mrs. A. Fashion. 2
Noah, M. She would be a
soldier; or, The plains
of Chippewa.   1
Payne, J. Brutus; or, The
fall of Tarquin.   2
Rogers, R. Ponteach; or,
The savages of America. 1
Tayleure, C. Horseshoe
Robinson.   2
Thomas, A. In Mizzoura. 3
Tyler, R. The contrast. 1
Walter, E. The easiest
way.   3
Warren, Mrs. M. The
group.   1
Willis, N. Tortesa, the
usurer.   2

MUMFORD, LEWIS. See AME
American caravan...

MURP Murphy, Charles T.;

254

Guinagh, Kevin and Oates, Whitney J., eds. Greek and Roman classics in translation... New York, Longmans, Green [c1947] 1052p
Aeschylus. Prometheus bound
Aristophanes. The clouds
Euripides. Hippolytus
Sophocles. Oedipus the king

MURRAY, GILBERT. See TEN Ten Greek plays...

MYB My best play... London, Faber & Faber [1934] 590p
Bax, C. The Venetian
Coward, N. Hay fever
Dane, C. Granite
Maugham, W. The circle
Milne, A. Success
Munro, C. The rumour
Robinson, L. The whiteheaded boy
Van Druten, J. After all

N

NAGE Nagelberg, Munjou Moses. Drama in our time. ... New York, Harcourt, Brace [c1948] 478p
Arent, A. One-third of a nation
Čapek, K. R.U.R.
Corwin, N. El Capitan and the corporal
Hellman, L. Watch on the Rhine
Howard, S. Yellow Jack
Saroyan, W. The human comedy
Sherwood, R. Abe Lincoln in Illinois
Wilder, T. Our town

NATHAN, GEORGE JEAN. See CRIT The Critics' prize plays... FIG Five great modern Irish plays... WORP World's great plays...

NEI Neilson, William Allan, ed. The chief Elizabethan dramatists, excluding Sah speare... Boston, Houghton Mifflin [1911] 878p
Beaumont, F., and Fletcher, J. The knight of the burning pestle
Beaumont, F., and Fletcher, J. The maid's tragedy
Beaumont, F., and Fletcher, J. Philaster
Chapman, G. Bussy D'Ambois
Dekker, T. The honest whore, pt. I
Dekker, T. The honest whore, pt. II
Dekker, T. The shoemakers' holiday
Fletcher, J. The faithful shepherdess
Fletcher, J. The wild-goose chase
Ford, J. The broken heart
Greene, R. The honourable history of Friar Bacon and Friar Bungay
Heywood, T. A woman killed with kindness
Jonson, B. The alchemist
Jonson, B. Every man in his humour
Jonson, B. Sejanus, his fall
Jonson, B. Volpone; or, The fox
Kyd, T. The Spanish tragedy; or, Hieronimo is mad again
Lyly, J. Endymion, the man in the moon
Marlowe, C. The Jew of Malta
Marlowe, C. Tamburlaine, pt. I
Marlowe, C. The tragical history of Doctor Faustus
Marlowe, C. The troublesome reign and lamentable death of Edward the second
Marston, J. The malcontent
Massinger, P. A new way to pay old debts
Middleton, T. A trick to

NEI (continued)
catch the old one
Middleton, T., and Rowley,
W. The changeling
Peele, G. The old wives'
tale
Shirley, J. The cardinal
Shirley, J. The lady of
pleasure
Webster, J. The Duchess of
Malfi

NELS Nelson, John Herbert
and Cargill, Oscar, eds.
Contemporary trends; A-
merican literature since
1900. Revised edition.
New York, Macmillan
[c1949] 1263p (American
literature; a period anthology. [v4] Oscar Cargill,
gen. ed.)
Anderson, M. Winterset
MacLeish, A. The fall of the
city
O'Neill, E. Bound east for
Cardiff
O'Neill, E. Lazarus laughed

NER Nero (Tragedy)... Nero &
other plays; edited... by
Herbert P. Horne; Have-
lock Ellis; Arthur Symons
and A. Wilson Verity...
New York, Scribner [1904-
48] 488p
Day, J. Humour out of breath
Day, J. The parliament of
bees
Field, N. Amends for ladies
Field, N. Woman is a
weathercock
Nero
Porter, H. The two angry
women of Abington

NET Nettleton, George Henry
and Case, Arthur Ellicott,
eds. British dramatists
from Dryden to Sheridan...
Boston, Houghton Mifflin
[c1939] 957p
Addison, J. Cato

Buckingham, G. The rehears-
al
Cibber, C. The careless hus-
band
Colman, G. The jealous wife
Congreve, W. The way of
the world
Cumberland, R. The West In-
dian
Dryden, J. All for love; or,
The world well lost
Dryden, J. The conquest of
Granada by the Spaniards.
pt. I
Etherege, G. The man of
mode; or, Sir Fopling
Flutter
Farquhar, G. The beaux'
stratagem
Fielding, H. Tom Thumb
Garrick, D. The lying valet
Gay, J. The beggar's opera
Goldsmith, O. She stoops to
conquer; or, The mistakes
of a night
Home, J. Douglas
Lillo, G. The London mer-
chant; or, The history of
George Barnwell
Otway, T. Venice preserved;
or, A plot discovered
Rowe, N. The tragedy of
Jane Shore
Sheridan, R. The critic; or,
A tragedy rehearsed
Sheridan, R. The rivals
Sheridan, R. The school for
scandal
Steele, R. The conscious
lovers
Vanbrugh, J. The relapse; or,
Virtue in danger
Wycherley, W. The plain
dealer

NEVI Neville, Mark Anthony
and Herzberg, Max J.,
eds. This England... Chi-
cago, Rand McNally
[c1956] 786p
Shakespeare, W. Macbeth
Wilde, O. The importance of
being earnest

NEWV (continued)
Miller, A. Death of a sales-
man
Williams, T. A streetcar
named desire
Wouk, H. The Caine mutiny
court-martial
NEWW New world writing... New
York, New American li-
brary 1952-1956. 10v
Bellow, S. The wrecker.   6
Bercovici, E. The heart of
age.   4
Brunson, B. A bastard of the
blood.   10
Denney, R. September lemon-
ade.   7
Eberhart, R. The visionary
farms.   3
García Lorca, F. Don Cristo-
bita and Doña Rosita.   8
Ionesco, E. The bald so-
prano.   9
MacDonagh, D. Happy as
Larry.   6
Meldon, M. Purple path to
the poppy field.   5
Picasso, P. Desire trapped
by the tail.   2
Williams, T. I rise in flame,
cried the Phoenix.   1

NIC Nicoll, Allardyce, ed. Les-
ser English comedies of the
eighteenth century... London,
Oxford university press
[1927] [537]p (The world's
classics)
Colman, G. The jealous wife
Inchbald, E. Every one has
his fault
Morton, T. Speed the plough
Murphy, A. The way to keep
him
Reynolds, F. The dramatist

NINE GREEK DRAMAS. See
HARC Harvard classics, v8

NOY Noyes, George Rapall, ed.
and tr. Masterpieces of
the Russian drama... New
York, Appleton-Century,

1933. 902p
Andreyev, L. Professor Stor-
itsyn
Chekhov, A. The cherry or-
chard
Fonvízin, D. The young hope-
ful
Gogol, N. The inspector
Gorky, M. Down and out
Griboyedov, A. Wit works woe
Mayakóvsky, V. Mystery-
Bouffe
Ostrovsky, A. The poor bride
Pisemsky, A. A bitter fate
Tolstoy, A. The death of Ivan
the terrible
Tolstoy, L. The power of
darkness
Turgenev, I. A month in the
country

O

OAT Oates, Whitney Jennings
and O'Neill, Eugene Glad-
stone, eds. The complete
Greek drama... New York,
Random house [c1938] 2v
Aeschylus. Agamemnon.   1
Aeschylus. The choephori. 1
Aeschylus. The eumenides. 1
Aeschylus. The Persians.   1
Aeschylus. Prometheus
bound.   1
Aeschylus. The seven against
Thebes.   1
Aeschylus. The suppliants. 1
Aristophanes. The Acharni-
ans.   2
Aristophanes. The birds.   2
Aristophanes. The clouds. 2
Aristophanes. The ecclesi-
azusae.   2
Aristophanes. The frogs.   2
Aristophanes. The knights. 2
Aristophanes. Lysistrata. 2
Aristophanes. Peace.   2
Aristophanes. Plutus.   2
Aristophanes. Thesmophori-
azusae.   2
Aristophanes. The wasps.   2
Euripides. Alcestis.   1
Euripides. Andromache.   1

Euripides. The bacchae. 2
Euripides. The cyclops. 2
Euripides. Electra. 2
Euripides. Hecuba. 1
Euripides. Helen. 2
Euripides. The Heracleidae.1
Euripides. Heracles. 1
Euripides. Hippolytus. 1
Euripides. Ion. 1
Euripides. Iphigenia in Aulis. 2
Euripides. Iphigenia in
Tauris. 1
Euripides. Medea. 1
Euripides. Orestes. 2
Euripides. The Phoenissae. 2
Euripides. Rhesus. 2
Euripides. The suppliants. 1
Euripides. The Trojan wo-
men. 1
Menander. The arbitration. 2
Menander. The girl from
Samos. 2
Menander. The shearing of
Glycera. 2
Sophocles. Ajax. 1
Sophocles. Antigone. 1
Sophocles. Electra. 1
Sophocles. Oedipus at
Colonus. 1
Sophocles. Oedipus the king 1
Sophocles. Philoctetes. 1
Sophocles. The trachiniae. 1

OATE Oates, Whitney Jennings
and Murphy, Charles The-
ophilus, eds. Greek litera-
ture in translation... New
York, Longmans, Green,
1944. 1072p
Aeschylus. Agamemnon
Aeschylus. The Eumenides
Aeschylus. Prometheus bound
Aristophanes. Lysistrata
Euripides. The bacchae
Euripides. Hippolytus
Menander. The arbitration
Sophocles. Oedipus the king
Sophocles. Antigone

OATH Oates, Whitney Jennings
and O'Neill, Eugene, jr.,
eds. ...Seven famous Greek
plays...New York, Modern

library [c1950] 446p (Mod-
ern library college editions)
Aeschylus. Agamemnon
Aeschylus. Prometheus bound
Aristophanes. The frogs
Euripides. Alcestis
Euripides. Medea
Sophocles. Antigone
Sophocles. Oedipus the king

OBERUFER, CHRISTMAS PLAYS
FROM. See HARW Har-
wood, A. C., tr.

OBSE The observer plays, with
a preface by Kenneth Ty-
nan. London, Faber and
Faber [c1958] 475p
Beynon, R. The shifting heart
Campbell, M., and Athas, D.
Sit on the earth
Cavan, R. All my own work
Davis, A. Four men, a tragi-
comedy
Jellicoe, A. The sport of my
mad mother
John, E. Moon on a rainbow
shawl
Simpson, N. A resounding
tinkle

O'CONNOR, JOSEPH. See GRE
Great plays (English)...

OLH Oliphant, Ernest Henry
Clark, ed. Elizabethan
dramatists other than Shake-
speare...New York, Pren-
tice-Hall, 1931. 1511p
Arden of Feversham
Beaumont, F., and Fletcher,
J. The knight of the burn-
ing pestle
Beaumont, F., and Fletcher,
J. The maid's tragedy
Beaumont, F., and Fletcher,
J. Philaster
Brome, R. A jovial crew
Dekker, T. The honest whore,
pt. II
Drayton, M. The merry devil
of Edmonton
Ford, J. The broken heart

259

OLH (continued)
Greene, R. Friar Bacon and
Friar Bungay
Heywood, T. A woman killed
with kindness
Jonson, B. The alchemist
Jonson, B. Bartholomew fair
Jonson, B. Volpone
Jonson, B., Chapman, G.,
and Marston, J. Eastward
hoe!
Kyd, T. The Spanish tragedy
Lyly, J. Campaspe
Marlowe, C. Edward II
Marlowe, C. Faustus
Massinger, P. A new way to
pay old debts
Middleton, T. Women, beware
women
Middleton, T., and Rowley,
W. The changeling
Milton, J. Comus
Peele, G. The old wives' tale
Porter, H. The two angry wo-
men of Abington
Rowley, W., and Middleton, T.
A fair quarrel
Shirley, J. The traitor
Tourneur, C. The revenger's
tragedy
Webster, J. The Duchess of
Malfi
Webster, J. The white devil
A Yorkshire tragedy

OLI Oliphant, Ernest Henry
Clark, ed. Shakespeare and
his fellow dramatists... New
York, Prentice-Hall, 1929.
2v
Arden of Feversham.   1
Beaumont, F., and Fletcher,
J. The knight of the burn-
ing pestle.   2
Beaumont, F., and Fletcher,
J. The maid's tragedy. 2
Beaumont, F., and Fletcher,
J. Philaster.   2
Brome, R. A jovial crew. 2
Dekker, T. The honest whore,
pt. II   1
Drayton, M. The merry devil
of Edmonton.   1

Ford, J. The broken heart. 2
Greene, R. Friar Bacon and
Friar Bungay.   1
Heywood, T. A woman killed
with kindness.   1
Jonson, B. The alchemist. 2
Jonson, B. Bartholomew
fair.   2
Jonson, B. Volpone.   1
Jonson, B., Chapman, G.,
and Marston, J. Eastward
hoe!   1
Kyd, T. The Spanish tragedy.
                             1
Lyly, J. Campaspe.   1
Marlowe, C. Edward II.   1
Marlowe, C. Faustus.   1
Massinger, P. A new way to
pay old debts.   2
Middleton, T. Women, be-
ware women.   2
Middleton, T., and Rowley,
W. The changeling.   2
Milton, J. Comus.   2
Peele, G. The old wives'
tale.   1
Porter, H. The two angry
women of Abington.   1
Rowley, W., and Middleton,
T. A fair quarrel.   2
Shakespeare, W. Antony and
Cleopatra.   2
Shakespeare, W. As you like
it.   1
Shakespeare, W. Coriolanus.
                             2
Shakespeare, W. Cymbe-
line.   2
Shakespeare, W. Hamlet. 1
Shakespeare, W. Henry IV,
pt. I.   1
Shakespeare, W. Julius
Caesar.   1
Shakespeare, W. King Lear.1
Shakespeare, W. Macbeth. 2
Shakespeare, W. The mer-
chant of Venice.   1
Shakespeare, W. Midsummer
night's dream.   1
Shakespeare, W. Othello. 1
Shakespeare, W. Romeo and
Juliet.   1
Shakespeare, W. Twelfth

night.   1
Shakespeare, W. The winter's
   tale.   2
Shirley, J. The traitor.   2
Tourneur, C. The revenger's
   tragedy.   2
Webster, J. The Duchess of
   Malfi.   2
Webster, J. The white devil.
                                2
A Yorkshire tragedy.   2

ORI Oriental literature...Rev.
   ed. New York, Colonial
   press [c1900] 4v (The
   world's great classics)
Abstraction.   2
Kálidás. Šakoontalá.   3
Nakamitsu.   2
The sorrows of Han.   4

OULD Ould, Herman, ed. The
   book of the P.E.N. ...Lon-
   don, Arthur Barker [1950]
   254p
Farjeon, E. The plane-tree
Jameson, S. William the defeated
Johnson, P. The Duchess at
   sunset

OXF Oxford anthology of American literature, chosen and
   edited by William Rose Benét and Norman Holmes
   Pearson. New York, Oxford
   university press, 1938.
   1705p
O'Neill, E. Lazarus laughed
               P
PAR Parks, Edd Winfield, and
   Beatty, Richard Croom,
   eds. The English drama,
   an anthology, 900-1642...
   New York, Norton [c1935]
   1495p
Abraham and Isaac
Beaumont, F., and Fletcher,
   J. Philaster; or, Love lies
   a-bleeding
Daniel, S. The vision of the
   twelve goddesses
Dekker, T. The shoemakers'

holiday
Everyman
Fletcher, J., and Shakespeare,
   W. Two noble kinsmen
Ford, J. 'Tis a pity she's a
   whore
Greene, R. The honorable his-
   tory of Friar Bacon and
   Friar Bungay
Heywood, J. A merry play be-
   tween John John the hus-
   band
Heywood, T. A woman killed
   with kindness
Jonson, B. Every man in his
   humour
Jonson, B. Oberon, the fairy
   prince
Jonson, B. Sejanus, his fall
Jonson, B. Volpone; or, The
   fox
Kyd, T. The Spanish tragedy
Lyly, J. Endymion
Marlowe, C. Edward II
Marlowe, C. The Jew of Malta
Marlowe, C. The tragical his-
   tory of Dr. Faustus
Massinger, P. A new way to
   pay old debts
Milton, J. Comus
Oxfordshire St. George play
Peele, G. The old wives' tale
Plautus, T. The miles glori-
   osus
The quem quaeritis
Robin Hood and the friar
The second shepherds' play
Seneca, L. Thyestes
Shetland sword dance
Shirley, J. The cardinal
Sidney, P. The Lady of May
Udall, N. Ralph Roister
   Doister
Webster, J. The white devil

PARNASSUS PLAYS (1598-1601)
   ...See LEIS Leishman, J.
   B., ed.

PARR Parry, W. Dyfed. Old
   plays for modern players
   ...London, Arnold [1930]
   156p

PARR (continued)
Abraham and Isaac
Heywood, J. The four p's
Jonson, B. Volpone; or, The
fox
Noah's flood
Peele, G. The old wives' tale
The shepherds' play

PARV Patt, Beatrice P., and
Nozick, Martin, eds. The
generation of 1898 and after
...New York, Dodd, Mead,
1961. 427p
Garcia Lorca, F. La casa de
Bernarda Alba

PATT Pattison, Walter Thomas.
Representative Spanish authors...New York, Oxford
university press, 1942. 2v
in 1
Rivas, A. Don Alvaro; o, La
fuerza del sino
Rueda, L. Paso séptimo: de
las aceitunas
Ruiz de Alarcón y Mendoza, J.
Las paredes oyen

PEARSON, NORMAN HOLMES.
See OXF Oxford anthology
of American literature...
edited by William Rose Benét and Norman Holmes
Pearson

PEN Pence, Raymond Woodbury,
ed. Dramas by present-
day writers...New York,
Scribner [c1927] 690p
Bennett, A., and Knoblock, E.
Milestones
Davies, M. The slave with
two faces
Drinkwater, J. Cophetua
Dunsany, E. A night at an inn
Galsworthy, J. Loyalties
Glaspell, S. Trifles
Gregory, I. Spreading the news
Jacobs, W. A love passage
Jones, H. The goal
Kaufman, G., and Connelly, M.
Merton of the movies

Mackay, C. Counsel retained
Morley, C. Thursday evening
O'Neill, E. "Ile"
Sutro, A. A marriage has
been arranged
Tarkington, B. Monsieur
Beaucaire
Wilde, P. Confessional

PENNSYLVANIA GERMAN SO-
CIETY. See BUFF Buff-
ington, Albert F., ed.
The Reichard collection of
early Pennsylvania German
plays...

PERRIN, BERNADOTTE. See
GREE Greek dramas...

PIE Pierce, Frederick Erastus
and Schreiber, Carl Fred-
erick, eds. Fiction and
fantasy of German romance.
New York, Oxford univer-
sity press, 1927. 392p
Kleist, H. Kaethchen of Heilbronn

PLAA Playbook: Five plays for
a new theatre. [New York]
New Directions [c1956] 298p
Abel, L. The death of Odys-
seus
Hivnor, R. The ticklish acro-
bat
Kinoshita, J. Twilight crane
Merrill, J. The immortal
husband
Richards, I. A leak in the
universe

PLAB Plays by Greek, Spanish,
French, German and Eng-
lish dramatists...Rev. ed.
New York, Colonial press
[c1900] 2v (The world's
great classics)
Aeschylus. Prometheus bound.
1
Aristophanes. The knights. 1
Calderón de la Barca, P.
Life a dream.   1
Euripides. Medea.   1

262

Goethe, J. Faust, pt. I. 2
Goldsmith, O. She stoops to
 conquer. 1
Ibsen, H. A doll's house. 2
Molière, J. The misanthrope.
   1
Racine, J. Phaedra. 1
Sardou, V. Les pattes de
 mouche. 2
Schiller, F. Mary Stuart. 2
Sheridan, R. The rivals. 2
Sophocles. Oedipus rex. 1

PLAD Plays of a half-decade...
 [London] Gollancz [1933]
 1008p
Anthony, C. Autumn crocus
Bax, C. The rose without a
 thorn
Berkeley, R. The lady with a
 lamp
Besier, R. The Barretts of
 Wimpole street
Delafield, E. To see ourselves
Fagan, J. The improper
 duchess
Hoffe, M. Many waters
Mackenzie, R. Musical chairs
Sherriff, R. Journey's end
Van Druten, J. After all
Van Druten, J. Yound Woodley

PLAG ...Plays of the Greek
 dramatists... New York,
 Caxton house [c1946] 360p
Note: Variant title: Eleven plays
of the Greek dramatists...
Aeschylus. Agamemnon
Aeschylus. Choephoroe
Aeschylus. The Eumenides
Aristophanes. The clouds
Aristophanes. The frogs
Aristophanes. Lysistrata
Euripides. The cyclops
Euripides. Iphigenia in Tauris
Sophocles. Antigone
Sophocles. Electra
Sophocles. Oedipus, the king

PLAM Plays of the Moscow art
 theatre musical studio...
 English translation from the
 Russian by George S., and

Gilbert Seldes, with introductions by Oliver M. Sayler. New York, Brentano
 [c1925] v.p.
Aristophanes. Lysistrata
Lecocq, C. The daughter of
 Madame Angot
Lipskeroff, C. Carmencita
 and the soldier
Offenbach, J. La périchole
Pushkin, A. Love and death,
 featuring "Aleko," by Rachmaninoff

PLAN Plays of the year, chosen
 by J. C. Trewin... London,
 Paul Elek [c1949-62] 24v
Abse, D. House of cowards. 23
Achard, M. Rollo. 20
Ackland, R. Before the
 party. 2
Ackland, R. A dead secret.
   16
Albery, P. Anne Boleyn. 14
Anouilh, J. The ermine. 13
Anouilh, J. Medea. 15
Anouilh, J. The waltz of
 the toreadors. 8
Arden, J. The party. 18
Boland, B. Cockpit. 1
Boland, B. The prisoner. 10
Boland, B. The return. 9
Braddon, R. Naked island. 22
Browne, W. The holly and
 the ivy. 3
Chetham-Strode, W. Back-
 ground. 4
Christie, D., and Christie,
 C. His excellency. 4
Coffee, L., and Cowen, W.
 Family portrait. 1
Dighton, J. The happiest days
 of your life. 1
Dighton, J. Who goes there!
   6
Dinner, W., and Morum, W.
 The late Edwina Black. 2
Dobie, L., and Sloman, R.
 The tinker. 24
Dowling, J., and Letton, F.
 The young Elizabeth. 7
Fairchild, W. The sound of
 murder. 20

POLL   Pollard, Alfred William,
    ed. English miracle plays,
    moralities and interludes...
    8th edition revised. Oxford,
    Clarendon Press, 1927.
    250p
  Abraham and Isaac
  The castell of perseverance
  The creation and the fall of
    Lucifer
  Everyman
  The four elements
  The harrowing of hell
  Ludus super iconia Sancti
    Nicolai
  Mary Magdalen
  Mysterium resurrectionis D. N.
    Jhesu Christi
  Noah's flood
  The sacrifice of Isaac
  The salutation and conception
  Secunda postorum
  Thersytes
  Bale, J. King John
  Heywood, J. The pardoner
    and the frere
  Skelton, J. Magnyfycence

POOL   Pooley, Robert C. ;
    Farmer, Paul; Thornton,
    Helen and Anderson, George
    K. , eds. England in litera-
    ture... Chicago, Scott,
    Foresman [c1953] 752p
  Fry, C. The boy with a cart
  Goldsmith, O. She stoops to
    conquer
  Shakespeare, W. Macbeth

PRAT   Pratt, Robert A. [and
    others] eds. Masters of
    British literature... Second
    edition. Boston, Houghton
    Mifflin [c1958, 1962] 2v
  Arnold, M. Empedocles on
    Etna.   2
  Arnold, M. The strayed
    reveler.   2
  Shakespeare, W. The first
    part of Henry the fourth.1
  Shakespeare, W. The tragedy
    of King Lear.   1
  Shakespeare, W. The winter's

    tale.   1
  Shelley, P. Prometheus un-
    bound.   2

PROB   Prose and poetry for ap-
    preciation... edited by H.
    Ward McGraw... Syracuse,
    N. Y. , Singer [c1934] 1071p
    (The prose and poetry se-
    ries)
  Dunsany, E. A night at an
    inn
  Gregory, A. The rising of
    the moon
  Monkhouse, A. The grand
    cham's diamond
  Tarkington, B. Monsieur Beau-
    caire

PROC   Prose and poetry for ap-
    preciation, edited by Eliza-
    beth Frances Ansorge [and
    others] Syracuse, N. Y. ,
    Singer [c1942] 787p (The
    prose and poetry series)
  Corwin, N. They fly through
    the air
  Gregory, A. Spreading the
    news
  Kaufman, G. , and Hart, M.
    The American way
  Knight, E. Never come Mon-
    day
  Knight, V. Cartwheel

PROD   Prose and poetry for ap-
    preciation, edited by Har-
    riet Marcelia Lucas [and
    others] Fourth edition.
    Syracuse, N. Y. Singer
    [c1950] 822p (The prose
    and poetry series)
  Corwin, N. The odyssey of
    Runyon Jones
  Gilbert, W. and Sullivan, A.
    The Mikado
  Glaspell, S. Trifles
  Sherwood, R. Abe Lincoln in
    Illinois

PROF   Prose and poetry of A-
    merica; edited by H. Ward
    McGraw... Syracuse, N. Y. ,

Singer [c1934] 1034p (The prose and poetry series)
Fitch, C. Nathan Hale
Glaspell, S. Trifles
Hopkins, A. Moonshine

PROG Prose and poetry of A-merica...edited by H. Ward McGraw...Syracuse, N.Y., Singer [c1934] 1198p (The new prose and poetry series. Southwestern edition)
Bowen, M. Crude and unre-fined
Fitch, C. Nathan Hale
Fortune, J. The cavalier from France
Glaspell, S. Trifles
Hopkins, A. Moonshine
Rogers, J. Judge Lynch

PROH Prose and poetry of A-merica; edited by H. Ward McGraw [and others] Catho-lic edition...Syracuse, N.Y., Singer [c1940] 1133p (The new prose and poetry series)
Fitch, C. Nathan Hale
Hopkins, A. Moonshine
Kelly, G. Poor Aubrey

PROI Prose and poetry of A-merica...edited by Julian L. Maline...Wilfred M. Mallon [and others] Syra-cuse, N.Y., Singer [c1949] 822p (At head of title: The St. Thomas More series)
Connelly, M. The green pas-tures
Hopkins, A. Moonshine
Mulvey, T. Letter to Tuffy

PROM Prose and poetry of Eng-land...edited by H. Ward McGraw. Syracuse, N.Y., Singer [c1934] 1196p (The new prose and poetry se-ries)
Dunsany, E. The lost silk hat
Goldsmith, O. She stoops to conquer

Shakespeare, W. Macbeth

PRON Prose and poetry of Eng-land; edited by H. Ward McGraw. Catholic edition ...Syracuse, N.Y., Singer [c1940] 1150p (The new prose and poetry series)
Benson, R. The upper room
Dunsany, E. The lost silk hat
Shakespeare, W. Macbeth

PROW Prose and poetry of the world; edited by John R. Barnes [and others] Syra-cuse, N.Y., Singer [c1941] 1010p (The prose and po-etry series)
Euripides. Medea
Ibsen, H. A doll's house
O'Neill, E. Where the cross is made
Sachs, H. The wandering scholar from Paradise
Synge, J. Riders to the sea

PROX Prose and poetry of the world; edited by James K. Agnew and Agnes L. Mc-Carthy...Syracuse, N.Y., Singer [c1954] 788p
Capek, K. R.U.R.
Miller, A. Pussycat and the expert plumber who was a man
Williams, E. Corn is green

PUCC Pucciani, Oreste F., ed. The French theater since 1930...Boston, Ginn and Company [c1954] 400p
Camus, A. Le malentendu
Cocteau, J. La machine in-fernale
Giraudoux, J. La guerre de Troie n'aura pas lieu
Montherlant, H. Le reine morte
Sartre, J. Les mains sales

THE PULITZER PRIZE PLAYS. See CORD, CORE, CORF
Cordell, Kathryn (Coe) and

267

THE PULITZER PRIZE PLAYS
(continued)
Cordell, William Howard,
eds.

Q

QUI Quinn, Arthur Hobson, ed.
Contemporary American
plays... New York, Scribner
[c1923] 382p
Crothers, R. Nice people
Emery, G. The hero
Kaufman, G., and Connelly,
M. To the ladies!
O'Neill, E. The Emperor
Jones
Williams, J. Why marry?

QUIG Quinn, Arthur Hobson, ed.
Representative American
plays from 1880 to the
present day... Modern drama
ed. New York, Century
[c1928] 495-1052p
Belasco, D., and Long, J.
Madame Butterfly
Crothers, R. He and she
Fitch, C. Her great match
Gillette, W. Secret service
Howard, B. Shenandoah
MacKaye, P. The scarecrow
MacKaye, S. Hazel Kirke
Mitchell, L. The New York
idea
Moody, W. The faith healer
O'Neill, E. Beyond the hori-
zon
Sheldon, E. The boss
Thomas, A. The witching hour
Vollmer, L. Sun-up

QUIJ Quinn, Arthur Hobson, ed.
Representative American
plays... New York, Century,
1917. 968p
Barker, J. Superstition
Belasco, D. and Long, J.
Madame Butterfly
Bird, R. The broker of Bo-
gota
Boker, G. Francesca da Ri-
mini

Boucicault, D. The octoroon;
or, Life in Louisiana
Crothers, R. He and she
Custis, G. Pocahontas; or,
The settlers of Virginia
Dunlap, W. André
Fitch, C. Her great match
Gillette, W. Secret service
Godfrey, T. The prince of
Parthia
Howard, B. Shenandoah
Howe, J. Leonora; or, The
world's own
MacKaye, P. The scarecrow
MacKaye, S. Hazel Kirke
Mitchell, L. The New York
idea
Moody, W. The faith healer
Payne, J. and Irving, W.
Charles the second
Rip Van Winkle
Ritchie, A. Fashion
Sheldon, E. The boss
Smith, R. The triumph at
Plattsburg
Thomas, A. The witching hour
Tyler, R. The contrast
Willis, N. Tortesa the usurer

QUIK Quinn, Arthur Hobson, ed.
Representative American
plays, 1767-1923... 3rd. ed.
rev. and enl. New York,
Century, 1925. 1052p
Barker, J. Superstition
Belasco, D. and Long, J.
Madame Butterfly
Bird, R. The broker of Bo-
gota
Boker, G. Francesca da Ri-
mini
Boucicault, D. The octoroon;
or, Life in Louisiana
Crothers, R. He and she
Custis, G. Pocahontas; or,
The settlers of Virginia
Dunlap, W. André
Fitch, C. Her great match
Gillette, W. Secret service
Godfrey, T. The prince of
Parthia
Howard, B. Shenandoah
Howe, J. Leonora; or, The

world's own
MacKaye, P. The scarecrow
MacKaye, S. Hazel Kirke
Mitchell, L. The New York
idea
Moody, W. The faith healer
O'Neill, E. Beyond the hori-
zon
Payne, J. and Irving, W.
Charles the second
Rip Van Winkle
Ritchie, A. Fashion
Sheldon, E. The boss
Smith, R. The triumph at
Plattsburg
Thomas, A. The witching hour
Tyler, R. The contrast
Vollmer, L. Sun-up
Willis, N. Tortesa the usurer

QUIL Quinn, Arthur Hobson, ed.
Representative American
plays from 1767 to the
present day... 5th ed. rev.
and enl. New York, Cen-
tury [c1930] 1107p
Barker, J. Superstition
Barry, P. Paris bound
Belasco, D. and Long, J.
Madame Butterfly
Bird, R. The broker of Bo-
gota
Boker, G. Francesca da Ri-
mini
Boucicault, D. The octoroon;
or, Life in Louisiana
Crothers, R. He and she
Custis, G. Pocahontas; or,
The settlers of Virginia
Dunlap, W. André
Fitch, C. The girl with the
green eyes
Gillette, W. Secret Service
Godfrey, T. The prince of
Parthia
Herne, J. Margaret Fleming
Howard, B. Shenandoah
Howard, S. The silver cord
MacKaye, P. The scarecrow
MacKaye, S. Hazel Kirke
Mitchell, L. The New York
idea
Moody, W. The faith healer

O'Neill, E. Beyond the hori-
zon
Payne, J. and Irving, W.
Charles the second
Rip Van Winkle
Ritchie, A. Fashion
Sheldon, E. The boss
Thomas, A. The witching hour
Tyler, R. The contrast
Vollmer, L. Sun-up
Willis, N. Tortesa the usurer

QUIM Quinn, Arthur Hobson,
ed. Representative plays
from 1767 to the present
day... 6th ed. rev. and enl.
New York, Appleton-Cen-
tury [c1938] 1157p
Anderson, M. Wintorsot
Barker, J. Superstition
Barry, P. Paris bound
Belasco, D. and Long, J.
Madame Butterfly
Bird, R. The broker of Bo-
gota
Boker, G. Francesca da Ri-
mini
Boucicault, D. The octoroon;
or, Life in Louisiana
Crothers, R. He and she
Custis, G. Pocahontas; or,
The settlers of Virginia
Dunlap, W. André
Fitch, C. The girl with the
green eyes
Gillette, W. Secret service
Godfrey, T. The prince of
Parthia
Herne, J. Margaret Fleming
Howard, B. Shenandoah
Howard, S. The silver cord
MacKaye, P. The scarecrow
MacKaye, S. Hazel Kirke
Mitchell, L. The New York
idea
Moody, W. The faith healer
O'Neill, E. Beyond the hori-
zon
Payne, J. and Irving, W.
Charles the second
Rip Van Winkle
Ritchie, A. Fashion
Sheldon, E. The boss

QUIM (continued)
Thomas, A. The witching hour
Tyler, R. The contrast
Vollmer, L. Sun-up
Willis, N. Tortesa the usurer

QUIN Quinn, Arthur Hobson, ed.
Representative American
plays from 1767 to the
present day... 7th ed., rev.
and enl. New York, Apple-
ton-Century-Crofts [c1953]
1248p
Anderson, M. Winterset
Barker, J. Superstition
Barry, P. Paris bound
Belasco, D. and Long, J.
Madame Butterfly
Bird, R. The broker of Bo-
gota
Boker, G. Francesca da Ri-
mini
Boucicault, D. The octoroon;
or, Life in Louisiana
Crothers, R. He and she
Custis, G. Pocahontas; or,
The settlers of Virginia
Dunlap, W. André
Fitch, C. The girl with the
green eyes
Gillette, W. Secret service
Godfrey, T. The prince of
Parthia
Haines, W. Command deci-
sion
Hammerstein II, O.; Rodgers,
R.; Logan, J. and Michen-
er, J. South Pacific
Herne, J. Margaret Fleming
Howard, B. Shenandoah
Howard, S. The silver cord
Jefferson, J. Rip Van Winkle
MacKaye, P. The scarecrow
MacKaye, S. Hazel Kirke
Mitchell, L. The New York
idea
Moody, W. The faith healer
O'Neill, E. Beyond the hori-
zon
Payne, J. Charles the second
Ritchie, A. Fashion; or, Life
in New York
Sheldon, E. The boss

Thomas, A. The witching hour
Tyler, R. The contrast
Vollmer, L. Sun-up
Willis, N. Tortesa the usurer

QUINTANA, RICARDO. See
EIGH Eighteenth century
plays...

QUIO Quinn, Arthur Hobson;
Baugh, Albert Croll and
Howe, Will David, eds.
The literature of America
... New York, Scribner
[c1929] 2v
Belasco, D. and Long, J.
Madame Butterfly.   2
Boker, G. Francesca da
Rimini.   1
Howells, W. The unexpected
guests.   2
O'Neill, E. Lazarus
laughed.   2
Tyler, R. The contrast.   1

R

RAY Ray, Gordon Norton; Edel,
Leon; Johnson, Thomas H.;
Paul, Sherman and Simp-
son, Claude, eds. Masters
of American literature...
Boston, Houghton [c1959] 2v
O'Neill, E. Desire under the
elms,   2
O'Neill, E. The long voyage
home,   2

READINGS FOR LIBERAL EDU-
CATION, v.2. See LOCLA,
LOCLB Locke, Louis
Glenn [and others] eds. In-
troduction to literature...

REDM Redmond, Crosby E.,
comp. Drama II... New
York, Macmillan [c1962]
357p
Barrie, J. The admirable
Crichton
Rattigan, T. The Winslow boy
Shakespeare, W. Julius Caesar
Van Druten, J. I remember

mama

REED, HARRY B. See HAP
Harbrace omnibus...

REEV Reeve, Franklin D., ed.
and tr. An anthology of
Russian plays...New York,
Vintage Books [c1961, 1963]
2v
Andreyev, L. He who gets
slapped.   2
Blok, A. The puppet show. 2
Bulgakov, M. The days of
the Turbins.   2
Chekhov, A. The sea gull. 2
Fonvizín, D. The minor.   1
Gogol, N. The inspector
general.   1
Gorky, M. The lower depths.2
Griboyedov, A. The trouble
with reason,   1
Mayakóvsky, V. The bed-
bug.   2
Ostrovsky, A. The storm.   1
Pushkin, A. Boris Godunov.1
Shvarts, E. The shadow.   2
Tolstoy, L. The power of
darkness,   1

REIN Reinert, Otto, ed. Drama,
an introductory anthology...
Boston, Little, Brown
[c1961] 652p
Everyman
Brecht, B. The good woman
of Setzuan
Chekhov, A. Three sisters
Ibsen, H. The wild duck
Ionesco, E. The lesson
Miller, A. A view from the
bridge
Molière, J. Tartuffe
Shakespeare, W. Macbeth
Shaw, G. Arms and the man
Sophocles. Oedipus rex
Strindberg, A. The ghost
sonata
Yeats, W. Purgatory

REIP Reinert, Otto, ed. Modern
drama, nine plays...Bos-
ton, Little, Brown [c1961,

1962] 491p
Brecht, B. The good woman
of Setzuan
Chekhov, A. Three sisters
Ibsen, H. The wild duck
Ionesco, E. The lesson
Pirandello, L. Six characters
in search of an author
Shaw, G. Arms and the man
Strindberg, A. The ghost
sonata
Williams, T. The glass me-
nagerie
Yeats, W. Purgatory

RELIGIOUS DRAMAS, 1924-25.
See FED Federal council
of the churches of Christ
in America.

REST Restoration plays; with an
introduction by Brice Har-
ris...New York, Modern
library [c1955] 674p
Congreve, W. The way of the
world
Dryden, J. All for love
Etherege, G. The man of
mode
Farquhar, G. The beaux'
stratagem
Otway, T. Venice preserved
Vanbrugh, J. The relapse
Villiers, G. The rehearsal
Wycherley, W. The country
wife

RHO Rhodes, Solomon Alhadef,
ed. The contemporary
French theatre...New York,
Crofts, 1942. 431p
Bernard, J. Martine
Claudel, P. L'annonce faite à
Marie
Curel, F. Le repas du lion
Lenormand, H. L'homme et
ses fantômes
Maeterlinck, M. Pelléas et
Mélisande
Porto-Riche, G. Amoureuse
Raynal, P. Le tombeau sous
l'Arc de triomphe
Romains, J. Cromedeyre-le-

271

RHO (continued)
Vieil
Sarment, J. Les plus beaux
yeux du monde

RICH Rich, Mabel Irene... A
study of the types of literature... New York, Century
[c1921] 542p
Gibson, W. The family's pride
Milton, J. Comus
Shakespeare, W. The tragedy
of Hamlet, Prince of Den-
mark
Wilde, P. The traitor

RICK Richardson, Lyon Norman;
Orians, George H., and
Brown, Herbert R., eds.
The heritage of American
literature... Boston, Ginn
[c1951] 2v
O'Neill, E. Anna Christie. 2

ROB Robbins, Harry Wolcott
and Coleman, William Har-
old, eds. Western world
literature... New York, Mac-
millan, 1938. 1422p
Aeschylus. Agamemnon
Aristophanes. The frogs
Calderón de la Barca, P.
Keep your own secret
Euripides. Iphigenia at Aulis
Everyman
Goethe, J. Faust, pt. I
Ibsen, H. Ghosts
Molière, J. Misanthrope
O'Neill, E. Beyond the hori-
zon
Plautus, T. The captives
Racine, J. Phaedra
Shakespeare, W. King Lear
Sheridan, R. The rivals

ROBI Robinson, Charles Alexander, jr., ed. An anthology of Greek drama, first
series... New York, Rine-
hart [c1949] 269p (Rinehart
editions)
Aeschylus. Agamemnon
Aristophanes. Lysistrata

Euripides. Hippolytus
Euripides. Medea
Sophocles. Antigone
Sophocles. Oedipus the king

ROBJ Robinson, Charles Alex-
ander, Jr., ed. An anthol-
ogy of Greek drama, sec-
ond series... New York,
Rinehart [c1954] 398p
(Rinehart editions)
Aeschylus. Choëphoroe
Aeschylus. Eumenides
Aeschylus. Prometheus bound
Aristophanes. The clouds
Aristophanes. The frogs
Euripides. The bacchae
Euripides. The Trojan women
Sophocles. Oedipus at Colonus
Sophocles. Philoctetes

ROBJA Robinson, Charles Alex-
ander, Jr., ed. The spring
of civilization, Periclean
Athens. New York, Dutton,
1954, 464p
Aeschylus. Agamemnon
Euripides. Medea
Euripides. The Trojan women
Sophocles. Antigone
Sophocles. Oedipus at Colonus
Sophocles. Oedipus the king

ROBK Robinson, Cyril Edward,
tr. The genius of the
Greek drama... Oxford,
Clarendon press, 1921. 96p
Aeschylus. Agamemnon
Euripides. Medea
Sophocles. Antigone

ROBM Robinson, Donald Fay,
ed. The Harvard Dramatic
Club miracle plays; ten
plays translated and adapted
by various hands... New
York, French, 1928. 241p
The Benediktbeuren play
Bourlet, K. The nativity
The Hessian Christmas play
The Maastricht play
The pageant of the shearmen
and the tailors

The provençal play
The star
The Towneley play
The Umbrian play
The wisemen

ROE   Roberts, Carl Eric Bech-
hofer, tr.   Five Russian
plays, with one from the
Ukrainian... New York,
Dutton, 1916. 173p
Chekhov, A. The jubilee
Chekhov, A. The wedding
Evreinov, N. The beautiful
despot
Evreinov, N. A merry death
Fonvizin, D. The choice of a
tutor
Ukrainka, L. [pseud.]   The
Babylonian captivity

ROET   Roby, Robert C., and
Ulanov, Barry, eds. Intro-
duction to drama... New
York, McGraw-Hill, 1962.
704p
Anouilh, J. Le voyageur sans
baggage
Chekhov, A. The cherry or-
chard
Congreve, W. The way of the
world
Euripides. Medea
Giraudoux, J. Tiger at the
gates
Ibsen, H. Rosmersholm
Jonson, B. The alchemist
Kaiser, G. From morn to
midnight
Lindsay, D. The satire of the
three estates
Molière, J. The misanthrope
Plautus, T. Miles gloriosus
Racine, J. Phaedra
Shaw, G. Man and superman
Sophocles. Oedipus rex
Strindberg, A. The dance of
death
Webster, J. The Duchess of
Malfi

ROGE   Rogers, Winfield Heyser;
Redinger, Ruby V., and

Haydn II, Hiram C., eds.
Explorations in living...
New York, Reynal & Hitch-
cock [c1941] 783p
Ibsen, H. An enemy of the
people
Shakespeare, W. Hamlet
Wilder, T. Our town

ROHAN, PIERRE de. See FEE,
FEF   Federal theatre
project.   Federal theatre
plays... ["Edited for the
Federal theatre by Pierre
de Rohan"]

ROLF   Rolfe, Franklin Prescott;
Davenport, William H. and
Bowerman, Paul, eds. The
modern omnibus... New
York, Harcourt, Brace
[c1946] 1071p
Anderson, M. Key Largo
Kaufman, G. and Ryskind, M.
Of thee I sing
Sherwood, R. Abe Lincoln in
Illinois
Thurber, J. and Nugent, E.
The male animal

ROSENFIELD, JOHN. See THX
Three Southwest plays...

ROSENFIELD, PAUL. See
AME   American caravan...

ROSS   Ross, Ralph Gilbert;
Berryman, John and Tate,
Allen, eds. The arts of
reading. New York,
Thomas Y. Crowell [c1960]
488p
Chekhov, A. A marriage
proposal
Shakespeare, W. The tragedy
of Macbeth

ROWE   Rowell, George, ed.
Nineteenth century plays...
London, Oxford university
press [c1953] 567p
Albery, J. Two roses
Boucicault, D. The colleen

273

ROWE (continued)
bawn
Bulwer-Lytton, E. Money
Grundy, S. A pair of spec-
tacles
Hazlewood, C. Lady Audley's
secret
Jerrold, D. Black-ey'd Susan
Lewis, L. The bells
Robertson, T. Caste
Taylor, T. The ticket-of-
leave man
Taylor, T. and Reade, C.
Masks and faces

RUA Rubinstein, Harold Frederick, ed. Four Jewish
plays... London, Gollancz,
1948. 303p
Bernhard, E. The Marranos
Block, T. You must stay to
tea
Hemro. Poor ostrich
Scott, P. Pillars of salt

RUB Rubinstein, Harold Fred-
erick, ed. Great English
plays... New York, Harper,
1928. 1136p
Beaumont, F. and Fletcher,
J. The maid's tragedy
Congreve, W. The way of the
world
Dekker, T. The shoemaker's
holiday
Everyman
Farquhar, G. The recruiting
officer
Fletcher, J. The chances
Ford, J. 'Tis pity she's a
whore
Goldsmith, O. She stoops to
conquer
Heywood, J. John, Tyb, and
the curate
Jones, H. Judah
Jonson, B. The silent woman
Jonson, B., Chapman, G. and
Marston, J. Eastward ho!
Kyd, T. The Spanish tragedy
Marlowe, C. Doctor Faustus
Marlowe, C. Edward the sec-
ond

Massinger, P. The bondman
Massinger, P. A new way to
pay old debts
Otway, T. Venice preserved
Peele, G. The old wives' tale
Robertson, T. Society
Sheridan, R. The school for
scandal
Vanbrugh, J. The provoked
wife
A Wakefield nativity
Webster, J. The white devil
Wilde, O. Lady Windermere's
fan
A Yorkshire tragedy

RUSS Russell, Harry Kitsun;
Wells, William and Stauffer,
Donald A., eds. Literature
in English... New York,
Holt [c1948] 1174p
Shakespeare, W. King Lear
Sheridan, R. The school for
scandal

RYL Rylands, George Humphrey
Wolfestan, ed. Elizabethan
tragedy... London, Bell,
1933. 623p
Chapman, G. Bussy d'Ambois
Ford, J. 'Tis pity she's a
whore
Heywood, T. A woman killed
with kindness
Marlowe, C. Tamburlaine the
great, pt. I
Tourneur, C. The revenger's
tragedy
Webster, J. The white devil

S

SAND Sanderlin, George. Col-
lege reading... Boston,
Heath [c1953] 849p
Ibsen, H. An enemy of the
people
O'Neill, E. Bound east for
Cardiff
Shaw, G. Androcles and the
lion

SATA Satan, Socialites, and

Solly Gold: Three new
plays from England. New
York, Coward-McCann
[c1961] 280p
Duncan, R. The death of Sa-
tan
Jupp, K. The socialites
Kops, B. Enter Solly Gold

SAYLER, OLIVER MARTIN,
See also MOS, MOSA Mos-
cow art theatre series of
Russian plays... and PLAM
Plays of the Moscow art the-
atre musical studio...

SAY Sayler, Oliver Martin, ed.
The Eleonora Duse series
of plays... New York, Bren-
tano [c1923] v.p,
Annunzio, G. d'. The dead
city
Gallarati-Scotti, T. Thy will
be done
Ibsen, H. Ghosts
Ibsen, H. The lady from the
sea
Praga, M. The closed door

SCAN ...Scandinavian plays of
the twentieth century...
Princeton, N.J., Princeton
university press, 1944-1951.
3v
Abell, K. Anna Sophie Hedvig.   2
Bergman, H. Mr. Sleeman is
coming.   1
Bergman, H. The Sweden-
hielms.   3
Dagerman, S. The con-
demned.   3
Grieg, N. The defeat; a play
about the Paris Com-
mune.   2
Josephson, R. Perhaps a
poet.   1
Krog, H. The sounding
shell.   2
Lagerkvist, P. Let man
live.   3
Lagerkvist, P. The man
without a soul.   1

Munk, K. Niels Ebbesen.   2
Schildt, R. The Gallows man:
a midwinter story.   1

SCH Schelling, Felix Emmanuel,
ed. Typical Elizabethan
plays... New York, Harper,
1926. 797p
Beaumont, F. and Fletcher,
J. The maid's tragedy
Beaumont, F. and Fletcher,
J. Philaster; or, Love
lies a-bleeding
Chapman, G., Jonson, B. and
Marston, J. Eastward ho!
Dekker, T. The pleasant
comedy of Old Fortunatus
Fletcher, J. Rule a wife and
have a wife
Ford, J. The chronical his-
tory of Perkin Warbeck, a
strange truth
Greene, R. A pleasant con-
ceited comedy of [George a
Greene], the pinner of
Wakefield
Heywood, T. A woman killed
with kindness
Jonson, B. The hue and cry
after cupid
Jonson, B. The sad shepherd
Jonson, B. Volpone; or, The
fox
The lamentable and true trage-
dy of Master Arden of
Feversham in Kent
Lyly, J. Endymion, the man
in the moon
Marlowe, C. The tragical his-
tory of Doctor Faustus
Marlowe, C. The troublesome
reign and lamentable death
of Edward II
Massinger, P. A new way to
pay old debts
Middleton, T. and Rowley, W.
The changeling
Munday, A. Sir Thomas More
(An ill May-day)
The return from Parnassus;
or, The scourge of simony,
pt. II
Shirley, J. The lady of pleas-

SCH (continued)
ure
Webster, J. The tragedy of
the Duchess of Malfi

SCI Schelling, Felix Emmanuel
and Black, Matthew W.,
eds. Typical Elizabethan
plays...Rev. and enl. ed.
New York, Harper [c1931]
1033p
Beaumont, F. and Fletcher,
J. The knight of the burn-
ing pestle
Beaumont, F. and Fletcher,
J. The maid's tragedy
Beaumont, F. and Fletcher,
J. Philaster; or, Love lies
a-bleeding
Chapman, G., Jonson, B. and
Marston, J. Eastward ho!
Dekker, T. The pleasant com-
edy of Old Fortunatus
Dekker, T. The shoemaker's
holiday; or, The gentle
craft
Fletcher, J. The faithful
shepherdess
Fletcher, J. Rule a wife and
have a wife
Ford, J. The broken heart
Greene, R. The honorable his-
tory of Friar Bacon and
Friar Bungay
Heywood, T. A woman killed
with kindness
Jonson, B. Every man in his
humor
Jonson, B. The hue and cry
after cupid
Jonson, B. Volpone; or, The
fox
Kyd, T. The Spanish tragedy
Lyly, J. Endymion, the man
in the moon
Marlowe, C. Tamburlaine the
great, pt. I
Marlowe, C. The tragical his-
tory of Doctor Faustus
Marlowe, C. The troublesome
reign and lamentable death
of Edward II
Massinger, P. A new way to

pay old debts
Middleton, T. Michaelmas
term
Middleton, T. and Rowley, W.
The changeling
Munday, A. Sir Thomas More
(An ill May-day)
Peele, G. The old wives' tale
The return from Parnassus;
or, The scourge of simony,
pt. II
Shirley, J. The lady of pleas-
ure
Webster, J. The tragedy of
the Duchess of Malfi

SCJ Schelling, Felix Emmanuel
and Black, Matthew W.,
eds. Typical Elizabethan
plays... Third edition, re-
vised and enlarged... New
York, Harper [c1949]
1065p
Beaumont, F. and Fletcher,
J. The knight of the burn-
ing pestle
Beaumont, F. and Fletcher,
J. The maid's tragedy
Beaumont, F. and Fletcher,
J. Philaster; or, Love lies
a-bleeding
Chapman, G., Jonson, B. and
Marston, J. Eastward ho!
Dekker, T. The shoemaker's
holiday; or, The gentle
craft
Fletcher, J. The faithful
shepherdess
Ford, J. The broken heart
Greene, R. The honorable his-
tory of Friar Bacon and
Friar Bungay
Heywood, T. A woman killed
with kindness
Jonson, B. Every man in his
humor
Jonson, B. The hue and cry
after cupid
Jonson, B. Volpone; or, The
fox
Kyd, T. The Spanish tragedy
Lyly, J. Endymion, the man
in the moon

276

Marlowe, C. Tamburlaine the great, pt. I
Marlowe, C. The tragical history of Doctor Faustus
Marlowe, C. The troublesome reign and lamentable death of Edward II
Massinger, P. A new way to pay old debts
Middleton, T. Michaelmas term
Middleton, T. and Rowley, W. The changeling
Munday, A. Sir Thomas More (An ill May-day)
Peele, G. The old wives' tale
The return from Parnassus; or, The scourge of simony, pt. II
Shirley, J. The lady of pleasure
Webster, J. The tragedy of the Duchess of Malfi

SCN Schinz, Albert; Robert, Osmond Thomas and Giroud, Pierre François, eds. Nouvelle anthologie française. New York, Harcourt, Brace, 1936. 680p
Corneille, P. Le cid
La farce de maître Pierre Pathelin
Hugo, V. Ruy Blas
Labiche, E. et Martin, É. La poudre aux yeux
Molière, J. Le bourgeois gentilhomme
Racine, J. Andromaque

SCNN Schneider, Elizabeth W.; Walker, Albert L. and Childs, Herbert E., eds. The range of literature... New York, American Book Company [c1960] 732p
Chekhov, A. The cherry orchard
Rice, E. The adding machine
Shakespeare, W. Othello, the Moor of Venice
Shaw, G. Arms and the man
Sophocles. Oedipus rex

SCW Schweikert, Harry Christian, ed. Early English plays... New York, Harcourt, Brace [c1928] 845p
Abraham and Isaac
Banns
Dekker, T. The shoemaker's holiday
Everyman
The fall of Lucifer
Greene, R. The honorable history of Friar Bacon and Friar Bungay
Jonson, B. Every man in his humor
The judgment day
Kyd, T. The Spanish tragedy
Lyly, J. Endymion
Marlowe, C. Tamburlaine the great, pts. I and II
Marlowe, C. The tragical history of Doctor Faustus
Noah
Peele, G. The old wives' tale
Quem quaeritis
Robin Hood and the friar
Sackville, T. and Norton, T. Gorboduc
Saint George and the dragon
The second shepherd's play
Udall, N. Ralph Roister Doister

SCWE Schweikert, Harry Christian; Inglis, Rewey Belle and Gehlmann, John, eds. Adventures in American literature... New York, Harcourt, Brace [c1930] 1064p
Fitch, C. Nathan Hale
O'Neill, E. Where the cross is made
Tarkington, B. The trysting place

SCWG Schweikert, Harry Christian; Inglis, Rewey Belle; Gehlmann, John and Foerster, Norman, eds. Adventures in American literature. Rev. ed. New York, Harcourt Brace, 1936. 1217p

SCWG (continued)
Kelly, G. Poor Aubrey
O'Neill, E. The Emperor
Jones
Tarkington, B. The trysting
place

SCWI Schweikert, Harry Christian; Miller, Harry Augustus and Cook, Luella Bus-
sey, eds. Adventures in
appreciation... New York,
Harcourt, Brace, 1935.
1065p
Dunsany, E. The lost silk hat
Howard, S. and DeKruif, P.
Yellow jack
Shakespeare, W. As you like
it

SEA Searles, Colbert, ed. Seven
French plays (1730-1897)
... New York, Holt [c1935]
749p
Augier, É. Le gendre de M.
Poirier
Beaumarchais, P. Le mariage
de Figaro
Becque, H. Les corbeaux
Hugo, V. Hernani
Marivaux, P. Le jeu de
l'amour et du hasard
Rostand, E. Cyrano de Ber-
gerac
Voltaire, F. Zaïre

SEAVER, EDWIN. See CROZ
Cross-section...

SEBO Seboyar, Gerald Edwin
and Brosius, Rudolph
Frederic, eds. Readings in
European literature. New
York, Crofts, 1928. 876p
Aeschylus. Prometheus bound
Aristophanes. The frogs
Euripides. Medea
Ibsen, H. Ghosts
Molière, J. The high-brow
ladies
Plautus. The crock of gold
Racine, J. Phaedra
Sophocles. Antigone

Terence. Andria; the fair
Andrian

SEBP Seboyar, Gerald Edwin
and Brosius, Rudolph Fred-
eric, eds. Readings in
European literature [Second
edition] New York, Crofts,
1946. 900p
Aeschylus. Prometheus bound
Aristophanes. The frogs
Euripides. Medea
Ibsen, H. Ghosts
Molière, J. The high-brow
ladies
Plautus. The Menaechmi
Racine, J. Phaedra
Sophocles. Antigone
Terence. Andria; the fair
Andrian

SECK Secker, Martin. The
eighteen-nineties... London,
Richards [1948] 616p
Dowson, E. The pierrot of
the minute
Yeats, W. The countess Cathleen

SECOND AMERICAN CARAVAN.
1928. See AME American
caravan. v2

SELDES, GEORGE S. See
PLAM Plays of the Moscow
art theatre musical studio
...

SELDES, GILBERT. See PLAM
Plays of the Moscow art
theatre musical studio...

SER Seronde, Joseph and Peyre,
Henri, eds. ... Nine clas-
sic French plays... Boston,
Heath [c1936] 748p
Corneille, P. Le cid
Corneille, P. Horace
Corneille, P. Polyeucte
Molière, J. Le précieuses
ridicules
Molière, J. Le misanthrope
Molière, J. Le Tartuffe

278

Racine, J. Andromaque
Racine, J. Esther
Racine, J. Phèdre

SERD Seronde, Joseph and
Peyre, Henri, eds. ...
Three classic French plays
...Boston, Heath [c1935]
253p
Corneille, P. Le cid
Molière, J. Les précieuses
ridicules
Racine, J. Andromaque

SET Setchanove, L. J. Five
French comedies... Boston,
Allyn and Bacon [c1925]
276p
Bernard, T. L'anglais tel
qu'on le parle
La farce de maitre Pathelin
Forest, L. Par un jour de
pluie
France, A. La comédie de
celui qui épousa une femme
muette
Maurey, M. Rosalie

SEV Seven plays... London,
Heinemann [1935] 775p
Coward, N. Conversation
piece
Dane, C. Moonlight is silver
Kennedy, M. Escape me
never!
Lonsdale, F. Aren't we all?
Priestley, J. Laburnum grove
Winter, J. The shining hour
Wooll, E. Libel

SEVD Seven plays of the modern
theatre. With an introduc-
tion by Harold Clurman.
New York, Grove Press
[c1962] 548p
Beckett, S. Waiting for Godot
Behan, B. The quare fellow
Delaney, S. A taste of honey
Gelber, J. The connection
Genet, J. The balcony
Ionesco, E. Rhinoceros
Pinter, H. The birthday party

SEVE Seven sacred plays with
an introduction by Sir
Francis Younghusband and
notes by A. H. Debenham.
London, Methuen [1934]
v. p.
Bulkley, A. The crown of light
Debenham, A. Good will to-
ward men
Debenham, A. The Prince of
Peace
Gonne, F. In the city of
David
Hines, L. Simon
Mell, M. The apostle play
The passion play of Alsfeld

SEVP Seven Soviet plays... with
introductions by H. W. L.
Dana. New York, Mac-
millan, 1946. 520p
Afinogenov, A. On the eve
Korneichuk, A. The front
Leonov, L. The orchards of
Polovchansk
Rokk, V. Engineer Sergeyev
Simonov, K. The Russian
people
Solovyov, V. Field Marshall
Kutuzov
Tur, L., Tur, P. and Sheinin,
L. Smoke of the father-
land

SHA Shafer, Robert, ed. American literature... New York,
Doubleday, Doran [c1926]
2v
Fitch, C. The girl with the
green eyes.   2
O'Neill, E. "The hairy
ape."   2

SHAH Shafer, Robert, ed. From
Beowulf to Thomas Hardy
... New York, Doubleday,
Page [c1924] 2v
Dryden, J. All for love.   1
Everyman.   1
Goldsmith, O. She stoops to
conquer.   1
Marlowe, C. The tragical
history of Doctor Faustus. 1

279

SHAI Shafer, Robert, ed. From
Beowulf to Thomas Hardy...
Rev. ed. New York, Double-
day, Doran [c1931] 2v
Congreve, W. The way of the
world.   1
Everyman.   1
Marlowe, C. The tragical his-
tory of Doctor Faustus.   1
Sheridan, R. The rivals.   2

SHAJ Shafer, Robert, ed. From
Beowulf to Thomas Hardy.
New ed. ...New York,
Doubleday, Doran [c1939] 2v
Dekker, T. The shoemakers'
holiday.   1
Dryden, J. All for love; or,
The world well lost.   1
Everyman.   1
Marlowe, C. The tragical his-
tory of Doctor Faustus.   1
The second shepherds'
play.   1
Sheridan, R. The rivals.   2
Wilde, O. The importance of
being earnest.   2

SHAR Sharp, Russell, A.; Brew-
ton, John E.; Lemon, Ba-
bette, and Abney, Louise,
eds. English and continental literature... Chicago,
Laidlaw [c1950] 800p (Cul-
tural Growth series)
Gregory, I. The rising of the
moon
Molière, J. The physician in
spite of himself
Shakespeare, W. Macbeth

SHAW Shaw, Harry, ed. A com-
plete course in freshman
English... Fifth edition. New
York, Harper & Brothers
[c1959] 1306p
Shakespeare, W. The tragedy
of Romeo and Juliet
Shaw, G. Pygmalion
Wilder, T. The long Christ-
mas dinner

SHAY Shay, Frank, ed. A

treasury of plays for wo-
men...Boston, Little,
Brown, 1922, 443p
Clements, C. Columbine
Clements, C. The siege
Dransfield, J. The lost
Pleiad
Emig, E. The china pig
Gerstenberg, A. Ever young
Gerstenberg, A. A patroness
Knox, F. For distinguished
service
Kreymborg, A. Manikin and
Minikin
Kreymborg, A. Rocking chairs
McCauley, C. The conflict
Maeterlinck, M. The death of
Tintagiles
Millay, E. The lamp and the
bell
Morley, C. Rehearsal
O'Neill, E. Before breakfast
Pillot, E. My lady dreams
Smith, H. Blackberryin'
Strindberg, A. Motherly love
Strindberg, A. The stronger
woman

SHERWOOD, GARRISON P. See
BEST plays of 1894/1899
...etc.

SILM Simonson, Harold Peter,
ed. Trio; a book of sto-
ries, plays, and poems...
New York, Harper &
Brothers [c1962] 489p
Chekhov, A. The cherry or-
chard
Ibsen, H. Ghosts

SIM Simpson, Claude Mitchell
and Nevins, Allan, eds.
The American reader...
Boston, Heath [c1941] 866p
Connelly, M. The green pas-
tures
Riggs, L. Green grow the
lilacs
Wilder, T. Our town

SIXB Six great modern plays...
[New York, Dell, c1956]

512p
Chekhov, A. Three sisters
Ibsen, H. The master builder
Miller, A. All my sons
O'Casey, S. Red roses for me
Shaw, G. Mrs. Warren's pro-
    fession
Williams, T. The glass me-
    nagerie

SIXC Six modern American
    plays. Introduction by Allan
    G. Halline... New York,
    Modern library [c1951] 419p
Anderson, M. Winterset
Heggen, T. and Logan, J.
    Mister Roberts
Hellman, L. The little foxes
Kaufman, G. and Hart, M.
    The man who came to
    dinner
O'Neill, E. The Emperor
    Jones
Williams, T. The glass me-
    nagerie

SIXD Six plays... London, Gol-
    lancz, 1930. 672p
Bax, C. Socrates
Connelly, M. The green pas-
    tures
George, E. Down our street
Glaspell, S. Alison's house
Rice, E. Street scene
Sherriff, R. Badger's green

SIXH Six plays... London, Heine-
    mann [1934] 746p
Coward, N. Design for living
Dane, C. Wild Decembers
Kaufman, G. and Ferber, E.
    Dinner at eight
Maugham, W. Sheppey
Priestley, J. Dangerous cor-
    ner
Winter, K. The rats of Norway

SIXL Six plays of 1939... [Lon-
    don] Hamilton [1939] v.p.
Behrman, S. No time for
    comedy
Hellman, L. The little foxes
Jones, J. Rhondda roundabout

Lyndon, B. The man in Half
    moon street
McCracken, E. Quiet wedding
Rattigan, T. After the dance

SIXP Six plays of today... Lon-
    don, Heinemann [1939]
    716p
Coppel, A. I killed the count
Coward, N. Point Valaine
Hodge, M. The island
Priestley, J. Cornelius
Sherwood, R. Idiot's delight
Wolfe, H. The silent knight

SMI Smith, Robert Metcalf, ed.
    ... Types of domestic trage-
    dy... New York, Prentice-
    Hall, 1928. 576p (World
    drama series)
Annunzio, G. d'. Gioconda
Hebbel, F. Maria Magdalena
Heywood, T. A woman killed
    with kindness
Ibsen, H. Hedda Gabler
Lillo, G. George Barnwell;
    or, The London merchant
Pinero, A. Mid-channel
Strindberg, A. The father

SMK Smith, Robert Metcalf, ed.
    ... Types of historical dra-
    ma... New York, Prentice-
    Hall, 1928. 635p (World
    drama series)
Hebbel, C. Agnes Bernauer
Ibsen, H. The pretenders
Kleist, H. The prince of Hom-
    burg
Schiller, F. William Tell
Shakespeare, W. King Henry
    the fourth, pt. I
Tennyson, A. Becket

SML Smith, Robert Metcalf, ed.
    ... Types of philosophic
    drama... New York, Pren-
    tice-Hall, 1928. 524p (World
    drama series)
Aeschylus. Prometheus bound
Andreev, L. The life of man
The book of Job
Byron, G. Manfred

SML (continued)
Everyman
Marlowe, C. Dr. Faustus
Milton, J. Samson Agonistes
Shelley, P. Prometheus un-
bound

SMN   Smith, Robert Metcalf, ed.
... Types of romantic dra-
ma... New York, Prentice-
Hall, 1928. 621p (World
drama series)
Corneille, P. The Cid
Dryden, J. All for love
Grillparzer, F. Sappho
Maeterlinck, M. Pelléas and
Mélisande
Phillips, S. Paolo and Fran-
cesca
Rostand, E. Cyrano de Ber-
gerac
Shakespeare, W. Rome and
Juliet

SMO   Smith, Robert Metcalf, ed.
... Types of social comedy
... New York, Prentice-Hall,
1928. 759p (World drama
series)
Congreve, W. The way of the
world
Goldsmith, O. She stoops to
conquer
Massinger, P. A new way to
pay old debts
Maugham, W. Our betters
Molière, J. Tartuffe
Pinero, A. The gay Lord
Quex
Sheridan, R. The school for
scandal
Wilde, O. Lady Windermere's
fan

SMP   Smith, Robert, Metcalf,
ed. ... Types of world
tragedy... New York, Prent-
ice-Hall, 1928. 667p
(World drama series)
Euripides. Medea
Gorki, M. The lower depths
Hauptmann, G. The weavers
Ibsen, H. Ghosts

Racine, J. Phaedra
Shakespeare, W. Othello, the
Moor of Venice
Shelley, P. The Cenci
Sophocles. Oedipus the king

SMR   Smith, Robert Metcalf and
Rhoads, Howard Garrett,
eds. ... Types of farce
comedy... New York, Pren-
tice-Hall, 1928. 598p
(World drama series)
Aristophanes. The frogs
France, A. The man who
married a dumb wife
Gay, J. The beggar's opera
Gilbert, W. and Sullivan, A.
Patience
Molière, J. The doctor in
spite of himself
Pinero, A. The magistrate
Plautus, T. The Menaechmi
Shakespeare, W. The taming
of the shrew
Wilde, O. The importance of
being earnest

SNYD   Snyder, Franklyn Bliss
and Martin, Robert Grant,
eds. A book of English
literature... 4th edition.
New York, Macmillan
[c1942-43] 2v
Abraham and Isaac.   1
Dryden, J. All for love.   1
Everyman.   1
Galsworthy, J. Loyalties.   2
Marlowe, C. Doctor
Faustus.   1
Noah's flood.   1
O'Casey, S. Juno and the
paycock.   2
Sheridan, R. The rivals.   1

SPC   Spearhead. 10 years' ex-
perimental writing in A-
merica [New York, New
directions, c1947] 604p
Hutchins, M.   Aunt Julia's
Caesar
Stein, G.   Daniel Webster
eighteen in America
Williams, T. 27 wagons full

282

of cotton

SPE Spencer, Hazelton, ed.
Elizabethan plays...Boston,
Little, Brown, 1933. 1173p
Beaumont, F. [and Fletcher,
J.] The knight of the burn-
ing pestle
Beaumont, F. and Fletcher, J.
The maid's tragedy
Beaumont, F. and Fletcher, J.
Philaster; or, Love lies a-
bleeding
Chapman, G. Bussy d'Ambois
Chapman, G.; Jonson, B. and
Marston, J. Eastward ho!
Dekker, T. The honest whore,
pt. I
Dekker, T. The honest whore,
pt. II
Dekker, T. The shoemakers'
holiday
Fletcher, J. The wild-goose
chase
Ford, J. The broken heart
Greene, R. The honourable
history of Friar Bacon and
Friar Bungay
Heywood, T. A woman killed
with kindness
Jonson, B. The alchemist
Jonson, B. Bartholomew fair
Jonson, B. Every man in his
humor
Jonson, B. Volpone; or, The
fox
Kyd, T. The Spanish tragedy;
or, Hieronimo is mad again
Lyly, J. Endymion, the man in
the moon
Marlowe, C. The Jew of Malta
Marlowe, C. Tamburlaine, pt.
I
Marlowe, C. The tragical his-
tory of Doctor Faustus
Marlowe, C. The troublesome
reign and lamentable death
of Edward the second
Marston, J. The malcontent
Massinger, P. A new way to
pay old debts
Middleton, T. A trick to catch
the old one

Middleton, T. and Rowley, W.
The changeling
Shirley, J. The lady of pleas-
ure
Webster, J. The white devil;
or, Vittoria Corombona

SPER Sper, Felix, ed. Favorite
modern plays...New York,
Globe Book Company
[c1953] 530p
Barrie, J. The admirable
Crichton
Besier, R. The Barretts of
Wimpole Street
Galsworthy, J. Loyalties
Lindsay, H. and Crouse, R.
Life with father
Rattigan, T. The Winslow boy

SPES Sper, Felix, ed. Living
American plays...New York,
Globe Book [c1954] 454p
Hart, M. and Kaufman, G.
You can't take it with you
Howard, S. The late Christo-
pher Bean
Lavery, E. The magnificent
Yankee
Van Druten, J. I remember
Mama
Williams, T. The glass me-
nagerie

SPF Spencer, Hazelton; Hough-
ton, Walter E. and Barrows,
Herbert. British literature
...Boston, Heath [c1951,
1952] 2v
Congreve, W. The way of the
world.   1
Dekker, J. The shoemakers'
holiday.   1
Marlowe, C. Doctor
Faustus.   1
The second shepherds'
play.   1
Sheridan, R. The school for
scandal.   1
Webster, J. The Duchess
of Malfi   1

283

SPI Spiller, Robert Ernest, ed.
The roots of national culture; American literature to
1830... New York, Mac-
millan, 1933. 758p (American literature: a period
anthology; Oscar Cargill,
general editor, v1)
Tyler, R. The contrast

SRY Srygley, Ola Pauline and
Betts, Otsie Verona, eds.
Highlights in English litera-
ture and other selections...
Dallas, Texas, Banks,
Upshaw [1940] 868p
Goldsmith, O. She stoops to
conquer
Milne, A. The boy comes
home
Shakespeare, W. Macbeth

SRYG Srygley, Ola Pauline and
Betts, Otsie Verona, eds.
Highlights in English litera-
ture... Dallas, Texas, Banks
Upshaw [c1940] 868p
Goldsmith, O. She stoops to
conquer
Milne, A. The boy comes
home
Shakespeare, W. Macbeth
Tolstoy, L. What men live by

SSST Stallman, R. W. and Wat-
ters, R. E. The creative
reader... New York, Ronald
[c1954] 923p
Chekhov, A. The cherry or-
chard
Coxe, L. and Chapman, R.
Billy Budd
Ibsen, H. The wild duck
Shakespeare, W. The tempest
Sophocles. Antigone

SSSU Stallman, R. W. and Watters, R. E. The creative
reader... Second edition.
New York, Ronald [c1962]
992p
Anouilh, J. Antigone
Coxe, L. and Chapman, R.

Billy Budd
Ibsen, H. The wild duck
Shakespeare, W. The tempest
Sophocles. Antigone

SSTA Stamm, Rudolf, ed. ...
Three Anglo-Irish plays...
Bern, Switzerland, A.
Francke, 1943. 114p (Bib-
liotheca Anglicana... v5)
Gregory, I. The rising of the
moon
Synge, J. Riders to the sea
Yeats, W. Deirdre

SSTE Stanford University.
Dramatists' Alliance. Plays
of the southern Americas
... Stanford Univ., Drama-
tists' Alliance, 1942. v. p
Acevedo Hernanandez, A.
Cabrerita
Sanchez, F. La Gringa
Vargas Tejada, L. Las con-
vulsiones

SSTG Stanton, Stephen S., ed.
Camille and other plays...
New York, Hill and Wang
[1957] 306p (Mermaid dra-
mabook)
Augier, É. Olympês marriage
Dumas, A. Camille
Sardou, V. A scrap of paper
Scribe, E. The glass of water
Scribe, E. and Bayard, J. A
peculiar position

STA Stauffer, Ruth Matilda,
comp. The progress of
drama through the centuries
... New York, Macmillan,
1927. 696p
Bulwer-Lytton, E. The lady
of Lyons; or, Love and
pride
Calderón de la Barca, P. The
constant prince
Corneille, P. Polyeucte
Euripides. The Trojan women
Everyman
Fitch, C. The truth
Goldsmith, O. She stoops to

conquer; or, The mistakes
of a night
Ibsen, H. An enemy of the
people
Jonson, B. Epicoene; or, The
silent woman
Marlowe, C. Faustus
Molière, J. L'avare
Plautus, T. Aulularia; or, The
pot of gold
Racine, J. Berenice
Schiller, J. William Tell
The second shepherds' play
Shakespeare, W. Hamlet
Sheridan, R. The school for
scandal
Sophocles. Antigone

STAT Stauffer, Ruth Matilda and
Cunningham, William H.,
eds. Adventures in modern
literature. New York, Har-
court, Brace [c1939] 1170p
Anderson, M. The feast of
Ortolans
Galsworthy, J. The silver box
Gibney, S. and Collings, P.
The story of Louis Pasteur
Glaspell, S. Trifles
Goodman, K. and Hecht, B.
The hand of Siva
Sherriff, R. Journey's end

STAU Stauffer, Ruth Matilda and
Cunningham, William H.,
eds. Adventures in modern
literature... Second edition.
New York, Harcourt, Brace,
1944. 1042p
Čapek, K. R.U.R.
Gibney, S. and Collings, P.
The story of Louis Pasteur
Glaspell, S. Trifles
Goodman, K. and Hecht, B.
The hand of Siva
Sherriff, R. Journey's end
Wilde, P. Blood of the
martyrs

STAUFFER, R.M. See also
FREI Freier, Robert...
Adventures in modern lit-
erature

STAV Stauffer, Ruth Matilda;
Cunningham, William H.
and Sullivan, Catherine J.,
eds. Adventures in mod-
ern literature. Third edi-
tion... New York, Harcourt,
Brace, 1951. 747p
Corwin, N. My client Curley
Glaspell, S. Trifles
O'Casey, S. The end of the
beginning
Sherriff, R. Journey's end
Van Druten, J. I remember
mama

STE   Steeves, Harrison Ross,
ed. Plays from the mod-
ern theatre... Boston, Heath
[c1931] 526p
Chekhov, A. The cherry or-
chard
Donnay, M. Lovers
Hauptmann, G. The beaver
coat
Ibsen, H. Ghosts
Molnár, F. Liliom
O'Neill, E. The great god
Brown
Pinero, A. The second Mrs.
Tanqueray
Schnitzler, A. Intermezzo
Wilde, O. The importance of
being earnest

STEI Steinberg, M.W., ed.
Aspects of modern drama
...[New York] Henry Holt
[c1960] 633p
Anderson, M. Elizabeth the
queen
Galsworthy, J. Strife
Miller, A. Death of a sales-
man
O'Neill, E. The great god
Brown
Saroyan, W. The time of
your life
Shaw, G. Candida
Shaw, G. Man of destiny
Synge, J. The playboy of the
western world
Synge, J. Riders to the sea
Wilde, O. The importance of

285

STEI (continued)
being earnest
Williams, T. The glass menagerie
Yeats, W. The dreaming of
the bones

STI Steinhauer, Harry, ed. Das
Deutsche drama, 1880-1933
...New York, Norton
[c1938] 2v
Hauptmann, G. Das friedens-
fest. 1
Hofmannsthal, H. Der tor und
der tod. 1
Kaiser, G. Gas I. 2
Schnitzler, A. Lebendige
stunden. 1
Toller, E. Masse mensch. 2
Unruh, F. Heinrich aus
Andernach. 2
Wedekind, F. Der kammer-
sänger. 1
Wiechert, E. Das spiel vom
deutschen bettelmann. 2

STJ Steinhauer, Harry and
Walter, Felix, eds. Omni-
bus of French literature...
New York, Macmillan,
1941. 2v
Beaumarchais, P. Le barbier
de Seville. 1
Becque, H. Les corbeaux. 2
Corneille, P. Le cid. 1
Hugo, V. Ruy Blas. 2
Marivaux, P. Le jeu de
l'amour et du hasard. 1
Molière, J. Le misanthrope. 1
Racine, J. Andromaque. 1

STJM Steinmann, Martin, Jr.
and Willen, Gerald, eds.
Literature for writing...
Belmont, Cal., Wadsworth
Publishing Co. [c1962] 692p
Gay, J. The beggar's opera
Miller, A. Death of a sales-
man
Shakespeare, W. Henry IV

STL Stern, Milton R. and Cross,
Seymour L., eds. Ameri-

can literature survey...
New York, Viking [c1962]
4v
O'Neill, E. The hairy ape. 4
Tyler, R. The contrast. 1

STM Stevens, David Harrison,
ed. Types of English dra-
ma, 1660-1780...Boston,
Ginn [c1923] 920p
Addison, J. Cato
Buckingham, G., and others.
The rehearsal
Congreve, W. Love for love
Congreve, W. The way of the
world
Dryden, J. All for love; or,
The world well lost
Dryden, J. Aureng-Zebe
Etherege, G. The man of
mode; or, Sir Fopling
Flutter
Farquhar, G. The beaux'
stratagem
Fielding, H. The tragedy of
tragedies; or, The life and
death of Tom Thumb the
great
Gay, J. The beggar's opera
Goldsmith, O. The good-
natured man
Goldsmith, O. She stoops to
conquer; or, The mistakes
of a night
Home, J. Douglas
Lillo, G. The London mer-
chant; or, The history of
George Barnwell
Otway, T. Venice preserved;
or, A plot discovered
Rowe, N. Jane Shore
Shadwell, T. Bury fair
Sheridan, R. The critic
Sheridan, R. The duenna
Sheridan, R. The rivals
Sheridan, R. The school for
scandal
Steele, R. The conscious
lovers

STOC Stock, Dora and Stock,
Marie, eds. ...Recueil de
lectures...Boston, Heath

286

[c1950] 240p
Labiche, E. La grammaire

STRASBERG, LEE. See FAM
Famous American plays of
the 1950's...

SUL Summers, Hollis Spurgeon
and Whan, Edgar, eds.
Literature: An introduction.
New York, McGraw-Hill,
1960. 706p
Jonson, B. Volpone; or, The
fox
MacLeish, A. The music crept
by me upon the waters
Miller, A. The crucible
Shaw, G. The devil's disciple
Sophocles. Antigone
Wilder, T. The matchmaker
Williams, T. Something un-
spoken

SUM Summers, Montague, ed.
Restoration comedies...
London, Cape, 1921. 400p
Crowne, J. Sir Courtly Nice;
or, It cannot be
Killigrew, T. The parson's
wedding
Ravenscroft, E. The London
cuckolds

SUMB Summers, Montague, ed.
Shakespeare adaptations...
London, Cape, 1922. 282p
D'Avenant, W. and Dryden, J.
The tempest; or, The en-
chanted island
Duffett, T. The mock-tempest;
or, The enchanted castle
Tate, N. The history of King
Lear

SURR Surre, Willard, ed.
Three distinctive plays a-
bout Abraham Lincoln...
New York, Washington
Square Press [c1961] 208p
Conkle, E. Prologue to glory
Drinkwater, J. Abraham
Lincoln
Van Doren, M. The last days

of Lincoln

SWIT Switz, Theodore MacLean
and Johnston, Robert A.,
eds. Great Christian
plays...Greenwich, Conn.,
Seabury, 1956. 306p
Abraham and Isaac
Conversion of St. Paul
Everyman
Resurrection
Totentanz

SYMONS, ARTHUR. See NER
Nero (Tragedy). Nero &
other plays.

T

TAFT Taft, Kendall B. Minor
knickerbockers...New
York, American book com-
pany [c1947] 410p
Payne, J. Charles the second

TAT Tatlock, John Strong Perry
and Martin, Robert Grant,
eds. Representative Eng-
lish plays...New York,
Century, 1916. 838p
Abraham and Isaac
Addison, J. Cato
Beaumont, F. and Fletcher,
J. Philaster; or, Love
lies a-bleeding
Browning, R. A blot in the
'scutcheon
Bulwer-Lytton, E. The lady
of Lyons; or, Love and
pride
Congreve, W. The way of the
world
Dekker, T. The shoemakers'
holiday; or, The gentle
craft
Dryden, J. Almanzor and
Almahide; or, The conquest
of Granada
Everyman
Fielding, H. The tragedy of
tragedies; or, The life and
death of Tom Thumb the
great

287

TAT (continued)
Fletcher, J. The wild-goose
chase
Goldsmith, O. She stoops to
conquer; or, The mistakes
of a night
Heywood, T. A woman killed
with kindness
Jonson, B. The alchemist
Lyly, J. Mother Bombie
Marlowe, C. The troublesome
reign and lamentable death
of Edward the second
Middleton, R. and Rowley, W.
The changeling
Noah's flood
Otway, T. Venice preserved;
or, A plot discovered
The second shepherds' play
Shelley, P. The Cenci
Sheridan, R. The school for
scandal
Steele, R. The conscious
lovers
Webster, J. The Duchess of
Malfi
Wilde, O. Lady Windermere's
fan

TAU Tatlock, John Strong Perry
and Martin, Robert Grant,
eds. Representative Eng-
lish plays... 2d ed. rev.
and enl. New York, Apple-
ton-Century [c1938] 914p
Abraham and Isaac
Addison, J. Cato
Beaumont, F. and Fletcher, J.
Philaster; or, Love lies a-
bleeding
Bulwer-Lytton, E. The lady of
Lyons; or, Love and pride
Congreve, W. The way of the
world
Dekker, T. The shoemaker's
holiday; or, The gentle
craft
Dryden, J. Almanzor and
Almahide; or, The conquest
of Granada
Everyman
Fielding, H. The tragedy of
tragedies; or, The life and

death of Tom Thumb the
great
Fletcher, J. The wild-goose
chase
Goldsmith, O. She stoops to
conquer; or, The mistakes
of a night
Heywood, T. A woman killed
with kindness
Jonson, B. The alchemist
Lillo, G. The London mer-
chant; or, The history of
George Barnwell
Lyly, J. Mother Bombie
Marlowe, C. The troublesome
reign and lamentable death
of Edward the second
Middleton, T. and Rowley, W.
The changeling
Noah's flood
Otway, T. Venice preserved;
or, A plot discovered
Pinero, A. The second Mrs.
Tanqueray
Robertson, T. Caste
The second shepherds' play
Shelley, P. The Cenci
Sheridan, R. The school for
scandal
Steele, R. The conscious
lovers
Webster, J. The Duchess of
Malfi
Wilde, O. Lady Windermere's
fan

TAV Taylor, Joseph Richard,
ed. European and Asiatic
plays... Boston, Expression
co., 1936. 730p
Aristophanes. The frogs
Calderón de la Barca, P.
Life is a dream
Corneille, P. The cid
Dekker, T. The shoemakers'
holiday
Enamai No Sayemon. The
cormorant fisher
Esashi Jūō. The bird catcher
in hell
Euripides. Medea
Everyman
Heywood, J. The four p's

288

Hroswitha. Dulcitius
Kālidāsā. Shakuntala
Massinger, P. A new way to
pay old debts
Plautus, T. The Menaechmi
Sackville, T. and Norton, T.
Gorboduc
Seami, M. Atsumori
The second shepherds' play
Seneca, L. Medea
Shakespeare, W. The comedy
of errors
Shirley, J. The traitor
The sorrows of Han
Udall, N. Ralph Roister
Doister

TAY Taylor, William Duncan,
ed. Eighteenth century
comedy... London, Oxford
university press [1929]
413p (The world's classics)
Farquhar, G. The beaux'
stratagem
Fielding, H. The tragedy of
tragedies; or, The life and
death of Tom Thumb the
great
Gay, J. The beggar's opera
Goldsmith, O. She stoops to
conquer
Steele, R. The conscious
lovers

TEN Ten Greek plays, trans-
lated into English by Gilbert
Murray and others; with an
introduction by Lane Cooper,
and a preface by H. B. Dens-
more. New York, Oxford
university press, 1930.
475p
Aeschylus. Agamemnon
Aeschylus. The choephoroe
Aeschylus. The eumenides
Aristophanes. The frogs
Aristophanes. Plutus, the god
of riches
Euripides. Electra
Euripides. Iphigenia in Tauris
Euripides. Medea
Sophocles. Antigone
Sophocles. Oedipus, king of

Thebes

THA Thayer, William Roscoe,
ed. The best Elizabethan
plays... Boston, Ginn
[c1890] 611p
Beaumont, F. and Fletcher,
J. Philaster; or, Love
lies a-bleeding
Fletcher, J. and Shakespeare,
W. The two noble kinsmen
Jonson, B. The alchemist
Marlowe, C. The Jew of
Malta
Webster, J. The Duchess of
Malfi

THEA Theatre. 1953-56. Edited
by John Chapman... New
York, Random House
[c1953-56] 4v
Abbott, G. and Bissell, R.
The pajama game.   54
Anderson, M. The bad
seed.   55
Anderson, R. Tea and sym-
pathy.   54
Axelrod, G. The seven year
itch.   53
Bagnold, E. The chalk
garden.   56
Behrman, S. and Logan, J.
Fanny.   55
Chase, M. Bernardine.   53
Chodorov, E. Oh, men!
Oh, women!   54
Christie, A. Witness for the
prosecution.   55
Denker, H. and Berkey, R.
Time limit!   56
Eliot, T. The confidential
clerk.   54
Fields, J. and Chodorov, J.
The ponder heart.   56
Fields, J. and Chodorov, J.
Wonderful town.   53
Gazzo, M. A hatful of
rain.   56
Giraudoux, J. Ondine.   54
Giraudoux, J. Tiger at the
gates.   56
Hackett, A. and Goodrich, F.
The diary of Ann Frank. 56

THO   Thomas, Russell Brown,
      ed.   Plays and the theatre
      ...Boston, Little, Brown,
      1937. 729p
Anderson, M. Elizabeth the
      queen
Besier, R. The Barretts of
      Wimpole street
Ibsen, H. An enemy of the
      people
Kelly, G. Poor Aubrey
Master Pierre Patelin
Molière, J. The miser
Morton, J. Box and Cox
O'Neill, E. In the zone
Shakespeare, W. Romeo and
      Juliet
Sheridan, R. The school for
      scandal
Sophocles. Antigone
Steele, W. The giant's stair

THOM Thompson, Stith, ed.
      Our heritage of world liter-
      ature...New York, Dryden
      press [c1938] 1246p
Aeschylus. Agamemnon
Aristophanes. The frogs
Chekhov, A. The cherry or-
      chard
Euripides. Alcestis
Goethe, J. Faust, pt. I
Ibsen, H. A doll's house
Molière, J. The miser
Plautus, T. The captives
Racine, J. Phaedra
Shakespeare, W. Hamlet
Sophocles. Antigone
Wilde, O. The importance of
      being earnest

THON Thompson, Stith and Gass-
      ner, John, eds. Our herit-
      age of world literature...
      Rev. ed. New York, Dryden
      press [c1942] 1416p
Aeschylus. Agamemnon
Aristophanes. The frogs
Chekhov, A. The cherry or-
      chard
Euripides. Alcestis
Goethe, J. Faust, pt. I
Hauptmann, G. The weavers

Ibsen, H. A doll's house
Molière, J. The miser
Plautus, T. The captives
Racine, J. Phaedra
Shakespeare, W. Hamlet
Sophocles. Antigone
Wilde, O. The importance of
      being earnest

THP   Three great Greek plays
      ...Selected [with an intro-
      duction] by Lyman Bryson.
      Greenwich, Conn., Faw-
      cett [c1960]
Aeschylus. Agamemnon
Euripides. Hippolytus
Sophocles. Oedipus the king

THR   Three modern plays from
      the French...New York,
      Holt, 1914. 272p
Donnay, M. The other danger
Lavedan, H. The prince
      d'Aurec
Lemaître, J. The pardon

THU   Three plays. London,
      Gardner, Darton [1926] v. p
Ouless, E. Our pageant
Pakington, M. The queen of
      hearts
Paul, Mrs. C. The fugitive
      king

THX   Three Southwest plays...
      With an introduction by
      John Rosenfield. Dallas,
      Southwest review, 1942.
      326p
Acheson, S. We are besieged
Rogers, J. Where the dear
      antelope play
Witherspoon, K.   Jute

THY   Three soviet plays...Mos-
      cow, Foreign Language
      Publishing House [1961]
      247p
Arbuzov, A. It happened in
      Irkutsk
Korneichuk, A. Platon Krechet
Pogodin, N. Kremlin chimes

291

TICK Tickner, Frederick James, ed. Restoration dramatists... London, Nelson [1930] 229p
Dryden, J. Aurangzebe
Farquhar, G. The beaux' stratagem
Otway, T. Venice preserved; or, A plot discovered
Vanbrugh, J. A journey to London

TICO Tickner, Frederick James, ed. Shakespeare's predecessors... London, Nelson [1929] 278p
Greene, R. Friar Bacon and Friar Bungay
Heywood, J. The four p's
Kyd, T. The Spanish tragedy
Marlowe, C. Tamburlaine the great. [pt. I]

TOBI Tobin, James Edward; Hamm, Victor M. and Hines, William H., eds. College book of English literature... New York, American book co. [c1949] 1156p
Marlowe, C. The tragical history of Doctor Faustus
The second shepherds' play
Synge, J. Riders to the sea

TOD Today's literature... edited by Dudley Chadwick Gordon, Vernon Rupert King and William Whittingham Lyman... New York, American book co. [c1935] 998p
Bernard, L. Lars killed his son
Flavin, M. Amaco
Ford, H. Youth must be served
Galsworthy, J. The silver box
Green, P. In Abraham's bosom
Gregory, I. The workhouse ward
Hopkins, A. Moonshine
Jennings, T. No more frontier
O'Neill, E. Where the cross is made

Riggs, L. Knives from Syria

TRE A treasury of the theatre ...from Aeschylus to Eugene O'Neill; edited by Burns Mantle and John Gassner. New York, Simon and Schuster, 1935. 1643p
Aeschylus. Agamemnon
Anderson, M. Elizabeth the queen
Anderson, M. and Stallings, L. What price glory?
Aristophanes. Lysistrata
Chekhov, A. The cherry orchard
Congreve, W. The way of the world
Connelly, M. The green pastures
Euripides. Electra
Everyman
Galsworthy, J. Escape
Goethe, J. Faust, pt. I
Gorki, M. The lower depths
Hauptmann, G. The weavers
Ibsen, H. Hedda Gabler
Job
Jonson, B. Volpone
Kālidāsā. Shakuntala
Kaufman, G. and Ryskind, M. Of thee I sing
Kiyotsugu, K. Sotoba Komachi
Molière, J. The misanthrope
Molnár, F. Liliom
O'Neill, E. Anna Christie
Pirandello, L. Six characters in search of an author
Racine, J. Phaedra
Rostand, E. Cyrano de Bergerac
Shakespeare, W. Hamlet
Shaw, G. Candida
Shelley, P. The Cenci
Sherriff, R. Journey's end
Sophocles. Antigone
Strindberg, A. The father
Synge, J. Riders to the sea
Webster, J. The Duchess of Malfi
Wilde, O. The importance of being earnest

TREA A treasury of the theatre
...[edited by Burns Mantle
and John Gassner] rev. and
adapted for colleges by
Philo M. Buck, jr., John
Gassner [and] H. S. Alber-
son. New York, Simon and
Schuster [c1940] 2v (v1,
From Ibsen to Odets; v2,
Aeschylus to Hebbel)
Abraham and Isaac. 2
Aeschylus. Agamemnon. 2
Anderson, M. Elizabeth the
queen. 1
Anderson, M. and Stallings,
L. What price glory? 1
Aristophanes. Lysistrata. 2
Chekhov, A. The cherry
orchard. 1
Congreve, W. The way of
the world. 2
Connelly, M. The green
pastures. 1
Euripides. Electra. 2
Everyman. 2
Galsworthy, J. Escape. 1
Goethe, J. Faust, pt. I. 2
Gorki, M. The lower depths. 1
Hauptmann, G. The weavers. 1
Hebbel, F. Maria Magda-
lena. 2
Ibsen, H. Hedda Gabler. 1
Job. 2
Jonson, B. Volpone. 2
Kālidāsa. Shakuntala. 2
Molière, J. The misan-
thrope. 2
Molnár, F. Liliom. 1
Odets, C. Awake and sing. 1
O'Neill, E. Anna Christie. 1
Pirandello, L. Six characters
in search of an author. 1
Plautus, T. The Menaech-
mi. 2
Racine, J. Phaedra. 2
Rostand, E. Cyrano de Ber-
gerac. 1
Shakespeare, W. Hamlet. 2
Shaw, G. Candida. 1
Sherriff, R. Journey's end. 1
Sophocles. Antigone. 2
Strindberg, A. The father. 1
Synge, J. Riders to the sea. 1

Webster, J. The Duchess of
Malfi. 2
Wilde, O. The importance of
being earnest. 1

TREC A treasury of the the-
atre...Revised edition for
colleges. Edited by John
Gassner...New York, Si-
mon and Schuster [c1950-
51] 2v (v1, From Aeschy-
lus to Turgenev; (v2,
From Henrik Ibsen to Ar-
thur Miller)
Abraham and Isaac. 1
Aeschylus. Agamemnon. 1
Anderson, M. Elizabeth the
queen. 2
Aristophanes. The frogs. 1
Barrie, J. The admirable
Crichton. 2
Becque, H. The vultures. 2
Brecht, B. The private life
of the master race. 2
Büchner, G. Danton's death.
1
Čapek, K. R.U.R. 2
Chekhov, A. The cherry or-
chard. 2
Congreve, W. The way of
the world. 1
Connelly, M. The green pas-
tures. 1
Coward, N. Blithe spirit. 2
Euripides. The Trojan wo-
men. 1
Everyman. 1
Galsworthy, J. Escape. 2
García Lorca, F. Blood
wedding. 2
Goethe, J. Faust. 1
Gogol, N. The inspector. 1
Gorki, M. The lower
depths. 2
Gregory, I. The workhouse
ward. 2
Hauptmann, G. The
weavers. 2
Hebbel, F. Maria Magda-
lena. 1
Hellman, L. The little
foxes. 2
Ibsen, H. Ghosts. 2

TREC (continued)
Ibsen, H. Hedda Gabler. 2
Jonson, B. Volpone. 1
Kālidāsa. Shakuntala. 1
Kiyotsugu, K. Sotoba Ko-
machi. 1
Maeterlinck, M. The in-
truder. 2
Marlowe, C. The tragical
history of Doctor Faustus. 1
Maugham, W. The circle. 2
Miller, A. Death of a sales-
man. 2
Molière, J. The misan-
thrope. 1
Molnár, F. Liliom. 2
Musset, A. No trifling with
love. 1
O'Casey, S. The plough and
the stars. 2
Odets, C. Golden boy. 2
O'Neill, E. Anna Christie. 2
O'Neill, E. The hairy ape. 2
Pirandello, L. Six characters
in search of an author. 2
Plautus. The Menaechmi. 1
Racine, J. Phaedra. 1
Rostand, E. Cyrano de Ber-
gerac. 2
Saroyan, W. My heart's in
the highlands. 2
Sartre, J. The flies. 2
The second shepherds' play. 1
Shakespeare, W. Hamlet. 1
Shaw, G. Candida. 2
Sheridan, R. The school for
scandal. 1
Sherriff, R. Journey's end. 2
Sophocles. Oedipus the king. 1
Stallings, L. and Anderson,
M. What price glory? 2
Strindberg, A. The father. 2
Strindberg, A. There are
crimes and crimes. 2
Synge, J. Riders to the sea. 2
Terence. The brothers. 1
Tolstoy, L. The power of
darkness. 2
Turgenev, I. A month in
the country. 1
Vega Carpio, L. Fuente ove-
juna. 1
Webster, J. The Duchess of

Malfi. 1
Wedekind, F. The tenor. 2
Wilde, O. The importance of
being earnest. 2
Wilder, T. Our town. 2
Williams, T. The glass me-
nagerie. 2

TREE A treasury of the the-
atre... Revised edition,
edited by John Gassner.
New York, Simon and Schu-
ster [c1951] 3v (v1, World
drama: From Aeschylus to
Turgenev; v2, Modern Euro-
pean drama: From Henrik
Ibsen to Jean-Paul Sartre;
(v3, Modern British and
American drama: From Os-
car Wilde to Arthur Miller)
Abraham and Isaac. 1
Aeschylus. Agamemnon. 1
Anderson, M. Elizabeth the
queen. 3
Aristophanes. The frogs. 1
Barrie, J. The admirable
Crichton. 3
Becque, H. The vultures. 2
Brecht, B. The private life
of the master race. 2
Büchner, G. Danton's death. 1
Čapek, K. R. U. R. 2
Chekhov, A. The cherry or-
chard. 2
Congreve, W. The way of the
world. 1
Connelly, M. The green pas-
tures. 3
Coward, N. Blithe spirit. 3
Euripides. The Trojan wo-
men. 1
Everyman. 1
Galsworthy, J. Escape. 3
García Lorca, F. Blood
wedding. 2
Goethe, J. Faust. 1
Gogol, N. The inspector. 1
Gorki, M. The lower depths.
2
Gregory, I. The workhouse
ward. 3
Hauptmann, G. The
weavers. 2

Hebbel, F. Maria Magdalena. 1
Hellman, L. The little foxes. 3
Ibsen, H. Ghosts. 2
Ibsen, H. Hedda Gabler. 2
Jonson, B. Volpone. 1
Kālidāsā. Shakuntala. 1
Kiyotsugu, K. Sotoba Komachi. 1
Maeterlinck, M. The intruder. 2
Marlowe, C. The tragical history of Doctor Faustus. 1
Maugham, W. The circle. 3
Miller, A. Death of a salesman. 3
Molière, J. The misanthrope. 1
Molnár, F. Liliom. 2
Musset, A. No trifling with love. 1
O'Casey, S. The plough and the stars. 3
Odets, C. Golden boy. 3
O'Neill, E. Anna Christie. 3
O'Neill, E. The hairy ape. 3
Pirandello, L. Six characters in search of an author. 2
Plautus. The Menaechmi. 1
Racine, J. Phaedra. 1
Rostand, E. Cyrano de Bergerac. 2
Saroyan, W. My heart's in the highlands. 3
Sartre, J. The flies. 2
The second shepherds' play. 1
Shakespeare, W. Hamlet. 1
Shaw, G. Candida. 3
Sheridan, R. The school for scandal. 1
Sherriff, R. Journey's end. 3
Sophocles. Oedipus the king. 1
Stallings, L. and Anderson, M. What price glory? 3
Strindberg, A. The father. 2
Strindberg, A. There are crimes and crimes. 2
Synge, J. Riders to the sea. 3
Terence. The brothers. 1
Tolstoy, L. The power of darkness. 2
Turgenev, I. A month in the country. 1

Vega Carpio, L. Fuente ovejuna. 1
Webster, J. The Duchess of Malfi. 1
Wedekind, F. The tenor. 2
Wilde, O. The importance of being earnest. 3
Wilder, T. Our town. 3
Williams, T. The glass menagerie. 3

TRES Tres dramas románticos ... Garden City, New York, Doubleday, 1962. 319p
García Gutiérrez, A. El trovador
Rivas, A. Don Álvaro; ó, La fuerza del Sino
Zorrilla y Moral, J. Don Juan Tenorio

TREWIN, J. C. See PLAN Plays of the year...

TUCD Tucker, Samuel Marion, ed. Modern American and British plays... New York, Harper [c1931] 946p
Anderson, M. Saturday's children
Barry, P. In a garden
Brighouse, H. Hobson's choice
Colton, J. and Randolph, C. Rain
Coward, N. The vortex
Crothers, R. Mary the third
Dane, C. Granite
Emery, G. The hero
Ervine, St. J. John Ferguson
Glover, H. The king's jewry
Granville-Barker, H. Waste
Green, P. The field god
Houghton, S. Hindle wakes
Howard, S. The silver cord
Kaufman, G. and Connelly, M. To the ladies!
Maugham, W. The circle
Millay, E. The king's henchman
Milne, A. The truth about Blayds
Moeller, P. Madame Sand

295

TUCD (continued)
O'Neill, E. The great god
Brown
Pinero, A. The thunderbolt
Vollmer, L. Sun-up
Wilde, O. The importance of
being earnest

TUCG Tucker, Samuel Marion,
ed. Modern continental
plays... New York, Harper,
1929. 836p
Andreyev, L. He who gets
slapped
Annunzio, G. d'. Francesca
da Rimini
Benavente y Martínez, J. La
malquerida
Bjørnson, B. Beyond our
power
Bracco, R. Phantasms
Brieux, E. False gods
Čapek, K. R. U. R.
Chekhov, A. The cherry or-
chard
Claudel, P. The tidings brought
to Mary
Gorki, M. The lower depths
Hauptmann, G. The rats
Kaiser, G. The coral
Kaiser, G. Gas, pt. I
Kaiser, G. Gas, pt. II
Maeterlinck, M. Pelléas and
Mélisande
Molnár, F. Liliom
Pérez Galdós, B. Electra
Rostand, E. Cyrano de Ber-
gerac
Schnitzler, A. Light-o'-love
Strindberg, A. Comrades
Vildrac, C. S. S. Tenacity
Wedekind, F. Such is life

TUCJ Tucker, Samuel Marion,
ed. Modern plays... New
York, Macmillan [c1932]
400p
Bennett, A. and Knoblock, E.
Milestones
Crothers, R. Mary the third
Hughes, H. Hell bent fer
heaven
Milne, A. The ivory door

O'Neill, E. The Emperor
Jones

TUCM Tucker, Samuel Marion,
ed. Twenty-five modern
plays... New York, Harper
[c1931] 1045p
Andreyev, L. He who gets
slapped
Annunzio, G. d'. Francesca
da Rimini
Barry, P. In a garden
Benavente y Martínez, J. La
malquerida
Čapek, K. R. U. R.
Chekhov, A. The cherry or-
chard
Coward, N. The vortex
Crothers, R. Mary the third
Ervine, St. J. John Ferguson
Green, P. The field god
Hauptmann, G. The rats
Howard, S. The silver cord
Kaiser, G. The coral
Kaiser, G. Gas, pt. I
Kaiser, G. Gas, pt. II
Maeterlinck, M. Pelléas and
Mélisande
Maugham, W. The circle
Milne, A. The truth about
Blayds
Molnár, F. Liliom
O'Neill, E. The great god
Brown
Pinero, A. The thunderbolt
Rostand, E. Cyrano de Ber-
gerac
Schnitzler, A. Light-o'-love
Strindberg, A. Comrades
Vildrac, C. S. S. Tenacity
Vollmer, L. Sun-up
Wilde, O. The importance of
being earnest

TUCN Tucker, Samuel Marion
and Downer, Alan S., eds.
Twenty-five modern plays
...Revised edition by Alan
S. Downer, New York,
Harper [c1948] 1009p
Andreyev, L. He who gets
slapped
Auden, W. and Isherwood, C.

The ascent of F6
Benavente, [y Martínez, J.] La malquerida
Čapek, K. R.U.R.
Chekhov, A. The cherry orchard
Cocteau, J. The infernal machine
Ervine, St.J. John Ferguson
Gorky, M. The lower depths
Green, P. The field god
Haines, W. Command decision
Hauptmann, G. The rats
Howard, S. The silver cord
Ibsen, H. Rosmersholm
Kaiser, G. The coral
Kaiser, G. Gas I
Kaiser, G. Gas II
Maeterlinck, M. Pelléas and Mélisande
Molnár, F. Liliom
O'Casey, S. The plough and the stars
O'Neill, E. The great god Brown
Pinero, A. The thunderbolt
Riggs, L. Roadside
Rostand, E. Cyrano de Bergerac
Schnitzler, A. Light-o'-love
Strindberg, A. Comrades
Synge, J. Riders to the sea
Wilde, O. The importance of being earnest

TUCO Tucker, S. Marion and Downer, Alan S., eds. Twenty-five modern plays ... Third edition... New York, Harper [c1953] 1008p
Andreyev, L. He who gets slapped
Benevente, J. La Malquerida
Čapek, K. R.U.R.
Chekhov, A. The cherry orchard
Cocteau, J. The infernal machine
Eliot, T. Murder in the cathedral
Ervine, St. J. John Ferguson
Gorky, M. The lower depths
Hauptmann, G. The rats

Howard, S. The silver cord
Ibsen, H. Rosmersholm
Kaiser, G. The coral
Kaiser, G. Gas, Parts 1 and 2
Maeterlinck, M. Pelléas and Mélisande
Miller, A. Death of a salesman
Molnár, F. Liliom
O'Casey, S. The plough and the stars
O'Neill, E. The great god Brown
Pinero, A. The thunderbolt
Riggs, L. Roadside
Rostand, E. Cyrano de Bergerac
Schnitzler, A. Light-o'-love
Strindberg, A. Comrades
Synge, J. Riders to the sea
Wilde, O. The importance of being earnest
Williams, T. A streetcar named desire

TUP Tupper, Frederick and Tupper, James Waddell, eds. Representative English dramas from Dryden to Sheridan... New York, Oxford university press, 1914. 460p
Addison, J. Cato
Congreve, W. The way of the world
Dryden, J. All for love
Dryden, J. The conquest of Granada
Farquhar, G. The beaux' stratagem
Fielding, H. Tom Thumb the great
Gay, J. The beggar's opera
Goldsmith, O. She stoops to conquer
Otway, T. Venice preserved
Sheridan, R. The rivals
Sheridan, R. The school for scandal
Steele, R. The conscious lovers

297

TUQ Tupper, Frederick and
Tupper, James Waddell,
eds. Representative Eng-
lish dramas from Dryden
to Sheridan...New and enl.
ed. New York, Oxford uni-
versity press [c1934] 722p
Addison, J. Cato
Cibber, C. Love's last shift
Congreve, W. The way of the
world
Dryden, J. All for love
Dryden, J. The conquest of
Granada
Etherege, G. The man of
mode
Farquhar, G. The beaux'
stratagem
Fielding, H. Tom Thumb the
great
Gay, J. The beggar's opera
Goldsmith, O. She stoops to
conquer
Lillo, G. The London merchant
Otway, T. Venice preserved
Rowe, N. The tragedy of Jane
Shore
Sheridan, R. The rivals
Sheridan, R. The school for
scandal
Steele, R. The conscious
lovers
Vanbrugh, J. The relapse
Wycherley, W. The country
wife

TUQH Turkish literature...tr.
into English for the first
time, with a special introduction by Epiphanius Wilson. ...Rev. ed. New York,
Colonial press [1901] 462p
(The world's great classics)
Mirza Feth-Ali, A. The
magistrates

TUR Turrell, Charles Alfred,
ed. and tr. Contemporary
Spanish dramatists...Bos-
ton, Badger [c1919] 397p
Álvarez Quintero, S. and Alvarez Quintero, J. The women's town

Dicenta y Benedicto, J. Juan
José
Linares Rivas, M. The claws
Marquina, E. When the roses
bloom again
Pérez Galdós, B. Electra
Zamacois, E. The passing of
the magi

TWE Twelve famous plays of
the restoration and eigh-
teenth century...New York,
Modern library [c1933]
952p
Congreve, W. Love for love
Congreve, W. The way of the
world
Dryden, J. All for love; or,
The world well lost
Farquhar, G. The beaux'
stratagem
Garrick, D. The clandestine
marriage
Gay, J. The beggar's opera
Goldsmith, O. She stoops to
conquer; or, The mistakes
of a night
Otway, T. Venice preserv'd;
or, A plot discover'd
Sheridan, R. The rivals
Sheridan, R. The school for
scandal
Vanbrugh, J. The provok'd
wife
Wycherley, W. The country
wife

U

UHL Uhler, John Earle, ed.
The best eighteenth century
comedies...New York,
Knopf, 1929. 480p
Farquhar, G. The beaux'
stratagem
Gay, J. The beggar's opera
Goldsmith, O. She stoops to
conquer
Sheridan, R. The rivals
Sheridan, R. The school for
scandal

ULAN Ulanov, Barry, ed.

Makers of the modern the-
ater... New York, McGraw-
Hill [c1961] 743p
Anouilh, J.   Antigone
Betti, U.   The queen and the
rebels
Chekhov, A.   Ivanov
García Lorca, F.   Yerma
Giraudoux, J.   Sodom and
Gomorrah
Giraudoux, J.   Song of songs
Hauptmann, G.   Hannele
Ibsen, H.   John Gabriel Bork-
man
Ionesco, E.   The bald soprano
Marcel, G.   Ariadne
Miller, A.   A view from the
bridge
Montherlant, H.   The master
of Santiago
O'Casey, S.   Purple dust
O'Neill, E.   The long voyage
home
Pirandello, L.   Henry IV
Shaw, G.   Getting married
Strindberg, A.   To Damascus,
part 1
Synge, J.   The well of the
saints
Toller, E.   Hoppla! Such is
life!
Williams, T.   Camino real
Yeats, W.   On Baile's strand
Yeats, W.   Purgatory

UNTE   Untermeyer, Louis, ed.
The Britannica library of
great American writing...
Chicago, J.B. Lippincott
[c1960] 2v
O'Neill, E.   The Emperor
Jones.   2

V

VAN DOREN, CARL CLINTON.
See also AMI American
omnibus... LON London
omnibus...

VAN   Van Doren, Carl Clinton,
ed. The Borzoi reader...
New York, Knopf, 1936.

1033p
Kaufman, G., Ryskind, M.
and Gershwin, I.   Of thee
I sing

VANM   Van Doren, Carl, ed.
Modern American prose...
New York, Harcourt, Brace
[c1934] 939p
Anderson, M. and Stallings,
L.   What price glory?

VENEZKY, ALICE.   See GRIF
Griffin, Alice Sylvia
(Venezky), ed. ...

VOAD   Voaden, Herman Arthur,
ed.   Four good plays to
read and act... Toronto,
Longmans Green [c1944]
297p
Coward, N.   Cavalcade
Jerome, H.   Pride and prejudice
MacLeish, A.   The fall of the
city
Saroyan, W.   My heart's in
the highlands

W

WAGC   Wagenheim, Harold H.;
Brattig, Elizabeth Voris
and Dolkey, Matthew, eds.
Our reading heritage...
New York, Henry Holt
[c1956] 4v
Bennett, A. and Knoblock, E.
Milestones.   4
Cohan, G.   Pigeons and
people.   3
Gilsdorf, F. and Gibson, P.
The ghost of Benjamin
Sweet.   1
Gordon, R.   Years ago.   1
Hoote, H.   The dancers.   2
Kelly, G.   Finders-keepers.   3
O'Neill, E.   In the zone.   2
Osborn, P.   Point of no re-
turn.   3
Rattigan, T.   The Winslow
boy.   2
Shakespeare, W.   Macbeth.   4

WAGC (continued)
Shaw, G. Saint Joan.   4

WAGE   Wagenheim, Harold H.;
Brattig, Elizabeth Voris
and Flesch, Rudolf, eds.
Read up on life...New York,
Henry Holt, 1952. 507p
(Holt literature series)
Gordon, R. Years ago

WAIT   Waite, Harlow O. and
Atkinson, Benjamin P.,
eds.   Literature for our
time...New York, Henry
Holt [c1953] 998p
Anderson, M. Winterset
Barry, P. The Philadelphia
story
Behrman, S. Biography
MacLeish, A. The fall of the
city
O'Neill, E. The hairy ape
Williams, T. The glass me-
nagerie

WAIU   Waite, Harlow O. and
Atkinson, Benjamin P.,
eds.   Literature for our
time...New York, Henry
Holt [c1958] 1009p
Barry, P. The Philadelphia
story
Giraudoux, J. Tiger at the
gates
O'Neill, E. The hairy ape
Shaw, G. Major Barbara
Williams, T. The glass me-
nagerie

WALB   Wall, Vincent and Mc-
Cormick, James Patton,
eds.   Seven plays of the
modern theater...New York,
American book co.   [c1950]
521p
Anderson, M. Winterset
Chekhov, A. Uncle Vanya
Coward, N. Blithe spirit
Ibsen, H. Hedda Gabler
Maugham, W. The circle
O'Neill, E. The hairy ape
Williams, T. The glass me-

nagerie

WALJ   Walley, Harold Reinoehl.
The book of the play...
New York, Scribner [c1950]
699p
Chekhov, A. The sea gull
Congreve, W. The way of the
world
Ibsen, H. An enemy of the
people
Molière, J. The misanthrope
O'Neill, E. Desire under the
elms
Racine, J. Phaedra
Rostand, E. Cyrano de Ber-
gerac
Shakespeare, W. The tragedy
of Hamlet, Prince of Den-
mark
Shakespeare, W. Twelfth night;
or, What you will
Sophocles. Oedipus the king
Strindberg, A. The dream
play
Synge, J. The playboy of the
western world

WALL   Walley, Harold Reinoehl
and Wilson, John Harold,
eds.   Early seventeenth
century plays, 1600-1642...
New York, Harcourt, Brace
[c1930] 1120p
Beaumont, F. and Fletcher,
J. A king or no king
Brome, R. A mad couple well
matched
Chapman, G. The revenge of
Bussy D'Ambois
Chapman, G., Jonson, B.
and Marston, J. Eastward
ho!
D'Avenant, W. Love and honor
Dekker, T. and Middleton, T.
The honest whore, pt. I
Fletcher, J. The wild-goose
chase
Ford, J. 'Tis pity she's a
whore
Heywood, T. A woman killed
with kindness
Jonson, B. Volpone; or, The

300

fox
Marston, J. The Dutch cour-
tesan
Massinger, P. A new way to
pay old debts
Middleton, T. A chaste maid
in Cheapside
Shirley, J. The cardinal
Webster, J. The white devil

WALPOLE, HUGH. See MAL
Malvern festival plays...

WAR Warfel, Harry Redcay;
Gabriel, Ralph Henry and
Williams, Stanley Thomas,
eds. The American mind
...New York, American
book co [c1937] 1520p
O'Neill, E. The Emperor Jones

WARH Warnock, Robert. Rep-
resentative modern plays...
American. Chicago, Scott,
Foresman [c1952] 758p
Anderson, M. Valley Forge
Behrman, S. Biography
Howard, S. The late Christo-
pher Bean
Kaufman, G. and Connelly, M.
Beggar on horseback
Miller, A. Death of a sales-
man
Odets, C. Waiting for Lefty
O'Neill, E. Mourning becomes
Electra
Williams, T. The glass me-
nagerie

WARI Warnock, Robert, ed.
Representative modern plays,
British. Chicago, Scott,
Foresman [1953] 710p
Barrie, J. The admirable
Crichton
Coward, N. The blithe spirit
Eliot, T. Murder in the ca-
thedral
Fry, C. A phoenix too fre-
quent
Galsworthy, J. Loyalties
Maugham, W. The constant
wife

O'Casey, S. Juno and the paycock
Shaw, G. The doctor's dilemma
Synge, J. Riders to the sea

WARN Warnock, Robert and
Anderson, George K., eds.
The world in literature...
Chicago, Scott, Foresman
[c1950] 2v in 1
Aeschylus. Agamemnon.   1
Aristophanes. The clouds. 1
Euripides. Hippolytus.   1
Kālidāsa. Shakuntala.   1
Shakespeare, W. Hamlet,
Prince of Denmark.   2
Sophocles. Oedipus the
king.   1
Vega Carpio, L. The sheep
well.   2

WAT Watrous, George Ansel,
ed. Elizabethan dramatists
...New York, Crowell
[1903] 293p
Beaumont, F. and Fletcher,
J. Philaster
Jonson, B. Every man in his
humour
Marlowe, C. Dr. Faustus

WATA Watson, Ernest Bradlee
and Pressey, Benfield, eds.
Contemporary drama: A-
merican, English and Irish,
European...New York,
Scribner [c1959] 577p
Chekhov, A. Uncle Vanya
Eliot, T. Murder in the ca-
thedral
Frings, K. Look homeward,
Angel
García Lorca, F. Blood wed-
ding
Ibsen, H. Hedda Gabler
Inge, W. Come back, little
Sheba
Miller, A. The crucible
O'Casey, S. Purple dust
O'Neill, E. Ah, wilderness!
Pirandello, L. Henry IV
Shaw, G. Man and superman

303

Kotzebue, A. Pharaoh's
daughter
Mackay, C. The prince of
court painters
Tarkington, B. and Wilson,
H. The Gibson upright
Webber, J. Frances and
Francis

WEE Week-end library. 3rd is-
sue [1930] Garden City,
N.Y., Doubleday Page,
1930. v.p.
Maugham, W. The circle
Morley, C. Really, my dear...
Morley, C. Wagon-lits

WHE Wheeler, Charles Bicker-
steth, ed. Six plays by
contemporaries of Shake-
speare... London, Oxford
university press [1928]
595p (The world's classics)
Beaumont, F. and Fletcher, J.
The knight of the burning
pestle
Beaumont, F. and Fletcher,
J. Philaster
Dekker, T. The shoemakers'
holiday
Massinger, P. A new way to
pay old debts
Webster, J. The Duchess of
Malfi
Webster, J. The white devil

WHITING, B.J. See COL College survey of English literature. [Edited by B.J.
Whiting... and others]

WHI Whitman, Charles Hunting-
ton, ed. Representative
modern dramas... New York,
Macmillan, 1936. 1121p
Anderson, M. Elizabeth the
queen
Barry, P. Hotel Universe
Behrman, S. Biography
Benavente y Martínez, J. The
bonds of interest
Brieux, E. The red robe
Chekhov, A. The cherry or-

chard
Galsworthy, J. Strife
Gorki, M. The lower depths
Green, P. In Abraham's
bosom
Hauptmann, G. The weavers
Howard, S. The silver cord
Ibsen, H. The wild duck
Maeterlinck, M. Pelléas and
Mélisande
Maugham, W. Our betters
Molnár, F. Liliom
O'Casey, S. Juno and the pay-
cock
O'Neill, E. The hairy ape
Pinero, A. Mid-channel
Pirandello, L. Six characters
in search of an author
Rostand, E. Cyrano de Ber-
gerac
Schnitzler, A. The lonely way
Strindberg, A. The father
Synge, J. Riders to the sea
Wilde, O. The importance of
being earnest

WHK Whitman, Charles Hunting-
ton, ed. Seven contempo-
rary plays... Boston, Houghton Mifflin [c1931] 565p
Chekhov, A. The cherry orchard
Galsworthy, J. Strife
Hauptmann, G. The sunken
bell
Ibsen, H. An enemy of the
people
O'Neill, E. Beyond the horizon
Rostand, E. Cyrano de Bergerac
Synge, J. Riders to the sea

WHT Whittaker, Charlotte C.,
ed. Youth and the world
... Chicago, Ill., Lippincott [c1955] 512p (Reading
for life series)
Ibsen, H. A doll's house

WILS Wilson, John Harold, ed.
Six Restoration plays...
Boston, Houghton Mifflin

WILS (continued)
[c1959] 463p
Congreve, W. The way of the
world
Dryden, J. All for love; or,
The world well lost
Etherege, G. The man of
mode; or, Sir Fopling
Flutter
Farquhar, G. The beaux'
stratagem
Otway, T. Venice preserved;
or, A plot discovered
Wycherley, W. The country
wife

WILSON, EPIPHANIUS. See
TUQH Turkish literature...

WINN Winny, James, ed. Three
Elizabethan plays... London,
Chatto and Windus [c1959]
223p
Mucedorus
The reign of King Edward III
Lyly, J. Midas

WISD Wise, Jacob Hooper;
Congleton, J. E.; Morris,
Alton C. and Hodges, John
C. ... College English: the
first year... New York, Har-
court, Brace [c1952] 959p
Kingsley, S. Darkness at
noon
Rostand, E. Cyrano de Ber-
gerac
Thurber, J. and Nugent, E.
The male animal

WISE Wise, Jacob Hooper;
Congleton, J. E.; Morris,
Alton C. and Hodges, John
C. ... College English: the
first year... Revised edition.
New York, Harcourt, Brace
[c1956] 982p
Miller, A. Death of a sales-
man
Rostand, E. Cyrano de Ber-
gerac
Shaw, G. Pygmalion

WISF Wise, Jacob Hooper;
Morris, Alton C. and
Hodges, John C., eds.
College English: the first
year. Third edition... New
York, Harcourt, Brace
[c1960] 982p
Anouilh, J. Antigone
Capote, T. The grass harp
Miller, A. Death of a sales-
man
Shaw, G. Androcles and the
lion

WOO Woods, George Benjamin;
Watt, Homer Andrew and
Anderson, George Kumler,
eds. The literature of
England... Chicago, Scott,
Foresman [c1936] 2v
Dekker, T. The shoemakers'
holiday.   1
Galsworthy, J. Strife.   2
Marlowe, C. The tragical his-
tory of Doctor Faustus. 1
The second shepherds' play.1
Sheridan, R. The rivals.   1
Wilde, O. The importance of
being earnest.   2

WOOD Woods, George Benja-
min; Watt, Homer Andrew
and Anderson, George Kum-
ler, eds. The literature of
England... [Rev. ed.] Chicago, Scott, Foresman
[c1941] 2v
Everyman.   1
Jonson, B. Epicoene; or, The
silent woman.   1
Marlowe, C. Doctor Faustus.
                                       1
Sheridan, R. The school for
scandal.   1
The second shepherds' play.1
Synge, J. Riders to the sea.
                                       1
Wilde, O. The importance of
being earnest.   2

WOOE Woods, George Benjamin;
Watt, Homer A. and Ander-
son, George K., eds. ...

The literature of England...
[Third edition] Chicago, Ill.,
Scott, Foresman, [1947] 2v
Congreve, W. The way of the
world.   1
Dryden, J. All for love   1
Everyman.   1
Marlowe, C. The tragical his-
tory of Doctor Faustus.   1
The second shepherds' play.1
Shakespeare, W. The tragedy
of Antony and Cleopatra. 1
Sheridan, R. The school for
scandal.   1
Synge, J. Riders to the sea.2
Wilde, O. The importance of
being earnest.   2

WORL   The world in literature
[edited by] Elizabeth Col-
lette; Tom Peete Cross and
Elmer C. Stauffer. Boston,
Ginn [c1949] 4v
Barrie, J. Shall we join the
ladies?   4
Shakespeare, W. Julius
Caesar.   2
Shakespeare, W. Macbeth. 4
Wilder, T. Our town.   3

WORLD DRAMA SERIES.   See
SMI, SMK, SML, SMN,
SMO, SMP, SMR Smith,
Robert Metcalf, ed.

THE WORLD'S GREAT BOOKS.
See GRE Great plays (Eng-
lish) ...GREA Great plays
(French and German)...
GREE Greek dramas...

THE WORLD'S GREAT CLASSICS.
See ORI Oriental literature
...PLAB Plays by Greek,
Spanish, French, German
and English dramatists...
TUQH Turkish literature...

WORP World's great plays; with
an introduction by George
Jean Nathan. Cleveland,
Ohio, World publishing co.
[1944] 491p

Aristophanes. Lysistrata
Chekhov, A. The cherry or-
chard
Goethe, J. Faust
Ibsen, H. The master builder
O'Casey, S. The plough and
the stars
O'Neill, E. The Emperor
Jones
Rostand, E. Cyrano de Ber-
gerac

THE WORLD'S GREATEST LIT-
ERATURE. See DRA
Dramatic masterpieces...

WRIGHT, JOHN HENRY. See
MAST Masterpieces of
Greek literature...

X, Y, Z

YOHA Yohannan, John D., ed.
A treasury of Asian litera-
ture...New York, John Day
[c1956] 487p
Kālidāsa. Shakuntala
Motokiyo, S. Atsumori

ZDA Zdanowicz, Casimir Douglas, ed. Four French
comedies of the eighteenth
century...New York, Scribner [c1933] 488p (The modern student's library)
Beaumarchais, P. Le barbier
de Séville
Lesage, A. Turcaret
Marivaux, P. Le jeu de l'a-
mour et du hasard
Sedaine, M. Le philosophe
sans le savoir

Almighty dollar, The. See
Woolf, B. The mighty dollar
Alone. Alyoshin, S.
L'alouete. See Anouilh, J. The
lark
Alsfeld, passion play. See Anony-
mous plays. The passion play
of Alsfeld
Amaco. Flavin, M.
L'amant ridicule. Bois-Robert,
F.
Amantes de Teruel, Los. Hartz-
enbusch, J.
Amants, Les. See Donnay, M.
The lovers
Amar despuês de la muerte. See
Calderón de la Barca, P.
Love after death
Amazing Dr. Clitterhouse, The.
Lyndon, B.
Ambush. Richman, A.
Amends for ladies. Field, N.
American, The. James, H.
American liberty triumphant.
See Leacock, J. The fall of
British tyranny
American orphan in Germany,
The. See Dunlap, W. False
shame
American way, The. Kaufman,
G. and Hart, M.
Americans in England. See
Paulding, J. The bucktails
Americans in Tripoli. See
Jones, J. S. The usurper
L'ami des lois. Laya, J.
Aminta. Tasso, T.
Amor de don Perlimplin. See
Garcia Lorca, F. Love of
don Perlimplin and Belisa in
the garden
L'amore dei tre re. See Be-
nelli, S. The love of the
three kings.
Amorous prawn, The. Kimmins,
A.
Amoureuse. Porto-Riche, G.
Amphitryon. Plautus, T.
Amphitryon 38. Behrman, S.
Amphitryon 38. Giraudoux, J.
See Behrman, S. Amphitryon
38
Anarchy. See MacKaye, S. Paul

Kauvar
Anastasia. Maurette, M.
Anatol. Schnitzler, A.
Anatomist, The; or, The sham
doctor... with the loves of
Mars and Venus. Ravens-
croft, E. and Motteux, P.
An der lumpa parti. Barba, P.
Andersonville trial, The. Levitt,
S.
Andronic. See Campistron, J.
Andronicus
Andronicus. Campistron, J.
And so ad infinitum. Čapek, K.
and Čapek, J.
And so they were married. See
Williams, J. Why marry?
And that's the truth. See Pi-
randello, L. Right you are!
If you think so
André. Dunlap, W.
Andria, The. See Terentius
Afer, P. The woman of An-
dros
Andria, the fair Andrian. See
Terentius Afer, P. The wo-
man of Andros
Androcles and the lion. Shaw, G.
Andromache. Euripides
Andromaque. Racine, J.
Angel on the ship, The. Wilder,
T.
Angel street. Hamilton, P.
Angels of war. Box, M.
L'anglais tel qu'on le parle.
Bernard, T.
Animal kingdom, The. Barry, P.
Ann Rutledge. Corwin, N.
Ann Veronica. Gow, R.
Anna Christie. O'Neill, E.
Anna Kleiber. Sastre, A.
Anna Lucasta. Yordan, P.
Anna Sophie Hedvig. Abell, K.
Anne Boleyn. Albery, P.
Anne Frank, the diary of a
young girl. See Hackett, A.
and Goodrich, F. The diary
of Anne Frank
Anne of the thousand days. Ander-
son, M.
Anniversary, The. See Chekhov,
A. The jubilee
L'annonce faite à Marie.

Claudel, P.
Annunciation, The. Anonymous
plays
Another language. Franken, R.
Another part of the forest. Hell-
man, L.
Antichrist. Anonymous plays
Antigone. Anouilh, J.
Antigone. Sophocles
Antigone and the tyrant. See
Anouilh, J. Antigone
Antigone et le tyrant. See
Anouilh, J. Antigone
Antipodes, The. Brome, R.
Antony. Dumas, A., père
Antony and Cleopatra. Shake-
speare, W.
Any other business. Ross, G.
Apius and Virginia. Anonymous
plays
Apollinaris. Second, L.
Apollo. Pixley, F.
Apollo of Bellac, The. Girau-
doux, J.
L'Apollon de Bellac. See Girau-
doux, J. The Apollo of Bellac
L'Apollon de Marsac. See Girau-
doux, J. The Apollo of Bellac
Apostle play, The. Mell, M.
L'apoticaire devalisé. Villiers,
C.
Appearance is against them.
Inchbald, E.
Appius and Virginia. See Anony-
mous plays. Apius and Vir-
ginia
Arbitration, The. Menander
Archives of Palermo, The. See
Stone, J. Tancred, King of
Sicily
Ardèle. Anouilh, J.
Ardèle; ou, La Marguerite. See
Anouilh, J. Ardèle
Arden of Feversham. Anonymous
plays
Aren't we all? Lonsdale, F.
Aria da capo. Millay, E.
Ariadne. Marcel, G.
Aristocrats. Pogodin, N.
Arm of the law, The. Brieux, E.
Arms and the man. Shaw, G.
Arraignment of Paris, The.
Peele, G.

Arrant knave, An. MacKaye, S.
Arsenic and old lace. Kessel-
ring, J.
Art of being bored, The. See
Pailleron, E. Le monde ou
l'on s'ennuie
Arvers' secret. See Bernard,
J. Le secret d'Arvers
As a man thinks. Thomas, A.
As husbands go. Crothers, R.
As it was in the beginning. See
Hodge, M. The wind and the
rain.
As long as they're happy. Syl-
vaine, V.
As the leaves fall. See Gia-
cosa, G. Like falling leaves
As you desire me. Pirandello,
L.
As you like it. Shakespeare, W.
Ascent of F 6, The. Auden, W.
and Isherwood, C.
Asinaria. See Plautus, T. The
comedy of asses
Asmodée. Mauriac, F.
Assumption of Hannele, The.
See Hauptmann, G. Hannele
At Mrs. Beam's. Munro, C.
At the bottom. See Gorki, M.
[pseud.] The lower depths
At the gate beautiful. Mason, H.
At the hawk's well. Yeats, W.
Athaliah. Racine, J.
Atonement of Pan, The. Red-
ding, J.
Atsumori. Seami, M.
En attendant Godot. See Beck-
ett, S. Waiting for Godot
Attentat. See Somin, W. Close
quarters
Attilio Rigolo. Metastasio, P.
Attowell's jig. Anonymous plays
Les aubes. See Verhaeren, É.
The dawn
Augustus in search of a father.
Chapin, H.
Aulularia. Plautus, T.
Aunt Julia's Caesar. Hutchins,
M.
Auprès de ma blonde. Achard,
M. See Behrman, S. I know
my love

311

Beggars' bush. Fletcher, J.,
Massinger, P. [and Beaumont,
F.]

Beggar's opera, The. Gay, J.

Behind the curtain of the soul.
See Evreinov, N. The theatre
of the soul

Behold the bridegroom. Kelly, G.

Behold we live. Van Druten, J.

Bell, book and candle. Van Druten, J.

Bell for Adano, A. Osborn, P.

Belle Lamar. Boucicault, D.

La belle Russe. Belasco, D.

La belle sauvage. See Baker, J.
The Indian princess

Belle's stratagem, The. Cowley,
Mrs. H.

Dells, The. Lewis, L.

Belshazzar. Milman, H.

Belshazzar. More, H.

Belshazzar's feast. Calderón de
la Barca, P.

Beneath four eyes. See Fulda,
L. Tête-à-tête

Benediktbeuren play, The.
Anonymous plays

Benjamin Franklin, journeyman.
Mackay, C.

Bérénice. Racine, J.

Berkeley square. Balderston, J.

Bernardine. Chase, M.

Best man, The. Vidal, G.

Besuch der alten dame, Der.
See Duerrenmatt, F. The visit

Betrayal, The. (Wakefield).
Anonymous plays

Betrayal of Christ, The (Chester)
Anonymous plays

Betraying of Christ, The (Coventry). Anonymous plays

Between the battles. Bjørnson,
B.

Beyond human power. See
Bjørnson, B. Beyond our power

Beyond our power. Bjørnson, B.

Beyond the horizon. O'Neill, E.

Bianca Viconti; or, The heart
overtasked. Willis, N.

Bias of the world, The. See
Benavente y Martínez, J. The
bonds of interest

Der biberpeiz, eine diebskomödie.

See Hauptmann, G. The
beaver coat

Biedermann and the firebugs.
Frisch, M.

Biedermann und die brandstifter.
See Frisch, M. Biedermann
and the firebugs

Big bonanza, The. Daly, A.

Big fish, little fish. Wheeler, A.

Big house, The. Robinson, L.

Big knife, The. Odets, C.

Bilker bilk'd, The. Anonymous
plays

Bill of divorcement, A. Ashton,
W.

Billy Budd. Coxe, L. and Chapman, R.

Billy the kid. Woods, W.

Bilora. Beolco, A.

Bilsen play. See Anonymous
plays. The star

Biography. Behrman, S.

Bird catcher in hell, The.
Esashi Jūō

Bird child, The. White, L.

Bird of contention, The. Clausen, S.

Birds, The. Aristophanes

Birth of Jesus, The (York).
Anonymous plays

Birth of Merlin, The; or, The
child hath found his father.
Anonymous plays

Birthday honours. Jones, P.

Birthday party, The. Piner, H.

Birthright. Murray, T.

Bishop Jon Arason. Sveinbjörnsson, T.

Bishop's candlesticks, The.
Rickert, V.

Bitter fate, A. Pisemkiĭ, A.

Bitter harvest. Turney, C.

Bitter oleander. See Garcia
Lorca, F. Blood wedding

Bjaerg-Ejvind og hans hustru.
See Sigurjónsson, J. Eyvind
of the hills

Black chiffon. Storm, L.

Black man, The; or, The spleen.
Payne, J.

Black Rip Van Winkle, The.
See Gold, M. Hoboken blues

Blackberryin'. Smith, H. F.

313

Brome plays. See Anonymous plays. Abraham and Isaac
Brothers, The. See Terentius Afer, P. Adelphi
Brothers in arms. Denison, M.
Brothers Karamazoff, The. Nemirovich-Danchenko, V.
Brott och brott. See Strindberg, A. There are crimes and crimes
Brutus; or, The fall of Tarquin. Payne, J.
Bucktails, The; or, Americans in England. Paulding, J.
Buggbears, The. Jeffere, J.
Bunch of keys, A; or, The hotel. Hoyt, C.
Bunthorne's bride. See Gilbert, W. and Sullivan, A. Patience.
El burlador de Sevilla. Téllez, G.
Burlesque. Watters, G. and Hopkins, A.
Bury fair. Shadwell, T.
Bury the dead. Shaw, I.
Bus stop. Inge, W.
Bushido. Idzumo, T.
Business is business. See Mirbeau, O. Les affaires sont les affaires
Busman's honeymoon. Sayers, D. and Byrne, M.
Bussy D'Ambois. Chapman, G.
Bussy D'Ambois, The revenge of. Chapman, G.
Butter and egg man, The. Kaufman, G.
By accident. Williams, H. and Williams, M.
By ourselves. See Fulda, L. Tête-à-tête
Bygmester Solness. See Ibsen, H. The master builder

C

Cabrerita. Acevedo Hernanandez, A.
La caccia al lupo. See Verga, G. The wolfhunt
Caesar and Cleopatra. Shaw, G.
La Cagnolte. See Labiche, E. and Delacour, A. Pots of money
Cain. Byron, G.
Cain and Abel. Anonymous plays
Caine mutiny court-martial, The. Wouk, H.
Caligula. Camus, A.
Calisto and Melibaea. See Anonymous plays. The beauty and good properties of women
Call it a day. Smith, D. G.
Calline browierts, Die. Iobst, C.
Cambises, King of Persia. Preston, T.
Cambyses. See Preston, T. Cambises, King of Persia
Camilla; or, The fate of a coquette. See Dumas, A., fils. La dame aux camélias
Camille. See Dumas, A., fils. La dame aux camélias
Camino real. Williams, T.
Camp of Wallenstein, The. Schiller, J.
Campaspe. Lyly, J.
Campion, Edmund. See Breen, R. and Schnibbe, H. "Who ride on white horses"
Campo dei fiori. See Ilyenkov, V. The square of flowers
Canavans, The. Gregory, I.
Canción de cuna. See Martínez Sierra, G. and Martínez Sierra, M. The cradle song
Candida. Shaw, G.
Candide. Hellman, L.
Candle in the wind. Anderson, M.
La cantatrice chauve. See Ionesco, E. The bald soprano
Cantique des cantiques. See Giraudoux, J. Song of songs
Capitan and the corporal, El. Corwin, N.
Les caprices de Marianne. Musset, A.
Captain Jinks of the horse marines. Fitch, C.
Captain O'Blunder. See Sheridan, T. The brave Irishman
Captives, The. Plautus, T.
Captivi. See Plautus, T. The captives

315

Cardinal, The. Shirley, J.
Career. Lee, J.
Career for Ralph. Richmond, S.
Careless husband, The. Cibber,
C.
Caretaker, The. Pinter, H.
Caridorf; or, The avenger. Bird,
R.
Carmencita and the soldier.
Lipskeroff, K.
Carthaginian, The. Plautus, T.
Cartwheel. Knight, V.
La casa de Bernarda Alba. See
García Lorca, F. The house
of Bernarda Alba
Casa paterna. See Sudermann,
H. Magda
Case of Astrolable, The. Phelps,
M.
Case of rebellious Susan, The.
Jones, H.
Casina. Plautus, T.
Casket, The. Plautus, T.
Cassilis engagement, The. Han-
kin, St. J.
Caste. Robertson, T.
Castle in the air. Melville, A.
Castle of perseverance, The.
Anonymous plays
Cat and the canary, The. Willard,
J.
Cat on a hot tin roof. Williams,
T.
Cathleen ni Houlihan. Yeats, W.
Cato. Addison, J.
Cavalcade. Coward, N.
Cavalier from France, The.
Fortune, J.
Cavalleria rusticana. Verga, G.
Cave man, The. Field, C.
Cave of Salamanca, The. Cer-
vantes Saavedra, M.
Cecile; or, The school for
fathers. Anouilh, J.
Cécile; ou, L'école des pères.
See Anouilh, J. Cecile
Celestina; or, The tragi-comedy
of Calisto and Melibea. Rojas,
F.
Célimare. Labiche, E. and
Delacour, A.
Célimare le bien-aimé. See
Labiche, E. and Delacour, A.

Célimare
La cena de Baltasar. See
Calderón de la Barca, P.
Belshazzar's feast
La cena delle beffe. See Be-
nelli, S. The jest
Cenci, The. Shelley, P.
Centenarian, The. See Álvarez
Quintero, S. and Álvarez Quin-
tero, J. A hundred years old
Centenario. See Álvarez Quin-
tero, S. and Álvarez Quintero,
J. A hundred years old
Chains. Baker, E.
Chalk circle, The. Anonymous
plays
Chalk garden, The. Bagnold, E.
Champion north. Wilson, T.
Champions of morality. See
Thomas, L. Moral
La chance de Françoise. See
Porto-Riche, G. Françoise'
luck
Chances, The. Fletcher, J.
Chandelier, The. Musset, A.
Changeling, The. Middleton, T.
and Rowley, W.
Changelings, The. Dodd, L.
Chantilly play, The. See
Courlet, Katherine. The na-
tivity
Charity ball, The. Belasco, D.
and De Mille, H.
Charles the second; or, The
merry monarch. Payne, J.
and Irving, W.
Charlotte Corday. Jerome, H.
Chaste maid in Cheapside, A.
Middleton, T.
Chatterton. Vigny, A.
Le chemin de Crête. See Mar-
cel, G. Ariadne
Cherry orchard, The. Chekhov,
A.
Chester play of the deluge. See
Anonymous plays. The deluge
Chester plays. See Anonymous
plays: Abraham, Melchisedec
and Isaac; The adoration of
the magi; The adoration of
the shepherds; Antichrist; The
betrayal of Christ; Christ's
ascension; Christ's ministry;

Christ's passion; Christ's resurrection; The creation of man: Adam and Eve; The death of Herod; The deluge; The fall of Lucifer; The last judgment; The magi's oblation; The nativity; The prophets; The resurrection, harrowing of hell, and the last judgment; The sacrifice of Isaac; Simon the leper; The slaying of the innocents
Le cheval Tartare. See Payne, J. Mazeppa
Le chevalier à la mode. Dancourt, F.
Chicago. Watkins, M.
Chicken feed. Bolton, G.
Chicken soup with barley. Wesker, A.
Child hath found his father, The. See Anonymous plays. The birth of Merlin
Child of Grace. See Funt, J. The magic and the loss
Child wife, The. See Ibsen, H. A doll's house
Children in uniform. Winsloe, C.
Children of darkness. Mayer, E.
Children of Heracles, The. See Euripides. The Heracleidae
Children's hour, The. Hellman, L.
Chimes of the Kremlin, The. Pogodin, N.
China pig, The. Emig, E.
Chinese white. Gielgud, V.
Choephori, The. See Aeschylus. Choephoroe
Choephoroe. Aeschylus
Choice of a tutor, The. Fonvízin, D.
Choosing company. Schwartz, D.
Chosroes. Rotrou, J.
Christmas carol, A. Shay, F.
Christmas mumming, A. Anonymous plays
Christmas play of St. George. See Anonymous plays. A Christmas mumming
Christopher Blake. Hart, M.
Christ's ascension (Chester). Anonymous plays

Christ's ministry (Chester). Anonymous plays
Christ's passion (Chester). Anonymous plays
Christ's resurrection (Chester). Anonymous plays
Chronicle history of Perkin Warbeck, The. Ford, J.
Church street. Robinson, L.
Churl, The. See Plautus, T. Truculentus
Ciascuno a suo modo. See Pirandello, L. Each in his own way
Le cid. Corneille, P.
Cid, The. See Corneille, P. Le cid
Cigale chez les fourmis, La. Legouvé, E. and Labiche, E.
Cinna; or, The mercy of Augustus. Corneille, P.
Circle, The. Maugham, W.
Circular staircase, The. See Rinehart, M. and Hopwood, A. The bat
Cistellaria. See Plautus, T. The casket
Cit turned gentleman, The. See Molière, J. Le bourgeois gentilhomme
La città morta. See Annunzio, G. d'. The dead city
City, The. Fitch, C.
Clandestine marriage, The. Colman, G. and Garrick, D.
Clarence. Tarkington, B.
Claudia. Franken, R.
Claws, The. Linares Rivas, M.
Clean kill, A. Gilbert, M.
Clearing in the woods, A. Laurents, A.
Clérambard. Aymé, M.
Climate of Eden, The. Hart, M.
Climbers, The. Fitch, C.
Clive of India. Lipscomb, W. and Minney, R.
Clod, The. Beach, L.
Close quarters. Somin, W.
Closed door, The. Praga, M.
Clouds, The. Aristophanes
Clutterbuck. Levy, B.
Cobler of Preston, The. Johnson, C.

Cock of the village, The. See
Smith, R. The last man
Cock-a-doodle dandy. O'Casey,
S.
Cockpit. Boland, B.
Cocktail party, The. Eliot, T.
Coelina; ou, L'enfant du mystère.
Pixérécourt, R.
Cold wind and the warm, The.
Behrman, S.
Coliphizacio (Wakefield). Anony-
mous plays
Colleen bawn, The; or, The
brides of Garryowen. Bouci-
cault, D.
College widow, The. Ade, G.
Colonel's lady, The. Sherriff, R.
Columbine. Clements, C.
Come back, little Sheba. Inge,
W.
Come le foglie. See Giacosa, G.
Like falling leaves
Come tu mi vuoi. See Piran-
dello, L. As you desire me
Comedia Himenea. See Torres
Naharro, B. Hymen
La comédie de celui qui épousa
une femme muette. France,
A.
Comedy called Misogonus, A.
See Anonymous plays. Miso-
gonus
Comedy of asses, The. Plautus,
T.
Comedy of errors, The. Shake-
speare, W.
Coming of peace, The. See
Hauptmann, G. Das friedens-
fest
Command decision. Haines, W.
Commercial drummer, The.
See Jessop, G. Sam'l of Posen
Commissioner, The. Courteline,
G.
Common conditions. Anonymous
plays
Complaisant lover, The. Greene,
G.
Comrades. Strindberg, A.
Le comte D'Essex. See Cor-
neille, T. The earl of Essex
Comus. Milton, J.
Conceited count, The. See

Destouches, P. Le glorieux
Concert, The. Bahr, H.
Condemnation. Tolstoi, L.
Condemned, The. Dagerman, S.
Confederacy, The. Vanbrugh, J.
Confessional. Wilde, P.
Confidential clerk, The. Eliot,
T.
Conflagration of the opera house,
The. See Kaiser, G. The
fire in the opera house
Conflict, The. McCauley, C.
Connais-toi. See Hervieu, P.
Know thyself
Conquering hero, The. Monk-
house, A.
Conquest of Granada, The. See
Dryden, J. Almanzor and
Almahide
Conscience. Iffland, A.
Conscious lovers, The. Steele,
R.
Conspiracy, The. See Bulwer-
Lytton, E. Richelieu
Constant prince, The. Calderón
de la Barca, P.
Constant wife, The. Maugham,
W.
Consuelo. López de Ayala, A.
Contract of marriage between
wit and wisdom, The. Anony-
mous plays
Contrast, The. Tyler, R.
Conversation piece. Coward, N.
Conversion of St. Paul, The.
Anonymous plays
Convulsiones, Las. Vargas Te-
jada, L.
Cophetua. Drinkwater, J.
Copper pot, The. Healey, F.
Copperhead, The. Thomas, A.
Le coq de village. Décour, C.
and Théodore, A. See Smith,
R. The last man
Coquette. Abbott, G. and
Bridgers, A.
Coral, The. Kaiser, G.
Les corbeaux. Becque, H.
Coriolanus. Shakespeare, W.
Cormorant fisher, The. Enamai
No Sayemon
Corn is green, The. Williams,
E.

Cornelius. Priestley, J.
Cornish play of the three Maries,
The. See Anonymous plays.
The three Maries
Corruption in the palace of jus-
tice. Betti, U.
Corruzione al Palazzo di Gius-
tizia. See Betti, U. Corrup-
tion in the palace of justice
Cose è se vi pare! See Piran-
dello, L. Right you are! If
you think so
Cosi sia. See Gallarati-Scotti,
T. They will be done
Cosroès. See Rotrou, J. Chos-
roes
Cottage on the cliff, The. See
Wood, H. East Lynne
Council of women, The. See
Aristophanes. The ecclesi-
azusae
Council retained. Mackay, C.
Counsellor-at-law. Rice, E.
Count your blessings. Jeans, R.
Countess Cathleen, The. Yeats,
W.
Countess Julie. See Strindberg,
A. Miss Julia
Country girl, The. Odets, C.
Country wake, The. See Dog-
get, T. Hob
Country wife, The. Wycherley,
W.
County chairman, The. Ade, G.
La course du flambeau. Her-
vieu, P.
Court singer, The. See Wede-
kind, F. Der kammersänger
Cousin Billy. See Labiche, E.
and Martin, E. Le voyage
de Monsieur Perrichon
Coventry plays. See Anonymous
plays. The annunciation; The
betraying of Christ; The death
of Pilate; The fall of Lucifer;
Herod and the magi; The
magi, Herod and the slaughter
of the innocents; The mystery
of the redemption; The pageant
of the shearmen and tailors;
The salutation and conception;
The shepherd's play; The trial
of Christ

Coward, The. Lenormand, H.
Cowled lover, The. Bird, R.
Cradle song, The. Martínez Si-
erra, G. and Martínez Sierra
M.
Cradle will rock, The. Blitz-
stein, M.
Craig's wife. Kelly, G.
Creation and the fall of Lucifer,
The (York). Anonymous plays
Creation of Adam and Eve, The
(York). Anonymous plays
Creation of Eve, The, with the
expelling of Adam and Eve
out of Paradise. Anonymous
plays
Creation of man: Adam and Eve,
The (Chester). Anonymous
plays
Creditors. Strindberg, A.
Crépuscule du théatre. See
Lenormand, H. In Theatre
street
Cretan woman, The. Jeffers, R.
Cricket and the hearth, The.
Smith, A.
Criminal code, The. Flavin, M.
Crispin médecin. Hauteroche, N.
See Ravenscroft, E. and
Motteux, P. The anatomist
Crispin, rival de son maître.
See Le Sage, A. Crispin rival
of his master
Crispin, rival of his master.
Le Sage, A.
Critic, The; or, A tragedy re-
hearsed. Sheridan, R.
Crock of gold, The. See Plautus.
Aulularia
Crock of gold, The; or, The
toiler's trials. Steele, S.
Cromedeyre-le-vieil. Romains,
J.
Crown of light, The. Bulkley, A.
Crows, The. See Becque, H.
Les corbeaux
Crucible, The. Miller, A.
Crucifixion, The (Wakefield).
Anonymous plays
Crucifixion, The (York). Anony-
mous plays
Crude and unrefined. Bowen, M.
Cruel fate. See Pisemskiĭ, A.

Deadly game, The. Yaffe, J.
Dear Brutus. Barrie, J.
Dear Charles. Melville, A.
Dear delinquent. Popplewell, J.
Dear Ruth. Krasna, N.
Death and the fool. See Hofmannsthal, H. von. Der tor und der tod
Death dance, The. Duncan, T.
Death of a salesman. Miller, A.
Death of Alexander the great, The. See Lee, N. The rival queens
Death of Eve, The. Moody, W.
Death of García Lorca, The. Whittington, R.
Death of Herod, The (Chester). Anonymous plays
Death of Ivan the terrible, The. Tolstoi, A.
Death of Odysseus, The. Abel, L.
Death of Pilate, The (Cornish). Anonymous plays
Death of Satan, The. Duncan, R.
Death of Tintagiles, The. Maeterlinck, M.
Death of Titian, The. Hofmannsthal, H. von
Death of Wallenstein, The. Schiller, J.
Death stone, The. Anonymous plays
Death takes a holiday. Casella, A.
Deburau. Guitry, S.
Decision. Chodorov, E.
Declassee. Akins, Z.
Deep are the roots. Gow, J. and D'Usseau, A.
Deep blue sea, The. Rattigan, T.
Defeat, The; a play about the Paris Commune. Grieg, N.
Deidre of the sorrows. Synge, W.
Deirdre. Russell, G.
Deirdre. Yeats, W.
Del'rey abajo, ninguno. Rojas Zorrilla, F.
Deluge, The (Chester). Anonymous plays
Deluge, The (Wakefield). Anonymous plays
Le demi-monde. See Dumas, A., fils. The outer edge of society
Den dödsdörnde. See Dagerman, S. The condemned
Depositio cornuti typographici. See Anonymous plays. The printer's apprentice
Los derechos de la salud. Sánchez, F.
La dernière nuit de Don Juan. See Rostand, E. The last night of Don Juan
El desdén con el desdén. Moreto y Cavana, A.
Design for living. Coward, N.
Le désir attrapé par la queue. See Picasso, P. Desire trapped by the tail
Desire trapped by the tail. Picasso, P.
Desire under the elms. O'Neill, E.
Desperate hours, The. Hayes, J.
Destinies of Haman and Mordecai, The. See Tyler, R. The origin of the feast of Purim; or, The destinies of Haman and Mordecai
Destruction of Jerusalem, The. Crowne, J.
Detective story. Kingsley, S.
Detour, The. Davis, O.
Les deux gendres. Étienne, C. See Payne, J. The two sons-in-law
Deux orphelines, Les. See D'Ennery, A. and Cormon, E. The two orphans
Devil and his dame, The. See Anonymous plays. Grim the collier of Croydon
Devil of a wife. Jevon, T. See Jevon, T.; Coffey, C.; Mottley, J.; and Cibber, T. The devil to pay
Devil passes, The. Levy, B.
Devil to pay, The; or, The wives metamorphos'd. Jevon, T.; Coffey, C.; Mottley, J. and Cibber, T.
Devil's disciple, The. Shaw, G.
Devil's general, The. Zuckmayer, C.
Devourer of dreams, The. See Lenormand, H. The dream doctor

321

Dial "M" for murder. Knott, F.

Diamond cut diamond. Williamson, H.

Diary of a scoundrel, The. Ostrovsky, A.

Diary of a young girl. See Hackett, A. and Goodrich, F. The diary of Anne Frank

Diary of Anne Frank, The. Hackett, A. and Goodrich, F.

Die ausnahme und die regel. See Brecht, B. The exception and the rule

Diff'rent. O'Neill, E.

Digby plays. See Anonymous plays. The conversion of St. Paul

Dinner at eight. Kaufman, G. and Ferber, E.

Disenchanted, The. Schulbert, B.

Disraeli. Parker, L.

Distaff side, The. Van Druten, J.

Distant point. See Afinogenyev, A. Far taiga

Divorce. Daly, A.

Divorcio nupcial. Eichilbaum, S.

Divorcons. See Sardou, V. and Najac, E. Let's get a divorce!

Em docktor Fogel sie offis schtunn. Birmelin, J.

Le docteur amoureux. Anonymous plays

Doctor and the devils, The. Thomas, D.

Doctor Faustus. See Marlowe, C. The tragical history of Doctor Faustus

Doctor in spite of himself, The. Molière, J.

Dr. Knock. Romains, J.

Dr. Kranich's sprechstunde. See Anonymous plays. Em Doctor Fogel sei offis schtunn (based on book by John Birmelin)

Doctor's daughter, The. See Goetz, R. and Goetz, A. The heiress

Doctor's delight. Molière, J.

Doctor's dilemma, The. Shaw, G.

Dodsworth. Howard, S.

Dog beneath the skin, The. Auden, W. and Isherwood, C.

Dog in the manger, The. Vega Carpio, L.

Les doigts de fée. Scribe, A.

Doll's house, A. Ibsen, H.

Dolly reforming herself. Jones, H.

Il domatore Gastone. See Morselli, E. Gastone the animal tamer

Domestic picture, A. Ostrovskii, A.

Dominant sex, The. Egan, M.

Dominion of darkness, The. See Tolstoi, L. The power of darkness

Don Álvaro; ó la fuerza del sino. Rivas, A. Don Álvaro ó la fuerza del sino

Don Carlos. Schiller, J.

Don Cristobita and Doña Rosita, The. García Lorca, F.

Don Juan in hell. Shaw, G.

Don Juan Tenorio. Zorrilla y Morae, J.

Don Juan's last night. See Rostand, E. The last night of Don Juan

Doña Clarines. Álvarez Quintero, S. and Alvarez Quintero, J.

Donna Diana. See Moreto y Cavaña, A. El desdén con el desdén

Don't listen, ladies! Guitry, S.

Doomsday circus. See Basshe, E. The dream of the dollar

Door should be either open or shut, A. Musset, A. de

Dot. Boucicault, D.

Double discovery, The. See Dryden, J. The Spanish fryar

Double yolk. Williams, H. and Williams, M.

Doughgirls, The. Fields, J.

Douglas. Home, J.

Dover road, The. Milne, A.

Down and out. See Gorki, M. [pseud.] The lower depths

Down our street. Wise, E.

Dragon, The. Gregory, I.

Dragon's mouth. Priestley, J. and Hawkes, J.

Un drama nuevo. Tamayo y

Baus, M.
Dramatic sequel to Hamlet, A;
or, The new wing at Elsinor.
"Mr. Punch" [pseud.]
Dramatic sequel to The lady of
Lyons, A; or, In the Lyons
den. "Mr. Punch" [pseud.]
Dramatist, The; or, Stop him
who can! Reynolds, F.
Dream doctor, The. Lenormand,
H.
Dream girl. Rice, E.
Dream of Scipio, The. Metas-
tasio, P.
Dream of the dollar, The.
Basshe, E.
Dream play, The. Strindberg, A.
Dreaming of the bones, The.
Yeats, W.
Dreamy kid, The. O'Neill, E.
Dreigroschenoper. See Brecht,
B. The threepenny opera
Drifting apart. Herne, J.
Ett drömspel. See Strindberg,
A. The dream play
Dronning gaar igen. See Abell,
K. The queen on tour
Dronningen og hennes menn. See
Kielland, T. Queen Margaret
of Norway
Drums of Oude, The. Strong, A.
Duchess at sunset, The. John-
son, P.
Duchess of Malfi, The. Webster,
J.
Duchess of San Quentin, The.
See Pérez Galdós, B. La de
San quintín
Duel of angels. Giraudoux, J.
Duenna, The. Sheridan, R.
Duk Moraud. Anonymous plays
Duke and no duke, A; or, Tra-
polin's vagaries. Tate, N.
Duke and the actress, The. See
Schnitzler, A. The green
cockatoo
Duke's motto, The; or, I am
here! Brougham, J.
Et dukkehjem. See Ibsen, H.
A doll's house
Dulcitius. Hrotsvit
Dulcy. Kaufman, G. and Con-
nelly, M.

Dumb waiter, The. Pinter, H.
Dupe, The. Ancey, G. [pseud.]
Dust in the eyes. See Labiche,
E. and Martin, É. La
poudre aux yeux
Dust of the road. Goodman, K.
Dutch courtesan, The. Marston,
J.
Dybbuk, The. Rappoport, S.
Dyskolos. See Menander. The
grouch

E

Each his own wilderness. Les-
sing, D.
Each in his own way. Piran-
dello, L.
Earl of Essex, The. Corneille,
T.
Earth-spirit, The. See Wede-
kind, F. Erdgeist
Easiest way, The. Walter, E.
East Lynne. Wood, H.
Easter resurrection play, An.
Anonymous plays
Eastward ho! Chapman, G.,
Jonson, B. and Marston, J.
Eastward hoe. See Chapman,
G., Jonson, B. and Marston,
J. Eastward ho!
Eastward in Eden. Gardner, D.
Easy virtue. Coward, N.
Eb refschneider un Susi Leim-
bach. Wollenweber, L.
Ecclesiazusae. Aristophanes
L'école de maris. See Molière,
J. School for husbands
L'école de pères. See Anouilh,
J. Cecile
Edmund Campion. See Breen,
R. and Schnibbe, H. "Who
ride on white horses"
Educating Josefina. Villa, L.
Edward, my son. Morley, R.
Edward II. See Marlowe, C.
The troublesome reign and la-
mentable death of Edward the
second
Edward III. See Anonymous
plays. The reign of King Ed-
ward the third
Edwardians, The. Gow, R.

Egelykke. Munk, K.
Egg, The. Marceau, F.
Egmont. Goethe, J.
Der egoist und kritikus. See
Kotzebue, A. Egotist and
pseudo-critic Herr Gottlieb
Merks
Egotist and pseudo-critic Herr
Gottlieb Merks. Kotzebue, A.
Eigensinn. See Benedix, R.
Obstinacy
Ein gesprach. Wollenweber, L.
Einsame menschen. Hauptmann,
G.
Der einsame weg. See Schnitz-
ler, A. The lonely way
El capitan and the corporal.
Corwin, N.
Elckerlijk. See Anonymous
plays. Everyman
Electra. Euripides
Electra. Giraudoux, J.
Electra. Hofmannsthal, H. von
Electra. Pérez Galdós, B.
Electra. Sophocles
Electre. See Giraudoux, J.
Electra
Elijah. Davidson, R.
Elizabeth the queen. Anderson,
M.
Elvira. See Calderón de la
Barca, P. No siempre lo
peor es cierto
Empedocles on Etna. Arnold, M.
Emperor Jones, The. O'Neill, E.
Emperor of the moon, The.
Behn, A.
Emperor's clothes, The. Tabori,
G.
Empress of Morocco, The.
Settle, E.
En gespräch zwischen zweb demo-
krate über politiks. Miller, D.
En idealist. See Munk, K.
Herod the king
En kvinde er overflodig. See
Sonderby, K. A woman too
many
Enchanted, The. Giraudoux, J.
Enchanted castle, The. See
Duffett, T. The mock-tempest
Enchanted island, The. See Dry-
den, J. and D'Avenant, W.

The tempest
End of summer. Behrman, S.
End of the beginning, The.
O'Casey, S.
Endgame. Beckett, S.
Endimion. See Lyly, J. Endy-
mion
Endymion, the man in the moon.
Lyly, J.
Enemy, The. Pollock, C.
Enemy, The. See Wincelberg,
S. Kataki
Enemy of society, An. See
Ibsen, H. An enemy of the
people
Enemy of the people, An. Ibsen,
H.
L'enfant du mystère. See Pix-
érécourt, R. Coelina
Engineer Sergeyev. Rokk, V.
English as it is spoken. See
Bernard, T. L'anglais tel
qu'on le parle
Enough stupidity in every wise
man. See Ostrovsky, A. The
diary of a scoundrel
Enrico IV. See Pirandello, L.
Henry IV
Enter madame. Varesi, G. and
Byrne, D.
Enter Solly Gold. Kops, B.
Entertainer, The. Osborne, J.
L'envers d'une sainte. Curel,
F. de
Epicoene; or, The silent woman.
Jonson, B.
Epicurean, The. See Wedekind,
F. The Marquis of Keith
L'epidémic. See Mirbeau, O.
The epidemic
Epidemic, The. Mirbeau, O.
Epidicus. Plautus, T.
Epitaph for George Dillon. Os-
borne, J. and Creighton, A.
Epitrepontes. See Menander.
The arbitration
Equal match, An. See Fletcher,
J. Rule a wife and have a
wife
Equites. See Aristophanes.
The knights
Erasmus Montanus. See Hol-
berg, L. Rasmus Montanus

G. d'
Francesca da Rimini. Boker, G.
Francis' new jig. See Anonymous plays. Attowell's jig
Françoise' luck. Porto-Riche, G.
Freedom of Jean Guichet, The. Mackay, L.
French without a master. See Bernard, T. L'anglais tel qu'on le parle
French without tears. Rattigan, T.
Friar Bacon and Friar Bungay. See Greene, R. The honorable history of Friar Bacon and Friar Bungay
Das friedensfest. Hauptmann, G.
Frock and thrills. See Scribe, A. Les doigts de fée
Frogs, The. Aristophanes
Fröken Julie. See Strindberg, A. Miss Julia
Frolic wind. Pryce, R.
From morn to midnight. Kaiser, G.
From rags to riches. Taylor, G.
From the depths. See Gorki, M. [pseud.] The lower depths
Front, The. Korneichuk, A.
Front page, The. Hecht, B. and MacArthur, C.
La frontière de Savoie. See Scribe, E. A peculiar position
Fruen fra havet. See Ibsen, H. The lady from the sea
Fuenteovejuna. Vega Carpio, L.
La fuerza del sino. See Rivas, A. Don Álvaro
Fugitive king, The. Paul, C.
Fulgens and Lucrece. Medwall, H.
Full moon in March, A. Yeats, W.
Fumed oak. Coward, N.
Fun after supper. Smith, B.
Furies, The. See Aeschylus. Eumenides

G

Galatea. See Gilbert, W. and

Sullivan, A. Pygmalion and Galatea
Galgamannen: en midvintersaga. See Schildt, R. The gallows man
Galileo. Brecht, B.
Galley slave, The. Campbell, B.
Gallows man, The: a midwinter story. Schildt, R.
Gamblers. Gogol, N.
Gambler's fate, The. See Dunlap, W. Thirty years
Game at chess, A. Middleton, T.
Game of love and chance, The. See Marivaux, P. Le jeu de l'amour et du hazard
Gammer Gurton's nedle. See Stevenson, W. Gammer Gurton's needle
Gammer Gurton's needle. Stevenson, W.
Gardener's dog, The. See Vega Carpio, L. The dog in the manger
La garra. See Linares Rivas, M. The claws
Gas I. Kaiser, G.
Gas II. Kaiser, G.
Gaslight. See Hamilton, P. Angel street
Gastone the animal tamer. Morselli, E.
Gauntlet, A. Bjørnson, B.
Gay invalid, The. See Molière, J. Doctor's delight
Gay Lord Quex, The. Pinero, A.
Le gendre de M. Poirier. Augier, E. and Sandeau, J.
Generous Portugal, The. See Fletcher, J. The island princess
Gengangere. See Ibsen, H. Ghosts
Le gentilhomme Guespin. Donneau de Visé, J.
Gentle craft, The. See Dekker, T. The shoemaker's holiday
Gentle gunman, The. MacDougall, R.
Gentle savage, The. See Brougham, J. Pocahontas
George a Greene, the pinner of

Herr Gottlieb Merks Government inspector, The. See Gogol, N. The inspector

Gracious ones, The. See Aeschylus. Eumenides

La grammaire. Labiche, E. and Leveaux, A.

El gran Galeoto. Echegaray y Eizaguirre, J.

Gran teatro del mundo. See Calderón de la Barca, P. The great theater of the world

Grand cham's diamond, The. Monkhouse, A.

Grand cham's necklace. See Monkhouse, A. The grand cham's diamond

Grand hotel. Baum, V.

Granite. Ashton, W.

Granny Maumee. Torrence, F.

Grass harp, The. Capote, T.

Grass is greener, The. Williams, H. and Williams, M.

Grasshopper at the home of the ants. See Legouvé, E. and Labiche, E. La cigale chez les fourmis

Great adventure, The. Bennett, A.

Great Broxopp, The. Milne, A.

Great diamond robbery, The. Alfriend, E. and Wheeler, A.

Great divide, The. Moody, W.

Great Galeoto, The. See Echegaray y Eizaguirre, J. El gran Galeoto

Great god Brown, The. O'Neill, E.

Great highway, The. Strindberg, A.

Great theater of the world, The. Calderón de la Barca, P.

Green bay tree, The. Shairp, M.

Green cockatoo, The. Schnitzler, A.

Green goddess, The. Archer, W.

Green grow the lilacs. Riggs, L.

Green hat, The. Arlen, M.

Green knight, The. Garnett, P.

Green pastures, The. Connelly, M.

Grief goes over. Hodge, M.

Grim the collier of Croydon; or, The devil and his dame. Anonymous plays

Grouch, The. Menander.

Group, The. Warren, M.

Gruach. Bottomley, G.

Der gruene kakadu. See Schnitzler, J. The green cockatoo

La guarda Cuidadosa. See Cervantes Saavedra, M. The vigilant sentinel

Guárdate del agua mansa. See Calderón de la Barca, P. Keep your own secret

Guerillas of the Ukrainian Steppes. Korneichuk, A.

La guerre de Troie n'aura pas lieu. See Giraudoux, J. Tiger at the gates

Guilty party. Ross, G.

Gunpowder, treason and plot. Williamson, H.

Der gute mensch von Sezuan. See Brecht, B. The good woman of Setzuan

Guys and dolls. Swerling, J.; Burrows, A. and Loesser, F.

Guzmán el Bueno. Gil y Zárate, A.

Gypsy. Anderson, M.

H

H.M.S. Pinafore; or, The lass that loved a sailor. Gilbert, W. and Sullivan, A.

Hairy ape, The. O'Neill, E.

Haiti. Dubois, W.

Half a loaf. See Lonsdale, F. Let them eat cake

Hamadryads, The. Irwin, W.

Hamlet. Shakespeare, W.

Hamlet of Stepney Green, The. Kops, B.

Hamlet; or, The new wing at Elsinore. See "Mr. Punch" [pseud.] A dramatic sequel to Hamlet

Hand of Siva, The. Goodman, K. and Hecht, B.

Hands around. See Schnitzler,

330

A. Round dance
Hannele. Hauptmann, G.
Hannele's assumption. See
Hauptmann, G. Hannele
Hanneles himmelfahrt. See
Hauptmann, G. Hannele
En hanske. See Bjørnson, B.
A gauntlet
Happiest days of your life.
Dighton, J.
Happiness in a nook. See
Sudermann, H. The vale of
content
Happy as Larry. MacDonagh, D.
Happy day, A. Kock, C.
Happy haven, The. Arden, J.
and D'Arcy, M.
Happy journey to Trenton and
Camden, The. Wilder, T.
Happy man, The. Williams, H.
and Williams, M.
Happy time, The. Taylor, S.
Hard fate, A. See Pisemskii,
A. A bitter fate
Harriet. Ryerson, F. and
Clements, C.
Harrowing of hell, The (Chester).
Anonymous plays
Harrowing of hell, The; or, The
extraction of souls from hell
(Wakefield). Anonymous plays
Harvest in the north. Hodson, J.
Harvey. Chase, M.
Haste to the wedding. See La-
biche, E. and Marc-Michel,
L. An Italian straw hat
Hasty heart, The. Patrick, J.
Hatful of rain, A. Gazzo, M.
Haunted house, The. Plautus, T.
"Having wonderful time." Kober,
A.
Hay fever. Coward, N.
El haz de leña. Núñez de Arce,
G.
Hazel Kirke. MacKaye, S.
He and she. Crothers, R.
He who gets slapped. Andreev, L.
Headshrinkers, The. See Reg-
nier, M. Paddle your own
canoe
Heart of age, The. Bercoveci,
E.
Heart of Bruce. Williamson, H.

Heart of Maryland, The. Be-
lasco, D.
Heart overtasked, The. See
Willis, N. Bianca Visconti
Heat wave. Pertwee, R.
Heautontimorumenos. Terentius
Afer, P.
Heaven and earth. Byron, G.
Hecuba. Euripides
Hecyra. See Terentius Afer, P.
The mother-in-law
Hedda Gabler. Ibsen, H.
Das heilige experiment. See
Hochwalder, F. The strong
are lonely
Heimat. See Sudermann, H.
Magda
Heinrich aus Andernach. Unruh,
F.
Heinrich und Heinrichs geschlecht.
See Wildenbruch, E. von
King Henry
Heiress, The. Goetz, R. and
Goetz, A.
Helen. Euripides.
Helena's husband. Moeller, P.
Hell-bent fer heaven. Hughes,
H.
Hello out there. Saroyan, W.
Héloise. Forsyth, J.
Henri III et sa cour. Dumas,
A., père
Henrietta, The. Howard, B.
Henry IV. Pirandello, L.
Henry IV. See Shakespeare, W.
King Henry the fourth
Henry IV of Germany, pt. I.
See Wildenbruch, E. von.
King Henry
Henry the fifth. See Anonymous
plays. The famous victories
of Henry the fifth
Hepta epi Thebas. See Aeschy-
lus. The seven against The-
bes
Her great match. Fitch, C.
Her master's voice. Kummer,
C.
Heracleidae, The. Euripides
Heracles. Euripides
Hercules furens. See Seneca,
L. Mad Hercules
Heracles mad. See Euripides.

331

Hope for a harvest. Treadwell,
S.
Hoppla! See Toller, E. Hoppla!
Such is life!
Hoppla! Such is life! Toller, E.
Hoppla, wir leben. See Toller,
E. Hoppla! Such is life!
Horace. Corneille, P.
Horizon. Daly, A.
Horse-shoe Robinson. Tayleure,
C.
Horse thief, The. Sachs, H.
Hostage, The. Behan, B.
Hotel, The. See Hoyt, C. A
bunch of keys
Hotel Universe. Harry, P.
Hour-glass, The. Yeats, W.
House by the lake, The. Mills,
H.
House in the square, A. Morgan,
D.
House of Atreus, The (Trilogy).
See Aeschylus. Agamemnon;
Choephoroe; Eumenides
House of Bernarda Alba, The.
García Lorca, F.
House of Connelly, The. Green,
P.
House of cowards, Abse, D.
Household peace, The. Mau-
passant, G. de
Houseparty. Britton, K. and
Hargraves, R.
How to succeed in business with-
out really trying. Burrows,
A., Weinstock, J. and Gil-
bert, W.
Die huchzich um kreitz waig?
Wieand, P.
Hue and cry after cupid, The.
Jonson, B.
Huis clos. Sartre, J.
Die huldigung des künste. See
Schiller, J. The homage of
the arts
Human comedy, The. Estabrook,
H.
Humour out of breath. Day, J.
Hundred years old, A. Álvarez
Quintero, S. and Álvarez
Quintero, J.
Hurricanes. Howard, B.
Hyacinth Halvey. Gregory, I.

Hymen. Torres Naharro, B.
Hymn to the rising sun. Green,
P.
Hypochondriac, The. See
Molière, J. Le malade imag-
inaire
Hypocrite, The. See Molière,
J. Le Tartuffe

I

I am a camera. Van Druten, J.
I am here! See Brougham, J.
The duke's motto
I fantasmi. See Bracco, R.
Phantasms
I killed the count. Coppel, A.
I know my love. Behrman, S.
I remember mama. Van Druten,
J.
I rise in flame, cried the
Phoenix. Williams, T.
I suppositi. Ariosto, L. See
Gascoigne, G. Supposes "I
want!" Holme, C.
Icebound. Davis, O.
Iceman cometh, The. O'Neill, E.
Ideal husband, An. Wilde, O.
Ideas of Madame Aubray, The.
See Dumas, A., fils. Les
idées de Madame Aubray.
Les idées de Madame Aubray.
Dumas, A. fils
Idiot's delight. Sherwood, R.
Idyl of San Francisco. See
Hoyt, C. A trip to Chinatown
If. Dunsany, E.
If a claw is caught the bird is
lost. See Tolstoĭ, L. The
power of darkness
If I were king. McCarthy, J.
Il faut qu'une porte soit ouverte
ou fermée. See Musset, A.
A door should be either open
or shut
Il reduce. See Beolco, A. Ruz-
zante returns from the wars
"Ile." O'Neill, E.
Ill May-day, An. See Anony-
mous plays. Sir Thomas
More
Imaginary invalid, The. See
Molière, J. Le malade imagi-

naire
Immoralist, The. Goetz, R. and Goetz, A.
Immortal husband, The. Merrill, J.
Impassioned wife, The. See Porto-Riche, G. Amoureuse
Impatient poverty. Anonymous plays
Importance of being earnest, The. Wilde, O.
Imposter, The. See Molière, J. Le Tartuffe
L'imposteur. See Molière, J. Le Tartuffe
Improper duchess, The. Fagan, J.
In a balcony. Browning, R.
In a garden. Barry, P.
In Abraham's bosom. Green, P.
In camera. Sartre, J.
In Mizzoura. Thomas, A.
In spite of all. MacKaye, S.
In the city of David. Gonne, F.
In the depths. See Gorki, M. [pseud.] The lower depths
In the frame of don Cristóbal. Garcia Lorca, F.
In the Lyons den. See 'Mr. Punch" [pseud.] A dramatic sequel to The Lady of Lyons
In the shadow of the glen. Synge, J.
In the summer house. Bowles, J.
In the train. O'Donovan, M.
In the zone. O'Neill, E.
In Theatre Street. Lenormand, H.
In time to come. Kock, H. and Huston, J.
Indian princess, The; or, La belle sauvage. Barker, J.
Indian queen, The. Dryden, J. and Howard, R.
Indomitable blacksmith. Law, W.
Ines Mendo; or, The triumph of prejudice. Mérimée, P.
Infernal machine, The. Cocteau, J.
Informer, The. O'Flaherty, L.
Inga. Glebov, A.
Inherit the wind. Lawrence, J. and Lee, R.

Innocent voyage, The. Osborn, P.
Innocents, The. Archibald, W.
Die inschurens bissness. See Grumbine, E. Die insurance bissness
Insect comedy, The. See Čapek, K. and Čapek, J. And so ad infinitum
Insect play, The. See Čapek, K. and Čapek, J. And so ad infinitum
Inspector, The. Gogol, N.
Inspector calls, An. Priestley, J.
Inspector-general, The. See Gogol, N. The inspector
Insurance business, Die. Grumbine, E.
Intellectual ladies, The. See Molière, J. Les femmes savantes
Intelligence comes to grief. See Griboiedov, A. Wit works woe
Los intereses creados. See Benavente y Martínez, J. The bonds of interest
Interests created. See Benavente y Martinez, J. The bonds of interest
L'intérieur. See Maeterlinck, M. Interior
Interior. Maeterlinck, M.
Interlude of Godley Queen Hester, An. See Anonymous plays. Godley Queen Hester
Interlude of impatient poverty, An. See Anonymous plays. Impatient poverty
Interlude of John the evangelist, The. See Anonymous plays. John the evangelist
Interlude of wealth and health, An. See Anonymous plays. Wealth and health
Interlude of youth, The. See Anonymous plays. Youth
Intermezzo. See Giraudoux, J. The enchanted
Intermezzo. Schnitzler, A.
Intimate relations. Cocteau, J.
Intimate strangers, The. Tarkington, B.
Intruder, The. Maeterlinck, M.
L'intruse. See Maeterlinck, M.

334

and Sir John
John loves Mary. Krasna, N.
Joseph Smith, jr., A play about.
  Phelps, M.
John the Baptist. Sudermann, H.
John the evangelist. Anonymous
  plays
John, Tyb and Sir John. Hey-
  wood, J.
John, Tyb and the curate. See
  Heywood, J. John, Tyb and
  Sir John
Johnny Johnson. Green, P.
La joie fait peur. Girardin, D.
Jonathan. Ewing, T.
Joseph and his brethren. Tyler,
  R.
Joshua Whitcomb. See Thomp-
  son, D. The old homestead
Le joug. See Guinon, A. and
  Marnière, J. The yoke
Die journalisten. See Freytag,
  G. The journalists
Journalists, The. Freytag, G.
Une journée de bonheur. See
  Kock, C. A happy day
Journey to heaven of Hannele,
  The. See Hauptmann, G.
  Hannele
Journey to Jerusalem. Ander-
  son, M.
Journey to London, A. Van-
  brugh, J.
Journey's end. Sherriff, R.
Jovial crew, A. Brome, R.
Joyous season, The. Barry, P.
Juan José. Dicenta y Benedicto,
  J.
Juan Lorenzo. Garcia Gutíerrez,
  A.
Juan Moreira. Manco, S.
Jubilee, The. Chekhov, A.
Judah. Jones, H.
Judge, The. Branner, H.
Judge Lynch. Rogers, J.
Judgment day. Rice, E.
Judgment Day, The (York).
  Anonymous plays
Judgment of Solomon, The.
  Tyler, R.
Die Jüdin von Toledo. See
  Grillparzer, F. The Jewess
  of Toledo

Judith. Giraudoux, J.
Julius Caesar. Shakespeare, W.
June moon. Lardner, R. and
  Kaufman, G.
Junior miss. Fields, J. and
  Chodorov, J.
Juno and the paycock. O'Casey,
  S.
Jupiter in disguise. See
  Plautus, T. Amphitryon
Just neighborly. Dean, A.
Justice. Galsworthy, J.
Jute. Witherspoon, K.

K

Kaethchen of Heilbronn; or, The
  test of fire. Kleist, H.
Kaga-Sodo. See Anonymous
  plays. The fatal error
Kamiano, the story of Damien.
  Lavery, E. and Murphy, G.
Der kammersänger. Wedekind,
  F.
Kamraterna. See Strindberg, A.
  Comrades
Kanske en diktare. See Joseph-
  son, R. Perhaps a poet
Kataki. Wincelberg, S.
Das Käthchen von Heilbronn;
  oder, Die feuerprobe. See
  Kleist, H. Kaetchen of Heil-
  bronn
Katie Roche. Deevy, T.
Keep an eye on Amélie. Fey-
  deau, G.
Keep, The. Thomas, G.
Keep your own secret. Calde-
  rón de la Barca, P.
Key Largo. Anderson, M.
Killing of Abel, The (Wakefield).
  Anonymous plays
Das kind der liebe. See Kotze-
  bue, A. Lovers' vows
Kind lady. Chodorov, E.
Kindling. Kenyon, C.
King Argimenes and the unknown
  warrier. Dunsany, E.
King Darius. Anonymous plays
King Edward the third. See
  Anonymous plays. The reign
  of King Edward the third
King Henry. Wildenbrugh, E.

King Henry the eighth. Shake-
speare, W.
King Henry the fifth. Shake-
speare, W.
King Henry the fourth. Shake-
speare, W.
King Henry VI, pt. I. Shake-
speare, W.
King Henry VI, pt. II. Shake-
speare, W.
King John. Bale, J.
King John. See Shakespeare, W.
The life and death of King
John
King Lear. Shakespeare, W.
King Lear. See Tate, N. The
history of King Lear
King of Friday's men, The.
Molloy, M.
King or no king, A. Beaumont,
F. and Fletcher, J.
King Stag, The. Gozzi, C.
King, the greatest Alcalde, The.
Vega Carpio, L.
Kingdom of God, The. Martínez
Sierra, G. and Martínez Sier-
ra, M.
King's daughter. See Lewis, S.
Siwan
King's henchman, The. Millay,
E.
King's jewry, The. Glover, H.
King's threshold, The. Yeats, W.
Kirflugen. See Clausen, S. The
bird of contention
Kiss and tell. Herbert, F.
Kiss in Zanadu, A. Ames, W.
Kiss the boys good-bye. Boothe,
C.
Kitchen, The. Wesker, A.
Kjaerlighedens tragedie. See
Heiberg, G. The tragedy of
love
Knave and queen. Young, C. and
Howard, B.
Knight of the burning pestle, The.
Beaumont, F. and Fletcher, J.
Knights, The. Aristophanes
Knives from Syria. Riggs, L.
Knock about, The. See And-
reev, L. He who gets
slapped
Know thyself. Hervieu, P.

Kongsemnerna. See Ibsen, H.
The pretenders
König Nikolo. See Wedekind, F.
Such is life
König Ottokars glück und ende.
Grillparzer, F.
Konkylien. See Krog, H. The
sounding shell
Das konzert. See Bahr, H.
The concert
Die koralle. See Kaiser, G.
The coral
Kremlin chimes. See Pogodin,
N. The chimes of the Krem-
lin
Kynge Johan. See Bale, J.
King John

L

"L." Atlas, L.
La la noo. Yeats, J.
Laburnum grove. Priestley, J.
Lace on her petticoat. Stuart,
A.
Le lâche. See Lenormand, H.
The coward
Lady Audley's secret. Hazle-
wood, C.
Lady from the sea, The. Ibsen,
H.
Lady in the dark. Hart, M.
Lady Julie. See Strindberg, A.
Miss Julia
Lady Margaret. See Scribe, A.
Les doigts de fée
Lady of Lyons, The; or, In the
Lyons den. See "Mr. Punch"
[pseud.] A dramatic sequel to
The Lady of Lyons
Lady of Lyons, The; or, Love
and pride. Bulwer-Lytton, E.
Lady of May, The. Sidney, P.
Lady of pleasure, The. Shirley,
J.
Lady of the camelias, The. See
Dumas, A., fils. La dame
aux camélias
Lady Windermere's fan. Wilde,
O.
Lady with a lamp, The. Berke-
ley, R.
Das lager. See Schiller, J.

337

The camp of Wallenstein
Lamentable and true tragedie of
M. Arden of Feversham in
Kent, The. See Anonymous
plays. Arden of Feversham
Lamentable tragedy of Locrine,
The. Anonymous plays
Lamp and the bell, The. Mil-
lay, E.
Lancashire witches, The, and
Tegue O. Divelly, the Irish
priest. Shadwell, T.
Land, The. Colum, P.
Land of happiness, The. Crocker,
C.
Land of heart's desire, The.
Yeats, W.
Laodice. Corneille, T.
Lark, The. Anouilh, J.
Larola. Willcox, H.
Lars killed his son. Bernard,
L.
Lass that loved a sailor, The.
See Gilbert, W. and Sullivan,
A. H. M. S. Pinafore
Last duel in Spain, The. Calde-
rón de la Barca, P. See
Payne, J. The last duel in
Spain
Last duel in Spain, The. Payne,
J.
Last judgment, The (Chester).
Anonymous plays
Last man, The; or, The cock of
the village. Smith, R.
Last mile, The. Wexley, J.
Last night of Don Juan, The.
Rostand, E.
Last of Mrs. Cheyney, The.
Lonsdale, F.
Last of the De Mullins, The.
Hankin, St. J.
Last of the Turbins. See Bulga-
kov, M. Days of the Turbins
Last of the Wampanoags, The.
See Stone, J. Metamora
Last refuge, The. Gardiner, W.
Låt människan leva. See Lager-
kirst, P. Let man live
Late Christopher Bean, The.
Fauchois, R.
Late Edwina Black, The. Dinner,
W. and Morum, W.

Late George Apley, The. Mar-
quand, J. and Kaufman, G.
Laughing woman, The. MacKin-
tosh, E.
Lazarus laughed. O'Neill, E.
Leah Kleschna. McLellan, C.
Leak in the universe, A.
Richards, I.
Lebendige stunden. Schnitzler,
A.
Left bank, The. Rice, E.
Legend of the rood, The (Corn-
ish). Anonymous plays
Le légataire universel. Reg-
nard, J.
Leicestershire St. George play.
Anonymous plays
Leonce and Lena. Büchner, G.
Leonora; or, The world's own.
Howe, J.
Lesson, The. Ionesco, E.
Lesson, The. See Kelly, G.
Finders-keepers
Let man live. Lagerkirst, P.
"Let my people go!" Hay, I.
Let them eat cake. Lonsdale,
F.
Let us be gay. Crothers, R.
Let's get a divorce! Sardou, V.
and Najac, E.
Letter of the law, The. See
Brieux, E. La robe rouge
Letters to Lucerne. Rotter, F.
and Vincent, A.
Letter to Tuffy. Mulvay, T.
Liar, The. See Corneille, P.
Le menteur
Liars, The. Jones, H.
Libation-bearers, The. See
Aeschylus. Choephoroe
Libel! Wooll, E.
Liebelei. See Schnitzler, A.
Light-o'-love
Das lied von der union. Wollen-
weber, L.
Life a dream. See Calderón de
la Barca, P. La vida es su-
eño
Life among the little folks. See
Payne, J. The boarding
schools
Life among the lowly. See
Aiken, G. Uncle Tom's cabin

338

Life and death of King John, The.
Shakespeare, W.

Life and death of Lord Cromwell, The. See Anonymous
plays. Thomas Lord Crom-
well

Life and death of Tom Thumb
the great, The. See Fielding,
H. The tragedy of tragedies

Life in Louisiana. See Boucicault, D. The octoroon

Life in New York. See Ritchie,
A. Fashion

Life is a dream. See Calderón
de la Barca, P. La vida es
sueño

Life of Cambises, King of Percia,
The. See Preston, T.
Cambisco, King of Persia

Life of King Henry the Fifth,
The. See Shakespeare, W.
King Henry the fifth

Life of man, The. Andreev, L.

Life of the insects, The. See
Capek, K. and Capek, J.
And so ad infinitum

Life with father. Lindsay, H.
and Crouse, R.

Life with Mother. Lindsay, H.
and Crouse, R.

Light up the sky. Hart, M.

Lightnin'. Smith, W. and Bacon,
F.

Light-o'-love. Schnitzler, A.

Like falling leaves. Giacosa, G.

Likes of her, The. McEvoy, C.

Liliom. Molnár, F.

Lily, The. See Molnar, F.
Liliom

Lily among the thorns, A. Martínez Sierra, G. and Martínez
Sierra, M.

Lima beans. Kreymborg, A.

Lion's share, The. See Curel,
F. de. Le repas du lion

Lirio entre espinas. See Martínez
Sierra, G. and Martínez Sierra,
M. A lily among thorns

List of assets, A. Olesha, Y.

Literatur. See Schnitzler, A.
Literature.

Literature. Schnitzler, A.

Litre becchi. See Anonymous
plays. The three cuckolds

Little accident. Dell, F. and
Mitchell, T.

Little foxes, The. Hellman, L.

Little glass clock, The. Mills,
H.

Little minister, The. Barrie, J.

Little poor man, The. Copeau,
J.

Live corpse, The. Tolstoi, L.

Live like pigs. Arden, J.

Living corpse, The. See
Tolstoi, L. The live corpse

Living hours. See Schnitzler,
A. Lebendige stunden

Living mask, The. See Pirandello, L. Henry IV

Living newspaper, A. See
Arent, A. Power

Living room, The. Greene, G.

Loaves and fishes. Maugham,
W.

La locandiera. See Goldoni, C.
The mistress of the inn

Locrine. See Anonymous plays.
The lamentable tragedy of
Locrine

London assurance. Boucicault,
D.

London cuckolds, The. Ravenscroft, E.

London merchant, The; or, The
history of George Barnwell.
Lillo, G.

London prodigal, The. Anonymous plays

London wall. Van Druten, J.

Lonely lives. See Hauptmann,
G. Einsame menschen

Lonely way, The. Schnitzler, A.

Long and the short and the tall,
The. Hall, W.

Long Christmas dinner, The.
Wilder, T.

Long day's journey into night.
O'Neill, E.

Long sunset, The. Sherriff, R.

Long voyage home, The.
O'Neill, E.

Look back in anger. Osborne, J.

Look homeward angel. Frings, K.

Loquacious barber, The. Holberg, L.

Lord Chumley. Belasco, D. and De Mille, H.
Lord's will, The. Green, P.
Lorenzaccio. Musset, A.
Lost horizons. Hayden, J.
Lost in the stars. Anderson, M. and Weill, K.
Lost pleiad, The. Dransfield, J.
Lost silk hat, The. Dunsany, E.
Lost son, The. See Buckstone, J. Luke the labourer
Lot and Abraham. See Anonymous plays. Abraham, Melchisedec and Isaac
Lottery, The. Duffield, B.
Louis XI. Boucicault, D.
Love after death. Calderón de la Barca, P.
Love and death, featuring "Aleko." Nemírovích-Danchenko, V.
Love and honor. Davenant, W.
Love and pride. See Bulwer-Lytton, E. The lady of Lyons
Love-chase, The. Knowles, J.
Love feast, The. See Benelli, S. The jest
Love for love. Congreve, W.
Love in a Dutch garden. See Housman, L. and Granville-Barker, H. Prunella
Love in idleness. See Rattigan, T. O mistress mine
Love in '76. Bunce, O.
Love lies a-bleeding. See Beaumont, F. and Fletcher, J. Philaster
Love of Don Perlimplin and Belisa in the garden. Garcia Lorca, F.
Love of four colonels, The. Ustinov, P.
Love of the three kings, The. Benelli, S.
Love passage, A. Jacobs, W.
Love-rogue, The. See Téllez, G. El burlador de Sevilla
Love thief, The. See Benelli, S. The jest
Lovers. Donnay, C.
Lovers' leap. Johnson, P.
Lovers of Teruel, The. See Hartzenbusch, J. Los amantes

de Teruel
Lovers' vows; or, The natural son. Kotzebue, A.
Love's labour's lost. Shakespeare, W.
Love's last shift; or, The fool in fashion. Cibber, C.
Loves of Mars and Venus. See Ravenscroft, E. and Motteux, P. The anatomist
Love's victory; or, The school for pride. See Moreto y Cavaña, A. El desdén con el desdén
Loving wife, A. See Porto-Riche, G. Amoureuse
Low bridge. Elser, F.
Lower depths, The. Gorki, M. [pseud.]
Loyalties. Galsworthy, J.
Lucky Sam McCarver. Howard, S.
Ludua super iconia Sancti Nicolai. Anonymous plays
Ludus super iconia Sancti Nicolai. See Hilarius. The statue of Saint Nicholas
Luke the labourer. Buckstone, J.
Lumie di Sicilia. See Pirandello, L. Sicilian limes
Lunatics and lovers. Kingsley, S.
Lute song. Howard, S. and Irwin, W.
Le luthier de Crémone. See Coppée F. The violin maker of Cremona
Lying-in room, The. Holberg, L.
Lying valet, The. Garrick, D.
Lysistrata. Aristophanes
Lyubov Yarovaya. Trenev, K.

M

Maastricht play, The. Anonymous plays
Macbeth. Shakespeare, W.
Machinal. Treadwell, S.
Machine infernale, La. See Cocteau, J. The infernal machine
Machine-wreckers, The. Tol-

340

ler, E.

Mactacio Abel (Wakefield).
Anonymous plays

Mactatio Abel. See Anonymous
plays. The murder of Abel

Mad couple well matched, A.
Brome, R.

Mad Hercules. Seneca, L.

Madam, will you walk. Howard,
S.

Madame Butterfly. Belasco, D.
and Long, J.

Madame Legros. Mann, H.

Madame Sand. Moeller, P.

Madness of Heracles, The. See
Euripides. Heracles

Madras house, The. Granville-
Barker, H.

Madwoman of Chaillot, The.
Giraudoux, J.

Maedchen in uniform. See Winsloe, C. Children in uniform

Maeve. Martyn, E.

Magda. Sudermann, H.

Magi, Herod, and the slaughter
of the innocents, The (Coventry). Anonymous plays

Magic and the loss, The. Funt,
J.

Magico Prodigioso, El. See
Calderón de la Barca, P. The
wonder-working magician

Magi's oblation, The (Chester).
Anonymous plays

Magistrate, The. Pinero, A.

Magistrates, The. Fath'Ali, A.

Magnificent Yankee, The. Lavery,
E.

Magnus Herodes (Wakefield).
Anonymous plays

Magnyfycence. Skelton, J.

Magpie and the maid, The. See
Payne, J. Trial without jury

Mahomet. Voltaire, F.

Maid of honor, The. Massinger,
P.

Maid who wouldn't be proper,
The. Mick, H.

Maid's tragedy, The. Beaumont,
F. and Fletcher, J.

Main line, The; or, Rawson's Y.
De Mille, H. and Barnard, C.

Les mains sales. Sartre, J.

Maitlands, The. Mackenzie, R.

Le maître des forges. See Ohnet, G. The iron manufac-
turer

Le maître de Santiago. See
Montherlant, H. The master
of Santiago

Major Barbara. Shaw, G.

Maker of dreams, The. Down,
O.

Le malade imaginaire. See
Molière, J. Doctor's delight

Malcontent, The. Marston, J.
and Webster, J.

Male animal, The. Thurber, J.
and Nugent, E.

Le Malentendu. Camus, A.

La malquerida. See Benavente
y Martínez, J. The passion
flower

Malvaloca. Alvarez Quintero,
S. and Alvarez Quintero, J.

Mamma's affair. Butler, R.

Man and his phantoms. See
Lenormand, H. L'homme et
ses fantômes

Man and the masses. See
Toller, E. Masse mensch

Man and wife. Daly, A.

Man for all seasons, A. Bolt, R.

Man from home, The. Tarkington, B. and Wilson, H.

Man in Half Moon street, The.
Lyndon, B.

Man in the forest, The. Field,
C.

Man in the moon, The. See
Lyly, J. Endymion

Man of destiny, The. Shaw, G.

Man of mode, The; or, Sir Fopling Flutter. Etherege, G.

Man of the world, A. See
Vega, V. El hombre de
mundo

Man who came to dinner, The.
Kaufman, G. and Hart, M.

Man who died at twelve o'clock,
The. Green, P.

Man who had all the luck, The.
Miller, A.

Man who married a dumb wife,
The. See France, A. La
comédie de celui qui épousa

une femme muette
Man who was dead, The. See
Tolstoĭ, L. The live corpse
Man with a load of mischief, The.
Dukes, A.
Man with the heart in the high-
lands, The. See Saroyan, W.
My heart's in the highlands
Man without a soul, The. Lager-
kvist, P.
Mañana de sol. See Álvarez
Quintero, S. and Álvarez
Quintero, J. A bright morn-
ing
Mandragola. Machiavelli, N.
La mandragola. See Machiavel-
li, N. Mandragola
Mandrake, The. See Machia-
velli, N. Mandragola
Manfred. Byron, G.
Le mangeur des rêves. See
Lenormand, H. The dream
doctor
Maniac, The. See Conway, H.
The battle of Stillwater
Manikin and minikin. Kreym-
borg, A.
Mankind. Anonymous plays
Manlius Capitolinus. La Fosse,
A.
Mannen utan själ. See Lager-
kvist, P. The man without
a soul
Man's disobedience and the fall
of man (York). Anonymous
plays
Many waters. Hoffe, M.
La marca de fuego. Alsina, A.
Marching song. Whiting, J.
Marco millions. O'Neill, E.
Marchands de gloire, Les. Pag-
nol, M. and Nivoix, P.
Margaret Fleming. Herne, J.
Margareth und die Lea, Die.
Wollenweber, L.
Margin for error. Boothe, C.
La Marguerite. See Anouilh,
J. Ardèle
Maria Magdalena. Hebbel, C.
Le mariage de Figaro. Beau-
marchais, P.
Le mariage d'Olympe. Augier,
E.

Mariamne. Hermite, l'T.
La Mariane. See Hermite, l'T.
Mariamne
Marido de su vinda, El. See
Benavente y Martinez, J.
His widow's husband
Les mariés de la Tour Eiffel.
Cocteau, J.
Marino Faliero. Delavigne, J.
Marius, Fanny and César. See
Behrman, S. and Logan, J.
Fanny
Marodörer. See Strindberg, A.
Comrades
Marquis of Keith, The. Wede-
kind, F.
Die marquis von Arcis. See
Sternheim, C. The mask of
virtue
Marranos, The. Bernhard, E.
Marranos, The. Cohn, E.
Marriage, The. Gogol, N.
Marriage bells, The. See
Wood, H. East Lynne
Marriage has been arranged, A.
Sutro, A.
Marriage of Figaro, The. See
Beaumarchais, P. Le mari-
age de Figaro
Marriage of Sobeide, The. Hof-
mannsthal, H. von
Marriage of wit and science,
The. Anonymous plays
Marriage of wit and wisdom,
The. See Anonymous plays.
The contract of marriage be-
tween wit and wisdom
Marriage proposal, A. Chekhov,
A.
Mars and Venus. See Ravens-
croft, E. and Motteux, P.
The anatomist
Martine. Bernard, J.
Marty. Chayefsky, P.
Martyrdom of Ali, The. Anony-
mous plays
Mary Bonaventure. See Hast-
ings, C. Bonaventure
Mary Broome. Monkhouse, A.
Mary loves. See Williams, W.
Trial horse no. 1
Mary Magdalene. Anonymous
plays

Mary Magdalene and the apostles. See Anonymous plays. The mystery of Mary Magdalene and the apostles

Mary, Mary. Kerr, J.

Mary of Scotland. Anderson, M.

Mary Rose. Barrie, J.

Mary Stuart. Schiller, J.

Mary Surratt, The story of. Patrick, J.

Mary the third. Crothers, R.

Maschera ed il volto, La. See Chiarelli, L. The mask and the face

Die maschinen-stuermer. See Toller, E. The machine-wreckers

Mask and the face, The. Chiarelli, L.

Mask of virtue, The. Sternheim, C.

Masks. Corneau, P.

Masks and faces; or, Before and behind the curtain. Taylor, T. and Reade, C.

Masks of angels. Peryalis, N.

Masque of kings, The. Anderson, M.

Masque of reason, A. Frost, R.

Masqueraders, The. Jones, H.

Massacre of the innocents, The. See Anonymous plays. The magi, Herod and the slaughter of the innocents

Masse mensch. Toller, E.

Massnahme, Die. See Brecht, B. The measures taken

Master builder, The. Ibsen, H.

Master of Palmyra, The. Wilbrandt, A. von

Master of Santiago, The. Montherlant, H.

Master Pierre Patelin. See Anonymous plays. La farce de Maître Pierre Pathelin

Master salesman, The. Upson, W.

Masters of time. Kocherga, I.

Matchmaker, The. Wilder, T.

Mayor of Garret, The. Foote, S.

Mazeppa; or, The wild horse of Tartary. Payne, J.

Mazeppa; ou, Le cheval Tartare. Chandezon, L. and Cuvelier de Trye, J. See Payne, J. Mazeppa

Me and Molly. Berg, G.

Measure for measure. Shakespeare, W.

Measures taken, The. Brecht, B.

Le méchant. Gresset, J.

Medea. Anouilh, J.

Medea. Euripides

Medea. Grillparzer, F.

Medea. Seneca, L.

Le médecin malgré lui. See Molière, J. The doctor in spite of himself

Médée. See Anouilh, J. Medea

Meet a body. Launder, F. and Gilliat, S.

Meineidbauer. See Anzengruber, L. The farmer forsworn

Der meister von Palmyra. See Wilbrandt, A. von. The master of Palmyra

El mejor Alcalde el rey. See Vega Carpio, L. The king, the greatest Alcalde

Member of the wedding, The. McCullers, C.

Men and women. Belasco, D. and De Mille, H.

Men in white. Kingsley, S.

Menaechmi, The. Plautus, T.

Menschen im hotel. See Baum, V. Grand Hotel

Menschenhass und reue. See Kotzebue, A. The stranger

Le menteur. Corneille, P.

Mercadet. Balzac, H.

Mercator. See Plautus, T. The merchant

Merchant, The. Plautus, T.

Merchant of Venice, The. Shakespeare, W.

Merchant of Yonkers, The. See Wilder, T. The matchmaker

Mercy Dodd; or, Presumptive evidence. Boucicault, D.

Mercy of Augustus, The. See Corneille, P. Cinna

Merlin gascon. Raisin, J.

Merrily we roll along. Kaufman,

343

G. and Hart, M.
Merry death, A. Evreinov, N.
Merry devil of Edmonton, The.
Anonymous plays
Merry go round. See Schnitzler,
A. La ronde
Merry monarch, The. See
Payne, J. and Irving, W.
Charles the second
Merry play, A. See Heywood,
J. John, Tyb and Sir John
Merry wives of Windsor, The.
Shakespeare, W.
Merton of the movies. Kauf-
man, G. and Connelly, M.
Mery play betweene Johan Johan,
the husbande, Tyb his wife,
and Syr Jhan, the preest, A.
See Heywood, J. John, Tyb
and Sir John
Mery play betweene Johan Johan,
Tyb, his wife and Syr Jhan,
the preest, A. See Heywood,
J. John, Tyb and Sir John
Mery playe betwene the pardoner
and the frere, the curate and
neybour Pratte. See Hey-
wood, J. The pardoner and
the friar
Mester Gert Westphaler eller
den meget talende barbeer.
See Holberg, L. The loqua-
cious barber
Metamore; or, The last of the
Wampanoags. Stone, J.
Michael and his lost angel.
Jones, H.
Michael and Mary. Milne, A.
Michael Kramer. Hauptmann, G.
Michaelmas term. Middleton, T.
Michel Auclair. Vildrac, C.
Midas. Lyly, J.
Mid-channel. Pinero, A.
Midnight bell, A. Hoyt, C.
Midsummer night's dream.
Shakespeare, W.
Midwinter story, A. See
Schildt, R. The gallows man
Mighty dollar, The. Woolf, B.
Mikado, The; or, The town of
Titipu. Gilbert, W. and Sul-
livan, A.
Miles gloriosus. Plautus, T.

Milestones. Bennett, A. and
Knoblock, E.
Milk white flag, A. Hoyt, C.
Miller's daughter of Manchester,
The, with the love of William
the conqueror. See Anony-
mous plays. Fair Em
Minick. Kaufman, G. and Fer-
ber, E.
Minna von Barnhelm; or, The
soldier's fortune. Lessing,
G.
Minnie Field. Conkle, E.
Minor, The. Fonvizín, D.
Minuet, A. Parker, L.
Minute men of 1774-1775, The.
Herne, J.
Miracle at Verdun, The. Chlum-
berg, H.
Miracle of Saint Nicholas and
the image, The. Hilarius
Miracle of Saint Nicholas and
the schoolboys, The. Anony-
mous plays
Miracle of Saint Nicholas and
the virgins, The. Anonymous
plays
Miracle of the blind man and
the cripple, The. La Vigne,
A. de
Mirandolina. See Goldoni, C.
The mistress of the inn
Mir-i-nisa. Sicam, G. and
Casiño, J.
Le misanthrope, Molière, J.
Misanthrope, The. See Molière,
J. Le misanthrope
Miser, The. Molière, J.
Misfortune of being clever, The.
See Griboíedov, A. Wit
works woe
Misfortunes of Arthur, The.
Hughes, T.
Misogonus. Anonymous plays
Miss Julia. Strindberg, A.
Miss Julie. See Strindberg, A.
Miss Julia
Miss Lulu Bett. Gale, Z.
Miss Sara Sampson. Lessing,
G.
Miss Thompson. Maugham, W.
Mistake at the manor, A. Frank,
M.

344

Mistake upon mistake; or, Appearance is against them.
See Inchbald, E. Appearance is against them
Mistakes of a night, The. See Goldsmith, O. She stoops to conquer
Mr. and Mrs. North. Davis, O.
Mr. Attowell's jig. See Anonymous plays. Attowell's jig
Mr. Jiggins of Jigginstown. Longford, C.
Mister Johnson. Rosten, N.
Mr. Pickwick. Young, S.
Mr. Pim passes by. Milne, A.
Mister Roberts. Heggen, T. and Logan, J.
Mr. Sleeman is coming. Bergman, H.
Mr. Thing. See Chase, M. Mrs. McThing
Mrs. Bumpstead-Leigh. Smith, H. J.
Mrs. Dane's defence. Jones, H.
Mrs. McThing. Chase, M.
Mrs. Moonlight. Levy, B.
Mistress Nell. Hazelton, G.
Mistress of the inn, The. Goldoni, C.
Mrs. Partridge presents. Kennedy, M. and Hawthorne, R.
Mrs. Warren's profession. Shaw, G.
Mixed marriage. Ervine, St. J.
Las mocedades del Cid. Castro y Bellvis, G.
Mock emperor, The. See Pirandello, L. The mock emperor
Mock-tempest, The; or, The enchanted castle. Duffett, T.
Moderskärlek. See Strindberg, A. Motherly love
Mollusc, The. Davies, H.
Le monde où l'on s'ennuie. Pailleron, É.
Money. Bulwer-Lytton, E.
"Money makes the mare go." See Hoyt, C. A Texas steer
Monna Vanna. Maeterlinck, M.
Monsieur Beaucaire. Tarkington, B.
M. Poirier's son-in-law. See

Augier, É. and Sandeau, J. Le gendre de M. Poirier
Le mont sauvage; ou, Le solitaire. Pixérécourt, R. See Payne, J. Mount Savage
La montaña de las brujas. See Sánchez Gardel, J. The witches' mountain
Monte Cristo. Fechter, C.
Montezuma. Robertson, L.
Month in the country, A. Turgenev, I.
Moon for the misbegotten, A. O'Neill, E.
Moon in the Yellow river, The. Johnston, D.
Moon is blue, The. Herbert, F.
Moon is down, The. Steinbeck, J.
Moon of the Caribbees, The. O'Neill, E.
Moon on a rainbow shawl. John, E.
Moonlight is silver. Ashton, W.
Moonshine. Hopkins, A.
Moor of Venice, The. See Shakespeare, W. Othello
Moral. Thoma, L.
Moral play of Albion, knight, A. Anonymous plays
Moral play of Everyman, The. See Anonymous plays. Everyman
More, Sir Thomas (An ill Mayday). Anonymous plays
Morning's at seven. Osborn, P.
La mort de Tintagiles. See Maeterlinck. M. The death of Tintagiles
La morte in vacanze. See Casella, A. Death takes a holiday
Moses in the bulrushes. More, H.
Most beautiful eyes in the world, The. See Sarment, J. Les plus beaux yeux du monde
Most happy fella, The. Loesser, F.
Most likely to succeed. See Kanin, F. Goodbye, my fancy
Most pleasant comedie of Mucedorus the kings sonne of Val-

345

346

Optimistic tragedy, An. Vish-
nevskiĭ, V.
Orchards of Polovchansk, The.
Leonov, L.
Oresteia (trilogy). See Aeschy-
lus. Agamemnon; Choepho-
roe; Eumenides
Orestes. Euripides
Origin of the feast of Purim,
The; or, The destinies of
Haman and Mordecai. Tyler,
R.
Orléans sepulcher, The. Anony-
mous plays
Oroonoko. Southerne, T.
Orphans of the storm. See
D'Ennery, A. and Cormon,
E. The two orphans
Orphée. Cocteau, J.
Orpheus descending. Williams, T.
L'osteria della posta. See
Goldoni, C. The post-inn
Othello, the Moor of Venice.
Shakespeare, W.
Other danger, The. Donnay, C.
Other side of a saint, The. See
Curel, F. de L'envers d'une
sainte
Other tomorrows. Palarca, J.
Our betters. Maugham, W.
Our boarding house. Grover, L.
Our lord of the ships. Piran-
dello, L.
Our pageant. Ouless, E.
Our town. Wilder, T.
Outer edge of society, The.
Dumas, A., fils
Outrageous fortune. Franken, R.
Outward bound. Vane, S.
Over evnc. See Bjørnson, B.
Beyond our power
Over 21. Gordon, R.
Overtones. Gerstenberg, A.
Overture. Bolitho, W.
Owl and cave, The. Field, C.
Oxfordshire St. George play,
The. Anonymous plays

P

Paachspel. See Anonymous
plays. The Maastricht play
Paddle your own canoe. Diamant-

Berger, M.
Paddle your own canoe. Regnier,
M.
Pageant of shearmen and tailors,
The (Coventry). Anonymous
plays
Painted laugh, The. See And-
reev, L. He who gets slapped
Pair of drawers, A. See Stern-
heim, C. The underpants
Pair of spectacles, A. Grundy,
S.
La paix du ménage. See Mau-
passant, G. de. The house-
hold peace
Pajama game, The. Abbott, G.
and Bissell, R.
Pantagleize. Ghelderode, M.
Pantomime for Easter day, A.
Anonymous plays
Paolo and Francesca. Phillips,
S.
Papa is all. Greene, P.
Papa Juan: centenario. See
Álvarez Quintero, S. and
Álvarez Quintero, J. A hun-
dred years old
Paphnutius. Hrotsvit
Le paquebot Tenacity. Vildrac,
C.
Par un jour de pluie. Forest, L.
Paradise play (Oberufer), The.
Anonymous plays
Paragon, The. Pertwee, R. and
Pertwee, M.
Le pardon. See Lemaître, J.
The pardon
Pardon, The. Lemaître, J.
Pardoner and the friar, The.
Heywood, J.
Les paredos oyen. Ruiz de
Alarcón y Mendoza, J.
Les parents terribles. See
Cocteau, J. Intimate rela-
tions
Paris and Helen. Schwartz, D.
Paris bound. Barry, P.
Paris Commune, A play about
the. See Grieg, N. The de-
feat
La Parisienne. Becque, H.
Parliament of bees, The. Anony-
mous plays

Parnassus plays (1598-1601).
See Anonymous plays: The
pilgrimage to Parnassus; The
return from Parnassus
Parnell. Schauffler, E.
Parra kumpt, Der. Wieand, P.
Parson's wedding, The. Killi-
grew, T.
Partisans on the steppes of the
Ukraine. See Korneichuk, A.
Guerillas on the Ukrainian
Steppes
Party, The. Arden, J.
Party spirit, The. Jones, P.
and Jowett, J.
Paso de las olivas, E. See
Rueda, L. The olives
Paso séptimo: de las aceitunas.
See Rueda, L. The seventh
farce
Passenger to Bali, A. St. Joseph,
E.
Il Passero. See Lopez, S. The
sparrow
Passing of the magi, The. Za-
macois, E.
Passing of the torch, The. See
Hervieu, P. La course du
flambeau
Passion flower, The. Benavente
y Martínez, J.
Passion play of Alsfeld, The.
Anonymous plays
Pasteur. Guitry, S.
Pastor sang. See Bjørnson, B.
Beyond our power
Los pastores. See Martínez Si-
erra, G. and Martínez Sierra,
M. The two shepherds
Patate. See Achard, M. Rollo
Patchwork quilt, The. Field, R.
Patelin, Pierre. See Anonymous
plays. La farce de Maître
Pierre Pathelin
Pathelin, Pierre. See Anony-
mous plays. La farce de
Maître Pierre Pathelin
Patience; or, Bunthorne's bride.
Gilbert W. and Sullivan A.
Patrie! Sardou, V.
Patriot, The. Neumann, A.
See Dukes, A. Such men are
dangerous

Patriots, The. Kingsley, S.
Patroness, A. Gerstenberg, A.
Patterns. Serling, R.
Les pattes de mouche. Sardou,
V.
Paul Kauvar; or, Anarchy.
MacKaye, S.
Pax. See Aristophanes. Peace
Payment deferred. Dell, J.
Peace. Aristophanes
Peace comes to Peckham. Del-
derfield, R.
La pecadora. See Guimerá, A.
Daniela
Le pêcheur d'ombres. Sarment,
J.
Peculiar position, A. Scribe, E.
Peer and the peri, The. See
Gilbert, W. and Sullivan, A.
Iolanthe
Peer Gynt. Ibsen, H.
Peg o' my heart. Manners, J.
Peggy. Williamson, H.
Pelléas and Mélisande. See
Maeterlinck, M. Pelléas et
Mélisande
Pelléas et Mélisande. Maeter-
linck, M.
Penny for the poor, A. See
Brecht, B. The three-penny
opera
Penthesilea. Kleist, H.
People in love. Reid, A.
People with light coming out of
them, The. Saroyan, W.
People's lawyer, The. See
Jones, J.S. Solon Shingle
Pepa la frescachona. Vega, R.
Le père de famille. Diderot, D.
Perhaps a poet. Josephson, R.
Peribanez and the commander of
Ocana. See Vega Carpio, L.
Peribáñez y el comendador de
Ocaña
Peribáñez y el comendador de
Ocaña. Vega Carpio, L.
La périchole. Offenbach, J.
Pericles, Prince of Tyre.
Shakespeare, W.
Perikeiromene, The. See
Menander. The shearing of
Glycera
Period of adjustment. Williams, T.

350

354

Rehearsal, The. Baring, M.
Rehearsal, The. Buckingham, G.
Rehearsal. Morley, C.
Reign of King Edward the third,
  The. Anonymous plays
Le reine morte. Montherlant, H.
El reino de Dios. See Martínez
  Sierra, G. and Martínez Si-
  erra, M. The kingdom of God
Relapse, The; or, Virtue in
  danger. Vanbrugh, J.
Remains to be seen. Lindsay,
  H. and Crouse, R.
Remarkable Mr. Pennypacker,
  The. O'Brien, L.
Remote. See Afinogenyev, A.
  Far taiga
Le repas du lion. Curel, F.
Requiem for a nun. Ford, R.
  and Faulkner, W.
Residuary légatee, The. See
  Regnard, J. Le légataire
  universel
Resounding tinkle, A. Simpson,
  N.
Respublica. Anonymous plays
Resurrection, The. Kimball, R.
Resurrection, The. Yeats, W.
Resurrection, harrowing of hell,
  and the last judgment. Anony-
  mous plays
Resurrection of Christ, The
  (Wakefield). Anonymous plays
Retnavali; or, The necklace.
  Harsha, son of Hira
Return from Parnassus, The;
  or, The scourge of Simony,
  pt. II. Anonymous plays
Return of Peter Grimm, The.
  Belasco, D.
Return of the prodigal, The.
  Hankin, St. J.
Reunion in Vienna. Sherwood, R.
Revenge of Bussy D'Ambois,
  The. Chapman, G.
Revenger's tragedy, The. Tour-
  neur, C.
Reverend Griffith Davenport, The.
  Herne, J.
Revesby sword play, The.
  Anonymous plays
Revisor. See Gogol, N. The
  inspector

Los reyes pasan. See Zama-
  cois, E. The passing of the
  Magi
Rhadamiste et Zénobie. Crébil-
  lon, P.
Rhadamistus and Zenobia. See
  Crébillon, P. Rhadamiste et
  Zénobie
Rhesus. Euripides
Rhinoceros. Ionesco, E.
Rhondda roundabout. Jones, J.
Richard of Bordeaux. Daviot, G.
  [pseud.]
Richelieu; or, The conspiracy.
  Bulwer-Lytton, E.
Les ricochets. Picard, L.
Rider of dreams, The. Tor-
  rence, F.
Riders to the sea. Synge, J.
Ridiculous précieuses, The.
  See Molière, J. Le précieu-
  ses ridicules
Rifle ball, The. See Wallach,
  L. Rosedale
Right you are! If you think so.
  Pirandello, L.
Rip Van Winkle. Burke, C.
Rip Van Winkle, as played by
  Joseph Jefferson. Anonymous
  plays
Rising of the moon, The.
  Gregory, I.
Il rittrato. See Scala, F. The
  portrait
Rival queens, The; or, The
  death of Alexander the great.
  Lee, N.
Rivals, The. Sheridan, R.
Road to Rome, The. Sherwood,
  R.
Roadside. Riggs, L.
La robe rouge. Brieux, E.
Robert Emmet. Boucicault, D.
Robin Hood and the friar.
  Anonymous plays
Robin Hood and the knight.
  Anonymous plays
Robin Hood and the potter.
  Anonymous plays
Robin Hood and the sheriff of
  Nottingham. Anonymous plays
Robust invalid, The. See Moli-
  ère, J. Doctor's delight

Saint John the evangelist. See
Anonymous plays   John the
evangelist
Saint Nicholas and the image.
See Hilarius. The miracle of
Saint Nicholas and the image
Saint Nicholas and the school-
boys   See Anonymous plays.
The miracle of Saint Nicholas
and the schoolboys
Saint Nicholas and the three
scholars. Anonymous plays
Saint Nicholas and the virgins.
See Anonymous plays. The
miracle of Saint Nicholas and
the virgins
Saint of Bleecker Street, The.
Menotti, G.
St. Patrick at Tara. Stephens, H.
Saint's day. Whiting, J.
Šakoontalá. See Kālidāsa. Sha-
kuntala
Sally Bowles. See Van Druten,
J. I am a camera
Salome's head. Ortiz de Mon-
tellano, B.
Salutation and conception, The
(Coventry). Anonymous plays
Salzburger grosse welttheater,
Das. Hofmannsthal, H.
Sam average. MacKaye, P.
Same sky, The. Mitchell, Y.
Samia. See Menander. The
girl from Samos
Sam'l of Posen; or, The com-
mercial drummer. Jessop, G.
Samson Agonistes. Milton, J.
Sandbox, The. Albee, E.
Santos vega. Bayón Herrera, L.
Sappho. Grillparzer, F.
Sara und die Betz, Die. Wollen-
weber, L.
Satin slipper, The; or, The
worst is not the worst.
Claudel, P.
Satire of the three estates, The.
Lindsay, D.
Saturday's children. Anderson,
M.
Saul. Alfieri, V.
Saul. Du Ryer, P.
Savages of America, The. See
Rogers, R. Ponteach

Le savetier calbain. Anony-
mous plays
Savonarola. Nagle, U.
Scaevola. Du Ryer, P.
La scala. See Rosso di San
Secondo, P. The stairs
Scarecrow, The. Mackaye, P.
Scenes from New York life and
the Pacific railroad. See
McCloskey, J. Across the
continent
School for fathers, The. See
Anouilh, J. Cecile
School for husbands. Molière,
J.
School for pride, The. See
Moreto y Cavaña, A. El
desdén con el desdén
School for scandal, The. Sheri-
dan, R.
Scourge of Simony, The. See
Anonymous plays. The re-
turn from Parnassus, pt. II
Scrap of paper, A. See Sardou,
V. Les pattes de mouche
Sea-gull, The. Chekhov, A.
Seagulls over Sorrento. Hastings,
H.
Searching wind, The. Hellman,
L.
Season in the sun. Gibbs, W.
Second lie, The. Mackay, I.
Second man, The. Behrman, S.
Second Mrs. Tanqueray, The.
Pinero, A.
Second part of the return from
Parnassus, The. See Anony-
mous plays. The return from
Parnassus
Second play of the shepherds,
The. See Anonymous plays.
The second shepherds' play
Second shepherds' play, The
(Wakefield). Anonymous plays
Second threshold. Barry, P.
Le secret. Bernstein, H.
Secret d'Arvers, Le. Bernard,
J.
Secret service. Gillette, W.
Secular masque, The. Dryden,
J.
Secunda pastorum. See Anony-
mous plays. The second

357

shepherds' play
See Naples and die. Rice, E.
Seeker, The. McCauley, C.
Sei personaggi in cerca d'autore. See Pirandello, L.
Six characters in search of an author
Sejanus, his fall. Jonson, B.
Self. Bateman, S.
Self avenger, The. See Terentius Afer, P. Heautontimorumenos
Self-tormentors, The. See Terentius Afer, P. Heautontimorumenos
Selskabsrejsen. See Fischer, L. The mystery tour
Sentinels, The; or, The two sergeants. Smith, R.
Separate tables. Rattigan, T.
Septem contra Thebas. See Aeschylus. The seven against Thebes
September lemonade. Denney, R.
Serenade, The. Jullien, J.
Serious charge. King, P.
Serpiente, La. Moock Bousquet, A.
Sertorius; or, The Roman patriot. Brown, D.
Servant of two masters, The. Goldoni, C.
La servante de Palaisseau. Caiginez, L. and Baudouin, J. See Payne, J. Trial without jury
Service. Smith, D. G.
Settlers of Virginia, The. See Custis, G. Pocahontas
Seven against Thebes, The. Aeschylus
7-1/2 cents. See Abbott, G. and Bissell, R. The pajama game
Seven keys to Baldpate. Cohan, G.
Seven year itch, The. Axelrod, G.
Seventh farce, The. Rueda, L.
Sganarelle. Molière, J.
Shadow, The. Shvarts, E.
Shadow and substance. Carroll, P.
Shadow fisher, The. See Sarment, J. Le pêcheur

d'ombres
Shadow of a gunman, The. O'Casey, S.
Shadow of doubt, The. King, N.
Shadow of heroes. See Ardrey, R. Stone and star
Shakespeare amoureux; ou, La pièce à l'étude. Duval, A. See Smith, R. Shakespeare in love
Shakespeare in love. Smith, R.
Shakuntala. Kālidāsa
Shall we join the ladies? Barrie, J.
Sham. Tompkins, F.
Sham doctor, The. See Ravenscroft, E. and Motteux, P. The anatomist
She stoops to conquer; or, The mistakes of a night. Goldsmith, O.
She who was shorn. See Menander. The shearing of Glycera
She would be a soldier; or, The plains of Chippewa. Noah, M.
Shearing of Glycera, The. Menander
Sheep well, The. See Vega Carpio, L. Fuenteovejuna
Shenandoah. Howard, B.
Shenandoah. Schwartz, D.
Shepherds, The. Coold, M.
Shepherds, The. See Anonymous plays. The second shepherds' play
Shepherds' play, The (Coventry). Anonymous plays
Sheppey. Maugham, W.
Sherlock Holmes. Gillette, W.
Shetland sword dance. Anonymous plays
Shewing up of Blanco Posnet, The. Shaw, G.
Shifting heart, The. Beynon, R.
Shining hour, The. Winter, J.
Shoemaker's holiday, The; or, The gentle craft. Dekker, T.
Shoptalk. Turque, M.
Shore acres. Herne, J.
Show-off, The. Kelly, C.
Shred of evidence, A. Sherriff, R.

Shrike, The. Kramm, J.
El sí de las niñas. Moratín, L.
Sicilian limes. Pirandello, L.
Siege, The. Clements, C.
Siege of Numantia, The. See
  Cervantes Saavedra, M. La
  Numancia
Siege of Rhodes, The. D'Ave-
  nant, W.
Siegfried. Giraudoux, J.
Siegfried's death. Hebbel, C.
No siempre lo peor es cierto.
  Calderón de la Barca, P.
Signor Marc. Wilkins, J.
Silent knight, The. Wolfe, H.
Silent woman, The. See Jon-
  son, B. Epicoene
Silver box, The. Galsworthy, J.
Silver cord, The. Howard, S.
Silver weddings. See Geraldy,
  P. The nest
Silver whistle, The. McEnroe,
  R.
Simon. Hines, L.
Simon and Laura. Melville, A.
Simon the leper. Anonymous
  plays
Simoom. See Lenormand, H.
  Le simoun
Le simoun. Lenormand, H.
Singer, The. Pearse, P.
Singing birds. See Offenbach,
  J. La périchole
Sinner, The. See Guimerá, A.
  Daniela
Sinner beloved, A. Osgood, P.
Sir Courtley Nice; or, It cannot
  be. Crowne, J.
Sir Fopling Flutter. See Ethe-
  rege, G. The man of mode
Sir John Oldcastle, pt. I.
  Anonymous plays
Sir Thomas More (An ill May-
  day). Anonymous plays
Sister Cecilia. See Hastings,
  C. Bonaventure
Sit on the earth. Campbell, M.
  and Athas, D.
Siwan. Lewis, S.
Six characters in search of an
  author. Pirandello, L.
Six cylinder love. McGuire, W.
Six men of Dorset. Malleson,

M. and Brooks, H.
Six of Calais, The. Shaw, G.
Sixteen. Stuart, A.
Skin game, The. Galsworthy,
  J.
Skin of our teeth, The. Wilder,
  T.
Skipper next to God. Hartog, J.
Skylark. Raphaelson, S.
Slander. See Echegaray y
  Eizaguirre, J. El gran Ga-
  leoto
Slaughter of the innocents, The.
  See Anonymous plays. The
  magi, Herod and the slaughter
  of the innocents
Slave with two faces, The.
  Davies, M.
Slaying of the innocents, The.
  Anonymous plays
Slipknot, The. See Plautus.
  Rudens
Small hotel. Frost, R.
Smoke of the fatherland. Tur,
  L.; Tur, P. and Sheinen, L.
Der snob. See Sternheim, C.
  A place in the world
Snob, The. See Sternheim, C.
  A place in the world
Snow goose, The. Gallico, P.
So ist das leben. See Wede-
  kind, F. Such is life
Social success, A. Beerbohm,
  M.
Socialites, The. Jupp, K.
Society. Robertson, T.
Socrates. Bax, C.
Socrates. Voltaire, F.
Sodom and Gomorrah. Girau-
  doux, J.
Il sogno di Scipione. See Me-
  tastasio, P. The dream of
  Scipio
Soldier's fortune, The. See
  Lessing, C. Minna von Barn-
  helm
Soldier's wife. Franken, R.
Solid gold cadillac, The. Teich-
  mann, H. and Kaufman, G.
Le solitaire. Pixérécourt, R.
  See Payne, J. Mount Savage
Solon Shingle. Jones, J. S.
Somebody knows. Van Druten, J.

Something unspoken. Williams,
T.
Sometimes even now. Chetham-
Strode, W.
Son-in-law of M. Poirier, The.
See Augier, É. and Sandeau,
J. Le gendre de M. Poirier
Song of songs. Giraudoux, J.
Song of songs which is Solomon's,
The. Francis, A.
Sons of Baldur, The. Scheffauer,
H.
Sophonisba. Mairet, J.
Sorrows of Han, The. Anony-
mous plays
Søskende. See Branner, H.
The judge
Sotoba Komachi. Kiyotsugu, K.
Le soulier de satin: ou, La pire
n'est pa toujours sûr. See
Claudel, P. The satin slipper
Sound of murder, The. Fair-
child, W.
Sounding shell, The. Krog, H.
South. Green, J.
South Pacific. Hammerstein,
II, O.
Spanish fryar, The; or, The
double discovery. Dryden, J.
Spanish gipsie, The. Middleton,
T. and Rowley, W.
Spanish husband, The; or, First
and last love. Payne, J.
Spanish play, The. See Anony-
mous plays. The Wisemen
Spanish student, The. Longfel-
low, H.
Spanish tragedy, The; or, Hier-
onimo is mad again. Kyd, T.
Sparrow, The. Lopez, S.
Sparrow falls, A. Williams, H.
and Williams, M.
Special providence. See Willi-
ams, H. and Williams, M.
By accident
Speed the plough. Morton, T.
Das spiel vom deutschen bettel-
mann. Wiechert, E.
Spirochete. Sundgaard, A.
Spleen, The. See Payne, J.
The black man
Splendid outcasts, The. Sisson,
R.

Spogelses-sonaten. See Strind-
berg, A. The ghost sonata
Spook sonata, The. See Strind-
berg, A. The ghost sonata
Sport of my mad mother, The.
Jellicoe, A.
Spreading the news. Gregory, I.
Springtime for Henry. Levy, B.
Spy, The. Clinch, C.
Square of flowers, The. Ilyen-
kov, V.
Squaring the circle. Kataev, V.
Squaw man, The. Royle, E.
Squire of Alsatia, The. Shad-
well, T.
Stable and the grove, The.
Geddes, V.
Stage door. Kaufman, G. and
Ferber, E.
Stairs, The. Rosso di San Se-
condo, P.
Star, The (Bilsen play). Anony-
mous plays
Star of Seville, The. See Vega
Carpio, L. La estrella de
Sevilla
Starke mitteln. Rosen, J. See
Daly, A. Needles and pins
Starter, The. Spence, E.
Star-wagon, The. Anderson, M.
State of the union. Lindsay, H.
and Crouse, R.
Statue of Saint Nicholas, The.
Hilarius.
Steamer Tenacity, The. See
Vildrac, C. Le paquebot Ten-
acity
Steamship Tenacity, The. See
Vildrac, C. Le paquebot
Tenacity
Stella. Goethe, J.
Step-in-the-hollow. MacDonagh,
D.
Stichus. Plautus, T.
Stone and star. Ardrey, R.
Stone guest, The. Pushkin, A.
Stop him who can! See Reyn-
olds, F. The dramatist
Stop it, whoever you are.
Livings, H.
Stora landsvägen. See Strind-
berg, A. The great highway
Storm, The. See Ostrovskiĭ, A.

The thunderstorm
Storm operation. Anderson, M.
Storm within, The. See Cocteau,
  J. Intimate relations
Story of Louis Pasteur, The.
  Gibney, M. and Collings, P.
Story of Mary Surratt, The.
  Patrick, J.
Strange case of Dr. Jekyll and
  Mr. Hyde. Sieveking, L.
Strange interlude. O'Neill, E.
Strange orchestra. Ackland, R.
Stranger, The. Kotzebue, A.
Stranglers of Paris, The.
  Belasco, D.
Strayed reveler, The. Arnold,
  M.
Street scene. Rice, E.
Street singer, The. Echegaray
  y Eizaguirre, J.
Streetcar named desire, A.
  Williams, T.
Strictly dishonorable. Sturges, P.
Strife. Galsworthy, J.
Strings, my Lord, are false,
  The. Carroll, P.
Strong are lonely, The. Hoch-
  walder, F.
Stronger, The. See Strindberg,
  A. The stronger woman
Stronger woman, The. Strind-
  berg, A.
Submerged. See Gorki, M.
  [pseud.] The lower depths
Success. Milne, A.
Success story. Lawson, J.
Such is life. Wedekind, F.
Such men are dangerous. Dukes,
  A.
Such stuff as dreams are made
  of. See Calderón de la Bar-
  ca, P. La vida es sueño
Sugar cane. Wilson, F.
Suitors, The. See Racine, J.
  Les plaideurs
Summer and smoke. Williams,
  T.
Summer of the 17th doll. Law-
  ler, R.
Summoning of Everyman, The.
  See Anonymous plays. Every-
  man
Sunken bell, The. Hauptmann, G.

Sunny morning, A. See Alva-
  rez Quintero, S. and Alva-
  rez Quintero, J. A bright
  morning
Sunshine follows rain. See
  Girardin, D. La joie fait
  peur
Sunshine through the clouds.
  See Girardin, D. La joie
  fait peur
Sun-up. Vollmer, L.
Superstition. Barker, J.
Supper for the dead. Green, P.
Supper of pranks, The. See
  Benelli, S. The jest
Suppliant maidens, The. See
  Aeschylus. The suppliants
Suppliant women, The. See
  Euripides. The suppliants
Suppliants, The. Aeschylus
Suppliants, The. Euripides
Supposes. Gascoigne, G.
Suppositi, I. Ariosto. See
  Gascoigne, G. Supposes
Susan and God. Crothers, R.
Suspecting truth, The. See
  Ruiz de Alarcón y Mendoza,
  J. La verdad sospechosa
Suspicious husband, The.
  Hoadly, B.
Swan, The. Molnár, F.
Swan song, The. Chekhov, A.
Swedenhielms, The. Bergman,
  H.
Sweeney Agonistes. Eliot, T.
Sweet bird of youth. Williams,
  T.
Sweethearts. Gilbert, W. and
  Sullivan, A.
Sword and queue. Gutzkow, K.
Sword of the Samurai, The.
  Mygatt, T.

T

Tails up. Roberts, C.
Take a giant step. Peterson,
  L.
Tale of Robin Hood, A. See
  Jonson, B. The sad shepherd
Tamburlaine the great. Mar-
  lowe, C.
Taming of the shrew, The.

Shakespeare, W.
Tancred and Gismund; or, Gismond of Salerne. Wilmot, R.
Tancred, King of Sicily; or, The archives of Palermo. Stone, J.
Tantris the fool. See Hardt, E. Tristram the jester
Tarnish. Pottle, E.
Tartuffe. See Molière, J. Le Tartuffe
Le Tartuffe; ou, L'imposteur. Molière, J.
Taste of honey, A. Delaney, S.
Taxes. Tolstoi, L.
Ta'ziya. See Anonymous plays. The martyrdom of Ali
Tea and sympathy. Anderson, R.
Tea for three. Locher, J.
Teahouse of the August moon, The. Patrick, J.
Tegue O. Divelly, The Irish priest. See Shadwell, T. The Lancashire witches and Tegue O. Divelly, the Irish priest
Telescope, The. Sherriff, R.
Temperance town, A. Hoyt, C.
Tempest, The. Shakespeare, W.
Tempest, The; or, The enchanted island. D'Avenant, W. and Dryden, J.
Tempo. Pogodin, N.
Le temps est un songe. See Lenormand, H. Time is a dream
Tender trap, The. Shulman, M. and Smith, R.
Ten-minute alibi. Willis, A.
Tenor, The. See Wedekind, F. The court singer
Tenth man, The. Chayefsky, P.
Teresa of Avila. Williamson, H.
Test of fire, The. See Kleist, H. Kaethchen of Heilbronn; or, The test of fire
Tête-à-tête. Fulda, L.
Texas steer, A; or, "Money makes the mare go." Hoyt, C.
Textiles. Anderson, S.
Theatre of the soul, The. Evreinov, N.
There are crimes and crimes.

Strindberg, A.
There shall be no night. Sherwood, R.
There's always Juliet. Van Druten, J.
Thérèse Raquin. Zola, E.
Thérèse, the orphan of Geneva. Payne, J.
Thersites. Anonymous plays
These cornfields. Courteline, G.
They came by night. Lyndon, B.
They fly through the air. Corwin, N.
They knew what they wanted. Howard, S.
They shall not die. Wexley, J.
Thieves' carnival. Anouilh, J.
Third person. Rosenthal, A.
Thirteenth chair, The. Veiller, B.
37 sous of M. Montaudoin, The. See Labiche, E. and Martin, É. Les trente-sept sous de M. Montaudoin
Thirty years; or, The gambler's fate. Dunlap, W.
This bondage. Popplewell, O.
This bored world. See Pailleron, É. Le monde où l'on s'ennuie
This bull ate nutmeg. Niggli, J.
This earth is ours. Kozlenko, W.
This gentle ghost. See Patrick, J. The story of Mary Surratt
This year, next year. Ronder, J.
Thistle and the rose, The. Horne, W.
Thomas Jefferson. See Kingsley, S. The patriots
Thomas, Lord Cromwell. Anonymous plays
Thomas Cranmer of Canterbury. Williams, C.
Thomas Muskerry. Colum, P.
Those familiar spirits. See Miller, A. The crucible
Thousand clowns, A. Gardner, H.
Three cuckolds, The. Anonymous plays

362

Three daughters of M. Dupont, The. See Brieux, E. Les trois filles de M. Dupont
Three-fold path, The. Rye, E.
Three kings' play (Oberufer), The. Anonymous plays
Three Maries, The. Anonymous plays.
Three men on a horse. Holm, J. and Abbott, G.
Three penny day, The. Plautus, T.
Three pieces of money, The. See Plautus, T. The three penny day
Three sisters. See Chekhov, A. The three sisters
Three sisters, The. Chekhov, A.
Three weddings of a hunchback. Borsook, H.
Threepenny opera, The. Brecht, B.
Thrice promised bride, The. Hsiung, C. C.
Thunder-bolt, The. Pinero, A.
Thunder rock. Ardrey, R.
Thunderstorm, The. Ostrovskiĭ, A.
Thurber carnival, A. Thurber, J.
Thursday evening. Morley, C.
Thy will be done. Gallarati-Scotti, T.
Thyestes. Seneca, L.
Ticket-of-leave man, The. Taylor, T.
Ticklish acrobat, The. Hivnor, R.
Tidings brought to Mary, The. See Claudel, P. L'annonce faite à Marie
Tiger at the gates. Giraudoux, J.
Till the day I die. Odets, C.
Time and again. See Duerrenmatt, F. The visit
Time is a dream. Lenormand, H.
Time limit. Denker, H. and Berkey, R.
Time of the cuckoo, The. Laurents, A.
Time of your life, The. Saroyan, W.

Timon of Athens. Shakespeare, W.
Tinker, The. Dobie, L. and Sloman, R.
'Tis a pity she's a whore. Ford, J.
'Tis all a notion. See Bird, R. 'Twas all for the best
Titus Andronicus. Shakespeare, W.
To Damascus, part 1. Strindberg, A.
To Dorothy, a son. MacDougall, R.
To love and to cherish. Egan, M.
To see ourselves. De La Pasture, E.
To the ladies! Kaufman, G. and Connelly, M.
To traade. See Soya, C. Two threads
Tobacco road. Kirkland, J. and Caldwell, E.
Tobias and Sara. Claudel, P.
Die tochter Pharaonis. See Kotzebue, A. Pharaoh's daughter
Der tod des Tizian. See Hofmannsthal, H. von. The death of Titian
Toiler's trials, The. See Steele, S. The crock of gold
Tom Thumb the great. See Fielding, H. The tragedy of tragedies.
Tom Tyler and his wife. Anonymous plays
Tomb beneath the Arc de triomphe, The. See Raynal, P. Le tombeau sous l'Arc de triomphe
Le tombeau sous l'Arc de triomphe. Raynal, P.
Tomorrow and tomorrow. Barry, P.
Tomorrow the world. Gow, J. and D'Usseau, A.
Top of the ladder. Guthrie, T.
Der tor und der tod. Hofmannsthal, H. von
Torch race, The. See Hervieu, P. La course du flambeau

363

Torquato Tasso. Goethe, J.
Tortesa, the usurer. Willis, N.
Totentanz. Anonymous plays
Touch it light. Storey, R.
Touch of the poet, A. O'Neill, E.
Touch wood. Smith, D. G.
Tovarich. Deval, J.
Tower of Babel, The. Goodman, P.
Town of Titipu, The. See Gilbert, W. and Sullivan, A. The mikado
Towneley play, The. Anonymous plays
Toys in the attic. Hellman, L.
Trachiniae, The. Sophocles
Tragedy of Hamlet, Prince of Denmark, The. See Shakespeare, W. Hamlet
Tragedy of Jane Shore, The. Rowe, N.
Tragedy of King Lear, The. See Shakespeare, W. King Lear
Tragedy of King Richard II, The. Shakespeare, W.
Tragedy of love, The. Heiberg, G.
Tragedy of Macbeth, The. See Shakespeare, W. Macbeth
Tragedy of Mustapha, the son of Solyman the magnificent. Orrery, R.
Tragedy of Pompey the great, The. Masefield, J.
Tragedy of the Duchess of Malfi. See Webster, J. The Duchess of Malfi
Tragedy of tragedies, The; or, The life and death of Tom Thumb the great. Fielding, H.
Tragedy or interlude manifesting the chief promises of God unto man, A. See Bale, J. God's promises
Tragedy rehearsed, A. See Sheridan, R. The critic
Tragi- comedy of Calisto and Melibea, The. See Rojas, F. Celestina
Tragical history of the life and death of Doctor Faustus, The. See Marlowe, C. The tragi-

cal history of Doctor Faustus
Tragical history of Doctor Faustus, The. Marlowe, C.
Tragidie of [Gorboduc; or of]
Ferrex and Porex, The. See Sackville, T. and Norton, T. Gorboduc
Trail of the torch, The. See Hervieu, P. La course du flambeau
Traitor, The. Shirley, J.
Traitor, The. Wilde, P.
Transfiguration. Toller, E.
Transformation. See Toller, E. Transfiguration
Translation of John Snaith, The. Cooke, B.
Trapolin's vagaries. See Tate, N. A duke and no duke
Trappolin suppos'd a prince. Cokain, A. See Tate, N. A duke and no duke
Traum ein leben, Der. Grillparzer, F.
Tre maa man vaere. See Locher, J. Tea for three
Tread the green grass. Green, P.
Trelawny of the "Wells." Pinero, A.
Trente ans; ou, La vie d'un joueur. Goubaux, P. and Ducange, V. See Dunlap, W. Thirty years
Les trente-sept sous de M. Montaudoin. Labiche E. and Martin, É.
Tres clerici. See Anonymous plays. Saint Nicholas and the three scholars
Trespassers. Reid, L.
Trial and error. Horne, K.
Trial horse no. 1: Many loves. Williams, W.
Trial of Christ, The (Coventry). Anonymous plays
Trial of treasure, The. Anonymous plays
Trial without jury; or, The magpie and the maid. Payne, J.
Trick to catch the old one, A. Middleton, T.
Trickster, The. See Plautus.

364

Pseudolus
Trickster of Seville, The. See
Téllez, G. El burlador de
Sevilla
Trickster of Seville and his guest
of stone, The. See Téllez, G.
El burlador de Sevilla
Trifles. Glaspell, S.
Trinummus. See Plautus, T.
The three penny day
Trip abroad, A. See Labiche,
E. and Martin E. Le voyage
de Monsieur Perrichon
Trip to Chinatown, A; or, Idyl
of San Francisco. Hoyt, C.
Trip to Niagara, A. See Bird,
R. News of the night
Triple-A plowed under. Staff of
the Living Newspaper
Tristram the jester. Hardt, E.
Triumph at Plattsburg, The.
Smith, R.
Triumph of Bohemia, The. Stir-
ling, G.
Triumph of prejudice, The. See
Mérimée, P. Ines Mendo
Troades. See Euripides. The
Trojan women; Seneca, L.
The Trojan women
Troilus and Cressida. Shake-
speare, W.
Les trois filles de M. Dupont.
Brieux, E.
Trojan women, The. Euripides
Trojan women, The. Seneca, L.
Trouble with reason, The.
Griboyedov, A.
Troublesome reign and lament-
able death of Edward the sec-
ond, The. Marlowe, C.
Truculentus. Plautus, T.
True and honorable historie of
the life of Sir John Oldcastle,
the good Lord Cobham, The.
See Anonymous plays. Sir
John Oldcastle, pt. I
True chronicle history of the
whole life and death of Thom-
as Lord Cromwell, The. See
Anonymous plays. Thomas
Lord Cromwell
Truth, The. Fitch, C.
Truth about Blayds, The. Milne,

A.
Truth suspected, The. See
Ruiz de Alarcón y Mendoza,
J. La verdad sospechosa
Try! Try! O'Hara, F.
Trysting-place, The. Tarking-
ton, B.
Tsar Fyodor Ivánovitch. Tolstoí,
A.
Turcaret. Le Sage, A.
'Twas all for the best; or, 'Tis
all a notion. Bird, R.
Twelfth night; or, What you will.
Shakespeare, W.
Twelve months. Marshak, S.
Twelve-pound look, The. Barrie,
J.
Twenty-fourth of February, The.
See Werner, F. Der vierund-
zwanzigste Februar
27 wagons full of cotton. Willi-
ams, T.
Twilight crane. Kinoshita, J.
Twin brothers, The. See Plau-
tus, T. The Menaechmi
Twin Menaechmi, The. See
Plautus, T. The Menaechmi
Twisting of the rope, The. Hyde,
D.
Two angry women of Abington,
The. See Porter, H. The
pleasant history of the two
angry women of Abington
Two bacchides, The. Plautus, T.
Two blind mice. Spewack, S.
Two bouquets, The. Farjeon, E.
and Farjeon, H.
Two crooks and a lady. Pillot,
E.
Two gentlemen of Verona, The.
Shakespeare, W.
Two noble kinsmen, The.
Fletcher, J. and Shakespeare,
W.
Two orphans, The. D'Ennery,
A. and Cormon, E.
Two roses. Albery, J.
Two sergeants, The. See Smith,
R. The sentinels
Two shepherds, The. Martínez
Sierra, G. and Martínez Sier-
ra, M.
Two sides of the door. Cropper, M.

Two sons-in-law, The. Payne,
    J.
Two thieves, The. Bates, E.
Two threads. Soya, C.
2 x 2 = 5. Wied, G.
Tyranny of love, The. See
    Porto-Riche, G. Amoureuse
Tzu forwitsich. Wieand, P.

U

Ubu Roi. Jarry, A.
Ultimo. Moser, G. von. See
    Daly, A. The big bonanza
Ulysses in Nighttown. Barken-
    tin, M.
Umbrian play, The. Anonymous
    plays
Uncertain joy. Hastings, C.
Unchastened woman, The. Ans-
    pacher, L.
Uncle Harry. Job, T.
Uncle Tom's cabin. Aiken, G.
Uncle Vanya. Chekhov, A.
Uncle's been dreaming. Voll-
    möller, K.
Under cover. Megrue, R.
Under milk wood. Thomas, D.
Under the sycamore tree. Spe-
    wack, S.
Underpants, The. Sternheim, C.
Une famille bien unie. See Pré-
    vert, J. A united family.
Unexpected guests, The. How-
    ells, W.
Uniform of flesh. See Coxe, L.
    and Chapman, R. Billy Budd
United family, A. Prévert, J
Unknown warrior, The. See Ray-
    nal, P. Le tombeau sous l'-
    Arc de triomphe
Unter vier augen. See Fulda, L.
    Tête-à-tête
Unto such glory. Green, P.
Upper room, The. Benson, R.
Usurper, The; or, Americans in
    Tripoli. Jones, J.S.

V

Vagabond king, The. See Mc-
    Carthy, J. If I were king
Vale of content, The. Sudermann,

H.
Valiant, The. Hall, H. and
    Middlemass, R.
Valley Forge. Anderson, M.
La valse de toréadors. See
    Anouilh, J. The waltz of the
    toreadors
Venceslas. See Rotrou, J.
    Wenceshaus
Venetian, The. Bax, C.
Venice preserv'd; or, A plot
    discover'd. Otway, T.
Il ventaglio. See Goldoni, C.
    The fan
Venus and Adonis. Obey, A.
Venus observed. Fry, C.
La verdad sospechosa. Ruiz de
    Alarcón y Mendoza, J.
Verhor des Lukullus, Das.
    Brecht, B.
Le verre d'eau. Scribe, A.
Verrechelte rechler, Die.
    Barba, P.
Die versunkene glocke. See
    Hauptmann, G. The sunken
    bell
Very special baby, A. Aurthur,
    R.
Vespae. See Aristophanes. The
    wasps
Vested interests. See Bena-
    vente y Martínez, J. The
    bonds of interest
Vestire gl'ignudi. See Piran-
    dello, L. Naked
Viceroy Sarah. Ginsbury, N.
Victoria Regina. Housman, L.
La vida es sueño. Calderón de
    la Barca, P.
Vigilant sentinel, The. Cer-
    vantes Saavedra, M.
La vie d'un joueur. Goubaux,
    P. and Ducange, V. See
    Dunlap, W. Thirty years
Das vierte gebot. Anzengruber,
    L.
Der vierundzwanzigste Februar.
    Werner, F.
View from the bridge, A.
    Miller, A.
Vildanden. See Ibsen, H. The
    wild duck
Violin maker of Cremona, The.

366

plays
Weather breeder, The. Denison,
M.
Weavers, The. Hauptmann, G.
Die weber. See Hauptmann, G.
The weavers
Wedding, The. See Barry, P.
Paris bound
Wedding, The. Shirley, J.
Wedding bells. Field, E.
Wedding day. See Ronder, J.
This year, next year
Wedding march, The. See La-
biche, E. and Marc-Michel.
An Italian straw hat
Wednesday's child. Atlas, L.
Weekend in May. See Gow, R.
The Edwardians
Weevil, The. See Plautus, T.
Curculio
Der weisse heiland. See Haupt-
mann, G. The white Saviour
Well of the saints, The. Synge,
W.
Well-remembered voice, A. Bar-
rie, J.
Wenceshaus. Rotrou, J.
Wept of the wish-ton-wish, The.
Anonymous plays
West Indian, The. Cumberland,
R.
What a life. Goldsmith, C.
What every woman knows. Barrie,
J.
What men live by. Church, V.
What price glory? Anderson, M.
and Stallings, L.
What you will. See Shakespeare,
W. Twelfth night
When a girl says yes. See Mora-
tín, L. El sí de las niñas
When ladies meet. Crothers, R.
When roses bloom again. Mar-
quina, E.
Where the cross is made.
O'Neill, E.
Where the dear antelope play.
Rogers, J.
White château, The. Berkeley,
R.
White devil, The; or, Vittoria
corombona. Webster, J.
White dresses. Green, P.

White redeemer, The. See
Hauptmann, G. The white
saviour
White saviour, The. Haupt-
mann, G.
White slave, The. Campbell, B.
White steed, The. Carroll, P.
Whiteheaded boy, The. Robinson,
L.
Whither goest thou? Currie, C.
Who goes there! Dighton, J.
"Who ride on white horses, " the
story of Edmund Campion.
Breen, R. and Schnibbe, H.
Whole truth, The. Mackie, P.
Why marry? Williams, J.
Why not? Williams, J.
Widow of Watling street, The.
See Anonymous plays. The
puritan
Wife, The. Belasco, D. and De
Mille, H.
Wife at a venture, A. Smith, R.
Wild birds. Totheroh, D.
Wild Decembers. Ashton, W.
Wild duck, The. Ibsen, H.
Wild-goose chase, The.
Fletcher, J.
Wild horse of Tartary, The.
See Payne, J. Mazeppa
Wilhelm Tell. See Schiller, J.
William Tell
Will, The. Barrie, J.
Will this earth hold? Buck, P.
William Penn. Smith, R.
William Tell. Schiller, J.
William the defeated. Jameson,
S.
Wind and the rain, The. Hodge,
M.
Winged victory. Hart, M.
Wingless victory, The. Ander-
son, M.
Wings over Europe. Nichols, R.
and Browne, M.
Winslow boy, The. Rattigan, T.
Winter journey, A. See Odets,
C. The big knife
Winter soldiers. James, D.
Winter's tale, The. Shakespeare,
W.
Winterset. Anderson, M.
Wisdom tooth, The. Connelly, M.

Wise virgins and the foolish virgins, The. Anonymous plays
Wisemen [The Spanish play], The. Anonymous plays
Wish you were here. Kobler, A. and Logan, J.
Wisteria trees, The. Logan, J.
Wit and science. See Anonymous plays. The marriage of wit and science; Redford, J. The play of wit and science
Wit and wisdom. See Anonymous plays. The contract of marriage between wit and wisdom
Wit works woe. Griboïedov, A.
Witch of Edmonton, The. Ford, J., Dekker, T. and Rowley, W.
Witches' mountain, The. Sánchez Gardel, J.
Witching hour, The. Thomas, A.
With intent. Williams, H. and Williams, M.
Within an inch of his life. Herne, J.
Within the law. Veiller, B.
Witness for the prosecution. Christie, A.
Wits, The. D'Avenant, W.
Wives metamorphos'd, The. See Jevon, T.; Coffey, C.; Mottley, J. and Cibber, T. The devil to pay
Woe from wit. See Griboïedov, A. Wit works woe
Wolf-hunt, The. Verga, G.
Woman and the walnut tree, The. Box, S.
Woman is a weathercock. Field, N.
Woman killed with kindness, A. Heywood, T.
Woman of Andros, The. Terentius Afer, P.
Woman of no importance, A. Wilde, O.
Woman of Paris, The. See Becque, H. La Parisienne
Woman of Samos. See Menander. The girl from Samos
Woman taken in adultery, The (N. town). Anonymous plays
Woman too many, A. Sønderby, K.

Woman's craze for titles. Dancourt, F.
Woman's revenge. Payne, J.
Women, The. Boothe, C.
Women, beware women. Middleton, T.
Women celebrating the Thesmophoria, The. See Aristophanes. Thesmophoriazusae
Women have their way, The. See Álvarez Quintero, S. and Álvarez Quintero, J. The women's town
Women of Trachis, The. See Sophocles. The Trachiniae
Women's town, The. Álvarez Quintero, S. and Álvarez Quintero, J.
Won at last. MacKaye, S.
Wonder-working magician, The. Calderón de la Barca, P.
Wonderful town. Fields, J. and Chodorov, J.
Wood demon, The. See Chekhov, A. Uncle Vanya
Words of the window pane, The. Yeats, W.
Workhouse ward, The. Gregory, I.
World a mask, The. Boker, G.
World and his wife, The. See Echegaray y Eizaguirre, J. El gran Galeoto
World and the child, The. Anonymous plays
World of boredom, The. See Pailleron, É. Le monde où l'on s'ennuie
World we live in, The. See Čapek, K. and Čapek, J. And so ad infinitum
World we make, The. Kingsley, S.
World well lost, The. See Dryden, J. All for love
World's own, The. See Howe, J. Leonora
Worm's eye view. Delderfield, R.
Worst is not the worst, The. See Claudel, P. The satin slipper
Worst not always true, The.

369